SPORTS
AND
RECREATIONAL ACTIVITIES
FOR MEN AND WOMEN

SPORTS
—— AND ——
RECREATIONAL ACTIVITIES
FOR MEN AND WOMEN

DALE MOOD

Professor of Kinesiology,
Associate Dean, College of Arts and Sciences,
University of Colorado, Boulder

FRANK F. MUSKER

Formerly Professor of Physical Education,
Boston University; Supervisor of Physical Education,
Peabody Public Schools, Peabody, Massachusetts

JUDITH E. RINK

Associate Professor,
Department of Physical Education,
University of South Carolina,
Columbia, South Carolina

TENTH EDITION

with 1097 illustrations

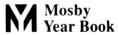
**Mosby
Year Book**

St. Louis   Baltimore   Boston   Chicago   London   Philadelphia   Sydney   Toronto

**Mosby
Year Book**

Editor **Donna Sokolowski**
Editorial Assistant **Loren Stevenson**
Project Supervisor **Barbara Merritt**
Editing and Production **Steve Rudloff, Kathleen Teal**
Designer **Laura Steube**

TENTH EDITION

Copyright © 1991 by Mosby–Year Book, Inc.
A Mosby imprint of Mosby–Year Book, Inc.

Mosby–Year Book, Inc.
11830 Westline Industrial Drive, St. Louis, Missouri 63146

Previous editions copyrighted 1953, 1958, 1963, 1967, 1971, 1975, 1979, 1983, 1987

Printed in the United States of America

Library of Congress Cataloging-in-Publication Data

Mood, Dale

   Sports and recreational activities for men and women/Dale Mood,
Frank F. Musker, Judith E. Rink.—10th ed.

     p.   cm.
   Includes bibliographical references.
   ISBN 0-8016-6202-8

    1. Sports.   2. Group games.   3. Physical education and training—
Study and teaching.   I. Musker, Frank F.   II. Rink, Judith.   III. Title.
GV704.M66   1991
   796'.0194—dc20
                                         90-46030
                                           CIP

GW/GW/VHP 9 8 7 6 5 4 3 2 1

Contributors

AEROBIC DANCE
Lorna L. Francis, Ph.D.
Instructor
Department of Physical Education
San Diego State University
San Diego, CA

KARATE
Rick Schmidt, Ph.D.
Assistant Professor
School of Health, Physical Education, and Recreation
University of Nebraska
Lincoln, NE

KAYAKING AND CANOEING
Peter Werner, Ph.D.
Professor
Department of Physical Education
University of South Carolina
Columbia, SC

Consultants

ARCHERY

Jean A. Barrett, Professor
Department of Health, Physical Education, and
   Recreation
California State University
Fullerton, CA

BACKPACKING

Jeff Steffen, Assistant Professor
Department of Physical Education
University of Northern Colorado
Greeley, CO

BADMINTON

Bob Erickson, Public Relations, Director
United States Badminton Association
Papillion, NE

BASKETBALL

James D. LaPoint, Associate Professor
Department of Health, Physical Education, and
   Recreation
University of Kansas
Lawrence, KS

BICYCLING

David R. Bassett, Jr., Assistant Professor
Department of Physical Education and Dance
University of Tennessee
Knoxville, TN

BOWLING

Gerald P. Carlson, Professor
Department of Health, Physical Education, and
   Recreation
University of Southwestern Louisiana
Lafayette, LA

DANCE: CONCERT AND RECREATIONAL

Judith Woodruff, Adjunct Instructor
Department of Physical Education and Recreation
East Tennessee State University
Johnson City, TN

FENCING

Anne Klinger, Department Head
Department of Physical Education
Clatsop Community College
Astoria, OR

FIELD HOCKEY

Susan Caples, Athletic Coach
Department of Athletics
Harvard University
Cambridge, MA

GOLF

A. Craig Fisher, Professor
Department of Exercise and Sport Science
Ithaca College
Ithaca, NY

GYMNASTICS

Carolyn Cody, Professor
Department of Physical Education
University of Northern Colorado
Greeley, CO

JOGGING

Wendell Liemohn, Professor
Department of Physical Education and Recreation
Baylor University
Waco, TX

MOUNTAINEERING

Norman L. Gilchrest, Associate Professor
Department of Health, Physical Education, and
   Recreation
Baylor University
Waco, TX

ORIENTEERING

Jerry D. Andrew, Lecturer
Department of Health and Physical Education
Texas A&M University
College Station, TX

PHYSICAL FITNESS

Cheryl Norton, Associate Professor
Department of Human Performance, Sport, and
   Leisure Studies
Metropolitan State College
Denver, CO

RACQUETBALL, PADDLEBALL, AND HANDBALL

Gene Ezell, Professor
Department of Health, Physical Education, and
   Recreation
University of Tennessee
Chattanooga, TN

RUGBY

John A.W. Baker, Associate Professor
Department of Physical Education
Southern Illinois University
Carbondale, IL

SELF-DEFENSE

Lawrence McGill, Adjunct Professor
Department of Human Performance, Sport, and
   Leisure Studies
Metropolitan State College
Denver, CO

SKIING: ALPINE

Tim LeValle, Ski Coach
Department of Athletics
University of Colorado
Boulder, CO

SKIING: CROSS COUNTRY

George Atkinson, Assistant Professor
Department of Health, Sport, and Leisure Studies
Northeastern University
Boston, MA

SKIN AND SCUBA DIVING

Joe Mottashed, Owner
Scuba Joe, Incorporated
Boulder, CO

SOCCER

A.I. Clifford Singh, Associate Professor
Department of Physical Education
California State University
San Bernardino, CA

SOFTBALL

Ronald F. Kirby, Professor
Department of Physical Education
Southeast Missouri State University
Cape Girardeau, MO

SPRINGBOARD DIVING

Gerald DeMers, Assistant Professor
Department of Physical Education and Recreation
   Administration
California Polytechnic State University
San Luis Obispo, CA

SWIMMING

Patricia Van Volkinburg, Instructor
Department of Kinesiology
University of Michigan
Ann Arbor, MI

TABLE TENNIS

Don Casady, Professor
Department of Physical Education
University of Iowa
Iowa City, IA

TEAM HANDBALL

March L. Krotee, Professor
Department of Physical Education
University of Minnesota
Minneapolis, MN

TENNIS

Robert Gensmer, Professor
Department of Sport Science and Physical Education
Denver University
Denver, CO

TOUCH AND FLAG FOOTBALL

Fred Murphy, Associate Professor
Department of Kinesiology
University of Colorado
Boulder, CO

TRACK AND FIELD

Harry Marra, Head Track Coach
Department of Physical Education
San Francisco State University
San Francisco, CA

VOLLEYBALL

Linda Delk, Assistant Professor
Department of Athletics
University of Northern Colorado
Greeley, CO

WATER POLO

George Weiny, Professor
Department of Physical Education
California State University
San Bernardino, CA

WEIGHT TRAINING, CIRCUIT TRAINING, WEIGHT LIFTING

Thomas Miller, Teacher
L.J. Schultz Middle School
Cape Girardeau, MO

WRESTLING

Doug Parker, Wrestling Coach
Department of Athletics
Springfield College
Springfield, MA

Preface

PURPOSE OF THE BOOK

The purpose of the tenth edition of *Sports and Recreational Activities for Men and Women* is to provide current fundamental knowledge about a broad spectrum of physical activities. The physiological, psychological, and social values of participation in physical activities have long been proclaimed by physicians, physical educators, and recreation directors, and it appears that their efforts are now being rewarded. Most evidence suggests that the number of people engaging in regular physical activity continues to increase. For reasons of safety, enjoyment, and motivation, it is important that these people start out correctly and that they are exposed to a variety of possibilities. We believe that participation in physical activities can enrich the quality of life and that use of the basic concepts provided in this book will promote this enrichment.

Sports and Recreational Activities for Men and Women is written for two groups of readers—participants and instructors (or instructors-to-be). People who decide to embark on a personal program of sports and recreation can benefit from this book's excellent overview of 39 popular physical activities. Physical educators, recreation leaders, playground directors, and camp counselors, no matter how well trained, seldom have the time to learn the fundamentals of the many activities covered in this book. For these instructors or students who will become instructors, the book should serve as a valuable resource when they are called upon to teach an unfamiliar activity.

In most cases, each chapter includes a brief historical perspective of the activity, information about the selection and care of required equipment, a digest of the basic rules, a discussion of the fundamental skills and techniques needed, ideas about strategies, safety concerns, a list of teaching considerations, terminology, and selected references. Armed with this knowledge both the participant and the instructor should find increased enjoyment in physical activities.

CHANGES IN THE TENTH EDITION

The revision process for this tenth edition was extensive. Although much about sports and recreational activities remains constant over the years, there also is much that changes. For example, we have updated the text to reflect the invention of new equipment, changes in the rules, the discovery of new techniques, and the increase in available references. The increasing participation of women in sports and recreational activities has brought about many rule changes during recent years (consider basketball, for example). The conversion of various dimensions to metric units and the simple need to update photographs as new apparel becomes available are other reasons revision is necessary. Along with these updating needs, many other changes have been made in this tenth edition to make it a more useful book.

CHAPTER CONSISTENCY

Particular attention has been given to present this wealth of diverse material as consistently as possible from chapter to chapter. In general and where appropriate, each chapter proceeds from behavioral objectives, to history, to equipment and facilities, to rules and etiquette, to fundamental skills and techniques, to strategies, to teaching considerations, and finally to ancillary information such as a glossary, suggested readings, and audiovisual materials.

NEW ILLUSTRATIONS

Many new photographs and drawings have been added and others replaced or modified to illustrate the latest developments in technique and instruction. If a picture is worth a thousand words, then the hundreds of illustrations in the book provide an efficient method for communicating a great deal of information. However, it is not always a simple task to obtain just the right photograph or drawing to capture the intent. A great deal of effort was spent on improving the illustrations for this edition so that the reader can truly "see" the nuances of each activity.

NEW CHAPTERS

Three new chapters have been added to the tenth edition of *Sports and Recreational Activities for Men and Women*. They are Aerobic Dance, Karate, and Kayaking and Canoeing. The increasing popularity of these activities warrants their inclusion in this book.

ANNOTATED REFERENCES

Recognizing that a book such as this cannot present every facet of every activity, we present for each chapter a list of suggested readings. Beginning in the ninth edition and continuing in this edition, we have provided a short annotation for many of these references. This will allow readers who wish further details about an activity to select readings that are germane to their particular interests.

VIDEOTAPES

New to the tenth edition is information at the end of most chapters specifying where relevant videotapes may be found. Videotapes of talented performers and of classic events are being used for instructional purposes at an increasing rate. We hope this additional resource will prove helpful.

NEW APPENDIX MATERIAL

We have augmented, in the appendix material, the list of companies who manufacture or distribute equipment relevant to the various activities described in this book. Addresses and brief descriptions of types of equipment are provided. This should serve as a handy resource for those interested in comparing information and purchasing equipment, clothing, and other paraphenalia required to participate or teach the activities covered in this book.

INSTRUCTOR'S MANUAL

An instructor's manual has been prepared for use with the tenth edition. It includes chapter outlines, test questions, and suggestions for discussion. The chapter outlines can be used to obtain a quick synopsis of the chapter contents. They are useful for organizing class lectures and could be reproduced for students as study guides. Objective test questions (true-false, matching, and multiple choice) are provided as a source of ideas from which an instructor may build a valid examination over the factual materials presented in each chapter. The suggestions for discussion include questions that can be used either as essay questions on examinations or as stimuli for discussions. They generally require the student to demonstrate comprehension of the chapter information by applying learned material for summarizing important concepts contained in the chapter.

ACKNOWLEDGMENTS

A book with as diverse and broad a scope as this is obviously the result of the work and ideas of many people. We wish to thank all the consultants and contributors, with a special tip of the hat to Lorna Francis, Rick Schmidt, and Peter Werner for their contributions of the new chapters on Aerobic Dance, Karate, and Kayaking and Canoeing, respectively.

We also extend our appreciation to Raili Mood and to many of the contributors and consultants for providing the many new photographs for this edition. Special thanks go to the officials of the various sporting goods companies and publishers for giving us permission to reproduce many drawings and photographs.

We wish to express our gratitude to Donna Sokolowski, Loren Stevenson, Barbara Merritt, and all the other folks at Mosby–Year Book for providing feedback and guidance and for keeping us to our deadlines. Their suggestions and gentle reminders are much appreciated.

Dale Mood
Frank F. Musker
Judith E. Rink

Contents

SPORTS
AND
RECREATIONAL ACTIVITIES
FOR MEN AND WOMEN

Introduction

There is almost unanimous agreement that optimum health is our most prized possession. Schopenhauer, the German philosopher, expressed this idea when he remarked, "The greatest of follies is to neglect one's health for any other advantage of life."

To improve and maintain optimum health, it is necessary for people of all ages to participate in physical exercise. However, there is wide variation in the types of exercises recommended for different age groups.

A good example of the importance of exercise in maintaining health is the emphasis placed on it in the health regimen of presidents of the United States. Along with close medical supervision, recent White House physicians have included exercises such as walking, jogging, hiking, golfing, swimming, and horseback riding in the presidents' conditioning programs.

In addition to the value of exercise in maintaining optimum health, there are often social and recreational benefits as well. In this age of increased leisure time these benefits are becoming even more important than in the past.

Although in many colleges and universities students are required to participate in physical education classes, several institutions have eliminated this requirement and instituted a totally elective program. In a large percentage of these cases the number of students taking physical activity classes has remained constant or increased.

There is little doubt that, in addition to students on college campuses, the number of people participating in sports and recreational activities in the United States has been increasing dramatically in recent years although this number is still far short of goals set by national health agencies. In part the increases in activity participation that have been noted can be attributed to an increase in the amount of leisure time available to most Americans. We have shorter work weeks and more and longer vacations than in the past. In additon, sports and recreational facilities have become increasingly abundant and accessible to larger and more diverse segments of the population.

The increased leisure time, however, does not explain why Americans choose to use this time engaged in sports and recreational activities; it merely provides the opportunity to do so. Increased facilities also reflect only that larger segments of the population choose to participate, but do not supply a reason for this choice.

A great number of theories have been proposed by educators, sociologists, medical personnel, and others to explain why we engage in physical activity. These theories are diverse yet contain many overlapping ideas. The satisfaction of creative desires, expression of inherent animal instincts, use of excess energy, preparation for other types of life situations, and exposure to risk to provide excitement are a few of the concepts that have been proposed.

People have become aware of several benefits of physical activity, particularly in the physiological area. Some of these benefits and relevant considerations are presented in the Physical Fitness chapter. In addition to the physiological benefits, the following are other areas believed to be affected positively by participation in sports and recreational activities.

PSYCHOLOGICAL FACTORS

Many life situations are conducive to producing tension and emotional stress resulting in worry, anxiety, fear, frustration, and the like. Although the evidence is not as definite because the factors involved are more difficult to measure, there is some indication that exercise under the proper conditions can be helpful in improving emotional stability and mental fitness, just as it aids in developing physical fitness. Participation in an interesting sport takes the mind from other things and from concentration on problems. Thus a healthful sport may be more valuable than walking in maintaining health. Exercise also helps release emotions through socially approved channels. It is a means of satisfying certain primitive urges that all people have, and it provides for self-expression. Experiencing success in developing skills and participating in a physical activity are excellent means of developing confidence and reaping satisfaction that comes from successful accomplishment. Through individual activities such as archery, bowling, running, swimming, gymnastics, and golf, it is possible to compete against oneself as well as against others.

KNOWLEDGE

A dominant factor in the American way of life is the ability of the average citizen to understand sports, if not as a participant, then as a spectator. Therefore, it is beneficial for the individual to learn the rules and strategies of various sports. In addition, knowledge of etiquette, safety, equipment, history, values, techniques, and other factors can enhance the enjoyment of watching or participating in team, dual, or individual activities.

SOCIAL VALUES

One important aspect of education is the attempt of educators to provide a program of activities that helps in the socialization of the individual. Because we are living in an age of great social conflict, it is highly important that teachers use every means possible to instill positive social habits in their students. A program of physical activities offers unlimited opportunities for developing broad social understandings. In fact, initial contacts between previously distant cultures or societies are sometimes made through a common interest in sports, as illustrated years ago by the "Ping-Pong diplomacy" that led to closer relations between China and the United States.

One facet of common social interests of Americans is shown by the wide publicity given to sports through radio and television, sports pages of newspapers, magazines, conversations, and discussions between individuals of all ages. There is possibly no better way to learn how to get along with and to live with others than through participation in sports. In sports the individual must show the same qualities that are necessary for successful and happy living in a democratic society. To be most successful, habits and attitudes of courtesy, self-control, initiative, cooperation, and loyalty must be acquired. The experience of being both a follower and a leader can be gained. Successful participation in sports implies that the participant must learn to be a good sport and to give credit where it is due, regardless of who wins or loses. Participation in term games, particularly, teaches the individual to work with others to the best advantage of the team and to control emotions.

College students are often motivated by the social instinct of belonging. One way the desire to associate with fellow students can be satisfied is through participation in sports. The congenial atmosphere of sports presents the opportunity to develop friendships that may have lasting value.

RECREATION

Technology has liberated us from much physical work, and recreation has assumed an important place in modern life as a result of the increasing amount of leisure time available to all.

It is evident that people can use leisure time constructively or destructively. One of the aims of a physical activities program is to teach the wise use of leisure time. People should be made aware of the vital place that wholesome recreation, and especially sports, can play in the full enjoyment of life.

Recreation, to be helpful, need not be elaborate or expensive. Many of the simple forms of recreation available to all are the most satisfying and of the greatest help in maintaining physical, mental, and emotional health.

FACTORS ASSOCIATED WITH A PHYSICAL ACTIVITY PROGRAM

To profit most from participation in sports and physical activities, a number of things should be considered.

Training and conditioning

Some physical educators and sports directors make a distinction between "conditioning" and "training." Conditioning is usually considered to be related to such things as proper eating, resting, relaxing, sleeping, and exercising regularly, as well as working toward the improvement of skills in an activity. Training, on the other hand, is considered by some to be the practice of certain movements by constant repetition until a skill is established or mastered. An example of this would be attempting to improve, and master to the greatest possible extent, skills required in such sports as swimming, golf, tennis, or track. The meanings of the words "training" and "conditioning" overlap, for gains in one generally lead to increases in the other.

It is necessary to participate in vigorous physical activity at regular intervals to develop and maintain maximum body efficiency. It is generally recommended by the American College of Sports Medicine that at a minimum one should participate in a moderately intense physical activity for 30 minutes at least 3 times per week. To reach this state it is best to begin with mild exercise and to gradually increase the intensity during subsequent periods. A main reason this is recommended is prevention of undue stress and strain on muscles of the body. The duration of exercise periods should be governed by the response of the individual to exercise and past training periods. Other factors such as age and physical condition will dictate the initial intensity and duration of exercise periods. To develop the greatest overall muscular efficiency, one should participate in activities that require some use of all the major muscles of the body. Many sports require repeated use of a limited set of muscles; thus it is best to take part in a wide variety of sports.

It is very important to follow a regular training routine. It is unwise to engage in any strenuous activity before the body is in condition for it. To increase the condition of the body requires application of a stress or overload. However, it is generally true that maintaining a particular state of physical condition requires less intense activity than is required to get to that level. It is also generally accepted that if participation is discontinued the degree of physical condition will decline at about the same rate required to build it.

Good physical condition is sufficient for participation in most sports. However, it must be kept in mind that certain sports require special training. Age makes a difference in conditioning and training; younger people can train and condition more rapidly than older people.

A well-chosen sequence of conditioning exercises is valuable in developing flexibility and should involve exercises for the (1) shoulders, chest, and back, (2) arms and shoulders, (3) neck, (4) lateral trunk, (5) back and buttocks, (6) legs and buttocks, (7) abdomen, (8) lower back and buttocks, (9) chest and arms, and (10) legs, ankles, and feet.

Physical examination

No one should participate in prolonged and strenuous physical activity without first having a complete medical examination by a physician. A medical examination including an exercise stress test is so important that it cannot be overemphasized, especially after the age of 35, and regular examinations should be repeated periodically throughout life. The results of medical examinations show that most people do not need to restrict physical activity; however, if certain defects are present, such as a defective heart, participation in unrestricted strenuous exercise can be very damaging.

Precautions

It should be apparent that an exercise program needs to be structured to fit each individual. Beginning level of fitness, medical condition, interests, age, and availability of facilities are examples of factors to be considered.

Before one engages in strenuous physical activity, there should be a period of gradual warming up and stretching of the muscles to eliminate some of the danger of muscle injury. Large-muscle groups, including the arms, legs, and trunk, should be warmed up first. In fact, they should receive major attention throughout the warming-up and limbering-up period.

It is usually recommended that vigorous and strenuous physical activity be tapered off. Sudden and complete relaxation after vigorous exertion without tapering off can cause dizziness, nausea, and even fainting if the exercise has been particularly strenuous. Giving the body processes a chance to slow down gradually is a precautionary measure observed by practically all champion athletes.

There are good reasons for tapering off following vigorous or stenuous exercise. During exercise the heart rate speeds up to keep the muscles supplied with sufficient oxygen and nutrients. The increased heart rate sends the arterial blood into the veins. Because the venous system has no forceful mechanism like the heart to help move blood back to the heart, the action of muscles must be depended on to help the return flow of blood. When the veins fill with blood, the pressure of contracting muscles produces a pumping action on the thin-walled veins to propel the blood back toward the center of the body. If vigorous exercise ends abruptly, the heart continues for a time to send extra amounts of arterial blood to the muscles. Because the muscles are suddenly quiet, there is not sufficient force for returning the extra blood to the heart. Consequently, the extra blood tends to pool in the muscles, and the imbalance may leave some organs with an inadequate supply of blood. During the tapering-off process following strenuous exercise, the muscles continue to squeeze blood from the extremities of the body back to the main circulation.

Sudden stopping of vigorous exercise without tapering off may also result in cramps, although research has not yet determined why. Stiffness may also be avoided or reduced by the tapering-off process.

Regardless of the care taken in beginning training and conditioning for sports, muscles may become sore and stiff. Mild exercise, in cases of this sort, helps the pumping action of the heart that is necessary to bring blood to the sore muscle and thereby speeds up the carrying away of waste products.

Another precaution is avoidance of overstraining and overdoing. Excess emotional stress can greatly add to the seriousness of overexertion. The ability to recuperate after strenuous exercise is a good guide at any age to the amount and extent of exercise to participate in at one time. Recuperation should be reasonably prompt. However, if the breathing and heart rate are still greatly accelerated 10 minutes after exercise, and if there is marked fatigue or weakness after a few hours' rest or a sense of definite fatigue the day following, the exercise likely has been too severe or prolonged.

As a last precaution following strenuous exercise, an adequate cooling-off period should follow the tapering-off process. From 3 to 6 minutes should elapse between tapering off and entering the shower. Otherwise, the warm water will prevent loss of heat from the body, and it will continue to perspire. Heavy perspiration following a shower and dressing may cause chilling, with the same results as chilling after being drenched by a cold rain.

Rest and sleep

Sufficient rest and sleep are necessary to maintenance of good physical, mental, and emotional health. Although it is thought that the average person needs 8 to 9 hours of sleep each night, the amount varies with the individual and with age. Growing children require more sleep than adults. Some people require more sleep than others who have similar activity levels. Regularity in rest and sleep is very important. If one is not getting sufficient rest and sleep, participation in strenuous and vigorous physical activities can be more harmful than helpful. It is recommended that each individual learn to judge the amount of sleep and rest necessary to maintain physical and mental alertness and a feeling of well-being.

Diet and nutrition

A balanced diet is necessary for maintenance of good nutrition. Nutrition is basic to physical, mental, and emotional health. Those who participate in physical activity usually require more food than those who lead sedentary lives. Participation in physical activities requires energy, and food is the main source of energy in the body.

It is usually best not to eat heavy meals before strenuous physical activity, especially if emotional stress is present as in a competitive activity. It is difficult for the body to digest and assimilate food under such circumstances.

Finally, together with exercise, diet is a controlling factor in body weight. Exercise is sometimes helpful in weight reduction; however, the number of calories eliminated through exercise is minimal when compared with the number of calories that can be eliminated through a sensible diet. If the overweight person uses exercise to reduce and then refrains from overeating, the exercise can be helpful.

Clothing and cleanliness

Proper clothing is important when participating in sports. It is essential to change from street clothes to gymnasium clothing when participating in vigorous activities that will cause perspiration and body odor. Even sports and gymnasium clothing can become so soiled by dirt and perspiration that they become objectionable to others. Therefore, it is important to have sufficient sports and gymnasium clothing and to keep it as clean as possible. It is particularly important that shoes and socks be properly selected. Gymnasium or other sports shoes should fit properly to safeguard the feet. Blisters form easily if shoes or socks do not fit properly. Clothing that fits too tightly and that may hinder performance should be avoided.

A shower should be taken after participation in vigorous physical activity for both hygienic and social reasons. Showers not only cleanse the skin but also reduce chances of infection. Some people like a warm shower followed by a short, cold shower; others prefer that water temperature be tapered from warm to comfortably cool. Hot showers are not recommended.

Injuries and illness

People often ask whether they should participate in physical activities during or following periods of mild illness such as colds, flu, and other infectious diseases. In most cases it is best to refrain from participation in physical activities during any illness caused by infection.

Care should be given to even slight injuries received while participating in physical activities. Small scratches and cuts should be treated as soon as possible. Any cut or scratch that seems to have become infected should have the attention of a physician immediately. Various infections can be contracted in gymnasiums and shower rooms. Participants should be careful in taking showers and drying in the dressing rooms to avoid "athlete's foot." Sprains and bruises of any seriousness should be given immediate first aid and then seen by a physician.

Safety

Sports and physical activities should be as safe as possible. Participants should take every precaution to prevent injury to themselves and to others. Equipment and rules and regulations of games and sports generally are designed to protect players as much as possible. Some sports (for example, football) and activities require special protective equipment, and playing them without protective equipment risks serious injury.

The beginner in certain sports should recognize that some advanced activities may be dangerous to attempt. For example, a beginner attempting advanced tumbling stunts would be in danger of injury because of a lack of skill. Everyone should give attention to safety, since a high percentage of the deaths and injuries from accidents can be prevented.

2

Aerobic Dance

Completion of this chapter should enable the reader to:

■ Recognize the benefits associated with regular participation in aerobic dance
■ Organize and design a safe and effective aerobic dance program, including the sequencing of activities
■ Select appropriate music, movement patterns, and exercises for an aerobic dance program

HISTORY

Aerobic dance, defined as continuous and rhythmic movement to music, was introduced by Jackie Sorenson in 1969. The combination of vigorous dance steps and exercises performed to popular music in a group setting soon became one of the fastest growing leisure activities in the United States. Today more than 20 million exercise enthusiasts participate in this multimillion dollar industry. Virtually every community offers some form of aerobic dance class. Even home exercisers can participate in this physically demanding activity by following popular aerobic dance leaders on television programs and videotapes.

Aerobic dance has evolved from rigidly choreographed dance routines intended for female participants to free-style routines that incorporate random combinations of dance, sport, and exercise movements designed to attract men and women. To further challenge enthusiasts, creative instructors have developed innovative aerobic dance programs that include water aerobics, bench stepping, sports conditioning, and interval and circuit training.

Professional aerobic dance associations are helping meet the demand for qualified instructors. Organizations such as the International Dance Exercise Association (IDEA) and the Aerobic and Fitness Association of America (AFAA) provide their members with services that include subscriptions to exercise journals, access to aerobic conventions and workshops, and opportunities to become certified as an aerobic dance instructor.

BENEFITS OF AEROBIC DANCE

Aerobic dance is an excellent activity for developing overall physical fitness. Balancing the health-related components of fitness, aerobic dance can improve a participant's flexibility, strength, cardiovascular fitness, and body composition. The rhythmic movements performed to music also help develop coordination and balance. In addition, exercising in a group setting provides opportunities for social interactions not afforded by many other aerobic activities (Fig. 2-1).

FACILITY

The ideal aerobic dance setting includes:

1. Good ventilation with a temperature of 60° to 70° F.
2. A floor that will absorb shock while controlling lateral motions of the foot and providing adequate traction. A hardwood sprung floor is an ideal aerobic dance surface.
3. Space for each participant to move comfortably. A good guide is enough space for each participant, with arms outspread, to take two large steps in any direction without touching anyone.
4. Acoustics that will allow the instructor's voice to be heard over the music.
5. For large groups, a raised platform for the instructor.
6. Mirrors to help participants observe and correct their posture and exercise positions.

Fig. 2-1. The aerobics dance class.

EQUIPMENT

Equipment needs vary according to the type of facility and the size of the class. All programs require a sound system and a collection of audio tapes or records. A wireless microphone for the instructor may be necessary if teaching in a large space. In addition, mats and certain strength training equipment such as light hand weights and rubber bands are useful during the floor exercise segment of the class.

APPAREL AND SHOES

Participants should wear lightweight, well-ventilated clothing. Cotton fabrics are recommended because they absorb moisture while allowing air to circulate through the material. Many of the fabrics used for aerobic dance apparel are made of cotton blends. Knee-length tights or fitness shorts worn with a leotard or T-shirt provide the greatest comfort and mobility. Wearing cotton socks will help absorb perspiration and reduce the likelihood of blisters. Participants should be encouraged to layer their clothing in cool facilities and remove outer garments (such as a warm up suit) as the body temperature rises with increased levels of activity.

Shoes are perhaps the most important item worn by the aerobic dancer. Since certain aerobic dance steps can generate vertical forces on the feet of up to four times ones body weight, participants need to select a shoe designed to dissipate these impacts. A well-constructed aerobic dance shoe has an adequately cushioned sole, especially under the ball of the foot, to help absorb the shock of forefoot movements characteristic of most aerobic dance steps. Proper support and stability are particularly important for lateral movements. The traction provided by the shoe should match the surface on which activities are being performed. For example, less traction is needed on a carpeted surface while greater traction is necessary on a hardwood floor. Finally, a shoe should be selected for its durability, flexibility, and lightweight characteristics.

FUNDAMENTAL SKILLS AND TECHNIQUES
Components of an aerobic dance class

A well-designed aerobic dance class consists of:
1. Warm-up and prestretch (10 minutes)
2. Aerobic activity (20 to 30 minutes)
3. Cool-down (2 to 5 minutes)
4. Strength work (5 to 10 minutes)
5. Final stretch (5 to 10 minutes)

Warm-up and prestretch

The purpose of the warm-up is to increase blood flow to the muscles, increase the rate of oxygen exchange between blood and muscles, increase the speed and force of muscle contraction, increase muscle elasticity as well as the flexibility of tendons and ligaments, and reduce the risk of cardiac abnormalities. Using a moderate tempo, movements during the warm-up should include rhythmic, full range-of-motion exercises designed to prepare the body for movements used during the aerobic routines. The initial warm-up should concentrate on large movements for the shoulders, arms, and legs. A warm-up routine might consist of shoulder rolls, arm circles, marches, step-touches, and toe and heel raises. After the muscles have been warmed, static stretching exercises should be performed to increase joint range of motion. Stretching positions should be held for at least 10 seconds, paying special attention to muscles of the shoulders, chest, hips, low back, thighs, calves and feet.

Aerobic activity

The purpose of the aerobic dance segment is to improve cardiovascular endurance. The physiological benefits of aerobic activity include increased heart and lung efficiency and decreased body fat. Aerobic benefits are achieved by using prolonged and continuous movement of the large muscles. Ideally, the aerobic segment of class will last 20 to 30 minutes performed at an intensity of 60% to 75% of the heart rate reserve.

To determine appropriate exercise intensity, participants need to determine their resting heart rates (RHR) and then calculate their target heart rate zones. Upon waking in the morning, the RHR can be determined by lightly placing the middle and index finger on either the carotid artery (at the neck) or the radial artery (on the thumb side of the wrist) and counting the number of beats occurring in 60 seconds. The target heart rate zone is then calculated by completing Karvonen's formula twice, once to establish the 60% value and again to establish the 75% value. The target heart rate zone lies between these two values. The formulas are:

220 − age − RHR × .6 (training percentage) + RHR ÷ 6
(to provide a 10 second heart rate) = 60% value

220 − age − RHR × .75 + RHR ÷ 6 = 75% value

For example, the target heart rate zone for a 40-year-old person with a resting heart rate of 72 beats per minute would be 23-26.

$$[(220 - 40 - 72) \times .60 + 72] \div 6 = 22.8$$
$$[(220 - 40 - 72) \times .75 + 72] \div 6 = 25.5$$

Exercise heart rate is taken for 10 seconds at the end of the aerobic segment (heart rate should be taken more frequently than this for beginners) and should be within the target zone (Fig. 2-2). Participants above the target heart rate can reduce the intensity of exercise by keeping the feet closer to the floor, by decreasing the amount of arm movement or by minimizing the extent of traveling. Conversely, exercise intensity can be increased by lifting the feet higher off the floor, by increasing the amount of arm motion, or by adding directional movement.

The aerobic segment consists of movement patterns choreographed to music. Movement patterns can be extremely varied ranging from calisthenic exercises such

Fig. 2-2. Taking the exercise heart rate.

as jumping jacks to dance movements such as leaps and lunges. Instructors can enhance their movement repertoire by using steps common to other dance forms including jazz, modern, folk, and ballet, or by borrowing movement patterns used in sports and games (such as basketball dribbling).

Common basic steps used in aerobic dance include jogs, marches, hops, jumps, knee lifts, kicks, twists, step touches, jumping jacks, and lunges. These steps can be varied by changing the rhythm (half time, double time), the direction of movement (forward, backward, sideways, diagonally, or in circles) and by adding arm positions to accompany the leg movements (Figs. 2-3 and 2-4).

Steps can be combined into movement patterns in several ways. Routines can be rigidly choreographed repeating the same movements each time the routine is performed. Choreographed routines help participants become secure with a movement sequence, allowing them to concentrate on the intensity of exercise and correct exercise positions. However, choreographed routines require a great deal of preparation by the instructor and can take extra class time to teach. Many instructors prefer to use a freestyle approach to combine movement patterns with music. Rather than using routines, instructors using the freestyle technique select movements in a random fashion, building combinations of step patterns as the music progresses. When skillfully led, participants enjoy the movement variety associated with the freestyle method. If, however, the step patterns are too complex for the group, participants may be unable to maintain appropriate exercise intensity as they struggle with unexpected and unfamiliar movements.

Foot pattern: 8 knee lifts in place.

Foot pattern with arms: 4 knee lifts in place while pressing the arms overhead, 4 knee lifts in place while pressing the arms down to the feet.

Fig. 2-3. Leg kick.

Fig. 2-4. Knee lift.

Foot pattern with arms and traveling: 4 knee lifts moving forward while pressing the arms overhead, 4 knee lifts moving backwards while pressing the arms down to the feet.

The first aerobic dance routine following the warm-up should be performed at a moderate pace to give the cardiovascular system ample time to adjust to the increasing demands of exercise. As the class progresses through the aerobic segment, the intensity and music tempo should be increased. Participants should be instructed to adjust the intensity of their movements to correspond with their level of cardiovascular fitness.

Cool-down

The purpose of the cool-down is to lower the heart rate gradually toward normal, prevent excessive pooling of blood in the lower extremities, and promote removal of metabolic waste products from the muscles. Slow but continued rhythmic contraction of the leg muscles is important to help return the blood from the lower extremities to the heart. A cool-down of 2 to 5 minutes can consist of walking around the room while gently swinging the arms or a slow aerobic dance routine.

It is wise to take a recovery heart rate at the end of the cool-down. A decrease in recovery heart rate over time is a measure of improved cardiovascular fitness. For comparative purposes, the recovery heart rate must be taken the same number of minutes following the end of the aerobic segment. A record sheet for recording exercise and recovery heart rates is useful for observing the progress of participants.

Strength exercises

Muscular strength is important for preventing injuries by helping the participant maintain proper alignment and body mechanics. It is therefore important to strengthen the muscles that help maintain good posture and aid in the proper execution of aerobic dance routines and floor exercises. Weak upper back muscles (upper trapezius and rhomboids) contribute to rounded shoulders while weak abdominals can lead to a swayback posture. Aggravated by vigorous movements on the feet, these anatomical deviations can result in neck, shoulder, and low back pain. Therefore it is prudent to strengthen the upper back muscles and abdominals in each class session. Rowing exercises and prone shoulder raises can be used to strengthen the upper back while curl-ups, diagonal curls, reverse curls, and pelvic tilts will help strengthen the abdominals.

It is also important to strengthen muscles of the shins (tibialis anterior). The most common injury reported by aerobic dancers is shin splints. While there are many causes for shin pain, a typical problem results from a muscle imbalance between the strong calf muscles (gas-trocnemius) that contract vigorously for a prolonged period of time during the aerobic dance segment and the weak shin muscles which are used less frequently during class. Various forms of toe tapping, walking on the heels, and ankle flexion with light weights or rubber bands can help to strengthen tibialis anterior muscles.

If time allows, instructors can include strength exercises for other parts of the body. These include side leg lifts for the hip abductors and adductors, leg curls and lifts for the hamstrings and gluteals, knee extensions for the quadriceps, arm curls for the biceps, elbow extensions for the triceps, lateral pull downs for latissimus dorsi, and lateral raises for the deltoids. Muscular strength is achieved by overloading the muscle with adequate resistance so that the student can complete 12 to 15 repetitions of an exercise. Surgical tubing, elastic bands, or light hand and ankle weights can provide appropriate resistance. In addition, holding a contraction for 5 seconds at different points in the movement pattern can provide added resistance to the muscles. To continue strength gains, the resistance for each exercise should be increased when participants can comfortably complete three sets of 12 to 15 repetitions.

To encourage controlled movements during the strength exercises, music tempos should be moderately paced and participants should be instructed to adjust the tempo (half time or double time) and on the number of repetitions required to meet their personal levels of strength. To encourage proper exercise technique, the instructor should move around the room providing appropriate exercise cues while observing and critiquing performance.

Final stretch

The purpose of the final stretch is to improve overall flexibility, which helps maintain good posture and proper body mechanics throughout the day. Stretching after a vigorous exercise session is often easier than stretching before since the joints are well lubricated and the temperature of the muscles is increased following the aerobic workout. It is best to perform these stretches on the floor allowing participants an opportunity to relax and concentrate on each stretch. The final stretch is most effective when performed to slow background music that does not have a strong beat. Flexibility exercises, held for 10 to 30 seconds, should include stretches for muscles of the arms, shoulders, chest, back, hips, thighs, and calves (Figs. 2-5 and 2-6).

Low, moderate, and high impacts

In the past, most aerobic dance routines consisted of high impact movements including variations of jogs, hops, and jumps. High impact aerobics (HIA), characterized by movements that require both feet to leave the

Fig. 2-5. Leg stretch.

Fig. 2-6. Stretching.

floor frequently, can produce vertical forces of up to four times the weight of the body. Researchers reporting on injuries suffered by aerobic dancers found a fairly high incidence of pain to the shins, feet, knees, and lower back. Although the injuries were seldom serious enough to require medical attention, concern that high impact movements were in part responsible for these aches and pains led to the development of a new form of aerobic dance called Low Impact Aerobics (LIA). LIA, characterized by movements that use a wide base of support while keeping one foot on the floor at all times, have not been without their share of unique problems and injuries.

In an attempt to stay close to the floor during LIA, the use of a wide base of support and the extreme lowering and raising of the center of gravity produces a great deal of prolonged and often extreme knee flexion. This can result in a number of knee injuries for individuals already suffering from structural knee problems. In addition, the larger arm movements used to maintain exercise intensity during LIA have resulted in shoulder injuries among participants using uncontrolled arm flinging motions.

Generally, LIA is not recommended for anyone who complains of knee discomfort during prolonged knee flexion or for well-conditioned individuals who are unable to achieve appropriate intensity levels using low impact movements. On the other hand, HIA are generally not recommended for individuals who are deconditioned, especially if they are obese, for women in the latter stages of pregnancy, for anyone who is susceptible to injuries related to impact shock such as shin splints, or for individuals who are uncomfortable with high impact steps, such as people suffering from incontinence. To accommodate individual differences in each class, many programs use a combination of high and low impact steps throughout the aerobic routines. This results in a decrease in the number of high impact steps being performed.

Aerobic dance instructors are also beginning to use a new technique which combines the best elements of HIA and LIA. It is called moderate impact aerobics (MIA). MIA movements require that one foot remain on the floor most of the time as in LIA, although the base of support is narrower and the center of gravity is lifted up and down as in HIA. MIA steps are therefore characterized by a springlike motion. All MIA movements should begin by lifting the body upward, rising onto the balls of the feet. Each step should be completed by gently pressing the heels against the floor. The advantages of MIA include less prolonged and extreme knee flexion often associated with LIA and smaller vertical impacts found in many HIA movements.

Aerobic training modes

Traditionally, the aerobic segment of an aerobic dance class consisted of continuous exercise. Today, interval and circuit training have become common.

Aerobic interval training involves high intensity work bouts (near maximal heart rate) followed by active rest or recovery periods of an equal length of time. Exercise and rest intervals vary from 3 to 5 minutes in length and are repeated four to six times during the aerobic segment of class. Since interval training requires high intensity exercise during the work bouts, high impact movements such as jumps and runs are commonly choreographed to fast-paced music. During the active rest, moderately paced movements such as walks and step touches are performed. Some programs incorporate light weights or rubber bands to develop upper body strength during the active rest. Due to the fast-paced, high-intensity nature of interval training, this activity is recommended only for the more advanced aerobic dancer. Interval training is associated with greater physical pain than experienced in continuous forms of training because more metabolic waste products are produced and accumulated in the muscles during the near maximal efforts of the activity.

Circuit training is another popular technique used in aerobic dance programs. A circuit consists of a specified number of exercise stations used to promote all-around physical fitness. The emphasis is on development of muscular strength and endurance, cardiovascular endurance, flexibility, and sometimes coordination and balance. Most circuits have between 10 to 20 stations. Each area is posted with a sign indicating the task to be completed. Participants are instructed to remain at a station for a given number of seconds, moving to the next station on command. The circuit moves in a clockwise or counterclockwise direction and can be repeated two to three times. Time spent at each station can vary from 30 to 60 seconds. A typical aerobic dance circuit includes strength exercises with light weights or rubber bands, aerobic exercise such as knee lifts, jumping jacks, and lunges, and agility and coordination stations such as running drills and rope jumping. Instructors should encourage participants to work as hard as possible at each station.

TEACHING CONSIDERATIONS
Patterns of class organization

An aerobic dance class should be arranged so that everyone can hear the instructor's verbal cues and see the demonstrations. Above all, it is important that the instructor be able to observe all class participants. In a typical aerobic dance class, the instructor stands at the front of the room with the participants facing forward. The disadvantage of this system is that the advanced participants usually stand at the front of the room while the less skilled stay at the back. The instructor cannot clearly observe those who are in greatest need of feedback. To resolve this problem, the instructor can periodically move from the front of the room to the back or the sides, asking participants to turn and face the instructor. A system of rotation is another effective way of observing class participants. At the end of each song the teacher instructs the participants to rotate. The front line moves to the back of the room while every other line moves forward one row. Other patterns of class organization include circle formations (where the instructor stands at the center) and movement patterns that travel from one end of the floor to the other.

Cuing

Cuing is a very important part of teaching aerobic dance. Participants depend on the instructor's verbal and nonverbal cues for every step they take. Each verbal cue should be brief and called on the preceding measure, giving ample time to move smoothly from one step to the next. Instructors can use a combination of types of cuing including footwork cuing (indicates whether to move the right or left foot), directional cuing (refers to the direction of movement such as forward, backward, left or right), rhythmic cuing (indicates the correct rhythm of the routine such as slow or quick), numerical cuing (refers to counting the rhythm such as "one, two, three and four"), and step cuing (indicates the name of the step such as "step touch"). Initially, participants will be most dependent on footwork, directional, and numerical cuing. Once they become somewhat skilled and learn the names of each step or movement pattern, the participants will rely more on step cues and pay most attention to nonverbal cues such as hand signals indicating direction.

When leading aerobic dance routines, the instructor should face the class using mirroring techniques (the instructor moves to the left when the class moves to the right). To avoid potential collisons between students, instructors should begin lateral movements to the same side each time. Most instructors prefer moving first to the right followed by movements to the left.

Music

Music provides the timing and style for exercise movements. In addition, it adds fun, variety, and excitement to an aerobic dance class. The tempo, or rate of speed, at which music is played determines the progression and intensity of exercise. Aerobic dance instructors determine the tempo of the music by counting the beats per minute (bpm). Over the years, the following guidelines have been adopted by instructors for selecting appropriate music tempo for aerobic dance:

Warm-up, prestretch and cool-down: 100 to 120 bpm

Floor exercise: 110 to 130 bpm
Aerobic activity: 130 to 144 bpm (LIA)
144 to 160 bpm (HIA)
Final stretch: under 100 bpm

Instructors must be cautious when using fast music tempos (more than 160 bpm). To avoid uncontrolled movements, participants should be encouraged to use the arms through a small range of motion and take short steps. Since beginners are not proficient enough to perform fast movements under control, they should not be expected to dance to fast-paced music. When using music with fast tempos, instructors should be aware that participants with long arms and legs need more time than participants with short limbs to cover the same spatial area. For example, people with short arms can raise them above their heads more quickly than people with long arms. Tall participants should therefore be encouraged to bend their arms in order to keep in time with fast music. The most efficient way to use music in class is to record a 40 to 60 minute audiotape which includes music for the warm-up, prestretch, the aerobic segment, the cool-down, the floor exercises, and the final stretch. However, instructors reproducing and playing music in an aerobic dance class should be familiar with the copyright laws. The Copyright Act of 1976 states that a person wishing to play copyrighted music for a "public performance" must obtain permission from the copyright owner. Using music during an aerobic dance class constitutes a public performance. Since it would be time consuming to obtain permission from the copyright owner of each piece of music used in a class, instructors can save valuable time by joining performing rights societies including ASCAP and BMI. These societies have been assigned the nondramatic rights of copyright owners and grant their members permission to play the music of numerous artists. Under the "fair use" doctrine, instructors teaching in the public schools or at institutions of higher education may be exempt from having to obtain copyright permission. It is wise, however, for instructors to consult with an attorney to determine if their use of music qualifies as "fair use."

Developing music tapes can be one of the most time consuming tasks for the aerobic dance instructor. To save valuable time and to stay current with popular music selections, instructors can subscribe to a number of music services that provide complete aerobic dance tapes classes (see the Resource Section of this chapter).

SAFETY CONCERNS

To ensure the safety of class participants, instructors should comply with the following guidelines:

1. Screen participants for common anatomical problems such as kyphosis, lordosis, and excess pronation of the feet. Also evaluate them for tight and

weak muscles. Early detection and correction of such problems can reduce the risk of aerobic dance injuries.

2. Encourage appropriate body alignment throughout the class period. Proper posture includes: head up, shoulders back, chest up, buttocks tucked under the hips, and knees relaxed.

3. Avoid or minimize the use of the following potentially harmful exercise positions: (1) sustained and unsupported forward flexion in a standing position, (2) unsupported forward flexion in a standing position with rotation, (3) trunk rotation against a fixed axis, (4) neck hyperextension, (5) fast head circles, (6) the yoga plough, (7) deep knee bends, (8) hurdler stretch, (9) hyperextension of the elbows and knees, (10) straight leg sit-ups, (11) double leg raises, and (12) side leg lifts supported on the knees and hands or elbows.

4. Avoid ballistic stretching. Static stretching is effective and tends to be safer than bobbing or bouncing techniques.

5. Insist that participants wear shoes during the aerobic segment of class.

6. Be aware of the placement of class members to avoid collisions during rapid movements across the floor.

7. Encourage participants to control the placement of their arms, avoiding any flinging motions. Shoulder injuries are becoming increasingly common in aerobic dance.

8. Avoid having the participants keep the arms at or above shoulder level for a prolonged period of time. This increases blood pressure, places stress on the tendons and muscles of the shoulder, and increases heart rate in a manner not related to increased cardiovascular conditioning.

9. Avoid prolonged and excessive deep knee flexion. Make sure the knees of participants remain over the first and second toes.

10. Be cautious of lateral movements on carpeted surfaces. The added friction associated with carpet can result in ankle inversion sprains.

11. Avoid dancing on concrete surfaces.

12. Reduce the risk of common musculoskeletal injuries during aerobic activity by progressing slowly and by not exceeding intensity levels of 75% heart rate reserve, exercise durations of 30 minutes and exercise frequencies of 4 days per week on alternate days.

13. Avoid too many consecutive movements on one foot such as dozens of hops.

14. Avoid rapid changes of direction.

15. Do not require participants to stay on the balls of the feet for extended periods of time. The lowering of the heels to the floor provides additional shock absorption for the feet.

16. Face the class as often as possible to effectively observe everyone's performance.

17. Do not allow the participants to hold their breath while performing strength exercises. Encourage them to exhale on exertion.

18. Control the movement of light hand and ankle weights at all times.

19. Be aware of exercise restrictions and modifications for special populations. For example, people with high blood pressure should not perform isometric contractions and should avoid keeping the arms above shoulder level for extended periods of time.

GLOSSARY

aerobic dance Continuous and rhythmic movement to music intended to improve cardiovascular fitness.

choreographed routines Formally arranged step patterns taught in the same sequence each time the routine is performed to the same music.

circuit training A form of exercising that promotes all around physical fitness by incorporating various stations involving strength, aerobic, and agility activities.

continuous training A form of aerobic training that requires the continuous performance of moderate to vigorous movement over a specified period of time.

cuing Verbal and nonverbal techniques used to inform aerobic dance participants of upcoming movements.

duration of exercise The total time of each exercise session.

flexibility The range of motion possible at a joint.

freestyle routines Teaching aerobic dance movements in a random fashion, building combinations of step patterns as the music progresses.

frequency of exercise The total number of exercise sessions per week.

HIA (High Impact Aerobics) An aerobic dance style characterized by movement that frequently requires both feet to leave the floor simultaneously.

intensity of exercise A form of aerobic and anaerobic training that involves performing a series of high intensity work bouts alternating with active rest periods.

LIA (Low Impact Aerobics) An aerobic dance style that minimizes the amount of vertical impacts by keeping one foot on the floor at all times while covering a larger spatial area with the feet and arms.

MIA (Moderate Impact Aerobics) An aerobic dance style requiring that one foot remain on the floor most of the time while lifting the body high onto the balls of the feet and then gently pressing the heels to the floor.

muscular strength Maximum force exerted by a muscle or muscle group against resistance.

target heart rate zone The number of heart beats per specified period of time necessary to achieve aerobic benefits while minimizing possible musculoskeletal injury.

tempo Rate of speed music is played; determined by counting the number of beats per minute (bpm).

SUGGESTED READINGS

Collins D, Hodges P, and Kelly J: Practical aerobic conditioning, Bloomingdale, Ind, 1987, Tichenor Publishing.

Cooper P, (editor): Aerobic and Fitness Association of America: Aerobic theory and practice, Costa Mesa, Calif, 1988, HDL Publishing.

Copeland C: Moves: The foolproof formula for choreography, Los Angeles, 1987, CompuThink, Inc.

Jacobson PC: Aerobic dance, Glenview, Ill, 1989, Scott, Foresman & Co. Contains exercise programs for the novice, occasional participant, or highly conditioned performer and routines of low-, medium- and high-intensity levels. Instructions for assessing progress are also included.

Kan E and Kraines M: Keep moving! it's aerobic dance, Palo Alto, Calif, 1987, Mayfield Publishing Co.

Kravitz L: Anybody's guide to total fitness, Dubuque, Iowa, 1986, Kendall/Hunt Publishing Co.

Mazzeo KS and Kisselle JK: Aerobic dance: a way to fitness, ed. 2, Englewood, Colo, 1987, Morton Publishing Co.

Stoll SK and Beller MB: Complete manual of aerobic instruction, Englewood Cliffs, NJ, 1989, Prentice Hall.

VanGelder N, (editor): Aerobic dance-exercise instructor manual, San Diego, 1987, International Dance Exercise Association Foundation.

RESOURCES
Aerobic dance associations

Aerobic and Fitness Association of America (AFAA), 15250 Ventura Boulevard, Suite 310, Sherman Oaks, CA 91403.

International Dance Exercise Association (IDEA), 6190 Cornerstone East, Suite 204, San Diego, CA 92121.

Reebok Professional Instructor Alliance, (a free service to aerobic dance instructors), 100 Technology Center Drive, Stoughton, MA 02072.

Films and videotapes

Brick L: *How to teach aerobics*. Brick Bodies 212 W. Padonia Rd, Titonium MD, 21093

Fitness currents: video magazine for the fitness professionals. Current Video Publishing, Inc., 9540 E Jewell, Suite D, Denver, CO, 80231

Kooperman S: *Chicago jazz'd funk: Instructor Training Video*, Sara's City Workout 1876 N. Sheffield, Chicago, IL, 60614

Ottis R: *Sportsmoves: instructor video*. Ottis Training Organization, P.O. Box 402203, Austin, TX, 78704

Twombly G: *Creative instructors aerobics*, 2314 Naudian Street, Philadelphia, PA 19146

Music services

The Aerobic Beat, 7985 Santa Monica Blvd., Suite 109, Los Angeles, CA 90046

David Shelton Productions, P.O. Box 310, Mendon, UT 84325

Fitnet, 1131 Harbor Bay Parkway, Suite 121, Alemeda, CA 94501

Mix Music International Inc., P.O. Box 2452, Kankakee, IL 60901

Muscle Mixes, 2934 Northwood Blvd., Orlando, FL 32803

3

Archery

Completion of this chapter should enable the reader to:

- Recognize and select appropriate archery equipment
- Understand rules and scoring procedures
- Describe correct techniques for stringing the bow, drawing, anchoring, aiming, and shooting
- Identify and use proper safety procedures
- Instruct a group of students in the fundamentals of archery
- Recognize and use archery terms correctly

HISTORY

The bow and arrow is one of the oldest mechanical weapons and remains the weapon of many aboriginal races and tribes in certain parts of the world. The bow and arrow was first used by primitive peoples for hunting. It was the chief weapon of the American Indians, both for hunting and for war. It was used as a weapon of war by the Egyptians in overthrowing Persia and in many other successful wars.

With the discovery of powder and the use of firearms in comparatively recent times, the bow and arrow has been retired to the realm of sport. In this capacity it has sporadically interested groups in various parts of the civilized world, particularly in England and the United States, but archery has not flourished to the same extent as many other sports.

The earliest contest in archery, "The Ancient Scorton Arrow," was held in England in 1673, created by the Ancient Scorton Arrow Society. This tournament is still in existence.

In the United States the first archery club, the United Bowmen of Philadelphia, was organized in 1828. The first tournament was held in Chicago in 1879, and tournaments sponsored by this club are still being held.

The formation of the Federation Internationale de Tir a l'Arc (FITA) in 1931 gave a great boost to target archery.

Archery, which had been a demonstration sport in the 1900 and 1904 Olympics, was given full status in 1908 but then dropped after the 1920 Games. Through the efforts of the FITA, archery was reinstated as a gold medal sport in the 1972 Olympic Games. Since this time the United States has done extremely well in this competition, with the men winning the gold medal in every Olympics since 1972 except in 1980, when the United States boycotted the Moscow Games (gold won by Tomi Poikolainen). John Williams started the string by winning gold in 1972, Darrell Pace won in 1976 and in 1984, and Jay Barrs placed first in 1988. The United States women archers dominated the 1972 (gold to Doreen Wilbur) and 1976 (gold to Luann Ryon) Olympics but since the boycott of the 1980 Moscow Olympics (won by Keto Losaberidze of the USSR) the dominance has shifted to the South Korean women. They picked up the gold in 1984 (Hyang-Soon Seo) and in 1988 (Kim Soo Hyung).

In 1986 the FITA introduced a new scoring system to be used in the Olympics called the Grand FITA round in an attempt to make competition more exciting. The same total number of arrows (288) are shot as in the previously used Double FITA round. However, in the new system each archer shoots 72 arrows on the first and second day as before, but then an elimination process begins with previous scores being thrown out after every 36 arrows. On the third morning, the leading 24 archers shoot 36 arrows to determine the best 18 to shoot 36 arrows that afternoon. The final 12 archers shoot 36 arrows on the fourth morning to bring the field to six.

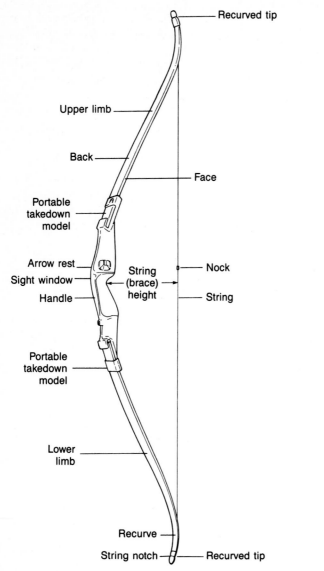

Recurved tip

Upper limb

Back

Face

Portable takedown model

Arrow rest

Sight window

Handle

String (brace) height

Nock

String

Portable takedown model

Lower limb

Recurve

String notch

Recurved tip

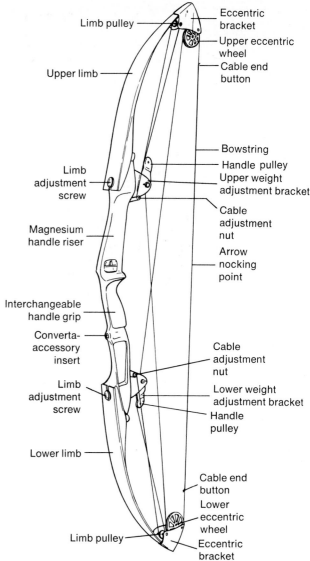

Limb pulley

Eccentric bracket

Upper eccentric wheel

Cable end button

Upper limb

Bowstring

Handle pulley

Upper weight adjustment bracket

Limb adjustment screw

Cable adjustment nut

Magnesium handle riser

Arrow nocking point

Interchangeable handle grip

Converta-accessory insert

Cable adjustment nut

Limb adjustment screw

Lower weight adjustment bracket

Handle pulley

Lower limb

Cable end button

Lower eccentric wheel

Limb pulley

Eccentric bracket

Fig. 3-2. Compound bow.

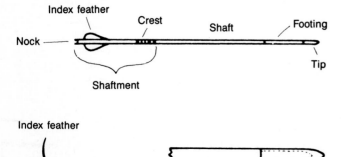

Index feather

Crest

Shaft

Footing

Nock

Tip

Shaftment

Index feather

Hen feathers

Tip

Fig. 3-1. Parts of the bow and arrow.

These six, starting from scratch, shoot 36 arrows on the fourth afternoon to determine the Olympic champion.

In 1971 the College Division of the National Archery Association was founded. It serves to coordinate and promote collegiate archery throughout the United States.

Along with the revival of interest in all individual sports, archery is being enjoyed by an increasing number of men, women, and children.

Today, archery continues to hold interest for several reasons: (1) the evolution of a new method of shooting, which is easier to learn and more accurate than the old, (2) development of more efficient bows and arrows, and (3) the fascination many people find in the activities possible to the archer, ranging from target shooting, clout, roving, field shooting, and novelty shoots to the hunting of small and large game.

EQUIPMENT
The bow

The two types of bows most commonly used by the beginner are the recurved bow (Fig. 3-1) and the relatively recently developed compound bow (Fig. 3-2). The compound bow's pulley system and its sophisticated weighting, balancing, and sighting devices have completely revolutionized the sport of archery. Of course, these advances increase the financial cost of the sport substantially, so the recurved bow is still popular, especially among beginners. A bow should be selected that can be pulled back full draw and held steady while aiming. This is determined by the weight of the bow—that is, the number of pounds of pull it takes to pull the arrow to its full length. Proper bow weight varies with age, sex, and strength of the archer. General recommendations for bow weights are: teen-age girls–20 to 25 lb; teen-age boys–20 to 30 lb; women–20 to 30 lb; men–25 to 40 lb.

The proper length of the bow is related to the length of the draw.

Draw length (in.)	Recommended bow length (in.)
24 or less	60 to 64
25 to 26	65 to 66
27 to 28	67 to 68
29 or more	69 to 70

The string consists of varied numbers of Dacron threads coated with beeswax, with loops at both ends. This type of bowstring is the most economical and re-quires least maintenance. New strings which increase the velocity of the arrow without increasing the bow weight are called fast strings and are made of Kevlar and other materials.

Points to look for in selecting a bow include:
1. The drawn bow bends evenly from the handle to the tips.
2. The upper and lower arms bend similarly.
3. When the bow is strung, the string divides it in half.
4. The cut of the bow follows the grain of the wood.
5. It feels comfortable in the hand.
6. It returns to its original shape after it is unstrung.
7. Pins and knots are plugged or there is extra wood around them.
8. Its weight and strength are suitable for the intended purpose.

The arrow

In the selection of arrows the beginning archer should make sure that the arrow is straight and that its length is appropriate for the length of his or her arm. To determine the proper arrow length measure the arm span (Fig. 3-3) and then refer to the following chart.

Arm span (in.)	Arrow length (in.)
57 to 59	22 to 23
60 to 62	23 to 24
63 to 65	24 to 25
66 to 68	25 to 26
69 to 71	26 to 27
72 to 74	27 to 28
75 to 77	28 to 29
Over 77	30 to 32

Fig. 3-3. Selection of arrow length. Measure arm span from fingertip to fingertip and refer to chart.

Another method for approximating correct arrow length is to place one end of an arrow against the sternum and, while keeping the shoulders back, reach straight forward with both arms and use an arrow of such length that it extends 2 to 3 inches past the fingertips.

The proper arrow length is very important. If the shaft is too short, it is possible to overdraw the arrow beyond the arrow rest on the bow, possibly resulting in injury to the archer or to someone else.

Port Oxford cedar is the best wood for arrows and should be purchased unless the cost is prohibitive. If so, birchwood is cheap and sufficiently durable. Aluminum and fiberglass have proved to be quite satisfactory for more advanced shooting.

The quiver is used to hold arrows.

Protective devices

Finger protection (Fig. 3-4) is necessary for all archers. Without it the archer's shots will be inaccurate and painfully executed. There are two types of finger protection: (1) the finger tab, a leather pattern cut to cover index, middle, and ring fingers, and (2) the shooting glove, similar to an ordinary glove without the thumb and little finger.

The armguard protects the forearm of the bow arm from string contact.

The target

Homemade targets and stands are usually considered best and are least expensive.

The tripod stand should consist of three pine boards, 3 inches × 1 inch × 6 feet long. It should incline backward about 10 to 15 degrees from the vertical.

The target butt is approximately 48 inches (1.2 m) in diameter and 4 to 5 inches (11 to 12 cm) thick. It is constructed from rye straw or marsh hay wound tightly in a coil and held firmly together with tarred cord.

The target face is made of heavy reinforced paper. On the face are painted five colored circles. The center is painted gold and is 9.6 inches (24 cm) in diameter. The other circles are 4.8 inches (12 cm) wide and are painted, from the center out, red, blue, black, and white. The target should be hung so that the exact center of the gold circle is 4 feet (1.22 m) from the ground.

RULES (USA)

The three major organizations governing the sport of archery are the National Archery Association (NAA), the

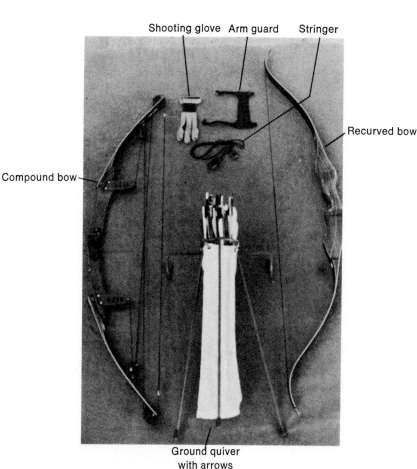

Fig. 3-4. Archery equipment.

National Field Archery Association (NFAA), and the Professional Archers Association (PAA).

NAA tournaments are conducted under International Rules (FITA), which place limitations on the equipment used; for example, compound bows, sight magnification, and release aids are not allowed. The NFAA tournament structure also includes many classifications and categories (such as limited and unlimited) that govern the equipment each archer may add to the bow. The PAA, a separate and complete association was formed when archery was officially inducted into the Olympics.

Crossbow archers compete in competitions organized by the National Crossbow Association; they do not compete officially against recurve or field shooters.

SCORING

Six arrows (an "end") are usually shot at one time. An arrow hitting the wrong target counts as a shot, but its score is forfeited. A loosened arrow may be retrieved if it can be reached by the archer with the aid of the bow without moving the feet. However, it is counted as a shot if it falls beyond the archer's reach.

An arrow that cuts two colors is always given the higher value of the two, even though the greater part of the arrow is in the ring of lower value. In tournament shooting all arrow holes are marked when arrows are drawn from the target. If an arrow rebounds or passes through the target mat, the hole is not marked and the score is recorded as the value of the unmarked hole. Local clubs or schools may elect to count rebounds and pass-throughs as 7 points, providing they are witnessed. When an arrow hits the petticoat, it counts for neither score nor hit. Scores are always listed with the highest score first, awarding 9, 7, 5, 3, or 1 point for the gold, the red, the blue, the black, and the white, respectively. Arrows must remain in the target until all are scored (Fig. 3-5).

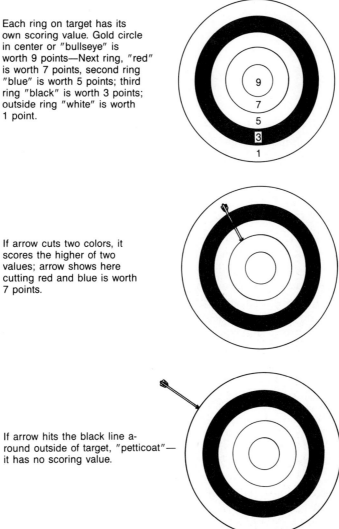

Each ring on target has its own scoring value. Gold circle in center or "bullseye" is worth 9 points—Next ring, "red" is worth 7 points, second ring "blue" is worth 5 points; third ring "black" is worth 3 points; outside ring "white" is worth 1 point.

If arrow cuts two colors, it scores the higher of two values; arrow shows here cutting red and blue is worth 7 points.

If arrow hits the black line around outside of target, "petticoat"— it has no scoring value.

Fig. 3-5. Scoring.

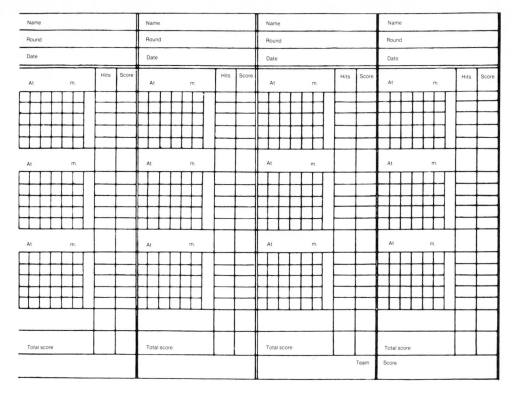

Fig. 3-6. Sample score sheet.

To call back to the archer the location of the arrow, the scorer reads the target like the face of a clock, for example, "6 o'clock red" if the arrow is in that location of the target.

Fig. 3-6 shows a typical score sheet.

SAFETY PRECAUTION WHILE SHOOTING IN GROUPS

Each archer shoots the end or flight of arrows and waits until the last arrow is shot. Following two blasts of a whistle, all archers retrieve their arrows, and no more shooting is permitted until all arrows are retrieved and all archers have returned to the shooting line. When this condition exists, the range supervisor permits shooting with one blast of the whistle. Three or more blasts of the whistle mean that a dangerous situation exists. The archers should stop shooting and remove all arrows from the bows.

TOURNAMENT SHOOTING

In NAA rounds the 5-color, 10-ring face is used, and score is counted from the center out: 10, 9, 8, 7, 6, 5, 4, 3, 2, 1 (Fig. 3-7). Shooting is in one direction only, beginning from the farthest range and finishing from the closest range. Table 3-1 shows the number of arrows, the distance, and size of target for various target rounds.

Arrows are scored in groups of 6. A perfect score for 144 arrows is 1440.

Competition in a tournament usually consists of double rounds. Scores are tabulated after each end of six arrows is shot.

Archers are classified as follows:

Men	18 years old or older
Women	18 years old or older
Intermediate boys	15 to 18 years old
Intermediate girls	15 to 18 years old
Junior boys	12 to 15 years old
Junior girls	12 to 15 years old
Cadet boys	Less than 12 years old
Cadet girls	Less than 12 years old

Field shooting

Because of the vast increase of bow hunting in this country, the National Field Archers' Association of Redlands, Calif., sponsors a type of tournament and practice range called field shooting. Fourteen or 28 targets of different sizes are placed at random over a course with both hills and valleys (Fig. 3-8).

Groups of four archers shoot a "field round" and advance from target to target. Targets are black and white and have a bull's-eye that counts 5 points and an outer ring that has a 3-point value. Four arrows are shot at

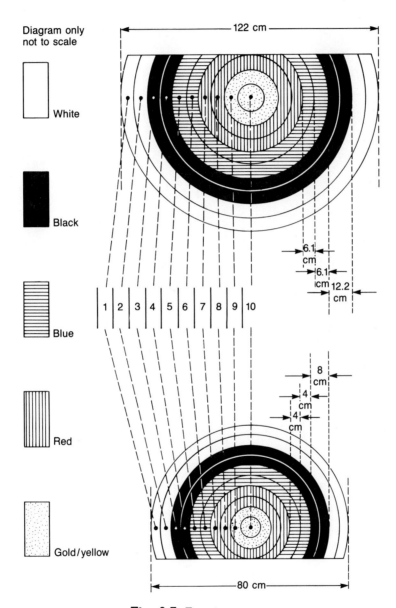

Fig. 3-7. Ten-ring target.

Table 3-1. TARGET ROUNDS

FITA round	Number of arrows	Distance (m)	Face (cm)	FITA round	Number of arrows	Distance (m)	Face (cm)
Men and intermediate	36	90	122	Easton 600 round*	20	60	122
boys	36	70	122		20	50	122
	36	50	80		20	40	122
	36	30	80	Collegiate 600 round*	20	50	122
Women and intermediate	36	70	122		20	40	122
girls	36	60	122		20	30	122
	36	50	80	Indoor FITA round I†	30	18	40
	36	30	80	Indoor FITA round II†	30	25	60
Junior metric round	36	60	122	Miniature round (indoor)‡	60	15	2 ft.
	36	50	122	Range round (indoor)‡	60	§	2 ft.
	36	40	80	Junior scholastic round‡	24	30¶	122
	36	30	80		24	20¶	122
Cadet metric round	36	45	122	Columbia round‡	24	50¶	122
	36	35	122		24	40¶	122
	36	25	80		24	30¶	122
	36	15	80	Junior Columbia round‡	24	40¶	122
900 m. round, men,	30	60	122		24	30¶	122
women, intermediate	30	50	122		24	20¶	122
boys and girls	30	40	122				
Junior 900 round	30	50	122	Clout round‖			
	30	40	122	Men and intermediate	36	165¶	—
	30	30	122	boys			
Cadet 900 round	30	40	122	Women and intermedi-	36	125¶	—
	30	30	122	ate girls			
	30	20	122	Junior and Cadet boys	36	110¶	—
				and girls			

*Four ends of five arrows per end at each distance.

†Arrows are shot in ends of three arrows, and scoring is tallied after each end. A 2½ minute limit is allowed for each end.

‡Not an official NAA round but may be used in school or camp tournaments.

§Sixty arrows from a single distance of 50, 40, 30, or 20 m.

‖The clout target is circular, 12.2 m. (48 feet) in diameter, divided into five concentric scoring zones each 1.22 m. in width. The target may be marked on the ground, or the scoring lines may be determined by a steel tape or nonstretch cord marked off at the dividing lines. The center is marked with a white marker, not more than 36 nor less than 30 inches square, standing perpendicular to the ground. Scoring values of each scoring zone from the center outward are 9, 7, 5, 3, 1.

¶Yards

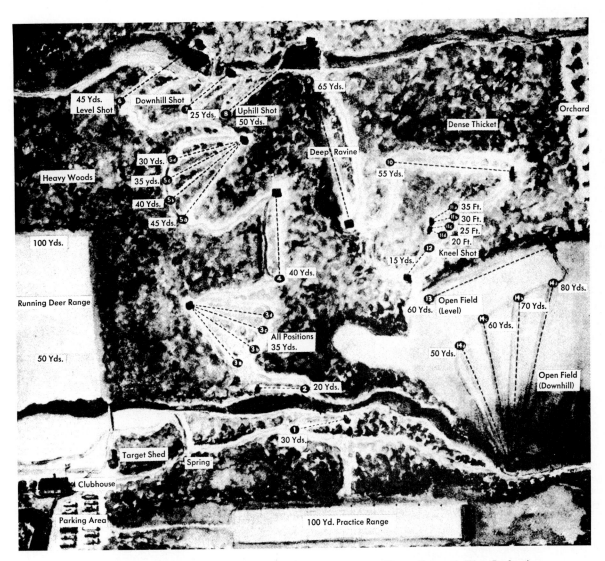

Fig. 3-8. Example of a 14-target field shooting course. (From Bear, F: The Archer's Bible, 1986, 1980 Doubleday & Co., Inc., New York, NY. Reprinted by permission.)

each target. The archer with the highest score is the winner.

FUNDAMENTAL SKILLS AND TECHNIQUES
Stringing the bow (bracing)
Push-pull method

Grasp the handle of the bow in the dominant hand with the back of the bow uppermost. Place the lower end against the inside of the arch of the foot on the same side, making sure that the tip does not touch the ground. Place the heel of the opposite hand on the back of the bow (Fig. 3-9) so that the loop of the string may be held between the thumb and first finger. By pulling on the handle with the dominant hand and pressing with the heel of the opposite hand, the bow may be bent and the string pushed up with the thumb and forefinger until it drops in to the nock. A bow stringer can also be used (Fig. 3-10).

Step-through method

Grasp the bow with the dominant hand (bow hand) and the string with the other hand (string hand). Put the back of the lower limb of the bow across the ankle of the foot on the string hand side. Step through the bow with the leg on the bow hand side. Put the bow handle high on the thigh of the leg on the bow hand side. Push the upper limb of the bow forward with the bow hand and guide the string into the nock with the string hand.

Checking the bow after stringing

Make sure that the loop is slipped completely into the nock and that the bowstring is centered. The distance from the string to the deepest part of the handle should measure about 6 inches, which may be measured roughly by making a fist and letting the thumb extend perpendicularly from it. This is called the fistmele or brace height.

Unstringing the bow (unbracing)

The process is exactly the same as stringing, except that the string is pulled out of the nock and the loop is slid down over the upper limb.

PREPARATION FOR THE DRAW
Stance

The archer stands astride the shooting line with the target directly out from the bow arm side. The archer's feet should be spread enough to give a firm and comfortable footing. The body and the head should be in a normally erect, comfortable position; the posture should allow complete absence of tension at any point.

Possible errors in stance
1. Both feet on the same side of the line
2. Feet too close or too far apart
3. Too much weight on one foot

Position of the bow hand

As you raise the bow to position, allow the hand to tip up so that the pressure of the bow is against the part of the palm just inside the base of the thumb. Allow the thumb and fingers to encircle the bow only very lightly—

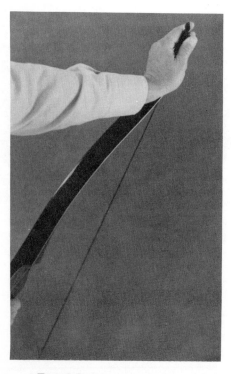

Fig. 3-9. Stringing the bow.

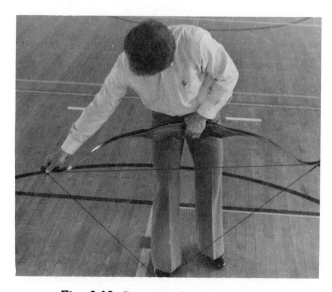

Fig. 3-10. Stringing the recurved bow.

just enough to keep it from falling. Never grip it (Fig. 3-11).

Position of the string hand

Reach under the string and hook the first, second, and third fingers of the right hand onto the string, allowing the whole first joint to hook over the string. The index finger should be above the arrow, the other two fingers below it.

NOCKING

Be sure that the index feather (different colored) is up and the arrow is at a right angle to the string. Make a nocking (reference) point on the string by wrapping masking tape around the string about three times. Always nock the arrow below the tape each time. Hold the bow down and inside while nocking, with the index feather facing away from the bow (Fig. 3-12).

THE DRAW AND ANCHOR

With simultaneous movement of the arms, slight pushing with the bow arm, and pulling with the string arm, the bow is brought to the desired position. As the draw is made, the outward pressure with the bow arm and the pull with the string arm should be equalized.

At the full draw, the bow arm is raised to shoulder height, with the elbow slightly bent and rotated downward to a 9 o'clock position.

The string hand is brought back to the face. In sight shooting (free style), the index finger is placed under the chin and lies in contact with the jawbone (low anchor). The string bisects both the nose and the chin for additional reference points. This point is known as the anchor point, and it is of prime importance that the string hand placement be exactly the same each time an arrow is drawn. At full draw the elbow of the string hand should be in line with the arrow.

In point-of-aim shooting, the string hand is brought back to the face; the string passes the nose to the side, and the index finger is locked in place under the cheekbone (high anchor) (Fig. 3-13). Fig. 3-14 illustrates the low or under-the-chin anchor employed in target shooting when using a sight.

Possible errors in the draw

Bow arm:
1. Elbow straight or hyperextended
2. Elbow bent too much
3. Left shoulder hunched

String arm:
1. Anchor point too far forward, too high, or below the chin
2. Some part of the hand other than the end segment of the forefinger or the string touches the anchor point
3. Elbow too high or too low

Fig. 3-11. Bow hand position.

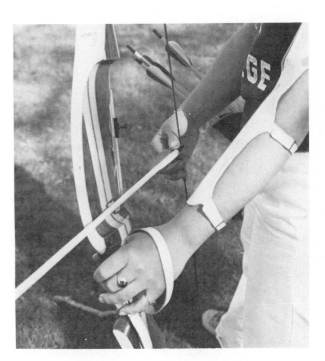

Fig. 3-12. Correct nocking position.

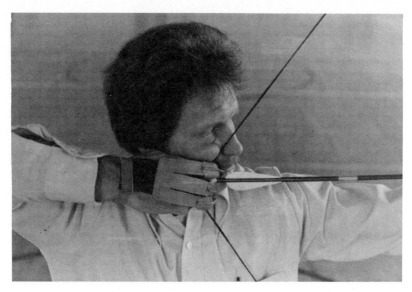

Fig. 3-13. High anchor point for field shooting with point of aim.

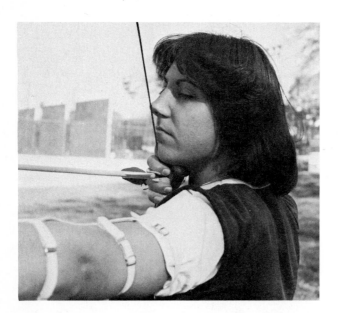

Fig. 3-14. Anchor position (low or under-the-chin anchor).

Aim, release, and follow through
Point of aim

Point of aim is a satisfactory method of aiming for the beginner, although sights may be used. With any bow and arrow there is only one distance at which a person may shoot and hit the center of the target by aiming directly at it while using point of aim. This will vary with the weight of the bow and with the length and weight of the arrow (Fig. 3-15). In order that the arrows may be grouped on the target at distances farther or closer than this point-blank range, the archer must use some auxiliary object in the background or foreground. This auxiliary object is known as the point of aim. At the completion of the draw, the point of the arrow should appear to be somewhere near the point of aim. The left hand is then moved slowly and steadily until the point of aim appears to be resting exactly on top of the point of the arrow (Fig. 3-16).

At the instant the aim is adjusted to your satisfaction, release the string by allowing the fingers to quit holding. But allow only the fingers to relax; the muscles of the string shoulder and back must keep pulling, and the muscles of the bow arm and shoulder must remain steady until the arrow has hit the target.

Note the location of the group formed by the arrows that were properly shot. If they are high on the target, the point of aim must be lowered or brought toward the archer. If they are low on the target, the point of aim must be raised or moved toward the target. If the point of aim is in proper line and they group to the right or left or scatter over the target, check for faults other than in point of aim.

Possible errors in aiming and releasing
1. Shift in position
2. Both arms and shoulders relaxed at the moment of release
3. Point of aim not reached before releasing string
4. Point of aim to the right or left of a line directly between the archer and the center of the target
5. Aiming with the left eye

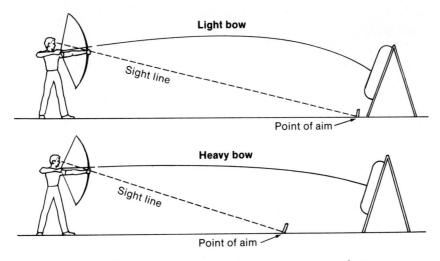

Fig. 3-15. Effect of weight of bow upon point of aim.

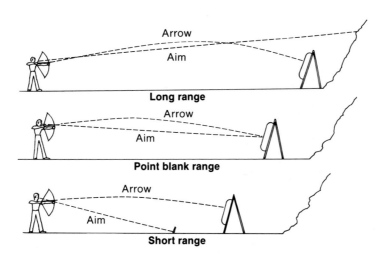

Fig. 3-16. Theory of the point of aim.

6. Sighting with both eyes
7. "Wrong arrow" used

Range finder

A device used for recording the established point of aim is called a range finder. It might be a piece of wood about 6 inches long. To record the point of aim, hold the finder at arm's length (Fig. 3-17) from the body toward the target, with the bull's-eye appearing just over the top of it. With the finder in this position, move the thumb up the stick until it is in line with the point of aim already established. At this point place a mark on the stick. In future shooting at this same distance, the point of aim can be reestablished by sighting through the mark recorded on the finder.

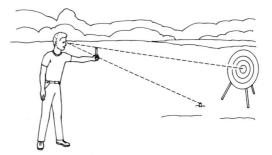

Fig. 3-17. The range finder.

Bow sight (free style)

A device that is used for sighting and is attached to the back of the bow is termed a "bow sight." It has vertical and horizontal adjustments and is good for all ranges. In use, the line of vision is through the sight to the center of the target. For a right-handed archer (one who draws the string back with the right hand), the left eye should be closed, and the sight should be placed by the target's center. For a left-handed archer, the left eye is used.

Pin sight

One of the most economical types of bow sights today is the pin sight, in which the shooter uses masking tape or weather stripping with one or two large pins for sighting. Other shooters may use a tongue depressor held to the bow by adhesive tape and a pin or match stick for sighting.

When adjusting the sight:

1. Always start about 10 yards (9.14 m.) from the target.
2. Set the pin about 4 inches (0.1 m.) above the arrow rest. Sight through the pin to the yellow of the target.
3. Shoot a group of three arrows. If the arrows land high on the target, set the pin higher; if low, set the pin lower.
4. After resetting the pin, try again. Aim at the gold (yellow) and shoot.
5. When changing distances, adjust the pin sight. As the archer moves away from the target, the pin sight should be moved closer to the grip of the bow.

Drawing arrows from the target

The back of one hand is placed against the target in such a way that the arrow is between the first and second fingers (Fig. 3-18). Grasp the arrow close to the target with the other hand and pull the arrow from the target. Care must be taken to draw the arrow straight out so that it will not be bent or kinked. After being drawn out,

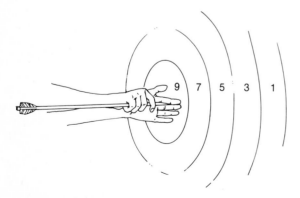

Fig. 3-18. Drawing the arrow from the target.

drop the arrow on the ground, leaving the hands free for removing the remaining arrows. If an arrow penetrates to where the feathers have entered the target, it must be drawn on through the back of the target to prevent roughing or stripping off the feathers. If the arrow has penetrated one of the wooden legs or the wooden support of the target, it should be loosened with a pair of pliers before removal. At times, arrows that miss the target slither along the ground and into the grass. These must be pulled from the point end, much in the same manner as removing an arrow that has penetrated the target past the feathers. In looking for arrows that have missed target, keep the eyes on the ground as it is easy to step on an arrow and break it.

SAFETY PRECAUTIONS

Archery contains certain elements of danger if participants become negligent or careless. Proper conduct and behavior while shooting or taking care of equipment off range are exceedingly important. Safety rules are as follows:

1. Do not go to the target while others are shooting. All participants go at the same time to retrieve arrows.
2. When finished shooting, step back three paces and wait.
3. Draw an arrow only when directed at the target.
4. Shoot at targets only from the shooting line.
5. Remember that bows and arrows are not toys.
6. Faithfully obey the starting and stopping signals.
7. On the field range, shout "Timber" before the arrow is released so that persons nearby receive adequate warning.
8. While shooting, be certain that there is an adequate backstop behind the target or, if there is no backstop, that the area is clear behind target.
9. Never leave bows and arrows unguarded where children or careless persons might handle them.
10. Never shoot straight up into the air under any circumstance.
11. Never shoot with a faulty bow or arrow or permit others to do so.
12. Never take chances or be in the least careless or negligent.
13. Do not pinch the arrow between the thumb and finger to shoot. Always use three fingers for drawing the arrow. This way you cannot accidentally release the arrow.

TEACHING CONSIDERATIONS

1. Teach safety procedures with no flexibility and strong consequences for any rule infractions. Establish and use consistent signals.
2. When teaching school populations, have the bows

strung before the first class so that time is not wasted on this procedure and students get an opportunity to shoot during the first class period.

3. Assign bows and arrows to students the first day that they will use the entire unit unless adjustments need to be made.

4. Teach stringing and unstringing of bows on the second day.

5. Give students the whole idea of the skill before breaking it down into parts. This can be done through demonstration or the use of audiovisual aids with a description of cues during the demonstration.

6. Practice stance, draw, and aim without an arrow, establishing clearly that the string is not to be released. Practice until each of these aspects is done correctly and with proper form. Do not go on until students have mastered the basics of each of these principles. Walk through each step if need be one at a time until mastered. In large classes use partners for feedback on:
   a. Straddling the line
   b. Raising the bow with the bow weight on the palm of the hand
   c. String hand position using first three fingers and whole first joint
   d. Level, straight pathway of elbow as it draws string back (9 o'clock position)
   e. Slightly flexed elbow on bow arm
   f. Correct anchor position

7. When students have mastered these steps, add nocking arrow, draw, anchor, aim, and release. Walk students through each step using cues before going to self-paced practice. Reemphasize rules for stepping in front of the shooting line before students release any arrows.

8. Teach students how to retrieve arrows and how to score arrows at one target before directing them to retrieve and score their own arrows.

9. Reemphasize point of aim and form after students have had an opportunity to shoot an end.

10. Help students analyze their errors in form based on clustering of arrows after enough practice results in consistent errors.

11. In longer units develop skills for shooting rounds and add novelty shooting (balloons, golf archery, etc.).

GLOSSARY

addressing the target Assuming the proper stance; ready to shoot. Feet should straddle the shooting line.

anchor point A definite point on one's face to which the hand is brought on the draw.

archer's golf An archery game simulating golf; sometimes played on a golf course.

arm guard A protective cover for the lower part of the bow arm.

back The side of the bow away from the body and facing the target.

belly The inside of the bow; the side facing the string.

bow arm The arm that is extended in preparation for release.

bow sight A device attached to the bow used to assist in aiming.

brace To loop the string in the nock when stringing the bow.

broadhead An arrow point used for shooting live game.

cast The distance an arrow may be shot.

clout shooting Usually 36 arrows shot at a 48-foot (15 m.) target placed or marked on the ground, 120 or 140 yards (110 or 128 m.) for women and 180 yards (165 m.) for men.

Columbia round A women's round consisting of 24 arrows shot at 50, 40, and 30 m.

crest The marks identifying the arrow.

double round A round shot twice in succession.

drift The motion of the arrow caused by wind or weather.

end Usually the shooting of six arrows, either in succession or in two groups of three.

eye The string loop.

field captain Usually the tournament director.

fistmele The height of the fist with the thumb raised (brace height).

fletch The placing of feathers on an arrow.

flight shooting The contest of distance shooting.

grouping Shooting a group of arrows close together on the target.

head The pile tip of the arrow.

hen feathers The two similar-colored feathers.

hit To hit the target anywhere.

index feather That feather of an arrow set at right angles to the nock; the odd-colored feather.

instinctive shooting Shooting without the aid of any sighting device.

jerking Jolting caused by too much recoil of the shooting hand on release.

Junior Columbia round For boys and girls; 24 arrows shot at each of 30 and 20 m.

Junior Scholastic round For boys and girls; 24 arrows shot at each of 30 and 20 m.

keeper A piece of binding used to keep the loose end of the string fastened to the unstrung bow.

lady paramount Woman directing a tournament.

let fly To release an arrow.

limbs Upper and lower parts of the bow.

loose The release of the bowstring after the draw.

low strung Less than a fistmele between the string and bow.

miniature round Indoor shooting; 60 arrows shot from 15 m. on a 2-foot target.

nock The groove at the end of the arrow.

nocking point The point on the string at which the arrow is placed.

overbowed Using a bow too heavy in draw weight.

perfect end To put six shots in the gold.

petticoat On the target face but outside the rings; beyond the white ring. If hit, no score is given.

pin sight A device on the bow to help in aiming.

point of aim The auxiliary object used in hitting the center of the target when the archer is not at point-blank range.

point-blank range The single distance where the true aim is on the bull's eye.

point The metal tip of the arrow.

quiver A device to hold arrows.

range Shooting distance.

range finder A device used to determine various distances.

range round Indoor shooting; 60 arrows shot from a single distance—50, 40, 30, or 20 m.

reflexed bow A bow with limbs that curve out.

release To shoot an arrow.

round To shoot a definite number of arrows at specific distances.

roving Shooting a given number of arrows at targets placed at varied distances over an outside course.

Scholastic round Twenty-four arrows shot at each of 40 and 30 m.

self arrow An arrow made from one piece of wood.

self bow A bow made from one piece of wood, as opposed to a composite bow.

serving The thread wrapped around the bowstring.

shaft The long center part of the arrow.

shaftment That part of the arrow holding the crest and feathers.

shooting line The line where one stands to shoot. The archer straddles this line.

shooting tab A protective device for fingers.

sight An aiming device that enables the archer to aim directly on the gold.

snake An arrow lost in deep grass.

spine A characteristic of the arrow's strength and flexibility.

stringing To place the string on the bow and make ready to shoot.

tackle Archery equipment.

tassel A bunch of fabric or a piece of cloth to wipe off wet arrows.

timber "Heads up"; a call of warning that an arrow is to be released. Used in field archery.

toxophilite One who has studied and mastered the art of shooting.

trajectory The flight of the arrow; the path that the arrow takes.

underbowed Using a bow that is too light in draw weight.

unit A 14-target course, including all official shots.

vane A plastic feather on an arrow.

wand shoot Shooting at an upright stick.

weight The number of pounds it takes to fully draw a bow.

windage The adjustment on the sight for right and left errors.

wobble Erratic motion of an arrow as it travels in flight.

SUGGESTED READINGS

Archery: a planning guide for group and individual instruction, Washington, DC, 1982, American Alliance for Health, Physical Education, and Recreation. Practical suggestions for initiating group and individual archery instruction. Useful for physical education and recreation classes in schools and colleges and in programs conducted by camps, recreation departments, and other agencies.

Archery: A sport for everyone, North Palm Beach, Fla, 1988, The Athletic Institute. Describes the rules and basics of archery.

Baier P, Bowers J, Fowkes CR, and Schoch S: The National Archery Association instructors manual, ed 3, Colorado Springs, 1982, National Archery Association.

Barrett J: Archery, Glenview, Ill, 1980, Scott, Foresman & Co. For beginning or intermediate archers. Research-based suggestions for refining technique, psychological aspects of archery, tear-out cards for self-evaluation and diagnosis of technique and program cards.

Bear F: Fred Bear's world of archery, Garden City, NY, 1979, Doubleday & Co, Inc.

Butler D: The new archery, New York, 1978, AS Barnes.

Gillan GH: Complete book of the bow and arrow, Harrisburg, Pa, 1971, Stackpole Books. Treats every facet of archery in illustrated detail: target archery, field archery, bow hunting, and fishing, how to shoot with a sight or without one. Contains a complete listing and comparison of available equipment.

Haywood KM and Lewis CF: Archery: steps to success, Champaign, Ill, 1989, Human Kinetic Publishers, Inc.

Kinton T: The beginning bowhunter, Merrillville, Ind, 1985, ICS Books, Inc.

McKinney WC and McKinney MW: Archery, ed 6, Dubuque, Iowa, 1990, WC Brown Publishers. Includes the latest tackle and techniques for target archery, bow hunting, and bow fishing, plus a brief introduction to the rich heritage of archery in literature, art, and history. Contains a unique chapter on physical conditioning for archers and more than 130 illustrations.

National Field Archery Association: Official handbook of field archery, Palm Springs, Calif, 1984, The National Field Archery Association.

Official Sports Library for Women: Individual sports—archery, fencing, golf, and riding, Washington, DC, 1980-1982, American Alliance for Health, Physical Education, and Recreation, National Association for Girls' and Women's Sports.

Pszczcola L and Mussett L: Archery, Dubuque, Iowa, 1984, WC Brown Publishers. An introduction to the basic skills, rules, strategies, and equipment of the sport of archery.

FILMS AND VIDEOTAPES

Archery. A five part series produced under the direction of Al Henderson, U.S. Olympic Coach, 1989, $129.00. Takes the viewer from the beginning to advanced competition. The Athletic Institute, 200 North Castlewood Rd., North Palm Beach, CA 33408.

Archery. Ten minute video by Fred Schuette. Basic skills, nock, anchor and release, aiming, pre-gap, and sight methods. Sports Video, 745 State Circle, Box 1941, Ann Arbor, MI 48106.

Archery Videos: Bows and arrows, 72 minutes, $139.95; *Bull's eye archery*, 50 minutes, $19.95; *How to tune your compound bow*, 60 minutes, $29.95; *You should know*, 105 minutes, $34.50. Available from "How-To" Sport Videos, 790 W. Tennessee Ave., Denver, CO 80223.

Archery right on, 12 minutes, 16 mm, sound, color. Rental $10. Archery from caveman to the Olympics. A complete overview. Fred Bear Sports Club Film Library, 25921 West Eight Mile Rd., Detroit, MI 48235.

A return to the Olympics, 32 minutes, 16 mm, sound, color. Rental $5; sale $200. Shows beginners to advanced archers preparing for the Olympic Games. Archery Manufacturers' Organization, c/o S.G.M.A., 200 Castlewood Rd., North Palm Beach, FL 33408.

Men's archery or *Women's archery*, color. Sale $24.95 each. Three loop films depicting the 7 steps of shooting form. The Athletic Institute, 200 Castlewood Rd., North Palm Beach, FL 33408.

7 steps to gold, 16 mm, sound, color. Rental $10. John Williams, 1972 Olympic Gold Medalist, demonstrates the seven basic steps. Covers freestyle and instinctive methods. Orange County Film Service, 2111 S. Standard, Santa Ana, CA 92707.

The best of the best, 28 minutes, 16 mm, sound, color. Free loan. Scenes from the 1976 Olympic Games. Fred Bear Sports Club Film Library, 25921 West Eight Mile Rd., Detroit, MI 48235.

The world of archery, 30 minutes, 16 mm, John Lanigan, c/o American Archery Council, Chicago, Ill.

25th World Archery Championships, 16 mm, sound, color. Rental $10. Shows international archers competing for world championship titles at Valley Forge, Pa. Fred Bear Sports Club Film Library, 25921 West Eight Mile Rd., Detroit, MI 48235.

Olympic archery/the inner contest, 13 minutes, 16 mm, sound, color. Scenes from the 1976 Montreal Olympics. Rental $5. Archery Manufacturers' Organization, c/o S.G.M.A., 200 Castlewood Rd., North Palm Beach, FL 33408. Free loan: Modern Talking Picture Service, Inc., 2323 New Hyde Park Rd., New Hyde Park, NY 11042.

Several hunting films are available from Fred Bear Sports Club Film Library, 25921 West Eight Mile Rd., Detroit, MI 48235.

4

Backpacking

Completion of this chapter should enable the reader to:

- Select and care for proper backpacking equipment
- Plan a safe backpacking trip
- Recognize the importance of conditioning and safety in backpacking
- Understand trail etiquette
- Teach a group of beginners the fundamentals of backpacking

HISTORY

Since the very early days of mankind, people have carried loads on their backs as a basic means of transporting the necessities of life. With the coming of horses, wagons, railroads, motor vehicles, airplanes, and other more efficient forms of transportation, the need to carry loads long distances has disappeared. The backpacker of today transports basic necessities in primitive fashion as a means of independence, recreation, and fun. With only a minimum of equipment and a little knowledge, the hiker can reach places that are inaccessible by any other form of transportation. The rewards of the backpacker are magnificent scenery, solitude, and a sense of awe inspired by the magnitude of natural surroundings. There is a great thrill and feeling of accomplishment in "doing it the hard way." There is challenge in the unknown and adventure on the trail. With a reasonable amount of preparation, any person in normal health who is willing to exert the effort can enjoy the vigorous life of the backpacker. To move about freely in the wilderness is to experience the adventures of our heritage and to learn of some of the most important lessons Earth has to offer.

EQUIPMENT

Modern backpacking equipment (Fig. 4-1) is highly efficient and well designed to minimize the weight that must be carried. It is also rather expensive, and a full outfit may call for an investment of several hundred dollars. Such an investment calls for judicious scrutiny of

Fig. 4-1. Backpacking with modern equipment.

all items before purchase, and it may be found that alternatives to large cash outlays can be achieved. If at all possible, equipment of the desired type should be borrowed, or perhaps rented, to find out whether it lives up to expectations. Only the necessary pieces of equipment should be bought at first, and additions can be made as experience and resources allow.

Hiking boots and socks

Good quality leather hiking boots are essential for the serious backpacker. All sorts of footgear may be seen on the trail, even gym shoes, but good boots offer protection and comfort. The boot selected should be sufficiently durable to last over many miles and should have a sole that will withstand wear from rocks and gravel and provide traction for walking on nearly any surface encountered. Most boots manufactured today have soles made of a synthetic rubber product known as Vibram, which is very durable. Recent developments in lightweight hiking shoes also offer protection at a reasonable cost.

Beginners tend to buy boots that are heavier and more expensive than necessary; a reputable outfitter selling quality merchandise can be of great help. It is extremely important that boots fit properly and that they be long enough so that the toes do not contact the front of the boot while one is walking downhill. Proper fitting procedure should include standing on a slant board to check toe position. In all instances, boots must be well broken in before attempting to hike on the trail. They should be worn at every opportunity before making a long hike, to make sure that they will not cause blisters. Opinions vary regarding the best way to break in boots, but wearing them frequently is recommended.

Socks are important companion pieces to boots, and most hikers use two pairs. The inner pair is usually lightweight wool, polypropylene, or similar material to wick moisture away from the feet, and the outer pair is usually heavyweight wool to provide cushioning of the feet within the boots. Clean socks should be worn every day, and at least one extra set of socks is needed. They can usually be laundered and dried at night, and even pinned to the outside of the pack if they are not dry by the time to start hiking.

Packs

The pack (Fig. 4-2) is a major investment and should meet the needs of the person using it. Most packs are mounted on a frame, with the pack and frame becoming an integral unit. Some packs have interior frames, and some have none at all, but the combination used most often consists of a lightweight frame with an attached pack containing several compartments. It should be possible to remove the pack from the frame, in case it becomes desirable to use the frame for carrying loads other

Fig. 4-2. Pack and hiking boots.

than the pack. The frame should be of lightweight metal, usually tubular aluminum alloy, with all joints sturdily welded, preferably by the heliarc process. Frames come in various sizes and should fit the wearer comfortably. Backbands prevent the frame from contacting the back of the wearer and should be adjustable for maximum comfort.

Packs are most often made of nylon and usually consist of a compartmentalized main body with exterior pockets for small items. Most manufacturers rate packs in terms of cubic inches of capacity, which is often of assistance in making selections. Pack sizes, number of compartments, color, and similar characteristics are matters of individual choice, and a wide variety should be examined before making the final selection.

It is important that the pack and frame have a good belt, preferably a padded one. The belt serves as a bottom backband to bear much of the weight of the pack and also maintains the pack and frame in position close to the body of the hiker. The length of the shoulder straps must be adjustable. When the pack is properly adjusted, part of the weight will rest on the shoulders and part on the hips of the wearer. The amount of weight distributed to hips and shoulders is a matter of wearer preference, but it is advisable to change the distribution from time to time while hiking. It is important that frame and pack be compatible, and if purchased separately, they should be properly joined. In buying a pack and frame, probably the best source of information and assistance is a reliable outfitter who sells quality merchandise.

Clothing

The major requirements for clothing used for backpacking are that it be comfortable and that it be adequate for temperatures likely to be encountered on the trail. Most backpacking is done in fairly cool climates, and wool clothing is usually welcome at night and in the early morning. In some instances, a set of long underwear can provide extra warmth during the day and as a sleeping garment at night. Wool has an advantage over most other materials in that it will maintain some of its insulating qualities when wet. Clothes made from various synthetic materials such as polypropylene have recently been introduced to the market and are excellent for the backpacker. It is usually best to "layer" clothing and adjust the number of layers to suit the temperature and degree of physical activity. When "layering" it is best to put insulating materials next to the body and cover with a nylon or gortex shell. Down jackets and vests are lightweight and highly efficient in retaining body heat, but they lose their insulating qualities when wet.

Some type of adequate rainwear is necessary if rain is likely to be encountered, and it should be compatible with other clothing worn. Lightweight rain suits are available that protect the wearer from the elements. Some types of rain suits are made of materials that permit body moisture to accumulate inside, but newer "breathable" fabrics are becoming available that eliminate this problem. As might be expected, they are generally higher in cost. Rain chaps—sleeves that cover the legs and tie to the belt—are often used with rain parka or poncho. The poncho is a large waterproof sheet of fabric or plastic with a hole in the middle through which the head is thrust to form a cloak-type garment. The poncho may also double as a ground cloth to prevent absorption of ground moisture by the sleeping bag or tent. Lightweight plastic raincoats or jackets likely to tear easily should be avoided, as they may fail at the time they are most needed.

For cooler weather, a wool watch cap or ski hat is advisable. Approximately 50% of the body heat can be lost through the head, neck, and ears if uncovered. Also, such a hat can be worn while sleeping if the sleeping bag does not cover the head.

It is wise to include in the clothing some reflective material that can be seen in the dark when a light shines on it. This could be very important if one of the party becomes lost.

Sleeping bags

The memories of minor discomforts of a hard day's hiking can be quickly erased by a good night's sleep. A sleeping bag adequate for temperatures encountered will contribute to such a night. Sleeping bags come in all sizes and shapes and with several types of insulation. Remember that no sleeping bag generates heat but only serves to stop heat loss from one's body. The mummy-style bag is probably most popular with backpackers, and down seems to be the most often selected insulating material. However, down loses its efficiency when wet, and it is then of little value to stop heat loss. The synthetic fibers used for insulating sleeping bags, such as Dacron, Hollofil II, Polarguard, Fiberfil II, and Hollowbound II, are almost as efficient as down and have the added advantage of being less influenced by moisture. However, synthetic-insulation-filled bags are approximately 30% heavier than down bags of equivalent warmth. Regardless of whether the sleeping bag is filled with down or synthetic fibers, it should never be stored tightly stuffed or rolled. Such storage will compress and break the insulating fibers. Sleeping bags should not be stored in stuff sacks. Most sleeping bag covers are made of rip-stop nylon and are available in numerous colors. Although color is of little importance for other than esthetic purposes, a light, tough cover that will permit body moisture to escape is essential. Sleeping bag covers should never be made of waterproof material, as large amounts of body moisture will collect in the bag and cause rapid heat loss.

Sleeping pads and air mattresses

In addition to a ground cloth to prevent ground moisture from being absorbed by the sleeping bag or tent floor, some means of blocking heat loss through the ground is desirable. This can be accomplished through the use of foam sleeping pads or air mattresses. Most regular air mattresses will not block heat loss as well as foam pads, but air mattresses specially designed for backpacking can be purchased. The two basic types of foam pads are of closed-cell or open-cell construction. Closed-cell pads need no additional cover and can serve as ground cloths, but open-cell pads will absorb moisture, and a ground cloth is needed. Foam pads enclosed in waterproof material are also available and they offer added protection from wetness. Where ground temperatures are not critically low, many people prefer to use no pad, and some are sufficiently hardy to sleep on the ground without the benefit of pad or mattress.

Tents and shelters

One of the heavier items frequently carried in a backpack is a small tent, usually made of nylon or similar lightweight material, with aluminum poles and stakes. In some situations, no shelter at all may be needed, but it is highly advisable to have some sort of covering to remain dry during rain or snow. A lightweight tarp (or tube tent) is the choice of some hikers, while others prefer a tent. The tarp works well in light rain, but it is not nearly so effective as a tent in avoiding mosquitoes or other insects. It is advantageous if the tent has a waterproof floor to serve as a moisture barrier and to eliminate the need for carrying a special ground cloth. The walls and roof of some tents are also made of waterproof material, which causes moisture to condense inside the tent, usually near the top. A more desirable arrangement is a tent with waterproof floor and walls and roof of material porous enough for moisture to escape. This makes an additional covering necessary, that is, a tent fly stretched over the entire top of the tent. Tents are often described as "two person," "three person," and so on. The prospective buyer should always see the tent set up before buying, to make sure that space in the tent is as extensive as described. Most "two person" tents provide barely enough space for two average-sized people, and little or no room for packs or other gear. Tent seams should be well-stitched, with reinforcement at points of strain. The typical tent designed for backpacking weighs 5 to 10 pounds, depending on size, type of material, and weight of poles and stakes. Tent closures should fit tightly and are usually of the zipper type. It is important that zippers are of high quality. Mosquito netting that closes tightly is a must if the tent flaps are to be left open in warm weather.

Cooking and eating equipment

Many types of cooking and eating utensils are available at most outfitters. While these are designed for light weight and compactness, fancy utensils are not necessary. An ordinary No. 10 can works well as a cooking pot and can be obtained from nearly any place that prepares food in large amounts. Restaurants, cafeterias, and similar places receive large quantities of food canned in these containers and are usually happy to give them away. The addition of a wire bail makes it possible to suspend the pot over a fire and to remove it easily. Heavy-duty aluminum foil can be used to fashion frying pans and small ovens and can be used to wrap food for cooking directly on a fire. It can be reused several times.

Regular stainless steel tableware is adequate, and if one has a pocketknife or sheath knife, a table knife may be considered unnecessary. An ordinary metal pie tin makes a satisfactory plate, provided it is cleaned well after each use. In all cases, cooking and eating equipment must be kept clean and should be sterilized by boiling after each use.

In addition to knife, fork, and spoon, some sort of cup is needed. Special types of cups are available such as the Sierra cup, which has a large-diameter top and a small-diameter base and can be used to heat water in as well as serving as a drinking cup. Some ordinary measuring cups will suffice, as will a tin, aluminum, or plastic cup. Metal cups freely transmit heat from hot liquids, and without care, burned lips may result. Cups made of Styrofoam or similar plastics have little value and are too delicate to withstand the rigors of trail use.

Experience will assist the hiker in deciding on the type of equipment to take, and after a few trips such selection will pose no problem. The fancier kits are desirable but certainly not essential to an enjoyable trip.

Trail stoves

Most backpackers prefer to cook over an open fire, and where this is possible, it offers maximum enjoyment of the outdoors. The cooking fire should be kept small, and wood that will provide coals should be used where possible. Most woods found in mountain country are softwoods and burn rather quickly, with almost no coals. Cooking pots blacken as a result of cooking over such fires, but such blackening in no way affects the quality of cooking, and it may actually increase the ability of the pot to absorb heat. If it is desirable to keep a cooking utensil bright and shiny, a coating of soap on the outside before its use over the open fire will help prevent permanent blackening.

However desirable the open cooking fire may be, there are places and times when such fires are not permitted, such as in areas of high danger of forest fire or where fuel is unavailable. At such times a small trail stove is indispensable for heating water and cooking. Most such stoves are lightweight and perform fairly well, but they lack the heat of the open fire. Trail stoves burn several types of fuel, including white gasoline, kerosene, compressed propane gas, or butane gas. Other fuels such as Sterno or hexamine may be used, but these usually deliver considerably less heat. In the case of butane fuel, the fuel tank must be kept above freezing for effective use. This may make it necessary for the hiker to take the fuel tank to bed with him or her in order to have usuable fuel to cook breakfast! Transporting stoves and fuels can be dangerous, and they should always be stored in the pack properly. Liquid fuel such as white gasoline should be transported only in metal bottles designed for the purpose. These should be carried in an outside pocket of the pack, so that leaks may be observed in time to prevent the pack from becoming a torch through accidental ignition. Be sure to carry a stove repair kit and to try out the stove prior to an overnight trip.

Whenever a fire is used, extreme care must be taken to make sure that only those things are burned that are intended to be burned. Burnable materials must be removed from the proximity of open fires, and every fire must be "dead out" before leaving the campsite. Garbage that will burn should be consumed completely by the fire, and all traces of the fire should be removed. Items that will not burn completely should be packed out and placed in a proper receptacle at the end of the trip. "Let no one say, and say it to your shame, that all was beauty here until *you* came!" It is the mark of the conscientious backpacker to "camp without a trace" and to protect the surroundings for the future enjoyment of others.

Pocket equipment

Several items should be carried in the hiker's pants pockets. A reserve supply of wooden matches, enclosed in a waterproof container, should be carried in the pocket, in addition to a supply in the pack. A folding pocketknife should also be carried, and special effort must be made to know the whereabouts of the knife at all times. Knives are probably the most "losable" items carried, and they are also one of the most important. A small metal referee's whistle should also be carried in the pants pocket, to use as an emergency signal if needed. The whistle can be heard over greater distances than the voice, and the whistle will still make noise long after the sound production of the vocal cords has been diminished to a whisper. In areas unfamiliar to the hiker, a compass is desirable, and it should also be carried in the pocket. These items must be carried on the person in the event that the pack is lost. These are items of prime importance to survival in an emergency and must be kept readily available in a location separate from the pack.

Equipment selection

The prospective backpacker with limited funds will be forced to make many careful choices when buying equipment. It is generally better to buy fewer items of good quality than to buy a larger number of items and compromise on quality. Again, it is advisable to borrow or rent equipment and actually use it before investing in an item intended for long-term service. Gaps in noncritical equipment can be filled in with simple makeshift gear until further knowledge is gained and the right equipment is bought.

The following list is offered to aid the novice in planning and acquiring equipment. The list is intended to present equipment needed in most areas of the United States, but additions or deletions may be appropriate depending on local conditions. Always consider quality of construction, weight, bulk, and durability. Remember, there are no equipment stores in the wilderness!

Essential equipment

Pack
Cooking kit or pot
First aid kit
Sleeping bag
Stuff sack
Tent or tarp
Ground cloth
Rainwear
Cup, plate, fork, and spoon
Knife, matches, compass, whistle (carried in pockets, not in pack)
Flashlight
Canteen
Trail guidebook(s)/maps
Prescription medication (if needed)
Extra socks
Soap
Small towel
Toilet tissue

Optional equipment

Frying pan
Aluminum foil
Pot tongs
Backpacker grill
Stove and fuel
Gym shoes
Nylon cord
Foam pad or air mattress
Camera and film
Books
Notebook and pencil or pen
Needles, thread
Extra flashlight batteries and bulb
Candles
Plastic bags
Dimes and quarters (for phone call in emergency)
Rubber bands
Hiker's staff
Safety pins
Tweezers
Sunglasses
Water treatment chemicals
Insect repellent
Lip balm
Sunburn lotion
Personal toilet articles

PLANNING THE TRIP
Where to go

A major decision confronting the hiker planning a trip is the selection of a suitable area. One of the great features of backpacking is the freedom it offers, within limits of particular areas. Many people enjoy the "bushwhack," that is, cross-country travel in any direction desired without confinement to established trails. In areas where this is permitted, it can offer solitude that may not be attainable otherwise. The beginning packer will quickly find that characteristics of the landscape may make the "bushwhack" difficult and that established trails offer better routes. Generally it is considered best to stick to existing trails until experience has been gained that would benefit the hiker in the cross-country venture. Some areas of the country have become well known for excellent trails and beautiful scenery, so much so that agencies in charge of many areas have been forced to establish a quota system that permits a limited number of people on a trail at a given time. Otherwise, the trails literally become worn out from excessive use and the abuse of overcrowding in campsite areas. Persons wishing to hike in such areas should determine whether permits are required and make application, if needed. Most areas open for backpacking are public use areas and include land controlled by state parks, the U.S. Forest Service, the National Park Service, conservation departments, or similar agencies. Many of the controlling agencies publish information about their respective areas and will furnish it on request. When selecting an area, it is wise to consider the nature of the terrain, existing trails, area rules, and the availability of such things as water and places to camp. Established trails originate at a place called a trailhead, and parking facilities are usually provided for at least a limited number of vehicles. If plans call for the trip to end at the same place it begins, it may be desirable to leave vehicles at that point. Should it end at some other access to the trail, it will be necessary to enlist the aid of someone to deliver hikers to the start of the hike and pick them up at its end.

For "first timers," a good approach is to camp out in the backyard, using the equipment to be taken on the trail. Thus, if something goes badly, experience can be gained without the discomfort or danger of being miles from home. Another good idea is to make a short overnight hike near home to "shake down" equipment and determine its adequacy. The things that the hiker can carry will be limited; needed things not carried will be unavailable, and things carried and not needed only add useless weight to the pack. There is no substitute for an actual trial to determine those things that must be taken and those things that are better left at home.

Checklists

One of the most valuable things that the beginner can do is make a list of things that are to be taken on the trip and check them off as the pack is loaded. This helps avoid leaving a critical item of equipment at home and brings organization to the process of preparation.

Food

An adequate supply of food is essential. The planner must realize that energy expenditure in hiking is much greater than in normal daily routine activity, and thus appetites are often much greater than normal on the trail. Certainly a good practice for the novice is to take what seems to be an adequate amount of food and then add a little more. A matter for prime consideration is the weight of the food. Much of the weight of most food is water, and any process to reduce water contained in food will aid in reducing the total load to be carried.

The major place where weight can be reduced is food, and dehydrated foods of some sort are essential if the trip is to be of more than a few days' duration. Well-prepared foods are available that have been freeze dried or have had the major portion of water removed by some other process. Wide choices are available from the typical outfitter. The major hindrance to such foods is their high cost. Freeze-dried foods may be the only resource for

long trips, but many equally nutritious foods that weigh only slightly more can be purchased at a supermarket. Pretrip activities should include a visit to a supermarket to determine the dry foods available that will suit the palate of the particular persons involved. When such foods are selected, they should be removed from their bulky commercial wrappings and repackaged into smaller space-saving units. Preparation instructions should be retained for each item. One means of food acquisition often espoused by backpackers is "living off the land." Not only is this uncertain, but it may be impossible because of low availability of natural food or local regulations that prohibit it. It is true that in some areas the diet may be supplemented by fish, berries, and sometimes fruit, but the wise packer will take an adequate supply of food along until sufficient experience is gained to be able to forage effectively.

Menus

Although some hikers detest any sort of formal organization, it will aid the beginner to take a written plan for each meal to be eaten on the trip. Changes can always be made, but it may be difficult to determine the amount of food needed without such a specific plan. When food is purchased, a good precedure is to group the items to be eaten at each specific meal. Then each of these groups should be placed in a plastic bag and labeled according to its intended time of consumption, such as "breakfast Saturday" or "supper Sunday." Such organization may not appeal to everyone; but it will ensure an orderly approach to the problem of providing adequate meals. Although unusual diets will probably not cause significant problems over a few days, the general procedure should be to follow the same guidelines in meal planning as one would if at home; that is, plan a balanced diet that contains a variety of foods. Because energy expenditure will be high, a diet containing large portions of carbohydrates is desirable, but other food elements should not be neglected. Extra salt should be included. The consumption of small amounts of salt with water at frequent intervals along the trail will aid in preventing leg cramps and in hot weather will minimize salt depletion resulting from heavy perspiration.

Trail food

It is usually desirable to plan lunches that require little or no cooking. In addition, most hikers find it advantageous to eat small amounts of high-energy foods during the course of the day's hike. A favorite is a mixture called "gorp." The origin of this word is obscure; it is sometimes said to mean "good old raisins and peanuts." Whatever the origin of the term, the mixture is often a creation of art. Depending on the taste of the preparer, it may include such items as dried fruit, chocolate, nuts of various kinds, cereals, and any other food that is high in energy but that will not become sticky when warm.

Water

Water is essential for the hiker, and it should be consumed with regularity and frequency. There is a tendency for the inexperienced hiker to drink less water than is desirable, and effort may be necessary to ensure adequate consumption. It is better to drink more than is needed than to chance becoming dyhydrated. This is particularly true in hot weather, and regular "water stops" should be planned. Small amounts of salt added to water or other liquids such as orange juice made from powdered concentrate can assist in maintaining salt balance. Salt and water that are not needed are excreted by normal body processes, and the better choice is to consume more than is needed rather than too little. Sources of safe water along the trail may be difficult to find, but proper pretrip planning involving use of available maps, trail guidebooks, and local inquiries can make this task easier. In some instances water must be carried for long distances; in others it may be readily available from springs, streams, or lakes. Where the safety of water is questionable, it should be treated with chemicals carried in the pack. Commercial preparations such as halazone are available from drugstores and outfitters. It is always advisable to check the date on the container of such preparations, as their effective life is limited. The amount of treated water consumed should always be in accordance with instruction on the container. Equally effective treatment can be accomplished with materials readily available in the typical household. Both tincture of iodine and ordinary laundry bleach may be used at the rate of 3 drops per quart of clear water (double the amount if the water is not clear). The chemical should be thoroughly dissolved in the water by vigorous shaking, and the treated water should then be left to stand for at least 30 minutes before being consumed. Although there will be a slight taste of the chemical used, it will be far superior to drink treated water than to contract gastrointestinal disorders or other serious malady.

Maps and guidebooks

These guides are of great help in assessing terrain and general physical characteristics of the area selected for hiking. They give many features of the land areas represented, including elevations, contours, water sources, campsites, area histories, and much more. Such maps can be purchased from many outfitters, and if not available locally they may be obtained from the Geological Survey and Water Resources Agency in each state. For information on maps of areas east of the Mississippi River, contact the Geological Survey Office in Washington, D.C.; for areas west of the Mississippi, contact the Geo-logical Survey Office in Denver. Index maps of each state are available; maps for specific areas may be ordered after consulting the index map.

Loading the pack

Once all of the items to be taken are assembled, they should be placed in the pack in some sort of order related to their function. Generally, lighter items are loaded near the bottom of the pack, and heavier items should be loaded near the top and close to the front. It is important to keep the greater portion of weight high on the back near the shoulders. Items that are likely to be used frequently or those that might be needed quickly should be placed in the side pockets on the pack to avoid the process of unpacking when the item is needed. Certainly rainwear should be readily accessible, and many packs provide special pockets for rainwear and maps. The most effective organization of the pack can best be learned through experience.

Try to keep the basic pack unit to a weight of 20 pounds or less. This weight includes all necessities that must be carried such as pack, tent, sleeping bag, and the like, and excludes expendable items, primarily food. The total maximum weight carried may vary considerably from one person to another, but a general rule of thumb is for the total weight to be carried not to exceed one third the body weight of the person carrying it. This is a *heavy* load, and the beginner will do well to limit loads to a considerably lower weight.

First aid kit

A first aid kit should be a basic part of the backpacker's equipment. Commercially prepared kits are available, but a satisfactory one can be put together from items readily available from a local drugstore. The following is a suggested list of items for such a kit:

  Antiseptic
  Band-Aids (several sizes, including extra large)
  Sterile gauze pads
  Moleskin
  Adhesive tape
  Lip balm
  Tweezers
  Needle
  Safety pins
  Triangular bandage
  Snakebite kit
  Other items as anticipated needs may indicate

ON THE TRAIL
Conditioning and safety

It is important that the hiker be in good physical condition and able to walk for extended periods while carrying a pack. Conditioning before the hike will improve stamina and make the process more enjoyable. Conditioning should be accomplished over a reasonable period of time and may include walking, jogging, and similar activities that promote overall conditioning. In any event the hiker should build up to the activity and not attempt greater distances than can be covered in the time allotted. Enjoyment, not exhaustion, is the objective. During the first few miles of a hike, it is wise to start slowly and "warm up" to the task. This is especially advisable if there is considerable increase in altitude in the first portion of the trail. Particular care must be given the feet, and at the first sight of irritation, action must be taken. The first warning is a burning sensation, often on the heel or toes. When this warning signal occurs, *stop!* Continued walking will quickly result in a blister, and the hiker may be "crippled" with the hike hardly started. Boot and socks should be removed and the area of irritation inspected. A moleskin plaster may be applied over the area affected. This material, available at drugstores, has a smooth surface to reduce friction and an adhesive backing that causes it to stick to skin. After applying moleskin, the hiker can apply foot powder and replace socks and boot, paying close attention to the way the foot feels after walking is resumed. It is much better to avoid blisters than to treat them, but if one occurs, it should be taken care of at once. A Band-Aid and powder can be applied if the blister is small. Opening the blister should be avoided if possible. If the blister must be opened, this should be done with a needle that has been heated until the point is red hot to sterilize it. The skin should be disturbed as little as possible, antiseptic applied, and the spot covered with a Band-Aid or similar dressing. It may be necessary to delay hiking a day or so if blisters become severe, and care must be taken to avoid infection and otherwise making them worse. Applications of a commercial preparation of benzoin (Tuf-Skin) several days in advance of the trip will help to toughen the skin on the feet and reduce the likelihood of blisters. Blisters are a real pain; avoid them!

When hiking in groups, there are usually some individuals who wish to walk faster than others. It is irritating to walk behind a person who walks slower than you do, and it is good to let the sprinters pass but to keep the party together! One rule is to keep the person behind you in sight by looking back frequently and stopping to rest when the group gets spread out farther than is desirable. Although it may cause some irritation on the part of those who wish to walk faster, a sure way to keep the group together is to put the slowest hiker in front and allow no one to pass. Some experienced packers make solo hikes into deep wilderness areas, and once in a while one remains there permanently. A much safer arrangement is to hike with at least one partner and to know the whereabouts of each other at all times. The "buddy" system allows one person to go for help in case of serious emergency.

Falls are a primary source of injury to backpackers, and precautions should be taken to avoid unnecessary risks. A broken leg or sprained ankle is no fun at any time, and on the trail deep in a wilderness area it becomes a serious problem. Travel over ice, wet rocks, and loose rocks poses special problems and should not be attempted without special knowledge and training. Each hiker must be responsible for his or her own safety and be ready to assist others.

A trip schedule should be left with someone before starting, in case a hiker must be located in an emergency and to enable emergency aid to be directed to the proper place if it should become necessary. Most established trails have some sort of registration procedure, either at a ranger station or a drop box a short distance up the trail from the trailhead. A good plan is to have someone start looking for you if you are not in contact with them at a specified time. In the event of a delay that is not an emergency, the party with whom you have the arrangement should be notified of your safety as soon as possible.

Extra precaution should be observed when descending trails, especially near the end of a trip, when fatigue is most evident and mishaps are most likely to occur. During downhill travel, hazards may be more likely to be hidden by vegetation, and loose rocks, rotten logs, and other dangers may appear without warning. Lightning in the mountains poses an extremely dangerous threat, and in the event of an electrical storm, hikers should retreat to the lowest available area and avoid high ridges and lone trees.

Trail pests

The degree of irritation caused by trail pests is usually inversely proportional to the size of the pest. The uninitiated hiker may fear mountain lions, grizzly bears, and other wild creatures, but mosquitoes, black flies, "no see-ums," and similar insects can cause far more discomfort than the larger animals. Generally, it must be understood that it is the hiker who is the interloper in any confrontation with an animal. Most animals wish only to be left alone. Snakes are often feared, but most are harmless. Small common garter snakes frequent springs in some mountain ranges, but they are there for the same purpose as the packer—to get a cool drink. Rattlesnakes are dangerous, and most can be avoided by careful observation during walking and especially when sitting down beside the trail or reaching along a rocky ledge. A good insect repellent will help considerably in dealing with insects, and common sense should prevail in dealing with other animals. No animal should be teased or antagonized. Remember, you are the intruder in the animal's home!

Personal hygiene

Habits of personal hygiene should not vary markedly from those practiced at home. It is important to maintain personal cleanliness, and although baths may not be taken as regularly as at home, they may be even more necessary. Small mountain streams should not be used as bathtubs or as a place to wash dishes or clothes. The water is usually cold, and the aquatic balances that influence fish and other life can be easily affected. Water can be heated in the cooking pot and used for washing clothes or for bathing. Use biodegradable soap, because the soil can break it down much more rapidly than ordinary soaps. Soapy water should not be discarded where it can run into a stream. The idea of washing socks and cooking in the same pot may not be attractive to some, but the matter of weight makes it essential to leave the wash basin at home. A thorough rinsing and boiling of water in the pot after use for washing will make it safe and ready for the next meal. Thorough rinsing of the pot is essential, because soap acts as a strong laxative if ingested.

Good toilet habits should be practiced and consist of depositing fecal material in a small hole at least 50 feet from the trail and at least 100 feet from any surface water and covered with 6 inches of soil.

Trail etiquette

All travelers on the trail have the same rights and privileges, and all should respect other travelers. On a narrow trail, let faster hikers pass by simply stepping off the trail and greeting them cordially. In many areas, horse pack trains use the same trails as backpackers, and often the packers do not rate very highly with the horse wrangler. Even though the packhorses see hikers frequently, they are often "spooked" by them. If you see a pack train approaching or one overtakes you, move off the trail at least 20 feet on the downhill side and stand quietly as the animals pass. Sudden movement or loud noise may cause horses to bolt and may result in runaways or horses falling down the side of the mountain.

Campsites

On some trails, camping may be permitted in designated areas only. It is important to adhere to such regulations to prevent damage to the surroundings and to keep the area in a near natural state for others who will follow. When camping is unrestricted, it is convenient if the campsite can be located near water. Level ground is also desirable, but it may be difficult to find in some areas. Fires must be used with great discretion, and the campsite must be made as natural as possible before leaving. Fires must be completely extinguished and the fire scar covered. All garbage that will not burn completely must be packed out. Backpackers are the self-appointed guardians of the wilderness, and they must use it with the least possible damage and leave no evidence of their presence in the area.

Hypothermia

The greatest killer of people in the outdoors is hypothermia. This condition occurs when the body core temperature falls below normal. Unless the condition is reversed, death results. Hypothermia is not freezing to death! Most often hypothermia occurs when the outdoor temperature is between 30° and 50° *above* zero. Hypothermia may be a problem at lower temperatures, but usually a person prepares more effectively for such situations. Sudden changes in weather may occur, and hikers caught unprepared in cold rainstorms are prime candidates for hypothermia. The combination of wet clothing and exposure to wind most frequently causes the problem. Such conditions remove heat from the body surface faster than it can be generated by normal body functions, and the decrease in temperature results. The hiker should be familiar with windchill factors.

It is extremely important that early symptoms of hypothermia—continued shivering, loss of alertness, and loss of control of the hands—be recognized and treatment started immediately. All of these things occur without the victim being aware of what is happening. The four basic defenses against hypothermia are:

1. Stay dry and out of the wind.
2. If chilling has already started, get out of wind and rain, give up objectives for the day if necessary, and "hole up" in a sheltered spot. Erect a tent and take advantage of such natural shelter as may be available.
3. Detect hypothermia by checking party members for uncontrolled shivering, slurred speech, memory lapses, stumbling, drowsiness, and apparent exhaustion.
4. Treat hypothermia as follows: get the victim to shelter, strip off his or her wet clothes and put on dry ones, get the victim into a warm sleeping bag, give warm drinks, and if at all possible build a fire. Keep the victim awake, and if necessary place the victim in a sleeping bag with another person, both naked. Remember, *think* hypothermia and be prepared to deal with it at the first sign of difficulty. Don't wait!

Heat stress

Another problem that can confront the hiker is heat stress. Precautions should be taken to avoid heat exhaustion and heat stroke, but it is equally important to recognize their symptoms and to treat them should they occur.

Heat is eliminated from the body by conduction, convection, radiation, and evaporation. The most important process for regulation of body temperature is sweating, which promotes cooling through evaporation. While hiking, some heat is lost through respiration, but it is minimal. Evaporation of sweat is influenced by the relative humidity, wind velocity, and outside temperature. High humidity is especially troublesome, because it reduces the rate of evaporation that can take place.

The steps of prevention, recognition, and treatment of heat stress are as follows:

1. Carry and ingest adequate amounts of liquid and salt to prevent depletion of these basic body requirements.
2. Ensure adequate rest and opportunity for cooling. Take frequent rest stops in shady areas.
3. Detect heat exhaustion from such symptoms as fatigue, muscle cramps, abdominal pain, and nausea. The pulse will be normal, the skin will be moist and pale, and there may not be an increase in temperature, although more commonly there will be. The tongue and mouth will be dry, and the hiker will feel weak and uncoordinated and may appear mentally dull.
4. Treat heat exhaustion by moving the hiker to a cool area, replenishing the liquid content of the body, and supplementing salt with this intake. Salt tablets are better than saltwater if nausea is present.
5. Detect heat stroke from symptoms such as fever; a rapid pulse rate; hot, dry, flushed skin; involuntary limb movements; and possible unconsciousness.
6. Treat heat stroke immediately by lowering body temperature through use of cold water, fanning, and massaging the limbs. Seek medical help as soon as possible.

TEACHING CONSIDERATIONS

Only instructors with a great deal of experience in backpacking and familiar with an area should guide others on a trip. This is particularly true in wilderness areas where help in emergency situations is not likely to be available. All instructors should consider the conditioning and experience of their group in planning a trip and should not consider more than casual day trips with unconditioned, unprepared, or ill-equipped backpackers.

GLOSSARY

benzoin A commercial preparation used in advance to toughen the skin of the hands.

biodegradable soap A type of soap that should be used when backpacking because the soil can break it down very quickly.

campsite An area for sleeping and/or fire building. On some trails camping may only be permitted in designated areas.

checklist A list of things that are to be taken. This is critical so that nothing is left behind.

cooking utensils An ordinary No. 10 can works well and is light for carrying.

dead out The condition every fire must be in before leaving the campsite.

first aid kit A kit that contains all the immediate remedies for the hazards encountered along the trail.

foam sleeping pad A means of blocking heat loss through the ground.

gorp A high energy food eaten during the course of the day's hike; "good old raisins and peanuts."

halazone A product used to treat water where its safety is questionable. Can be purchased in drugstores.

heat stress A common problem that confronts the hiker. High humidity is especially troublesome.

hypothermia A condition that occurs when the body core temperature falls below normal. It is the greatest killer of people in the outdoors.

leather boots An essential item for a serious backpacker both for safety and comfort.

liquid fuel One source of fuel for camping; should be kept in a metal container and carried in a pocket on the outside of the pack.

maps Guides for assessing the terrain and general physical characteristics of the area selected for hiking.

menus Written plans for food consumption for each meal.

mummy-style bag A sleeping bag adequate for temperatures encountered and most popular with hikers.

pack A compartmentalized bag mounted on a metal frame.

rain chaps Sleeves that cover the legs and may be tied to the belt.

trail etiquette Observance of respect for other travelers.

trailhead A place where established trails originate.

trail pests Animals that may cause discomfort or danger; remember that the hiker is the interloper in any confrontation with an animal, and that good insect repellent will help dealing with insects.

SUGGESTED READINGS

Forgey W: Wilderness medicine, Harrisburg, Pa., 1979, Stackpole Books.

Forgey W: Hypothermia: death by exposure, Merrillville, Ind., 1985, ICS Books, Inc.

Jensen CR and Jensen CJ: Backpacking for fun and fitness, Champaign, Ill., 1981, Leisure Press. Gives information on backpacking gear, food, navigation, and emergency treatment.

Manning H: Backpacking: one step at a time, New York, 1977, Vintage Books, Random House, Inc.

Maughan JJ and Collins K: Outdoor woman's guide to sports, fitness and nutrition, Harrisburg, Pa., 1983, Stackpole Books. Contains information tailored to women on climbing, hiking, skiing, kayaking, and canoeing.

Maughan JJ and Puddicombe A: Hiking the backcountry: a do-it-yourself guide for the adventurous woman, Harrisburg, Pa., 1981, Stackpole Books. Covers nearly every situation and type of terrain that any backpacker might run into, offering the kind of practical advice that comes from long experience.

Meier J: Backpacking, Dubuque, Iowa, 1980, W.C. Brown Publishers. Contains the latest information on backpacking and back-country hiking and safety equipment, and off-trail hiking. Off-trail travel techniques, tips for survival and step-by-step photographs demonstrate key skills.

Rustrum C: Backcountry, Harrisburg, Pa, 1981, Stackpole Books. Volume of adventures, trips, and events from the northern wilderness during the first part of this century.

Rustrum C: Hiking, Harrisburg, Pa, 1983, Stackpole Books. Comprehensive, procedural coverage from the short, cumulative urban walks to the long wilderness trek, with analysis of equipment, outdoor living methods, and other pertinent information.

Satterfield A and Bauer E: The Eddie Bauer guide to backpacking, Reading, Mass, 1983, Addison-Wesley Publishing Co. Offers advice on route finding, first aid, muscle exercises, hiking boots and other equipment, and much more.

PERIODICAL

Backpacker, 23 West 44th St., New York, N.Y. 10036.

FILM

Backpacking, West Wind Productions, Inc., 855 Broadway, Boulder, Colo.

5

Badminton

Completion of this chapter should enable the reader to:

- Appreciate the versatility of the game of badminton
- Be cognizant of the important considerations for selecting and caring for badminton equipment
- Understand the rules and scoring procedures of the game
- Describe the correct grip, wrist action, ready position, footwork, strokes, and shots
- Understand badminton strategy and etiquette
- Instruct a group of students in the fundamentals of badminton
- Emphasize skill, stamina, and athletic ability necessary for badminton competition
- Recognize and use badminton terms correctly

HISTORY

A game with some sort of racquet and a feathered object goes far back into history. A game similar to badminton (shuttlecock kicking) was played in China as early as the fifth century AD, and there is mention of the game as long ago as the twelfth century in the Royal Court records of England.

Battledore shuttlecock was popular in King James I time, so it is not surprising that the game was played by early English settlers in America.

The portrait "Young Prince Sulkonsik" by Adam Mangoki, who lived about 1700, shows young members of the Royal Family of Poland holding a shuttlecock and racquet with a stance similar to that used by a modern expert preparing to serve. A portrait by Jean Simeon Chardin (1699-1779) hanging in the Uffizi Gallery in Florance depicts a girl with a racquet and shuttle.

"Portrait of Master Stephen Crossfield" hangs in the Metropolitan Museum of Art, New York. Painted by American William Williams (1727-1791), it depicts a young man holding a battledore (racquet) and shuttlecock.

It is generally accepted that the modern game of badminton, involving court boundries and a winning objective, was named when a group of British army officers home on leave from India around 1873 played the game at Badminton, the country estate of the Duke of Beaufort in Gloucestershire, England. In 1878 the Badminton Club of the city of New York was founded. Records in the New York City Museum of History substantiate that this is the oldest organized badminton club in the world. This club was the leading social rendezvous in New York for 25 years. Such names as Astor, Roosevelt, Rockerfeller, and Vanderbilt appeared on the membership list. Badminton was in its "heyday" in the United States in the 1930's when thousands of players, including famous athletes and Hollywood stars, enjoyed the game.

The American Badminton Association was founded in 1936. This association changed its name in 1977 to the United States Badminton Association.

The second organized badminton club was founded in Ireland in 1899. This organization was a founding member of the International Badminton Federation (IBF) in 1934. (The first badminton played internationally was a match between England and Ireland in Dublin in 1903.) The original IBF included nine national badminton organizations. By 1939 the tally had risen to 15; today there are more than 90. The Thomas Cup competition for men's teams was started in 1948; the Uber Cup competition for women's teams was started in 1956.

Strangely, no European country has yet won either trophy. Malaysia, Indonesia, and China have shared the 15 competitions for the men's trophy. The women's trophy was won three times by the United States, three times by Japan, and then by Indonesia and China. Additional international competition is provided by the Asian games, the British Commonwealth games, the South East Asian games, and the Pan American matches. In 1977 the first official world championship was held in Malmo, Sweden; tournaments are now scheduled every two years.

Badminton was a demonstration sport in the 1972 Olympics and an exhibition sport at the 1988 Olympics. It will be a full medal sport for the first time at Barcelona, Spain in 1992. Badminton is now part of the U.S. Olympic Festival which is held every non-Olympic year.

CARRYOVER VALUES

Badminton offers fun and fitness for everyone. It is a sport that is easy to learn but difficult to master. A beginning player receives pleasure and exercise immediately, and an advanced player can get an extremely vigorous workout by playing just one game with an equally skilled opponent. Research studies of movement show that a badminton player uses more arm action in one match than the average baseball pitcher does in a nine-inning baseball game. Also, a top-flight badminton player runs more in one match than a running back or end does in a 60-minute football game.

Badminton is played by women, men, and children. Thus it is often called the family sport. Adaptability to small areas, indoors and outdoors, at a minimal cost provides an opportunity for everyone to participate. For advanced players who wish to compete, tournament play is available almost anywhere in the United States. Tournaments sponsored by local badminton clubs (there are over 250) sanctioned by the U.S. Badminton Association provide tournament competition for juniors, women's singles, men's singles, women's doubles, men's doubles, mixed doubles, senior men's singles, senior doubles (men's and women's), and senior mixed doubles. In addition most tournaments provide play for persons aged 40 years and older. The United States has junior (18 and under), adult (19 to 39), senior (40+), masters (50+), grand masters (60+) and golden master (70+) championships.

SELECTION AND CARE OF EQUIPMENT

In all sports, good equipment is a prerequisite to good play. Badminton is no exception. For the beginner, good used equipment is often preferable to cheap new equipment.

The racquet

1. Weight depends on the strength of the individual and the feeling of comfort with the racquet.
   a. Most good racquets are between 3 and 4 ounces (85-113 g).
   b. Smaller players should select light racquets for better maneuverability.
2. Racquets should be evenly balanced or slightly lighter in the head.
   a. Doubles players usually prefer lighter racquets because quicker shots are possible.
   b. Point of balance is normally 11 to 13½ inches (28-24 cm) from the bottom of the handle.
3. Handle (grip):
   a. Size depends on size of hand.
   b. Normal racquet grips vary between 3½ and 3⅝ (8.9-9.2 cm) inches.
   c. The player should try several sizes and pick the one that feels best.
4. Strings:
   a. Nylon is relatively immune to moisture, inexpensive, longer lasting than gut, and preferred for class use and beginners because of its serviceability and cost.
   b. Gut is expensive, less durable than nylon, not moisture proof, and requires special care, but it is preferred by more advanced and tournament players because of its resiliency and "playability."
   c. Gut and nylon are normally strung to tensions around 20 pounds.
5. Care of the racquet:
   a. Frayed strings should be replaced before they break to prevent loosening of string tension.
   b. Racquets should be kept away from extreme heat or extreme cold.
6. Other types of racquets:
   a. Metal racquets are very durable. Most are some combination of carbon, ceramic, graphite, or other material.
   b. Graphite racquets are popular among advanced players because they are light, give a whipping action, and provide a subtle sensitivity to the shuttlecock.

Shuttlecocks

Shuttles are made either of goose feathers or nylon. There are several kinds of feather shuttles, and the price varies depending on the quality of the feathers and construction of the shuttle. Feather shuttles are usually used for tournaments, but because of feather breakage, these shuttles usually last only one or two games. Feathers can be pointed or rounded on the tip. The feather shuttle should be kept in a moist environment to prevent the feathers from drying out. This can be done by wrapping a moist towel around the tube 24 hours prior to use. Nylon shuttles are best for class use because they last several weeks and require no special environment.

The International Badminton Federation has defined the correct speed of a shuttlecock. Recorded in the IBF Statute Book, Law 4 states that "A shuttlecock shall be deemed to be of correct pace if, when a player of average strength strikes it with a full underhand stroke from a spot immediately above one back boundary line in a line parallel to the sidelines, and at an upward angle, it falls not less than 1 foot (30.5 cm) and not more than 2½ feet (76.2 cm) short of the other back boundary line." This statement needs to be further explained for those not accustomed to testing shuttles. The problem is to determine the shuttle speed at the particular time and place. The manufacturer has previously determined the speed by weighing the shuttle. The measure of weight is by grains (approximately ⅙ ounce). Shuttles weigh 73 to 85 grains.

In making the test (Fig. 5-1), attention should be given to the point of contact of the shuttle and the racquet. It should be directly above the back boundary line, which means that the person testing the shuttle should have both feet behind the back boundary line, that is, outside of the court area.

The distance between the long service line for doubles and the back boundary line is 2½ feet. A shuttle of correct pace when tested properly will fall within 9 inches of either side of the doubles service line.

Students and teachers of badminton should know how to test a shuttle and should test those in use. When ordering shuttles, whether feathered or nylon, indicate a shuttle speed to suit the particular time (winter, summer), altitude, and area of the country (north, east, south, west) in which they are to be used. The speed of the shuttle determines the type of game that results. It requires an undue amount of effort and strain to clear a slow shuttle overhead from back line to back line; to clear a backhand the length of the court is almost impossible. The game becomes one of brute force, and the stronger person will prevail. The game should be one of speed, finesse, deception, control, and power.

The net and standards

The net is 5 feet 1 inch (1.56 m) in height from the surface of the court at the post. The posts should be sufficiently firm to keep the net stretched and are placed on the side boundary lines of the court. Where this is not practicable, some method must be used for indicating the position of the side boundary line where it passes under the net, such as by the use of a thin post or strip of material, not less than 1½ inches (3.8 cm) in width, fixed to the side boundary line and rising vertically to the net cord. Where this is in use on a court marked for doubles, it should be placed on the side boundary line of the doubles court irrespective of whether singles or doubles are being played.

The net is made of fine natural cord or artificial fiber of a dark color and an even thickness not exceeding ⅝ to ¾ inch (1.5 to 2 cm) mesh. It should be firmly stretched from post to post and is 2 feet 6 inches (0.765 m) in depth. The top of the net is 5 feet (1.53 m) from

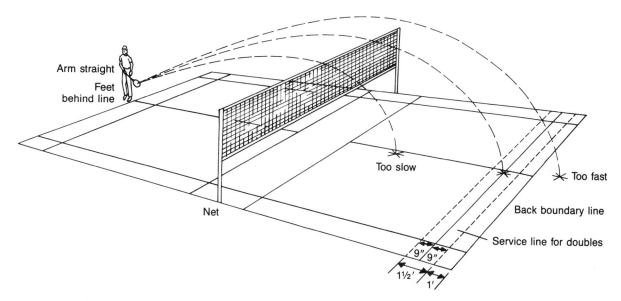

Fig. 5-1. Testing the speed of shuttlecocks. They should land within 9 inches of either side of the service line for doubles.

the floor at the center and 5 feet 1 inch (1.56 m) at the posts, and it is edged with 3-inch (7.62 cm) white tape doubled and supported by a cord or cable run through the tape and strained over and flush with the top of the posts.

HOW TO LAY OUT A COURT

If two or more courts are laid out side by side, a minimum of 6½ (2 m) feet should be allowed between them. In laying out a home court in the backyard, either tape or dry lime can be used for the boundary lines. For the gymnasium, the boundary lines are defined by white or yellow lines 1.5 inches (4 cm) wide. In laying out a badminton court at home, the singles and doubles courts can be combined. The doubles playing court is the same length (13.4 m) as the singles playing court but is 0.92 m wider.

The ceiling height of a court used for international competitive play is a minimum of 39 feet (12 m) from the floor over the full court (Fig. 5-2).

RULES

The object of the game is to hit the shuttlecock back and forth across the net with the racquet without permitting it to touch the ground, endeavoring to hit it into the opposing court so that it cannot be returned.

Scoring

The doubles and men's singles games consist of 15 points. When the score is 13 all, the side that first reached 13

has the option of "setting" the game to 5, and if the score becomes 14 all, the side that first reached 14 has the option of "setting" the game to 3. After a game has been "set," the score is called "love all," and the side that first scores 5 or 3 points (whichever set has been exercised) wins the game. In either case the option to "set" the game must be made before the next service is delivered after the score has reached 13 all or 14 all.

The women's singles game consists of 11 points. When the score is 9 all the player who first reached 9 has the option of "setting" the game to 3, or when the score is 10 all the player who first reached 10 has the option of "setting" the game to 2.

The opposing sides contest the best of three games. The players change ends at the start of the second game and also at the start of the third game (if any). In the third game the players change ends when the leading score reaches 8 in a game of 15 points or 6 in a game of 11 points. When it has been agreed to play only one game the players change ends as provided for the third game.

If players forget to change ends, the ends are changed immediately as the mistake is discovered and the existing score stands.

Faults

A fault made by a player of the side that is "in" (has the serve) puts the server out; if made by a player whose side is "out," it counts a point to the "in" side.

It is a fault:

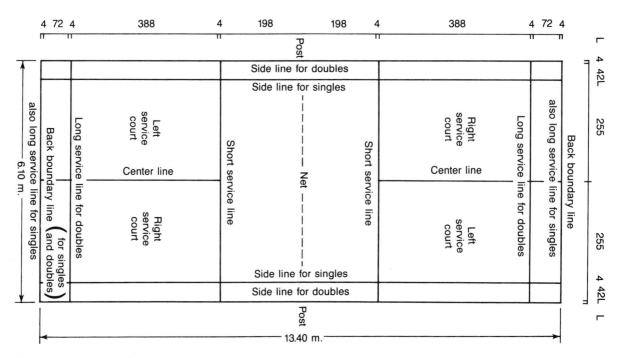

Fig. 5-2. Double and single badminton court dimensions (metric).

1. If, in serving, the shuttle at the instant of being struck is higher than the server's waist, or if at the instant of the shuttle being struck, the shaft of the racquet is not pointing sufficiently downward that the whole head of the racquet is discernibly below the whole of the server's hand holding the racquet (Fig. 5-3).

2. If, in serving, the shuttle falls into the wrong service court (into the one not diagonally opposite to the server) or falls short of the short service line, beyond the long service line, or outside the side boundary lines of the service court into which service is in order.

3. If the server's feet are not in the service court from which service is at the time being in order, or if the feet of the player receiving the service are not in the service court diagonally opposite until the service is delivered.

4. If before or during the delivery of the service any player makes preliminary feints or otherwise intentionally balks (tries to deceive) the opponent, or if any player deliberately delays serving the shuttle or getting ready to receive it, so as to obtain an unfair advantage.

5. If, either in service or play, the shuttle falls outside the boundaries of the court, or passes through or under the net, or fails to pass the net, or touches the roof or side walls, or touches the person or dress of a player. A shuttle falling on a line is deemed to have fallen in the court or service court of which such line is a boundary.

6. If the shuttle in play is struck before it crosses to the striker's side of the net. The striker may, however, follow the shuttle over the net with the racquet in the course of the stroke.

7. If, when the shuttle is in play, a player touches the net or its supports with racquet, person, or dress.

8. If the shuttle is held on the racquet (that is, caught or slung) during the execution of a stroke, or if the shuttle is hit twice in succession by the same player with two strokes, or if the shuttle is hit by a player and partner successively.

9. If a player obstructs an opponent.

General

The server may not serve until the opponent is ready, but the opponent is deemed to be ready if a return of the service is attempted.

The server and the player served to must stand within the limits of their respective service courts (as bounded by the short and long service, the center and side lines), and some part of both feet of these players must remain in contact with the surface of the court in a stationary position until the service is delivered. A foot on or touching a line in the case of either the server or the receiver is held to be outside the service court. The respective partners may take up any position, provided they do not unsight or otherwise obstruct an opponent.

If, in the course of service or rally, the shuttle touches and passes over the net, the stroke is not invalidated thereby. It is a good return if the shuttle, having passed outside either post, drops on or within the boundary lines of the opposite court. A "let" may be given by the umpire for any unforeseen or accidental hindrance.

If, in service or during a rally, a shuttle, after passing over the net, is caught in or on the net, it is a "let."

If the receiver is faulted for moving before the service is delivered or for not being within the correct service court, and at the same time the server is also faulted for service infringement, it is considered a "let."

When a "let" occurs, the play since the last service does not count, and the player who last served serves again.

If the server in serving misses the shuttle completely, it is a fault; but if the shuttle is touched by the racquet, a service is delivered.

If a player has the chance of striking the shuttle when quite near the net, the opponent must not extend the

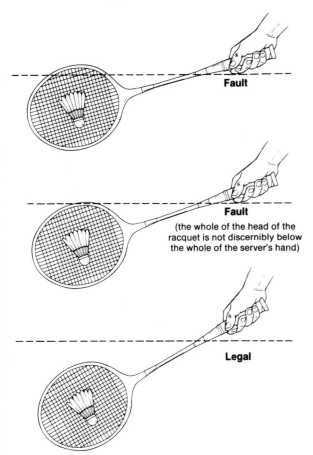

Fault

Fault

(the whole of the head of the racquet is not discernibly below the whole of the server's hand)

Legal

Fig. 5-3. Delivery of service.

racquet near the net. A player may, however, hold up the racquet for protection to avoid being hit in the face if this action does not result in obstructing the opponent's stroke.

It is the duty of the umpire to call "fault" or "let" should either occur, without appeal being made by the players, and to give a decision on any appeal regarding a point in dispute, if made before the net service, and also to appoint linesmen and service judges at the umpire's discretion. The umpire's decision is final, but the decision of a linesman or service judge should be upheld. This does not preclude the umpire also from faulting the server or receiver.

Singles play

The players serve from and receive service in their respective right-hand service courts only when the server's score is 0 or an even number of points, the service being delivered from and received in their left-hand service courts when the server's score is an odd number of points. "Setting" does not affect this sequence.

Both players change service courts after each point has been scored.

Doubles play

It having been decided which side is to have the first service, the player in the right-hand service court of that side commences the game by serving to the player in the service court diagonally opposite. If the latter player returns the shuttle before it touches the ground, it is to be returned by one of the "in" (serving) side and then returned by one of the "out" (receiving) side, and so on, until a fault is made or the shuttle ceases to be "in play." If a fault is made by the "in" side, its right to continue serving is lost, as only one player of the side beginning a game is entitled to do so, and the opponent in the right-hand service court then becomes the server; but if the service is not returned or the fault is made by the "out" side, the "in" side scores a point. The "in" side players then change from one service court to the other, the service now being from the left-hand service court to the player in the service court diagonally opposite. So long as a side remains "in," service is delivered alternately from each service court into the one diagonally opposite, the change being made by the "in" side when, and only when, a point is added to its score.

The first service of a side in each inning is made from the right-hand service court. A "service" is delivered as soon as the shuttle is struck by the server's racquet. The shuttle is thereafter "in play" until it touches the floor or playing surface or until a fault or "let" occurs. After the service is delivered, the server and the player served to may take up any position they choose on their side of the net, irrespective of boundary lines.

Only the player served to may receive the service, however, should the shuttle touch or be struck by his or her partner, the "in" side scores a point. No player may receive two consecutive services in the same game.

Only one player of the side beginning a game is entitled to serve in its first innings. In all subsequent innings, each partner has the right, and they serve consecutively. The side winning a game always serves first in the next game, but either of the winners may serve and either of the losers may receive the service.

If a player serves out of turn or from the wrong service court and the serving side wins the rally, it is a "let," provided that such "let" is claimed and allowed or ordered by the umpire before the next succeeding service is delivered.

If a player of the "out" side standing in the wrong service court is prepared to receive the service when it is delivered, and the receiving side wins the rally, it is a "let," provided that such "let" is claimed and allowed or ordered by the umpire before the next succeeding service is delivered.

If in either of the previous cases the side at fault loses the rally, the mistake stands and the players' position is not corrected.

Should a player inadvertently change sides incorrectly and the mistake not be discovered until after the next succeeding service has been delivered, the mistake stands, and a "let" cannot be claimed or allowed, and the players' position is not corrected.

FUNDAMENTAL SKILLS AND TECHNIQUES
Grip of the racquet

1. Forehand grip: The handle of the racquet is held as if the player were shaking hands with the racquet (Fig. 5-4, *A* and *B*).
2. Backhand grip: Similar to the forehand grip except the hand is rotated slightly to the left and the thumb is placed flat against the side bevel for additional power. The changing of grips during play becomes somewhat automatic (Fig. 5-4, *C* and *D*).
3. The racquet should be held at the extreme end of the handle with fingers well spread.
4. A standard grip may be secured by placing the racquet, as the player normally would, in front of the body, with the playing surface perpendicular to the floor and then grasping the racquet as one would grip the handle of a hatchet.
5. The standard grip can be used for both forehand and backhand strokes.
6. The hand, wrist, and arm should be entirely relaxed, but the fingers should tighten on the handle just before the racquet contacts the shuttle.

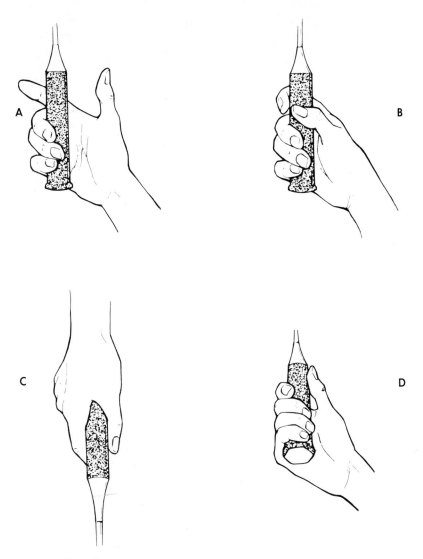

Fig. 5-4. Gripping the racquet (right-handed player).

Wrist action

1. Wrist action is used to disguise intentions. A simple flick of the wrist aids not only in directing the shuttle but also in sending the opponent in the wrong direction, since the flight is concealed until the last fraction of a second.
2. In starting all shots, the player should keep the racquet well back by cocking the wrist. The racquet's forward swing should not be checked; follow-through is important.

Ready position and footwork

To move properly on a badminton court, the player must start from a constantly maintained "ready" position. The ideal starting position on the court is approximately a step and a half from the short line and straddling the center line. The player who does not reach this ideal

position on the court before the opponent hits the shuttle should stop and react to where the shuttle is hit. A player should never be moving as the opponent is hitting the shuttle.

The correct stance is similar to that of an infielder in baseball expecting a grounder. Weight should be on the balls of the feet, with the feet far enough apart to assure stable balance. The body should be ready to spring in any direction. The knees should be slightly bent. The racquet head should be held at about shoulder height comfortably away from the body.

In the ready position the feet are in the 12 o'clock position (Fig. 5-5). To cover the court properly a speed line should be set up to get to the 1 o'clock, 3 o'clock, and 5 o'clock positions for a forehand stroke. Movement to the right, for a forehand stroke, at these positions on the court involves moving the body's center of gravity

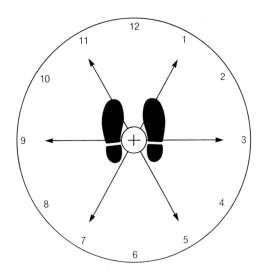

Fig. 5-5. Footwork.

in the direction of the shuttle. For the backhand stroke the speed line should be set up to 7 o'clock, 9 o'clock, and 11 o'clock positions.

STROKES
Service
High deep serve
The high deep serve is an underhand forehand serve hit high so that the shuttle will land in deep court, near the back line.

1. Starting position: Feet in stride position with left foot in front for right-handed players. Shift weight to the rear on backswing, then forward as racquet comes forward. Both feet must remain in contact with the court; "stepping" is a fault.
2. A full backswing is made with the wrist cocked.
3. The wrist is uncocked just prior to contact.
4. Follow-through: Shuttle contact is made well in front of the body, not at the side, on the follow-through of the underhand stroke.

Low short serve
The low short serve should be made in such a manner that the shuttle barely clears the net, is on a downward trajectory the moment it passes over the net, and lands close to the short line in the opponent's court.

All basic techniques for the low short serve—starting position, body rotation, shift in weight, and so on—are the same as for the deep high serve except:

1. This is a "push" type of serve, accomplished with the wrist remaining almost fully cocked throughout the serve, with little rotation of the forearm.
2. The server should attempt to contact the shuttle as close to the waist height as possible to achieve the desired flat trajectory.

Drive serve
The drive serve is comparable to hitting a line drive in baseball. This serve can be driven at the opponent preferably to hit just below shoulder level.

Basic techniques for the drive serve—starting position, body rotation, and so on—are the same as for the deep high serve except:

1. The racquet is partially uncocked at contact with the shuttle.
2. Inasmuch as the racquet does not go beyond half cock, there is not a complete follow-through in a full arc, as in the high deep serve.

Forehand overhead shots
Forehand overhead shots begin with the player's weight on the back foot, followed by shifting of weight from the right to the left foot. Body rotation occurs here.

Defensive clear shot
1. The racquet is angled slightly back from the perpendicular to attain a high trajectory (Fig. 5-6, A).
2. Contact with the shuttle is high and slightly in front of the player.
3. The player should hit the shuttle high and deep and assume proper court position as a receiver.

Attacking clear shot
1. This is the same shot as the defensive clear, except the head of the racquet is almost perpendicular to the floor on contact with the shuttle, giving it a flattened trajectory (Fig. 5-6, B).
2. This is a quick hit used primarily to place the shuttle deep and out of reach of the opponent.
3. The object of this shot is to get the shuttle past an out-of-position opponent.

Smash
1. Deception on this "put away" or kill shot is accomplished by making it appear that the return will be a "clear" or "drop."
2. The body should be facing the net on completion of the shot.
3. One should lead with the elbow as the body rotates. The arm should be straight on contact with the shuttle.
4. This shot is an extension of the overhead clear, except contact is made with the shuttle farther in front of the body and angle of the racquet is slightly forward (Fig. 5-6, C).
5. Vigorous wrist action just prior to contact provides the velocity for the smash.

Drop
1. For a fast drop, the racquet is held at approximately the same angle as for the smash at contact. It should

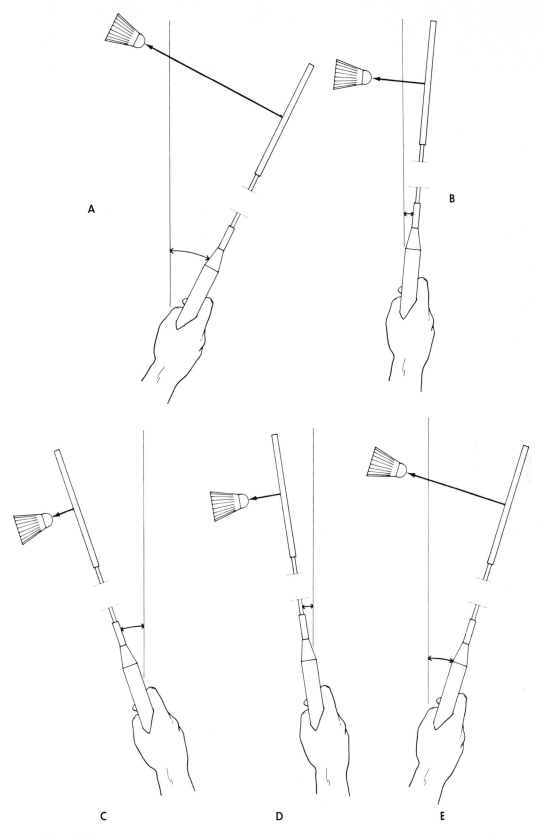

Fig. 5-6. Racquet contact points for various shots. **A**, Contact point for defensive clear. **B**, Contact point for attacking clear. **C**, Contact point for smash. **D**, Contact point for fast drop. **E**, Contact point for loop drop.

be hit like a smash, except with a softer touch (Fig. 5-6, *D*).

2. For a loop drop, the racquet angle is similar to that of a defensive clear (Fig. 5-6, *E*).

Backhand overhead shots

The player's back is to the net. The forearm is bent toward the chest for the "ready" position. On striking the shuttle, the arm is extended and the forearm is simultaneously rotated in a clockwise direction. The angles at contact, the placement of the shuttle in the opponent's court, and the use of backhand overhead shots are the same as for forehand overhead shots.

Drive shots

The shuttle is hit quickly, forehand or backhand, on a flat trajectory. The forearm drive action is similar to that of throwing a baseball sidearm.

1. In both forehand and backhand, one should lead with the elbow and hit from a cocked position.
2. The arm should be straight on contact with the shuttle.

Underhand clear shot

The player swings up and through with the wrist in a cocked position, using the same mechanics as in a high deep serve.

Net shots

Net shots require a delicate stroke. The racquet, therefore, does not need to be held as firmly as it is in power shots.

1. Contact the shuttle as near the top of the net as possible.
2. Use arm movement instead of forearm rotation.
3. Stretch and reach for the shuttle.

Around-the-head shots

Such shots are within an arc around the head, above the shoulder, and on the left side of the body.

1. Body faces net, with weight on left foot at contact.
2. Right leg swings forward at completion of stroke.
3. Basic stroke is rotation motion.
4. The angle of the racquet at the time the shuttle is hit determines whether a clear, smash, or drop shot can be executed.

STRATEGY
Singles

1. Serve long unless opponent is playing back for just such a serve; in that case, serve short to take advantage of opponent's poor position.
2. Base use of long or short serve on opponent's strengths and weaknesses.

3. Return a high serve with a drop or clear shot.
4. Use a clear shot for a low serve, or if it can be reached before falling too far below the net, use a net shot.
5. Use down-the-line smashes or smash at opponent's right hip or shoulder.
6. Return a smash with a drop to the point on the court farthest from the point at which the smash was made.
7. Drive down the sidelines.
8. Play your position; do not try to outguess your opponent.
9. Take advantage of your opponent's weaknesses, but not to the extent that such repeated effort improves the weakness.

Doubles

1. Play formations:
   a. Side by side: Each person is responsible for half the court, from front to back. Disadvantages are that it is hard to run from the net to the back court and make a good smash or a good attacking stroke, and returns to the center cause confusion as to who will hit them.
   b. Front and back: One person plays the front court and one the back, with the front player taking all net shots and any other shot that can be returned with a better shot than the partner can deliver. Although this is a popular formation for doubles, a disadvantage is the resulting poor defense against smashes and drives down the sidelines.
   c. Combination: This formation combines the best features of the other two. The partners rotate in a counterclockwise circle, so that the backcourt player need never return for a backhand shot in the near court. When the team using this formation is on the attack, the players should be playing front and back; when on defense, they should be playing side by side.
2. Play shots that will give an opening for your partner on his or her return. Do not leave your partner open to a heated attack from the opponents.
3. Serves low and short, preferably to the corner formed by the center line and short service line.
4. Smash long serves, but occasionally use a drop shot.
5. Rush short serves.
6. Do not play too close to the net. A position around the short service line is best for playing the net.
7. If servers are playing in front-and-back formation, the best return of a low serve is a half-court shot down the sidelines.
8. Make placements to the least obvious spots.

BADMINTON COURTESY

Sportsmanship is the foremost courtesy. Be gracious; never "needle" an opponent. If in doubt about a boundary decision, call it in favor of the opponent; the opponent, if a good sport, will disagree. If fouling occurs at the net, one should call it on one's self.

Hand a shuttle over to an adjoining court player at the end of a rally. Thank a player when your shuttle is returned.

Do not delay in calling a foul.

Do not play indifferently against an inferior opponent.

TEACHING CONSIDERATIONS

1. For school-age populations establish the grip and ready position as well as a basic underhand and overhead shot. It is not necessary to teach specialized shots until students can keep the shuttlecock going continuously across the net cooperatively with these basic shots.

2. Begin with singles, even if it means using half a court for practice.

3. Design experiences to have students change the placement, force levels, and trajectory of the shuttlecock from these basic shots.

4. Teach the short and high deep serve.

5. Introduce competitive play and stress placement of shuttlecock away from opponent. Introduce the clears and drop shot as students attempt to place the shuttlecock in front of the service line and near the back boundary. Practice the specialized skills and put them back into the game. Modify the games if need be by giving extra points for points won using one of these shots.

6. Begin doubles play with side-by-side strategies. Introduce combination up and back and side by side as soon as students are consistently returning to their home base position after being pulled out of position defensively.

7. Design warm-up activities that include combinations of skills using both forehand and backhand strokes.

GLOSSARY

alley The area on the sides of the court between the doubles and singles court; the alleys are 1½ feet wide.

back alley The shuttle may not be served into this area. It is 2½ feet wide.

backhand Hitting the shuttle on the left side of the body, if a player is right-handed.

bird The badminton "ball"; the shuttlecock.

carry Catching the shuttle on the racquet and then slinging it.

clear A high, deep shot.

crosscourt Hitting the shuttle diagonally over the net from one side of the court to the other side.

defensive clear A shot driven high to the backcourt.

drive A hard-hit shuttle that travels flat and close to the net.

drop A shot that barely clears the net and then falls into the opponent's front court.

face The hitting surface of the racquet.

fault Any violation of the rules.

flight The path of the shuttle.

forecourt The front of the court.

forehand Hitting the shuttle on the right side of the body, if a player is right-handed.

frame The part of the racquet that holds the strings.

high clear A shuttle that is hit very high and lands in the back of the opponent's court.

kill A hard-hit shuttle that is impossible to return.

long serve Any serve hit into the back alleys.

match Two of three games.

miss Failure of the racquet to come in contact with the shuttle.

net flight A shuttle that follows the net when hit.

on-guard stance Ready for the serve or return.

racquet The instrument, usually weighing about 3 ounces, used to hit the shuttle.

rally Hitting the shuttle back and forth.

receiver The player to receive the serve.

round-the-head stroke Circling the racquet clockwise around the head and hitting it with the overhand motion.

serve Putting the shuttle into play.

server The one who starts the volley.

setting Deciding on the score of the game if there is a tie.

short serve Hitting the shuttle over the net but not into the opponent's court.

side out To lose serve.

sling (See carry).

smash A high shot returned sharply; same as kill.

throw A carried shuttle; this is a fault.

toss serve A shuttle that is tossed or dropped out in front of the server.

volley Hitting the shuttle while it is in the air.

SUGGESTED READINGS

Ballou RB: Teaching badminton, Minneapolis, 1982, Burgess Publishing Co.

Bloss MV and Hales RS: Badminton, ed 6, Dubuque, Iowa, 1990, WC Brown Co.

Chafin MB and Turner M: Badminton everyone, Winston-Salem, NC, 1984, Hunter Textbooks, Inc. Contains material on techniques and strategies for all levels, drills and skill improvement, conditioning and fitness, and rules and terminology. Also includes tips for students, hundreds of illustrations, and chapter quizzes.

Gibbons-Hufty E: Badminton, Edina, Minn., 1985, Burgess International Group, Inc.

Krotee M and Turner E: Innovative theory and practice of badminton, Dubuque, Iowa, 1984, Kendall/Hunt Publishing Co.

Moore B and Henderson T: Shuttlecock action, Dubuque, Iowa, 1977, Kendall/Hunt Publishing Co.

Official rules book of badminton, Bergenfield, NJ, 1989, General Sportcraft Co., Ltd.

Poole J: Badminton, Glenview, Ill, 1982, Scott, Foresman and Co. Written by a champion player, this book includes step-by-step summary of mechanics for each movement, latest developments in equipment and mechanics, and drills.

Reznik J and Byrd R: Badminton, Scottsdale, Ariz, 1987, Gorsuch Scarisbrick Publishers.

Scheele HAE editor: World badminton, official publication No. 22, 1981, International Badminton Federation.

Skrivseth M, Haywood J, Dugas EA and Fabian L: Badminton made simple, Dubuque, Iowa, 1989, Eddie Bowers Publishing Co. Contains over 100 pictures, a complete list of drills and information for players of all ability levels.

United States Badminton Association: Official rules of play (U.S.B.A. Handbook), Papillion, Neb, 1989, The Association.

FILMS AND VIDEOTAPES

Badminton. Ideal Pictures, 417 N. State St., Chicago, IL 60611.

Poole J: *Badminton,* 14 min video, $32.50. Sports Video Champions on Film, 745 State Circle, Ann Arbor, MI 48106.

Badminton fundamentals, 16 mm, All American Productions and Publishers, Greeley, Colo.

Badminton series. The game is divided into three sections and covered completely from beginning to advanced play, $89.00, Athletic Institute, 200 Castlewood Drive, North Palm Beach, FL 33408.

Beginning badminton series. Athletic Institute, 805 Merchandise Mart, Chicago, IL 60654.

Let's play badminton. General Sportscraft Limited, New York.

Tips on better badminton. Sports Tips and Teaching Aids, Detroit.

6

Basketball

Completion of this chapter should enable the reader to:

- Appreciate the development of the game of basketball
- Explain the basic rules of the game and the slight differences that exist between the men's and women's game
- Demonstrate the fundamental skills of passing, dribbling, and shooting
- Explain the general principles of offensive and defensive strategy
- Instruct a group of students in the basic skills of basketball

HISTORY

Basketball was introduced in 1891 by Dr. James A. Naismith, then physical education director at the YMCA College in Springfield, Massachusetts. The first official game was not played until 1892. Basketball was principally designed as a game to create interest in the gymnasium during the winter months.

A peach basket was first used as the hoop. After each score the ball had to be taken out of the basket before play could be resumed.

The game spread rapidly to the nation's playgrounds, community centers, gymnasiums, schools, and colleges, until today nearly every boy and girl learns to play basketball.

In 1899 the women formulated their own rules, and in 1901 the first women's *Basketball Guide* was published.

Although basketball was included as a demonstration sport in the 1904 St. Louis Olympics, it was not finally adopted until 1936. The United States beat Canada (19 to 8) for the gold medal in 1936 but the game was played outdoors on a clay court in the rain. The United States dominated Olympic basketball by winning the gold medal in 1948 (65 to 21 over France), 1952 (36 to 25 over Russia), 1956 (85 to 55 over Russia), 1960 (81 to 57 over Russia), 1964 (73 to 59 over Russia), and 1968 (65 to 50 over Yugoslavia). The United States lost for the first time in Olympic history in the famous final game of the 1972

Munich Olympics when the Soviet team, after protesting, was awarded the chance to replay the final 3 seconds of the game and won 50 to 49. In 1976 the Americans regained the gold medal by defeating Yugoslavia 95 to 72. Yugoslavia defeated Italy 86 to 77 in 1980, the year the United States boycotted the Olympics. In Los Angeles the United States team once again claimed the gold medal by defeating Spain 96 to 65. In the 1988 Seoul Olympics the United States men's team had its worst finish ever by claiming the bronze medal.

Women's basketball was added to the Olympics in 1976, and the gold medal was claimed by the Soviets with the United States team picking up the silver medal. In 1980 the Soviet women defeated Bulgaria 104 to 73. The United States women's team won its first gold medal by defeating Korea 85 to 55 in 1984 and its second straight gold medal with a victory over Yugoslavia in 1988.

EQUIPMENT

The playing court is a rectangular surface free from obstructions, having maximum dimensions for college of 94 × 50 feet (28.65 × 15.24 m) and for high school of 84 × 50 feet (25.60 × 15.24 m) (Fig. 6-1). However, many courts are smaller. The court dimensions are the same for men's and women's basketball.

The backboard, 6 feet (1.83 m) wide and 4 feet (1.23 m) high (smaller for high school), is located at the center of each end of the court 4 feet (1.23 m) in from the end

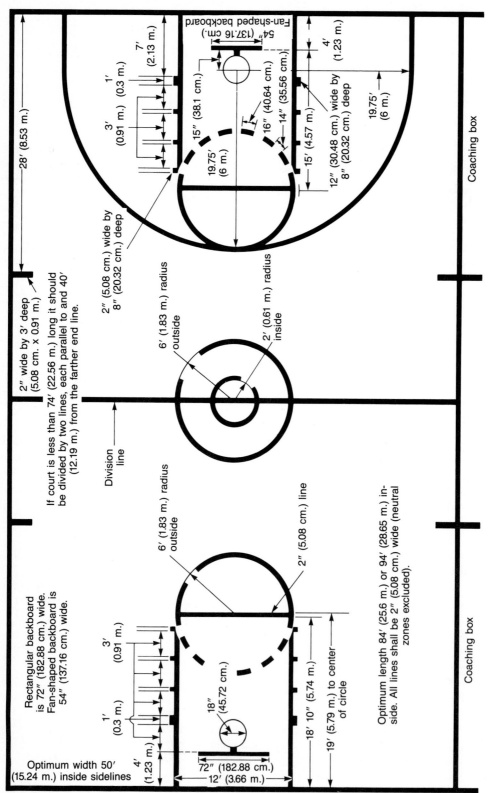

Fig. 6-1. Basketball court for men and women. Left end shows large backboard for college games; right end shows small backboard for high school games. For the broken semicircle in the free throw lane, it is recommended that there be eight marks 16 inches (40.64 cm) long and seven spaces 14 inches (35.56 cm) long. There should be a minimum of 3 feet (0.91 m) and preferably 10 feet (3.05 m) of unobstructed space outside the court. If this is impossible, a narrow broken 1-inch (2.54 cm) line should be marked inside the court parallel with and 3 feet (0.91 m) inside the boundary. Three point line is 19.75 feet (6 m) from the basket for high school and college courts.

line and 9 feet (2.74 m) above the floor. It can be made of hardwood, metal, or glass (Fig. 6-2).

The basket is an open hammock net, suspended from the backboard on a metal ring 18 inches (45.7 cm) in diameter, which must be 6 inches (15.2 cm) from the rigid surface to which it is fastened and 10 feet (3.05 m) above the floor.

The ball used by men is spherical, measuring 30 inches (76.2 cm) in circumference. The ball used by women is 28.5 to 29.0 inches (72.4 to 73.7 cm) in circumference.

Foot comfort and protection should be a primary concern of both coach and player. Shoes and socks that fit well and that are designed for use by basketball players help avoid unnecessary injuries and discomfort, including blisters, sprained ankles, and bruised heels.

GENERAL RULES

Rules governing the game are revised each year by the joint Basketball Rules Committee, representing the Amateur Athletic Union (AAU), National Association for Girls' and Women's Sports (NAGWS), National Collegiate Athletic Association (NCAA), Young Men's Christian Association (YMCA), National Federation of State High School Athletic Associations, Canadian Amateur Basketball Association, and chartered boards of officials.

The game

The home team provides the game ball, and traditionally the visiting team is given the choice of courts for the first half. If a neutral court is used, a coin toss determines home team and choice of courts. The teams change sides of the court at halftime. Half of the court is the frontcourt of one team and the backcourt of the other team.

The ball is passed, thrown, bounced, handed, or otherwise moved among players of one team, with the intent of scoring a basket and preventing the other team from scoring.

Teams consist of five players: two forwards, two guards, and one center. Generally the forwards play closest to the opponent's basket, the guards play closest to their team's basket, and the center plays between the forwards and the guards.

The game is started with a jump ball between any two opponents (usually the centers) at center court. After each field goal the ball is put into play by the team not scoring, from the out-of-bounds area behind the basket at which the score was made.

After a free throw awarded because of a personal foul, the ball is put into play by the opponent from behind the opponent's basket. If the free throw is the result of a technical foul, the ball is put into play from out of

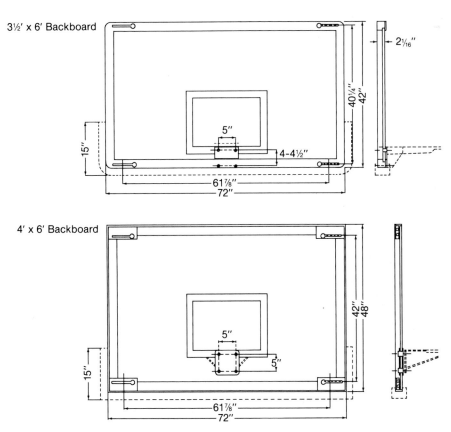

Fig. 6-2. Basketball goals.

bounds at midcourt by the free thrower's team.

A player is out of bounds if he or she touches the floor on or outside the boundary line. If a player causes the ball to pass over the boundary line, the ball is put into play by an opposing player from that spot. Any player can make the throw-in. The player throwing the ball in must stand out of bounds where the referee designates, may take one lateral step to the left or right, jump up or take two or more steps backward, and may use either one or two hands to make the throw-in, which must be completed within 5 seconds.

Rules common to men's and women's basketball

1. Numbers must be worn by players on front and back.
2. A jump ball is taken following a double foul.
3. The hand is considered to be a part of the ball on tie balls, shots, dribbles, interceptions, and the like.
4. The penalty for a violation is loss of possession of the ball.
5. The following are not considered dribbles:
   a. Successive tries for goals
   b. Fumbles
   c. Attempts to gain control of the ball by:
      (1) Tapping it from the control of another player
      (2) Tapping it from the reach of another player
      (3) Blocking a pass and recovering the ball
      (4) Blocking a shot and recovering the ball
6. During a free throw players from the defensive team shall occupy both lane spaces adjacent to the end line.
7. On jumb balls, opponents are entitled to alternate positions around the restraining circle if they so indicate before the official is ready to toss the ball.
8. On jump balls, the players must hold their established positions around the restraining circle until the ball has been tossed.

Rule differences

Two important differences in the rules for men's and women's basketball are:

1. Use of a 30-second clock in women's basketball and a 45-second clock in men's basketball. After securing possession of the ball, the offensive team must attempt a shot at the basket before the time clock goes to zero or give up possession of the ball.
2. In men's basketball the ball must be advanced into the frontcourt within 10 seconds but in women's basketball (with the shorter 30-second clock) there is no such rule.

Violations common to men's and women's basketball

1. Taking more than one step with the ball without passing, shooting, or dribbling
2. Kicking the ball with foot or lower leg

3. Stepping out of bounds with the ball
4. The center's leaving the circle before the ball is tipped in beginning play
5. Staying in one's own free-throw lane for more than 3 seconds
6. Failure to observe free-throw regulations
7. Failure to inbound the ball within 5 seconds
8. Double dribbling
9. Moving the ball into the backcourt once it has been advanced to the frontcourt (over-and-back)
10. Technical fouls include:
    a. Taking time out too often
    b. Failure of substitutes to report to proper officials
    c. Unsportsmanlike conduct
    d. Use of illegal numbers or uniforms
    e. Touching the backboard or rim illegally
11. Personal fouls include:
    a. Charging
    b. Blocking
    c. Pushing
    d. Holding
    e. Tripping
    f. Hacking or kneeing

When a violation is committed, the ball is given to the opponents out of bounds. When a foul is committed, the opponents may be given a free throw, an opportunity to make two free throws if the first one is made, or the ball out of bounds. The decision as to which of these options is awarded depends on the particular foul committed, the level of play (high school or college), and the number of fouls that the offending team has previously committed. A player fouled in the act of shooting gets two free throws. If the basket is made, one free throw is awarded and the basket is counted. Only personal fouls disqualify a player. A player is allowed only four personal fouls; a fifth sidelines the player for the remainder of the game.

Officials

The officials include a referee, an umpire, three timekeepers, and two scorers (one timekeeper and one scorer are assistants). The third timekeeper runs the 30- or 45-second shot clock.

Scoring

Two points are awarded for each basket from the floor, and 1 point is awarded for each free throw. Three points are awarded for field goals made from outside the three-point line.

Coaching box

A coaching box is outlined outside the side of the court on which the officials' table and players' benches are located. The area is bounded by the endline extended, sideline, midcourt marker extended, and the players' bench. The endline and midcourt mark lines are 3 feet long and 2 inches wide, and their color contrasts with that of the midcourt mark line and endline.

DURATION OF GAME
Men's game
College men play for two periods of 20 minutes each, with a 15-minute rest at halftime. If the score is tied at the end of the 40 minutes, as many 5-minute periods as needed to break the tie are played.

High school teams play four quarters of 8 minutes each, with a 10-minute halftime rest and 1 minute between quarters. If the score is tied at the end of the fourth quarter, as many 3-minute periods as needed to break the tie are played.

Women's game
Women play for two halves of 20 minutes each, with a 15-minute rest between halves. If the score is tied at the end of the game, as many 5-minute periods as needed to break the tie are played.

High school teams play four quarters of 8 minutes each, with a 2-minute rest between quarters and a 10-minute rest between halves. To break a tie, as many 3-minute extra periods as necessary are played.

FUNDAMENTAL SKILLS AND TECHNIQUES
Passing
Passing is the key to successful basketball. A successful team must be able to handle, control, and move the ball downcourt quickly and accurately to create scoring opportunities.

First, learn to catch as well as pass. When the ball is thrown to you, spread the fingers but keep them relaxed. When the ball hits the fingers, let the arms give slightly toward the body. When the ball is under control, finger it into passing position by placing the hands on each side of the ball so that you can get it away quickly or get set for a shot.

Some practical helps
1. Remember that the cause of most fumbling is holding the arms too stiff while catching.
2. Watch the ball all the way into the hands.
3. Do not fight the ball; that is, do not pass until you have full control of the ball.
4. Stay relaxed, and try not to rush passes.
5. Keep your head up and use peripheral vision to spot any free teammate.
6. When a teammate calls for the ball, check the position of the defender before making a pass, and make the pass to the side farthest from the deender.
7. Move toward a pass rather than away from it.

8. Passes to moving teammates should lead them so they do not have to slow down or reverse direction.
9. When some mastery in controlling the ball has been gained, learn to pass with deception, for example, looking one way and passing another, or faking high and passing low.
10. Rely on "split vision," actually looking straight ahead but seeing the receiver out of the corner of the eye.
11. Do not pass blindly.

Chest or push pass
Hold the ball with both hands, elbows close to the body, fingers spread with thumbs pointed inward. Step toward the receiver and whip the ball with a strong wrist snap and push of thumbs and fingers, making the arms follow through in the direction of the pass (Fig. 6-3).

Cross-body pass
Hold and throw the ball with both hands. Assume a crouched position and turn one side of the body to the opponent and bring the ball back to the other side by bending both elbows. Execute the pass across the chest with a strong wrist snap and extension of the arms, letting the hands follow through in the direction of the pass.

Bounce pass
A bounce pass can be executed with either one or two hands and is often used to get the ball past a defensive player between the passer and the teammate who is to receive the pass. For the two-handed bounce pass hold the ball in much the same manner as for the chest pass except somewhat lower, about waist high. Then push the ball out and down with enough force and at such an angle that the ball bounces to the teammate. The one-hand bounce pass is often executed directly from the dribble. The bounce pass should only be used for short passes and it should travel between one half and three quarters of the distance in the air.

Two-hand overhead pass
Hold and throw the ball with both hands. Bring the ball well above and slightly behind the head with both hands and release it with a strong wrist snap and extension of the arms. Arms and hands follow through in the direction of the pass (Fig. 6-4).

Shovel or underhand pass
Hold and throw the ball with both hands. Spread the legs and crouch, keeping the ball close to the floor; step toward the receiver and shovel the ball with both hands with a low underhand sweep.

This pass can also be executed from a semicrouched position, with the ball held waist high and close to the body, fingers pointing down on the ball, and the ball

Fig. 6-3. Chest pass.

Fig. 6-4. Two-hand overhead pass. **A**, Midway. **B**, End.

Fig. 6-5. Baseball pass.

brought back around to the side of the body. The ball is released with a shoveling motion, a wrist snap, and a step in the direction of the receiver.

Baseball pass

Shift the ball in front of the waist to the throwing hand, turn the opposite side of the body in the direction of the pass, and then whip the ball back, as in an infield throw. Step toward the receiver and throw the ball with a full arm motion and wrist snap. Permit the fingers to follow through without a twist so that the movement does not cause the ball to curve (Fig. 6-5).

One-hand hook pass

With the opposite side turned in the direction of the receiver, bring the ball from the hips, up and back. Cradle the ball on the wrist with the fingers well spread behind it for control and throw it with a hook motion of the arm and strong wrist action over the head, following through with the hand (Fig. 6-6).

Pivoting

Pivoting is a skill used to elude an opponent when a player has the ball. A forward pivot is executed by keeping one foot in place on the floor and moving the other forward and across the foot in place (Fig. 6-7). A reverse pivot is executed by keeping one foot in place and moving the other backward in a semicircle.

Dribbling

Learn to dribble with the body low for protection and the head up. Dribble with the hand farthest from the defender and use the body to protect the ball. Spread the fingers and relax the wrist and fingers. Control the ball with the fingers, pushing it down and forward; do not bat it.

Keep the ball low, below the waist. Avoid a high bounce dribble. The ball can be moved downcourt faster by passing than by dribbling, so never dribble when you can pass.

Fig. 6-6. One-hand hook pass.

Fig. 6-7. Pivot and pass.

Fig. 6-8. Fake right.

Up-and-under fake pass and dribble

Stand for the shot in front of the opponent and go through the motion of bringing the ball up for a jump shot. As the guard closes in or leaps to block the shot, duck low and drive past to one side, dribbling with the hand farthest from the opponent.

Fake pass and dribble

Hold the ball waist high on receiving it; then fake to the right with the ball and head. As the guard goes in that direction, turn quickly to the left and cross-step with the right foot and dribble the ball on the left side with the left hand, which is farthest from the guard (Fig. 6-8).

Shooting
Jump shot

The jump shot is the most common one in basketball. It is often executed from a dribble, but players should be able to accomplish it in almost any situation. Come to a stop from the dribble and execute a controlled jump. At the same time, bring the ball overhead, with the shooting hand behind and the elbow of the shooting arm under the ball and the other hand in front. At the peak of the leap, remove the balance hand and release the ball with extension of the right forearm and good wrist extension (Fig. 6-9).

One-hand set shot

Hold the ball chin high with both hands, the fingers spread along the sides and slightly behind the ball, the thumbs directed inward behind the ball, and the feet close together with one slightly ahead of the other. Turn the ball so that the shooting hand is behind and under the ball. Bend the knees, bring the ball up, removing the left hand if shooting with the right, and shoot with a strong wrist action and extension of the arm, letting the feet come off the floor, and follow through (Fig. 6-10).

Lay-up shot

Stop dribbling when the right foot is on the floor, step with the left foot, bring up the right knee and jump off the left foot, leap high into the air, shifting the ball to the shooting hand, and raise the shooting hand as high as possible above and in front of the head. Release the ball off the fingertips, laying it softly against the backboard (Fig. 6-11). *Note:* Use both hands to bring the ball up for the shot and do not remove the balancing hand too soon.

Hook shot

Hold the ball high with both hands, bring the ball to the right side opposite the basket, and remove the balance hand (left). Shoot with a full sweep of the right arm, keeping the arm perfectly straight. In starting the shot, take a short step with the left foot away from the basket and take off on it. The ball is released farthest from the guard, making the shot difficult to block (Fig. 6-12).

Defense

There are two principal types of defense: one-on-one and zone. In one-on-one defense, each player is responsible

Fig. 6-9. Jump shot.

Fig. 6-10. One-hand set shot.

Fig. 6-11. Lay-up shot.

Fig. 6-12. Hook shot.

for one opponent. In zone defense, each player is responsible for a certain area or zone.

One of the main reasons for using a zone defense is to tightly guard the opponent's free-throw-line area to prevent drive ins for easy lay-up shots. All players shift on defense as the ball moves, to cut off passing lanes to the basket. It is considered strategically sound to use a zone defense when:

1. You are playing on a small floor.
2. Your team is in foul trouble.
3. You have an exceptional rebounder you want to keep near the opponent's basket.
4. The opponents have a height advantage.
5. The opponents have weak outside shooting.
6. The opponents have an exceptional player or two that your best defenders cannot handle one on one.

Stance
The feet should be in a forward stride position, knees and hips slightly bent, and the back straight. If the left arm is raised and the right arm extended to the side, the left foot should be forward. If the right arm is up, the right foot should be forward. From this position one should be able to quickly move in any direction.

Role of defensive player
A defensive player should attempt to position the body between the opposing player and the player's own bas-

ket. If a pressing defense is being used, the defensive player should get into position so that one arm and hand are in the passing lane, between the ball and the player being guarded.

Objectives of defensive players
1. To harass your opponent by playing in close and moving arms in a distracting manner
2. To block the shot by staying with the ball as the opponent attempts to throw it (do not jump too soon)
3. If the opponent holds the ball unprotected, to tie up the ball by grabbing it
4. To knock an unprotected ball out of the opponent's hands
5. To steal a ball that is being dribbled
6. To deflect a ball that is being passed by an opponent to a teammate
7. To intercept a passed ball

Offense
Offensive tactics will vary with the defensive play patterns employed by an opposing team throughout a single game of basketball. One type of offensive tactic must be employed to meet a 2-1-2, 2-3, or a 3-2 zone defense and another type to meet a one-on-one defense.

The most common method of offense against the zone defense is to use quick sharp passing with the intent of penetrating the zone and forcing an opposing player out of an assigned position. Other tactics commonly used are mismatching (1-3-1 offense against a 2-1-2 defense) and overloading (putting an extra offensive player in a weakly defended area of the zone).

Basic maneuvers against the one-on-one defense are the give-and-go and the pick-and-roll. The intent is to screen a defensive player and then get the ball to the open offensive player. Spontaneous one-on-one offense, called free-lancing, is quite common, but it is more common to use sets of plays.

TIPS TO REMEMBER

1. Dribble only when necessary to set up a shot or pass.
2. Move the ball by passing rather than dribbling. It is faster.
3. Practice being able to pass and catch the ball with no wasted motion. This is essential to an effective offense.
4. Improve your shooting percentage by developing a consistent shooting form and concentration.
5. Become proficient at lay-ups and other short-range, high-percentage shots before working on more difficult shots.
6. Practice most often those shots you expect to get in games as a result of your team's offensive patterns.
7. Be aware of floor balance. Your team should always have one or more rebounders when a shot is taken and one player back on defense to prevent an easy fast-break basket by the opponents.
8. Make an extra effort to get the inside position on opponents at both ends of the court to improve your rebounding.
9. Learn to position yourself on defense so as not to lose sight of either the ball or the person being guarded.
10. Work on proper physical conditioning. It is equally as important to be able to get from one end of the court to the other and back again as it is to play good offense and defense.
11. Stay in condition year-round. Injuries result from inactivity followed by hard workouts with little or no adjustment period.
12. Remember that basketball is a team sport. The best individual players do not always make the best team players. Good team players develop an ability to help others play at their peak performance.

TEACHING CONSIDERATIONS

1. For younger learners use smaller and lighter balls to develop basic skills.
2. Develop individual skills of dribbling for control of the object in simple conditions first (in one spot; moving forward, to the left, to the right, and backward; changing speed and level of dribble; stopping and starting; and dribbling to avoid others or objects).
3. Develop passing skills in a stationary position first varying the level of pass. As soon as some degree of proficiency has been established practice passing to a moving receiver varying the distance and adding the pass on the move. Emphasize quick passes and the idea of the lead pass (passing the ball ahead of the moving receiver).
4. Combine dribbling and passing skills with an emphasis on a smooth transition from one skill to another (pass to a dribble and dribble to a pass). Add several players and emphasize cutting into a space to receive a pass in cooperative group work.
5. Teach basics of the foul shot, set shot, and lay-up. Combine the set and lay-up shots with combinations of dribble and pass as soon as basic proficiency in simple conditions has been established.
6. Begin offensive and defensive play with one-on-one situations. Teach students defensive position to get the ball from a dribbler and offensive strategies to maintain possession.
7. With large groups of learners decrease the amount of space for game play, particularly when less than five-on-five work is being developed.
8. Manipulate the rules to bring out better play (e.g., no dribbling, three passes) and to encourage continuous play (e.g., be flexible when calling traveling, eliminate foul shots and jump balls).
9. Consider introducing zone defense as a concept of defending space. Three defensive players can constitute a zone defense. Add different patterns of zone defense as the number of defensive players increases.
10. Mix some game play with skill work in each lesson once a unit gets started. Progress with skills over the unit. Do not establish units that do all the basic skill development in the first few lessons and all the play in the last few lessons.
11. See Fig. 6-13 for official signals.

Fig. 6-13. Official basketball signals.

GLOSSARY

alternate possession rule The rule where any jump ball situations after the opening jump ball result in each team gaining possession of the ball. The team losing the opening jump ball will be awarded the first possession, with teams alternating possession for the rest of the game.

assist A pass or handoff resulting in a basket by a teammate.

backboard The surface of wood, metal, or glass to which the basket is affixed, used to carom shots into the basket.

backcourt The half of the court away from the basket under attack; the guards are often called backcourt players.

basket (a) The iron hoop through which goals are scored; (b) a field goal.

bench The reserve strength of a team, apart from the starting five players.

blocking A foul by a defensive player who blocks the legal path of an offensive player.

center jump The method of putting the ball into play at the beginning of a game by having the referee toss up the ball between the rival centers.

charging A foul by an offensive player who runs into a defensive player having established legal court position.

dribble To bounce and control the ball continuously with one hand while walking or running. To double dribble is to stop and then resume dribbling, which is a violation.

dunk To leap to or above the basket and stuff the ball through the hoop. Such a movement with great vigor is called a slam dunk.

fast break A style of offense in which a team attempts to race to the offensive basket before the defense can get set.

field goal A basket scored from the floor.

free throw An unobstructed shot from the foul line, worth one point, awarded as a penalty for a foul by the opposing team.

free throw lane The area on the floor bounded by the free-throw line, the end line under the basket, and two connecting lines forming a 12-foot (3.66 m) (collegiate) or 18-feet (5.49 m) (professional) lane; also called foul lane.

free throw line A line, 15 feet (4.58 m) from the basket, behind which the shooter must stand in attempting a free throw; also called foul line.

frontcourt The half of the court in which a basket is under attack.

give and go A play in which one player passes to a teammate and drives toward the basket to receive a pass for a lay-up.

hand-off Handing the ball to a teammate (instead of passing it)

held ball Simultaneous possession of ball by opposing players, leading to use of the alternate possession rule.

hook shot A sweeping, one-handed field goal attempt, with the shooter's back at least partially to the basket.

hoop (a) The rim of the basket; (b) a basket or score.

jump ball A means of putting the ball into play by having an official toss it upwards between two players. This only occurs on the jump ball to start the game.

jump shot A field goal attempt in which the ball is released at the top of a vertical jump; also called jumper.

key The key-shaped area on the floor in front of each basket, usually painted in a contrasting color.

lay-up A shot from alongside the basket, using the backboard as a guide.

man-to-man defense A style of team defense in which each player is assigned a specific opponent to guard anywhere on the court.

offensive foul A personal foul committed by a member of the offensive team, usually not involving a free throw as part of the penalty.

palming An illegal means of carrying the ball along while dribbling.

personal foul Any of a variety of body-contact fouls; five, or in professional ball, six personals disqualify the player who commits them.

pick A legal method of providing shooting room for a teammate, by taking a position that "picks off" or blocks a defensive player.

pick-and-roll A maneuver in which a player moves suddenly (rolls) toward the basket for a pass from the teammate for whom a pick has been set.

pivot A position taken by a player with his/her back to the basket, at the head or alongside the free-throw lane, from which they can spin and shoot or hand-off to teammates moving past him/her toward the basket; also the floor area where pivot play is feasible.

post A synonym for pivot. "High post" means farther from the basket, "low post" means closer.

press A style of defense in which offensive players are closely guarded and harried. A "full-court press" is applied all over the floor; a "half-court press" only after the ball is brought across the midcourt line.

rebound A shot that caroms off the basket or backboard and remains in play, to be recovered by either team.

set shot A field-goal attempt from a stationary position, usually relatively far from the basket.

steal Capture of the ball from the hands of a player by the defender; also, an intercepted pass.

switch A defensive technique in which players who have man-to-man assignments switch responsibilities with each other as their offensive players cross paths.

technical foul A foul imposed for misbehavior or some technical rule infraction. The penalty is a free throw plus possession of the ball for the offended team.

ten-second rule The requirement that a team bring the ball across the mid-court line within 10 seconds after gaining possession.

three-pointer A field goal made by a player who is fouled in the act of shooting, plus the free throw that is made; also a basket scored from outside the three-point line on the court.

three-second rule The restriction against offensive players taking up set positions within the free-throw lane for more than 3 seconds.

tip-in A field goal made by tipping the ball into the basket while airborne for a rebound.

trailer A player who follows behind his/her teammates on a fast break as a passing option if they are unable to get off a shot.

trap Convergence of two or more defenders on a ball handler to force a turnover or steal.

traveling Illegally moving the ball by violating the dribbling rules.

turnover Loss of possession of the ball without attempting a field goal.

twenty-four second rule In the National Basketball Association (NBA) the requirement that a team make a field goal attempt within 24 seconds after gaining possession of the ball; in international amateur competition the limit is 30 seconds; in college basketball the limit is 45 seconds.

violation Any infraction not classified as a foul. The penalty is loss of possession of the ball.

zone A style of team defense in which each player is assigned to guard a designated floor area, rather than a specific opponent.

SUGGESTED READINGS

Barnes MJ: Women's basketball, Boston, 1980, Allyn & Bacon, Inc.

Bird L and Bischoff J: Bird on basketball, Reading, Mass., 1984, Addison-Wesley Publishing Co. Contains over 100 photos, charts, and diagrams covering passing, shooting, defense, dribbling, and rebounding. Also covers subtle points such as moving without the ball, rebound positioning, court sense, being a team player, and training.

Brown D: The LSU basketball organizational handbook, West Point, NY, 1984, Leisure Press. Provides an overview of skill development, conditioning, coaching, recruiting, and motivating.

Cooper JM: Basketball: player movement skills, Carmel, Ind, 1987, Benchmark Press, Inc. The author analyzes player movement skills in game situations for students and fans.

Cousy B, Power FG and Warren WE: Basketball: concepts and techniques, ed 2, Rockleigh, NJ, 1983, Allyn & Bacon, Inc. Using 124 photographs and 299 diagrams, this book contains material on analysis of coaching essentials, individual and team offensive techniques, the passing game, the fast break, and zone offenses and defenses.

Foster B: Conditioning for basketball: a guide for coaches and athletes, West Point, NY, 1983, Leisure Press. Presents step-by-step guidelines for developing fitness for basketball including weight training, agility, and quickness.

Fox RA: Basketball: the complete handbook of individual skills, Englewood Cliffs, NJ, 1988, Prentice Hall. The author breaks footwork, dribbling, passing, shooting, one-on-one moves, post moves, advanced scoring, and rebounding into their essentials and provides step-by-step instruction and skill-specific drills.

Krause J: Better basketball basics: before the X's and O's, ed 2, West Point, NY, 1984, Leisure Press. For basketball players of all ages, this book contains instructions for developing fundamental skills including team and individual drills with almost 600 photographs.

Krause J: The basketball bible, West Point, NY, 1982, Leisure Press. A cross-indexed compilation of more than 3000 basketball-related references from books, periodicals, research, theses, and dissertations.

Moore B and White J: Basketball theory and practice, Dubuque, Iowa, 1980, WC Brown Co.

The NCAA official basketball rules, Shawnee Mission, Kan, 1989, College Athletics Publishing Service.

Official basketball rules and guide, Reston, VA, 1984, American Alliance for Health, Physical Education, Recreation, and Dance, National Association of Girls' and Women's Sports.

Pruden V: A conceptual approach to basketball, Champaign, Ill, 1987, Human Kinetics Publishers, Inc. Contains basic components of successful offensive and defensive systems and how to apply these principles to game situations.

Scott J: Step-by-step basketball fundamentals for the player and coach, Englewood Cliffs, NJ, 1989, Prentice Hall. Contains more than 170 drills and exercises plus over 200 photos and illustrations.

Twelve great basketball offenses, Reston, VA, 1982, American Alliance for Health, Physical Education, Recreation, and Dance. Presents the basics of 12 of the greatest basketball offenses, each highlighted with supporting diagrams.

Whiddon S and Reynolds H: Teaching basketball, Edina, Minn, 1983, Burgess International Group.

Wilkes G: Basketball, ed 5, Dubuque, Iowa, 1990, WC Brown Publishers. Presents essential basketball skills, information on offensive and defensive patterns of play, strategy and rules of the game, sportsmanship.

VIDEOTAPES

Techniques of basketball (series). Athletic Institute, 200 Castlewood Dr., North Palm Beach, FL 33405.

Steve Alford's All-American Workout. Athletic Institute, 200 Castlewood Dr., North Palm Beach, FL 33405.

Forty-five videos including skills, strategies, famous coaches tips, drills and plyometrics. "How To" Sports Videos, Box 5852, Denver, CO 80217.

Ten individual NCAA instructional basketball videos including three for women's basketball. Karol Video, 22 Riverview Dr., Wayne, NJ 07470.

7

Bicycling

Completion of this chapter should enable the reader to:

- Be familiar with important considerations in the selection of bicycling equipment
- Know how to select a proper-sized bicycle and make appropriate adjustments
- Demonstrate the basic maneuvers of starting, braking, steering, and shifting gears
- Know the rules of the road and execute them for maximum safety when cycling

HISTORY

The first bicycles, developed in the 1800s, were unlike today's machines. They did not go well and were almost impossible to stop. They were heavy, crude, and inefficient. When approaching a corner, the rider had to dismount and turn the bike around by hand because there was no way to steer it. Needless to say, these first bicycles were not used for transportation.

However, even those first cumbersome contraptions did have a simple advantage over walking: they used muscle power to move horizontally rather than vertically. When walking, energy is expended to fight gravity by moving the body up in order to move the legs out to take a step. This upward movement is wasted because it is not in the direction we wish to go.

When we stand up, muscles must be tensed and bones compressed to support body weight. This muscle tension expends energy even though no motion takes place. Walking triples the load on the legs. By sitting on a seat or board with two wheels attached to it, we save much of the expended vertical energy lost through standing muscle tension. Thus the first bicyclists could sit on a seat and pedal the bike with their feet and glide along to their destination, using less energy than walking requires.

Increasing the size of the front wheel increased its circumference, which is the distance one revolution of the pedals propels the rider. High wheelers, or "ordinaries" or "penny-farthings," as they were called, were in use from 1870 to 1885.

The chain-driven-rear-wheel "safety" bicycle appeared in 1885. This removed the restriction of direct drive from pedals to wheel. Development of the derailleur, which enables a selection of different gear ratios, has changed bicycling drastically. Racing bicycles now commonly have 14 gear ratios and the even newer "mountain" bicycles have up to 21 gear ratios.

The bicycle of today (Fig. 7-1) is a remarkable. lightweight, efficient, versatile, and economical machine. In many countries it is used as the primary mode of transportation.

Cycling as an Olympic event has changed a great deal over the years, for the most part because of changes in equipment. In the 1896 Olympics six cycling events, including a 12-hour race, were held. In the next Olympics in 1900 at Paris there was only one cycling event. In 1908 in London the first cycling events on a banked 500 m oval track were conducted. European nations, especially England, France, and Holland, provided the best cyclists in the early Olympics. Until 1984 no United States cyclist had won a medal since 1908. With professional cycling increasing in popularity and attracting the finest Western European cyclists, the Eastern European countries and the Soviet Union began winning most of the medals from around 1960. Although the Soviet Union would have brought a very strong cycling team to Los Angeles had it not boycotted the 1984 Olympics, the outstanding success of the Americans came somewhat as a surprise.

The success of the U.S. cycling team at the 1984 Olym-

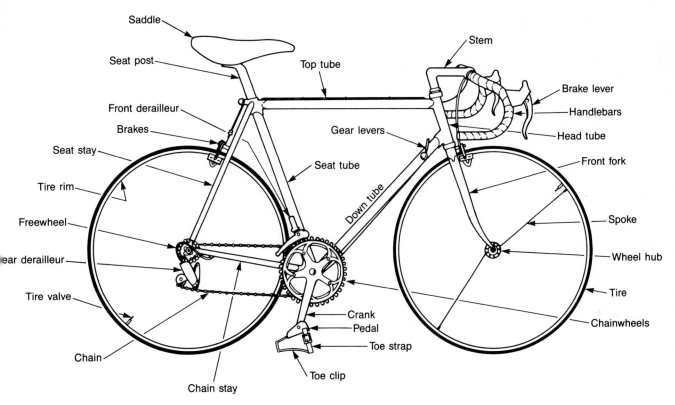

Fig. 7-1. Modern bicyle.

pics, where they won several medals in both the sprint and road race events, provided a needed boost for American cycling. Also, the recent success of American riders such as Greg LeMond and Andy Hampsten on the European professional circuit has increased interest in the sport. In 1989, LeMond staged an incredible performance to win the 2000-mile Tour de France stage race by 8 seconds!

THE BICYCLIST
Posture

One of the most important considerations in choosing a bicycle is its fit. A bicycle which does not fit will be uncomfortable and will not handle correctly. Most people believe that the bicyclist sits on the seat, pushes with the legs, bends the back, and steers with the hands. In reality, the cyclist straddles the seat, spins the pedals, leans forward from the hips, and steers by leaning.

Clothing

A great deal of specialized clothing is available today, designed and manufactured with racing and long-distance bicycling in mind. Cycling shorts are made from stretchable lycra material and are chamois lined to prevent saddle chafe and sores. Some are "anatomically designed," that is, they are curved to fit the cyclist in the seated position. Colored jerseys with pockets on the back

carry identification, a spare tire tube (flats are common), and energy snacks. A bottle is fitted to the frame and its contents used to replace body fluids. Fingerless gloves are worn by many bicyclists. They can be used to rub bits of glass off tires, and the gloves protect the palms of the hands should a fall occur.

Lightweight bicycling helmets are available in most bicycle shops. The newer ones made of lycra-covered styrofoam are well ventilated and weigh only about 8 ounces.

Although other specialized clothing is unimportant to commuters or short-distance riders, these are important. Almost all deaths and most serious injuries incurred in cycling accidents are caused by head injuries. Where there is the chance of the head striking an immovable object— as in football, hockey, auto racing, and other contact sports—protective headgear can save a life (Fig. 7-2).

Saddle selection

Because the rider does not sit on the seat but straddles it, the saddle (seat) is a prop for the pelvic bones. It is important that chafing be avoided, because the legs will be in constant motion. Therefore, a smooth, flexible saddle just wide enough for good support but not wide enough to chafe is best.

Most saddles today are made of flexible plastic covered

Fig. 7-2. Bicycle clothing.

with foam and leather and are quite comfortable. Women will probably find a saddle designed for wider pelvic bones to be more comfortable than a conventional saddle. The less expensive vinyl-covered saddles are often too hard and they do not absorb moisture. A mattress saddle with springs is only satisfactory for riding short distances in an upright position. It may feel better at first, but the longer the ride the more uncomfortable it gets.

Saddle height and bike size

To check the basic frame size of the bicycle, straddle it, and lift it until the top tube touches the crotch. If the bicycle is the proper size there should be 1 to 2 inches of clearance between the tires and the ground. The saddle should be positioned so that it is just possible to place the heels (without shoes) on the pedals at the bottom position and pedal backward without rocking the hips. The top of the handlebars should be about 1 inch lower than the saddle. After adjusting the seat and handlebar height, move the saddle forward or backward until a natural posture is felt when reaching forward to the top of the handlebars and the front hub is blocked from view by the handlebars: Often the stem length needs to be changed to achieve this ideal position.

Pedaling technique

The mark of a good bicyclist is the smooth steady way in which he or she pedals the bike. The foot must be placed on the pedal so it can push the pedal as far around the circle as possible. To do this you use the foot as a lever with the ankle as fulcrum while pedaling on the ball of the foot. At the bottom of the circle the heel is up and the toe is down. At the top of the circle the heel is down and the toe is up, thus pulling the pedal back. This is called ankling. Smooth ankling is achieved only by using toe clips and straps and shoes with cleats, but this technique should be practiced even if tennis shoes or rubber pedals are used.

The feet should rotate the pedals at a rhythmic, constant pace (cadence), twice as fast as walking. A slow cadence is 60 revolutions per minute, 80 is normal, and 90 to 100 is racing pace.

Care of equipment

Before starting a ride of any distance, be sure to give the bicycle a quick safety check. Grip the brake levers and make sure that the brakes work. Look for worn brake blocks and loose cables. Make sure the handlebars, seat, and wheels are not loose and see that the wheels are aligned, or "true." Check the tires for the proper pressure and for worn or cut places. Under-inflated tires greatly increase rolling resistance and increase the chance of damaging the rims. Lubricate the chain if necessary. Make sure to have a spare tube, tire irons, and a pump. Taking a few moments before a ride could save a long walk home, but more importantly, it could prevent an accident.

Tires

Tires fail more frequently than any other part of a bicycle. Knowing how to change tires and fix flats will save a lot of time and money.

There are two kinds of bicycle tires. The most common type—"wired-on" or clinchers—are so named because of the wire bead that seals the tires to the rim. The other kind, used almost exclusively by racers, are "tubulars." These tires are glued onto the wheel rim.

Changing wired-on tires is not difficult, and with a little practice one can become proficient. If a spare tube, some tire irons, and a pump are carried, a flat tire should never cause a delay of more than a few minutes.

Tubes within the tires also come in two types (actually it is the valves that are different), so it is important that the tire pump carried fits the type of valve on the bike. Schrader valves are large and thick, like automobile valves. Presta valves are narrow and require the little button on the valve tip to be unscrewed to use them. Each takes a different hand pump to fill with air.

Types of bicycles

There are many different types of bicycles, each designed for a different purpose. *Racing bikes* feature drop handlebars, short wheelbases, and are light in weight. *Touring bikes* are equipped for carrying loads—they have heavy-duty wheels, luggage rack attachments, and "granny gears" for climbing steep hills. *Mountain bikes* have wide, knobby tires and rugged construction; they were originally designed for use on dirt roads and trails, but their upright posture and ease of use has made them popular in cities as well. *Commuter bikes* are average "around-town" vehicles which come in all shapes and sizes. Often equipped with fenders and reflectors, they provide reliable transporation and recreation.

BASIC MANEUVERS
Starting

Grasp the top of the handlebars and swing a leg over the seat to straddle the bicycle. Backpedal until one pedal is forward and high. Place the ball of the foot on the high pedal and kick off with the other foot. This will start the bicycle moving. Place the other foot on its pedal and ease the crotch backward up onto the saddle.

Stopping

Apply the brakes to slow down. Put the pedals in the high and low positions, transfer your weight to the low pedal, and slide forward and off the seat. Remove the foot from the high pedal and reach for the ground while slowing to a stop. Just before the stop, turn the front wheel away from the free foot to tip the bicycle. If timed correctly, the bicyclist will stop and lean onto the free foot just as it touches the ground. Backpedal to the starting position.

Steering

Steering is accomplished more by leaning than by turning the handlebars. This effect can best be tested by walking along pushing the bike forward, holding onto only the saddle. A slight tip to the left or right will naturally turn the front wheel in the same direction. This action occurs when the bicyclist is in the saddle. The hands and arms on the handlebars primarily support the body's upper torso.

Gear shifting

The premise of variable bicycle gear ratios on 10-speed bikes is that the bicyclist is most efficient when pedaling at a constant rate in revolutions per minute. (One revolution is two complementary strokes, one from the left leg and one from the right.) Inasmuch as the bicyclist faces variable conditions during the ride, it would be impossible to keep a constant pace with only one gear. For example, the average bicyclist would be unable to keep the same pace going uphill as on the flat. Other variable conditions include wind and weight carried. Shifting gears allows the optimum in mechanical efficiency.

To shift the common 10-speed bicycle, the bicyclist should keep pedaling but with very little force. Move the level until the derailleur clatters and then quiets down. Move the lever only slightly to avoid shifting through two gears. The shift should occur before the cadence is slowed by a hill. Practice shifting smoothly on the flat so that it can be done quickly and safely in all situations.

Braking

Use both brakes to stop safely by applying pressure first to the rear brake and then to the front brake. Gradually brake harder until coming to a stop or until the rear wheel starts to skid. If this happens let up on both brake levers until the wheels start to turn again.

Never use only the rear brake in traffic. It cannot provide enough deceleration to stop in the event of trouble. Also never brake hard with only the front brake, as you may be thrown forward over the handlebars. Be careful when riding in rain. The brakes will not work until the brake blocks wipe the rims dry. Riding on steel rims in wet weather is much more dangerous than riding on alloy rims. In any case, remember to leave extra distance for stopping.

RULES OF THE ROAD

The rules of the road for bicyclists are the same as for automobile drivers. Automobile drivers cooperate with each other within the rules of the road, and motorists usually cooperate with bicyclists who obey these rules. Conflict arises when bicyclists or motorists, through ignorance or design, act unreasonably on the roadway.

Where to ride on the roadway

Bicyclists have a right to a safe corridor along the road. Care must be taken, however, not to interfere with other users of the road. Courtesy toward others will pay in increased respect and safety. Bicycles are vehicles, and the following are recommended rules governing the place of bicycles on the roadway. Unfortunately, some people do not recognize bicycles as legitimate vehicles. This belief often results in actions inconsistent with standard traffic engineering practice and commonsense rules of behavior in traffic situations.

When riding on a road of standard width, the bicyclist should ride inside the traffic lane at the right-hand side of the road. Cars will usually have ample room to pass within or nearly within this lane. On roads that are too narrow to permit safe passing either within the lane or over the centerline, the bicyclist should ride in the center of the right lane. If riding as fast or faster than the other traffic, use the lane as if operating a car. Do not weave in and around parked cars.

Never ride on the left side of the street, facing traffic. Very few bicyclists are hit by overtaking cars. Instead, the greatest number of car-bicycle collisions are caused by wrong-way riding. When approaching a motorist from an unexpected spot, the bicyclist could be hit without being seen. Riding on the wrong side of the road also causes bicycle-bicycle collisions. Bicyclists usually occupy the right portion of the roadway but going in the wrong direction, there exists a risk of a head-on collision with another bicyclist.

It is important not to ride in the motorist's blind spot, especially when approaching intersections or driveways, where a motorist might make a right turn. Overtake on the right only when the cars are stopped or are barely moving. Never overtake on the right where it is possible for the motorist to make a right turn, and never overtake on the right when the road is too narrow to do so safely.

Right turns

Make a right turn in the same manner as a car does—from the farthest right of the roadway.

Some roads have right-turn-only lanes. When riding in the right-hand portion of a right-turn-only lane, the bicyclist must turn right (Fig. 7-3, *B*). If the bicyclist attempts to go straight through, he or she could be hit by a motorist legally turning right. When a bicyclist encounters a right-turn-only lane but does not wish to follow it, the alternative is to merge to the left and ride on the righthand edge of the next straight-through lane (Fig. 7-3, *A*). Merge left by looking over your left shoulder

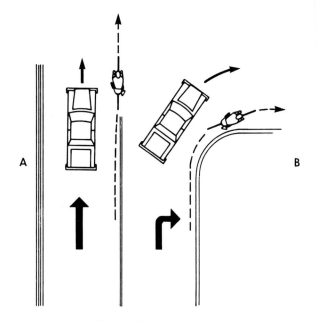

Fig. 7-3. Right turns.

before changing the path of travel. Change lanes only when overtaking traffic has cleared or slowed to allow you to move over.

Left turns

Never attempt a left turn from the right side of the street. The bicyclist stands a good chance of being hit by an overtaking car by making a left turn in front of it.

To make a safe left turn, the bicyclist must follow the same procedure as an automobile driver. The first step is to merge left. Look back over your shoulder for overtaking cars. It may help to signal, but the look is mandatory. Never signal without looking. A signal is a matter of courtesy; the look is a matter of life and death. After looking over the left shoulder for overtaking cars, move into the left lane if the way is clear. When occupying a left-turn-only lane, ride at the *right* edge of the lane (Fig. 7-4, *A*). This will allow motorists to also occupy the lane and turn simultaneously when the way ahead is clear. If the lane is not a left-turn-only lane, stay as close to the centerline of the road as possible (Fig. 7-4, *B*). This will allow motorists who wish to go straight through to pass on the right while the bicyclist is waiting for the oncoming traffic to clear.

After completing a left turn it is easiest to turn into the right lane of the new street. But before doing this, check for traffic in that lane. Remember to check for oncoming traffic that may make a right turn on red and be entering that inside lane just as the bicyclist does.

Sometimes on multilane streets the traffic is so heavy that it is not possible to make a left-hand turn in the

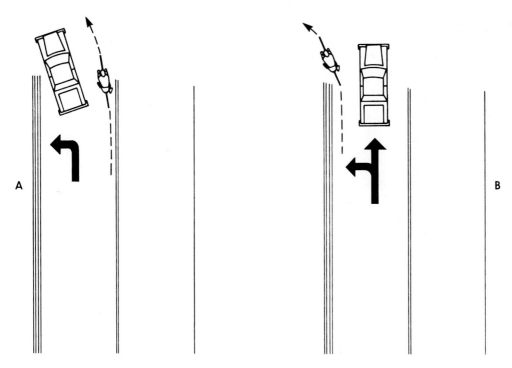

Fig. 7-4. Left turns.

manner described. If this happens it is best to use pedestrian rules, ride to the far corner of the intersection, and turn the bicycle in the proper direction and wait for the light to change. At an intersection without a signal, wait for the traffic to clear in all directions.

SAFETY

Statistics show that in the majority of bicycle accidents the rider simply falls off the bicycle for some reason. The remainder of accidents are collisions with automobiles, fixed objects, and other bicyclists. This implies that the greatest cause of accidental injury is inept bicyclists.

First, it is important to know how to ride a bicycle. That is, the bicyclist should adopt riding procedures that are reasonable and proper, always be observant, recognize potential problems, and be able to cope in emergency situations. Second, it is important to operate a bicycle as a vehicle. This provides operating procedures that are predictable and expected by drivers of automobiles and by other bicyclists. Because of unexpected turning and crossing maneuvers into streets from bike paths and sidewalks, it is much safer to ride a bicycle in the street than in these off-street facilities.

Studies have shown that experienced active bicyclists, such as those who belong to organized clubs, have one sixth to one seventh the accident rate of other bicyclists. It appears that, in the case of bicycling at least, a little knowledge is truly a dangerous thing.

BICYCLING ACTIVITIES

Safe and proper bicycling offers a lifetime of enjoyment and fitness. Social and other benefits are also possible by joining a local bicycle club. Bicycle club members can supply a wealth of knowledge and are happy to help newcomers become more knowledgeable and more skillful bicyclists. Usually club members are aware of the latest equipment. On club rides the novice can rapidly learn what others spent years finding out—where the best rides are, bicycling techniques that make riding easier, and favorite lunch stops.

There are two types of bicycle clubs: racing and touring (Figs. 7-5 and 7-6). Check with a local bicycle shop to find out about club activities. Initially, the novice is wise to investigate joining a touring club. Touring clubs usually have three levels of rides: short, medium, and long, or easy, moderate, and strenuous. Initially pick an easy ride and go with the club. The bicyclist should be self-sufficient by carrying water, a pump, a spare tube, and tire irons.

TEACHING CONSIDERATIONS

1. Define the purpose of the instruction in terms of bicycle touring, racing, or a combination of both.
2. Check equipment for safety and fit.
3. Teach bicycle safety and etiquette.
4. Combine more lecture-type material with opportunities for activity.

Fig. 7-5. Bicycle touring.

5. Provide opportunities to cycle in a touring or racing situation. Where possible conduct these activities in the environment to be used by the student.
6. Design an obstacle course in a parking lot for improving bike handling skills.
7. Hold a 5 to 10 mile time trial starting individual cyclists at 30-second intervals.
8. When planning initial trips organize a buddy system.
9. Do not take large groups of cyclists into heavy traffic.

GLOSSARY

bicycle clothing Special clothing such as chamois-lined shorts which prevent saddle chafe and sores.

braking Bringing the bicycle to a stop by using both brakes properly.

gear shifting (derailleur) Varying the gear ratios on 10-speed bikes; the bicyclist is most efficient when pedaling at a constant rate of revolutions per minute.

helmet Lightweight headgear designed for bicycle riding.

rules of the road Rules that apply to both cyclists and automobile drivers.

saddle A smooth leather seat just wide enough for good support and not wide enough to chafe.

safety check Checking that the parts of the bicycle are in good working order before a ride.

steering Guiding the bicycle more by leaning than turning the handlebars.

Fig. 7-6. Bicycle racing.

SUGGESTED READINGS

Basic bicycling, Reston, Va, 1982, American Alliance for Health, Physical Education, Recreation, and Dance. Presents informative tips on bicycle riding and maintenance.

Bicycle Magazine: Complete guide to bicycle maintenance and repair, Emmaus, Pa, 1980, Rodale Press. Puts basic bicycle repair and maintenance within the rider's reach. With many illustrations and photos, it provides clear step-by-step instructions for almost any repair.

Borysewicz E: Bicycle road racing, Brattleboro, Vt, 1985, Velonews Corp. A good reference for competitive cyclists by the former U.S. Olympic team coach.

Bridge R: Bike touring: the Sierra Club guide to outings on wheels, San Francisco, 1979, The Sierra Club.

Browder S: The American biking atlas and touring guide, New York, 1983, Workman Publishing Co., Inc.

Burke ER: Science of cycling, Champaign, Ill, 1986, Human Kinetics Publishers. A digest of the technical aspects of research affecting cycling, including the physiological, mechanical, biomechanical, psychological, and medical aspects.

Burkett LN and Darst PW: Cycling, Glenview, Ill, 1987, Scott, Forseman & Co. An introductory text which explores ways to incorporate bicycling into any lifestyle for fitness and fun as well as transportation.

DeLa Rosa DM and Kolin M; The ten-speed bicycle, Emmaus, Pa, 1979, Rodale Press. Explains in simple terms the function of bike components and how to keep them in adjustment. Contains 200 photos and illustrations.

Fariah I: Applied physiology of cycling, Sports Medicine I:187-204, 1984.

Hawkins K and Hawkins G: Bicycle touring in the Western United States, New York, 1982, Patheon Books.

Krause J and Krause V: Indoor cycling, Garden City, NJ, 1987, Doubleday. Describes the accident-free aerobic exercise.

Lemond G and Gordis K: Greg Lemond's complete book of cycling, New York, 1987, Putnam Publishing Corp.

Mariolle M: The woman cyclist, Chicago, 1988, Contemporary Books.

Sjogaard G, et al.: Physiology in bicycling, Ithaca, NY, 1984, Movement Publications, Inc. This well-illustrated book contains information useful to the coach and athlete.

Sloane E: The all-new complete book of cycling, New York, 1980, Simon & Schuster.

Woodland L: Cycle racing: training to win, ed 2, New York, 1988, Viking Penguin, Inc.

PERIODICALS

Bicycle Guide, published nine times a year by Rabden/Bicycle Guide Partners, 711 Boylston St., Boston, MA 02116.

Bicycling, published monthly by Rodale Press, Inc., 33 E Minor St., Emmaus, PA 18098.

Velo-News, published monthly by Velo-News Corp., Box 1257, Brattleboro, VT 05301.

Winning bicycle racing illustrated, 1127 Hamilton St., Allentown, PA 18102.

FILM

Only one road. AAA Foundation for Traffic, Falls Church, Va.

8

Bowling

Completion of this chapter should enable the reader to:

- Display a knowledge of the rules of bowling
- Demonstrate the correct grip, stance, approach, and delivery in bowling
- Identify three styles of delivery
- Instruct a group of students in the fundamentals of bowling
- Recognize and use bowling terminology correctly

HISTORY

Through existing records, bowling can be traced back as far as 7000 years ago. This easily establishes bowling as one of the oldest games known. Archaeologists trace its origin to the ancient Egyptians, with evidence of crudely shaped implements being used.

The game of modern tenpins had its inception in northern Italy, being derived from variations as played by the ancients. This the Italians called "bowls." Rounded stones without finger holes and held in the open hand were used as balls.

Later, in the thirteenth century, the game spread to Germany, Holland, and England and was known as ninepins. The playing area was known as the bowling green, because the game was usually played on grass. In 1623 early Dutch settlers introduced the game to America as ninepins. It was played on grass or clay and later on a single wide board. This game attracted considerable interest, and extensive betting centered about it. Laws banning ninepins were passed in several states in the 1840s.

Later, to circumvent the existing law and continue the activity, a Dutchman added one more pin and called it tenpins.

In 1895 the American Bowling Congress* was organized, and it formulated rules governing alleys, balls, and pins. Bowling is so popular in the United States that it can safely be said that it has more enthusiasts today than almost any other sports activity. It is estimated that nearly 60 million people bowl.

In recent years high school officials formulated the American High School Bowling Congress (AHSBC).* The Women's International Bowling Congress (WIBC) was formed before the AHSBC.

Colleges and universities often include lanes in their student recreation centers, and in many colleges bowling appears on the physical education curriculum as a basic sports skill. Large numbers of students have enrolled in such bowling courses.

Contests on television have done much to increase the popularity of bowling.

Bowling was a demonstration sport in the 1988 Olympics and will become a gold medal event in 1992.

SOCIAL VALUES

Bowling is a sport that appeals to everyone, weak or strong, young and old, men and women. It requires the learning of comparatively few skills. It requires only a change of shoes and no special uniform. One can bowl during lunchtime, after work, or in the evening. This is appealing to the average American. It requires no great strength; rather, rhythm, relaxation, and coordination are the essentials. Once mastered, it is an art. Around the bowling alley, social intercourse is pleasurable and

---

*2200 N. Third St., Milwaukee, WI

*8142 Indiana Ave., Chicago, IL

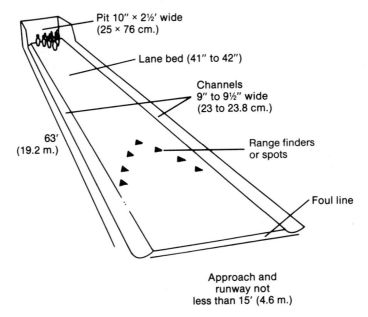

Fig. 8-1. The lane.

tensions seem to disappear. There is always the challenge, as in golf, to turn in a better score. That one single little pin seems to topple, but sometimes stands up there and wants to fight back. One can play alone for enjoyment or can easily join a local team. Bowling, because it uses many muscles, is one of the best recreational sports skills and it is relatively inexpensive.

EQUIPMENT AND FACILITIES

In bowling, 10 wooden or plastic pins are set in triangular position at the far end of a wooden runway called a lane (Fig. 8-1). The lane is 60 feet (18.3 m) long from the No. 1 pin to the foul line. It is 42 inches (105 cm) wide. On each side of the lane a channel approximately 9 inches (23 cm) wide runs from the foul line to the pit, behind the pins. Behind the foul line is the approach, which must not be less than 15 feet (4.6 m) long. The pit must have a drop of at least 9½ inches (24 cm) from the lane floor.

Pins are set 12 inches (0.3 m) apart from center to center (Fig. 8-2). A pin is 15 inches (38 cm) in height with a base diameter of 2¼ inches (5.6 cm). It is typically constructed of clear hard maple.

Balls are constructed of Bakelite or of a hardened rubber substance. The circumference is not more than 27 inches (68 cm), and the official ball weighs from 10 to 16 pounds (4.54 to 7.26 kg). Balls usually have either two or three bored holes for the bowler's fingers to aid in holding and accurately delivering the ball. Special balls with four or five finger holes are now available.

Other forms of bowling, such as duckpins, barrel pins, and candlepins, involve the use of small pins and small

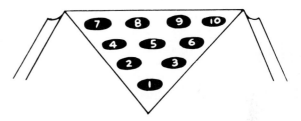

Fig. 8-2. Position of pins and their numbers.

balls. The fundamentals of all these games are essentially the same. In duckpins three balls are rolled per frame.

RULES

1. The bowler is allowed to roll two balls from behind the foul line down the lane at the pins in an attempt to knock down all the pins. If all the pins are knocked down with the bowler's first ball, it is called a strike (shown on the scorecard as an X in the upper right-hand corner of the frame in which it was made), and it is not necessary to roll the second ball.

2. A spare is made when a player bowls down all the pins with two balls in any frame; it is designated by a slash (/) in the upper right-hand corner of the frame in which it is made. The count in such frame is left open until the player bowls the first ball in the succeeding frame, when the number of pins knocked down thereby is added to the 10 earned by the spare, and the total is credited.

3. Pins that are knocked down by another pin rebounding in the play from the side partition or rear cushion are counted as pins down, except where pins rebound

off the body, arms, or legs of a human pinsetter. Pins that are bowled off the lane bed, rebound, and remain standing on the lane must be counted as pins standing. A pin knocked down by a human or mechanical pin-setter does not count and must be replaced on the spot where it stood before delivery of the ball.

4. A foul occurs when the bowler permits any part of the foot, hand, or arm, while in contact with the lane, to rest on or extend beyond the foul line, or if at any time after the ball leaves the hands and passes over the foul line, the bowler permits any part of the body to come in contact with the lane, division boards, wall, or uprights that are on or beyond the foul line.

5. No count is made on a foul ball, and any pins that are knocked down or displaced by it are respotted. A foul ball counts as a ball bowled by the player.

League bowling

1. Two adjoining lanes are used in all games of league or tournament play, and the bowling of ten complete frames on the pair of lanes on which the game was started constitutes an official game. The members of the contesting teams successively and in regular order bowl one frame on one lane, and the next frame on the other lane, so alternating each frame until the game is completed. Each player bowls two balls in every frame, except where a strike is made.

2. No pins may be conceded, and only those actually knocked down may be counted. Every frame must be completed at the time the player is bowling in regular order.

3. When a strike is made in the tenth frame, the bowler is then permitted to bowl two more balls on the same lane. When a spare is made in the tenth frame, the bowler is permitted to bowl one more ball on the same lane.

4. In case of a tie game, each team bowls one complete frame on the same lane on which its tenth frame was bowled, bowling and scoring said extra frame in the same manner as the tenth frame. If, at the completion of the first extra frame, a tie still exists, teams change lanes for additional frames that may be required to determine the winner.

5. Every ball delivered, unless it is declared a dead ball by the umpire, is counted against the player. If, when rolling at a full frame, it is discovered after the ball has been delivered that one or more pins are mis-placed, the ball and resulting pinfall are counted. It is the duty of the player to look at the pins before bowling, and if the setup is not satisfactory, to request that the pins be respotted.

6. Should a player by mistake bowl on the wrong lane or out of turn or be interfered with by another bowler or spectator, or should the ball come in contact with any obstacle on the lanes, then the ball is called a dead ball by the umpire and is immediately rebowled.

7. Pins that are knocked down or displaced by a ball that leaves the lane before reaching the pins, or from a ball rebounding from the rear cushions, do not count and they are immediately respotted. Removal or in-terference with pins by a human pinsetter before they stop rolling is cause for the umpire to order the pins respotted.

SCORING

Although many newer bowling establishments now pro-vide automatic scoring by computer, considerable en-joyment is added to the game if each participant is able to keep score accurately. A perfect score is 300 points. To score a game the results for each frame are recorded, and the cumulative total for the 10 frames is the final score. In each frame the total number of pins knocked down in two tries is recorded except when a strike or spare is made. In case of a strike, the score for the frame is 10 (marked with an X in the small square) plus the count of the next two balls bowled. In case of a spare, the score for the frame is 10 plus the number of pins knocked down with the next ball. If a foul is committed, the score for that ball is not counted. If the foul occurs on the first ball, all pins are reset and the next ball is scored as the second ball of that frame. A sample game (called a line) in which the correct method of scoring is illustrated is shown in Fig. 8-3.

Frame 1. The bowler, on the first ball, knocks down eight pins. An 8 is placed in the first square of the first frame. On the second ball, the bowler fails to hit either of the two remaining pins. The miss is indicated by a dash (—), which is called an "error." The bowler totals the number of pins knocked down with both balls and places the score 8 in the first frame.

Frame 2. The bowler knocks down seven pins with the first ball in this frame and places a 7 in the first squre to indicate the number of pins scored. The bowler gets the remaining three pins with the second ball and thus places the symbol for a spare (/), in the second square. The second frame cannot be scored until the results of the first ball of the third frame are known.

Frame 3. Six pins are knocked down with the first ball in the third frame. The score of 6 is added to the 10 gotten in the second frame to give a total of 16. The running score in the second frame is 8 (first frame) plus 16, or 24. Three pins are knocked down with the second ball, giving a total of nine pins for the third frame. The running score in the third frame is 24 plus 9, or 33.

Frame 4. Unfortunately, the bowler throws the first ball of the fourth frame into the channel. This is recorded in the first square as a C (channel ball), which has a zero value. The second ball of this frame knocks down all ten

Frames	1	2	3	4	5	6	7	8	9	10	TOTAL
Name	8 – 8	7 / 24	6 3 33	C / 43	F 9 52	X 79	X 98	7 2 107	⑧ – 115	9 / 5 130	*130*

Fig. 8-3. Sample method of scoring.

pins. However, as this is the second ball, it is scored as a spare. The running score in the fourth frame cannot be scored until the first ball of the fifth frame has been delivered.

Frame 5. The bowler crosses the foul line while delivering the first ball. Although the bowler knocks down nine pins, a zero score is received for the first ball because a foul is committed. The fourth frame can now be scored. The score for the fourth frame is 10 plus 0, or 10. The running score in the fourth frame is 43. The foul is indicated by placing an F in the first square. The pins are then reset and the bowler delivers the second ball, which knocks down nine pins. A 9 is placed in the second square, and 9 is added to the score of the previous frame to give a running score of 52 in the fifth frame.

Frame 6. The bowler knocks down all 10 pins with the first ball. This is indicated by placing an X in the first square. The running score cannot be recorded as a strike but is scored by adding 10 to the number of pins knocked down with the next two balls bowled.

Frame 7. The bowler again makes a strike with the first ball. The bowler now has two consecutive strikes, or a "double." The player cannot yet score the sixth or seventh frame.

Frame 8. In this frame the bowler gets seven pins with the first ball rolled and records the 7 in the first square. Now the score for the sixth frame can be computed. This score is 10 (strike in frame 6) plus 10 (strike in frame 7) plus 7 (number of pins gotten with the first ball in the eighth frame), or 27. The running score in the sixth frame is 52 plus 27, or 79. The second ball in frame 8 knocks down two pins, recorded by a 2 in the second square. Now the seventh-frame score can be computed. It is 10 plus 7 plus 2, or 19; the running score is 98 in the seventh frame and 107 in the eighth frame.

Frame 9. In this frame the first ball delivered hits the headpin (No. 1 pin) squarely, and a "split" results. The No. 7 and No. 10 pins remain standing. The split is indicated by encircling the 8, shown in the first square of the ninth frame. The second ball misses both pins and a miss (error) is indicated by the dash (—) in the second square. The ninth frame score of 8 is added to the running score of 107 to give a total of 115 in the ninth frame.

Frame 10. The bowler gets a spare with the second ball. Because this is the tenth frame, the bowler is entitled to another ball. The extra ball knocks down 5 pins, giving a score of 15 for the tenth frame. The 15 is added to the ninth frame's running score of 115 to give a total score of 130.

FUNDAMENTAL SKILLS AND TECHNIQUES
Ball selection

Select a ball, not too heavy or too light, that fits the fingers comfortably. Comfortable fit is essential to good delivery. Select a ball with finger holes that are neither too narrow nor too wide for finger spread, that is, from thumb to fingers. A good method to determine finger span is to insert the thumb into the thumb hole up to the second joint, or about four fifths of its length, then lay the hand flat on the surface of the ball with the fingers spread over the holes. The knuckle joints of the fingers should extend about ¼ inch beyond the inside near edge of the finger hole. This allows for proper looseness or slack, which is essential for a comfortable grip. This slack or play between the palm and the ball should be about ¼ inch. This is the recommended method of fitting the regular ball; it does not apply to fingertip or semifingertip balls.

Grip

Whether a two- or three-finger grip is used is a matter of individual preference. There are champion bowlers who use the two-finger grip, and champions who use the three-finger grip. The two-hole ball is rarely used today. If a person has an excessively weak grip, a four- or five-hole ball is recommended. Bowling balls supplied by bowling establishments are nearly always three-hole balls (Fig. 8-4). The three-finger grip is recommended for beginners or younger bowlers. It causes less strain on the wrist and arms and the popular hook ball can be delivered better with the three-finger grip.

When the ball is released, the thumb should come out of the hole first.

Stance

The bowler assumes a stance, before throwing, with body facing pins, erect or slightly crouched, about 15 feet back of the foul line (Fig. 8-5). The left foot is slightly in front of the right. The ball is held in the right hand, waist high. Some bowlers hold it higher with the idea of aiming, resting the weight of the ball on the left hand.

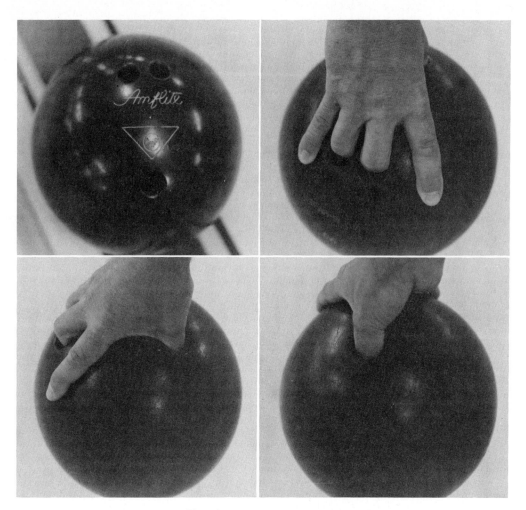

Fig. 8-4. Three-hole grip.

Footwork

The most essential and fundamental skills confronting the beginning bowler are footwork, balance, and rhythm. The bowler should take four or five steps before delivering the ball. There are many good bowlers using either style. Probably the most popular among bowlers is the four-step approach. However, each bowler should experiment until he or she finds the number of steps that fit. After this is accomplished, the bowler is ready to synchronize the footstep pattern with the arm movements while delivering the ball. The result of this practice is rhythm and timing. Practice footwork so that the feet move parallel to each other, remaining on the same board on which they start. Practice a fast walk, a slow run, or a gliding movement, rather than the walk or run. To find the correct starting spot in the approach, starting from the foul line, step off the number of steps desired and add 6 inches.

Delivery and approach to foul line

There are many styles of delivery. Usually the ball is carried anywhere from chest high to waist high and may be carried in the center of the body or in front of the right shoulder. In general, the approach has four phases: push-away, swing, forward swing, and release of the ball.

The bowler starts the approach toward the foul line by pushing the ball slightly down and away from the body so that it is extended outward between chest and waist height (Fig. 8-6). During this movement a step forward with the right foot is taken if the bowler is using the four-step delivery. If five-step delivery is used, the left foot starts first. The push-away places the ball forward about waist high, and the weight of the ball and gravity give the impetus in making the backward swing arc that is the next phase in the series of movements (Fig. 8-7).

In executing this arc, the bowler should not carry the ball too far backward at the end of the arc, but should

Fig. 8-5. The stance.

Fig. 8-6. The push-away.

Fig. 8-7. The swing.

Fig. 8-8. Forward swing.

Fig. 8-9. The release.

Fig. 8-10. The follow-through.

end a little above waist high. The ball is now poised in readiness to gain momentum from this pendulum swing downward and forward smoothly for the release and follow-through (Fig. 8-8).

Release

If the bowler has achieved perfect timing, the ball should be coming forward in its well-executed arc just as the last step (left foot) is being taken. The body weight should be perfectly balanced over this last step with the left foot (Fig. 8-9).

With continued practice the series of arm and feet movements blends into a graceful, coordinated, rhythmic pattern.

The approach starts slowly and accelerates toward the end. The last step must stop short of the foul line (see rules). The ball should contact the lane about 12 to 16 inches beyond the foul line.

Follow-through

At the finish of the arm movement, the bowler's left foot will be in front, the right foot balanced on the floor like a rudder behind, and the bowling arm extended forward and upward in the follow-through so essential in many sports skills. The final movement of the approach is an easy sliding glide that is controlled to stop about 2 to 4 inches short of the foul line (Fig. 8-10).

The bowler's posture at the finish should be smooth, easy, and relaxed, with a bend at the knees and very little at the hips. The opposite arm is used as an aid to balance. For a straight ball, the ball should be rolled smoothly onto the alley beyond the foul line and about 6 to 8 inches from the right channel. For a hook or curve ball this distance will vary depending on the amount of curve.

Delivery

The skill techniques just described are common to all delivery styles. The bowler is now confronted with the choice of three styles of delivery: straight ball, hook, and curve (Fig. 8-11). The beginner should first try the straight ball, as it is easiest, but should also experiment immediately with the hook, as it is the most efficient and is the one used by almost all professional bowlers.

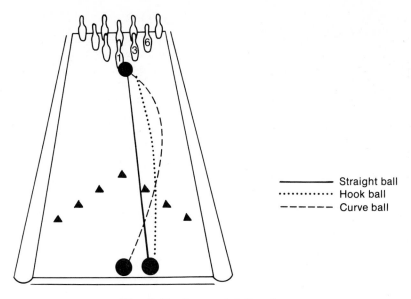

Fig. 8-11. Types of deliveries.

Straight ball

To throw a straight ball, the thumb is placed on top of the ball in a 12 o'clock position (Fig. 8-12, A), directed at the headpin so that the ball will roll in a straight line. The most universal approach is from the right corner of the lane, so that the aim is directed in a diagonal crosslane path between the No. 1 and No. 3 pins.

Hook ball

The hook ball is the most effective of all bowling styles for producing strikes. This style is universal with leading high-scoring teams. The technique recommended for the beginner's hook ball is as follows: The thumb is placed at the 9 o'clock position, so that the V formed by the thumb and forefinger points down the lane (Fig. 8-12, B). In a natural hook the wrist or fingers do not turn or rotate. The thumb's coming out first allows the fingers to lift their side of the ball, and a hook results. The ball is released near the right channel. The aim is at the 3-6 pocket. The ball then rolls with a forward motion and breaks sharply toward the left at the 1-3 pocket (Fig. 8-11). With the ball coming in at such a sideward angle, the pins are effectively swept off the lane. Unlike other styles, the hook ball, even thinly hitting the head pin, leaves few single pins remaining and few splits. There is no question of the effectiveness of the hook ball, and it can be mastered with long practice.

Curve ball

The curve ball is not recommended for beginners because of its inconsistency and the difficulty in controlling

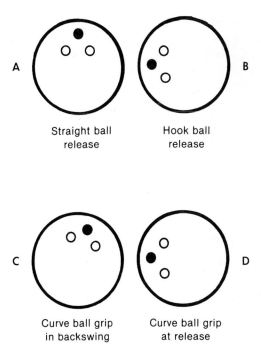

Fig. 8-12. Grips for various types of delivery.

it. Much practice is required for its mastery (Fig. 8-11).

The technique is as follows: On the backswing the wrist is rotated to the right, and on the forward swing to the left, which gives the ball a wide, sweeping curve (Fig. 8-12, C and D). The release is the same as for the hook ball. The ball is laid down near the center of the lane. The follow-through is forward.

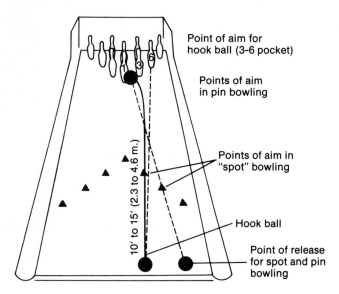

Point of aim for
hook ball (3-6 pocket)

Points of aim
in pin bowling

Points of aim in
"spot" bowling

Hook ball

Point of release
for spot and pin
bowling

10' to 15' (2.3 to 4.6 m.)

Fig. 8-13. Point of aim for various shots.

Aim

There are two methods of aiming: at the pin and at the spot. The most effective balls are rolled to hit the 1-3 pocket. For the beginner, the pin method is best, that is, aiming at the pin or pocket one desires the ball to hit. The eyes should be focused on that area throughout the entire delivery and follow-through (Fig. 8-13).

In the spot method the bowler usually aims to roll the ball over a definite spot on the lane or over an imaginary line from the foul line down the lane to coincide with the pin or pocket desired to be hit. To aid the spot bowler most lanes have triangularly shaped spots located at specific distances from the foul line (see Fig. 8-1).

TIPS TO REMEMBER

1. Develop an even speed in rolling all shots, and use whichever speed develops the most accuracy and consistency.
2. Concentrate on the spot desired to be hit.
3. Relax.
4. Be sure that the approach is not too fast or too slow.
5. Do not force a delivery; let the weight of the ball do the work. The arm merely serves as a pendulum.
6. In rolling the straight ball, be sure the fingers are behind the ball when it is released, to prevent the ball from curving.
7. Learn to let the thumb come out of the hole first.
8. Hold the wrist firm when releasing the ball.
9. Lay the ball on the lane smoothly.
10. In follow-through, let the arm continue in the direction of the pins.

BOWLING FOR SPARES

Spare bowling is extremely critical for good scores and requires practice to obtain accuracy and confidence. Improvement in bowling is directly related to mastering the techniques for picking up spares. The following points are important to this aspect of the game:

1. Determine the key pin (usually the one closest to the bowler) and where it must be hit to pick up the remaining pins.
2. Use the three basic alignments for the remaining pins:
   a. Center position for center pins
   b. Left position for right-side pins
   c. Right position for left-side pins
3. Roll the same style of ball for the spare as used for the first ball of the frame.
4. Concentrate harder on the second ball than the first, as there is less opportunity for pin action and less margin for error.

TEACHING CONSIDERATIONS

1. Basics of bowling can be taught in a gym without real balls by using softballs and a target area. Stance, footwork, approach, and delivery can be effectively practiced before going to the lanes.
2. If needed, lanes can be set up inside the gymnasium using hard rubber bowling balls, 2 × 4's, and plastic pins.
3. If lanes are available for instruction, begin with selection of the ball. Teach stance, delivery, and approach with proper footwork without using the ball. Then add the ball. Concentrate on the push-away action.
4. Teach a four-step approach and hook ball as the basic style, modifying later for individuals as needed.
5. Begin practice without the pins set up and initially disregard foul-line infractions. Add rule infractions as learners develop consistency in the coordination and rhythm of their delivery and are placing the ball onto the alley rather than dropping the ball onto the alley.
6. Once pins are set up the instructor may vary the approach to strike and spare bowling. Some instructors effectively teach strike bowling by setting up only the 1-3 pins and encouraging pin bowling at the 1-3 pocket. Students will not be successful unless they hit the pocket most desirable for strike bowling. Eventually all pins should be set up, and both strike and spare bowling strategies need to be communicated and practiced.
7. All aspects of scoring do not have to be introduced until learners are using two balls to get down all the pins. All students should be expected to learn how to score.

8. Spot bowling can be introduced to advanced beginners once consistency and some success in pin bowling has been achieved.

9. Introduce spare bowling by setting up different spare combinations with pins in front of the learner and having the learner make decisions about which pin to hit and where to hit it.

10. Handicap students and put them into teams for a unit tournament. If time permits, alternate instruction with actual games so students are bowling games early in the unit and are still receiving instruction throughout the unit.

GLOSSARY

anchor The last bowler on a team.

approach That part of the lane or runway on which the bowler takes the steps to proceed to the delivery point, the foul line.

average Total number of pins credited to a bowler divided by the number of games bowled in one season in a sanctioned league.

baby split The 3-10 pin split for right-handed bowlers and the 2-7 pin split for left-handed bowlers.

backup ball A ball delivered in such a manner as to curve toward the arm that delivered the ball. For a right-handed bowler the ball curves to the right.

bedposts The 7-10 split.

blow Same as error or miss.

box Same as frame.

Brooklyn or **crossing over** Hitting the headpin and adjacent pin on the opposite side of the lane from which the bowler released the ball on the delivery.

channel Another name for the gutter.

cherry Knocking down one or more of the front pins in a spare and leaving others standing.

convert To make a spare.

double Two consecutive strikes.

error A complete failure to knock down any remaining pins after the first ball is rolled.

foul The act of touching the foul line with the foot or hand. If a foul is made on the first throw, all 10 pins are respotted; if it occurs on the second throw, only the pins knocked down with the first ball count.

frame The box on the score sheet in which the scores are recorded. Ten frames constitute a game.

gutterball A ball that falls off the lane into the gutter.

headpin The No. 1 pin.

hook A ball that is caused to curve from outside in on its way to the pins.

kingpin The No. 5 pin.

lane A bowling alley.

leave Pins left standing after the first ball has been rolled.

line A complete game recorded in the ten frames across the score sheet.

mark A strike or a spare.

pocket The gap between the No. 1 and No. 3 pins for righthanders and between the No. 1 and No. 2 pins for lefthanders.

rack The trough holding the balls beside the runway.

return The ball returned from the pit to the bowler by way of a trough alongside or under the alley.

setup The arranging of ten pins in regular formation.

sleeper A pin that is hidden behind another pin.

spare Bowling down all pins with two balls in any one frame.

strike Bowling down all pins with the first ball rolled.

striking out Rolling strikes for any part of a remainder of a game.

tandem Any two pins in a spare formation arranged one behind the other.

triple or turkey Three consecutive strikes at any time in a game.

SUGGESTED READINGS

ABC Bowling guide, American Bowling Congress, 1989-90, 1572 E. Capitol Dr, Milwaukee, Wisc.

Bellisimo L and Bennet J: The bowlers manual, ed 4, Englewood Cliffs, NJ, 1982, Prentice-Hall, Inc.

Carlson G and Blackwell EH: Bowling basics: a step-by-step approach, ed 2, Dubuque, Iowa, 1988, Kendall/Hunt Publishing Co.

Grinfelds V and Hulstrand B: Right down your alley, ed 2, Champaign, Ill, 1985, Human Kinetics Publishers, Inc. Contains advice on how to improve bowling efficiency, accuracy, and consistency, and how to correct common errors.

Harrison JM and Maxey R: Bowling, Glenview, Ill, 1987, Scott/Foresman and Co. In addition to the skills and rules necessary to play the game, the text offers a dictionary of bowling terms, a self-test, and activities and resources for further instruction.

Hastings R: Let's go bowling, Dubuque, Iowa, 1982, Kendall/Hunt Publishing Co.

Kenny J: Strike touch bowling, Champaign, Ill, 1982, Leisure Press.

Mackey R: Bowling, Palo Alto, Calif, 1980, Mayfield Publishing Co. A concise bowling handbook that discusses auditory and visual cues to help students acquire basic skills when practicing on their own.

Martin JL, Tandy RE, and Agne-Traub CE: Bowling, ed 5, Dubuque, Iowa, 1990, William C. Brown Co. Presents the fundamental skills needed to be a good bowler and introduces special bowling events. Both basic and advanced bowling skills are covered, and common faults and their remedies are explained.

McIntyre F: Successful bowling, Edina, Minn, 1985, Burgess International Group, Inc.

National Bowling Council: Instructor's manual, Washington, DC, 1980, National Bowling Council.

Schunk C: Bowling, ed 3, New York, 1983, WB Saunders Co. An introduction to bowling with emphasis on development and improvement through body mechanics and timing. Includes a history section, updated terminology, and techniques.

Scott TM and Carpenter CL: Bowling everyone, Winston-Salem, NC 1983, Hunter Textbooks, Inc. Using easy-to-follow descriptions and numerous illustrations, the book covers footwork, targeting, ball delivery, and other bowling moves. Terminology, scoring, rules, conditioning, bowling aids, and left-hander problems are also covered. An error chart and end-of-chapter quizzes are included.

Showers N: Bowling, Glenview, Ill, 1980, Scott, Foresman & Co. For bowlers of all ability levels, this book covers all aspects of bowling and includes a diagnostic chart on common faults and symptoms and possible remedies.

Strickland RH: Bowling: steps to success, Champaign, Ill, 1989, Human Kinetics Publishers.

Williams GD: Developing your bowling potential, Dubuque, Iowa, 1983, Kendall/Hunt Publishing Co.

Women's International Bowling Congress, Inc.: Rules for WIBC, Inc., sanctioned leagues, Columbus, Ohio, 1988, Women's International Bowling Congress, Inc.

FILMS

Better bowling. Ned Day, Films Inc., New York.

Bowling aces. Joe Falcaro, Associated Films, YMCA Motion Picture Bureau, New York.

Bowling fundamentals. Teaching Films, Inc., New York.

Bowling skill. Teaching Films Custodians, Inc., New York.

Set 'em up. Teaching Films Custodians, Inc., New York.

Splits, spares and strikes. Teaching Films Custodians, Inc., New York.

VIDEOTAPES

Let's Bowl with Dick Weber, The Bowling Masters, and *Bowling with Marshall Holman and John Petraglia.* Karol Video, 22 Riverside Dr., Wayne, NJ 07470.

6 bowling videos available from Sports Video. Champions on Film, 745 State Circle, Box 1941, Ann Arbor, MI 48106.

A New Approach to a Great Old Game, Fundamentals of the Arm Swing, Fundamentals of Footwork and *Bowling Strikes and Spares.* The Athletic Institute, 200 N. Castlewood Dr., North Palm Beach, FL 33408.

A Pro's Guide to Better Bowling, Volumes I and II, each 60 min. "How To" Sport Videos, Box 5852, Denver, CO 80217.

9

Dance: Concert and Recreational

Completion of this chapter should enable the reader to:

- Distinguish among various forms of dance and appreciate their development
- Demonstrate the fundamentals of movement
- Understand how elements of movement (space, time, and force) and creativity apply to modern dance
- Organize and teach square dancing
- Organize and teach folk dancing
- Recognize forms of social dancing

Dance offerings today at all academic levels are increasingly broad in scope and rich in content. School programs regularly include two general types of dance: recreational forms and performing (or concert) forms. The former include folk, square, and social (or ballroom) dance, all of which are done for the recreation of the participants. They are leisure activities with a primary goal of social interaction through the use of dance skills.

Concert dance forms involve using the body as an instrument to communicate with (or entertain) an audience. The goals are esthetic rather than recreational. Although modern dance is the form most frequently found in schools, ballet and jazz are increasing in popularity, and tap dance is experiencing a revival of interest.

The growth of participation in recreational dance forms is indicated by the proliferation of clubs, classes, festivals, publications, shops, recordings, demonstrations, conferences, and professional teacher-leaders. Recreational forms of dance change mood every so often (e.g., disco and country swing) but remain a recreational outlet for millions of people. Ballroom and couple dances are currently enjoying a revival.

Experts tend to recommend freer forms of dance and exploratory movement in the early years, with emphasis on developing the ability to move in many ways so that the body can be used expressively as well as rhythmically. In later years there should be more emphasis on technique, style, and form. Each type of dance has a special contribution to make.

It is possible to gain knowledge and some appreciation of dance through reading. However, only through extensive dancing does a person develop the skills needed for teaching or fully understanding any form of dance. This is true primarily because the body is the instrument used in dance. Students of dance are not learning to hit a ball or hurdle an obstacle. The only model for their activity is the skill that dance teachers demonstrate in using their bodies, their "dance instruments."

Ideally, exposure to dance starts at the elementary level. Specialized training is necessary for the teacher who wishes to deal with this level, and in particular to relate dance to the elementary curriculum. This is the best time to involve boys in dance, as they quickly find that it is exciting and challenging to participate in dance classes and to explore movement through dance.

Concert forms

MODERN DANCE
History

People have always danced. They have used some form of rhythmic movement as a part of their life pattern from the beginning of time. History indicates that dance has been used in worship, as a part of ritualistic ceremonies, for entertainment, and as a means of expressing thoughts and ideas.

Fig. 9-1. Modern dance students improvise.

At the turn of this century, Isadora Duncan rebelled against what she considered to be the artificial movements of ballet. She felt that dancing should be free and natural.

Following closely upon Duncan and her free and natural dance style came Ruth St. Denis and Ted Shawn who reintroduced theatricalism and technique into dance and formed the Denishawn school in 1915. A major contribution of Ted Shawn's was bringing men into the art and providing a formalized technique for them. The Denishawn company helped keep alive the nation's interest in dance by making 13 cross-country tours in the 1920s while the school provided training for future teachers and performers. These included three major pioneers of what became known as modern dance; Martha Graham, Charles Weidman, and Doris Humphrey. All three of these artists performed, toured, and opened schools. The fourth pioneer to contribute to the development of modern dance in this country and to the musical theatre was Hanya Holm.

During this period many teachers of physical education participated in dance classes taught by these outstanding artists and in turn taught dance to the young people in their own classes. Today many universities house a dance department. Dance is taught to all age groups, is used as therapy, and is a performing art in theatres, television, and film.

Modern dance is of great importance in the total education, as it involves the individual mentally, physically, and emotionally. It stresses individualism and development of personal choreographic style (Fig. 9-1).

FUNDAMENTALS OF MOVEMENT

An understanding of the fundamentals of movement is necessary before dance can be used as a means of expression or communication. Movement may be axial or locomotor, using personal space or general space. Axial movement is movement of the body or any part of the body over a stationary base. This movement may take place on any level and with any part of the body as the base of support. Flexion, extension, rotation, bending, stretching, and twisting, or any combination of these movements plus a variation or forceful release of energy produces an interesting design pattern (Figs. 9-2 and 9-3).

Locomotor movements cause the body to travel from one spot to another. There are two categories of locomotor movements. The first includes moving the body with different parts of the body in contact with the floor, for example, rolling, crawling, creeping, or walking on the knees or possibly on the hands. The second includes all the foot patterns used in moving the body through space. Tempo and rhythm may vary with each pattern. There are only eight possible movements; anything else is a combination or variation of the basic eight.

walk Transfer of weight from one foot to the other foot.
run Transfer of weight from one foot to the other foot with a slight spring as the weight leaves the back foot to come down on the forward foot. The toes touch the floor first, and then the heel comes down. The movement of the legs and feet can cause the body to be carried upward as well as forward.
leap Transfer of weight from one foot to the other as in a run, but a greater spring causes the body to be in the air for a

Fig. 9-3. Layout.

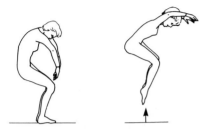

Fig. 9-2. Flexion.

Fig. 9-4. Leap.

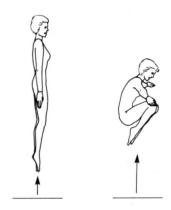

Fig. 9-5. Jump.

Fig. 9-6. Hop.

moment with both feet off the floor. The leap may be long and low or short and high (Fig. 9-4).

jump Movement in which the body springs into the air from one or both feet and lands on both feet (Fig. 9-5).

hop Transfer of weight on the same foot. The body springs into the air from one foot and lands on the same foot (Fig. 9-6).

skip Combination of a walk and a hop. The movement is performed on the same foot. The step, which is the first part of the movement, is rhythmically long, and the hop, the second part of the movement, is short.

slide Combination of two walking steps. The forward step or the first part of the movement is rhythmically long, and the second step, in which the other foot is brought up to the forward foot and the weight placed on it, is rhythmically short.

gallop Combination of a leap and a walk. The leap, the first part of the movement, is rhythmically long, and the walk onto the other foot is rhythmically short.

All dance forms employ these eight basic locomotor movements in some form or style. All eight may be performed in any tempo, meter, or direction in space, such as forward, backward, or sideward. Interesting combinations make challenging and delightful dance patterns. Changes in the space elements, such as level, focus, and size, with the individual's own stylization can be the beginnings of creative endeavors, for example:

Three long walks and two jumps, changing level and body direction

Two skips and two gallops, changing size and focus

Any combination of runs and hops, changing position of the arms

Movement properties

Theorists through the years have attempted to categorize movement properties for studying, teaching, and analyzing dance. Laban suggested that every human movement involves the four factors of space, force, time, and flow.

Dance takes place in space. Therefore, a knowledge of the basic space elements is a necessary part of the education of the modern dancer. Space is all around us; we live in it, we move in it constantly, we cannot exist without it. The dance, to be appreciated and to be creative, must concern itself with space, and the dancer must consider how space can be used to full advantage.

Dance must take direction in space. The individual is capable of moving forward, backward, sideward, and diagonally and of turning or spinning in one spot. Also, a particular dance pattern should be well placed in the space or area within which the dancer is moving, either on the stage or in a room. This means that the dancer travels toward or away from all sides or corners of the area.

The dancer must be concerned about the level in which movement occurs. The dancer may be lying flat on the floor, seated on the floor, on the knees, on the feet, or in the air. A combination of all these levels might be experienced during the dance pattern.

Force is concerned with concepts such as strength, manifested in downward movements, and lightness, shown in upward movements. This movement property, also described as weight, include such descriptions as weak, heavy, weighty, and resilient. The control of various muscular tensions gives an indication of the bodily awareness in the intent of the dancer's movement performances.

Time refers to the speed of movements. Usually quick and sudden movements are made in a backward direction while slow and sustained motions are correlated with reaching forward. The mood of a dance performance is most influenced by variations in the property of time.

Flow involves such aspects of movement as rigidity, stability, flexibility, and fluency. Expressions of feelings and emotions are connected to the flow of a dance performance.

Lockhart categorized movement qualities in a different way by using the mechanical properties and release of energy into the various parts of the body as criteria. She classifies movement qualities into swinging, sustaining, percussing, suspending, vibrating, and collapsing.

Swinging is the most frequently used and naturally occurring of the body's movements. Swings are characterized by a slight impulse, a giving away to gravity, and a pause prior to repetition. These movements convey feelings of freedom, openness, and ease.

Sustained movement is even, smooth, and free of sudden and sharp actions. This requires maximum muscular control. Sustained movement elicits feelings of calmness, self control, restraint, and sometimes, mystery.

Sharp, aggressive movement in which energy appears and disappears quickly symbolize percussive movement quality. Emotions of vigor, explosiveness, directness, and aggressiveness are evoked through percussive movement.

Movement is described as suspended when two opposing forces are equated. The instant at the peak of a leap when the upward force and the force of gravity are equal is an example of this movement quality. It is used to express anticipation, ecstasy, and breathlessness.

Vibrating movement results from quickly recurring small percussive movements. It is characterized by intermittent spurts of energy within a limited range. Most commonly this quality of movement is used to denote fear or rage.

Collapsing movements occur when muscular tension in the body is released and gravity is permitted to take over. This can be accomplished in a gradual and controlled manner or suddenly. Emotions such as acquiescence, resignation, and helplessness are elicited through this movement quality.

Rhythm and its relationship to dance

Rhythm is what makes the world go around; it is the pulsation of the universe, the foundation of the world. We would not and could not be alive today if rhythm was not a part of us. Beating of our hearts and exhalation of air from our lungs are excellent examples of rhythm. Changing of seasons, patterns in rock formations on the coast, stars in the heavens, tides, and patterns of trees and flowers are all rhythmic examples given to us by nature. We also find rhythm in the pattern of our lives. These rhythmic patterns may be seen in changes in the fashion world, politics, economics, and in the many social changes that come upon us during a lifetime.

Rhythm, by definition, is a series of pulsations that can be even or uneven, weak or strong. These are grouped in small groups of time. Some rhythmic elements a dancer is concerned with are:

accent Stress or force of movement which can vary from very strong and hard to light and weak.
underlying beat Constant pulsation that takes place throughout the dance. This beat is divided into units, thus designating the meter or time in which the dance is performed.
phrase A group of several meters giving a feeling of unity and completion to the rhythmic sentence and movement pattern.

Modern dance may be performed with or without accompaniment, but in either case the above rhythmic elements are always present and must be taken into consideration.

Technique

Modern dance technique develops control of the body and a kinesthetic awareness and increases the range of movement. Warm-up exercises prepare the body for the more demanding work to follow. Patterns in place develop strength and flexibility, alignment, and balance and expand the movement vocabulary. Combinations using the length of the studio develop a sense of air or lightness, timing, and a culmination in actually "dancing" all that has preceded. Each section is a preparation for the next.

To teach dance rather than a series of exercises to music, the leader must be technically skilled to the level of competent demonstration. Phrasing must be clear, with interesting rhythmic variations. Many kinds and variations of movement must be presented to increase the beginner's vocabulary of movement. A dance class is conducted in the same way whether students are taking a class for fun, career preparation, or body development. Students should dance in class as if they were on stage, with total concentration and intensity.

All individuals can be creative in movement to some degree, if only because we are creative in movement in the way we go about our daily tasks. Modern dance develops further the individual's creativity in movement. In a modern dance class the student learns to explore movement and then to solve movement problems. The student learns to improvise, or move on the spur of the moment without any previous plan, and then to plan a dance pattern or dance study. This study usually is based on some element of the dance the student is studying at the time: qualities of movement, one or several space elements, rhythmic elements, or various forms of axial or locomotor movements. Last, the dancer is prepared to create a composition. This composition has a theme or idea and has a beginning, a development, a climax, and an ending.

Sources of inspiration for creativity in modern dance come from the world around us. A dance study may be based on an idea, emotion, interesting design, or another art form, such as music, poetry, literature, painting or sculpture, or it may be centered around an everyday experience or even a sports event. In planning a dance composition or study, the dancer should develop the idea in a personal, perhaps unusual or unexpected manner, but always keeping the main idea present. Also remember that in planning a dance composition, all the elements of time, space, force, and the various types of movement and design, whether symmetric or asymmetric, are to be used and to be seen. In a dance composition there must be unity and harmony as well as variety and contrast and yet repetition for emphasis. The ending of one movement should be the beginning of the next. If this is accomplished, a smooth transition of movement and thought will take place, and the composition will relate a well-developed idea and not a series of unrelated and unstructured events.

The following are suggestions or sources of inspiration in composing a dance:

1. Select an experience such as shopping on a crowded Saturday afternoon at Christmastime. Show accomplishment as well as failure by stylizing the movements with changes in level and dimension.

2. Imagine you are caught in a very small tunnel and cannot find your way out. Express your reactions and fears in a movement pattern.

3. Find a unique way to greet a friend you have not seen for some time. Plan the sequence of movements in relation to various qualities of movement.

4. Draw an interesting design of heavy and light curves, circles, and wiggly lines. Then create a dance sequence to interpret the design.

5. Select a game or a sport. Analyze part of the movement patterns used in the sport. Stylize them as to success and failure based on changes in tempo.

6. Choose a simple gesture such as opening or closing a door. Do it as many different ways as you can and relate each to a different character study, such as a fearful shy individual, a fast-moving egocentric individual, a tough tomboy, or a demure little old lady.

In composing a dance, the dancer must explore over and over again the various movement patterns possible until one is found that the dancer likes and is comfortable performing. This takes practice. Movements must be clear and set well in space. Rhythmic changes must be exact and well defined. This is a mental, physical, and emotional challenge, but the final outcome is well worth the effort, because that is when the complete expression and discovery of the individual is realized.

BALLET

History

Ballet technique emerged from court dances of the sixteenth century. The basic steps were codified by Beauchamps at the Royal Academy of Dance in Paris in the seventeenth century. In the early nineteenth century Carlo Blasis published two books that described the theories and procedures of that day. His descriptions are the basis of ballet training of the intervening years and of today. Ballet moved through a period of acclaim in the eighteenth and early nineteenth centuries, but public interest declined in the latter part of the nineteenth century. When Serge Diaghelev's Ballet Russe, a group of emigres from Russia, came to Paris in 1909, western Europe was astonished by the artistic daring and innovation of Russian ballet. This created renewed interest throughout the western world. While it only functioned

Fig. 9-7. Ballet class.

for 20 years, in that time it transformed ballet into a vital art form.

By the 1940s America could claim two major companies, Ballet Theatre (later changed to American Ballet Theatre) and the New York City Ballet. Since that time ballet has flourished throughout the United States, with many ballet companies active today including a large number of civic and regional groups.

Ballet in education

Today ballet is much more frequently a part of the secondary school dance program than in the past. The highly disciplined training builds a strong technique (Fig. 9-7). Youngsters are most responsive to ballet, much to the surprise of some teachers who have been hesitant to include it in the school dance offerings. As in all other aspects of dance, the caliber of the teaching will determine the eagerness and enthusiasm of the students, the amount of progress made, and the suitability of the form in the total dance offerings.

JAZZ
History

Jazz dance grew out of the African heritage, the Irish clog dance, minstrel shows, vaudeville, social dances, and other sources. It is truly American in origin.

Syncopation makes jazz rhythmically stimulating.

Jazz dance in education

Jazz in the educational setting ranges from clichéd movements or steps taken from disco dancing to work that is original and varied, exciting for the movement style as well as the rhythm. It is changing continually because of its strong relationship to contemporary popular culture.

The way jazz is taught determines whether it will be a limited movement opportunity or an opportunity to improve and expand technique and to explore movement in this exuberant style.

TAP DANCING
History

Tap dancing is an American art form which includes African, Irish, and English influences. It developed in the mid-1800s in big city ghettos through minstrel shows and blackface characterization. From the intermingling of blacks and European immigrants, the Irish jig, English clog dancing, and African-based steps evolved into the current form of tap dancing. The songs and natural rhythms of Southern blacks who had adopted the jig movements from the Irish helped form the "buck and wing." The 1900s brought about a new and complex set of steps that were more rhythmic, smooth, and steady. Tap dancing was popularized during these times through vaudeville shows, on showboats, and especially on the Broadway stage in the Ziegfeld Follies and other shows. Recent films depicting the history of tap dancing such as *White Nights* and *Tap* have revived interest in this dance form. Personalities having a strong influence on the history and development of this art were Bill Robinson, Fred Astaire, Ginger Rogers, Gene Kelly, Paul Draper, Honi Coles, Ann Miller, Gregory Hines, Dan Dailey, and many others.

Tap dance in education

Tap dancing instruction began in public schools around the early 1900s. Today there are hundreds of teachers and instructional facilities for this art form. Tap dance terms have become standardized, and rhythm technique and execution analysis are essential to good instruction. Educators from the beginning recognized the values of this rhythmic movement. The 1980s produced a resurgence in the popularity of tap dancing (as evidenced by plays and movies such as *A Chorus Line*, *42nd Street*, *The Tap Dance Kid*, and *My One and Only*) causing the teaching of tap dancing to flourish once again.

Recreational forms

All recreational dance involves people moving together and enjoying the group or partner as well as the rhythmic movement. These forms are an ideal coeducational activity, as they provide an easy, casual basis for mixing and working together. There are dances suitable for every age level.

A major stimulus to the growth of recreational dance has been the development of good recordings. Having appropriate, inexpensive music readily available eliminates the cost and trouble of an accompanist. Moreover, authentic music is motivating to beginning dancers. They can tape music for home practice and small parties. Where once only large groups could afford dance music, now the individual can bring an "orchestra" home for a family swing session.

If teachers, recordings, and dances are up to date, students can move readily from the classroom to local clubs and recreational classes for leisure enjoyment. Some teachers take their classes to community dances or require attendance once during the semester to increase the likelihood of participation after graduation.

Fun is part of any recreational dance class from the first day. There is no long period of learning before the student can enjoy the satisfaction of accomplishment. At the same time, challenging new figures, steps, or dances should constantly be presented, as should more complicated combinations or more intricate rhythm. The range of skill possible in recreational dance forms is extremely wide.

Limitations of space preclude discussion of all the types of recreational dance, and new variations are constantly becoming popular. For example, country-western round dance, country-western swing, and round dancing are currently very popular. Thus only square dancing is presented in detail; folk and social dances are introduced briefly.

AMERICAN SQUARE DANCE
History

The American square dance (Fig. 9-8) had its beginning in England with the English country dance, a dance form that developed among the people in rural districts. In the early 1600s the dance did not enjoy tremendous popularity, especially in larger cities. The impetus that propelled it into prominence came in 1651 when John Playford published the first English country dance book. Most of the dances compiled for this first publication were known as "longways," or what the French later called *contra* dances. In the contra, participants arranged themselves in two lines facing each other. Through various sequences of movements, dancers moved from one position in the line to the next or from one line to the other.

Before the introduction of Playford's book, the dances of the royal court had been in vogue. These dances sometimes contained intricate dance steps and suggested a romantic or flirtatious attitude on the part of participants. To understand the significance of Playford's publication

Fig. 9-8. Square dancers doing a left-hand square.

in regard to the people's choice of dances, it is necessary to investigate the conditions that prevailed in England during the early part of the seventeenth century.

Segments of England's population had been agitating for change in government. This led to civil war and the eventual beheading of the king. Before this event, a group of Puritans, who had been urging separation of church and state, managed to sail to America in an attempt to set up their own government. As evidence of the desire for a government of their own and as a sign of their rebellion, the Puritans and other sympathetic groups refused to participate in the dances of the court, preferring the more simple English country dances. Playford, a Puritan, attempted to meet this need with his publication. Not only was this book accepted with great acclaim among England's discontented, but it also met with favor in America.

From this beginning the American square dance evolved. Instead of the pomp and circumstance attending the dances of the court and the social etiquette marked by favors given to the most prestigious persons at a dance, participants took their places in lines according to their order of arrival. Gone was the intricate, delicate footwork, and in its place was a steady, even movement of the feet to each beat of the music. The flirtatious attitude among participants of the court dances was replaced by emphasis on movement patterns and the coordination of all dancers in an attempt to work together to effect these patterns of movement. The dance emphasized the cohesiveness of the people and stressed democracy in action. Today the American square dance is still based on these principles.

From its beginning, the American square dance has exemplified the ideals on which the country was founded and that its citizens have attempted to realize in the intervening years. It is the folk dance of North America, not only because it has been a part of the culture since its colonial beginnings, but also because the essence of the dance reflects the philosophy and values of its people.

In the early 1700s the French, who had also found enjoyment in the longways, introduced the square formation. It was believed that the contra did not allow for sufficient activity or excitement. The French realized that they could effect figures similar to those used in the contra in the square formation, thereby assuring more activity for all participants. The new style of dance that emerged as a result of this innovation was called the *cotillion*.

The advent of the French Revolution added further innovations to the cotillion. A faster tempo and more intricate dance steps grew out of the cultural changes taking place in France. People were demanding change and excitement, and they found an outlet in their dance.

By the mid-1800s the cotillion no longer satisfied the people. Its rather short, simple movement patterns were not enough to sustain interest. All facets of the culture were becoming more complicated, and it was inevitable that the dance should also articulate this growing complexity. The French combined five to six cotillions into one dance for greater intricacy in dancing. The French *quadrille* became popular in England and America soon after its inception.

The first American innovation to the dance came with the introduction of the "caller". It is the caller that sets the American square dance apart from all other dances and that provides the major justification for labeling it the American folk dance. Before the advent of the caller in the early 1800s (during or soon after the War of 1812) participants memorized each dance. However, with a caller presiding over the dance program, it was possible to perform a new, unfamiliar dance as long as one knew its "basics" or dance patterns (circle, dos-a-dos, promenade, and such). This change heralded a new method of learning how to dance. Sequences of basics no longer needed to be committed to memory. The patter call evolved as an adjunct to this concept. The caller would make up dances as he or she went along. This introduced the element of anticipation—not knowing what will be called next—that has drawn many people to the square dance over the years. Participants rely on their knowledge of basics, listening ability, coordination, timing, and rhythm to successfully complete a dance.

In the mid to late 1800s the singing call emerged. Currently popular music was used (the practice when choreographing new dances), and a figure was developed by the choreographer in which there was an exchange of partners. This figure was constructed in such a way that if repeated three more times dancers would be back with their original partners in their home positions.

In the late 1800s the waltz, polka, and other couple dances became overwhelmingly popular in Europe and in the eastern United States. Consequently, ballroom dancing took over as the favorite form of social dancing in the cities, and the contra and square dances were eliminated from the dance program. In the eastern United States, the American square dance receded into small towns.

Meanwhile, it was enjoying tremendous popularity in the West. The visiting-couple figure predominated, as did rhyming patter depicting life on the plains. However, by the early 1900s ballroom dancing became popular in the newly formed cities of the West, and here too, square dancing became associated with the small town, the roundups, and the granges.

Little change occurred in the American square dance from the early 1900s until after World War II. For the most part, those who participated in dancing were content to perform the dances of yesteryear. A study of the evolution of the American square dance shows that change in the dance has occurred during times of social unrest and political upheaval. Thus it was inevitable that World War II would precipitate a new style of American square dance.

During the war, United Service Organizations, church groups, and other organizations presented social activities for service personnel. The square dance seemed a logical activity to inspire congenial social cohesiveness among strangers. After the war many of the young men who had enjoyed this experience turned to calling to provide hometown neighbors with a similar experience. Overnight, it seemed, the American square dance gained tremendous popularity, and with this popularity came many changes in the dance.

The wave of popularity grew in the West and quickly spread eastward. In southern California in 1941 there were approximately 10 clubs and 5 callers. By November 1948 there were some 30 callers and 75 square dance clubs. Six months later, in May 1949, the number had risen to some 400 active groups in the same area. By the end of 1950 there were an estimated 50,000 square dancers in Los Angeles alone and five million in the nation.

By the time the wave of popularity hit the east coast in the late 1940s and the early 1950s, a new dance style—the modern American square dance—had developed. There were few differences in dancing from one section of the country to the other. For this reason, dance historians believe it was at this point that the square dance finally emerged as the national dance—the American folk dance.

The square dance as it developed from the 1940s to the 1970s is vastly different from the square dance of the early twentieth century. From some 10 or 12 basic movements prior to 1940, there are now over 800. Twenty or more new singing calls are released each month from the 15-odd commercial square dance record companies now in existence. One to two years' instruction is required to prepare participants for community dancing. The simple visiting-couple figure of the Western square dance is no longer performed. Instead, the line, posting, and star-thru figures are used along with the traditional circle formation. Participants learn to perform basics, not dances. They rely on their ability to listen to the calls; to coordinate their movements with each other; to time each basic correctly while dancing; to move to the beat, tempo, and phrasing of the music; and to space their steps appropriately for the various formations and basics used in the dancing.

It is estimated that some 6 to 10 million people belong to square dance clubs in the United States. For many, square dancing takes up at least two to four evenings a month, while for others dancing two or three evenings a week is not unusual. The American folk dance knows more participants than any other national folk dance. It continually changes as the culture changes. It is a vibrant, living folk dance articulating the values of its people.

Objectives of square dancing

1. To provide satisfaction and self-pride by giving the participant a new "ability"
2. To promote gracefulness
3. To develop coordination
4. To help develop self-discipline
5. To help develop good timing and rhythm
6. To provide an opportunity to learn to relax with the opposite sex
7. To provide an opportunity to develop emotional and social values
8. To provide an activity that will promote "togetherness and fun" for everyone

Square dance formation

The square dance is performed by sets of 4 couples. The "lady" is always situated to the right of the man. The couple in front of the caller is couple 1. Couple 3 faces couple 1. These two couples are the *head* couples unless otherwise designated. Couple 2 is to the right of 1. Couple 4 is opposite 2. Couples 2 and 4 are the *side* couples. Home position is the starting position. If a mistake is made by a couple while performing a figure, "Square the set" is called, and all couples return to starting position.

Relative position of partners

The lady on the man's right is always his *partner;* the one to his left is his *corner.* The man to the lady's left is her *partner;* the man to her right is her *corner.* During the dance the man may be separated from his starting partner. If he is separated and the word *partner* is called, he must take the lady who at that time is to his right. Partners hold hands whenever possible.

Shuffle step

The dance should be performed in a light-footed, lively shuffle step, with the dancers changing from one basic to another. One step is taken on each beat or count. The feet slide forward on the floor. When moving to the right, as in "Circle right," dancers step right foot to the side, then step left foot in front of the right. They continue this sequence with toes pointed toward the center of the circle.

Square dance composition

basics Individual movements, for example, "Go forward and back."

phrase A number of basics making 8 or 16 counts.

figure A group of phrases, usually 64 counts, in which the couples start at and return to home position.

dance Enough figures to take a couple through a song.

name of square dance Usually the main figure, for example, "Ducking for the Oyster" or "Taking a Peek." The dance can be identified by the name of the music to which it is danced.

Starting the dance

The call "Honor your partner" starts the dance. Participants bow first to their corners and then to their partners.

Fundamental skills of the square dance

circle Eight beats halfway; 16 beats all the way. Designated dancers join hands, turn slightly in the direction designated, and shuffle-step around. This may be to the left or to the right. The call may be for ladies, for men, or for everybody

forward and back Eight beats or counts. Designated couples take four steps toward the center of the circle and then back out four steps.

dos-a-dos Eight counts. Partners, corners, or opposites shuffle forward, go back to right of each other past each other's right arm, go back to back, and then back out to starting position.

promenade Eight counts halfway; 16 counts all the way. Pairs take right hands as though shaking hands and position themselves side by side, facing counterclockwise with the man on the inside of the circle and the lady on the outside. The man reaches under his right arm with his left hand and grasps the lady's left hand. They then shuffle-step together around the circle.

ladies' chain Eight counts. Ladies, heads or sides, shuffle across the set, touching right hands as they pass each other in the center of the circle. They then extend their left hands to the men. The men take the ladies' left hands with their left hands, place their right hands on the ladies' waists, and all turn counterclockwise to home and starting position.

allemande left Eight counts. The man joins his left hand or arm with whomever allemande is to be made. Both then shuffle counterclockwise around each other, back to starting position.

star Eight counts. Designated partners extend designated hands into the center of the circle and shuffle around in an inner circle one full circle, returning to starting position. Dancers may be called to do a right or left star.

right and left thru Eight counts halfway; 16 counts all the way. Two couples face each other. Couples extend their right hands to the persons opposite them and pass them on the right, then immediately give their left hands to each other, and men put their right arm around their ladies to courtesy-turn them around to face each other (couples have exchanged places).

right hand round the partner Eight counts. Partners face each other holding right hands and go around each other moving in a clockwise direction, then return to starting position. This basic is opposite to allemande left (and is sometimes called allemande right).

grand right and left Eight counts halfway; 16 counts all the way. Partners face each other and hold right hands. They walk by each other and take the opposite hand of the dancer they are facing. They advance around the circle, alternating from side to side until they meet. Men go counterclockwise; ladies advance clockwise.

grand square Thirty-two counts. Simultaneously all dancers walk a small square in their corner of the full square (Fig. 9-9). Couples 1 and 3 walk forward four steps, meeting in the center of the set while partners in couples 2 and 4 face each other and walk four steps backward to the outside corners of the set (Fig. 9-9, *B*). Partners in couples 1 and 3 face each other with backs to side walls, join inside hands and walk back four steps (they will now be in home position of couples 2 and 4); at same time man 4 and lady 2 and man 2 and lady 4 face each other and walk four steps forward to arrive at original home position of couples 1 and 3 (Fig. 9-9, *C*. They continue this sequence as shown in Fig. 9-9, *D* and *E*, at which point all couples should be back in their home positions. The entire sequence is then reversed (first four counts shown in Fig. 9-9, *F*) by beginning with couples 2 and 4 walking to the center while couples 1 and 3 move backward to the outside corners of the set.

sashay round your corner Eight counts. Using sideward sliding steps and always facing the center, the man goes to the left, outside and around his corner, and returns to his original position.

seesaw round your own Eight counts. The man uses sideward sliding steps to the right, outside and around his corner, returning to his original position.

around that couple, take a peek Sixteen counts forward and back. Couple 1 faces couple 2. Couple 1 goes forward, splits, goes past couple 2, peeking at each other, and then backs up to starting position. The call may be for heads or for sides to take a peek.

dive for the oyster Sixteen counts. First and second couples face by shuffling together. All hold hands and circle halfway to the left. Second couple joins hands and raises arms while

the first couple goes four steps under and four steps back. Again all join hands and circle halfway around and back to starting position.

balance Dancers take two steps back from partner and curtsy.

balance and swing Couples balance as shown above; then take two steps forward, joining hands or arms, and rotate twice around each other.

weave the ring Eight counts halfway; 16 counts all the way. Same movement as the grand right and left except hands do not touch.

Construction of the figure

"Bow to your corner, bow to your partner, and all join hands."

Circle to the left halfway	8 counts
All go forward and back	8 counts
Circle right halfway	8 counts
Circle to the left all the way	16 counts
Circle to the right all the way	16 counts
All go forward and back	8 counts
	64 counts

"Bow to your corner, bow to your partner"

Dos-a-dos your corner	8 counts
Dos-a-dos	8 counts
All join hands and circle left	16 counts
Heads go forward and back	8 counts
Sides go forward and back	8 counts
All join hands and circle right	16 counts
	64 counts

"Take a peek"

Circle left all the way	16 counts
Heads "take a peek" round the couple on the right	16 counts
Sides "take a peek" round the couple on the right	16 counts
Circle right all the way	16 counts
	64 counts

Music for square dancing
Patter or hoedown music

Patter music is used for timing and rhythm. It usually does not have a familiar melody, and as a rule it is used to teach the basic skills.

Singing call

Singing call music has a definite melody, and there is a specific set of figures written for it. Examples of singing calls are: *Oh Johnny!*, *Hot Time in the Old Town Tonight*, *Hello, Dolly! Cabaret*, *Buffalo Girls*, and *Pop Goes the Weasel*.

FOLK DANCE

Folk dances (Fig. 9-10) are traditional dances, part of the cultural heritage of a group, nation, or religion. They

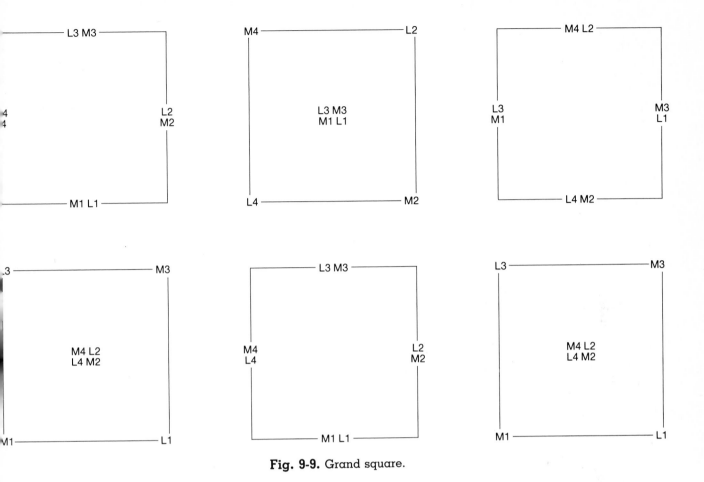

Fig. 9-9. Grand square.

Fig. 9-10. Folk dance students practice a line dance.

developed as ethnic dances in which ordinary folk participated. In contrast, some ethnic dances evolved as art forms danced by selected, highly skilled performers.

Sources

Folk dances are international. Some had their start as a means of celebrating some special occasion such as the harvest, a wedding, or a feast day. Others grew out of work practices, religious ceremonies, or military customs. But most evolved as recreational pastimes, a means of having fun.

Because folk dances are "of the people," they often are changed "by the people." Someone may add a clap here or a turn there to make a dance more enjoyable. Others follow along, and the change thus spreads. This continues today. There may be a local variation on almost any dance, but basic styles, steps, and formations tend to endure and give each dance its special flavor.

Forms

Folk dances take many forms. In some, individuals dance alone without touching anyone else. In others the individual is in a line or circle or broken circle (with a leader at one end) in contact with those on either side. Neighbors may join hands, hook arms, put hands to shoulders or about the waist, or just interlace little fingers. Sometimes they wear loose belts that are grasped by dancers on either side, especially in line dances for men where the action is very vigorous.

Dances for two, three, six, or eight are more structured. Group formations vary from short lines to single circles, double circles, parallel lines, squares, stars, and even triangles. In dances for partners there is a definite dance position or way they relate to each other, for example, closed (facing and close as for ballroom dance), open (side by side), shoulder-waist (man's hands at the woman's waist and her hands on his shoulders), and butterfly (partners facing, hands joined, and arms outstretched at shoulder height).

Currently, nonpartner dances for any number seem to be most popular. They are quickly organized and make it easy for anyone to join the group. They suit the casual atmosphere of many folk gatherings. Couple and group dances take more organization to get started, and some persons may be left out.

Basic dance steps

Basic movements used in folk dances are walking (or stepping), running, leaping, jumping, hopping, skipping, sliding, and galloping. Traditional folk dance steps are composed of combinations of these basic movements put to various rhythms. Following are brief descriptions of some common folk dance steps. ("Close" means to bring the feet together and step and L is left, R is right.)

two-step (2/4 or 4/4 meter) The rhythm is quick, quick, slow as the last count is held.

step	close	step	hold
L	**R**	**L**	

polka (2/4 meter) The hop is quick, coming on the pick-up beat just before count 1. The rhythm changes from the two-step to ah, quick, quick, slow.

hop	step	close	step
L	**R**	**L**	**R**

schottische (4/4 meter) Four movements on four counts with an even steady rhythm. Sometimes the action is step, close, step, hop; sometimes runs are used in place of steps:

step	step	step	hop
L	**R**	**L**	**L**

waltz box (3/4 meter) Six steps on six counts (two measures of music) with an even rhythm. The rhythm is slow, slow, slow.

step forward	side	close
L	**R**	**L**
step backward	side	close
R	**L**	**R**

mazurka (3/4 meter) Three actions on three counts in even time. Styling includes sweeping the left foot backward across the right shinbone on the hop.

step	close	hop
L	**R**	**R**

Combinations of the basic movements changing direction, rhythm, and style appear in amazing variety in the hundreds of folk dances recorded and performed. The steps described here are a small sampling that have become set through frequent use.

Regional dance characteristics

The following brief highlights point up some regional differences in dance styling. There is much fascinating material available (see sources listed) in this area for the student dancer.

England. Country dances for couples moving with light, springy, running steps have a smooth, gliding effect. With arms hanging freely and bodies erect, the dancers interweave in interesting patterns.

Germany. Couple dances with regular patterns such as waltzes, polkas, and schottisches are typical. Also there are dances featuring intricate clapping sequences and much slapping of the body with rhythmic precision.

Greece. Common are broken-circle dances led by a man waving his handkerchief to signal step changes. He improvises with much flamboyance as the line keeps the basic step. Often the women are in separate lines and are much more restrained in their movements.

Hungary. Sudden changes in tempo, clicking of the heels, stamping of feet, and individual improvisation are part of dances such as the csárdás.

Ireland. Intricate, exact footwork characterizes Irish solo dances such as jigs and hornpipes. Reels call for simpler, more gliding steps.

Israel. Religious dances express hope, joy, and courage. National dances serve to unify the many ethnic groups in Israel, blending movements from Europe, Asia, and the Mideast. The use of circle formations in Israeli dances reflects the strength of their ties. Accomplished choreographers create new dances based on traditional steps and forms. The hora is Israel's national dance.

Mexico. Fast footwork with crisp stamping and heel-toe tapping gives excitement to flirtatious couple dances. Action centers in the legs and feet as the man clasps his hands behind his back and the lady holds her full skirt.

Scandinavia. Smoothly turning couple dances are typical. Best known is the Swedish hambo. There are also vigorous dances for men and some clowning, light-hearted dances.

Scotland. To traditional bagpipe music, precise Scottish dancers perform with toes pointed, bodies erect, and hands carefully placed. Flings, reels, schottisches, and sword dances are familiar.

Yugoslavia. Most typical is the kolo, with a leader waving his handkerchief to signal step changes. The many kolos are as varied as the diverse Slavic peoples of this country. Some are quiet, some are bouncy, and some are lively and noisy as the dancers punctuate their steps with exuberant shouts.

SOCIAL DANCE

Popular couple dances without set patterns are classified as social or ballroom dances (Fig. 9-11). They have a casual, relaxed quality not possible in patterned dances. Each couple moves independently of others, and in some dances partners are quite independent of each other, improvising at will. But most social dances are characterized by the man leading and the woman partner following whatever steps, styling, and rhythmic variations he chooses and indicates.

Sources

Formal social dancing began with the European court dances of the Renaissance. Dance masters were employed to develop and teach proper steps to the aristocracy. Today dancers and dance teachers continually invent new steps and styles. Popular music, films, television, and stage shows have all inspired new dances that have swept the United States.

The social dances of one era tend to become the folk dances of following eras. Whenever pleasing combinations begin to be repeated and take set forms, the dance can be recorded and copied by others. The waltz, polka, schottische, and mazurka were all early social dances. Only the waltz continues as a modern ballroom dance, although the polka appears occasionally in the ballroom. The Charleston of the roaring twenties already is appearing in folk dance books. Probably some of the current fad dances will come to the same fate in time. Continual

Fig. 9-11. Social dance—the fox trot.

change seems to be the only certainty in popular social dancing. However, set standards and required steps are spelled out for established dance forms, especially those used in dance competitions.

BASIC STEPS

"Anyone who can walk to music can dance!" This common introduction to a social dance class points up the fact that every form of social dance is based on walking steps. Differences of style and rhythm and patterns set to distinctive music distinguish the different forms. A few variations on the basic steps that are common to all forms are listed here.

rocking Staying in place stepping forward and back or from side to side.
closing Stepping one foot next to the other and transferring the weight. Steps may be forward, backward, or sideways.
balancing Taking a long step followed by two closes. Often the shift of weight is minimal on the closes.
hesitating Pausing by touching the free foot to the floor without transferring weight.
pivoting Rotating in either direction. Dancers may stay in place or travel on a pivot.

Social dance forms

To indicate the rhythmic patterns of the common social dances listed below the symbol S indicates slow and the symbol Q indicates a quick step.

Fox-trot. The fox-trot is an American dance evolving from a trotting dance performed by Harry Fox in a Ziegfeld show in 1913. Present forms tend to be smooth, with dancers gliding around the dance floor with little up and down motion. Fox-trots may be dreamy and slow or quick and light. They can be adapted to in-place dancing in a small space or can be expansive where space permits (one step *QQQQ*, two step *QQS*, magic step *SSQQ*).

Swing. From the lindy of the 1920s and the jitterbug of the 1930s comes our modern swing. The basic step is still the six-count lindy with variations. Though the music may be bouncy, good swing dancers smoothly execute the individual turns, exchanges, and position variations typical of Eastern swing. On the West Coast a slower, more complicated swing form has developed.

Waltz. The oldest ballroom dance form and the first to be danced in closed (or waltz) position, the waltz was considered shocking when first introduced to Americans in the early nineteenth century. Previously it was the rage in Vienna, with Strauss waltzes filling the air. It probably originated in seventeenth-century Germany. The name comes from the German word "to revolve," and turning with smooth, gliding steps continues to be characteristic of waltzing *(SSS)*.

Cha-cha. A Cuban dance growing out of the earlier mambo in the mid-1950s, this dance is characterized by three quick steps. The dancers often are apart, allowing much freedom of movement around the basic "step, step, cha, cha, cha," of the dance. The Latin rhythm is catchy and distinctive *(SSQQQ)*.

Rumba. The rumba was introduced to the United States from Cuba in 1930. Like the cha-cha, action is from the waist down, with a subtle swaying of the hips resulting from careful knee and foot action. The dancers weave interesting patterns as they change positions in this relatively restrained Latin dance *(SQQ)*.

Tango. From Argentina this "dance with a stop," as it was called, came by way of Europe to the United States in 1913. Characterized by sudden changes of direction interrupting the catlike slow steps, the tango is a distinctive form with its many fan (flaring) and corté (dipping) steps *(SSQQS)*.

Samba. From Brazil comes this bouncy, vibrant dance. It involves much knee action, with the dancers' bodies resembling a swinging pendulum as they sway and turn. It was introduced to the United States at the New York World's Fair in 1939 *(QQS)*.

Contemporary dances. Always of interest to students are the currently popular dances. Now and then one endures to find its way into dance literature. For some years, through the 1960s and 1970s, discotheque, no-contact, partner dances were the fad. Then the line hustle came along, and there was no partner at all, just individuals doing essentially the same steps at the same time. At present, there is a resurgence in the popularity of ballroom and couple dancing. New steps come out regularly, with studios competing to create interesting combinations. These are enjoyable, stimulating dances that add a contemporary spice to the classroom scene.

TEACHING CONSIDERATIONS
Square dance

1. Explain the activity and let participants hear a recording of the fundamentals.
2. Use a blackboard, draw a "set," explain positions: home, head, sides, partner, corner.
3. Explain what is meant by "Honor your Partner," and have students practice: bow to the corner, bow to your partner.
4. Teach the class the shuffle step. Have them perform and repeat it until all students do this well. Have them hold hands, go forward and backward, and circle right and left.
5. Explain and demonstrate the beat or count of the square dance, and explain how square dances are phrased. Play a recording and let the class hear the beats and phrases as you count.
6. Teach each basic until all participants are familiar with the mechanics and the call and until they react quickly.

Folk and social dance

1. If possible provide students with the opportunity to see the dance performed with the music.
2. With complex step patterns, teach the basic step directly (not necessarily in the appropriate group formation). Slow down the speed if needed using word cues (e.g., step, close, step, hold). Increase speed of practice until it approaches correct speed. Add the music to practice. Allow sufficient individual practice to have the step be automatic before using the group formation of the dance.
3. With complex group formations (folk dance) teach the chorus first and then other patterns. Walk through parts of the dance with the students first slowly, then more quickly, and then with the music before adding parts to the whole.
4. Repeat parts as new ones are added.
5. Keep the atmosphere and learning climate informal but stress good technique. The dances are more enjoyable that way.
6. As the number of dances students learn increases, provide opportunities for review. Try not to have whole lessons of just new dances.
7. Intersperse regional information with learning dances (folk dance).
8. Use the names for the steps to provide later transfer to other dances that use the same steps.
9. Use mixers to provide opportunities for students to dance with different partners.

SUGGESTED READINGS
General

Anderson J: Ballet and modern dance: a concise history, Princeton, NJ, 1986, Princeton Book Co. Publishers.

Clarkson P and Skrinar M: Science of dance training, Champaign, Ill, 1988, Human Kinetics Publishers.

Gray JA: Dance instruction, Champaign, Ill, 1989, Human Kinetics Publishers. Integrates traditional perspectives of dance education with latest research and technology.

Jacob E: Dancing: a guide to the dancer you can be, Reading, Mass, 1981, Addison-Wesley Publishing Co.

Minton SC: Choreography, Champaign, Ill, 1986, Human Kinetics Publishers. Contains suggestions on selecting accompaniment, designing costumes, and planning lighting.

Minton SC: Body and self, Champaign, Ill, 1990, Human Kinetics Publishers. Designed to teach you how to move more gracefully, exercise without injury, detect habitual movement patterns, and create more imaginative movements.

Concert forms

American Alliance for Health, Physical Education, Recreation, and Dance: Children's Dance, Reston, Va., 1981, American Alliance for Health, Physical Education, Recreation, and Dance. Contains innovative ideas in the field of dance education.

Arnheim D: Dance injuries: their prevention and care, ed. 2, St. Louis, 1980, The CV Mosby Co.

Joyce M: Dance techniques for children, Palo Alto, Calif, 1984, Mayfield Publishing Co. Contains numerous age-graded activities, sample achievement chart, guidelines for developing a series of lessons, material on assessing students, and nearly 100 photos.

Kraus R and Chapman S: History of dance in art and education, Englewood Cliffs, NJ, 1981, Prentice-Hall.

Lane C: All that jazz and more: the complete book of jazz dancing, Champaign, Ill, 1983, Leisure Press. Designed for instructors; explains commonly used techniques for beginners and advanced students.

Minton S and Genoff K: Modern dance: body and mind, Englewood, Colo., 1984, Morton Publishing Co. Aimed at the beginning student, this book uses over 125 illustrations to describe the kinesiologic basis of dance movement and provide an understanding of the relationships between technique, improvisation, and composition.

Morgenwroth J: Dance improvisations, Pittsburgh, Pa, 1987, University of Pittsburgh Press.

Schlaich J and Dupont B, editors: Dance: the art of production, ed 2, St. Louis, 1988, The CV Mosby Co.

Shafranski P: Modern dance: twelve creative problem-solving experiments, Glenview, Ill, 1984, Scott, Foresman & Co. Designed to stimulate creativity and improvisation for the beginning modern dance student by using a workbook format with a detailed outline procedure for each experiment.

Sherbon E: On the count of one: a guide to movement and progressions in dance, ed 3, Palo Alto, Calif, 1982, National Press Books.

Washbourne D: Basic tap dancing, Montpelier, Vt, 1981, Penguin Books.

Recreational forms
General

Casey B: Dance across Texas, Austin, Tex, 1985, University of Texas Press.

Hager S: Hip hop: the illustrated history of break dancing, rap, music, and graffiti, New York, 1984, St. Martin's Press.

Harris J, Pittman A, and Waller MS: Dance a while, ed 6, Minneapolis, 1988, Burgess Publishing Co.

Livingston P: The complete book of country swing and western dance and a bit about cowboys, Garden City, NJ, 1981, Doubleday and Co., Inc.

Stinson S: Dance for young children: finding magic in movement, Reston, Va, 1988, AAHPERD.

Folk dance

Casey B: International folk dancing U.S.A., Garden City, NJ, 1981, Doubleday and Co., Inc.

Weikart PS: Teaching intermediate folk dance, Ypsilanti, Mich, 1982, High/Scope Press.

Social dance

Schild MM: Social dance, Dubuque, Iowa, 1985, Wm. C. Brown Group. Stresses the interrelationship between dances to help novices learn. For each dance, information on history, basic steps, variations, timing, styling, and turns is included. Suggested routines and musical selections are also presented.

Square dance

Casey B: The complete book of square dancing and round dancing, Garden City, NJ, 1985, Doubleday and Co., Inc.

Schild MM: Square dancing everyone, Winston-Salem, NC, 1987, Hunter Textbooks, Inc. Covers the background and development of square dance, resource materials, singing call drills, basics of clogging, and a checklist of basic square dance movements.

Tap dance

Marx T: Tap dance, Englewood Cliffs, NJ, 1983, Prentice-Hall.

PERIODICALS

Sets in Order, National Square Dance Magazine, 462 N. Robertson Blvd., Los Angeles, CA, 90048.

Journal of Physical Education, Recreation and Dance, American Alliance for Health, Physical Education, Recreation and Dance, 1900 Association Dr., Reston, VA, 22091.

Dance Teacher Now, SMW Communications, Inc., 3020 Beacon Blvd., West Sacramento, CA, 95691.

VIDEO TAPES

Series of five videotapes titled: *Social dance aerobics* and other series of three videos called *Learn to dance,* "How To" Sports Videos, Box 5852, Denver, CO, 80217.

Ballet class: intermediate and advanced and tap dancing for beginners. Sports Video, 745 State Circle, Box 1941, Ann Arbor, MI, 48106.

Preparing to dance, Sources for dance, Dance design: Shape and time, Dance design: Motion, and *Dance design: Space.* American Alliance for Health, Physical Education, Recreation and Dance, 1900 Association Dr., Reston, VA, 22091.

Many records, cassettes, filmstrips, and videos available from Kimbo Educational, P.O. Box 477K, Long Beach, NJ, 07740.

10

Fencing

Completion of this chapter should enable the reader to:

- Appreciate the historical development of fencing
- Recognize the various fencing weapons
- Understand the basic rules of the sport
- Demonstrate fundamental fencing skills
- Execute basic offensive and defensive fencing tactics
- Teach beginning fencing students using proper techniques and terminology

HISTORY

Fencing is defined as "the sport and act of swordplay". It originated as a form of deadly combat before the Christian era and has continued as such for more than 2000 years.

Fencing has a fascinating and exciting history. It had its beginning with a crudely shaped spear used as a deadly weapon in war. The invention of gunpowder changed its utility as a major weapon (also true of the bow and arrow). Later, gentlemen and nobility dueled to the death to avenge an insult or restore honor that had been smudged.

In the fourteenth century the Germans first attempted to make dueling a sport as well as a fight to the death, but made little headway. The first fencing school was established in Spain in the fifteenth century. Further influences in the development of fencing as a sport were creation of protective equipment and outlawing of dueling to the death throughout most of Europe in the eighteenth century.

Different swords and sabers were devised by the Italians, French, and Germans down through the years, to the modern foil, épée, and saber. Schools of instruction in fencing flourished throughout Europe. The early, heavier sword was replaced by a lighter weapon to obtain greater speed, dexterity, and precision. Surprisingly, this formerly deadly method of combat was converted into an excellent and popular modern sporting event of skill and precision.

Fencing has been a medal sport in the Olympics since 1896. The French and Italians won most of the fencing medals in the early years and through the 1960s. Edoardo Mangiarotti of Italy amassed an amazing total of 13 medals (six gold, five silver and two bronze) between 1932 and 1956. Since the 1960's the sport has been dominated by Eastern European and Soviet fencers.

The United States, though producing an occasional outstanding fencer, has not fared well in the Olympics. In fact, when Peter Westbrook won the Olympic bronze medal in the saber in 1984, it was the first individual fencing medal for the United States since 1960.

Fencing is important in a modern program of physical education and recreation. It is also well adapted for physically handicapped persons (even amputees). Age is no barrier. It is an excellent coeducational activity and therefore ranks very high socially.

In the United States both men and women fence with all three weapons: the foil, épée, and saber. The purpose of the sport is to hit, or score a clean touch on an opponent, without being hit.

In America, fencing other than intercollegiate is controlled by the United States Fencing Association (USFA).

EQUIPMENT

1. Competition uniforms of nylon and/or kevlar
2. Mask to protect the face and neck
3. Breast protector for women
4. Soft leather or chamois gloves

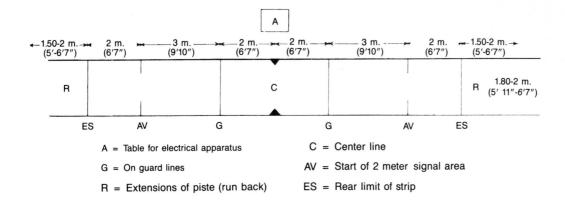

A = Table for electrical apparatus   C = Center line

G = On guard lines   AV = Start of 2 meter signal area

R = Extensions of piste (run back)   ES = Rear limit of strip

For electric foil and epee the metallic strip must cover the whole length and breadth of the strip, including its extensions (run back)

Note: Measurements given to nearest inch, the distance from ES to AV is 6'7"

Fig. 10-1. Regulation strip for all three weapons.

5. Saber elbow guard of leather or composite material
6. Underarm protectors
7. Foil
8. Épée
9. Saber
10. Mats: The strip on which the bouts take place, between 5 feet 11 inches and 6 feet 7 inches (1.8 to 2 m) wide and 45 feet 11 inches (14 m) in length; three parallel lines to be drawn across the strip—one in exact center, the other two warning lines 3 feet 3 inches (98 cm) from the ends (Fig. 10-1).

ABRIDGED RULES OF FENCING
Scoring

Individual competition. Individuals usually compete on a round-robin basis, but other formats such as single and double elimination are also common.

Intercollegiate team competition. A team consists of nine persons, three using each of the three weapons. Each contestant fences a bout with each of the three opponents in the same weapon, making a total of 27 bouts.

General procedures

1. When competition is nonelectric (now seldom except in classes) the contest is ruled by a jury of five judges (head judge is called the director), a scorer, and a timekeeper.
2. In nonelectric competition fencers change ends of the strip after 3 touches have been scored unless one fencer is left handed and the other is right handed, in which case the judges change ends of the strip.
3. With electronically scored competitions, the only officials required are a director, a scorer, and a timer.

4. The director calls "fencers ready" or "on guard," starts action with a call of "fence" or "play," and ends it with "halt." The clock runs only between "fence" and "halt."

Rules, requirements, and strategies

1. The objective in all fencing bouts is to score five hits on the opponent's valid target area, which differs for each of the three weapons.
2. If neither fencer scores five hits during the 6 minutes allotted for both men's and women's bouts, the winner is the fencer having the highest number of valid hits.
3. Although fencing places a premium on quickness, speed of reaction, finesse, agility, and dexterity, the sport has become increasingly aggressive and now also requires strength and endurance conditioning.
4. The foil and épée events are electronically scored in most competitions but the saber event still relies on a jury of five judges.
5. In general, fencers attempt to maintain a safe distance from the opponent until one decides to attack. The attack may be parried by the fencer on the defense who may then decide to counter-attack (called a riposte). Bouts, then, consist of attacks, parries, ripostes and counter-ripostes.

MODERN FENCING WEAPONS
Foil

The foil (Fig. 10-2) is the basic weapon of fencing. It is a thrusting weapon. Its maxiumum weight is 17.637 ounces (500 gm), and its maximum length is 33 inches (83.8 cm). It is rectangular and tapers out from the guard to a very thin, flexible upper section toward the button-like tip. The guard is circular and concave to protect the hand. The grip may be wood, cord wrapped, molded metal, or plastic.

The target in foil fencing includes the trunk from the collar to the groin lines in front or to a horizontal line passing across the tops of the hip bones in the back. Touches, to be valid, must arrive on the target as the result of a thrusting action clearly and cleanly with the point and in accordance with certain conventions, or rules of order, frequently called "right of way" or privilege of attack. The attacker is the individual who first extends the arm. The attacker is said to have the right of way. A successful parry gains for the defendant the right of way. When both fencers are hit simultaneously, the touch is awarded to the one who has the right of way. If neither fencer has the right of way, no touch is awarded. Touches made on the head, arms, or legs are called off-target hits but carry no penalty other than halting the bout.

The first person scoring five touches within 6 minutes wins the bout. If the time runs out and the score is tied, fencing continues without time restriction until one fencer scores a touch.

Épée

The épée (Fig. 10-2), is also a thrusting weapon. It is more pointed, heavier, and more rigid than the foil. It weighs 27.16 ounces (770 gm) and has a maximum length of 43.307 inches (108 cm).

Fig. 10-2. The various weapons. *Left to right:* Foil, épée, and saber.

The target for épée includes every portion of the body.

Épée has no right of way convention. If both fencers are touched simultaneously, each is considered to have scored a touch. If the score is tied after 6 minutes, no further fencing takes place, unless the format is one of elimination. In round robin competitions both fencers would lose and the bout would be scored as a double defeat. If, however, a score of 5-5 occurs before time expires, the bout continues until one fencer scores a single touch or time expires. The score on the score sheet remains 5-5, no matter how many touches are scored, and one fencer is credited with a defeat and the other with a victory.

Saber

The saber (Fig. 10-2) is a weapon with cutting edges along the entire front and one third of the back of the blade. Cuts as well as thrusts are valid.

The saber has a maximum weight of 17.637 ounces (500 gm) and a maximum length of 41.338 inches (103 cm).

The saber target includes all portions of the body, including the head, arms, and hands, above a horizontal line drawn through the greater trochanter (hip bone).

Saber has a right of way convention and is scored similarly to foil.

FUNDAMENTAL SKILLS AND TECHNIQUES

In fencing the student must acquire not only eye-hand coordination, but also the technique of the use of the body, legs, feet, arms, and hands and must coordinate them skillfully into the use of the weapon in hand. In addition, the student must also acquire a keen sense of distance, speed, force, and precision in all movements.

The French grip

The convex side of the curve of the handle should be placed in the palm at the heel of the thumb. The thumb is placed on the top of the broad surface of the handle close to the circular guard. The tip of the index finger is placed on the opposite side of the handle, so that the foil is controlled with the thumb and forefinger. The other three fingers curl around the handle so that the tips rest on the concave surface and press the handle firmly against the base of the thumb. The wrist is held slightly flexed and supinated so that the flat of the pommel rests flat against the wrist in such a manner that the sword will form a direct straight line of extension with the forearm (Fig. 10-3).

Fig. 10-3. The French grip (top view).

Fig. 10-4. Front and side views of on-guard position.

On guard

The on-guard position is designed to give the greatest balance and efficiency in performing either offensive or defensive movements in advancing, retreating, or directly attacking. The body in this position also offers the smallest possible target.

Using the proper grip, the weapon arm is extended toward the opponent, the elbow flexed in an obtuse angle and held closely in line with the body. The hand is about level with the lower sternum, the weapon pointing slightly upward, directly toward the opponent's chest (Fig. 10-4).

To assume this position the feet are approximately shoulder width apart and at right angles to each other, heels in line. The body weight is distributed evenly over both feet. The knees are bent so that they extend over the instep of the foot. The torso is held erect with the dominant side and toe of the leading foot facing the opponent. The head is erect and turned to face the opponent. The nondominant arm is raised behind so that the upper arm is horizontal, the forearm vertical, and the hand completely relaxed behind the head.

Advance and retreat

Advancing and retreating are the fundamental and basic movements from the on-guard position. To advance, the forward foot is first moved forward and the other foot follows. To retreat, the rear foot is moved back and then the forward foot is moved back. The steps are short, varying from a few inches to about 1 foot. The legs are maintained in the on-guard position. The purpose of the advance movement is to get within attacking distance of an opponent; the purpose of the retreat is to get out of reach of an opponent.

Another advancing step used is a jump, called the ballestra. In this jump, both feet leave the floor at the same time, with one foot slightly ahead, and regain contact with the floor at the same time. A back ballestra is sometimes used for retreating.

Lunge

The lunge is an important action in fencing. It is a method used to reach an opponent with the tip of the weapon to make a touch. It is executed from the on-guard position and is preceded by an extension of the weapon arm, followed by lunging, with the foremost leg while the rear foot remains in place. If well executed with speed and precision at the right moment in a bout, it is likely to make a score on an opponent.

The weapon arm should be extended as quickly as possible without locking the elbow. One does not rotate the wrist or hunch the shoulders. The body should be held erect, not leaning. Simultaneously with the lunge, one extends the back arm fully to the rear for balance.

Recovery from lunge

To recover to the on-guard position, one bends the left leg and simultaneously pushes back with the right, then brings the forward foot back quickly to the on-guard position. The back arm, by being brought back into its original on-guard position, also aids in recovery from the lunge. During recovery the body should remain low.

It is sometimes necessary to recover forward to take up ground given by an opponent who is retreating from a lunge. This action simply involves bringing the rear foot to the on-guard position. This enables the attacker to defend if the attack has failed, to attack again, or to retreat if the opponent counterattacks.

SIMPLE ATTACKS

A simple attack is a single movement without feint or previous threat to the opponent's target. The three main types are straight thrust, the disengage, and the cutover or coupe.

Straight attack

The straight attack is the lunge as already described, with a straight thrust of the arm preceding the lunge.

Disengage

The disengage is a change of line which is accomplished by passing the point of the weapon around the bell guard of the opponent's weapon. The movement is semicircular and is executed by the wrist and fingers. The weapon is kept close to the opponent's blade at all times. This action can be used as an attack resulting in a touch or can be followed by a lunge to score. During a bout, fencers continuously try to keep their opponents in a closed line while trying for an opportunity in an open line.

The disengage can be used as an attack in an effort to hit the target in an open line.

Cutover or coupé

This simple method of attack is the opposite of the disengage: the point is passed over the top of the opponent's blade when in the high line or under the opponent's blade when in the low line. It is another method of changing the line of engagement. It is principally used when an opponent has lowered the weapon or uses pressure with the weaker leverage of the blade nearer the tip of the weapon against the strong part of the attacker's blade. It is easier then to cut over than to disengage or to pass under. The action is executed by sharply lifting the top of the weapon over the opponent's weapon, using the fingers and wrist. The arm is extended as the weapon goes downward and forward to the target, followed immediately by an attack.

COMPOUND ATTACKS

Compound attacks are composed of more than one action. The first action is usually a feint, designed to draw a response from the opponent.

The beat

The beat is a quick sharp blow of the middle of the blade on the weak part of the opponent's blade to make an opening or feint before an attack.

The one-two (or double disengage)

The attacker makes a disengage as previously described, hoping that the defender will attempt to parry. If the defender responds with a simple parry, the attacker avoids the blade contact and makes a second disengage back to the original line. Ideally, an attack occurs with the second disengagement.

The doublement (double)

The double also begins with a disengage, again hoping to draw a parry from the defender. If the defender responds with a circular parry, the attacker follows the defender's bell-guard; that is, the defender passes the blade tip over and around the defender's bell to complete the attack in the line of the first disengage.

DEFENSE

Parries are movements of defense executed by the blade to deflect the blade of the opponent's offensive action at the target so that a touch is avoided. All parries are executed by the fingers and wrist with just enough movement to catch the opponent's blade and prevent a thrust to the target. One should always try to parry with the forte, not with the foible, of the blade. A successful parry (a parry that deflects the opponent's blade from the line of attack) takes the right of way from the offensive and permits an immediate counterattack. The counterattack is usually a simple extension of the weapon arm and is called a riposte.

The target is divided in half, at breast level, into high and low lines of defense. In the high line the foil is

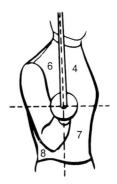

Fig. 10-5. Four areas to be protected by weapon.

pointed at chest level. In the low line the point is at the level of the knee. These positions of the weapon will give sufficient leverage to deviate the attacking blade to one side or the other.

The weapon hand must protect four major areas or lines: the inside-high, inside-low, outside-high, and outside-low, numbered 4, 7, 6, and 8, respectively, in Fig. 10-5. Parries are named by the area they protect (for example, parry 4 protects 4 line).

The eight fundamental parries are parries 4, 6, 7, and 8 and their counters. Parry 4 and parry 6 are the most common parries and consist of lateral movements of the blade to a position in front of the area named. The defender's blade makes a sharp light tap against the attacker's blade. A riposte follows immediately.

When an attack is directed to the 4 area, the defender uses his or her fingers to move the weapon point to the opposite side of the opponent's blade by passing under the bell-guard. The defender then moves to cover his or her 6 line.

Should the attack be directed to 6 line, the defender's point is moved to the opposite side of the attacker's blade by passing under, and the parry is completed to 4 line.

FENCING ETIQUETTE

1. Show respect for opponent by stopping the attack when he or she waves the back hand and calls for the director to stop the bout.
2. Show a high level of sportsmanship throughout the match. Call a "touch" on yourself whenever there is a question. Also call "off-target" when you hit an opponent in a nonlegal area.
3. Be totally familiar with the competition rules.
4. Acknowledge all touches.
5. Refuse all questionable scores.
6. Respect the decisions of the judges.
7. Always salute the opponent, the jury, and spectators before a bout.
8. If an opponent drops a weapon, withhold an attack until it has been recovered.

9. Shake hands with the opponent after the bout and thank the director for presiding.

TIPS TO REMEMBER

Fencing weapons are used quite differently from weapons in other sports. In fencing, the weapon is used for thrusting rather than for hitting or swinging. Thus it is essential for the beginner to learn the fundamental skills, because they are not skills that beginners ordinarily are accustomed to or carryovers from other sports. Fencing is a game of leverage. The defender uses the strong part of the weapon against the weak part of the attacker's blade.

Practice positions, movements, and footwork.

Emphasize safety. Do not allow "horseplay." Specifically do not point a weapon at anyone who is not wearing a mask. Always carry the weapon with the point down. Study the rules carefully.

TEACHING CONSIDERATIONS

1. Do not teach fencing unless proper protective equipment is available. Begin with foils to teach basics. Do not attempt to teach fencing to students who are likely to engage in horseplay or off-task behavior that could be dangerous. Establish safety rules regarding use of the foil when not engaged in practice and be firm and consistent with these rules.

2. Begin with the grip and on-guard position. Teach advancing and retreating movements. Conditioning exercises may be necessary for students who might experience muscle soreness from these activities.

3. All attacks can be practiced first at a wall target with the four areas clearly outlined, then with a passive defense responding in a predictable manner, and then with the defense responding in an unpredictable manner. In all cases do not move on until students have the fine control of the foil necessary to make the practice safe.

4. Begin with the lunge. Practice the lunge until the sequence of arm extension, the forward leg coming forward, and recovery is a natural action.

5. Work with specifying the area of attack and parry in a drill-like fashion. Attacks can be practiced first, followed by a responsive parry followed by a counterparry. Initially specify sequence and offensive and defensive roles and later move to self-initiated offensive roles.

6. Practice all possible combinations of offensive and defensive sequences. Develop the language so that communication between teacher and students can take place.

7. As soon as students have a sufficient repertoire of offensive and defensive moves, include some periods in each lesson for bouting.

GLOSSARY

advance Move forward on an opponent to gain ground.

attack Offensive movement that gains right of way.

attack on the blade Beat, pressure, and glide attacks used to deviate the defensive weapon point.

attack of second intention Attack intended to be parried, so that the attacker may parry the return and score on the counterattack.

ballestra or jump lunge A forward or backward movement employing a jump before the lunge.

beat attack An attempt to create an opening for an attack by giving a sharp blow to the opponent's blade.

blade parts:
    foible Weak and flexible portion of the blade, comprising the third of the blade nearest the tip.
    forte Strong inflexible third of the blade nearest the guard.
    middle Middle third of the blade.

bout A contest between two individuals.

circular parry A defensive move that deflects an attacking blade to avoid a touch.

counterattack A stop thrust in which the time is taken from the attacker by touching before the final action of the original attack begins.

engagement Crossing and touching of weapons.

feint A movement of the blade designed to draw a parry or other reaction from the opponent.

fleche An offensive movement made by crossing the back foot in front of leading foot usually followed by a short run.

jury Four judges and the director who conducts the fencing bout.

match The aggregate of bouts fenced between members of two teams.

off target An invalid touch.

on-guard The position taken by a fencer signaling a readiness to fence.

parry Defensive action made to prevent a touch.

president Director of a bout.

remise Following an attack, the defender delays the riposte. The attacker, without recovering from the lunge, may merely move the sword so that the point is replaced in the target area.

retreat To move backward, to open the distance from an opponent.

right of way Established by a fencer who first extends the weapon arm with point in line of attack.

riposte or **return** An offensive action after a successful defense; it may be a simple or compound return.

stop hit A counterattack made during the opponent's attack during a hesitation in that attack. To count as a valid touch, the counter attack must land before the final movement of the opponent begins.

strip The area on which a fencing bout is conducted.

touch A hit on the target that would puncture or wound if weapons were pointed.

SUGGESTED READINGS

Bower M: Foil fencing, ed., Dubuque, Iowa, 1990, Wm. C. Brown Group. Contains description of basic positions, essential techniques, and basic strategies for the beginner, as well as examples and drills for offensive and defensive techniques, material on informal bouting and advanced bouting techniques, and conditioning for fencing.

Curry NL: The fencing book, Champaign, Ill, 1984, Human Kinetics Publishers, Inc. A comprehensive manual on fencing skills and fundamentals including chapters on skill development, rules, strategy, and conditioning.

Gaugler WM: Fencing everyone, Winston-Salem, NC, 1987, Hunter Textbooks, Inc. Contains three sections—one each on foil, épée, and sabre. Has detailed descriptions of offensive, defensive, and counter-offensive action in fencing, hundreds of photos, and quizzes on each of the three sections.

Simonian C: Basic foil fencing, ed. 2, Dubuque, Iowa, 1982, Kendall/Hunt Publishing Co.

Sports Illustrated book of fencing, New York, 1984, JB Lippincott Co.

United States Fencing Association: Directing épée, and the official study guide, 1750 Boulder Ave, Colorado Springs, CO.

FILMS AND VIDEOTAPES

Basic training of foil fencing, 16 mm, sound, black and white, 22 minutes. Prepared by the Hungarian College of Physical Education in Budapest. Presents fundamentals from on-guard position illustrating advance, jump-lunge, distances, parries, ripostes, and various engagements in slow-motion; still and trick shots. Order from University of California, Extension Media Center, 2223 Fulton St., Berkeley, CA 94720.

Fencing. Featuring Coach Mike DeCicco of Notre Dame. $34.95. Karol Video, 22 Riverside Dr., Wayne, NJ 07470.

Fencing in French. United States Fencing Association, 1750 Boulder Ave., Colorado Springs, CO, 80904.

Fencing with foil, super 8 mm, color, cartridge loops. Sale per loop or complete set of 19. Prepared by Michael Alaux, 1968 U.W. Olympic foil team coach; Michael Gaylor, 1967 NCAA foil champion; and Anne Seppala, 1969 captain, Hunter College fencing team. Order from the Athletic Institute, 200 Castlewood Dr., North Palm Beach, FL, 33408.

Modern foil techniques, super 8 mm, color, cartridge loops. Prepared by Charles A. Selberg, world masters foil team champion. A study guide accompanies each loop. Subjects progress from grip and on guard to ballestra and attacks into tempo. Order from Bill Snyder Films, P.O. Box 2784, Fargo, ND 58102, or from American Fencer's Supply, 2122 Fillmore St., San Francisco, CA, 94115.

Training with Michael Marx. Colleen Olney, 2221 S.E. 117th St., Portland, OR, 97216.

Omnibus.16 mm, sound, black and white. Prepared by the Ford Foundation in 1956 for television. Suitable for general audiences to arouse interest in all types of fencing. Order from AFLA, 601 Curtis St., Albany, CA, 94706.

Sabre fencing. Super 8 mm, color, cartridge loops. Sale per loop or complete set of 21. Prepared by Csaba Elthes, fencing master, and Jack Keane, captain of the U.S. Olympic Team. Order from the Athletic Institute, 200 Castlewood Dr., North Palm Beach, FL, 33408.

11

Field Hockey

Completion of this chapter should enable the reader to:

- Describe the history and development of field hockey
- Be aware of important equipment selection and care considerations
- Understand the rules of field hockey and related games
- Execute the correct grip, dribble, strokes, and ball control skills
- Understand basic defensive and offensive strategies and formations
- Demonstrate fundamentals to a group of students
- Recognize and use field hockey terms correctly

HISTORY

About 2500 years ago, the early Greeks and other ancient nations played a game very similar to our present-day hockey. Centuries later the game was being played in France and was called "hoquet." Then the English began to play it under the name of "hokay." The French pronounced "hoquet" as we would pronounce hockey. The game became generally known as hockey by its English spelling and pronunciation. However, later when ice hockey, a similar game played on ice, became popular, the game of hockey was called field hockey, and so it remains today.

Between 1880 and 1890 field hockey was played exclusively by men in England, France, and other European countries and is still popular with them. In the United States, men tried the game, but it met with little favor.

A group of women who formerly lived in England formed the Livingston Association on Staten Island about this time, but it was short-lived. Then in 1901 Constance M.K. Applebee, of the British College of Physical Education, demonstrated the game of field hockey during a visit to Radcliff College. She recommended it as a health-building form of combative recreation for college women. Miss Applebee was then invited to several Eastern women's colleges (Smith, Vassar, Wellesley, Bryn Mawr, and Mount Holyoke), and on each campus field

hockey was accepted with high favor. Women's teams were formed, and the first interclass contest was held in 1902.

The women enjoyed the game so much that they adopted it and revised the rules to make them uniform and suitable for women's play. In 1920 an American women's team traveled to England, and later an English team visited the United States to play games in Philadelphia, New York, Boston, and Baltimore, thereby establishing field hockey as an international game.

In 1922 the United States Field Hockey Association (USFHA) was formed in Philadelphia to govern the sport for women, its purpose being to advance the interests of hockey for women and girls. The game's popularity spread rapidly among schools, colleges, and clubs.

In 1927 this widespread interest throughout the world brought about an International Federation of Women's Hockey Associations (IFWHA), and tournaments were held in Philadelphia and Denmark.

In 1963 the USFHA hosted 18 of the 25 IFWHA member nations. Plans were made for this Federation to meet every 4 years for conference games and discussion of international rules and hockey problems.

The next conference, in 1967, was held in Cologne, Germany, with the format unchanged. The first unofficial IFWHA World Championship was held in 1971 in Auckland, New Zealand. The Netherlands won the tournament, and the United States finished eighth. The first official World Championship was held in Edinburgh, Scotland, in 1975; England won the title, and the United States finished eleventh.

The second World Championship was held in Vancouver, Canada, in 1979. The United States improved to an amazing third in world standings. The Netherlands finished first and West Germany second.

Another world hockey organization has been in existence for many years and until 1930 was a men's group. The Fédération Internationale de Hockey (FIH) controls Olympic hockey and has well over 50 members. Members conduct world championships between Olympics for both men and women. Many national women's teams belong to both organizations.

With women's hockey introduced into the Olympics for the first time in 1980, a combined committee from both world organizations was formed to organize the methods, standards, and procedures for qualifying. The team from Zimbabwe won the round robin tournament (six teams) to capture the first women's field hockey Olympic gold medal. The decision of the United States to boycott the Moscow Olympics cost our national team the chance to compete, which they had earned in the 1979 World Championship. The appearance of both the men's and women's field hockey teams in the 1984 Olympics marked the first time in 28 years for them in this competition. Although they had been ranked among the top six teams in the world in the early 1980s, it nevertheless came as a mild surprise when the women's field hockey team took the bronze medal in the 1984 Olympics by winning a stroke-off against Australia to break the tie for third place.

In 1988, the men's team from Great Britain won the Olympic gold medal as did the women's team from Australia. The U.S. women's team finished eighth.

The IFWHA and the FIH united in 1981 to form a single world-governing body.

Men's field hockey is popular around the world and has been in the Olympics since 1908. India and Pakistan dominated for years, but Germany, the Netherlands, New Zealand, and Australia have emerged as consistent world-class teams. The United States men's team, under the direction of the Field Hockey Association of America, has never been an influence in world competition.

In the United States the USFHA played a national championship tournament for the first time in 1974.

One of the most significant steps in field hockey was undertaken in the colleges by the Association of Intercollegiate Athletics for Women (AIAW) in 1975. They organized regional championships throughout the country, with the winners moving on to a national collegiate championship. West Chester (Pa.) State College won in 1975, 1976, and 1977.

In 1981 both the AIAW and the NCAA offered independent national championships for Division I, II, and III colleges.

Indoor hockey is making huge strides in Europe. The United States is just beginning in this sport, but it is rapidly becoming popular and organized.

GENERAL DESCRIPTION

The official game is played by two teams of 11 players on a grass field or artificial surface. Each player has a stick with which to propel and receive the ball. Each team attempts to put the ball into the opponent's goal, which is defended by a goalkeeper, the only player with special privileges and equipment.

The game should be modified in a variety of ways for youngsters, physical education classes, and intramural sports for maximum participation and fun. Games having two, three, or four players on each team in limited space, using cones as goals, are appropriate in these situations.

EQUIPMENT
Sticks

The implement for propelling and receiving the ball in field hockey is a stick (Fig. 11-1), which is commonly divided into two parts—the handle and the head—for discussion and selection purposes. The head, which is the playing part of the stick, is curved and must be flat on the left side and rounded on the right. Only the flat side may be used to play the ball. It is referred to as the face of the stick. The handle is thin and round for a comfortable grip. The handle is generally covered with toweling, rubber, or leather; the head of the stick is uncovered and is usually made of mulberry. The legal maximum stick weight is 23 ounces (652 gm) for women and 28 ounces (793 gm) for men; the minimum is 12 ounces (340 gm). Most players choose a stick weighing 18 to 21 ounces. The thin handle is preferred so that the stick's weight is in the head. The heavier the head, the easier it is to hit hard, but the more difficult it is to quickly and deftly maneuver the ball. The length can vary from 30 to 38 inches (0.76 to 0.96 m). Most high school and adult players should use 35-inch (0.89 m) sticks. Youngsters and junior high players use 30- to 34-inch (0.76 to 0.86 m) sticks. If the stick is slightly too long, the player can choke down a little. Care of the stick includes treating the head with linseed oil and replacing the covering when it wears out and becomes uncomfortable. To prevent drying and warping, the sticks should be stored in a horizontal position in a well-ventilated place.

Ball

The official ball is composed of cork and twine and covered with white leather (although coverings of other ma-

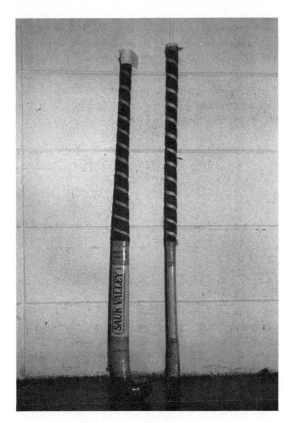

Fig. 11-1. Hocky sticks.

terials and colors are acceptable) or the more commonly used (because of low cost and high durability) composition ball covered with hard rubber. The circumference is not more than 9¼ inches (23.1 cm) or less than 8¹³⁄₁₆ inches (21.95 cm), and the weight is between 5½ and 5¾ ounces (156 to 163 gm).

Shin guards

Many types of leg protectors are available. Most are plastic with light padding inside. Like soccer guards, they fit comfortably into knee socks, and some have elastic straps that fit around the calf of the leg. Sockguards, ¾-inch foam rubber inserts in the sock, are popular. Players should wear shin guards to prevent injury.

Shoes

Cleated shoes are best for play on grass. The cleats may be rubber or plastic but not metal. On hard surfaces basketball shoes are recommended. Turf shoes are now available for play on artificial turf.

Clothing

The uniform consists of comfortably fitting shorts or kilts, shirts or blouses, and knee socks or stirrup socks. The player should be able to use full extension of the body without restrictions.

Gloves

If players like to keep their hands warm and protected, golf-type gloves are best, because they allow the players to have a good feel of their sticks.

Goalkeeper's equipment

Pads. The goalkeeper needs to protect the legs up to midthigh. Canvas or bamboo pads are the most common. Pads come in sizes to accommodate the size of the goalkeeper.

Kickers. These are padded and fit over and around the shoe and may or may not be attached to the pads. They have straps that go under the shoe, or they have a leather cleated sole that the shoe slides into, and they buckle behind the heel. The toe in the newer and preferred models is flat and hard.

Gloves. Special gloves, padded on the outside and on the left palm, are necessary for handling aerial shots.

Chest protector. Lacrosse protectors, made of foam rubber, should always be used.

Face mask. Face masks are mandatory. Form fitting ice hockey masks with a cage are preferred.

DIMENSIONS OF FIELD

The hockey field (Fig. 11-2) is about the size of a football field (100 x 60 yards) (91.5 x 54.9 m), with a goal at each end. Goalposts are 4 yards (3.66 m) apart and 7 feet (2.13 m) high, joined by a crossbar. The goal is enclosed by a net or wire screen supported by two additional posts 4 to 6 feet (1.2 to 1.8 m) behind the goal. A spot is marked 7 yards (6.4 m) in front of the center of each goal. A smaller field can be used for junior play.

RULES
Basic rules

The game is played by two teams of no more than 11 players each. One player is designated goalkeeper.

Time of play varies according to the level of competition, but no more than two halves of 35 minutes each, with a 5-minute halftime, are played. To play off a tie, up to two 10 minute overtimes are played. If after the first 10 minutes the score is still tied, a second sudden-death period is played. If no goals are scored in the sudden-death period, the game is recorded as a tie.

Pass-back

To start the game, to resume play after halftime, and after each goal is scored, a pass-back is played at the center of the field. The pass-back for the start of the game is made by a player of the team that did not make the choice of ends, after halftime by a player of the opposing team, and after a goal has been scored by a player of the team which the goal was scored against. Teams may cross the centerline at first touch. The pass-

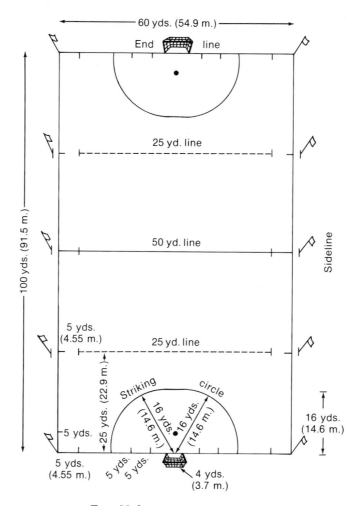

Fig. 11-2. Plan of field of play.

back may not be directed over the centerline.

Players, other than the player making the pass-back, must be in their own half of the field. Players on the opposing team must be at least 5 yards (4.55 m) from the ball. Wasting time is not permitted. The clock is stopped on the official's signal for a goal and restarted on the official's whistle for a pass-back. The team has 5 seconds to put the ball in play.

Toss

The captains toss a coin for choice of start or ends. The winner of the toss has the choice either of possession of the ball at the start of the game or of which end of the field to attack in the first half. The loser of the toss has the option not selected by the winner of the toss.

Bully

A bully is taken when time has been stopped by the official and neither team was in possession of the ball.

The bully is started by one player from each team, standing with feet parallel and square, toes pointing to the sideline, and left shoulder facing his or her goal line. With their sticks they alternately tap the ground to the right of the ball and each other's stick above the ball three times. After the third tap above the ball, both players try to initiate an attack. For any violation of this procedure the bully is repeated.

Scoring

Putting the whole ball over the goal line into the opponent's goal is a score. The ball must be touched by a member of the attacking team in the circle to count. A rule modification for college and school girl's play allows a goal to be scored from anywhere on the field. Except in the case of a direct free hit, side-in or long corner hit, the ball must first be touched by another player of the team in possession for the goal to count. Each goal counts 1 point.

Fouls

A player may not:
1. Play the ball with the round side of the stick
2. Raise the stick in a dangerous way
3. Propel the ball with any part of the body
4. Play dangerously, that is, wildly or deliberately hit into an opponent or uncontrolledly raise the ball
5. Interfere in any way with an opponent's stick
6. Trip, charge, shove, or interfere with any opponent's person or clothing
7. Interpose any part of the body between the ball and an opponent who is within playing distance
8. Be offside, that is, play ahead of a teammate with the ball and in a position with less than two defenders between the player and the goal line; a player cannot be offside until reaching the opposing 25-yard line
9. Use the hand to stop or catch the ball

A player may:
1. Play the ball with the flat side of the stick
2. Play the ball with no fear of obstruction when the feet are facing the opponent's goal line and the ball is in front of the player
3. Play anywhere without the ball up to the opponent's 25-yard line so long as two opponents, including the goalkeeper, are between the player and the goal line

Goalkeepers play by the same rules except that they may play the ball with their feet and may give an aerial ball slight impetus forward. Goalkeepers lose these privileges if they leave the circle.

No foul should be called when the fouled team is able to maintain an advantage and has the same or better opportunities than it had prior to the foul.

Penalties

1. When the foul *occurs outside the circle*, the opponents get a free hit from the spot where the foul occurred. An intentional, flagrant foul inside the 25-yard line results in a penalty corner.

2. When the foul occurs *inside the circle by an attacker*, the opponents have a free hit anywhere in the circle.

3. When the foul occurs *inside the circle by a defender*, the opponents have a penalty corner.

4. When a foul is committed *inside the circle by a defender and a certain goal was prevented*, a penalty stroke is awarded to the opponents.

5. For simultaneous fouls a bully is taken on the spot of the foul.

Free hit

The free hit is taken on the spot by any member of the fouled team. An exception is when the offense fouls in

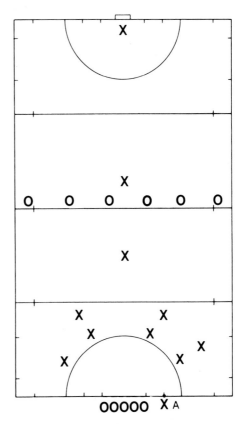

Fig. 11-3. Field hockey penalty corner.

the circle. In this case the opponents may take the free hit anywhere in the circle, but all players in the circle must be at least 5 yards (4.55 m) away.

The ball should be motionless, and the strike may use any legal stroke. The ball should not be raised in such a way as to be dangerous in itself or likely to lead to dangerous play. At the moment the free hit is taken no player of the opposing team may be within 5 yards of the ball. Should, however, the umpire consider that a player is standing within 5 yards in order to gain time, the free hit is not delayed.

For a free hit awarded to the attacking team for a breach of the rules within 5 yards of the circle, at the moment when the free hit is taken no player other than the striker may be within 5 yards of the ball. After a free hit is taken, the striker may not touch the ball again until it is touched by someone else.

Penalty corner

1. The corner hitter (Player XA in Fig. 11-3) hits or pushes the ball along the ground from a spot no closer than 10 yards (9.10 m) from the near goalpost on the side of the team's choosing. Lifting the ball is a foul. The hitter's feet may or may not be in bounds. The player

may not touch the ball again until it is touched by someone else.

2. Any of XA's teammates may be receivers. No member of the team may have any part of the body or stick in the circle until the ball is hit. No member may be closer than 5 yards (4.55 m) to the corner hitter. The receiver must control the ball before shooting, and passes or deflections must be controlled before the shot is taken unless a defender touches the ball. In college and international competition the ball must be stopped dead.

3. The defending team may have no more than five players on the endline. The remaining six must go to the 50-yard (45.72m) line and may go as low as the 25-yard (22.9m) line. Their bodies and sticks must be behind the line until the ball is hit; then they may move to defend. No defender may be closer than 5 yards to the corner hitter.

Penalty stroke

The penalty stroke is between the goalkeeper and any member of the fouled team:

1. The goalkeeper is not permitted any change in dress or equipment. The keeper must have part of the feet on the goal line and may not move them until the ball is stroked. At the moment the ball is stroked the goalkeeper may use all legal means to prevent the ball from going into the goal. The goalkeeper need not clear the ball.

2. The stroker is 7 yards (6.4 m) from the center of the goal line. The stroker may push, flick, or scoop but may not hit. The stroker lines up with the feet behind the ball and is permitted one stride prior to stroking the ball. Dragging or lifting the back foot is not considered a step unless it passes the front foot before the ball is shot. The ball may be touched only once, and the attacker must execute smoothly and continuously with no faking or deception. When the whistle blows, the attacker has 5 seconds to execute the stroke.

3. All other players of both teams shall be beyond the nearer 25-yard (22.9 m) line.

4. A successful goal is followed by a pass-back. An unsuccessful shot gives the defending team a 16-yard (14.6 m) hit opposite the center of the goal line.

Out of bounds

1. When the ball goes out of bounds *over the sideline*, the opponents receive a side-in.

2. When the defending team unintentionally sends the ball over the endline from within their 25-yard (22.9 m) area a hit shall be taken by the attacking team. A player from the attacking team shall hit the ball from a spot on the goal line within 5 yards (4.55 m) of the corner flag nearest to the point where the ball crossed the goal line.

3. When the ball is hit *over the endline by the attack*, a 16-yard (14.6 m) hit is awarded to the opponents.

Side-in

Any member of the team may push or hit the ball into play from the spot where it went out of bounds. The player's feet may or may not be in bounds. At the moment the side-in is taken, players on the opposing team must be 5 yards (4.55 m) away. After taking a hit-in, the player may not touch the ball again until it is touched or has been played by another player of either team.

16-yard hit

The ball is hit from any spot not more than 16 yards (14.6 m) from the endline opposite the point where the ball went out of bounds. In the men's game the hit may be taken at any spot along the line between the point where the ball left the field and 16 yards out. All rules of the free hit apply here.

Breach of push-in or free hits

1. When the breach is by the hitter, the opponents are awarded a hit-in or free hit on the same spot. The exception is a breach by a player taking a free hit in the circle, in which case the opponents are awarded a penalty corner.

2. When the breach is by the opposition, the play is repeated only if the breach gives the opposition an advantage.

Breach of penalty corners

1. When the breach is by the hitter on a penalty corner, the opposition has a 16-yard hit anywhere in the circle or 1 yard outside the circle in line with where the foul occurred.

2. When the breach is by the opposition, the play is repeated only if the violation gives the opposition an advantage.

Rules for outdoor hockey teams of five or seven players

All rules for teams of 11 apply except the following: (1) maximum duration for each half is 15 minutes, and (2) full field is used but with the 5-yard (4.55 m) lines forming the sidelines or with no offsides.

Rules for indoor hockey

The rules are generally the same as for field hockey unless noted otherwise. Two exceptions are no lifted balls (except on a goal) and no back swing strokes are allowed. The game is played by two teams of six players. Each team may have six substitutes. Each half lasts a maximum of 20 minutes.

Starting and restarting the game

At the start of the game a pass-back is made by the player of the team winning the toss, and after a goal it is made by a member of the team scored against. The pass may or may not be forward. All players must be in their half of the court, and no one except the passer may be closer than 3 yards (2.73 m) from the ball. No player shall cross the centerline until the ball is pushed.

Playing area

The court is rectangular, 40 x 20 yards (36.4 x 18.2 m). When possible, sideboards 4 inches wide and inclined slightly inward will surround the area.

Circle

The circle measures 10 yards (9.4 m) instead of 16 yards (14.6 m). On narrower than regulation playing areas the circles will meet the sideline. Penalty corner marks will be 7 yards (6.4 m) from goalposts and the penalty stroke 7 yards (6.4 m) from center of the goal mouth.

Bully

No bully shall be closer than 3 yards (2.73 m) from the endline and 1 yard (91 cm) from the sideboards.

Fouls

A player may not:
1. Hit or play the ball in the air
2. Take part in the play while lying on the ground unless the player is the goalkeeper
3. Hit the ball
4. Lift the ball in the field of play

A player may:
1. Be offside
2. Push the ball

Free hits

Free hits are referred to as free pushes. All players must be at least 3 yards (2.73 m) from the pusher.

Penalty corners

Offense.
1. The pusher is 7 yards (6.4 m) from the near goalpost.
2. No one may be within 3 yards (2.73 m) of the pusher.
3. The half or game shall be prolonged to complete a penalty corner.

Defense. All players may defend, but they are on the endline opposite the side of the pusher. No player other than the goalkeeper is allowed in the goal (Fig. 11-4).

Out-of-bounds over the sideboards

Any ball that goes over the sideboards is put in play by a member of the opposite team 1 yard (91 cm) from the

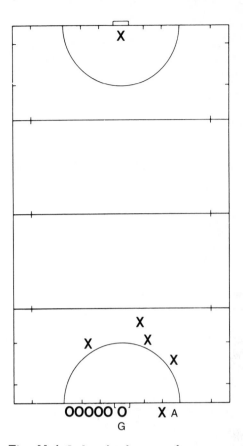

Fig. 11-4. Indoor hockey penalty corner.

sideboards but not in the circle. No one may be within 3 yards (2.73 m) of the pusher.

Out-of-bounds over the endboards

No matter who sends the ball over, the defending team gets a free push inside the circle. The exception is when a defender deliberately sends the ball over the endboard or makes no effort to keep it in play; then a penalty corner is awarded.

FUNDAMENTAL SKILLS AND TECHNIQUES
Grip

1. The stick is held in front of the body at an angle so that the head, with the toe pointing up, is on the ground about 1½ feet in front of the feet. The flat side of the stick should face left. The top of the handle will be about 6 to 8 inches in front of the thighs.
2. For the *traditional* grip one holds the stick as described above, then brings the left hand in from the left and grips the stick on the top of the handle. The back of the left hand should face left. Then the right hand is brought in from the right and grips the stick about 4 to 6 inches below the left. The back of the right hand faces right.
3. For the *continental* grip one holds the stick as shown in Fig. 11-5. If the left hand is under the chin with

Fig. 11-5. Continental grip.

Fig. 11-6. Dribble.

palm down and thumb pointing right, it can be moved straight down to grip the stick on top of the handle. The back of the left hand should be facing directly away. The right hand is the same as in the traditional grip.

Dribble

The ultimate objective is for each player to develop a rhythm and harmony between self and the ball, at speed, over varying distances, and against all kinds of opposition. The dribble (Fig. 11-6) is needed to gain ground, to set up a pass by drawing an opponent, and to beat or dodge an opponent. In open field the straight dribble (the ball moves in a straight line) is best. Before passing or beating an opponent, the Indian or zig-zag dribble (the ball moves ahead but in doing so it alternately moves diagonally left and right) is best because it is quicker and can be more deceptive.

Grip

Straight dribble (continental). The back of the left hand now faces obliquely up and over the right shoulder. The back of the right hand faces backward.

Indian or zig-zag dribble (continental). When the ball is moved left, the back of the left hand faces the same as in the straight dribble. When the ball is moved right, the back of the left hand faces the ground. The back of the right hand faces right throughout the dribble.

Wrists and arms

Straight dribble. The left wrist and forearm is a straight extension of the stick. The arm is at 90 degrees at the elbow, which is 10 to 12 inches from the body. The right wrist is hyperextended, and the right arm is straight.

Indian or zig-zag dribble. This is the same as the straight dribble except the left arm is almost straight out in front of the body, and the right wrist is also straight.

Body and head

Straight dribble. The body is slightly left of and behind the ball, and the center of gravity is slightly lower than when running without the ball. The head is up as often as possible for increased vision.

Indian or zig-zag dribble. The procedure is the same as in the straight dribble except the body is directly behind the ball. In a one-on-one play the player swerves down field rather than running in a straight line. Lifting the head frequently is essential.

Feet and legs

Straight dribble. Both feet are slightly left of and behind the ball. With balance, one can run quite fast without losing the ball.

Indian or zig-zag dribble. Both feet are directly behind the ball; the player runs fast, with sudden changes of pace and direction to get around opponents quickly.

Stick

Straight dribble. The stick is angled across the body at 45 degrees. The top of the handle is opposite the left thigh. The face of the stick faces the direction in which the player is moving and is ahead of and slightly to the right of the right foot.

Indian or zig-zag dribble. The stick is angled straight out in front of the body. When moving the ball left, the face of the stick faces diagonally left. When moving the ball right, the stick is turned over and the toe is down, moving the ball diagonally right. Playing the ball with the toe down is referred to as reverse stick. The stick is turned by the left hand through a relaxed right hand. The back of the right hand faces right throughout every move of the stick in the Indian dribble.

Ball

Straight dribble. The ball is 14 to 18 inches in front of and slightly to the right of the right foot. It is propelled forward in a series of short taps, imparted principally by the right hand.

Indian or zig-zag dribble. The ball moves alternately left and right diagonally 14 to 18 inches out in front of the body. The ball should not be allowed to get outside either foot.

Common faults

1. The wrist bends so that the forearm, wrist, and stick no longer form a straight line.
2. The player fails to keep the stick at 45 degrees.
3. The ball is too close to the feet.
4. The eyes become riveted to the ball.
5. The back of the left hand no longer faces obliquely up and over the right shoulder.

Push stroke

The push stroke (Fig. 11-7) is used for passing over short distances. It is characterized by the absence of a backswing, which allows for quickness in execution and disguising the direction of the pass until the last instant.

Grip

Using the continental grip, the back of the left hand faces obliquely up over the right shoulder. With the traditional grip the back of the left hand faces the intended direction of the pass. The back of the right hand faces backward. Unless a player is very strong, the right hand is at least halfway or farther down the stick.

Wrists and arms

The left wrist and forearm are a straight extension of the stick. The right wrist is hyperextended, and the arm is straight. The ball is pushed by a powerful, quick, whipping action of the right hand and wrist. The left hand lends guidance and control to the stick, and it ends up very much behind but in line with the right.

Body and head

The body is inclined forward with the head over the ball. The left shoulder faces the intended direction of the pass. The body weight is back on the right foot before the push. The weight shifts to the left foot as the right hand and wrist push the ball. The body on the follow-through is low and at full stretch.

Feet and legs

The left foot is forward a little more than shoulder's width from the right foot. The feet are parallel and slightly angled. The legs are bent, and the right leg extends on the follow-through.

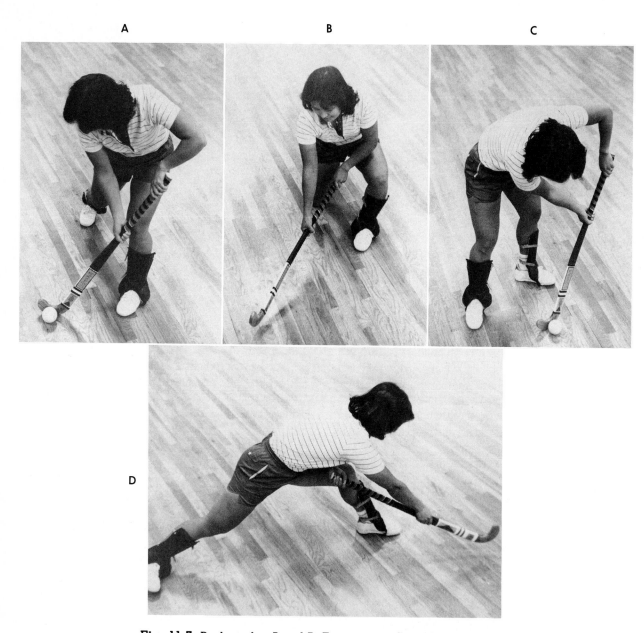

Fig. 11-7. Push stroke. **A** and **B**, Front views. **C** and **D**, Side views.

Stick

The stick is angled about 45 degrees across the body with the handle slightly ahead of the head of the stick. The face of the stick is directly behind and on the ball. The stick follows through the ball in the direction of the push as far as possible.

Ball

The ball is anywhere from midway between the feet up to the left foot.

Common faults

1. Player is unable to coordinate weight transfer.
2. Left shoulder is not brought around.
3. The stick is held vertically instead of angled.
4. Left hand and wrist hinder action and do not end up behind the right.
5. Player fails to follow through.
6. Right foot is forward.

Ball control skills

Ball control is the ability to bring any ball coming at you from any direction under control—to "catch" it. The ball's speed is deadened on the face of the stick. Ultimately, players should be able to play the ball immediately upon receiving it.

Grip

Ball coming toward the player. With the continental grip the back of the left hand faces obliquely over the right shoulder. With the traditional grip, the back of the left hand faces the oncoming ball. In both cases the right hand faces backward (see Fig. 11-6).

Ball coming from left. With the continental the back of the left hand faces obliquely up and away from the body in the same direction as the toe of the stick. With the traditional the back of the hand faces the oncoming ball. The back of the right hand in both cases faces right. Allow the ball to come across your body and receive it off your right foot. The stick is stationary. See Fig. 11-8.

Ball coming from right. Taking the ball in *midstride*, using the continental grip, the back of the left hand faces obliquely over the right shoulder; using the traditional, the back of the left hand faces the oncoming ball. The back of the right hand faces backward toward the body (Fig. 11-9). Allow the ball to come across your body and receive it off your left foot. The stick is stationary. Taking the ball *reverse stick*, the continental grip is used, and the back of the left hand faces down while the back of the right hand faces the oncoming ball (Fig. 11-10).

In receiving any ball the right hand, which is comfortably down the stick, is very relaxed so that it can move the face of the stick behind the ball and then act

Fig. 11-8. Ball control. Ball coming from left. Traditional grip.

Fig. 11-9. Ball control. Ball coming from right. Traditional grip.

Fig. 11-10. Ball control. Ball coming from right. Reverse stick. Continental grip.

as the major factor in cushioning the ball and preventing deflections.

Wrists and arms

Ball coming toward the player. The left wrist and forearm are straight extensions of the stick, with the left elbow bent at 90 degrees. The right wrist is hyperextended, and the right arm is comfortably straight.

Ball coming from left. The left wrist and arm are straight extensions of the stick. The right wrist and arm are straight.

Ball coming from right. Taking the ball midstride, both arms and wrists are the same as when the ball is coming toward the players. Taking the ball reverse stick, both arms and wrists are the same as when the ball is coming from left.

Body and head

When receiving any ball the player must concentrate enough to see the ball make contact on the face of the stick.

Ball coming toward the player. The body is behind and slightly left of the ball.

Ball coming from left. The body is inclined forward.

Ball coming from right. Taking the ball midstride, the body twists 90 degrees right from the waist to face the oncoming ball. Taking the ball reverse stick is the same as when the ball is coming from left.

Feet and legs

Except when taking a ball from the right in midstride, the feet must be sufficiently behind the ball to prevent overrunning it.

As in other sports, players must be prepared to go to meet the ball, or the pass will be intercepted.

Stick

When fielding any ball and at the moment of contact, the face of the stick must squarely meet the ball. The face of the stick must be inclined slightly toward the ball to trap it and keep it on the ground.

Ball coming toward the player. The stick is angled 45 degrees across the front of the body. The handle is opposite the left thigh, and the head is on the ground forward of and slightly right of the right foot.

Ball coming from left. The stick is angled forward in front of the right foot. The toe is up.

Ball coming from right. Taking the ball midstride, the stick is angled across the body with the handle slightly higher than and left of the left knee, and the head of the stick is on the ground out from but between the feet. In reverse stick the stick is angled forward opposite the left foot with the toe down.

Ball

The ball, after contact with the stick, is in position to be dribbled, pushed, hit, or shot. Deflections and rebounds are acceptable as long as they are not dangerous.

Common faults

1. Face of the stick is not square to the oncoming ball.
2. Left wrist is bent.
3. Right hand is too tight, so the player does not feel the ball on the stick.
4. The player moves the stick into the ball rather than absorbing its speed.
5. The face of the stick is not angled forward, creating upward deflections.

Hit

The hit moves the ball far, hard, and decisively to any part of the field. It is a necessary complement to the push because it allows for the big game by opening up and spreading the play. A "good ball" is a hard, accurate pass that hugs the ground and can be handled by the receiver. Although the following are components of the hit, successful execution is one action; that is, the backswing, downswing, hit, and follow-through combine in one continuous motion (Fig. 11-11).

Grip

Preliminary. The traditional grip is used with the back of the left hand facing the intended direction of the pass. The right hand is directly under and touching the left, with the back facing right. The Vs formed by the thumb and index fingers on both hands are in line with the toe of the stick. In most cases the right hand slides up to the left, but some prefer to slide the left hand down. Quickness, not power, is gained.

A   B   C

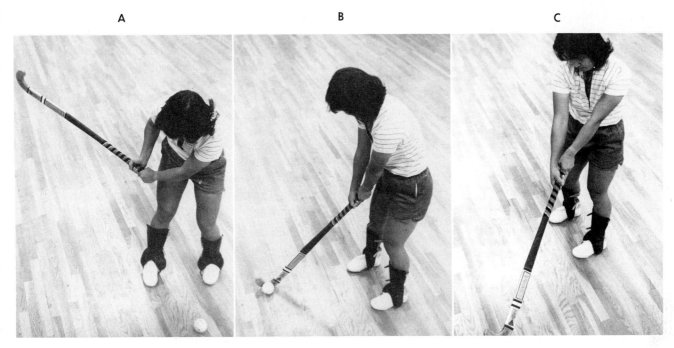

Fig. 11-11. Hit. **A**, Backswing. **B**, Contact. **C**, Follow-through.

Backswing. The same grip is used.

Hit and follow-through. The hands grip tighter at contact.

Wrists and arms

Preliminary. Wrists and arms are straight and out from the body.

Backswing. The stick is brought back with the arms and wrists, which do not touch any part of the body. The wrists are about waist height, firmly cocked, so that the head of the stick is higher than the wrists. The left arm has a slight bend in it on the backswing. The right wrist is cocked and the right arm is slightly and comfortably bent. The right elbow points back, about 6 inches away from the body. Hands are 5 to 7 inches off the hip. The toe of the stick should point up at the end of the backswing.

Hit and follow-through. Transfer the weight from the right foot to the left on the down swing with the left foot (even with the ball at contact). Snap the wrists on contact with the ball. The arms together with the wrists produce the hit, and they must be straight at contact. The muscles of the arms and wrists, like all muscles, must be tensed at impact. Follow through until the arms are parallel to the ground.

Body and head

The head is over the ball throughout.

Preliminary. The body is turned so that the left shoulder faces the intended direction of the pass.

Backswing. The weight is shifted to the rear foot.

Hit and follow-through. The weight is shifted to the front foot just before the stick makes contact with the ball. The force of the swing should naturally bring the body through in the direction of the hit.

Feet and legs

Preliminary. The feet are about shoulder width apart and pointed at right angles to the direction of the hit. The left foot is ahead of the right. The legs need to be firm, strong, and slightly flexed.

Backswing. Same feet and leg positions are used.

Hit and follow-through. At impact the leg muscles must be tense but not rigid, with the knees slightly bent.

Stick

Preliminary. The flat side of the stick is placed directly behind the ball, facing the intended direction of the pass.

Backswing. The stick goes straight back, not behind the right shoulder. The toe is above the wrists and pointing slightly upward.

Hit and follow-through. The stick is vertical at impact, and it clearly continues in the direction of the hit until the head reaches waist height and there is no more upward movement.

Ball

Preliminary. The ball is a comfortable distance from the body and is even with the left foot at the moment of impact.

Hit. After being struck by the middle of the face of the stick, the ball should travel smoothly along the ground.

Common faults

1. Choppy, lofted, or sliced hits because of poor placement of ball
2. Topping the ball because of not keeping the eyes on the ball throughout the hit
3. Left shoulder not around far enough, causing misdirection
4. Arms too tight in on the body, restricting their movement
5. Right elbow bent, weakening and making the hit awkward
6. Only the wrists or only the arms used
7. Failure to follow through
8. Carrying the stick in a backswing position for several yards, thus telegraphing intentions

Flick

The flick is a lofted stroke that is used to score goals and to clear over the opponents. The basics are the same as the push with the following differences:

1. The stick must not only be behind the ball but also slightly under it.
2. The ball is positioned slightly more forward just prior to the flick.

Tackle

The tackler wants to dispossess the opponent of the ball. If that is not possible, the player can, by the pressure exerted, force passes that can be intercepted by teammates.

Basic defensive stance

Grip. The left hand is on the top of the stick, and the back of it faces up. The right hand is more than halfway down the stick, gripping it firmly. The back of the right hand faces down.

Wrists and arms. The wrists are straight and the arms are bent so that the forearms are parallel to the ground.

Body and head. The eyes concentrate on the ball only. The body is inclined slightly forward with the center of gravity low.

Feet and legs. Legs are comfortably flexed, with the feet shoulder width apart. The feet should be in motion.

Stick. The stick is in a horizontal position close to the body with its blade facing up except before the tackle to the right (reverse stick), when the round side faces up.

Making the tackle

Wrists and arms. The right hand pushes the stick out toward the ball; the left hand, wrist, and arm carry the stick to the ball. The left arm and wrist become an extension of the stick. The right arm is back for balance. As soon as the ball is touched and in position to play, the right hand comes back on the stick.

Body and head. Eyes are on the ball. When the stick is thrust to the ball, the body is also extended, almost parallel to the ground, out over the left foot.

Feet and legs. The same moment the stick is thrust to the ball, the left leg reaches out in the same direction and the right leg is extended to the rear.

Stick. The face of the stick moves the ball out of the opponent's possession. The stick must contact the ball, not the opponent's stick or legs.

Turn

Tackles are often not possible from the front because the dribbler has good control. If the tackler sees that the front tackle is not going to be possible, the tackler gets out of the dribbler's path and makes a half turn to run side by side with the dribbler. The turn is crucial. The player must turn the hips and shoulder around far enough that the first step is toward the goal line. The tackle is now made while both players are running, and the tackler can afford a miss and still be in a position to tackle again. The tackler should influence the opponent in a particular direction by stepping to one side or the other.

Note: Players who are not strong enough to use one hand to tackle should slide their right hand up under their left and execute the same as with one hand. The player must be level with or ahead of the dribbler.

Common faults

1. Moving toward an opponent in control
2. Having center of gravity too high
3. Hitting opponent's stick or leg
4. Waiting too late to turn
5. Not turning far enough around
6. Not being forceful enough on the ball
7. Over committing

Passing

Passing is the heart of the game. It is the intentional movement of the ball by two teammates. Passes eliminate defenders.

Techniques

1. Pushing and hitting for delivering the ball
2. Controlling or fielding skills to receive the ball

Players without the ball

To receive a pass, teammates without the ball must take the initiative and get free of their opponents so they can receive a pass. Making hard cuts at speed is one way to lose an opponent.

Player with the ball

The passer makes the pass when he or she is sure there is no opponent in or close to the line of the intended pass. If the path of the pass is clear, then the passer must send the ball *accurately and properly paced* to a teammate. A ball hit too hard will go by the teammate, and too soft a hit gives the opponent time to move in and intercept. To make an accurate pass the passer must assess the teammate's speed and direction so that the receiver does not break stride. The passer must *time* the pass. Players who get free without the ball do not have much time before the defender recovers. If the passer is slow to recognize the moment the teammate is free, the pass will be late and likely intercepted. Conversely, the passer must recognize when to hold the ball momentarily because the teammate is getting free and will be available in a few steps. If the passer passes too soon, the teammate will not be there. Good vision, timing, and accuracy are important for successful passing.

Passing strategies

Upfield pass (Fig. 11-12, A). When possible, passes should always go to an open teammate closer to the goal than the player with the ball. Upfield passes will be at a variety of angles.

Through pass (Fig. 11-12, B). This is the ultimate upfield pass. It runs parallel to the sideline and is very penetrating because it eliminates two defenders.

Square pass (Fig. 11-12, C). This pass gains no field position, because it runs parallel to the endline. It should not be used if there is any chance of an interception. The square pass is best used in a "give and go" (Fig. 11-12, D). This passing combination is most often associated with basketball, but it is equally useful and effective in field hockey. The player with the ball takes it close to an opponent. The player "gives" a square pass to a teammate and "goes" quickly to the open space behind the opponent for a return pass.

Back pass. Passing backwards will often open up the field of play and allow the team to change the point of attack.

Shooting. Scoring a goal should be viewed as the final pass. It is a ball that goes by the goalkeeper into the goal.

BASIC DEFENSE

Simply stated, defense is the team not in possession of the ball. When the opponents have possession, the players on the defending team in the vicinity of the ball actively attempt to get it while their teammates not immediately involved move back into the best defensive position in case the ball suddenly shifts. Pressure, marking, and covering are the basic principles in defense (Fig. 11-13).

Pressure. Pressure must be exerted against the opponent with the ball in such a way that a tackle is possible if ball control is lost. If a tackle is not possible, pressure reduces the passing angles.

Marking. Defense must be such that opposing attack players without the ball cannot receive the ball or are under instant pressure if they do. To mark effectively the defender must be goalside and ballside of the opponent, and the defender must be able to see both the opponent and the ball. The farther the opponent is from the ball, the less tightly the defender has to mark.

Covering. At the point of attack where the opponent with the ball is pressured and near teammates are marked, there is space behind the defenders. A player must be assigned to cover this space should a pass suddenly come through or an opponent get by.

BASIC OFFENSE

The offense is the team with the ball. At the moment a player gets the ball every teammate thinks offense, and the players in the vicinity of the ball become active participants in the attack.

The following are the principles of offense.

Movement off the ball. The key to successful attacks is players without the ball seeking open space. The player with the ball should have a minimum of two open teammates to whom to pass.

Width. Crowding is one of the biggest problems in all team sports. The first move a player should make is wide—to the sidelines. This forces the defender into a decision. Does the defender go with the ball carrier or stay in position? By spreading out and stretching the defense, the ball carrier will be able to receive the ball and have some space to work with.

Depth. This principle encourages an uneven distribution of attack players rather than a straight line. This provides more passing opportunities for the player with the ball.

STATIC SITUATIONS
Free hit

Offensively, the first priority is to take a free hit fast, before the other team sets up. If this is not possible, the player can delay slightly to give teammates a chance to organize. Movement by the receivers and deception by the passer are essential. Usually a short pass is most effective and a long pass should only be used if a player is wide open.

Defensively, against the free hit, the team must re-

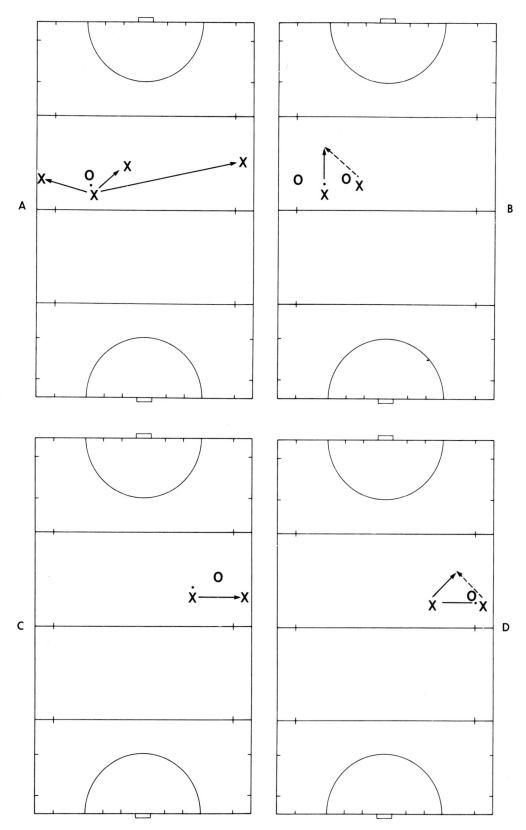

Fig. 11-12. Passing strategies. **A**, Upfield pass. **B**, Through pass. **C**, Square pass. **D**, Give and go.

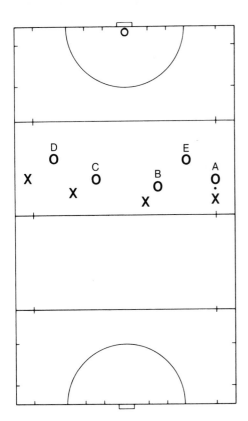

Fig. 11-13. Defense. OA is pressuring; OB, OC, and OD are marking. OE is covering.

cover quickly and set themselves up so there is no outlet for the free hit.

Side-in

Essentially, tactics of the side-in are the same as in the free hit. Offensively, it is important to keep possession of the ball and the pusher should not make a back or square pass if there is any chance of interception.

Penalty corner

Offense. The player who hits in must be able to accurately and smoothly hit the ball to the shooter. The shooter should be the player with the greatest ability to hit hard, accurately, and quickly. The other forwards are in a position to get a goal from a goalkeeper's rebound. At least three defenders should be in a backup position should the ball come out of the circle. Tactically, it is best to take the penalty corner on the left because the shot on goal is to the weak side (left) of the onrushing defender, making it difficult to stop.

  Defense. The fastest player should go to the shooter, hoping to get the ball or at least disrupting the shooter's rhythm and concentration. Two players, one on each side, come out a step behind to get any deflections or

dodges. One defender covers and one comes out on the opposite side from the corner in case the ball suddenly shifts. No one should block the goalkeeper, who comes out to reduce the angle of the shot.

GOALKEEPING

The goalkeeper is the last line of defense. The goalkeeper needs qualities of agility, quickness, strength, power, and the ability to anticipate. If all these qualities are evident but there are signs, no matter how small, of lack of courage, aggression, or confidence, the player is not meant to be a goalkeeper.

Skills

  Stopping. Pads should be together, with feet slightly turned out. Body is flexed, with the weight forward.

  Kicking or clearing. The kicking foot is swung rapidly into the ball, using the instep, the inside of the pad, or the toe.

  Hand stop. The goalkeeper catches the ball and releases it immediately, then follows with a kick.

Tactics

The basic tactic for goalkeepers is to take the shooting angles away from the forward. By coming off the goal line and being directly between the ball and goal, the goalkeeper reduces the shooter's opportunity for scoring, and the goalkeeper's chance for success is greater.

FORMATIONS

Other than the goalkeeper, whose position remains stable, the players can be arranged in any manner. The traditional formation (Fig. 11-14) of the remaining 10 players is five defenders and five attackers or, as is the common "system" one or two defenders or attackers are made midfielders or links who play both offense and defense (Figs. 11-15 and 11-16). It is thought that the defense is tighter and more secure and that the offense is more varied and unpredictable. Generally speaking, the team needs a sweeper, whose job it is to cover and to chase down through balls and take on breakaway forwards. The team needs three backs, whose job is primarily defense; two or three midfielders, who play about 60% defense and 40% offense; and three or four forwards, who are primarily responsible for scoring.

PROGRAM
General

All players must have equipment they can handle. A stick that is too long or heavy forces the player to compensate, producing bad technique. In the early stages it is not important for beginners to know all parts of every technique. The techniques can be learned and improved by making minor adjustments to many children's games.

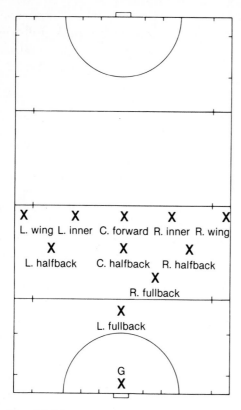

Fig. 11-14. Traditional formation or 5-3-2.

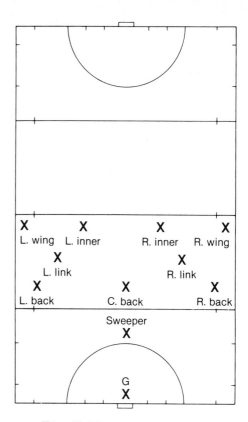

Fig. 11-15. The 4-2-3-1 system.

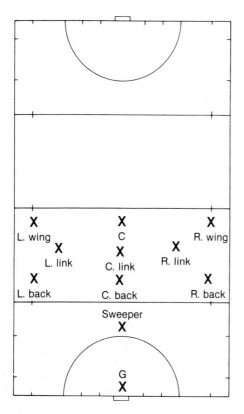

Fig. 11-16. The 3-3-3-1 system.

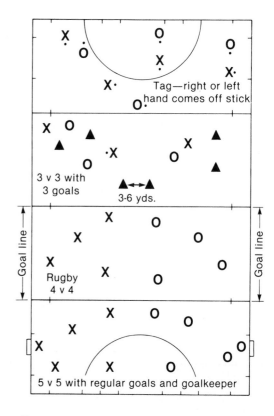

Fig. 11-17. Small games and competitions.

All kinds of tag, relays, obstacle courses, "keep away," and "steal the bacon" types of games are useful and fun.

Small games and competitions

In the beginning, the game can be played one versus one, and then gradually moved up to two versus two, three versus three, and so on. Interspersed with even sides should be uneven sides, such as two versus one, three versus two, four verses three, and the like, to work on specific group play and to give one team a good chance of succeeding. These types of games contain all the skills and tactics of eleven versus eleven, but they permit the players many more opportunities with the ball (Fig. 11-17).

Scoring. The scoring objectives in these small games and competitions are many and varied.

1. No goals—"keep away"—number of consecutive or sequence of passes.
2. One, two, or multiple goals (cones) placed on the lines or indiscriminately in the playing area where scoring can come from either side, with or without goalkeepers.
3. Regulation goals with or without goalkeepers in limited space, depending on number of players.
4. Rugby—successfully having possession of the ball over any part of a line up to 25 yards long. This game is excellent for spreading play. Players should think of that line as if it were the edge of the circle. If they control the ball over the line, then they can be certain they would have had a shot on goal.
5. Be creative.

FLOOR HOCKEY

Floor hockey is a popular game and is an excellent lead-in to field hockey. It is a combination of ice hockey and basketball, is strenuous, is ideal for boys and girls, and can be taught in a short time.

For safety, participants should play the puck—not the opponents. The stick must be carried below the waist at all times, and body checking is not allowed.

A basketball court can be used as the playing area, and either a puck or a floor hockey ball can be used. The midcourt line of the basketball court is the center line. The basketball midcourt jump circle is the center circle in which play always begins (after a goal or penalty). The goal area should not exceed 58 x 46 inches (117 x 147 cm); hockey nets are recommended. A restraining line 5 feet (1.52 m) from the front of the goal and 4 feet (1.22 m) on each side of the goal defines the goal box.

Each team consists of six players. One is the goalkeeper who can stop shots with the stick, feet, or hands. One is the center who is the only player allowed to move full court and is the offensive leader. The stick of the center must be striped with black tape. Two players are defensive and cannot go past the center line, and their main task is to keep the puck out of their half of the floor. Two players are forwards who work with the center player on offense. These two players cannot go into their defensive half of the court.

The game consists of three periods, each 8 minutes in length with 5-minute rest periods between them. A flip of a coin determines which team gets the puck to begin the game, and whichever team is behind gets the puck to start the second and third periods. Play begins with the referee's whistle. The center of the team in possession of the puck begins play with a pass. The center must have at least one foot inside the center circle during this pass, and all other players must be outside the 10-foot (3.05 m) restraining circle.

The clock begins when the puck is touched by any player following the center pass and runs continuously except for a roughing foul, a misconduct call, or the scoring of a goal. Any player that accumulates a total of five fouls or a combination of three roughing fouls and a misconduct must be substituted for immediately. Free substitution is allowed at any time.

TEACHING CONSIDERATIONS

1. Passing, fielding, and dribbling work should dominate practice sessions for beginners working alone and with partners for maximum practice opportunities. Combine dribbling and passing as soon as possible. Be firm about safety rules regarding use of the stick. Do not forget to help fielders receiving a pass from the right to adjust to using only one side of the stick.
2. As soon as some degree of ball control has been achieved work with two-on-one situations to emphasize opening up space, quick passes, dodging, tackling, and defensive and offensive strategy. Two-on-one experiences can be designed as a "keep away" situation or as two offensive players shooting against a goalie.
3. All essential skills and strategies can be taught in five-on-five games or practice situations of four-on-three or five-on-three. It is critical that hockey be learned as a "space" game, and reduced numbers make basic strategies easier for the beginner to utilize. Games with fewer numbers also give more practice opportunities. Teach how to avoid defense and how to defend with few players.
4. Save specialty rules (bully, penalty corner) for more advanced players. It tends to slow the game down.
5. Be strict in calling safety violations but be more flexible for beginners on fouls such as off sides and obstruction.

GLOSSARY

ball control Maneuvering or maintaining possession of the ball.

clear Removing the ball from the scoring area.

cover Defender stationed behind a teammate challenging for ball so that defender will be in a position should teammate be beaten.

defender A player whose major contribution is to get the ball from the opponents; prevents opponents from scoring.

dribble Individual technique of moving and maintaining control of the ball with short taps off end of stick.

fielding Absorbing the ball's speed on the end of the stick so that it is immediately under control.

flick Push that is lofted, primarily a shot for getting ball out of danger.

forwards Primarily offense; the first line of the attack.

goal (1) The unit of scoring; (2) the cage on the end line into which a team tries to put the ball.

hit Stroke used for moving the ball over great distances and for shooting.

Indian dribble Controlling ball in front of body and propelling it forward in a zig-zag pattern; ball is moved alternately with a regular dribble and reverse stick.

links Midfielders; play both offense and defense.

marking (1) Defender playing close enough to an opponent to prevent opponent from receiving a pass; (2) defender close enough to tackle or pressure an opponent immediately upon receiving the ball; (3) one-on-one defense.

pass Intentional moving of the ball from one teammate to another.

pressure Decreasing the time and space that an attacking player has in which to pass or dribble.

push The stroke used for short passes; no preliminary action before release, making it the quickest pass.

reverse stick Playing the ball with the toe of the stick down.

score Goal; the final pass.

square Pass that goes parallel to endline to a teammate moving forward and taking it on the run.

sweeper Free defender who covers and roams behind defense picking up all through passes and who must take on forward with ball who gets free.

system Arrangement of players on the field.

tactics Thinking level of play; the outwitting of opponents.

through pass Pass that goes parallel to sideline between opponents.

timing Releasing a pass at the right moment; involves good judgment of the positions of teammates and opponents.

weak side (1) The left side of the player; (2) the side of the field away from the ball.

width Players' taking a wide position toward sideline.

SUGGESTED READINGS

American Alliance for Health, Physical Education, Recreation, and Dance: Field Hockey Guild, Washington, D.C., 1982, National Association of Girls' and Women's Sports.

Fong D: The coaches' collection of field hockey drills, Champaign, Ill, 1982, Human Kinetic Publishers, Inc. A compilation of over 100 drills contributed by many of the most successful field hockey coaches in the country.

Hockey coach: the official manual of the Hockey Association, London, 1982, Hodden & Stoughton.

Martens R: Parent guide to USA junior field hockey, Champaign, Ill. 1982, Human Kinetics Publishers, Inc. Explains rules, skills, and strategies. Also contains information about the physical and psychological concerns surrounding youth sports.

United States Field Hockey Association manual for coaches. The official manual of the United States Field Hockey Association. North Chill, N.Y., 1989, United States Field Hockey Association.

Working rules of the game of hockey, London, 1980, Charles Mitchell, Ltd.

FILMS AND VIDEOTAPES

Field Hockey by Vonnie Gros. A 26-minute videotape available from Sports Video, 745 State Circle, Box 1941, Ann Arbor, MI 48106.

Field Hockey and *Floor Hockey*. Two videotapes available from Athletic Institute, 200 N. Castlewood Dr., North Palm Beach, FL 33408.

Field Hockey: the basics. A 45-minute videotape available from How To Sports Videos, Box 5852, Denver, CO 80127.

Goalkeeping techniques, 15 minutes. American Alliance for Health, Physical Education, and Recreation.

Hockey—improve your game. All England Women's Hockey Association, 60 minutes, American Alliance for Health, Physical Education, and Recreation.

Hockey strokes—fundamentals of the game. Scottish Women's Association, 40 minutes, American Alliance for Health, Physical Education, and Recreation.

12

Golf

Completion of this chapter should enable the reader to:

- Recognize the values and benefits of participation in golf
- Be knowledgeable in the selection of golf equipment and in the uses for each club
- Practice proper technique in executing the basic golf swing and the several specialized shots
- Know the rules of golf and be familiar with the etiquette that is so much a part of the game
- Teach a group of beginning students the fundamentals of golf
- Properly use the many and colorful terms associated with golf

Golf is one of the most challenging and fascinating of modern sports. The thrill of striking a ball well over 200 yards and the satisfaction of successfully executing the soft touch needed for a 4-foot putt are of lasting pleasure. Whether one learns to play golf for relaxation and fun or aspires to achieve a high competitive level is the privilege of the individual. Few sports offer playing fields with such great variety and beauty as golf courses.

HISTORY

The game of golf is one of the most ancient of the modern sports. Historians do not agree on its origin, but it appears certain that golf was played in Scotland more than 500 years ago. As early as 1457 the Scottish Parliament ordained that golf should not be played by the people because it was distracting from the practice of archery, which was deemed necessary for defensive purposes. Old paintings and drawings show that similar games were also played about that time in Holland, Belgium, and France. The Dutch term "kolf," meaning a club, is considered by some to have given rise to the name of the present-day game. Regardless of how much Scotland invented on her own and how much she borrowed from others, it appears certain that that country was the source from which the game as it is known today spread to all

parts of the world. St. Andrews in Fife, Scotland is believed to be the oldest existing golf course.

Courses or links of the early days differed greatly from those of the present. Golf was then distinctly a seaside game. It was played over stretches of land that linked the waterline of the seashore with tillable lands farther inland. It was this condition which led to calling the scene of play "links," which in fact means a seaside golf course.

Location of holes followed no definite plan. The landscape was partially covered by bushes, trees, and the like. Open areas were chosen as finishing points or putting greens. No official number of holes was adopted as standard for a round of play until 1858, when 18 holes were designated as a round.

Historical documents tell of the organization of golf clubs in the United States in the closing years of the eighteenth century. However, the game as we know it today had its start in the United States approximately 80 years ago. A few clubs were started in the eastern United States, and the rapid increase in popularity since then has greatly increased the number of private and municipal courses. Today, class instruction in golf is found in most secondary schools and colleges. Colleges and universities often own and operate golf courses; high schools use private and municipal courses. In recent years television coverage of major golf events has done much to stimulate interest in the game. In fact, in many urban areas of the country the number of golf courses has become insufficient to accomodate the demand. In 1980 the National Golf Foundation indicated that if a new golf course was built every day until 2000, there would still be a shortage. In 1989 they revised this statement to suggest that if five new courses were built every day until 2000, there would still be a shortage. It has been estimated that more than 16.5 million Americans play golf sometime during a year.

There are at least 16,000 golf driving ranges in America. Many people become enthusiasts and start playing golf as a result of experience on a driving range.

Golf today is no longer a game for those with a high income. It is played by individuals from a variety of economic backgrounds and includes the young and the old, duffers as well as masters.

Truly, golf is a sport that offers a life-long source of pleasure. One or two well-timed and well-directed shots often serve as the catalyst that causes the player to return for another round.

The social values and aspects of golf include the following: it encourages excellent compatibility of mixed groups; it clears and freshens the mind by diversion of interest; it brings urban dwellers into sunshine and nature; it provides restful activity for the working individual; the golfer is pitted against self as well as against opponents; each hole is a separate contest and challenge; and the game is played by people of all ages, sizes, and builds. As recreation, golf is one of the most desirable of all sports.

GENERAL DESCRIPTION

Eighteen holes make up the typical golf course. The first, ninth, tenth, and eighteenth holes are generally near the clubhouse. Any multiple of nine holes can be played, and each hole varies in length and general layout. Hazards are generally placed to penalize a poor shot. The object is to score as few strokes as possible for each hole. Play starts at the tee behind two markers, continues along the fairway, which is generally bounded by rough, and finishes at the green, which is often surrounded by bunkers. The ball is rolled into the hole marked by the pin or flagstick.

EQUIPMENT

The United States has contributed in large share to improvements in golf equipment, for example, the type of ball in use today: the steel-, graphite-, and titanium-shafted clubs and the peg tee.

Clothing

Dress should be comfortable and in accord with local custom on the course played.

Spiked golf shoes are an important part of a player's golfing equipment. However, if they are not available, a pair of tennis shoes will suffice.

Clubs

It is not necessary to have the best set of golf clubs on the market to enjoy playing golf and to play it satisfactorily. On the other hand, one should not handicap his or her game by playing with inferior equipment. Purchasing clubs that are suitable to your characteristics and that are made by a dependable manufacturer is a sound policy for assurance of satisfaction and long wear.

Golf clubs come in a variety of lengths, weights, shaft flexibility and other features (Fig. 12-1). Club length is usually determined by a person's height, and club weight is often selected on personal preference in relation to feel. Usually, the faster the swing, the less whip you should have in your club shafts. Ask your golf teacher or club professional for advice on the type of clubs to purchase.

The maximum number of clubs allowed to be carried by a golfer is 14.

Starter set

The beginning golfer should not invest in an expensive and complete set of clubs. Options include purchasing a set of used clubs or a starter set. The advantages of purchasing a set of used clubs rather than a starter set are usually in the quality and number of clubs obtained for a comparable cost. On the other hand, with a starter set it is possible to purchase a brand that can be added to later as needed. In either case the minimum clubs to start with include a 3 wood; a putter; and the 3, 5, 7, and 9 irons.

Woods

The four common woods are the driver, or no. 1 wood; the no. 3 wood; the no. 4 wood; and the no. 5 wood (Fig. 12-2). They have longer shafts and weigh more than the iron clubs and consequently can give more distance than an iron club having a similar loft or tilt to the club face. The driver is the longest hitting club and is usually used at the tee.

Driver. The driver hits 220 to 300 yards (201 to 275 m) (women, 150 to 200 yards [137 to 183 m]) and is used only on the tee.

No. 3 wood. This club hits 200 to 240 yards (183 to 220 m) (women, 150 to 170 yards [137 to 155 m]) and is used from a good lie for long shots.

No. 4 wood. This club hits 200 to 230 yards (183 to 210 m) (women, 145 to 160 yards [133 to 146 m]) and is used from a good lie where distance and height are needed.

No. 5 wood. The no. 5 wood hits 190 to 220 yards (174

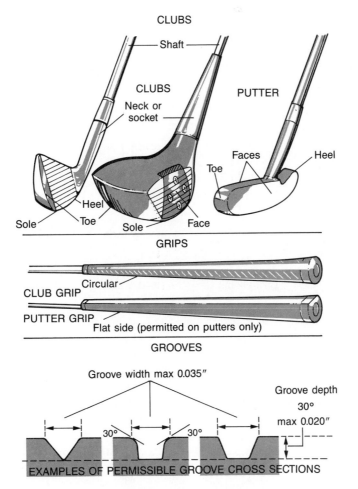

Fig. 12-1. Club features.

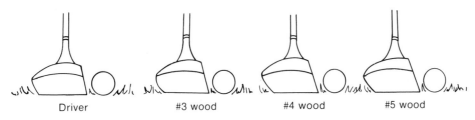

Fig. 12-2. The woods.

to 201 m)(women, 120 to 150 yards [109 to 137 m]) and is used from a poor lie or in place of a long iron.

Irons

Irons are used from the fairway or from the tee on short holes. The player selects the proper iron according to the distance required (Fig. 12-3). For various irons and distances achieved with each, see Figs. 12-3 and 12-4.

Putter. This club is used for putting on the green or from just off the green. Putters are manufactured in a great variety of styles and are chosen on the basis of individual preference.

Pitching or sand wedge. These clubs are used for short approaches from the rough and fairways, less than 125 yards (115 m), and as a trouble club from tall rough or sand traps. They are very versatile when properly used.

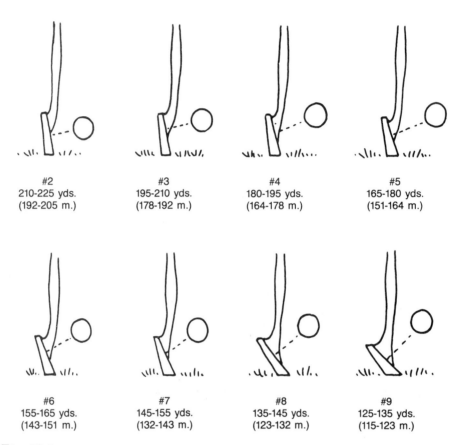

#2	#3	#4	#5
210-225 yds.	195-210 yds.	180-195 yds.	165-180 yds.
(192-205 m.)	(178-192 m.)	(164-178 m.)	(151-164 m.)

#6	#7	#8	#9
155-165 yds.	145-155 yds.	135-145 yds.	125-135 yds.
(143-151 m.)	(132-143 m.)	(123-132 m.)	(115-123 m.)

Fig. 12-3. Various irons showing angle of pitch of each club and approximate distance obtained by male golfers.

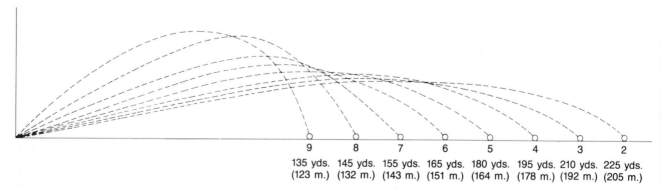

	9	8	7	6	5	4	3	2
	135 yds.	145 yds.	155 yds.	165 yds.	180 yds.	195 yds.	210 yds.	225 yds.
	(123 m.)	(132 m.)	(143 m.)	(151 m.)	(164 m.)	(178 m.)	(192 m.)	(205 m.)

Fig. 12-4. Distances and flight of ball using the same swing with each iron (male golfer).

Golf balls

Golf balls are made by many manufacturers. Their construction varies from a solid one-piece ball to a ball developed from a small hard core wound with rubber bands and sealed with a durable cover.

Ball preference is left up to individual feel and style of play. The better players usually prefer a wound ball of higher compression, where beginners would use a one- or two-piece ball with a durable cover that does not cut easily. One should have at least three balls in the golf bag when going out to play.

Plastic balls may be used for the gymnasium, small field, or backyard practice.

THE COURSE

A golf course is usually built and constructed to best conform to the locale of the land. A complete golf course consists of 18 holes, which requires not less than 100 acres. In many communities 9-hole or 18-hole courses are constructed on less acreage with shorter holes that require less time to play. Par-3 courses, on which 18 holes can be played in 3 hours or less, are becoming increasingly popular.

A well-constructed golf course is architecturally planned so that each hole differs from the rest, yet certain elements are common to all.

Each hole is composed of a tee and tee markers, fairway, rough, trees, boundary, sand bunkers and sometimes water hazards, and green, cup, and flag. The shape and size of the greens, as well as the placing of bunkers and water hazards, are left to the creativity of the golf course architect.

Par for the course is usually determined by the distance of the holes from the middle of the tee down the middle of the fairway to the middle of the green. Holes up to 250 yards (229 m) are usually designated as par 3, holes from 251 to 470 yards (230 to 430 m) as par 4, and holes from 471 to 600 yards (431 to 549 m) as par 5. Par 3 is a score usually obtained by reaching the green in one shot and rolling the ball into the cup with two putts. On a par 4, the golfer should reach the green in two; and on a par 5, reach it in three. A championship course usually has a par of 72, or an average of four strokes per hole. A typical course has four par-3 holes, 10 par-4 holes, and four par-5 holes.

Par for women differs somewhat from that for men, depending on the difficulty of each hole as to distance, hazards, and the like.

Refer to the sample scorecard (Fig. 12-5) with regard to par for men and women, distances of each hole, and hole handicap (a ranking of the holes by difficulty.)

FACILITIES FOR PRACTICE

1. Outdoor driving range and putting green
2. Any large room, preferably a gymnasium
3. Two or three large pieces of canvas hung in front of a wall with fish netting along sides to form a cage-type setup
4. Mats from which to hit
5. Clubs and balls (plastic balls may be used if nets are not available)
6. A large rug with short nap for putting
7. Putting cups for individual putting (water glasses can be used)

FUNDAMENTAL SKILLS AND TECHNIQUES

Because certain clubs and types of shots fall into natural groupings, the following material has been arranged to take advantage of these categories. For the left-handed player, it will be necessary to reverse the techniques as presented here because consideration has been given only to the righthanded player.

The golf grip

1. Ten-finger grip; sometimes used by players with small, weak hands or extremely short fingers (Fig. 12-6)
2. Interlocking grip; preferred by some players who like a solid feel (Fig. 12-7)
3. Overlapping or Vardon grip (Fig. 12-8); the most popular grip, used by most professional players (described below)

One opens the left hand, and with the thumb and fingers together, places the club diagonally across the hand from the middle joint of the index finger across the heel of the hand. The hand closes over the club so that it is held by the fingers. The V formed by the thumb and index finger should point approximately to the right shoulder. When the club is held in the position of address, you should see the first three knuckles of the fingers. The thumb is above, one quarter turn over the club with the pad of the thumb on the grip of the club formed by the first and second fingers of the left hand. The correct rotation of the left hand allows cocking of the wrist at the peak of the backswing. It also allows the left arm to deal a backhand blow to the ball. At this point the player should try swinging the club head with only the left arm, watching that the arm remains comfortably straight and that the wrist cocks at the top of the backswing.

To place the right hand in position, the club handle should first contact the middle joint of the right forefinger. When the hand is closed, this forefinger knuckle must be on the right side of the shaft, never under it. Then one closes the hand, placing the thumb to the left, diagonally across the shaft so that it helps the forefinger to grip. The feel of the club head is controlled mainly by the fingers, giving more power and control. The left thumb should fit snugly into the palm of the right hand. The little finger of the right hand should be wrapped

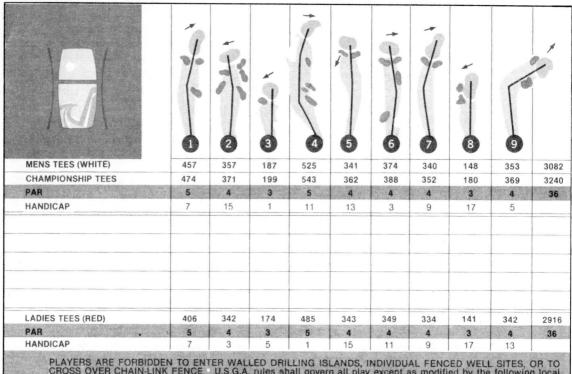

	1	2	3	4	5	6	7	8	9	
MENS TEES (WHITE)	457	357	187	525	341	374	340	148	353	3082
CHAMPIONSHIP TEES	474	371	199	543	362	388	352	180	369	3240
PAR	5	4	3	5	4	4	4	3	4	36
HANDICAP	7	15	1	11	13	3	9	17	5	
LADIES TEES (RED)	406	342	174	485	343	349	334	141	342	2916
PAR	5	4	3	5	4	4	4	3	4	36
HANDICAP	7	3	5	1	15	11	9	17	13	

PLAYERS ARE FORBIDDEN TO ENTER WALLED DRILLING ISLANDS, INDIVIDUAL FENCED WELL SITES, OR TO CROSS OVER CHAIN-LINK FENCE • U.S.G.A. rules shall govern all play except as modified by the following local rules. LOCAL RULES: • Ball may be dropped two club lengths from staked trees—no penalty. • Drop off all paved paths and roads—no penalty. • Walled drilling islands are out of bounds. • Wire fenced well sites—if within orange staked area drop straight behind point where ball lay and hole, no limit to distance behind—no penalty. • Water hazards: holes 3, 6, 10, 14, 15. • Rock drainage ditches—when rock interferes with stance or swing, drop two club

	10	11	12	13	14	15	16	17	18	IN	TOTAL	HDCP	NET
	404	348	487	166	366	363	375	178	439	3116	6198		
	411	369	506	184	380	381	394	203	466	3294	6534		
	4	4	5	3	4	4	4	3	5	36	72		
	2	10	14	16	6	8	4	12	18				
	383	340	418	149	351	347	358	155	441	2942	5858		
	4	4	5	3	4	4	4	3	5	36	72		
	4	14	2	18	10	12	8	16	6	LADIES COURSE RATING 72.4			

COURSE RATING
CHAMPIONSHIP TEES 70.1
MENS TEES 63.0

DATE _____

PLAYER _____

ATTEST _____

lengths—no penalty. • Out of bounds defined by white stakes or green stakes—white tops: No. 4 only—out of bounds right side as staked. • Driving range Out of Bounds as staked. COURSE RULES: • Players will at all times observe the rules of Golf etiquette. • Practicing prohibited anywhere on course. • Replace turf and fix ball marks on greens. • Keep electric carts off tees and 30 ft. from greens. • Keep electric carts on paths and designated areas. • Keep pull carts off tees, areas between traps and greens, and 10 ft. from greens. Lateral water hazard: Hole No. 4.

Fig. 12-5. Typical scorecard.

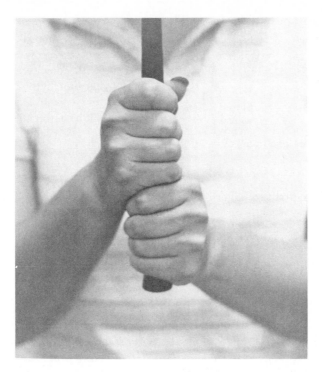

Fig. 12-6. Ten-finger grip.

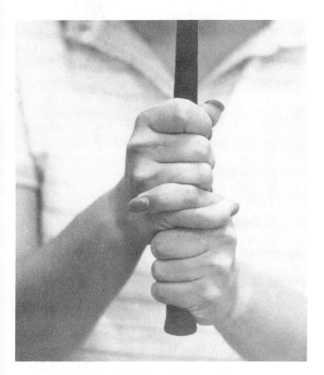

Fig. 12-7. Interlocking grip.

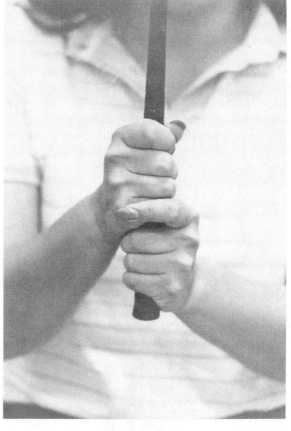

Fig. 12-8. Overlapping grip.

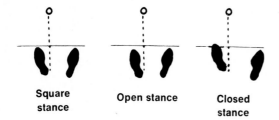

Fig. 12-9. Various foot positions.

around the crevice formed by the first two fingers of the left hand (overlapping grip).

It should be emphasized that, regardless of the grip used, the back of the left hand and the palm of the right should face squarely toward the target.

The stance

For various foot positions, see Fig. 12-9.

Square stance. The feet, knees, hips, and shoulders are parallel to the line of flight. This stance is used for almost all long shots of both woods and irons because it allows free movement of either side of the body. The knees are slightly bent, the toes turn slightly outward, and the weight is evenly distributed. The arms hang downward from the shoulders and away from the body but not forward. The body curves naturally, but not sharply, forward. The eyes are on the ball.

Open stance. The left foot is withdrawn slightly from the line of flight, but the knees, hips, and shoulders remain square. This stance is used rarely for wood shots but more often for the shorter iron shots. It tends to restrict the turning and pivoting of the left side but allows a better follow-through. This stance encourages the fade or slice but can result in increased distance.

Closed stance. The right foot is withdrawn slightly from the line of flight, but the knees, hips, and shoulders remain square. This stance is often used for wood shots and encourages a draw or hook.

The golf swing

For progressive steps in the golf swing see Fig. 12-10.

Tempo

Maintaining an even tempo is one of the most important aspects of developing a proper golf swing. A player who is able to maintain good rhythm and smoothness throughout the swing will be able to develop an efficient and consistent golf swing. Most beginners attempt to hit the ball too hard, which results in an improper tempo or an uneven rhythm and causes many faults. In fact, as a variable, strength is much less important than proper tempo and clubhead speed in the successful golf swing. Beginning golfers should strive to achieve a consistent

tempo or rhythm in all shots attempted. Often a simple key such as saying "Back," " Wait," and "Through" or "One, two, three" on the backswing and "One, two, three" on the downswing and follow-through will help to develop the rhythm necessary for success. Once the idea of tempo is understood and accomplished, the beginner will have the necessary basis for the development of a sound golf swing. Without proper rhythm it is difficult to hit the ball correctly, and much power is wasted. In general, the golf swing is developed by gradually increasing the speed. The golfer should begin slowly, then accelerate on the downswing, keeping a continuous rhythm throughout. It takes approximately the same time to take the club from the address to the top of the backswing as it does to complete the downswing and the follow-through.

Addressing the ball

When addressing the ball, the player takes the proper grip and places the head of the club on the ground, with the sole of the club parallel to the turf. The feet should be placed approximately shoulder width apart or in a relative position for the club used, for example, wider for the longer clubs. The arms should fall naturally from the shoulders and not so far away from the body that the individual is stretching. For the woods, the ball is generally placed in line with the inside portion of the left heel. As the length of the club and the required distance decrease, the ball is addressed farther to the right of the left foot but seldom farther back than in the center of the stance.

The waggle

The waggle is a preliminary movement that takes a variety of forms, depending on individual preference. It is designed to help the golfer relax, adjust the grip, check alignment, and get ready to begin the swing. Usually, it involves slight body movement and the lifting of the club head several inches to check balance and position. When the golfer feels ready, there is a slight hesitation before the beginning of the full swing. This preliminary move tends to ease tension in preparation for the shot.

The backswing

Before beginning the swing, the golfer must fix his or her eye on the ball. The swing is started with a rotation of the shoulder and hips, which starts the club head moving to the back. The left arm should be kept straight and the club head low to the ground. The wrists begin to cock approximately halfway back on the swing. The right elbow is kept close to the body, and the weight is shifted from a balanced position to the right foot. The left knee is turned inward, and the left foot rolls to the right, keeping the left heel low to the ground. At the

Fig. 12-10. Progressive steps of swing.   *Continued.*

7

8

Fig. 12-10. Progressive steps of swing (continued).

top of the backswing the left shoulder is pointing at the ball and the club is parallel to the ground and pointing toward the target.

The downswing

To make a smooth change of direction, the downswing is started with the left leg. The left foot comes down flat to the ground, and the knees and hips are moved forward toward the target. The knees are bent slightly to allow freedom of movement as the weight is shifted from the right side to the left. There should be a feeling of pulling from the left side. The wrists should remained cocked until the arms are parallel with the ground. The left leg straightens and the left side becomes firm to provide a strong hitting position. At impact, there should be a straight line from the ball or club head through the hands to the left shoulder. The head must remain stationary and the eyes remain focused on the ball after contact is made.

Follow-through

After impact, the right arm becomes just as straight as the left arm was on the backswing. The head rises naturally but does not move forward as the right shoulder comes under. Both arms should be stretched out as far as possible toward the target. The wrists will begin to turn over after the arms have reached their limit, finishing with the hands high above the head.

The swing plane

When the golfer takes the club back from the ball, the club should come slightly inside the line of flight, maintaining a plane that will run back approximately between the shoulders and neck. One of the keys in a successful golf swing is to maintain this same plane on the down-

swing. To accomplish this, the golfer must maintain the proper sequence of body movements. The swing is started with the legs and hips, then the arms come into play, then the wrists begin cocking. This same order must be maintained on the downswing if the plane is not to be broken. The downswing starts with the legs and hips, then the arms come into play and next the wrists uncock so that they are straight at the point of contact. This sequence will enable the golfer to swing from slightly inside the line of flight out through the ball, maintaining proper control of the shot. Any deviations from this sequence will allow the club head to break the plane and will cause inconsistency or initiate numerous faults or problems with the flight of the ball. This sequence and having the clubhead square to the intended line of flight at impact are the two most important factors in a successful golf swing.

Common errors

The following are errors often made by beginners when learning the golf swing:

1. Swaying or moving the head to the right instead of pivoting the body over the ball
2. Backswing that is too fast, eliminating good tempo and throwing the golfer off balance
3. Bending the left arm
4. Raising the left shoulder
5. Backswing with a too flat or too horizontal plane
6. Raising the head from its original position
7. Pausing too long or not long enough at the top of the swing.
8. Rushing the downswing
9. Uncocking the wrists too soon, which throws off the proper sequence and usually casts the club outside the correct plane

Fig. 12-11. Pitch shot.

10. Hitting too hard with the right hand, which drops the right shoulder, causing contact behind the ball
11. Relaxing the wrists at the moment of impact or slowing the downswing, impeding proper rhythm or tempo
12. Failing to complete the follow-through with the hands held high

The short swing

One of the consistent factors in golf is that it is not necessary to learn a different swing for each club. The plane varies slightly with the length of the club; however, there is no difference in what has to be learned to attempt the swing. When a shot requires less distance than produced by the shortest club in the bag, a shorter swing must be executed. The short swing is a breakdown of the full swing, and the distance of the shot is commensurate with the length of the backswing. If a half swing is required for a particular shot, then the golfer uses less body turn and less wrist action than in the full swing, where the wrist break is not completed until the club is brought to the top of the swing. The shorter the swing, the less wrist action and body movement occur. The follow-through is the same as in the backswing. A one-quarter backswing requires a one-quarter follow-through; a one-half backswing requires a one-half follow-through; and so on. The rest of the fundamentals are exactly the same as described for the full swing. The golfer should practice short swings of various lengths to determine how far the ball will travel and to obtain the correct feel for the distance required.

The pitch shot

The pitch shot (Fig. 12-11) is usually executed with a no. 9 iron, pitching wedge, or sand wedge. This shot will fly high and is used to hit the ball over a bunker or hazard of some type and will stop on the green with very little roll. The stance should be square or slightly open, with the length of the backswing determined by the distance needed as described for the short swing. Some golfers prefer to choke down on the club for greater control, particularly for the shorter shots. Inasmuch as the swing is shorter, body movement is kept to a minimum, there is little wrist cock, and the left arm is straight throughout the swing. It is important that the follow-through be carried the same distance as the backswing, with care taken not to make any special effort to meet or hit the ball hard. Tempo is just as important in the short swing or pitch shot as it is in the full swing. Regardless of the distance of the shot, it is important that one hit down through the ball and not try to scoop the ball into the air. The club is designed to give the proper lift to the ball.

The chip shot

The chip shot (Fig. 12-12) is usually executed with a no. 7 iron and is effective when the golfer has an open shot to the pin and does not have to hit over any type of hazard. The stance is similar to that for the pitch shot, with slightly more weight forward at the address. The less-lofted club face will allow the ball to travel low and run much farther than the pitch shot. Again, the distance of the shot is determined by the length of the backswing, and the follow-through should be commensurate with the backswing. One should practice taking the club back various distances to determine the proper length of the backswing for the distance required. Club selection for this shot is usually determined by selecting the club that will allow the ball to hit as close to the edge of the green as possible and roll the remainder of the way to the cup. A short chip shot can be executed in a manner similar

Fig. 12-12. Chip shot.

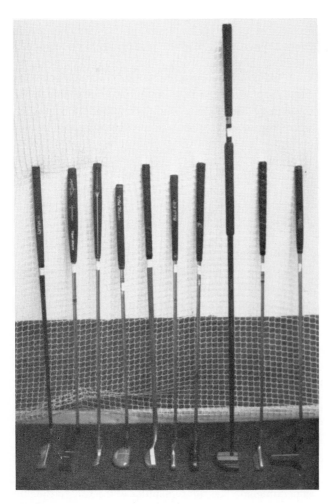

Fig. 12-13. Putters.

to a putting stroke. Again, the key to the chip shot is proper tempo and rhythm, with care not to chop at the ball with an uneven tempo.

Putting

Putting is individual in nature, although there are certain aspects of the stroke that must be maintained regardless of the golfer's style or the type of putter used. For examples of the many styles and designs in which putters are manufactured, see Fig. 12-13. The stance may be wide, narrow, open, or closed, depending on the individual preference. However, there must be no body or head movement and the putter blade should be taken straight back in line with the direction required for a straight-through motion toward the hole. Figs. 12-14 and 12-15 display two types of putting stances that can be used. The following description of putting can be used as a guide; however, technique can be varied according to personal preference. The distance of the putt is determined by the length of the backswing. A shorter putt requires a shorter backswing and a longer putt a longer backswing, but the tempo must be consistent throughout.

Stance

1. The stance is fairly upright, with the neck and shoulders bent slightly.
2. The feet are 8 to 12 inches apart.
3. The stance is square.
4. The weight is balanced.
5. The left arm is kept close to the torso.
6. The right forearm is close to the right thigh.
7. The ball is at the left instep.

Fig. 12-14. Upright putting stance.

Fig. 12-15. Crouched putting stance.

Grip

1. The back of the left hand and the palm of the right hand are square to the line.
2. Both thumbs are directly on top of the grip.

Swing (see box)

1. The swing is short and low to the ground.
2. It is in line with the intended roll of the ball.
3. It is completely relaxed, slow, and steady.
4. There is no body or head movement.
5. The club head follows through.
6. The ball should be struck firmly enough to reach the hole.

Reading the green

1. The player checks the grass to determine whether the putt will be with or against the grain.
2. The player sights the hole from behind the ball to determine the angle of roll.

Sand bunkers

Executing the bunker shot properly can save the golfer many strokes. To control this shot, the player must hit the sand about 2 inches behind the ball and let the sand throw the ball out of the trap. The distance the ball travels is relative to the distance hit behind the ball. The object is not to bury the club but to continue to swing smoothly through the sand and under the ball, with a strong follow-through and finish.

General principles

1. Because sand traps vary from deep, soft sand to shallow, hard clay and sand, each shot is different.
2. The trap is entered from the lowest point so as not to destroy the bank or unduly disturb the surface.
3. The player positions his or her feet and then moves them back and forth in order to sink into the sand and have a firm stance.
4. In addressing the ball, one should not touch the sand with the club head until the ball is hit.
5. On leaving the trap, all irregularities made in the sand should be covered by smoothing them out with the club head or rake.

The explosion shot (Fig. 12-16)

1. The grip, stance, and swing are about the same as for the short, high approach.

CHECKPOINTS FOR THE GOLF SWING

A. The overlapping grip
   1. Left hand is gripped with fingers to form V over right shoulder
   2. Right hand is not too far under shaft; the V formed should point over right shoulder
   3. The thumbs are placed on the side of the shaft
   4. The little finger of the right hand overlaps the first finger of the left hand
B. The stance
   1. Square: both feet are equidistant from the line of flight
   2. Open: the left foot is a little farther from the line of flight than the right foot
   3. Closed: the right foot is farther away from the line of flight than the left foot
C. The swing
   1. Backswing
      a. Fix the eye on the ball; determine the proper position of the head
      b. Start back with rotation of shoulder and hips
      c. Keep the left arm straight
      d. Keep the club head low to the ground
      e. Begin to cock the wrists approximately halfway back on the swing
      f. Keep the right elbow close to the body
      g. Shift weight from left foot to right foot
      h. At top of backswing the left shoulder will be pointing at the ball and the club will be parallel to the ground pointing toward the target
   2. Downswing
      a. Start with the left leg
      b. Left foot comes down flat to the ground
      c. Shift weight from right foot to left foot
      d. Bend the knees to allow freedom of movement
      e. There is a feeling of pulling from the left side
      f. Uncock the wrists when the hands are parallel with ground
      g. At the moment of impact the ball, the hands and the left shoulder are almost in a straight line
      h. The left leg straightens and becomes firm
   3. Follow-through
      a. The right arm is just as straight as the left was on the backswing
      b. The head rises naturally with the pulling of the right shoulder
      c. The grip must be firm but not tight throughout the swing
      d. Arms are stretched out as far as possible
      e. The wrists will begin to turn over after the arms have reached the limit
      f. Finish with the hands high
D. Suggestions for putting
   1. Keep the putter blade flat on the ground
   2. Keep both toes parallel with the line of flight
   3. Putt the ball off the left foot
   4. Keep the blade low to the ground
   5. Use no body or head action at any time

Fig. 12-16. The explosion shot.

2. The stance is open, with the feet fairly close together and well-set in the sand.
3. The grip must be firm but not tense.
4. The swing must be fairly long, upright, and U-shaped.
5. The club head must not stop in the sand because sand pushed ahead of the club will cause the ball to rise. The follow-through should be definite and powerful.
6. The amount of sand taken, or the distance back of the ball that the club head enters the sand, determines the distance the ball will travel. Thus the closer one is to the green, the more sand one must take.

Sidehill lies

When playing from sidehill lies, the golfer must adjust the stance and ball replacement to conform to the contour of the ground. The golfer should avoid trying to overswing and should first take one or two practice swings to become familiar with the changes in swing feel.

General principles
1. Do not overswing.
2. Play for accuracy.
3. Allow the club head to follow the contour of the ground.

Uphill
1. There is a tendency to pull or hook, so aim to the right.
2. Stand close to the ball with the feet almost together.
3. Put more weight on the right foot.
4. Play the ball forward of the normal position in stance.

Downhill
1. There is a tendency to slice, so aim to the left.
2. On a steep slope avoid wood clubs because it is difficult to achieve a rise.
3. Play the ball back of the normal position in stance.

4. Weight is naturally more on the left foot, which will restrict the action of the pivot to the left. Shift the weight to the right foot.

Ball below feet

1. There is a strong tendency to slice, so play to the left.
2. The weight is on the toes, so open the stance somewhat.
3. Avoid topping by moving the grip closer to the top end of the club and concentrating on staying down until after the ball is contacted.
4. Do not pivot as much as on level ground; more of a U-shaped swing is natural.

Ball above feet

1. The tendency is to pull or hook, so play to the right.
2. Hold the club short.
3. Swing slowly; a fast swing will throw you back, causing you to top the ball.
4. There is a tendency to toe the ball with the club, so play it close.

Playing from the rough

When playing from the rough, set yourself firmly with a slightly open stance. The club should be brought back in a more upright motion. Hit down through the ball and finish the swing strongly.

General principles

1. Do not press in trying for too much distance.
2. Use the U-shaped swing.
3. Play the shot safely rather than gamble on a "lucky one."
4. Open the face of the club slightly to cut the grass better and to give a quicker rise in long grass.
5. Each rough position will differ from the last, so judge each one as the occasion arises.

RULES

1. The ball must be played as it lies except as outlined by the rules. Local rules may permit preferred lies, or "winter rules," in which case the ball may be moved with the club head provided that it is not moved nearer the hole.
2. The ball must be fairly struck with the head of the club.
3. The player whose ball is farthest from the hole plays first.
4. If a ball goes out of bounds, the player must play the next stroke at the spot from which the ball was last struck. If the stroke was played from the tee, the ball may be teed; in all other cases it must be dropped. The penalty is loss of stroke and distance. (Add 2 strokes to score for the hole.) If any part of the ball lies in bounds, the ball remains in play.

5. In match play, if a player's ball knocks the opponent's ball into the hole, the opponent shall be considered to have holed out on the last shot. A ball that has been moved by an opponent's ball may be left at that point or replaced in its original spot. In stroke play, the ball moved must be replaced as near as possible to its original spot. The golfer playing the putt has the right to ask the opponent to mark the ball.

   The player has the option of having the flagstick attended or removed. If the putted ball strikes an attended flagstick or a person attending the flagstick in stroke play, there is a 2-stroke penalty. In match play, if the flagstick is held by an opponent or an opponent's caddy, the opponent loses the hole. If it is held by the player's caddy, the player loses the hole.

   Note: If a ball is believed to be out of bounds, a provisional ball may be played before the golfer leaves the point from which the first ball was played.
6. Irregularities of surface that might in any way affect the player's stroke may not be removed or pressed down by the player, any partner, or caddies. However, ball marks on a green may be repaired before putting.
7. A player may not move, bend, or break anything fixed or growing before striking at a ball in play. This applies to holding branches out of the way and to trampling weeds to improve the lie of the ball.
8. A ball lying or touching an obstruction, such as clothing, lumber, vehicles, ground under repair, and the like, may be lifted and dropped over the shoulder away from such an object without penalty but may not be moved closer to the hole.
9. If a player's stroke is interfered with by any object such as just mentioned, the ball may be moved two club lengths, no nearer the hole, without penalty.
10. When a ball lies in a hazard, nothing shall be done that can in any way improve its lie; the club may not touch the ground in addressing the ball or during the backswing; nor may anything be touched or moved by the player before the ball is struck.
11. If a ball lies or is lost in a recognized water hazard (whether the ball lies in water or not, or in casual water in a hazard) the player may drop a ball, under penalty of 1 stroke, either behind the hazard, keeping the spot at which the ball crossed the margin of the hazard between himself or herself and the hole, or in hazard, keeping the spot at which the ball entered the water between himself or herself and the hole. If the ball was played from the teeing ground, a ball may be teed under the penalty of 1 stroke, as near as possible to the spot from which the original ball was played.

    If a ball lies or is lost in casual water (unintentional

hazard), the player may drop a ball without penalty on dry ground as near as possible to the spot where the ball lay but not nearer to the hole.

12. A golfer may have no more than 14 clubs when playing.

13. A ball is considered lost if not found within 5 minutes.

ETIQUETTE

Students should study golf etiquette carefully and govern their conduct accordingly. Golf developed as a mannerly game, and it still remains so. One should play the game by the rules without exception.

1. There should be no more than four persons in one party, and each person should have a set of clubs.
2. No one should move or talk or stand close to or directly behind the ball or the hole when a player is making a stroke.
3. On the putting green, the player whose ball lies nearest the hole should hold the pin while other players putt.
4. No player should play until golfers playing ahead are out of range.
5. Players loooking for a lost ball should allow other players coming up to pass them. They should signal to the players following them to pass, and having given such a signal, should not continue their play until these players have passed ahead and are out of range.
6. A player should see that any turf cut or displaced (a divot) by him or her is at once replaced and *pressed down*.
7. No practice shots should be attempted on any part of the course when other golfers are following.
8. Slow players should allow a faster group to play through.
9. Local course rules should be observed.
10. All shots should be played according to the rules of the game.
11. The player farthest away from the hole shoots or putts first.
12. A player should avoid walking ahead of partners or opponents.
13. The tee shot should be played from behind the markers.
14. If any player or person on the course is in danger of being hit by your shot, "fore" should be called as a warning.
15. The golf bag should always be laid down off the green.
16. Footprints in a sand trap should be smoothed out after a shot.
17. When holding the flag on the green, a player should stand so that a shadow does not fall across the cup.
18. When all players have holed out, the party leaves the putting green immediately for oncoming players.
19. When one member of a twosome, threesome, or foursome has lost a ball, all members of the group should help look for it.
20. Above all, players should be courteous.

Golf teaches the highest principles of etiquette and consideration for others.

The game is no longer enjoyable when rules are broken at random. Golf etiquette is easily understood and, when correctly observed, affords pleasure and enjoyment of the game.

TEACHING CONSIDERATIONS

1. The basic swing is usually introduced with a no. 5 iron as a full swing. It is advisable to practice without the ball until basic form is established. Golf whiffle balls are useful once the ball is introduced. This enables students to get a great deal of practice with limited equipment. Repetition is critical. Nets to hit into avoid time wasted chasing balls.
2. As soon as possible give students a distance goal to swing toward so that maximum force can be attained and the importance of form can be established.
3. Introduce woods and other irons as only slight variations of the basic swing. Emphasize the basic elements as well as critical differences between use of the woods and other irons. One wood and a no. 9 or wedge are all that are necessary for basic instruction before learners are introduced to playing a hole (or toward a distance target area).
4. Teach principles of putting but permit variations in style.
5. After learners have had experience with a wood, several irons, and putting, introduce concepts regarding the short swing, pitch and chip shots, and strategies for different lies. Each of these situations should be practiced separately and not just alluded to in instruction.
6. If possible, have learners go to a golf course before the end of the unit and not just as a culminating event. Prepare them for a particular course and review golf etiquette and rules. Learners will return to instruction highly motivated and willing to share their experiences and problems when they have had an opportunity to actually play golf.

GLOSSARY

ace Making the hole in 1 stroke.

addressing the ball Placing the body and club in position to stroke the ball.

approach shot A shot played to the green.

apron The area immediately surrounding the green.

away Ball farthest from the hole, to be played first.

banana ball Slang term for a slice.

birdie Making a hole in 1 stroke less than par.

bogey A score of 1 over par on any hole.

bunker Hazard, usually artificial, of exposed ground or sand.

caddie Assistant to the player, who watches the ball, carries the clubs, and the like.

carry The distance the ball travels through the air.

casual water Not a permanent water hazard. A ball lying in casual water may be lifted without penalty.

clubs Implements used to propel the ball.

course rating Comparative course difficulty.

cup Hole into which the ball is played.

dead Ball does not roll after flight.

divot Slice of turf cut out with club.

driver Wood, club no. 1.

eagle Two under par for any hole.

face Contact surface of the club head.

fairway The mowed or well-kept part of the area between the tee and green.

flagstick Indicates number and position of hole. The flagstick is in the hole.

fore Warning signal.

foursome Four people playing as a group.

green Short-cropped grass around a hole.

grip Handle of the club or method of grasping.

gross score Actual score shot by a player in stroke play.

halved Tied score on a hole or a complete game.

handicap Strokes given to a player to enable him or her to shoot a score of par, computed on the basis of 80% of the difference between the player's average score and par.

hazard Natural or unnatural obstacle on a course.

head Part of club used for hitting.

heel Inside part of the club head at base of shaft.

hole The cup into which the ball is rolled.

holed A ball is "holed" when it is in the cup.

hole out Final stroke for a hole.

honor Right to play first from a tee by low score on the previous hole.

hook A shot that curves to the left if hit by a right-handed golfer.

iron A club with an iron head.

lie Position of the ball on the course.

links The entire course.

loft The elevation of a shot or angle of the club face.

match A game.

match play Competition based on a hole-by-hole basis.

medal play Competition based on total strokes per round (also called stroke play).

par Expected score for a hole; a set number of strokes.

penalty stroke A stroke added to the score of a player or team for a rules violation.

pin The flagstick in the hole marking it.

press Too much tensing of muscles or swinging too hard. Also, slight forward movement of the hands before putting or swinging the club.

pull-shot A shot hit diagonally to the left (right-handed golfer).

push-shot A shot hit diagonally to the right (right-handed golfer).

rim the cup The ball rolls around the edge of the cup without falling in.

rough Rough ground and long grass off the fairway.

round Any series of holes, generally 18.

shaft The stick that holds the club head.

slice The ball curves to the right (right-handed golfer).

stance Position of the feet.

stroke Act of swinging at the ball even though it may be missed.

tee An elevation, generally a wooden peg, on which the ball is placed and from which it is to be driven.

teeing-ground Starting point for each hole; a designated area behind markers.

toe Front portion of the club head away from the shaft.

topped A ball hit above the center that rolls on the ground.

trap Usually a sand pit in the fairway and around the green.

up The number of holes or strokes by which one leads an opponent.

waggle Preliminary movements with the club as the ball is addressed.

wood A club with a wooden head.

SUGGESTED READINGS

American Alliance for Health, Physical Education, Recreation, and Dance: Official rules of bowling/golf, Reston, Va., 1983, National Association of Girls' and Women's Sports.

Bowen B and Clemence B: Golf everyone, ed 2, Winston-Salem, NC, 1984, Hunter Textbooks, Inc. Written for all ability levels, this book contains illustrations, chapter evaluations, rules, drills, and sections on conditioning and the fitness values of golf. It is easy to read, gives step-by-step explanations, and uses checkpoints.

Bunker L and Owens D: Golf: better practice for better play, West Point, NY, 1984, Leisure Press. A guide to the mental and physical aspects of golf. Examples are provided on how to implement techniques developed through practice to playing skills on the course. Practice ideas and self-testing devices designed to improve the play of every golfer are included.

Bunker L and Rotella R: Mind mastery for winning golf, Englewood Cliffs, NJ, 1981, Prentice-Hall, Inc.

Cornish G and Whitten R: The golf course, Norwalk, Conn, 1981, Golf Digest Book Services.

Dobereiner P: The world of golf, Norwalk, Conn, 1981, Golf Digest Book Services.

Ewers JR: Golf, Glenview, Ill, 1989, Scott, Foresman & Co. Geared for beginning and intermediate golfers. The book contains practice drills, methods for correcting errors, and advice on how to choose a golf course.

Gallwey TW: The inner game of golf, Norwalk, Conn, 1981, Golf Digest Book Services.

Gensemer R: Beginning golf, Englewood, Colo, 1986, Morton Publishing Co. Contains a step-by-step approach for beginning golfers and more than 200 photographs and illustrations.

Hardy M and Walsh E: Golf, ed 2, Glenview, Ill, 1986, Scott, Foresman & Co. Pointers on how to correct errors and checkpoints on fundamentals such as short game and full swing are included. Exercises for developing essential endurance, flexibility, and strength are also offered along with suggested readings. Nearly 70 illustrations.

Keogh B and Smith C: Personal par: a psychological system of golf for women, Champaign, Ill, 1985, Human Kinetics Publishers, Inc. Presents a unique mental approach enabling golfers to analyze their game to set personally challenging, yet achievable goals. Includes relaxation techniques to minimize anxieties and mental practice exercies to improve concentration.

Mackey R: Golf, learn thru auditory and visual cues, Debuque, Iowa, 1981, Kendall/Hunt Publishing Co.

Nance V and Davis E: Golf, ed 6, Dubuque, Iowa, 1990, Wm. C. Brown Group. Presents golf in a practical, step-by-step progression. Includes material on safety, etiquette, rules, attitude and technique improvement, tips on correcting errors, and equipment selection as well as several photos and drawings.

National Golf Foundation: Golf teaching and coaching kit, 1981. Includes instructor's guide, coach's guide, lessons, visual aids for instruction, planning and conducting competitive events, easy way to learn rules. 200 Castlewood Dr, North Palm Beach, FL 33408.

New York Times Scrapbook: The complete book of golf, Norwalk, Conn, 1980, Golf Digest Book Services.

Owens D: Teaching golf to special populations, West Point, NY, 1984, Leisure Press. An easy-to-read guide on how to teach golf to special populations—the physically impaired, the mentally retarded, and the visually imparied.

Owens D and Bunker LK: Golf: steps to success, Champaign, Ill, 1989, Human Kinetics Books.

Nicklaus J: Golf my way, Norwalk, Conn, 1984, Golf Digest Book Services.

Nicklaus J and Bowden K: Jack Nicklaus' lesson tee, Norwalk, Conn. 1980, Golf Digest Book Services.

Sheehan L: The whole golf catalog, Norwalk, Conn, 1980, Golf Digest Book Services.

Stock E and Carleton J: Golf: from tee to green, Dubuque, Iowa, 1985, Eddie Bowers Publishing Co. Written for golfers at all levels but most helpful for beginning and intermediate level golfers. Contains over 50 photos and diagrams, descriptions of 10 stretching exercises, and a self-evaluation problem checklist.

United States Golf Association: A junior program for your club and district, Far Hills, NJ, 1989, United States Golf Association Golf House.

United States Golf Association: Rules of golf, Far Hills, NJ, 1989, United States Golf Association Golf House.

Watson T: Rules of golf, illustrated and explained, Norwalk, Conn., 1980, Golf Digest Book Services.

FILMS AND VIDEOTAPES
Distributors

Film Comm, 1980 West Grand Ave., Chicago, IL 60610.

Golfworks, 4820 Jacksontown Rd., Newark, OH 43055.

How to Sports Videos, Box 5852, Denver, CO 80217.

JK Production, P.O. Box 525, Peoria, IL 61651.

Ladies Professional Golf Association, 1250 Shoreline Dr., Sugarland, TX 77478.

The Athletic Institute, 200 Castlewood Dr., North Palm Beach, FL 33408. Provides complete free listing of competitive and instructional films.

Professional Golf Association, 100 Ave. of the Champions, Box 12458, Palm Beach Gardens, FL 33410. Audiovisual library.

Sports Video Champions on Film, 745 State Circle, Box 1941, Ann Arbor, MI 48106.

Sports Videos, Karol Media, 22 Riverside Dr., Wayne, NJ 07470.

United States Golf Association, Golf House, Library Corner Rd., Far Hills, NJ 07931. Films for rent or purchase.

13

Gymnastics and Tumbling

Completion of this chapter should enable the reader to:

- Appreciate the historical development of gymnastics and tumbling
- Understand the importance of safety and spotting techniques
- Know the basic rules for dual-meet competitions in gymnastics
- Explain fundamental skills in vaulting, pommel horse, parallel bars, high bar, still rings, floor exercise, uneven parallel bars, and balance beam
- Demonstrate fundamental skills and techniques in tumbling activities
- Teach basic gymnastics and tumbling skills safely

Gymnastics

HISTORY

The word "gymnastics" means naked art and comes from the early Greeks. It is believed that the Chinese were the first to develop activities that resembled gymnastics. The Greeks worked with an apparatus rather than on it, whereas the Romans used an apparatus in the form of a wooden horse on which to practice in preparation for combat. The word "gymnasium" is also a Greek word and means the ground or place for gymnastic performances.

Johann Basedow (1723-1790) was the first European to teach organized gymnastic exercises. Johann Guts Muths (1759-1839), the "great-grandfather of gymnastics," published the first book on gymnastics.

After the Napoleonic victories over the Germans, a plan for building up the national strength of Germany was formulated by Frederick Jahn during the period from 1810 to 1852. Jahn is credited with introducing the parallel bars, the horizontal bar, the side horse with pommels, and the vaulting buck. He wanted the Germans to be united to protect themselves, so he took the boys of Berlin to nearby woods on hikes and there they invented these different types of apparatus. In 1842, 10 years before Jahn's death, formally structured gymnastics was introduced into the German public school.

Mats were first used in Copenhagen, Denmark, when the Military Gymnastic Institute was opened to train teachers in gymnastics.

About 1850, a wave of German immigration brought gymnastics clubs to America, where they were called Turner Societies.

In 1865, the American Turners established a Normal College of the American Gymnastic Union for training gymnastic teachers.

Gymnastics took hold through these Turner Clubs and YMCAs, schools, and colleges. Heavy apparatus, such as parallel bars, horizontal bar, side horse, rings, and balance beams, is the equipment used in most schools, colleges, clubs, and YMCA gymnasiums; the more elementary jungle gyms, teeter-totters, slides, rings, swings, and the like are used in parks and community centers.

Gymnastics in modern usage and competition generally refers to body movements on apparatus and tumbling on mats.

The use of apparatus in American public schools and colleges was impeded by three factors:

1. Around 1800 Dio Lewis introduced exercises that did not require apparatus, and the schools accepted them enthusiastically.
2. The Swedish influence around 1900 emphasized calisthenics.
3. Between World War I and World War II gymnastics

did not occupy its rightful place in the total program of high schools and colleges in the United States. The trend was toward mild recreational activities for the majority, and strenuous competition was encouraged only for a few.

Following World War II, the pendulum swung back to resistive forms of exercise, including gymnastics. Today there is considerable emphasis on competitive gymnastics in the secondary schools, YMCAs, and colleges throughout the United States.

Noteworthy developments were the organization of the National Association of American Gymnastic Coaches in 1946 and the National Gymnastic Clinic in 1951. The current ruling body for gymnastics is the United States Gymnastics Federation (USGF).

Participation in gymnastics has increased dramatically in recent years. This increase is probably in part due to the impact of the televised Olympic games during which names such as Olga Korbut, Nadia Comaneci, Kurt Thomas and Mary Lou Retton became familiar. The tremendous success of the 1984 U.S. Olympic gymnastics team will undoubtedly continue this trend. Although the strong Soviet team was not present at the 1984 Los Angeles Olympics, the team gold medal won by the men was the first American gold medal in gymnastics since 1932, and Mary Lou Retton's gold medal in the all-around event was the first individual Olympic gymnastics medal of any kind to be won by a U.S. woman. By winning the team gold, all-around silver (Peter Vidmar), pommel horse gold (Vidmar) and bronze (Tim Dagget), rings bronze (Mitch Gaylord), and parallel bars gold (Bart Connors) and silver (Mitch Gaylord), the 1984 U.S. men's team by far surpassed any previous U.S. gymnastics success. But perhaps the most dramatic moment of the 1984 summer Olympics came when Mary Lou Retton "stuck" her vault for a rare perfect score of 10 to win the all-around event. This highlight capped the best U.S. women's gymnastics performance ever with a team silver medal, vault silver (Mary Lou Retton), uneven parallel bars silver (Julianne McNamara) and bronze (Mary Lou Retton), balance beam bronze (Kathy Johnson), and floor exercise silver (Julianne McNamara) and bronze (Mary Lou Retton).

The men and women Soviet teams returned to the 1988 Olympic games with outstanding teams. Both won the team gold medal and most of the individual medals. The U.S. men's team finished a disappointing eleventh and the women's an even more disappointing fourth, with Phobe Mills capturing the only individual medal (a bronze on the beam).

The women's bid for the team bronze was crushed by a controversial 0.5 point penalty assessed by the head of the technical committee. In fact, many tremendous gymnastic performances were overshadowed by such controversies and questions about judging. Forty perfect scores of 10 were awarded to 14 gymnasts, and in the men's pommel horse, a three-way tie for the gold was awarded.

SAFETY RULES

1. Apparatus should be inspected regularly to detect faults, make proper adjustments, and remove hazards.
2. Accidents on apparatus never "just happen." They are caused by carelessness.
3. An adequate number of clean mats should be placed around the apparatus. Mats should be carried, not dragged, and should not be overlapped when placed around the apparatus. They should be folded and put away when not in use.
4. Strength and skill are built progressively; the need for progression from the simple to the more complex must be recognized.
5. Participants should master the art of spotting through instruction and by practicing with supervision.
6. Magnesium chalk on the hands will help prevent slipping. To prevent hand tear, wearing leather grips should be encouraged.
7. Fooling and horseplay should be absolutely forbidden in the gymnastics area.
8. Flexibility exercises are essential before practicing stunts. Strength development should be done after the workout.

SPOTTING

Spotting is such an important safety and teaching skill that it deserves special attention. It involves the supporting, catching, or adjusting of the performer to aid in the completion of a stunt or to prevent possible injury from landing incorrectly. Spotting can aid the performer in "getting the feel" of a stunt or sequence of stunts. It is accomplished by hand spotting or with specialized equipment such as spotting belts. The most important purpose of spotting is for safety and to prevent injury, especially of the head, neck, and spine. Whether for teaching or for safety, the spotter should (1) know what the gymnast is about to perform, (2) know what and when possible mishaps might occur, (3) know what must be done to spot and when the spot must occur, and (4) be strong enough to assist if needed. Directions for spotting are given with many of the stunts described. Where required, the spot (●) shown on the figures illustrating most of the skills indicates the points at which the instructor should offer assistance.

DUAL-MEET COMPETITION

Competition rules for high schools and colleges are written by the National Federation of State High School

Associations and the National Collegiate Athletic Association (NCAA). The USGF writes rules for competitions other than those in schools. In some states rules for high school competition are formulated by state high school coaches' associations.

Order of competition
Men

The events, in order of competition, for a dual meet are floor exercises, pommel horse, still rings, long horse vaulting, parallel bars, and high bar. Usually a 2-minute warm-up period is allowed after the meet starts in championship meets; however, none is permitted in dual meets.

Number of entries. Each team shall be limited to a maximum of six entries per event. Four of the men must be designated as all-around contestants. A gymnastics team shall be limited to 12 men.

Women

For women the order of events in competition is vaulting, uneven parallel bars, balance beam, and floor exercise.

Number of entries. The number of gymnasts from each team to compete in each event should exceed the number of scores that will count for the final team totals (for example, five entries using three scores per team or four entries using three scores per team).

Score

The best three scores for each team in each gymnastics event are totaled to determine the team's score for that event. This includes the all-around score. The event scores are totaled to determine the final team score.

Judges

Four judges plus one superior judge conduct the competition. Each of the four judges flashes a score based on 10 points, 4 points for composition and 6 points for execution. Then the low and high scores are dropped and the other two averaged. If the middle two scores are too far apart, the superior judge's score is added to the average of these two scores and then this sum is divided by two to get the final score.

EQUIPMENT
1. Pommel horse
2. Long horse
3. Parallel bars
4. Uneven parallel bars
5. Horizontal bars
6. Still rings
7. Balance beam
8. Mats
9. Carbonate of magnesium
10. Emery paper to clean bars
11. Reuther board
12. Free exercise area: 40 × 40 feet (12 × 12 m)

FUNDAMENTAL SKILLS AND TECHNIQUES

The gymnastic exercised presented here are basic movements primarily for developmental purposes. Advanced stunts and routines may be found in other sources.

Vaulting

In all gymnastics events except vaulting, several stunts and movements are linked to produce a routine. In vaulting a single stunt is performed and judged.

The vaulting event is slightly different for men and women. For men the long horse over which the vaults are made is approximately 53 inches (1.35 m) in height, and the vaults are made over the length of the horse. In women's competition the vaults are made across the width of the horse, which is approximately 43 inches (1.09 m) in height.

The vaults described and illustrated in this chapter are fundamental and seldom used in anything but the most elementary gymnastics competition. On the other hand, they are fun to learn and in some cases require courage to try the first time. The use of a reuther board is optional with the vaults presented here.

Squat vault

Use a two-foot take off, and as the hands contact the horse, push downward and as the body begins to lift, pull the knees to the chest. When the body clears the horse, extend the body. At the landing, flex at the knees, bring the arms forward for balance, and finish by standing as if at attention. (See Fig. 13-1.)

Fig. 13-1. Squat vault.

Flank vault

This is also termed the "side vault." Use a two-foot take-off and vault so that the side of the body passes over the horse. Keep the legs extended and the toes pointed. Land in a partial knee bend with the arms extended to the side. (See Fig. 13-2.)

Fig. 13-2. Flank vault.

Face vault

Use a two-foot takeoff and pass the body over the horse by doing a quarter turn so that the body faces the horse as it passes over it. Land with the side to the horse, with one hand on the horse and the other extended to the side. (See Fig. 13-3.)

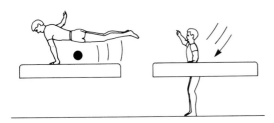

Fig. 13-3. Face vault.

Rear vault

In this vault the rear or back of the body passes over the end of the horse. If the vault is a rear vault to the right, the body makes a quarter turn to the right and passes over the horse in this position. After the body passes over the horse, place the left hand on the horse and extend the right to the side. (See Fig. 13-4.)

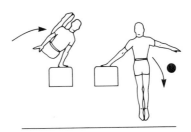

Fig. 13-4. Rear vault.

Straddle vault

Do not stop on top of the horse, but pass the body completely over it. Keep the head up. This vault should be spotted closely.

The spotter stands on the vaulter's right side and in front of the horse. Using both arms, the spotter supports the right arm of the vaulter until the vaulter jumps. The spotter then steps away from the horse to assist with the landing if required. (See Fig. 13-5.)

Fig. 13-5. Straddle vault.

Stoop vault

The stoop vault is the same as the squat vault except the legs are kept straight rather than tucked as the body passes over the horse. This requires more height, and a vaulting board should be used. A spotter should stand in front of the horse and to one side of the performer. The spotter should grasp and lift the near shoulder and use the other arm to help lift the performer's hips as they pass over the horse. (See Fig. 13-6.)

Fig. 13-6. Stoop vault.

Pommel horse

As with vaulting, the stunts described here are not normally seen in gymnastics competition but are rather fundamental to this apparatus and are lead-up activities to more advanced stunts.

Squat to rear support

Use a two-foot takeoff and pass over the horse by lifting the hips high, keeping the head up, and bringing the knees between the arms. After the feet pass over the horse, come to rest in a rear support. (See Fig. 13-7.)

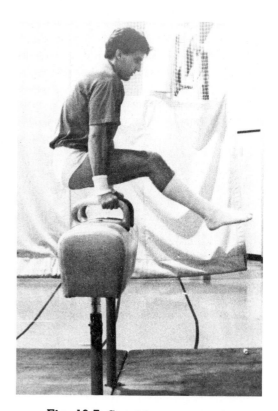

Fig. 13-7. Squat to rear support.

Feint left or right

Do this from the front support. Swing the leg up and over the end of the horse, either the right side (the croup) or the left side (the neck). If the right leg passes over the horse, turn the face to the left; if the left leg passes over the horse, turn to the right. Keep the arms fully extended, legs stiff, and toes pointed. Pass the leg over the horse and then bring it back. (See Fig. 13-8.)

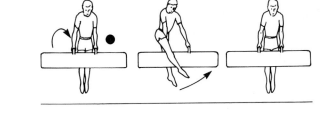

Fig. 13-8. Feint left or right.

Cut left or right

From the front-leaning support, pass the leg over the end of the horse and under one hand. To accomplish this, the weight of the body must be transferred to the opposite hand. Attempt to keep both arms and legs extended. (See Fig. 13-9.)

Fig. 13-9. Cut left or right.

Right flank to rear support, reverse flank left to front support

If the weight is kept over the horse as the flank is performed, the catch to the rear support is not difficult. To perform the reverse flank, put all the weight on the right arm. The secret of the vaults and catch is proper weight distribution. (See Fig. 13-10.)

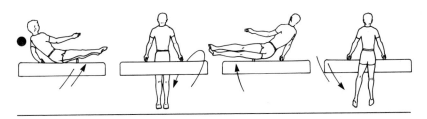

Fig. 13-10. Right flank to rear support, reverse flank left to front support.

One-half alternating single-leg circles and return

Jump to a support, lean to the left, and lift the right leg and arm. Bring the right leg forward, and replace the right hand on the right pommel. Lean on the right hand, lift the left leg and arm, swing the left leg forward, and replace the left hand on the left pommel. The performer should now be in a rear support position. Shift both legs to the right, separate them as the right arm is lifted, and return the right leg to its original position. Finally, lean on the right hand as the left leg is returned to its original position. (See Fig. 13-11.)

Fig. 13-11. One-half alternating single leg circles and return.

Parallel bars

Run and jump to cross support

Take the jump as in the dive and roll. Land in the forward-leaning position and then swing forward. *Spot for a collapse on the backswing.* Spot under the bar on the chest if a collapse takes place. (See Fig. 13-12.)

Fig. 13-12. Run and jump to cross support.

Hand traveling

1. Hand over hand, walk forward the length of the bars. Keep the chest out, head up, back arched, and toes pointed. (See Fig. 13-13.)
2. Hop the length of the bars in a straight-arm support position. In this hop forward the hands are moved simultaneously.
3. Riding a bicycle with the legs increases the difficulty. (See Fig. 13-14.)

Fig. 13-13. Hand traveling.

Fig. 13-14. Bicycle riding.

Intermediate swing

From a cross support position in the center of the bars, start to swing the body from the shoulders forward and backward. Learn to balance the center of body weight over the hand supports by leaning back when the legs are moving back.

Intermediate swing with hop

In doing the intermediate swing, keep the arms extended, flex the body on the front swing, and extend it to the back swing. The hop is executed on the front swing. *Spot this for a possible collapse right after the catch.* (See Fig. 13-15.)

Fig. 13-15. Intermediate swing with hop.

Forward swinging dips

1. Swing from the shoulders.
2. At the end of the rear swing, flex the arms, keeping the back arched and head up (Fig. 13-16).
3. Swing forward in a bent-arm position so that the chin is even with the bars in the middle of the swing.
4. At the front end of swing, straighten the arms and shoot the feet forward.

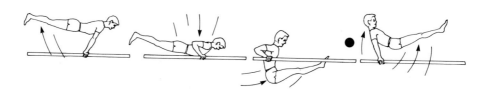

Fig. 13-16. Forward swinging dips.

Hip rise

Swing forward vigorously in the upper arm hang. Approaching the front end of the swing, pull forward with the arms and then push up to a cross support. (See Fig. 13-17.)

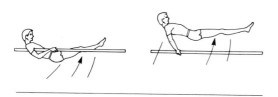

Fig. 13-17. Hip rise.

Back roll from sitting position

From a straddle-seat position in the center of the bar, grip the bar behind the back with the thumbs in. Spread the flexed elbows to make rockers. Slowly roll backward to a straddle-seat position.

Shoulder balance

Be in the center of the bar and extend elbows to be level with the shoulders. The forearms should be flexed at the elbow, with the hands on the bar. Flex the knees and place the feet on the bars. Roll the hips up first, then the legs, and arch the back to maintain balance. If you start to fall backward, keep the elbows well spread and swing downward, using the upper arms as rockers. *Always have a spotter on each side when practicing this.* (See Fig. 13-18.)

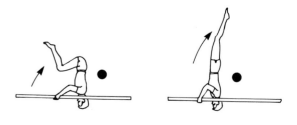

Fig. 13-18. Shoulder balance.

Dismounts

From a cross support at the center of the bars, execute one of the following dismounts over either bar:

1. Rear vault dismount, in front of hands (Fig. 13-19)
2. Front vault dismount, behind hands
3. Side vault dismount facing outward, in front of the hands

From the outside cross seat on one bar, execute a rear vault over the other bar.

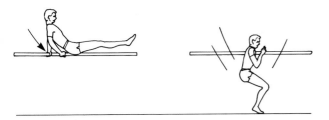

Fig. 13-19. Rear vault dismount.

Short underswing dismount

Stand under the bar; jump up and grasp the bar. From a hang position, pull the body up over the bar to a front rest, drop the trunk backward, and at the same time pike at the hips and raise the legs (straight at knees) forward until the ankles are at the bar. As the body swings downward under the bar, shoot the feet forward and pull backward and upward with the arms, shooting out forward to stand on the mat.

Single- and double-leg cut-offs

Single-leg cut-off. At the end of the forward swing, push back and cut off. *Keep the head back so that the face does not hit the bar. Spot this on both shoulders from the back.* The backward lean before the cut-off is very important. (See Fig. 13-20.)

Double-leg cut-off. Apply the same principle as in the singleleg cut-off. Cut off with both legs. Use the same spotting technique as for the single-leg cut-off (See Fig. 13-21.)

Fig. 13-20. Single-leg cut-off.

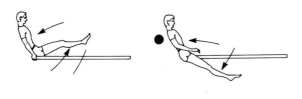

Fig. 13-21. Double-leg cut-off.

Split-off

This is nothing but a straddle vault. Be sure to keep the head up. Do not raise the hips too high. *Spot this forward on the chest and shoulders*. (See Fig. 13-22.)

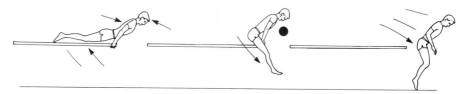

Fig. 13-22. Split-off.

High bar

Swing

Execute a short underswing from the hang and dismount.

Chins

1. Use the ordinary grasp and pull up to the chest six times.
2. Use the wide grasp and pull up to the back of the neck four times.
3. One hand grasps the bar and the other hand grasps the wrist of the chinning arm. Chin two times.
4. One hand grasps the bar and the other hand grasps the bicep of the chinning arm.

Skin the cat over the bar

From a hang position, pull the legs up through the hands and then over the bar; do not allow the body to swing.

Skin the cat

From a hang position, bring the legs up through the arms and over the head until the feet point toward the floor. Return to original position.

Monkey hang

From a hang position, bring the legs up through the arms and over the head until the feet point toward the floor. Release one arm, swing a complete turn on one arm, and then regrasp the bar.

Seat swing-up from swing

Pull the legs up through the hands and then over the bar. Arch the back and slowly pull the body up over the bar into a sitting position on top of the bar. (See Fig. 13-23.)

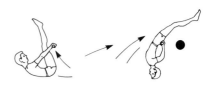

Fig. 13-23. Seat swing-up from swing.

Kip or upstart

Stress arching the back at the front of the swing and wait for the hips to start the return swing before bringing the instep to the bar. Bring the instep to the bar and shoot the legs up, out, and down. Press down and in with the shoulder muscles. Get a little wrist motion when going above the bar. Do not push away from the bar. Force the shoulders well forward. (See Fig. 13-24.)

Fig. 13-24. Kip or upstart.

Single-knee mount

From a hang position with an ordinary grasp, swing one knee over and hook it on the bar, outside or inside the arms, using either leg. Swing the other leg downward and backward and pull in with the arms, mounting to a cross seat on the top of the bar.

Hand and knee circles

From a cross-riding seat on the bar (one leg on each side of the bar) and with an ordinary grasp (thumbs in direction circle is made), reach back with the rear leg and swing it downward hard and forward. The other leg is hooked at the knee over the bar, and a complete circle backward around the bar is made. The spotter stands by to assist.

Hock swing dismount

Sit on the bar, then let the body back slowly with both knees hooked on the bar between the hands. Release the hand grip and make an underbar swing. At the end of the forward swing, snap the knees straight and swing the legs down to a stand on the mat. (See Fig. 13-25.) The spotter stands by for protection. (Wear long pants for knee hooks.)

Crotch circles

From a side-riding seat and an ordinary grasp, fall backward to start the circle. When the body is under the bar, flex and pull on the arms somewhat to complete the circle. This circle can also be executed forward with the reverse grasp, with the thumbs in the direction of the circle. This can also be performed sideways from a cross-riding seat, the hands grasping in front. Dismount with a short underswing.

Cast

From a hang position with a regular grasp, pull up to a half chin, lean the shoulders and head back, and at the same time raise the legs, holding the knees and ankles stretched and together. Shoot the legs forward and upward, at the same time extending the elbows. *Note:* As the legs swing upward and shoot outward, also shoot the body forward by pushing on the elbows for a big swing (See Fig. 13-26.) Practice this swing several times.

Fig. 13-25. Hock swing dismount.

Fig. 13-26. Cast.

Heel circle forward with reverse grip

Sit on top of and grasp the bar with a reverse or under-grip. Keep the legs extended, extend the arms, and raise the hips backward until the heels rest on the bar. Keep this position and let the body drop. Slightly alter the hand and leg relationship. Start the hip extension. Drive the legs over the bar. Return to a sitting position. (See Fig. 13-27.)

Fig. 13-27. Heel circle forward with reverse grip.

Stem rise

A requisite for this skill is a good cast. After the cast, swing down and back in an extended posture. At the end of the back swing, pike, raise the back and shoulders, and lift the body above the bar by pushing down with the hands. Place the body weight over the bar by leaning over the bar and arching. Come to the front-learning support. (See Fig. 13-28.)

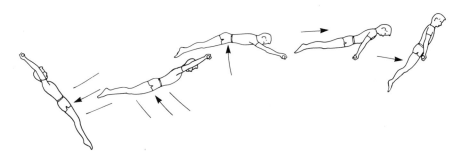

Fig. 13-28. Stem rise.

Hip circle forward

Pull over to a front-leaning support. Push down with the arms and raise the body so that the thighs rest on the bar. With the head held up, fall forward, keeping the thighs in contact with the bar. Hold this position. Shorten the radius on the upswing by forcing the head forward and bending the arms. Come to a rest over the bar.

Cast to handstand

Practice this first on the low bar. Practice with both grips. Assume a front-leaning support position. Slightly flex the arms so that the bar contacts the lower abdomen and swing the legs under the bar as the body leans forward. Forcefully hyperextend the body and push with the arms as the body weight remains over the bar. (See Fig. 13-29.)

Fig. 13-29. Cast to handstand.

Half giant swing

Use the overgrip (palms down). Start cast as for a handstand, but push back. Swing down fully extended. At the 5-o'clock position, break at the waist and come to a rest on the bar. (See Fig. 13-30.)

Fig. 13-30. Half giant swing (overgrip).

Still rings
Double front cut-off

From a pike hang position, rotate the body forward vigorously, bending the elbows, and at the same time bring the separated legs, with the knees bent, down across the elbows. Immediately after this, and while still rotating forward, release the rings and land standing on the mat (See Fig. 13-31.)

Fig. 13-31. Double front cut-off.

Double back cut-off

From a bent-arm hang, swing the legs and hips upward vigorously, spreading the legs held straight until the crotch is astride the wrists. While the body still has momentum, release the rings and land in a standing position. (See Fig. 13-32.) *Spot the back and shoulders.*

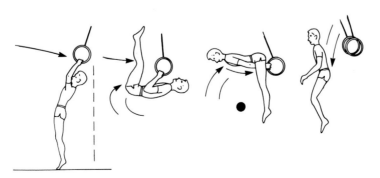

Fig. 13-32. Double back cut-off.

Front roll with arms flexed

This is a good stunt for the weight lifter, the body builder, or the student who has been working apparatus for quite a while. It takes strength. Use a low ring to spot. Jump to the cross support position. Lower the shoulders and raise the hips. Do not turn the hands as you perform this first move. As the body falls over, supinate the hands. Do not let the shoulders drop. As the body turns forward, pull up as high as possible and pronate the hands. This move should bring the weight above the rings and on the arms. Now perform a push-up. *Spot by lifting the performer above the rings*. (See Fig. 13-33.)

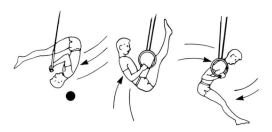

Fig. 13-33. Front roll with arms flexed.

Shoulder stand

Lower the rings to about 3 feet (0.91 m) from the floor. Now stand up on a chair or stool. Grasp the rings from the inside. Raise the hips slowly as the shoulders are lowered. On the first couple of tries steady the body by locking the legs around the ropes. Keep the eyes at all times on the mats: If the head is flexed, the body will somersault. Eventually arch the back and bring the feet together. Keep the rings close to the shoulders at all times. *Spot this by keeping the performer from turning over too quickly*. (See Fig. 13-34.)

Fig. 13-34. Shoulder stand.

Muscle-up

Grasp the rings with the false or high grip. The body should be suspended on the wrists. Execute a pull-up as high as the chest. As the height of the pull-up is completed, the feet should be raised to about a 30-degree angle. Now drop the legs down and pronate the hands as the arms are inwardly rotated. This action should place you above the rings. Now push up, arch the back, and hold the head up. *Spot this by helping to lift the performer above the difficult level.* (See Fig. 13-35.)

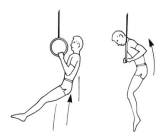

Fig. 13-35. Muscle-up or pull- and push-up.

Kip

Put the rings down to chest high. Grasp them from the outside. Now take a half step backward. Lift one leg and then the other into the pike position. Swing forward, and on the backward swing extend rapidly at the waist as you push down with the hands. Force the head and shoulders forward and up. This action should place the body in a cross-support position. *Spot this in the middle of the back through the waist extension.* (See Fig. 13-36.)

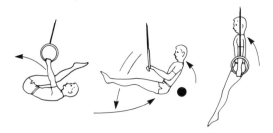

Fig. 13-36. Kip.

Standing back or reverse cut-off

This is not a difficult stunt to master. The important thing is the timing. The level of the rings should be just above the head. Grasp the rings from the outside. While holding the rings, fall off balance. Just as the body falls off balance, pull up to a half bend, throw the head back, and flex rapidly at the waist. Hold on as the body rotates until you can see the mat, and then release the hands. *Spot with the spotter's right hand over the performer's left arm and on the chest, the left hand in the small of the back to turn the performer.* (See Fig. 13-37.)

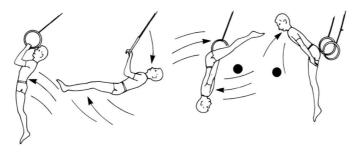

Fig. 13-37. Standing back or reverse cut-off.

Reverse uprise or back kip

Study the figures closely. On the forward swing, go into the pike. Immediately, without a swing in the pike position, lift the hips above the rings by quickly pulling up. Now, without losing momentum, hyperextend the head and shoulders. Push down forcefully with the hands. End in a cross-support position. This is accomplished most easily with the false grip. *Spot this under the shoulders.* (See Fig. 13-38.)

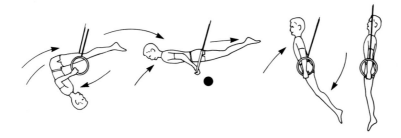

Fig. 13-38. Reverse uprise or back kip.

Stem rise

The important move in this stunt is from the pike to hyperextension. The hips should drop out of the pike first. After the hips drop, whip the legs back and then up. Push down hard with the hands, and bring the body to rest in the cross position. (See Fig. 13-39.) *Spot a possible overthrow.*

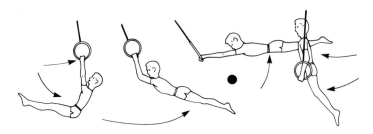

Fig. 13-39. Stem rise.

Floor exercise

Floor exercise is performed on a thin resilient pad or mat, within an area 40 × 40 feet (12 × 12 m).

Floor exercise contains dance movements, including leaps and poses, elements of dance combinations, acrobatics, and tumbling grouped in rhythmic and harmonious patterns. Through these and other movements, the gymnast explores tempo, height, distance, mood, direction, and precision or form. The basic elements of form are balance, good body alignment, and full body extension (including pointed toes).

The routines, which are performed to music for women and without music for men, generally begin and end with a sequence of tumbling. The main part, or body, of the routine consists of dance movements, balances, and flexibility stunts.

The gymnast tries to create an artistic image. The composition is developed into a coherent pattern showing a change of pace, vitality, expression, individuality, and originality.

A great part of an individual's success involves adhering to an established and well-defined routine that includes elements which are not too difficult for the performer. Once the routine is composed it must be practiced consistently.

Learning methods

The elementary movements as well as combinations must be adapted not only to the age and sex of the students but also to their mental and physical abilities.

1. Learn skills first—simple, fundamental, elementary movements.
2. Combine various skills into series; combine dance steps and tumbling and make them into a simple routine.
3. Set routines to music for women gymnasts.
4. Warm up properly with stretching and flexibility exercises before trying the routine.

A few movements that may be used in a floor exercise routine are described.

Toe rise or stand

Take a standing position. Rise up on your toes and extend your arms sideward and back with the palms of your hands facing up and out, chest up, shoulders down. Lower your heels to the floor as you drop your arms at your sides to return to a full stand. (See Fig. 13-40.)

Fig. 13-40. Toe rise.

Body wave

Start with the body partially flexed—knees, hips, back, and head. Balance on the toes, with arms reaching forward but relaxed; then hyperextend the body and drop the arms down and back and the head forward. Last, extend the head, raise the body tall, and elevate the arms. (See Fig. 13-41.)

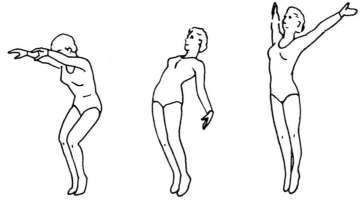

Fig. 13-41. Body wave.

Body sweep

Kneel on one knee and place your hand at a comfortable distance and on line with the knee to acquire equal distribution of weight. Swing the other arm forward and extend the other leg backward. (See Fig. 13-42.)

Balance seat

Sit on the floor with your back straight, legs together, and your hands on the floor in back of your hips. (Your arms may be raised outward from the shoulders.) Raise your legs to make a V with your trunk. (See Fig. 13-43.)

Fig. 13-42. Body sweep.

Fig. 13-43. Balance seat.

Split

Stand with one leg ahead of the other and slowly lower the body downward into a split. (See Fig. 13-44.)

Fig. 13-44. Split.

One-leg balance

Take a standing position. Raise one leg to the side and as high as possible. Grasp the instep of your raised leg with one hand and extend the other arm to a horizontal or upward position. (See Fig. 13-45.)

Fig. 13-45. One-leg balance.

Front scale

Take a standing position. Raise one leg backward and upward as the chest moves forward. As you balance on one foot, extend your arms horizontally in front of you. Keep your head up and arch your back. (See Fig. 13-46.)

Arabesque

Take a standing position. Raise one leg horizontally backward. Balance on one foot and hold your arms out to the side and slightly back for balance. (One arm may be raised, and one out to the side.) Allow your body to lean slightly forward and at the same time keep your head and chest almost vertical. (See Fig. 13-47.)

Fig. 13-46. Front scale.

Fig. 13-47. Arabesque.

Handstand

Place your hands on the mat, shoulder-width apart with your fingers pointing forward. Keep your arms straight, head up, and eyes forward. Kick upward. Extend the shoulders and hold stomach and buttocks tight. Do not arch the back. (See Fig. 13-48.)

Fig. 13-48. Handstand.

Back walkover

From a standing position with the arms raised over the head, bring one leg (extended) up parallel with the floor. As the hips shift forward reach back, arch the back, and place the hands with the fingers pointing forward on the mat. As the hands contact the mat, kick the leg that was originally raised and push with the other leg to complete the walkover. Spot by kneeling on the side of the raised leg, support the performer's back with an extended right arm, and use the left hand to assist the movement of the raised leg during the kicking portion of the stunt. (See Fig. 13-49.)

Fig. 13-49. Back walkover.

Front walkover

Take a standing position. Go into a handstand and let your feet continue on over to the floor. Land on one foot. Lift your hands off the floor, bringing your body to an upright position, and then bring your other foot to the floor. (See Fig. 13-50.)

Fig. 13-50. Front walkover.

Valdez to handstand

Sit on the floor. Place one hand on the floor in back of your hip and to the side; simulate a wide grip. Raise your other arm shoulder high and turn the palm of that hand upward. Bend one leg so that the sole of your foot is on the floor near your seat and your knee is near your chest. Extend the other leg. (A Valdez can be done on the same arm with either leg bent. For some it is easier to have the bent leg on the same side as the supporting arm.) From this position, throw your head straight back and your raised arm overhead and directly to the rear. (The hand is twisted, but the throw is directly back.) Lift the extended leg upward. (The move will be on one plane with one dimension—a straight line back like a flip-flop.) Speed is picked up with a vigorous leg push and a strong head and arm throw. A handstand is assured with an extended head throw. (See Fig. 13-51.)

Fig. 13-51. Valdez to handstand.

Uneven parallel bars

One of the last pieces of apparatus to be added to the sport of gymnastics was the uneven parallel bars. The routines performed on this apparatus are sort of a cross between those performed on the horizontal bar and on the parallel bars. Originally the routines included predominately pretty and graceful positions, but over the years the event has become one of fast, powerful swinging movements. The following stunts and their explanations are basic to more complex stunts but still require much time and practice to master.

Jump to front support

Stand facing the low bar. With the hands on the bar and with the hands in an over-grip, jump so that the body comes to rest on a straight-arm support. (See Fig. 13-52.)

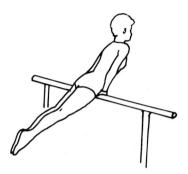

Fig. 13-52. Jump to front-leaning support.

Back pullover

Grasp the low bar with an overhand grasp. Kick one leg (extended) forward while pulling the hips toward the bar with the hands. Bring the two legs together and rotate around the bar to a front support position. (See Fig. 13-53.)

Fig. 13-53. Back pullover.

Cast to dismount

Start in a front support position on the low bar (facing the high bar), with an overhead grip. Pike at the waist around the low bar. Push back with the heels and against the bar with the thighs while pushing down on the bar with the arms. Continue to grip the bar until the body is parallel with the floor. As the descent from this position begins, push away from the bar, extending at the shoulders, release the grip, and land on the feet facing the bar. (See Fig. 13-54.)

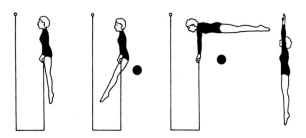

Fig. 13-54. Cast to dismount.

Forward mill circle

Start with one leg on either side of the bar (stride support) and an underhand grip (palms forward). Lift the body as high and as far forward as possible. As the rotation begins, extend the upper body out from the bar as far as possible. At the bottom of the downswing, curve the body slightly forward to shorten the radius and continue the rotation until the starting position is reached. (See Fig. 13-56.)

Fig. 13-56. Forward mill circle.

Back hip circle

Start from a front support position. Push away (cast) and then return to the bar. As the hips touch the bar, they allow the body to pike slightly at the waist and lean back with the shoulders as the legs come forward around the bar. Rotate around the bar and extend from the pike as the rotation is completed. Learn this stunt on the low bar before trying it on the high bar, and use a spotter during the learning phase. (See Fig. 13-55.)

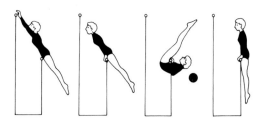

Fig. 13-55. Back hip circle.

Front hip circle

Use an overhand grip and start in the front support position. Lean forward while pushing against the bar to extend the upper body. As the bottom of the downswing is reached, begin to pike slightly at the waist and pull against the bar to shorten the radius for the upswing. Continue the rotation until the original starting position is attained. (See Fig. 13-57.)

Fig. 13-57. Front hip circle.

Single-leg stem rise

Start by sitting on the low bar and grasping the high bar with an overhead grip. Flex one leg and place that foot on the low bar while raising the other leg (extended) to the high bar. Pull with the arms, push against the low bar with the support foot, and extend the straightened leg up against the high bar. Finish in a support position on the high bar. (See Fig. 13-58.)

Fig. 13-58. Single-leg stem rise.

Glide kip

Facing the low bar and about 3 feet away from it, jump upward with the hips as the upper body reaches the bar. Grasp the bar with straight arms and begin the downswing with a pike at the hips. As the rotation continues, straighten at the hips so that an extended position is attained. As the height of the forward swing is reached, immediately pike at the hips and bring the legs to the bar, creating a pike position. Immediately "shoot the legs up the bar" as the body extends and the arms push down on the bar. Finish with a front support position on the bar. (See Fig. 13-59.)

Fig. 13-59. Glide kip.

Penny flip dismount

Sit in the low bar, reach up and grasp the high bar, and move backward until the knees are in contact with the low bar. Hook the knees around the low bar and lift the hips until the body is in a straight line from the shoulders to the knees. Release the grip on the high bar. As the rotation around the knees is completed (the upper body should travel beyond parallel to the floor) unhook the knees, bring the legs under the body, and stand facing away from the low bar. (See Fig. 13-60.)

Fig. 13-60. Penny flip dismount.

Balance beam

Routines on the balance beam involve many of the stunts that are performed in floor exercise except that they must be accomplished on a beam only 4 inches wide (10.2 cm) and approximately 16 feet long (4.88 m). The routine on the beam must be continuous and smooth and include tumbling, dance-type movements, and not more than three static or balance positions.

After mounting the beam (somtimes with the use of a reuther board) various tumbling stunts (described later in this chapter) are interspersed with locomotor combinations. The routine is completed with some form of dismount. The routine performed in competition has a minimum and a maximum time limit.

Any number of sequences can be developed from the positions illustrated in Fig. 13-61. Examples of elementary, intermediate, and advanced routines are shown in Figs. 13-62, 13-63, and 13-64.

Fig. 13-61. Balance beam; pass through positions.

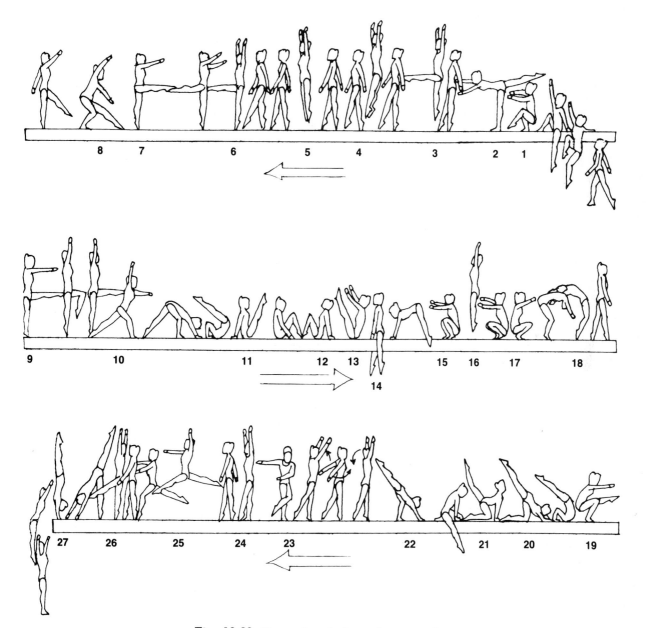

Fig. 13-62. Elementary balance beam routine.

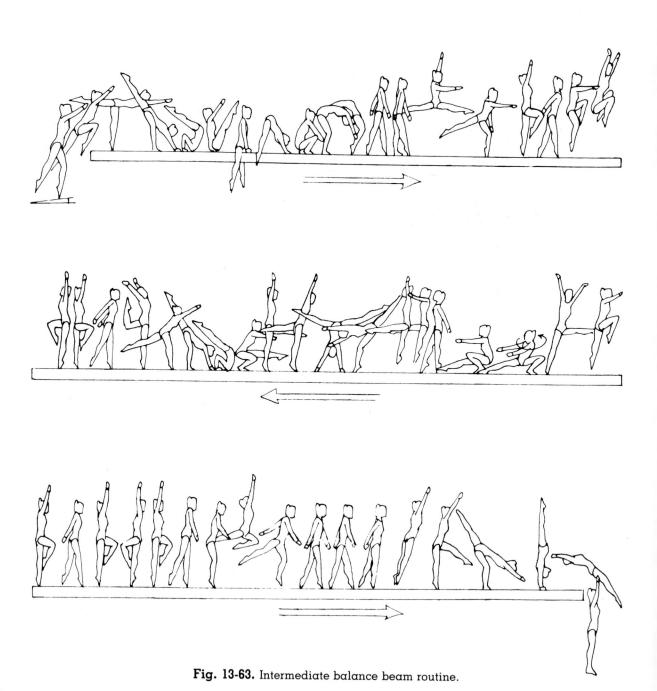

Fig. 13-63. Intermediate balance beam routine.

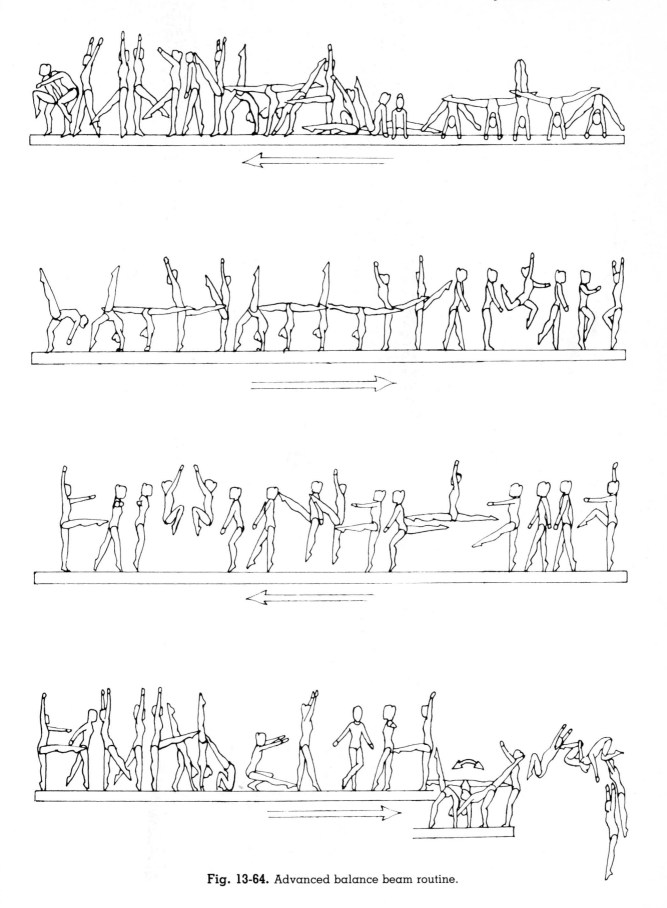

Fig. 13-64. Advanced balance beam routine.

Tumbling

Tumbling is the art of manipulating the body in feats of skill without the use of apparatus. Tumbling maneuvers include rolls, somersaults, twists, springs, balances on hands, and manipulation of the body in unusual positions.

From primitive times and through all stages of development, people have nurtured the desire to learn new ways to move the body. Tumbling offers such an outlet.

HISTORY

The earliest historical records, in the form of painting, sculpture, and literature, indicate that tumbling was connected with the dance, a most fundamental activity. Tumblers of early times had an important influence on entertainment and the theater, and in Greece and Rome tumblers entertained at private dinner parties and social occasions. Tumbling was also popular during the Middle Ages.

The word tumble is Teutonic in origin and means to dance violently or to dance with posturing, balancing, and contortions. The terms used by other nationalities showed similar spelling and embodied the same activities of somersaulting, rolling, and contorting the body.

There is no question that springboard diving in swimming pools and rebound tumbling on the trampoline have been influenced by the tumbling art.

EQUIPMENT

A firm, padded. nonslippery mat is all that is necessary.

Gymnastics slippers and a proper gymnasium uniform are adequate.

FUNDAMENTAL SKILLS AND TECHNIQUES

Tumbling provides an excellent means for developing agility, poise, balance, and coordination as well as being helpful in development of physical fitness. Success in learning new skills gives the individual self-confidence, courage, and determination.

A great number of stunts and tumbling skills can be learned. Those presented are individual, elementary, and fundamental and form a basis to advance to the more difficult skills. A vast number of companion (or pairs) exercises can be introduced into a program. Pyramid building can also be used. Also a routine in which several of the single stunts presented can be done in progression is a fun and rewarding exercise.

Lead-up developmental exercises

Animal walks (Figs. 13-65 to 13-72) should be used as part of the conditioning program. The snail drag is especially good for developing the upper body.

Fig. 13-65. Galloping dog. Run on all fours.

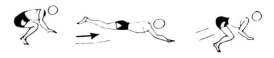

Fig. 13-66. Frog hop. Dive to hands and land in squat.

Fig. 13-67. Crab walk. Belly up.

Fig. 13-68. Elephant walk. Keep knees stiff and spread feet.

Fig. 13-69. Wet-cat footwalk. Walk on three limbs and shake one.

Fig. 13-70. Bear walk. Same as elephant walk but feet together.

Fig. 13-71. Kangaroo hop or donkey kick. Place hands on mat, kick feet in air, and land in squat position with hands still on mat. Reach forward and repeat.

Fig. 13-72. Snail drag. Keep legs inactive and drag body with arms.

First-level stunts

Beginning tumblers should never work without a spotter. Use safety belts when necessary. See that mats are always in place.

The following are considered progressive ability stunts of the first level of proficiency.

Spinal rock. Keep the head up, grasp the shins, pull tight, and rock. (See Fig. 13-73.)

Fig. 13-73. Spinal rock.

Forward roll. Reach forward, duck the head well under, round the back, roll, and tuck. (See Fig. 13-74.)

Fig. 13-74. Forward roll.

Forward roll to back. Complete the forward roll but do not lift the head after passing over it. (See Fig. 13-75.)

Fig. 13-75. Forward roll to back.

Forward roll—arms folded. Cross the arms, place the head on the mat, and then roll. Keep the arms folded until back on the feet. (See Fig. 13-76.)

Fig. 13-76. Forward roll—arms folded.

Forward roll—arms horizontal. Extend the arms to the side, place the head on the mat, and roll with a tight flexion. Keep the arms horizontal until completion of the roll. (See Fig. 13-77.)

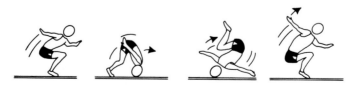

Fig. 13-77. Forward roll—arms horizontal.

Forward roll—legs crossed. Cross the legs. Reach well forward, duck the head well under, roll tight, and tuck. Make a half turn on ascending.

Forward roll—holding toes. Spread the knees apart and do a deep knee bend. Reach down between the knees and grasp the toes. Now place the back of the head on the mat and roll. Force the head and shoulders forward.

Backward roll over shoulder. Lie supine on the mat, place the right hand down by the side and the left arm out to the side, turn the head to the right, and bring the knees up and over the left shoulder. Land on the knees. (See Fig. 13-78.)

Fig. 13-78. Backward roll over shoulder.

Backward roll. Begin in a squat position with the fingers pointing forward. Put the hands behind the hips, make the back round and roll to the rear. Break the "fall" with the hands. As soon as the weight is off the hands move them to the top of the shoulders with the fingers pointing backward to take the weight off of the neck. Keep the chin tucked to the chest and the knees together throughout the movement.

Backward roll—pike. Bend forward with the knees stiff, place the hand behind the thighs, drop back to the seat, raise the legs, and roll straight over the head. (See Fig. 13-79.)

Fig. 13-79. Backward roll—pike.

Backward extension roll. Start as for the backward roll-pike, but when the weight is on the shoulders, shoot the legs to the ceiling and push hard with the hands (See Fig. 13-80.)

Fig. 13-80. Backward extension roll.

Football roll. Spread the feet apart, bend over, and place the left hand on the mat, Reach under the left arm with the right. Drop to the right shoulder, roll over, and roll across the back from the right shoulder to the left hip. Get up on the left knee and then step up on the right foot. (See Fig. 13-81.)

Fig. 13-81. Football roll.

Tripod. Make a triangle with the head and hands. Slowly place the knees on the elbows. (See Fig. 13-82.)

Fig. 13-82. Tripod.

Headstand. Be sure that the head and hands form a good triangle. Place the forehead, not the top of the head, on the mat. Raise the hips by straightening the back. Now raise the legs slowly. (See Fig. 13-84.)

Flying angel. Bottom performer lifts the top performer over the body slowly. Top performer then arches the back and raises the head. (See Fig. 13-83.)

Fig. 13-83. Flying angel.

Fig. 13-84. Headstand.

Cartwheel. Begin in a standing position with the side of the body facing down the length of the mat and the arms extended overhead. Rock back on the back leg and then to the forward leg. Place the front hand down on the mat. As the other hand comes over, place it on the mat in line with the first hand. At the same time push with the front leg and swing the back leg up and over the body. Keep the head up and watch the hands as they are placed on the mat. When the stunt is completed the performer should be facing the same way as at the start (See Fig. 13-85.)

Fig. 13-85. Cartwheel.

Cheststand on partner. Place the chest on the back of the partner, grasp the upper arm and thigh, kick slowly into position, hold tight, and arch the back slightly. (See Fig. 13-86.)

Fig. 13-86. Cheststand on partner.

Two high. The important move here is the hand position. Top performer stands in back of the bottom performer. Bottom performer reaches over the shoulders with the palms up. Top performer places the palms in the bottom performer's. Holding this hand position, the two face each other. The position now should be like shaking hands with the left hands, right hands over the head. Top performer places the left foot on the bottom performer's left thigh. This is done from the side with the toe of the top performer pointing in toward the middle of the bottom performer's body. As the bottom performer pulls with the right hand, the top performer steps up on the shoulder. (See Fig. 13-87.)

Fig. 13-87. Two high.

Handstand support. Keep the head up as you kick up. The catcher should stand to the side to prevent being kicked in the face. (See Fig. 13-88.)

Fig. 13-88. Handstand support.

Headstand in hands. Place the forehead in the hands and the forearms on the mat. Kick up slowly. (See Fig. 13-89.)

Fig. 13-89. Headstand in hands.

Second-level stunts

The following are exercises for those who have advanced to a more progressive level of tumbling skill. They represent the second level of proficiency.

Triple roll. From the three-performer lying position, the middle performer rolls to the left, and the performer on the left springs from the hands and knees over the middle performer, landing in the middle. The middle performer always rolls under and executes only one full turn and comes to rest on hands and knees. This is repeated from left to right. (See Fig. 13-90.)

Fig. 13-90. Triple roll.

Dive and roll over three performers. First teach a simple dive and roll. Use a two-foot takeoff. Be sure to dive high enough. Land first on the hands, then duck the head and roll. Flex the body tight and tuck if possible. (See Fig. 13-91.)

Fig. 13-91. Dive and roll over three performers.

Headspring over mat. The best way to learn this is to do a flexed handstand. Let the body fall off balance. Just as the balance is lost, kick hard and push with the hands. (See Fig. 13-92.)

Fig. 13-92. Headspring over mat.

Double roll with partner. Hold onto each other's ankles. Flex the knees and place the feet on the floor close to the thighs. Spread the knees apart so that the performer on top can duck the head and roll. This is important. Each person should work hard to help the other performer. (See Fig. 13-93.)

Fig. 13-93. Double roll with partner.

Fish dive. Take a standing position. Kick either foot backward and upward and jump off the other foot. Land on the hands, with the feet over the head (handstand position). Now bend the arms and let the body down, rolling from the chest to the knees. Flex at the waist and push hard with the hands until the weight is back over the feet. Lift the body to the squat stand. (See Fig. 13-94.)

Fig. 13-94. Fish dive.

Dive cartwheel. To do this stunt properly, take about a 10-yard run, finish with a short hop, dive about 5 feet, and do a cartwheel. (See Fig. 13-95.)

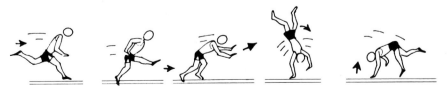

Fig. 13-95. Dive cartwheel.

Tiger stand. Try to keep the upper arm perpendicular to the floor and kick up slowly. (See Fig. 13-96.)

Fig. 13-96. Tiger stand.

Mule kick. The best way to start this is from the handstand. Slightly bend the knees and bend the arms. Snap the legs downward and push hard with the arms. This is the true landing position—body bent forward and arms reaching backward and upward. Immediately use the lift of the arms, and jump back up into the handstand position. As the jump is made, keep the head down. (See Fig. 13-97.)

Fig. 13-97. Mule kick.

Round-off. Facing the far end of the mat, take several running steps and do a skip step. Throw the arms downward and place the front hand on the mat about 18 inches in front of the front foot. The second hand is then placed in front and slightly forward (not on the same line) of the first hand. At the same time push with the front leg and drive the other leg upward. As the legs come overhead bring them together, turn the body and arch slightly to finish with a mule kick. At the finish, the performer should be facing the opposite direction from the start. (See Fig. 13-98.)

Fig. 13-98. Round-off.

Fifteen-second handstand. Kick into a good balance and lock. Keep the head in line and use the fingers. Point the toes and tighten the muscles through the hips.

Pitch-back flip. Top performer stands in the palms of the bottom performer. On the count of three, the top performer throws the arms straight for the ceiling and jumps with all his or her strength. The top performer then throws the head back and forcibly brings the knees up to give rotation. As the top performer jumps, the bottom performer lifts straight up and sits back to prevent being kicked in the face. The thing to watch for in this stunt is the overthrow. Be sure to have a spotter or safety belt. This is very important. Never attempt this skill without spotting. (See Fig. 13-99.)

Fig. 13-99. Pitch-back flip.

Pitch from belly. This is a handspring with the assistance of the bottom performer. The top performer places the stomach on the bottom performer's feet. The feet are placed in a V—heels together, toes apart. The bottom performer pulls the top performer forward, and as all the top performer's weight is felt, the bottom performer pulls the top performer's upper body forward and pushes hard with the feet. As the top performer's weight passes over, the bottom performer pushes with the hands. It is important to have at least one spotter assisting so that the top performer does not overthrow (See Fig. 13-100.)

Kip from mat. While in the lying position, place the hands over the shoulders on the floor and roll back until the weight is on the back of the head and shoulders. As the body is rolled forward slightly, shoot the legs up in the air and push hard with the hands. The legs should go up and forward. (See Fig. 13-101.)

Fig. 13-101. Kip from mat.

Fig. 13-100. Pitch from belly.

Roll-over kip from mat. Start this as a forward roll. Immediately on contact of the shoulders with the floor or mat, kip as in the preceding exercise. (See Fig. 13-102.)

Fig. 13-102. Roll-over kip from mat.

Headspring. This is executed from the top of the head. Place the head on the mat with the hands slightly forward. Keep the knees flexed as the body falls off balance. As the body rolls past center, kick hard as in the kip and push hard with the hands. (See Fig. 13-103.)

Fig. 13-103. Headspring.

Front handspring. Take about a 5-yard run, hop, and whip the hands to the mat. Kick one foot hard backward and upward and push hard with the other. Keep the head up and the arms extended. As the legs pass over the head, give a little kick, flex at the wrist, and land on the feet. (See Fig. 13-104.)

Fig. 13-104. Front handspring.

Back flip. Stand with the arms outstretched. Drop the arms down, and flex the knees to about a quarter knee bend. Throw the arms over the head as hard and fast as possible so that the body is lifted off the floor. Jump with the arm lifted as high as possible. Throw the head back and bring the knees up to the chest. Tuck and let out. This should never be done without a spotter. The overhead mechanic should be used. (See Fig. 13-105.)

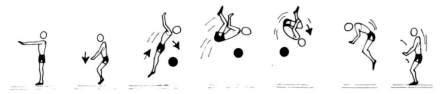

Fig. 13-105. Back flip.

Front flip. There are many different ways to throw this stunt, but the best is the two-arm backward-upward lift. Take about a 10-yard run. Use a two-foot take-off. From the take-off, which is executed in a one-quarter forward bend, jump hard and throw the arms with much force backward and upward. Roll over in the air into a tight tuck, and let out. (See Fig. 13-106.)

Fig. 13-106. Front flip.

Back handspring. This is performed as though sitting on a chair. Sit with the back straight and swing the arms down and back. Keep the feet flat on the floor. Just as the body falls off balance, whip the arms over the head and throw the head back. As the arms are thrown back, reach for the floor and throw the belly to the ceiling. Snap to the feet. (See Fig. 13-107.)

Fig. 13-107. Back handspring.

TEACHING CONSIDERATIONS

1. Although the apparatus activities described in this chapter are basic to more advanced skills, they require physical abilities not developed in many students. Particular amounts of arm strength, abdominal strength, and flexibility are necessary in many cases for students to be able to learn these skills successfully. Teachers must choose either to develop these prerequisites or to modify downward the expectations for learning. Students' attempting skills for which they do not have prerequisite abilities creates safety problems.

2. Many tumbling skills are basic to apparatus work. Because of this, many teachers choose to teach tumbling skills at first or build in tumbling skills with apparatus work. Tumbling skills permit more activity practice for larger numbers of students.

3. Checklists of skills on apparatus that go from simple to complex are often helpful for students to know what to work on and also for teachers to evaluate student progress. The emphasis must be on good form and not merely getting through an action.

4. It is often helpful to introduce a piece of apparatus to the whole group but then use stations of different apparatus to practice. Teachers can make the decision to be at one or two stations for a period or to rotate as needed. Stations can be organized so that groups rotate at a signal from the teacher, or individuals can move freely from one station to another.

5. Some students can perform some skills without spotters. Aerial skills in particular should be performed with trained spotters or should not be performed without the teacher. Instruction should continuously emphasize control of movement. Crashes and abandonment of control should never be permitted.

6. It is often desirable to have a culminating experience involving performance in gymnastics units toward which students can work. Students can choose one or two events and work to put sequences together. They can practice even the simplest moves until they perform them with smooth transitions and good form.

SUGGESTED READINGS

Brown JR and Wardell D: Teaching and coaching gymnastics for men and women, New York, 1980, John Wiley & Sons, Inc. Contains material on history, organizing programs, safety and spotting hints, workout schedules, organizing competitive meets, psychology of coaching, liability, and routines for all gymnastic events.

Cooper P: Feminine gymnastics, Minneapolis, 1980, Burgess Publishing Co.

Cornelius WL: Gymnastics, Englewood, Colo, 1983, Morton Publishing Co. Provides gymnastics progression from individual skills and short combinations to compulsory routines for men. Also contains material on equipment and strength and flexibility programs.

George GS: Bio-mechanics of women's gymnastics, Englewood Cliffs, NJ, 1980, Prentice-Hall, Inc.

Nobel DK: Gymnastics for kids age 3-7, Champaign, Ill, Human Kinetics Publishers, Inc. An illustrated guide for parents and instructors.

National Association for Girls' and Women's Sports: Gymnastics guide 1989-93, Reston, Va, American Alliance for Health, Physical Education, Recreation and Dance.

National Collegiate Athletic Association: Official gymnastics rules, Phoenix, 1989, College Athletics Publishing Service.

Sands B: Coaching women's gymnastics, Champaign, Ill, 1984, Human Kinetics Publishers, Inc. What coaches should know about setting reasonable goals, schedule and training load, facility and equipment, support staff, warm-ups, overtraining, and psychological and technical preparation.

Unestahl LE: The mental aspects of gymnastics, Ithaca, NY, 1983, Mouvement Publications. Describes a systematic approach to mental training and mental preparation as applied to gymnastics.

Warren M: The new book of gymnastics, London, 1980, Arthur Barker, Ltd.

FILMS AND VIDEOTAPES

Gymnastics films or videotapes may be obtained from the following: American Alliance for Health, Physical Education, Recreation, and Dance, 1900 Association Dr., Reston, VA 22091.

Association Films, 561 Hill Grove Ave., La Grange, IL 60525.

Athletic Institute, 200 Castlewood Dr., North Palm Beach, FL 33408. Six videos, including one on rhythmic gymnastics.

Donn Clegg, 501 S. Highland Ave., Champaign, IL 61820.

Frank Endo, 18011 La Salle, Gardena, CA 90248.

Gymnastics Aids, Inc., Northbridge, MA 01534.

How To Sports Video, Box 5852, Denver, CO 80127. Twelve videos, including three on beginning, intermediate and advanced tumbling.

Sports Film Library, U.S. Olympic Committee, Olympic House, 57 Park Ave., New York, NY 10016.

Sports Video: Champions on Film, 745 State Circle, Box 1941, Ann Arbor, MI 48106. Eight videos, including one each featuring the men's and women's USSR gymnastics team.

Glen Sundby, 410 Broadway, Santa Monica, CA 90406.

United States Gymnastic Federation, P.O. Box 7686, Fort Worth, TX 76111.

RECORDS

Records for artistic and rhythmic gymnastics may be obtained from the following:

Barry Nease Studio, R.D. 1, Box 114, Boalsburg, PA 16827.

Chiswichord, 18 Grosvenor Rd., Chiswick, London W44#H, England.

Hoctor Dance Records, Inc., P.O. Box 38, Waldwick, NJ 05463.

Kimbo Educational Records, Box 55, Deal, NJ 07723.

Orion Records, Inc., 614 Davis St., Evanston, IL 60436.

Hugo Sartorello, 5058 N. 83rd St., Scottsdale, AZ 85253.

Statler Records, Inc., Dept. IG, 1795 Express Dr., North Smithtown, NY 11787.

Gary Wachtel, 45 Englewood Ave., Buffalo, NY 14214.

WM Productions, 4950 Nome St., Unit C, Denver, CO 80239.

14

Jogging

Completion of this chapter should enable the reader to:

- Know the guidelines for starting a jogging program
- Select and care for proper jogging equipment, particularly shoes
- Demonstrate correct running form
- Construct a proper training schedule according to one's goals
- Prevent and treat jogging injuries
- Teach fundamental jogging principles and skills

HISTORY

For many years jogging has been a major acitivty in the YMCA, the Boston Young Men's Christian Union, Boys Clubs, and many college physical education programs. However, the benefits of jogging were never completely realized until a scientific study was conducted by Dr. Kenneth H. Cooper, Major, USAF Medical Corps, in the early 1960s. His research made a significant contribution by correlating oxygen consumption and pulse rate with various types of exercise and the vigor and duration of each. He described a sort of pharmacopoeia of exercise that describes the training effect of each of several types of exercise and gives the value of each in building cardiorespiratory efficiency. He differentiated between "aerobic" and "anaerobic" exercise, based on the oxygen consumption each requires, and substantiated the effectiveness of aerobic types, such as jogging.

Jogging is popular as an exercise medium for an increasingly fitness-conscious American public. Increasing numbers of participants seem to be joining in this activity for a variety of reasons.

Most beginning runners view jogging as a means to health and fitness, including prevention of heart disease and weight loss. Others use exercise to relieve tension and frustration built during daily activities. "It feels good to run," say most. The run itself may not always be pleasant, but the effects usually are. The physical and mental glow after running is real and important to the runner.

GETTING STARTED

Jogging is usually defined as running slowly at a comfortable pace of about 9 to 12 minutes per mile. Running is an individual activity, so some will be able to run farther and faster than others with seemingly the same effort. A good guideline for the beginning runner is to utilize the talk test: run just fast enough so that you are still able to carry on a conversation.

Running need not be a form of self-torture. To have a successful running experience, a sensible program should be initiated. The following guidelines are applicable to almost everyone:

1. Consult your physician before initiating any type of exercise program. (This guidelines increases in importance with an increase in age. After the age of 35 it is recommended that a novice jogger have an exercise stress test before embarking on a jogging program.)
2. Start slowly. If you overdo, your first day will probably be your last.
3. Be consistent. Set up a practical routine, and stick with it for at least 6 to 8 weeks.
4. Listen to your body. It will reveal your limits. Try not to become overly competitive and exceed those limits. If you become sore, back off for a day or two.
5. Take walking breaks frequently during the first few runs. Warm up and cool down by walking.

6. Get a pair of comfortable, properly fitting shoes (see next section). Clothing will be dictated by common sense and experience.

7. Do not always gear your schedule to how far you can run. Try using time as a guideline. Start with as little as 5 minutes of walking and easy running. Increase the time slowly, trying not to strain. By gearing your program to time, you allow the body to work to its own limits. Disappointment will not be part of your program when you fail to cover a set number of miles or kilometers.

Running can be enjoyable if it is done with a positive frame of mind.

SHOE SELECTION

Individual needs and requirements vary greatly from runner to runner, so that one brand of shoes cannot be recommended for everyone. Along with comfort and protection, various skill levels and competitive attitudes as well as differing body types and individual mechanical weaknesses must be considered.

The ideal shoe (Fig. 14-1) is designed to provide protection while leaving running motion unencumbered, so keep in mind that proper selection of a training shoe is essential for avoiding injuries while ensuring maximum performance and comfort.

The best place to start is with a good shoe specialist who offers a wide variety of brands and models. Try on several of the available choices and lace them up as if going for a run. Check the shoes for minor defects (which are common in this age of mass production), and then take them out for a short run. Take your time in making a selection.

Set your own requirements, keeping these questions in mind: Are you heavy on your feet, or do you run lightly with good form? What type of terrain will you run on (trails, roads, or grass)? As you strictly a fun runner, or training for a specific distance or time? Find the model shoe that fits your needs, then buy the pair that fits your feet best.

The sole should be durable yet soft enough to aid the body in absorbing the shock of each foot strike. You are seeking traction, flexibility, and good cushioning. The heel counter should be firm. Check the material used in the heel wedge and midsole. Is it soft and flexible yet not mushy? It too absorbs shock, but it should be firm enough to protect the foot from sharp objects and rocks. Check an older pair of shoes (if available) to see whether they have retained their softness.

The width of the heel is also important. Is the heel wide enough to provide good stability yet not change your normal running gait?

Check the ankle and Achilles tendon padding as well as the heel cup for the soft firm support that will help lock the heel in. They should be well-molded to prevent unnecessary side-to-side roll.

The side panel reinforcing should bring the arch support into proper position and fit snugly, yet not bind to the point of causing blisters, and be made of durable material.

The forefoot or toe area should be high and well rounded to provide enough room for the toes to move around. You should be able to pinch the front end of the shoe and there should be enough space to fit the width of a finger between the front of the longest toe and the front of the shoe. It is not uncommon to require a running shoe to be a half size larger than street shoes.

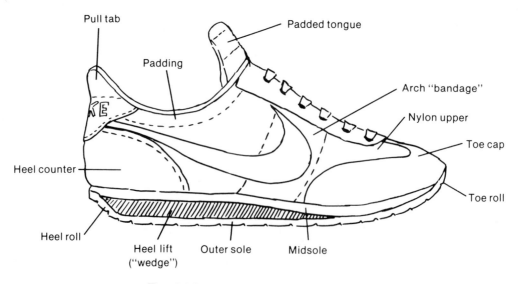

Fig. 14-1. Anatomy of a running shoe.

The insole should provide some cushioning and also prevent the foot from slipping around when it perspires. If the insole is unsatisfactory it can be taken out and replaced with a popular commercial brand. The tongue should be well padded.

A soft yet firm arch support that fits well the first time is important. However, as with the insole, it can be replaced with a commercial product.

Width sizing has become popular with the expansion of the running shoe market in the past few years. Price is also a factor, but one should remember that expense does not ensure good fit or quality.

A good pair of shoes are a runner's most critical investment (outside of time), yet they are not a cure-all. The anatomy of your foot may call for something not offered by today's mass-produced shoes. If you cannot find a pair of shoes that fit comfortably, you may need to seek professional help from a qualified podiatrist or orthopedist.

Reserve your running shoes for running. Using them for casual wear causes different wear patterns, which will affect the life of the shoe.

Beginners should purchase a pair of training shoes. They offer more cushioning than a racing shoe. Always remember that it is important to wear high quality socks when jogging. Socks capable of "wicking" moisture away from the feet are a must.

RUNNING FORM

Many people believe long-distance running requires little or no skill. Simple observation of different runners shows that some seem to float along almost effortlessly, whereas others pound along, struggling with each step and exhibiting contorted expressions. The obvious difference is cardiovascular conditioning, but technique and efficiency of movement are also involved to a great extent and require skill and practice.

Distance running is a natural activity, so a runner should do what comes naturally as long as it is mechanically sound. The slower a runner travels, the easier it is to get away with poor form. Problems arise when the tempo is increased and mechanical inefficiencies become compounded by the increase in speed.

The keys to improving running technique are simple.

Foot placement

The slower you go, the flatter the landing. Try to land lightly and gently; do not pound. As you run faster you move higher on the foot, toward the toes. All runners land first on the outside edge of the foot, then roll inward. This absorbs shock. The precise point of contact varies with speed.

Stride

This is also a function of speed. The short stride is more economical and also slower. As the pace increases, so does the length of stride. Keep in mind that you should lead with the knee first. The foot should follow and extend to meet the ground. Do not overstride; keep your feet under you. The point of foot contact should be directly under the knee, with the knee slightly flexed.

Body carriage

Run tall and with a straight back (See Fig. 14-2). The head should remain level. Do not look at the sky or at your feet but out in front of you. This approach assures you of an erect, balanced running stance. The head should be in line with the trunk and the trunk in line with the legs.

The hips should be directly over the legs. Try not to "sit" or lean forward. A runner tends to "sit" when fatigue sets in, and this leads to shorter, mechanically inefficient stride.

The arms should play an active role in running. They are there for balance and driving and should not be ignored. Arms help the legs go faster as long as they remain rhythmic. Hold the hands loosely cupped and relaxed, palms turned inward. Bend the elbow and bring the arms

Fig. 14-2. Running form.

parallel to each other, slightly inward but not across the midline of the chest.

The best time to practice technique is a short afternoon run. Stride six times over 50 to 60 yards (45 to 50 m) on a smooth, grassy surface, concentrating on any problem. Having someone watch you run several times before making suggestions. All runners have innocent quirks in running styles that are their trademarks. If they do not affect mechanical efficiency they should be left alone.

TRAINING

A phenomenon that has occurred along with the large increase in the number of joggers in the country is the availability of races in which to participate. Almost every weekend a run is sponsored by some organization. Some are for serious runners, some for fun, some for raising money for charitable causes, some for recognizing local traditions and many are a combination of reasons. While it is possible to be a jogger and never enter a race, these events are motivational much like the recital that piano teachers use to motivate students to continue practicing. These races also can be fun social events. If you desire to enter a race, it shouldn't be done without advance preparation and training for the event's demands.

The word "training" like the word "jogging," can be ambiguous. The difference is sometimes artificial. Training indicates effort toward completing a specific distance or race; jogging is usually done on a more casual basis for fitness or health reasons.

There are several methods of starting training. Most are fairly simple. There are guiding principles, terminology, and systems of training for the beginning racer.

Fundamental principles of training

Stress. The body must adapt to stress if it is to improve its general condition. Training stimulates the type of stress the body will encounter during a race. A fine line separates training from stress and strain during the run.

Overload. Overload means taking on a little more work than is comfortable. It should be done for brief periods at first, perhaps every other day. Stretch your limits gradually. If done too quickly it can result in injury or at least soreness.

Specificity of training. Training must resemble the type of race you are preparing for in both speed and distance.

Consistency. Body systems get into shape by regular training. Do not do a super workout one day and then be unable to walk the next. Be consistent.

Recovery. The body must be given adequate time to rejuvenate itself. Continuous hard training will bring you down eventually. Rest is just as important as stress.

Pacing. Take a long view toward running. Both in races and training, focus on gradual improvement. At first im-

provement comes quickly as mileage piles up. *Remember:* More does not always mean better.

Training schedules

Individualize your training schedule. Find a system that fits your life style and makes your running a part of you for the rest of your life. Keep yourself happy and eager. Undertrain rather than overtrain.

A program for a jogger who has been training for several months and is now interested in preparing for a 6- to 20-mile (9.7 to 32.2 km) run might look like this:

Sunday: Long easy run of 15 miles (24 km) or 1½ hours on relatively flat terrain.
Monday: MORNING—Easy 40-minute run. EVENING—Brisk 45-minute run followed by 8 to 10 strides on grass. Stretch and cool down. Do abdominal exercises.
Tuesday: EVENING—Medium to hard 1-hour run on fairly hilly terrain. Start easy, finishing with a long, hard sustained pace. Be sure to cool down.
Wednesday: MORNING—Easy 3 to 5 miles (4.8 to 8.0 km). EVENING—Forty-minute run according to the way you feel.
Thursday: MORNING—Forty-minute run. EVENING—Fartlek workout over hills, changing the pace often; 1 hour total time.
Friday: EVENING—Brisk 45-minute run.
Saturday: Try to find a race over 3 miles (4.8 km). Set a predetermined goal. Experiment. Easy afternoon run of 4 or 5 minutes (6.4 to 8.0 km).

This sample workout is equal to about 70 miles a week, adequate even for a marathon of less than 3 hours. Using time as the basis for your program will allow you to individualize your training and respond to the way your body feels. If you feel good, cover more miles. If you need more time to recuperate, you will achieve fewer total miles. Get to know your own fatigue symptoms, because continuous overstress will result in a reverse training effect.

Types of training systems

LSD, or long slow distance. In this method of training a runner concentrates on running longer and farther, with little attention to speed. At least 95% of the time you should be able to converse and feel comfortable while on a training run. Keep pulse rate and respiration well within your limits. Do all things in moderation.

Fartlek. "Fartlek" is a Swedish word meaning speed play. The basic principle is to change the pace endlessly by charging hills, stretching out going downhill, accelerating to a sprint, striding, jogging, and walking. Try to let changes in pace occur naturally, such as when forced to stop at an intersection or pausing the admire the mountain scenery. Do it off the track on uneven and changing terrain. Fartlek is not a long easy distance run in the country with a 50-yard burst thrown in every mile!

Interval training. This method of training has five basic components: (1) distance of each fast run, (2) interval or recovery between the fast runs, (3) number of repetitions to be run, (4) duration of each run, and (5) activity done between each run (walking, jogging, or complete rest). When trying to build endurance, run longer training runs with shorter rest periods or jog for recovery. To sharpen and become faster, run as fast or faster than race pace, with almost complete rest for recovery. Interval training can bring quick results, but unless it is used in conjunction with a good endurance base, the results can be quickly wiped out by illness or injury.

Hard-easy-hard. This is more a philosophy toward running and training. The body must be given the opportunity to recuperate and rest after being placed under stress. There should be days when the activity is varied or when little or no training is done. Supplemental activities such as swimming, cycling, or weight training may be incorporated.

Hill running. Most runners believe that hills should be an intergral part of the training routine. Hill work is actually speed work in disguise, in that the heart rate is elevated and resistance work is done. Few runners enjoy hills, and many fear them when they are part of a race. However, by placing them on your training schedule you may gain not only strength but confidence. Because of the force producing braking action of the striking leg, pain in the lower back, hip, or knee can result from downhill running. Downhill running should be done like sprinting or fast striding. Keep yourself balanced with the hips into the running action. Do not "sit"! Land on the ball of the foot. Keep the arms in rhythm.

INJURIES

Most running experts suggest that a stretching routine before and, perhaps more importantly, after jogging can reduce injuries. If you start your jog easily the initial stretching may not be as important, but a warm down routine is important. This is true not only for limbering up, but also to keep muscles constricting and pumping blood back to the heart. Even with adequate stretching, warming up and cooling down, injuries will occur to most runners. Most runners try to ease through their injuries by taking time off or running easier for a while.

Minor irritations are a way of life for most runners. As one disappears another arises, but they are usually not serious enough to make the runner give up the sport.

There are those who, through their own ignorance, are unwilling to heed the signs of trouble indicated by those minor irritations. Their excuse for avoiding medical attention is that the physician usually tells them to stop running for a while. However, the number of injuries to the lower limbs is on the rise and cannot be dismissed. Injuries present real problems, and the runner should seek a sensible solution based on fact rather than on hit-and-miss guesswork.

Problems with muscles or tendons are usually associated with fatigue or an aching pain. Burning or shooting pain may indicate nerve irritation. A consistent burning pain is probably caused by inflammation. Other injuries include blister, bone spurs, Morton's toe, muscle strain and tears, plantar fascia inflammation, and sciatic nerve problems.

It is necessary to isolate the location of an injury and determine the type of pain and its depth and point of maximum tenderness. Also important to note are: How did the pain start? Was it from new shoes or running a long way on roads or sharp downhills? Did you have a proper warm-up? Did you make unusual demands on the body?

Most injuries can be attributed to simple overuse or overstress. During training the foot can strike the ground 5000 times in 1 hour—a tremendous amount of stress for the leg to sustain.

Biomechanical deformities, structural susceptibilities, and postural malformations that may not be evident in everyday walking can show themselves as injury when the runner has been overstressed. Add to this poor running shoes, improper training methods, and poor running surfaces, and the runner is a risk of injuries.

The overuse syndrome usually is evidenced by shin splints, Achilles tendonitis, chondromalacia of the knee, stress fractures, or bursitis. This symdrome can be treated by proper training, which includes a well-organized stretching program with a hard-easy approach to training. A well-planned conditioning period, proper shoes, and varied running surfaces all contribute to lessening the problems of overuse.

The knee is a common area of injury because it is a vulnerable hinge joint that takes most of the punishment inflicted by hard surfaces. The bottom edge of the kneecap is often irritated, a condition medically termed chondromalacia. This condition indicates joint instability and usually affects the hyaline cartilage on the joint side of the kneecap. It can be a result of excessive rotation of the knee at foot strike. The best way to prevent this injury is by stabilizing the foot with heel or arch supports and by strengthening the quadriceps or thigh muscles through weight training.

The Achilles tendon connects the heel bone and the calf muscles. It is synonymous with vulnerability. Running tends to shorten this tendon and cause inflexibility and tightness. The best way known to prevent this is to stretch before and after a run. The inclined wall push-up is a good exercise to specifically work on the Achilles tendon. One method of reducing the stress placed on the affected tendon is to place a ¼-inch lift in the running shoes.

The term "shin splints" is a catchall for lower leg problems. Shin splints is a symptom, not a condition. It is primarily a swelling along the lower front of the legs and is usually a muscular problem. It results from (1) improper shoes, (2) insufficient shock absorption, (3) excessive training on hard surfaces, concrete, or all-weather tracks, (4) lack of flexibility, or (5) poor running form. Runners who suffer the last from shin splints are those who keep their feet and knees in line with their hips. Other potential causes include an imbalance between an overly strong calf muscle and weak anterior or front muscles. Soreness in the shins can be a common complaint of the beginning runner. The legs are not used to this type of muscular activity and should be given time to adjust.

Cryotherapy, or ice treatment, has been used for all of these problems with excellent results for many years. The primary effect of cold—vasoconstriction (decrease in size of blood vessels)—takes place in the first few minutes of application. This is strictly a reflex action with an accompanying decrease in the capillary blood pressure and an increase in the arterial blood pressure. Ice is used for the first 24 to 48 hours in acute muscular skeletal injuries. The secondary effect is vasodilation, an increase in the rate of blood flow to the injured area. A massive hyperemia is produced because of the increase in blood flow, with the peripheral blood vessels being constricted and the deeper blood vessels being dilated. (In contrast, with heat application there is dilation, with stagnation of blood in the area.) Cold also produces an anesthetic effect—a decrease in the spasticity of the muscles and an increase in the blood flow rate, rather than a gross increase in the circulation.

There are several methods of cold application. Crushed or shaved ice works best and produces a colder solution. A slush solution with a cold towel also works well. Massage with a frozen cup of ice is best for the knee and similar joint areas. The surface temperature when using ice treatments should be no higher than 55° F (31° C).

Remember: When ice therapy is first induced, the shock of the cold will cause an aching sensation. The skin will become numb in about 3 minutes and then redden. Therapy should be terminated at this point and repeated later.

These are some of the most common types of injuries and preventive measures as well as simple methods of treatment. If a problem persists, seek advice of a qualified podiatrist or orthopedic surgeon.

MISCELLANEOUS SUGGESTIONS

1. Do everything in moderation.
2. Start out by improving your cardiovascular efficiency. Work up gradually to at least a 30-minute jog three times per week.
3. Use the hard-easy-hard approach, allowing your body time to recuperate. Undertrain rather than overtrain.
4. Learn to calculate and measure your target heart rate (THR) and train at a pace to elicit this heart rate. THR is really a range and the object is to keep your heart rate in this range while jogging. THR can be calculated by subtracting your age from the value of 220. The resulting value is an estimate of your maximum heart rate. Multiply this value by .70 and by .85 to obtain the two end points of the THR range, which is appropriate for young adults in good health. These percentages would be lower for older adults. For example, the estimated maximum heart rate for a 20 year old is 200 (220 − 20). Multiplying this value by .70 and .85 results in a range THR range of 140 to 170. Jogging at a pace to elicit a heart rate between these two values will produce a training effect over time.
5. Keep an accurate record of your mileage. Find out how much stress your body can handle comfortably. Take your pulse before getting out of bed and about 1 or 2 hours after your evening workout. Place the numbers on a graph. This will allow you to see the progress being made toward cardiovascular efficiency.
6. The recovery phase is also important to the jogger. It will take between 3 and 5 hours for the heart rate to return to preexercise levels. By taking your pulse 1 to 2 hours after evening workouts, you will begin to see what type of adaptations your body is making to running stress.
7. Eat sensibly. With an increase in calorie expenditure expect an increase in appetite. Eat a well-balanced diet. Be wary of fad diets.
8. Take fluids early if you are planning on running more than 1 hour, especially in warm weather. Water seems to work best for everyone. Be prepared and do not overextend yourself, whatever your goal!
9. Vary the training program.
10. Run with someone. Making your jogging sessions enjoyable through social interaction will help ensure that you stick with them.

TEACHING CONSIDERATIONS

1. Instructional programs for groups must deal with two major factors:
   a. For clear training effects to be achieved students must exercise at least 3 days a week a minimum of 30 minutes for at least 5 to 6 weeks.
   b. Individuals will start at different levels of ability and will have different target goals.
2. If programs do not meet for the length of time required, additional work outside of the instructional period should be included.

3. Some type of preassesssment should be used to determine beginning levels of students. Several tests using time (a 12-minute run-walk) or heart rate for a given work load are available. Programs should then be designed on this basis.

4. Heart rate is the best simple indicator of workload. Teach students show to calculate their target heart rates as described earlier. Before set training programs are established, teach pacing for this rate. Begin increasing students' distance according to heart rate on a weekly basis. Have them keep records of progress. Give each student a target distance and time for the end of the program if possible.

5. Use the jogging experience to teach about the effects of exercise on the body and life-style of the student. Students are interested in this information. Jogging units can be combined with physical fitness experiences.

6. Provide a lot of encouragement, slow down overeager beginners, and be alert to adverse physical reactions. Become part of the class if possible.

7. Encourage students to be sensitive to their body to determine limits.

GLOSSARY

aerobic Running that allows a near-normal breathing pattern; literally, "with oxygen."

anaerobic Running involving labored breathing; literally, "without oxygen."

endurance Ability to run for a long time; created by long, slow, easy running.

fartlek A style of training employing frequent changes of pace; from the Swedish word meaning speed play.

fast distance Steady training running at slightly less than maximum speed.

interval training A formalized training program alternating fast running with rest periods.

lactic acid Chemical by-product of anaerobic or oxygen-debt running that produces fatigue.

long distance More than 6 miles or 10,000 m.

marathon 26 miles 385 yards; Olympic distance.

middle distance 880 yards to 6 miles (800 to 10,000 m).

overdistance Longer than one's racing distance.

oxygen debt Running faster than one's normal breathing pattern can sustain body needs; shortness of breath.

pace Average rate at which a distance is run.

recovery Rebuilding energy after a hard effort.

repetitions Series of runs with recovery breaks between, as in interval training.

resistance Body's ability to withstand stress.

specificity The principle that physiologic preparation for an activity must include training very similar to that activity.

steady state Maximum rate at which the body can operate aerobically.

training Running program designed to increase the level of fitness and improve a runner's performance in racing.

SUGGESTED READINGS

Cantlay J and Hoffman R: Running together: the family book of jogging, Champaign, Ill, 1981, Leisure Press. Contains chapters on mechanics of running, stretching, safety, nutrition, fitness, and competitive running.

Corbin DE: Jogging, Glenview, Ill, 1988, Scott, Foresman & Co. Emphasizes sensible and enjoyable exercise, stressing the physical and physiological benefits while recognizing potential hazards.

Davis M and VanWoerkom C: A safe change of pace for the beginning jogger, Dubuque, Iowa, 1981, Kendall/Hunt Publishing Co.

Dintiman G: How to run faster, West Point, NY, 1984, Leisure Press. Includes step-by-step instructions on how to increase foot speed.

Fisher GA and Allsen PE: Jogging, ed 2, Dubuque, Iowa, 1987, Wm C Brown Group. Presents the essentials of an easy-to-understand fitness program that allows the reader to master each theory and technique at his or her own pace. Contains special sections on warming up, training, and aerobic conditioning.

Fixx JF: Jim Fixx's second book of running, New York, 1980, Random House, Inc.

Henderson J: Running for fitness, for sport, and for life, Dubuque, Iowa, 1985, Wm C Brown Group. Presents guidelines for development of a sound program, physiological and psychological benefits of jogging, the effect of jogging on risk factors for chronic and degenerative diseases, the role of jogging on weight loss and maintenance, prevention and treatment of injuries, and motivational strategies.

Rosato F: Jogging for health and fitness, ed 2, Englewood, Colo, 1988, Morton Publishing Co. Presents, along with physiological and psychological benefits, information on risk factors for chronic and degenerative disease, weight loss and maintenance, jogging injuries, and motivational strategies.

Sachs MH and Sach ML: Psychology of running, Champaign, Ill, 1981, Human Kinetics Publishers, Inc. Focuses on the significance of running to runners, the positive and negative aspects of running addiction, the psychological state and the mind-body relationship of the runner, how obsessions with running can create psychological problems, and how therapists use running in treating emotional disorders.

Williams C and Moore C: Jogging everyone, Winston-Salem, NC, 1983, Hunter Textbooks, Inc. Provides information on jogging programs, warm-up and cool-down routines, shoe selection, and diet.

VIDEOTAPES

Running for fun and fitness, Cross country, Marathon challenge, by Bill Rodgers. Available from How To Sports Videos, Box 5852, Denver, CO 80217.

15

Karate

Completion of this chapter should enable the reader to:

- Appreciate the rich tradition behind this martial art
- Be familiar with the types of karate training
- Understand the ranking system in karate
- Be aware of etiquette and safety concerns of karate
- Be knowledgeable about the physical and psychological principles of karate

HISTORY

The martial art of karate as it is known today began in the late nineteenth and twentieth centuries in Japan. Its origin as a system of self-defense, however, dates back many centuries. Legend relates how a Buddhist priest named Bodhidharma traveled overland from India to China to instruct monks of the Liang dynasty at the Shaolin Temple regarding the tenets of Buddhism. There he taught the monks a combination of Indian fist-fighting and yoga which eventually became known as the kung-fu system of Shaolin-tsu (Shaoln "fist-way"). As the art spread throughout China many styles and systems appeared.

As cultural trade increased, the fighting techniques of China were carried to other Asian countries, the most significant of which was Okinawa. It was here that the empty-handed fighting systems of China were combined with the empty-handed fighting systems of Okinawa (known as *te*) and a rough form of karate was developed.

It was not until the twentieth century, when Gichin Funakoshi (an Okinawan karate instructor and school teacher) introduced Okinawa-te to Japan, that it acquired the name of karate. The original Chinese characters that made up the name "karate" translated as "Chinese hands." Mr. Funakoshi is credited with substituting the first character, *kara* (meaning "Chinese") to that of *kara* (meaning "empty"). The kara of "empty" has the meaning of not only empty-handed or weaponless fighting, but also of keeping one's spirit of inner self hollow (meaning selflessness and unselfishness).

Karate was introduced into the Okinwawn middle-school system in 1905 where it became a required part of the physical education curriculum. It was not until the years between 1917 (in Kyoto at the Butokuden-Hall of Martial Virtues) and 1923 (at the national Athletic Exhibtion in Tokyo) that karate began to proliferate into the colleges and universities in Japan. It was here that the art received its greatest impetus. Following World War II, from 1945 to 1965, many U.S. servicemen studied martial arts in Japan. On their return to the United States a number of these servicemen opened martial arts schools. Here, too the martial arts rapidly spread and today are practiced by thousands of students.

Today there are more than 100 styles of karate. The word style refers to a system or tradition in the way that karate is taught. Generally, styles of karate can be classified according to national systems such as Japanese, Korean, Chinese, and Okinawan. Table 15-1 is an overview of some of the major styles taught throughout the world today.

THE MEANING OF KARATE-DO

The modern Japanese martial arts of karate and judo are practiced the world over as forms of sport competition, self-defense, physical education, and aesthetics. However, their primary focus is to serve as systems of self-

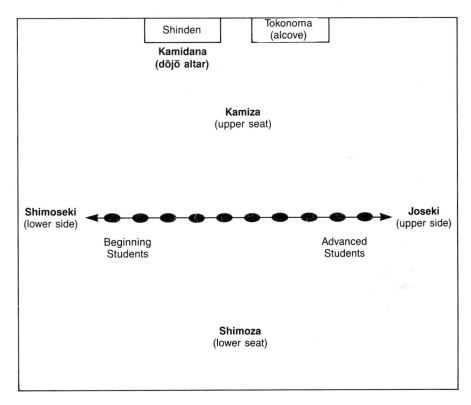

Fig. 15-1. Dojo schematic.

Table 15-1. MAJOR STYLES OF KARATE

Japanese	Okinawan	Korean	Chinese
Shotokan	Goju-ryu	Tae Kwon	T'ai Chi Ch'uan
Wado-ryu	Isshin-ryu	Do	Siu-Lum
Shito-ryu	Shorei-ryu	Hapkido	Hsing-I
Goju-ryu	Shorin-ryu	Tang Soo Do	Wing Chun
Kyokushinkai	Uechi-ryu	Taekyon	Hop Gar

cultivation and to transmit those ideals, norms, and behaviors associated with the traditional cultural setting of the martial arts. These include fostering ideals such as loyalty, bravery, and acceptance of physical and mental hardships through disciplined training. Of paramount importance is development of a strong fighting spirit.

The martial arts are considered to be both physical and mental disciplines that focus on self-cultivation by way of the combative mode. The *do* suffixed to the words karate-do and judo suggest that they are philosophical paths or ways to travel throughout life in the pursuit of self-perfection of character. Japanese culture is replete with such activities. Those more familiar to the Westerner include the tea ceremony (chado), calligraphy (shodo), and Zen meditation. The martial arts, however, serve as a unique system of *seishin kyoiku* (spiritual ed-

ucation) by way of the combative mode. The highest aim of all of the martial arts such as karate-do, kendo, judo, kyudo, and aikido is to develop character through physical, mental, and moral education.

DOJO

Every dojo (martial arts training hall) is arranged so that there is a front and back wall and an upper and lower side (Fig. 15-1). The point of reference for training activity and etiquette is the front wall (shomen). Located at the front wall in most traditional dojo is a Shinto or Buddhist diety shelf known as the *kamidana*. The kamidana is the focal point for training activity and etiquette. In place of the kamidana in dojo outside of Japan, many schools elect to place a national flag or a picture of the founder of their karate style. Some dojo also have a *to-*

Size	Measurements for children		Jacket length	Pants length	Belt length
0	under 4'9"	<150 lbs.	28"	26.5"	77"
1	4'10"-5'3"	106-120	30.5"	29"	79.5"
2	5'4"-5'6"	121-135	36"	31.5"	88"
3	5'7"-5'9"	136-165	38"	34"	95.5"
4	5'10"-6'0"	166-200	39.5"	37.5"	102"
5	6'1"	200+	40"	39"	111"
6			50.5"	41.5"	120"

Fig. 15-2. Karate uniform size chart.

konoma, or a special place on the front wall where a fine sword or piece of calligraphy *(kakemono)* depitcing a martial arts training concept may be placed.

The upper seat in the dojo is the *kamiza*, while the lower seat is the *shimoza*. The kamiza is the location that the teacher occupies at the beginning and end of class for formal salutation. The shimoza is the location where students line up before and after class for the same purpose. Generally, higher ranking students line up towards the right, or *joseki*, side of the dojo while lower ranking students line up towards the left, or the *shimoseki*, side.

Ideally, a dojo should be clean, simple and without ostentatious display of trophies or other encumberances. The floor should be of smooth wood and should be thoroughly cleaned by students at the end of each training period.

Uniform

The uniform worn while training is called the *karate-gi*. It consists of a jacket, pants, and belt about 8 feet long. Most traditional dojo require the karate-gi to be white, although there are exceptions. While the belt primarily serves to keep the jacket closed, its color also denotes level of expertise.

Karate-gi are manufactured in light, medium, and heavy weight material and are available in a vareity of costs and sizes. It is important that it fit somewhat loosely and not restrict movement while training. Figure 15-2 illustrates the most common sizes available.

RANKING SYSTEM USED IN KARATE

Karate uses the *kyu-dan* system to rank its exponents in terms of proficiency, knowledge, and experience. The *kyu* ranks, also known as the *mudansha* (ungraded) ranks, begin with either the tenth, ninth, or eighth kyu for beginners and proceed up to the first kyu (usually designated in most dojo by the brown belt). The *dan* ranks, also known as the *yudansha* (graded) ranks, begin with the first degree black belt *(shodan)* and progress up to the tenth degree black belt *(judan)*. In most traditional dojo it takes 4 to 5 years to achieve the rank of first degree black belt if a karateka (karate practitioner) trains three to five times per week with no breaks in training. Belt colors most often used in the mudansha class include white, orange, blue, purple, green, red, and brown. The black belt is used to denote those in the yudansha class. The Federation of All-Japan Karate-do Organizations (FAJKO) uses the ranking system shown in Table 15-2.

It is considered axiomatic in most karate circles that to progress from one martial arts rank to a higher one, the practitioner must demonstrate significant improvement in both martial arts skill and technique as well as character. This necessitates that karateka pursue not only physical training, but academic training as well if they are to acquire the skill and wisdom required for higher rank. In addition, examinees are tested on basics, *kata* (formal exercise), and *kumite* (sparring). More advanced karateka must demonstrate sufficient skill in *tameshiwari* (board-breaking) and self-defense. Some schools require that advanced karateka demonstrate technical profi-

Table 15-2. KARATE RANKING SYSTEM

Ranks	Age	Title
Ju-Dan (10th) over 10 years after Ku-Dan	70 years or over	*Hanshi (master) over 15 years after Kyoshi 55 years old or over
Ku-Dan (9th) 10 years after Hachi-Dan	60 years or over	
Hachi-Dan (8th) 8 years after Shichi-Dan	50 years or over	*Kysohi (teacher) over 10 years after Renshi 40 years old or over
Shichi-Dan (7th) 7 years after Roku-Dan	42 years or over	
Roku-Dan (6th) over 5 years after Go-Dan	35 years or over	*Renshi (instructor) over 2 years after 5th Dan 35 years old or over
Go-Dan (5th) over 3 years after Yo-Dan	under 35 years	
Yō-Dan (4th) over 3 years after San-Dan	under 35 years	
San-Dan (3rd) over two years after Ni-Dan	under 35 years	No formal title
Ni-Dan (2nd) over 1 year after Shō-Dan	under 35 years	No formal title
Shō-Dan (1st) at least three years**	under 35 years	No formal title
Ikkyū (1st Brown)		
Nikyū (2nd Brown)		
Sankyū (3rd Brown)		
Yonkyū (4th class)		Kyū (below brown identified by different colors) However,
Gokyū (5th class)	No age specified	all kyūs are considered white relative to the black
Rokkyū (6th class)		belt
Shichikyū (7th class) optional		
Hachikyū (8th class) optional		

[1]Ranking system adopted by FAJKO March 27, 1971. FAJKO—Federation of All Japan Karate-Dō Organizations
*TITLES: May not be given irrespective of how high the rank; awarded for exceptional achievement and outstanding character.
**Daily practice.

ciency in the use of a traditional martial arts weapon. The highest yudansha levels require that the karateka produce a written thesis or completed research on some aspect of martial arts theory or practice.

In addition to the kyu and dan ranks given in karate, karateka may also be awarded one of three honorary titles after reaching the rank of *yondan* (4th degree black belt). The three special titles are those of *renshi* (instructor), *kyoshi* (teacher), and *hanshi* (master). Refer to Table 15-2 for the requirements of these titles.

A head instructor of a style of karate is usually referred to as *Kancho* (literally, "building chief"). *Shihan* (master) is the term usually given to those of 6th degree black belt or higher. *Sensei* (teacher) is the term given to black belts who head an individual dojo or who have the primary responsibility of teaching within a dojo. *Sempai* (senior) is the term usually given to the more experienced and higher ranking students within a group while the term *kohai* (junior) is used to designate those karateka of lower rank and lesser experience. It is important to note that while Sensei, Sempai, and Shihan are used as formal forms of address, kohai is never used in this manner.

KARATE TRAINING

Karate training is generally divided into three basic aspects: kihon, kata, and kumite. Kihon training consists of fundamental practice in the execution of blocks, punches, strikes, kicks, stances, stepping, and body-shifting techniques. Generally, these are performed by karateka on an individual basis. Kata training consists of learning and executing prearranged traditional routines of attack and defense against imaginary opponents. Most schools require karateka to learn two to three kata per rank for advancement. Kumite training consists of learning and executing basic, intermediate, and advanced levels of fighting. Basic sparring, sometimes referred to as one-attack fight, or *yakusokugeika* ("promise" practice), consists of two opponents executing attack and defense techniques against prearranged targets.

Kihon (fundamental practice)

1. Blocking techniques: Blocking techniques are employed to defense vital areas of the body against punches, strikes, and kicks primarily by deflecting them from their intended target of attack. The more common techniques include the down block, the middle forearm chest block, the high block, and the knife-hand block. (See Fig. 15-3.)
2. Punching and striking techniques: Punching and striking techniques are used to attack vital areas of the body. The two basic techniques include the lunge punch (or straight punch) and the reverse punch. Basic striking techniques include the hammer-fist knife-hand strike, the knife-hand strike, and the back-fist strike. (See Fig. 15-4.)
3. Kicking techniques: The front, round, side, and back kicks comprise the basic kicking techniques used in karate. Like the punching and striking techniques, these may be delivered to vital target areas in attack or counterattack modes. (See Fig. 15-5.)
4. Stances: For the karateka, strong stances (tachikata) and combative postures (kamaekata) serve as the foundations from which to deliver strong offensive and defensive techniques. Some of the more common stances used in karate include the front stance, back stance, straddle-leg stance, rooted stance, cat-leg stance, and square stance. (See Fig. 15-6.)
5. Stepping and body-shifting techniques: Stepping techniques allow the karateka to move from one position to another for attack and defense. During basic

Fig. 15-3. Blocking techniques. **A,** Route of downward block. **B,** Route of forearm block against body attack. **C,** Route of upper block against head attack.

Fig. 15-4. Punches and strikes.

Fig. 15-5. Kicking techniques. **A,** Route of side thrust kick. **B,** Route of side snap kick. **C,** Route of front kick. **D,** Route of roundhouse kick.

Fig. 15-6. Karate stances. **A,** Front stance. **B,** Back stance. **C,** Straddle-leg stance. **D,** Rooted stance. **E,** Cat leg stance. **F,** Square stance.

practice the front stance is used to execute many attacking techniques while the back stance and rooted stance are used to execute many defensive techniques.

Kata (practice of forms)

Kata are exercises of offensive and defensive techniques arranged in formal sequences and executed against imaginary opponents. They are loosely analagous to compulsory gymnastics floor routines. Formulated and transmitted down through the ages by true masters of the art of karate, they consist of a number of movements that must be performed in a strict sequence with correct power, speed, focus, rhythm, and movement interpretation. Historically, they represent a condensation of the fighting knowledge of the master who developed the kata. Kata were originally designed to have no unnecessary movements. Each movement in the kata had a combative application. As the karateka practices each kata, the vast amount of information within the kata gradually begins to reveal itself to the practitioner.

In performing kata, execution of techniques must not be rigid and robotic-looking in nature but must effectively contrast the active (do) and passive (sei) elements of the kata to demonstrate proper rhythm and fluidity of human motion. Years of practice are required to master even the most basic kata. Figure 15-7 shows an example of a kata known as Heian Yondan.

Japanese karate kata are traditionally divided into the two styles of Okinawan karate from which they were derived, the Shorin-ryu and the Shorei-ryu. Kata from the Shorin-ryu tradition emphasize movements which are light and flexible, while those of the Shorei-ryu tradition emphasize movements which are strong and powerful. Generally, kata were commonly named by the originator according to a technique, movement, or philosophical meaning of the kata itself. At other times, the kata were assigned the name of the originator. Table 15-3 lists the Japanese names of some of the kata along with their associated meaning which are practiced by karateka who train in the Shotokan tradition of karate-do.

Kumite (fighting)

Kumite, or free-fighting, is the application of skills learned in kihon and kata practice to practical fighting and self-defense situations. This aspect of karate training allows karateka to practice their fighting skills against one another. Beginning karateka train to execute attacking and counterattacking techniques with maximum power and speed and stop just short (*Sun-dome* = about 3 cm) of actual contact to prevent intentional injury. More advanced karateka, after undergoing disciplined training and conditioning, are allowed to make light contact to restricted target areas during kumite. Kumite teaches the concepts of proper distancing and timing, the proper moment to initiate an attack or defense, and recognition of offensive and defensive maneuvers made by an opponent. Additionally, it is necessary to master effective body shifting (*taisabaki*) techniques and quick-witted changing techniques (*henka waza*).

Fig. 15-7. Heian Yondan   *Continued.*

Fig. 15-7, cont'd. Heian Yondan

Fig. 15-7, cont'd. Heian Yondan

Continued.

Fig. 15-7, cont'd. Heian Yondan

Table 15-3. NAMES OF KATA PRACTICED IN THE SHOTOKAN KARATE TRADITION

Name of Kata	"Meaning of Kata"	Outstanding Feature(s)
Ten-no Kata	"Form of the universe"	Basic attack and defense techniques
Taikyoku	"Chaos" or "Void"	Fundamental stances, blocks and punches
Heian	"Peaceful"	Comprehensive techniques, that when mastered, one should be "comfortable" in most basic self-defense situations
Bassai Sho and Dai	"To penetrate a fortress"	Strong movements intended to change disadvantage into advantage by employing differing degrees of power and rapidly switching blocks
Kanku Sho and Dai	"To view the sky"	Variation of fast and slow technique, jumping
Jion	name of originator	Turning, shifting, various stepping patterns
Jutte (sometimes "Jitte")	"10 hands"	Fast and slow movements, high and low blocking postures, reversal of body positions
Empi	"Flying swallow"	Fast and slow movements, high and low body positions, reversal of body positions
Hangetsu	"Cresent" or "Half moon"	Coordinating stepping and breathing with circular arm and leg movements
Gankaku	"Crane on a rock"	Balancing on one leg, side kick and back fist
Chinte	"Small hands"	Small, but powerful hand blocks and strikes
Unsu	"Cloud hand"	Strong forceful arm and hand blocks with stances and high level ridge hand strikes
Sochin	"Preservation of peace among men" ("immovable")	Low, powerful movements in stances
Nijushi	"24 hands"	Strong blocking and striking techniques
Tekki	"Iron horse"	Strong hand and leg techniques from horse stance
Jion	named after Chinese monk who visited Okinawa	Multiple hand punches, strong hand and foot techniques

Kumite is arbitrarily categorized into basic, intermediate, advanced and specialized levels. Basic kumite, also called *yakusoku* or "promise" (agreement to attack only a predesignated target area) kumite, consists of *sanbon* (three-step) kumite, *gohon* (five-step) kumite, and *ippon* kumite (one attack fight). In sanbon or gohon kumite the attacking karateka attacks either three to five times consecutively to the *jodan* (upper level), *chudan* (middle level), or *gedan* (lower level) with a lunge punch-front stance technique while the defending karateka steps backwards in a front stance at the same time executing the appropriate high, middle, or low blocking technique. On the last block, the defending karateka counters with a reverse punch technique.

In the initial attack in ippon kumite, the offensive karateka launches a prearranged attack to the face with a lunge punch-front stance technique while the defending karateka steps to the rear in a defensive stance (usually a rooted stance or a back stance) and executes a counteroffensive technique. It is important here for the offensive karateka to hold position after the attack so that the defending karateka has time to deliver a counteroffensive technique with good form. In the second attack, the offensive karateka executes a lunge punch-front stance technique to the middle level and the defending

karateka counters with an appropriate counteroffensive technique. In the third attack, the offensive karateka launches a prearranged front kick-front stance attack and the defending karateka again counters with an appropriate counteroffensive technique. At the completion of the first high, middle, and low attack-counter sequence, both karateka change roles to gain equal practice in attack and defense training.

Ippon jiyu kumite (one-attack fight from fighting stance position) is performed almost like ippon kumite. Two exceptions are that both karateka use a free-fighting stance position and the attacking karateka instantaneously returns to the original preattack position after attack delivery so the defending karateka does not have time to counter the initial attack.

Jiyu kumite allows both karateka to move about at will and execute offensive and defensive maneuvers as opportunities arise. Again, as in the other forms of kumite, punches, kicks, and strikes are stopped just short of contact to avoid injury. When training in a karate dojo, the kumite usually continues until one karateka scores which is considered to be a decisive blow on the opponent. A decisive blow is one in which good technique, posture, timing, balance, and power can be demonstrated. In competitive sport matches, kumite bouts usually last for a designated period (such as 3 or 5 minutes) or number of points scored (e.g., one to three).

Specialized free-fighting may include activities such as circle fighting (*enjin*) kumite or seated free-fighting (*suwari geiko*) kumite. In enjin kumite, one karateka is located in the center of a circle of six to eight other karateka. Each karateka on the circle takes turns in rapidly attacking the karateka in the center with a strong technique. The karateka in the center is responsible for avoiding, blocking, and countering each attack. In su-wari-geiko kumite, two karateka face each other about 1 meter apart in a formal Japanese kneeling posture known as *seiza*. The offensive and defensive karateka follow the same sequence of attack and defense as followed in ippon kumite described previously.

ETIQUETTE

Proper behavior in the dojo is considered to be the hallmark of a matrial art that is taught within traditional contexts. Dojo protocol and etiquette create a teaching and learning environment that is conducive to disciplined training according to Japanese customs and traditions. Rituals followed within the dojo have a purpose and it is not one of religious conversion. They serve to establish decorum, develop an attitude conducive to disciplined training, prepare for the learning process, and show respect for the karate tradition.

Although each dojo has specific rules, there is agreement among practitioners regarding behavior allowed when visiting or training. It is customary not to wear shoes on the training surface even if you are in everyday clothes. Prior to beginning a training session, karateka should present themselves with a clean body and clean *karategi* (uniform). This shows respect for those you are going to train with and for your martial art. While training it is inappropriate to wear jewelry, watches, or the like. Your training uniform must always be kept neat and clean. It is important to bow when entering and leaving a dojo, and before and after training with an opponent, or prior to or after speaking with an instructor or senior student. Acts of profanity, loud talking, laughing, so-cialzing, and misconduct are out of place. When in the dojo one should use the time to either train or meditate. Karate and other martial arts begin and end with courtesy.

SAFETY

Since the martial art of karate is a combative activity, safety is of paramount importance. Following a few basic rules will reduce the potential for injuries. When attacking or counterattacking during kumite one must remember to stop all techniques just short of contact. It is recommended that karateka, especially beginners, use protective equipment to cover the shins, forearms, and hands when engaged in free-fighting. It is strongly en-couraged that one wear a protective mouthguard and refrain from wearing eyeglasses or hard contacts when sparring. If eyeglasses are worn it is important to wear some type of associated protective device. Keeping toenails and fingernails trimmed and removing all jewelry during training will also reduce injury.

CONDITIONING

Karate makes balanced use of almost all major muscle groups. Speed, power, flexibility, balance, agility, and reaction time are important components of training sessions. While practicing kihon, kata, and kumite provides an adequate conditioning stimulus to the body, supplemental conditioning such as jogging, cycling, swimming, and weight training will enhance cardiorespiratory fitness, muscular strength, endurance, flexibility, and body composition.

Serious karateka make extensive use of the *makiwara* (straw-wrapped punching board) and the heavy bag to develop precision and power in performing effective punches, strikes, and kicks. Use of these two pieces of training equipment helps karateka develop the focus necessary in tensing and relaxing muscles during various techniques.

PHYSICAL AND PSYCHOLOGICAL PRINCIPLES

Being successful at karate requires an understanding and application of fundamental physical and psychological principles to training. The proper use of speed, strength, technique, balance, timing, distance, and focus is necessary to effectively use karate skills.

Tachikata (importance of stances)

To maintain balance, the center of gravity must be within the base of support. There are times in karate when you need a stable stance and times when you need an unstable stance. Stable stances are needed to strike with force or when you are receiving a strong attack. Unstable stances are required when it is necessary to change your stance and move rapidly from one position to another.

Chikara (power)

The ability to generate power is necesary in karate. Since power is a product of speed and strength, it is important to emphasize both of these in training. Energy generated from the slower but larger and more powerful muscles of the hips and trunk should be coupled with those of the smaller, weaker but faster muscles of the extremities to generate maximum power in blocking, puching, striking, and kicking.

Kime (focus)

The ability to focus (*kime* means to penetrate the spirit) your technique results from contracting muscles at the moment you make contact with your target. At the same time it is important to exhale forcefully to help augment the power generated.

Kiai (spirit cry)

Associated with karate is the traditional spirit cry known as the *kiai!* Kiai represents a willful activation and union of the karateka's vital energy and should not be misconstrued as merely "shouting."

Koshi Kaiten (hip rotation)

The importance of the lower central torso region in generating power and maintaining stability in karate and other martial arts cannot be overemphasized. This region, known as the *seika tanden* is the focal point of thought and motion. Without effectively employing the hips in karate techniques, there can be no true power.

Jun Kaiten (regular hip rotation)

This motion occcurs when the direction of rotation and direction of technique are the same. As an example, when the hips are rotated to the left, the right fist is used for punching. When the hips are rotated to the right, the left arm may be used for an outward-to-inward block.

Gyaku Kaiten (outward hip rotation)

This motion occurs when the direction of rotation and direction of the technique are opposite to one another. In this motion the hips rotate to the right and the technique is executed to the left. As an example, reverse rotation is used in executing the down block, middle block, and knife-hand block.

Kokyu (use of proper breathing)

As a general rule, when attempting to generate power to execute any technique, it is necessary to forcefully exhale only about two thirds of the air from the lungs. In doing so, less time is needed to refill the lungs prior to the next technique. Additionally, exhaling all of the air from the lungs may weaken the power of a technique.

Mizu no Kokoro (mind like water)

This refers to the need to make the mind calm and serene, similar to that of an undisturbed body of water. Just as undisturbed water accurately reflects objects, so does the undisturbed mind accurately reflect that which it sees. A composed mind, devoid of distractions and apprehensions, will accurately reflect the physical and mental posture of the opponent and thus, will be able to respond with appropriate offensive and counteroffensive techniques. Conversely, if the surface of the water is disturbed, the images it reflects will also be disturbed. In like manner, if the mind is preoccupied with thoughts of attack, defense, or apprehension, it will not be able to anticipate the opponent's intentions and thus create an opportunity for the opponent to attack.

Tsuki no Kokoro (mind like the moon)

Just as moonlight shines equally on everything within its range, this concept refers to the ability of being constantly aware of the totality of your opponent's movements and intentions. Clouds which block out the light of the moon are similar to nervousness and distractions which interfere with the interpretation of your opponent's intentions. This makes it impossible to find openings in your opponent's defenses to deliver an effective attack or counterattack. When watching an opponent, a karateka should envision looking at a distant mountain (*enzan no metsuke*). This insures that the opponent's entire body is in the field of vision, as well as the background. Better detection of the relative motion of the opponent's technique is then possible.

Ma (timing)

This deals with the principle of correct timing in attack and defense situations.

Maai (combative engagement distance)

This is the principle of correct distancing in delivering offensive and defensive techniques. For training, distancing is generally divided into close, middle, and far distance. Opponents practice modifying techniques so that they can be used at these ranges.

Kuzushi (off-balancing)

This refers to unbalancing your opponent, either psychologically or physically, to create an opening for an attack or counterattack.

Tsukuri (fitting-in)

This refers to "fitting in" or closing the combative engagement distance between you and your opponent with an appropriate technique.

Kake (the attack)

This is the attack or counterattack in a combative situation.

Ki, Ken, Tai Ichi (spirit, sword, and body are one)

Literally translated, this means "spirit, sword, and body are one." This combative concept comes from Japanese swordsmanship and indicates that for a technique to be effectively employed, one's resolute will, proper technique, and body must all be used simultaneously.

Suki (opening)

This refers to either a physical or psychological "opening" in your opponent through which to deliver an attack or counterattack.

Waza o Hodokoso Koki (proper moment to attack)

Closely related to the concept of suki is that of *waza o hodokoso koki*, which is the psychological moment to execute an effective technique. Generally, there are four instances in which a karateka may deliver a technique against an opponent. These are (1) at the start of the opponent's technique, (2) when the attack comes, (3) when the opponent's mind is motionless, and (4) when creating an opening in your opponent.

Kobo Ichi (appropriateness of attack)

This refers to the appropriate timing of offensive and defensive techniques. Three levels of timing are recognized.

1. *San no sen*—to take the initiative with one's attack.
2. *Tai no sen*—to take the initiative when the enemy attacks.
3. *Go no sen*—to take the initiative later. This is not the same as engaging in defensive karate. It refers to setting up or leading an opponent into a situation in which you have an advantage.

Zanshin (remaining heart)

This translates literally as "remaining heart" or "remaining mind." It refers to the psychological domination or awareness remaining or "lingering" over an opponent, even after an offensive or counteroffensive technique has been completed.

RULES FOR SPORT COMPETITION

The martial art of karate is an international sport and is practiced in almost every country of the world. In most karate tournaments karateka may participate in either kata or kumite competition, or both. The rules under which karateka compete vary according to the sponsoring organization. Some of the major organizations under whose auspicies competition is held are WUKO (World Union of Karate-do Organization), FAJKO (Federation of All-Japan Karate-do Organization), and the AAU (Amateur Athletic Union).

Kata

In kata competition, sequence of movements (*embusen*), good form, proper body rhythm (*unsoku*), proper speed (*waza no kamkyu*), development of power, proper tension and relaxation techniques (*karada no shin-shuku*), correct breathing, continuity (*renzoku-sei*), and awareness of imaginary opponents (*waza no imi*) are judged. Contestants usually perform either a preselected or self-chosen kata and are graded on an overall point system which ranges from 0 or 3 to

In some scoring systems each judge (the number of which may vary) awards a score and the highest and

Table 15-4. BASIS FOR AWARDING POINTS IN KATA COMPETITION

Perfect	10
Excellent	9
Very Good	8
Good	7
Average	6
Fair	5
Poor	4
Very Poor	3

lowest scores are deleted. The remainder of the scores are added together to form a total score. Deductions ranging from 0.1 to 1.0 may be made in each area. The karateka with the highest score at the end of the competition is the winner. One of the point systems used to judge kata is shown in Table 15-4.

Kumite

Kumite competition is conducted between two karateka usually matched according to sex, age, and experience level (belt rank). The competition area (*shiaijo*) is generally a flat surface, preferably a wood floor, with an area of about 8 meters square. The actual kumite consists of a free exchange of punches, blocks, strikes, and kicks with rapidly changing offensive and counteroffensive movements until one karateka scores an effective "hit" (stopped just short of actual contact) against a valid target area. Depending on the quality of the technique which is scored according to good posture (*shisei*), technique (*kihon waza*), timing, speed (*waza no kamkyu*), distance, and correct application of power (*chikara no kyojaku*) either a full point (*ippon*) or half point (*waza-ari*) is awarded. Generally two out of three points wins a kumite match which generally lasts 2 or 3 minutes. Within the match area are two to four judges and one referee. According to the rules used, either a flag or "mirror" system is used to award points. It is the duty of the judges to call points and act as arbitrators in awarding points. The referee conducts the match, awards points, announces fouls, and issues warnings and disciplinary actions.

Target areas of the human body

Effective attacks and counterattacks are aimed at a vital target area. In self-defense, this means that the technique delivered will strike an area in such a way as to cause the assailant to quit the assault. In sport competition, it means that if the technique were to make contact, it would cause the opponent to quit the assault also. Figure 15-8 outlines the most common target areas of the body against which techniques may be delivered to disable as assailant.

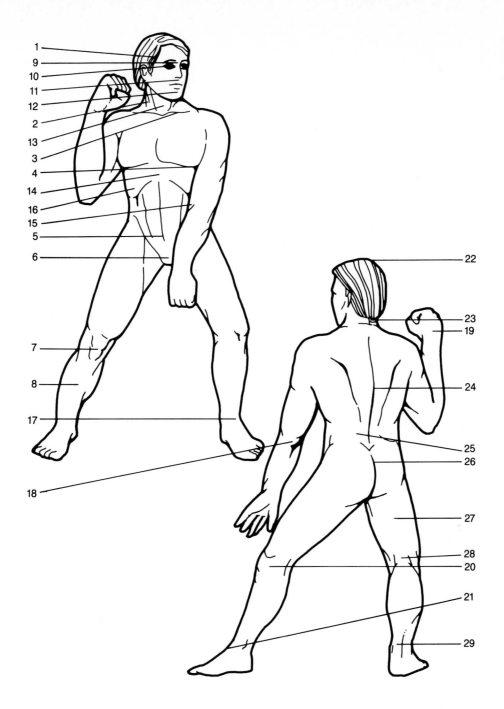

1. Chin
2. Side of neck
3. Collarbone
4. Armpit
5. Abdomen
6. Testicles
7. Knee
8. Shin
9. Bridge of nose
10. Eye
11. Just below nose
12. Chin
13. Throat
14. Solar plexus
15. Front of elbow

16. Ribs
17. Ankle
18. Back of elbow
19. Wrist
20. Side of knee
21. Instep
22. Skull
23. Back of neck
24. Center of back
25. Kidneys
26. Coccyx
27. Back of thigh
28. Back of knee
29. Achilles tendon

Fig. 15-8. Target areas.

GLOSSARY
Japanese/English
Tachikata (stances)

fudo-dachi Immovable stance
hachiji-dachi Open-leg stance
hangetsu dachi Half-moon stance
heiko-dachi Parallel stance
heisoku-dachi Attention stance
jiyu-dachi Free-fighting stance
kiba-dachi Horse stance
kokutsu-dachi Back stance
kosa-dachi Cross-legged stance
neko-ashi-dachi Cat-leg stance
renoji-dachi L-stance
sanchin-dachi Hourglass stance
shiko-dachi Square stance
shizentai-dachi Natural stance
sochin-dachi Diagonal straddle-leg stance
teiji-dachi T-stance
uchi-hachiji-dachi Inverted open-leg stance
yoi-dachi Preparatory stance
zenkutsu-dachi Front stance

Ukewaza (blocking techniques)

age-uke Rising block
gedan-barai Downward block
haishi-uke Back-hand block
juji-uke X-block
kake-uke Hooking block
kakiwake-uke Reverse wedge block
kakuto-uke Bent-wrist block
keito-uke Chicken head wrist block
morote-sukui-uke Two-hand scooping block
morote-tsukami-uke Two-hand grasping block
morote-uke Augmented forearm block
nagashi-uke Sweeping block
osae-uke Pressing block
otoshi-uki Dropping block
seiryuto-uke Ox-jaw block
shuto-uke Knife-hand block
sokumen-awase-uke Side two-hand block
soto-uke Outside block
sukui-uke Scooping block
teisho-awase-uke Combined palm-heel block
tekyubi-uke Wrist-hook block
tsukami-uke Grasping block
uchi-uke Inside block

Tsukiwaza (punching techniques)

age-zuki Rising punch
awase-zuki U-punch
choku-zuki Straight punch
dan-zuki Consecutive punching
gyaku-zuki reverse punch
hiraken-zuki Fore-knuckle fist straight punch
hasami-zuki Scissors punch
heiko-zuki Parallel punch
ippon-ken-zuki One-knuckle fist straight punch

kagi-zuki Hook punch
kizami-zuki Jab punch
morote-zuki Double-fist punch
nagashi-zuki Flowing punch
nakadaka ippon ken Middle finger one-knuckle fist
oi-zuki Lunge, or chase, punch
seiken choku-zuki Fore-fist straight punch
tate-zuki Vertical fist punch
teisho-zuki Palm-heel punch
ura-zuki Close punch
yama-zuki Mountain punch

Keriwaza (kicking techniques)

age-uke-kake-uke Upper block (reverse foot)
ashibo-kake-uke Leg hooking block
ashikubi-kake-uke Ankle hooking block
fumikiri Cutting kick
fumikomi Stomping kick
gyaku-mawashi-geri Reverse round kick
mae-geri Front kick
mae-tobi-geri Jumping front kick
mawashi-geri Round kick
mikazuki-geri Cresent kick
nidan-geri Double jump kick
sokutie-mawashi-geri Circular sole kick
sokutei-osae-geri Pressing sole block
tobi-geri Jumping kick
yoki-tobi-geri Jumping side kick

Uchiwaza (striking techniques)

empi-uchi Elbow strike
haishu-uchi Back-hand strike
haito-uchi Ridge-hand strike
hiji-uchi Elbow strike
kentsui-uchi Bottom-fist strike
nukite Spear hand
riken-uchi Back-fist strike
shuto-uchi Knife-hand strike
tettsui-uchi Bottom-fist strike
uraken-uchi Back-fist strike

Commands and directions

mae Front
ushiro Back
hidari Left
migi Right
hajime Begin
yame Stop
yoi Ready
mawatte Turn
yasume Relax
narande Line up
seiretsu Line up by rank
modotte Return to original position
rei Bow
sensei ni rie Bow to teacher
otagai ni rei Bow to each other
shomen ni rei Bow to the front of the dojo

Other important terms

aite Opponent
dan Black belt rank
dojo Martial arts school
embusen Kata performance line
enjin kumite Circle fight
jiyu kumite Free-fighting
kamae Posture
kancho Building chief ("chief instructor of organization")
karate Empty hand
kata Formal exercise
kiai Spirit cry
kihon Basic exercise
kohai Junior
kumite Sparring
kyu Colored belt rank
makiwara Punching post
mokuso Meditation
nagewaza Throwing technique
obi Belt
okyu teate First aid
osotu-gari Major outside reap
osu Greeting, shows respect
ouchi-gari Major inside reap
renzuki Alternate punching
ryu Tradition
sanbon-kumite Three-step sparring
seiza Formal sitting position
sempai Senior
senjin kumite Line fight
sensei Teacher
shihan Master
shotokan Pine-sea style ("kan" translates here as building)
suki Opening
suwari-geiko Seated sparring
teki Enemy
tori Attacker
uke Defender
ukemi Falling practice

SUGGESTED READINGS

Egami, S: The heart of karate-do, Tokyo, 1980, Kodansha Publishing Company.

Kim, D and Leland, TW: Karate, ed 2, Dubuque, Iowa, 1975, Wm C Brown Publishers.

Sawyer, M: Karate everyone, Winston-Salem, NC, 1985, Hunter Textbooks, Inc. Written for the college karate class, this text contains origins, conditioning tips on self-protection, and safety considerations.

Schmidt, RJ and Hesson, J: Karate: a sport for life, Glenview, Ill., 1989, Scott, Foresman & Company. Suitable for individual or group instruction, this book contains an overview of the sport, basic skill sequences, and a description of forms of competition. Also contains a pronunciation guide.

16

Kayaking and Canoeing

Completion of this chapter should enable the reader to:

- Appreciate the development of canoeing and kayaking
- Select and care for proper equipment
- Describe and execute fundamental canoe and kayak techniques
- Practice proper safety procedures
- Understand and practice boating etiquette
- Instruct a group of students in basic canoe and kayak techniques

HISTORY

Canoeing and kayaking have evolved over hundreds of years. The first boating vessels were probably single logs or logs strapped together (rafts). With the use of fire and primitive tools, crafts such as the dug-out canoe emerged. Natives from Central America, the Figi Islands, Africa, the Solomon Islands and Indian tribes from North America used the dugout canoe for travel, trade, and war.

The canoe and kayak can be traced to the Indian tribes and Eskimos of North America. In areas where trees were scarce, frame and skin craft were constructed. A wooden or bone frame was designed to form the gunwales, keel, and ribs and the skins of buffalo, moose, or cattle were sewn together and stretched over the frame. Seams were sealed with pitch or tallow. In the North Central parts of the United States and Canada where trees were more plentiful, bark from birch trees was stretched over a wooden frame.

Decked (covered) boats were used by Eskimos mainly in Alaska and Greenland. These boats were called kayaks or umiaks. Kayaks were smaller, for one person, and were paddled with double-blade paddles. Umiaks were larger (up to 30 feet) and were paddled by up to eight paddlers using single-blade paddles. Open boats were called canoes. Canoes for one person were 12 to 17 feet long, while those built up to 30 feet long could carry more people. They were mainly paddled with single-blade paddles. Sometimes poles were used for steering and navigating upstream.

The canoe and kayak were a primary source of transportation. They were used for hunting and for transporting furs to trading centers. When the settlers from Europe and Britain came to North America, they often had the help of Indians in facilitating travel. Canoes were fast, had maneuverability on the water, and were light weight for portaging between lakes or rivers. Many French immigrants settled in the Canadian north and found the adverturous life of hunting and trapping more attractive than clearing land and farming. They adopted the Indian lifestyle and became expert canoeists. Known as voyagers, they became renouned in history.

Unlike voyagers, other European and British settlers employed the Indians to help them. Samuel de Champlaign, Jacques Marquette, Louis Joliet, Lewis and Clark, and others had Indian guides and used Indians to paddle canoes. Therefore, paddling expertise was never learned by these explorers.

In time, western settlement of the United States and Canada passed through a sequence from frontier to settlements of farmers and ranchers, to a more urbane society. The art of canoeing nearly disappeared except for those few who pursued that lifestyle. By 1900 over two thirds of the population lived in the country and the demands of farming and tending animals left little time for leisure. Later, railroads and the automobile further lessened the canoe's importance as a means of transporation. Between 1920 and 1940 both Canada and the United States changed from being two thirds rural to three fourths urban. This led to the near disappearance of canoeing and kayaking in North America.

Interestingly, Europeans who traveled in the United States and Canada saw the canoe or kayak and popularized it as sport in their countries. In 1865 John MacGregor made his famous trip covering a thousand miles throughout England and Europe in the Rob Roy. Because the Rob Roy and others like it were closed or decked boats, kayaking became known as canoeing across Europe. Around the turn of the century, another person named Smith toured France in a canoe modeled after the Indian canoe. The term unCanadian or a Canadian became popular. These terms are still used throughout Europe. Whitewater paddling in Europe was pursued as a leisure activity. The Europeans have since dominated international canoe and kayak racing.

The resurgence of canoeing and kayaking in North America was influenced primarily by two things related to recreational pursuits. Sport fishing in the north became popular and fishermen hired Indian guides to paddle. However, the sport was fishing, not canoeing. The real thrust for recreational paddling has been in summer camps for children. Private camps, YMCA camps, military academies, and the like have done an excellent job of teaching the basics of flat water canoeing for several generations. However, with rules such as "no standing in the canoe" and "don't shoot the rapids", little was done to develop whitewater technique until the mid 1970s. During the time for the late 1930s through the early 1970s canoe and kayak building was limited to two or three models by two companies, Old Town and Grumman. Canoes were primarily made of wood strips and aluminum.

Development of synthetics such as plastic, fiberglass, Acrylonitrile Butadiene Styrene (ABS), and Kevlar, along with a maturing of social, economic, and environmental values, has resulted in a growing popularity of canoeing and kayaking. While the popularity of flatwater boating has stabilized, participation in whitewater canoeing and kayaking continue to increase. Interest in sea kayaking promises to lead the industry in the 1990s.

With the expansion of interest in canoeing and kayaking, Americans have also returned to racing to be competitive with the Europeans. In the 1988 Olympics, Greg Barton won the first U.S. Gold Medal in flatwater kayaking. The first World Whitewater competition in the United States took place on the Savage River in Maryland in 1989 after being held in Europe for decades. Kathy Hearn, Davey Hearn, Jon Lugbill, and others have lead the resurgence of whitewater slalom racers.

VALUES

Whereas most outdoor recreation and sports develop muscles of the lower limbs, canoeing and kayaking primarily develop muscles of the back, abdomen, shoulders, and arms. It is an excellent aerobic activity as most canoe and kayak outings last for at least half an hour and many take a half day, whole day, or even several days. Canoeing and kayaking may begin as recreational activities or as a sports interest. As skill is developed the number of options become almost limitless. One can canoe or kayak solo or with a partner. Canoeing and kayaking can offer solitude as well as the companionship of groups. Canoeing and kayaking is done by both sexes and people of all ages.

The versatility of canoes and kayaks is amazing. One can paddle on the smallest creek, river, or lake, while the fastest growing aspect of the sport is sea kayaking. After developing skill in a selected vessel, it is possible to combine paddling with picture taking, sight seeing, fishing, hunting, bird watching, and the like. If one wishes to become competitive, there is flatwater racing or whitewater slalom and downriver racing competition. Competition varies in nature from citizens races (friendly, novice racing) to Olympic events.

EQUIPMENT

Paddles, boats, personal gear, and clothing has changed greatly in recent years. Natural materials in clothing and boats have given way to synthetics. The differences have brought about changes in the sport.

In the past equipment such as an aluminum canoe served many purposes. Today specialized equipment exists for different boating and paddling styles. Since the diversity of selection in equipment can be overwhelming, asking instructors or boat outfitters appropriate questions concerning equipment and gear will enhance the chance of making good choices.

CLOTHING

On a hot summer day it may be comfortable in a swimsuit or cotton shirt and shorts. However, during the spring or fall and on cold water rivers or lakes, always consider the prospect of hypothermia.

Layering clothes increases warmth and comfort. A wicking layer next to the body transfers moisture from the skin to the outer layers. Silk and polypropylene serve this purpose. Absorbing material should be the middle layer. Wool, pile, and bunting moves moisture to the outer layer. The outer layer protects against wind and water and is usually made of nylon or Gore-tex. While it may not be necessary to wear all these clothes at all times, weather conditions should always be considered. Clothes not needed immediately should be packed in a dry bag. Wetsuits and drysuits are often worn by paddlers in extreme conditions.

Shoes should also be considered. Entry, exit, or portage conditions can't be predicted. Old sneakers, hiking boots, river shoes, and booties are all choices. Many accidents have been caused by poor traction or stepping on cut glass. It is important to protect the feet from injury.

Other personal choices are hats and sunglasses. Hats help keep the body warm and protect the eyes from the sun's glare. Sunglasses protect eyes from glare and from harmful ultraviolet rays.

ACCESSORY GEAR

Accessories for canoeing and kayaking include paddles, lifevests, flotation, spray covers, first aid kits, and rescue equipment. Next to choosing a proper canoe or kayak, the choice of a paddle is most critical. Paddles are constructed of wood, fiberglass, carbon fiber, plastic, and aluminum. Grips are either pear-shaped or T-shaped. Shafts are straight or angled from 5 to 15 degrees. Blade width may vary from 6 to 9 inches or more. Length is determined by the paddler's height and whether the paddle will be used from a sitting or kneeling position. High-performance paddles are light and expensive, but sometimes not very durable. Paddles used on rugged, remote trips should be heavy and durable. Aluminum shafts are light and durable, but may feel cold to bare hands. Beginning paddles use whatever the outfitter provides, but as one becomes serious about canoeing or kayaking it is important to learn about the choices before buying.

Paddlers should always wear a U.S. Coast Guard approved lifevest for adequate buoyance, physical protection, and warmth. Type III and Type V personal flotation devices (PFDs) are most commonly used. Persons who paddle decked boats (kayaks, C-1's, etc.) or open boats in difficult rivers with a probability of capsizing should use helmets. Helmets have a plastic or fiberglass shell with a liner to cushion blows.

Flotation is a necessity for canoes and kayaks so they will not sink when swamped. Many aluminum and fiberglass canoes have flotation in sealed compartments in the bow and stern. Closed boat flotation includes airbags and ethafoam or styrofoam walls which also prevent the deck from collapsing on the boater's legs in the case of a pin. Open boat flotation may include inflatable air bags, styrofoam blocks, and tire inner tubes. Extra flotation causes greater displacement of water when the boat is capsized, making rescue easier.

Spray covers and spray skirts are used in some canoeing conditions and most kayaking conditions to keep water from entering the vessel. Spray covers and skirts must release reliably, but not prematurely, under normal boating conditions so the paddler can get free of the boat should the need arise.

First aid equipment is a must for all boaters. The extent of preparedness depends on the qualifications of the personnel in the group and the nature of the trip.

Long distance or wilderness trips require additional preparedness. At a minimum, a first aid kit should contain dressings, ointments, disinfectants, pain medication, emergency phone numbers, and health forms for each participant.

Rescue equipment is important for unexpected emergencies. Throw lines or rescue bags are often necessary for rescuing people or boats. "Painter lines" on canoes and grab loops on kayaks are helpful in rescue because they allow a person to get away from the boat while still maintaining contact. Other rescue equipment could include pulley and rope systems and repair kits for remote travel.

BOATS

The characteristics of canoes and kayaks vary widely. Paddlers can select boats geared to their strength, body size, and purpose (racing, touring, or pleasure). The most important features of canoes, kayaks, and paddles are shown in Fig. 16-1.

Length

The overall length of a boat is the distance from one end to the other. If the width remains the same, an increase in length will increase the speed and tracking ability of the craft.

Width (beam)

Width is measured at two points for canoes—the molded beam and the waterline. The molded beam width is the distance between the tops of the two sides. The narrower this width, the easier it is to paddle because the canoeist does not have to reach out as far. The waterline width is the widest point when a boat rests in the water. More weight added to a boat will generally increase its waterline width. Kayak width is measured at the widest point. Whitewater models generally are widest near the middle. This allows for increased maneuverability. Touring and downriver kayaks are widest somewhat back of the middle. This increases straight-line tracking ability, but inhibits maneuverability.

Depth

In a canoe, depth is measured at the centerline from the gunwale down. A taller boat deflects spray and waves, but may catch more wind than one with less depth. A shallow boat minimizes wind resistance, but increases the probability of shipping water. Depth in a kayak influences the amount of room for the legs.

Rocker

The rocker is the shape of the hull along the underwater keel line (Fig. 16-2). A straight keel line improves tracking ability. Turning is made easier (less drag) as a rocker is added.

Parts of a Canoe

Parts of a Kayak

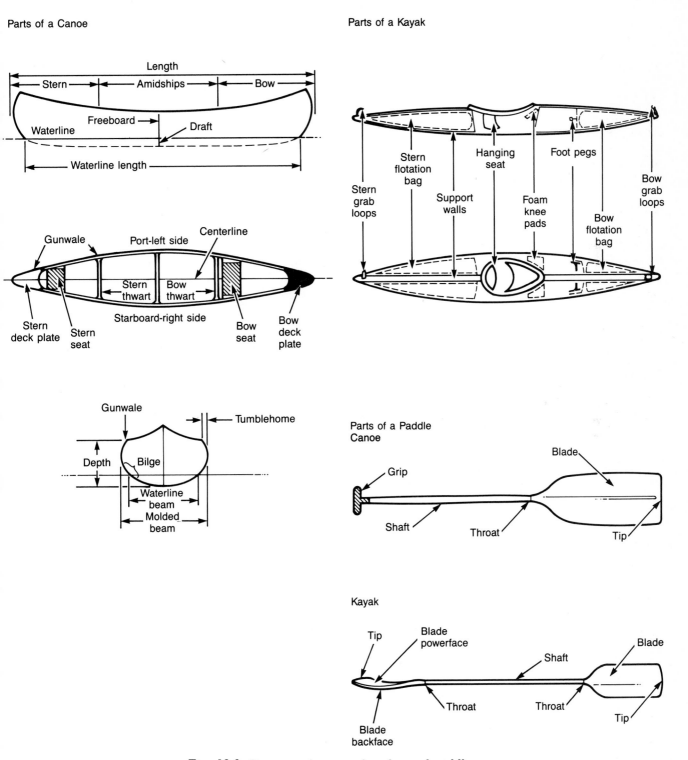

Parts of a Paddle
Canoe

Kayak

Fig. 16-1. Features of canoes, kayaks, and paddles.

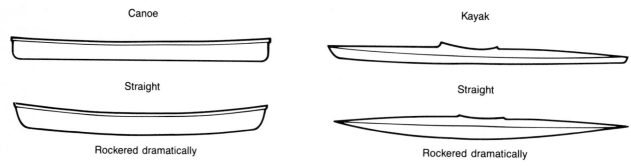

Fig. 16-2. Canoe and kayak rocker.

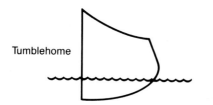
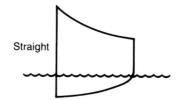
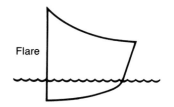

Fig. 16-3. Flare and tumblehome.

Flare and tumblehome

These terms refer to the shape of the boat above the waterline (Fig. 16-3). Flared sides provide increased stability. Boats with tumblehome have less molded beam width than waterline width. When boats with tumblehome are leaned extremely, stability is decreased dramatically.

Symmetry

Symmetry refers to the shape of the boat from front to back at the waterline (Fig. 16-4). Symmetry affects a boat's movement through the water and its ability to turn. Symmetrical boats are used for quick maneuverability. Asymmetrical boats usually lengthen and streamline the shape of the bow to increase the efficiency of passage through the water. In asymmetrical boats directional control is increased, but turning ability is decreased.

Vees, arches, and flat bottoms

These terms describe the bottom shape of the boat (Fig. 16-5). Flat bottom boats tend to be very stable. Rounded hulls are initially less stable than flat bottoms if they have flare. They have good stability and are forgiving, however, when the boat is leaned. The greater the boat's vee shape, the better the directional ability but the poorer its stability.

Volume

Volume indicates the fullness of a boat's shape and how much weight it can carry. High performance vessels for racing have low volume. Medium volume boats can carry some gear and are suited for general recreational paddling. High volume boats can carry more than 200 pounds and are used for extended travel.

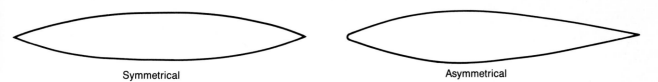

Symmetrical   Asymmetrical

Fig. 16-4. Symmetry.

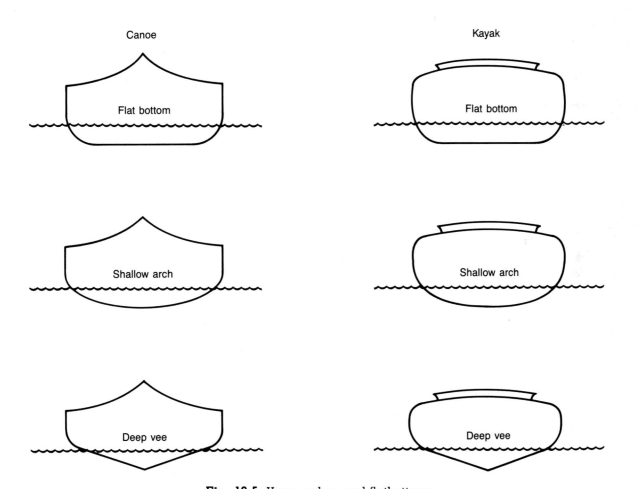

Fig. 16-5. Vees, arches, and flatbottoms.

Boat types

Canoes are classed into two divisions—tandem (for two people) and solo. Each division has several classes based on the purposes for which the canoe may be used. Within the tandem division the casual recreation, day tripper, touring, and downriver boats are the most popular. Casual recreation canoes are generally built with cost a primary consideration along with low maintenance, casual storage, and safety. Performance is not a primary consideration (Fig. 16-6, *A*). Tripper and touring canoes are medium volume (Fig. 16-6, *B*). They are designed to carry two paddlers with gear, yet have low profiles, are lightweight for portability, and are fairly quick in the water. Downriver canoes are valued primarily for their directional integrity or fast straight-ahead paddling (Fig. 16-6, *C*). They are good performers in waters ranging from millponds and open bays to nontechnical class II and class II whitewater rivers. Competition cruising, whitewater playboat, whitewater slalom, and Olympic flatwater are further types of tandem canoes used for racing in various conditions.

Solo canoes are the second division of canoes. Types of solo canoes are cruising, racing, sport, whitewater, and Olympic flatwater (Fig. 16-7). Cruising canoes are designed for the traveler. Sport canoes are ideal for day tripping or "just messing around" on a lake or millpond. They combine maneuverability and directional integrity.

Kayaks likewise have many designs or types (Fig. 16-8). They include casual recreation, touring, sea cruising, downriver, whitewater slalom, whitewater playboat, squirt, and Olympic flatwater. Casual touring kayaks are primarily touring boats, but will handle nicely in moderate whitewater. Touring kayaks are high-volume boats designed to carry generous loads with compromising handling qualities or moderately rough water. Sea cruising kayaks are long, high-volume boats designed to cover long stretches of unpredictably rough open water with comparative ease. Because of the interest in exploring the open water and coastline, this is the fastest growing segment of the kayak industry. The remaining kayaks are generally for racing or recreation in whitewater.

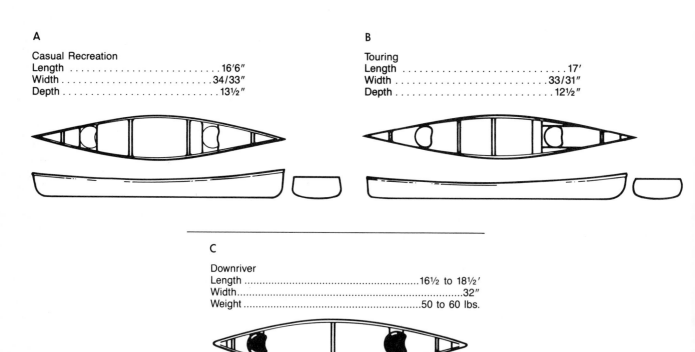

A

Casual Recreation
Length . . . . 16′6″
Width . . . . 34/33″
Depth . . . . 13½″

B

Touring
Length . . . . 17′
Width . . . . 33/31″
Depth . . . . 12½″

C

Downriver
Length . . . . 16½ to 18½′
Width . . . . 32″
Weight . . . . 50 to 60 lbs.

Fig. 16-6. Types of tandem canoes.

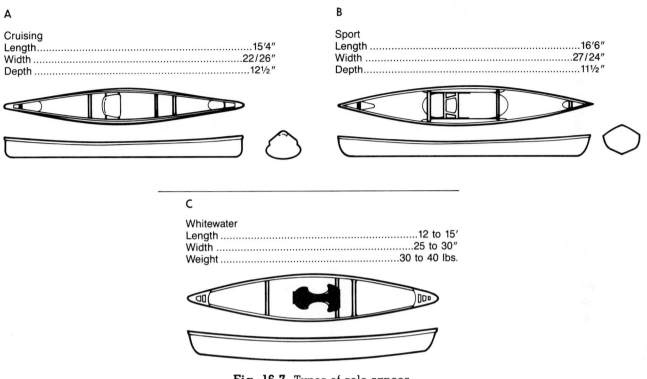

A

Cruising
Length...15'4"
Width ....22/26"
Depth ....12½"

B

Sport
Length ....16'6"
Width ....27/24"
Depth...11½"

C

Whitewater
Length ....12 to 15'
Width ....25 to 30"
Weight ....30 to 40 lbs.

Fig. 16-7. Types of solo canoes.

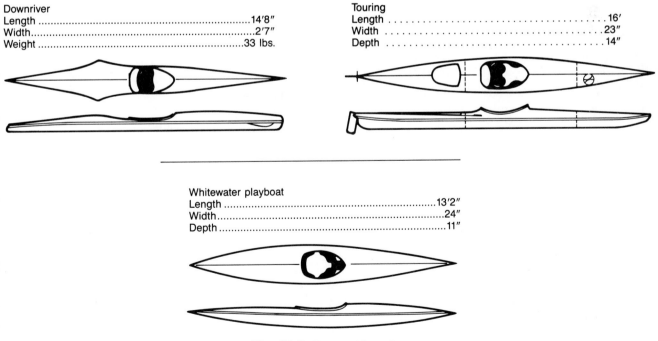

Downriver
Length ....14'8"
Width...2'7"
Weight ....33 lbs.

Touring
Length . . . . 16'
Width . . . . 23"
Depth . . . . 14"

Whitewater playboat
Length ....13'2"
Width...24"
Depth ....11"

Fig. 16-8. Types of kayaks.

GENERAL RULES AND WATER ETIQUETTE
Be kind to others

There is an old rule that good friends or spouses should never paddle together because of disagreements over route selection, fault for capsize, and so on. Communicate with your partner. Help or compensate for your partner. Offer assistance when asked. Don't be loud and obnoxious. Don't hog the best practice place, view, and the like.

Stay with your group

If you are in a group, paddle as fast or as slow as the rest while maintaining a reasonable distance between boats. Getting too far ahead or behind puts you in a position to get lost, reduces the safety of the group as a whole, and generally causes ill feeling toward you. If necessary, break your group into two units—one faster, one slower.

Respect other's property

Make sure you have permission to put your boats in the water and take them out. When stopping along a lake or river to eat, rest, or sleep, get permission and respect property such as trees, animals, fences, and land. Don't litter and when you can, clean up the litter of others.

Follow established rules

The U.S. Coast Guard and other governing bodies, such as the American Whitewater Affiliate of the American Canoe Assoication, have rules for safety on the water. Know and follow them. Some general rules are:

1. Boats propelled by oars or paddles have the right-of-way over motor boats.
2. In a crossing situation the boat to the starboard (right) has the right-of-way.
3. Use the universal river signals to communicate to others (Fig. 16-9).

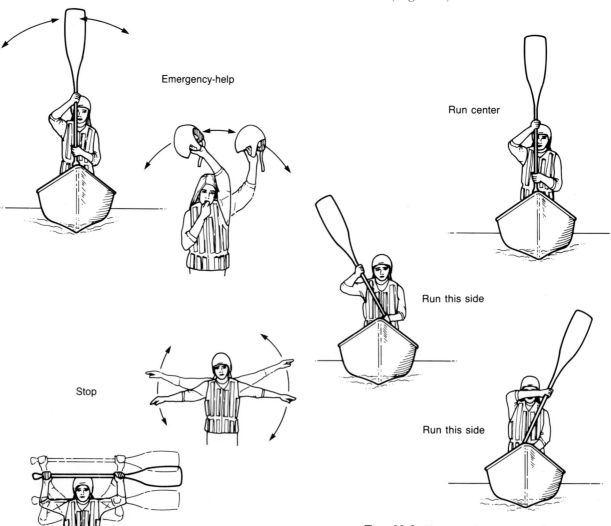

Fig. 16-9. Universal river signals.

FUNDAMENTAL SKILLS AND TECHNIQUES
Orienting the paddler to the boat

Canoes and kayaks are lightweight and shallow-draft craft. They are sensitive to weight distribution (fore and aft as well as side to side). The key is to keep the center of gravity (CG) over the center of buoyancy (CB). As weight in the form of packs or paddlers is added to a canoe or kayak, there is a potential for both the CG and CB to shift fore, aft, or to one side.

Maintaining balance in a canoe or kayak is regulated by keeping the CG over the base of support (CB) and by keeping the CG as low as possible. A sudden change in trim caused by an outside force such as a wave, collision, or by leaning to one side results in a shift where the CG may begin to fall outside the CB. As this happens it is necessary to use a righting action called a "hip flip" to recenter the CG over the CB.

The recommended position for canoe paddling is kneeling. This offers a low center of gravity with three points of contact with the canoe. The knees are spread wide and the buttocks rest against the seat or thwart. One can also perform the righting action (hip flip) from this position quite well. Other paddling positions such as sitting, high-kneel, or standing are possible but should not be tried until one has a feel for the canoe and has become competent in basic paddling strokes.

Kayakers always sit in their vessel with their legs out in front. To get a good fit or to "wear the kayak," the knees should be bent up and out to fit snugly on the upper walls of the kayak. Foot braces should be adjusted so the balls of the feet press against the braces. This snug fit gives a low center of gravity and allows a good hip flip for maintaining stability.

A good stability drill is to get into position in the boat, lean slightly to one side, and then flip the hips back under to correct the base of support and regain equilibrium. Another is to rock from side to side while keeping the navel, shoulders, and head in a centered position. In both instances the paddlers can get a good feel for the boat and learn that by making adjustments the craft can maintain stability under changing conditions.

Correct launching and docking (getting in and out) of canoes and kayaks are essential to a successful experience. Canoes may be boarded end first with the canoe perpendicular to shore or from the side with the side parallel to shore. When two people board a canoe, the bowman usually boards first to maintain trim. The stern person assists by straddling the canoe and holding the gunwales. The bow person places the first foot on the center or keel line of the canoe while keeping the weight centered over the leg on the bank or dock. Next, while keeping low by bending at the hips and knees, the hands grasp each of the gunwales. Then the trail leg is brought into the canoe at which time the canoeist assumes the kneeling position ready to assist the stern person in getting in (Fig. 16-10). When getting out, the process is reversed. Launching and docking a canoe from a position parallel to the dock involves the same procedures. Step into the center. Grasp both gunwales. Keep weight low (Fig. 16-11).

Getting into and out of a kayak with its tiny cockpit is more of a challenge. The best way is to place the kayak parallel and next to shore. Place the paddle across the kayak, just behind the cockpit, with one of the blades lying flat on shore for support. With the hand nearest the kayak grip the junction of the kayak paddle and the cockpit to keep the boat steady. While keeping your weight leaning towards shore, place the lege nearest the kayak just to the front of the seat. Follow it with the other leg. Then lower yourself into the seat, being careful not to scrape your shins across the top of the cockpit (Fig. 16-12). Exiting is a reversal of the process.

Fig. 16-10. Launching.

Fig. 16-11. Launching parallel to dock.

Fig. 16-12. Launching the kayak.

In both canoeing and kayaking it may be necessary to perform what is called a wet entry and exit. The exit part is easy. In a canoe, rather than jumping out or capsizing, it is safer to place both hands on one gunwale, maintain contact and slip over the side of the canoe into the water. When doing a wet entry it is important for a partner or another canoe to provide support and assistance. With this assistance being provided from the opposite side, place both hands on the gunwale, perform a scissors kick to gain lift, and push up with the arms into a support position with the hips near the gunwale. Next swing the legs one at a time over the gunwale and into the canoe. Staying low through this process is important. A wet exit from a kayak is accomplished by capsizing, removing the skirt from the cockpit rim with a pulling action and carefully withdrawing the hips and legs from the boat. After

righting the kayak and approaching it diagonally from the rear, a wet entry can be performed by placing both hands on the cockpit and using the arms to pull up onto the back deck of the kayak in straddle position. Then, by placing both hands behind the hips, both legs are lifted simultaneously (bilaterally) and smoothly back into the kayak and slide back down into a sitting position.

The mechanics of paddling

There are three major types of canoe and kayak strokes. They are power strokes; turning, lateral, or corrective strokes; and bracing strokes. Power strokes primarily provide forward or reverse momentum. Turning, lateral, or corrective strokes turn the boat so that it veers from its straight course or is brought back onto its straight course. Bracing strokes provide stability for the craft.

Strokes are also divided into onside and offside strokes. Onside strokes are executed on the selected paddling side. Offside strokes are executed on the other side. There are two phases to all strokes. The *propulsion phase* is application of force on the paddle against the water. The *recovery phase* is return of the paddle to a "catch" position where the blade is braced against the water ready to begin the propulsion phase. Recoveries can be feathered above the water or sliced through the water.

Strokes can be dynamic or static. A dynamic stroke moves the blade actively against the current. A static stroke is a fixed-position stroke used to turn or veer the boat. Static strokes require the boat to be moving faster than the current to be effective.

Many paddling strokes use a third-class lever system for propulsion. A third-class lever has the fulcrum on one end, the power or force in the middle or shaft, and the resistance at the end of the blade (water). The use of a third-class lever assists the paddler in gaining speed and range of motion at the blade end of the paddle. As a result, the paddler gains a mechanical advantage. The larger the paddle (within reason) the better the mechanical advantage. The disadvantage of a third-class lever is the relatively high energy expenditure required. First-class levers are used in one or two selected strokes such as the J and pry or pushaway. In the pry stroke the water is again the resistance. The fulcrum moves to the middle of the shaft at the function between the bottom paddle hand and the gunwale. The force is provided by the top paddle hand. This allows the paddler to transfer the stroke's power directly to the canoe as in rowing with an oar and make the stroke effective in its purpose.

The powerface (P) is that side of the blade which is pressed against the water during a forward stroke. The backface (B) is the reverse side of the paddle and is pressed against the water during a backstroke. Turning, lateral, correcting, and bracing strokes will be identified as to whether they use the powerface or backface of the paddle for execution.

To establish linear motion in a canoe or kayak it is best to have the paddle in a vertical position and follow a straight path parallel to the keel line of the boat (Fig. 16-13). To establish rotary motion (Fig. 16-14) in a vessel it is best to apply force to the paddle as far forward or aft of midships as possible to establish an arc around a pivot point.

Newton's Third Law of Motion states that for every action there is an equal and opposite reaction. In paddling, the action is the application of force to the blade. The reaction is the movement of the craft in the opposite direction. To go forward, pull the water back. To go to the right, push or pull the water to the left.

The most powerful stroking action is accomplished with the arms in a relatively fixed, straight, extended position and by using the large, strong muscles of the

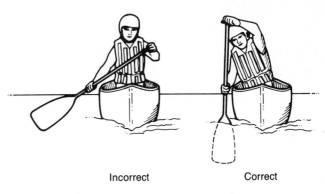

Incorrect   Correct

Fig. 16-13. Paddle position for linear motion.

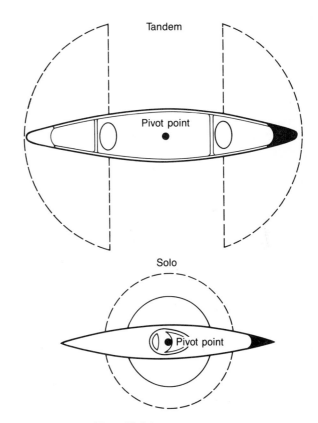

Fig. 16-14. Rotary motion.

back and torso. This concept is called torso rotation (Fig. 16-15). During the recovery phase, the shoulder of the onside arm is rotated forward to "coil" the body. During the power phase of the stroke the torso is unwound.

Three types of wind and water resistance that can affect a craft are frontal, surface, and eddy resistance (Fig. 16-16). Frontal resistance occurs where the force of wind or water strikes a craft first. It exerts the greatest pressure against a boat. Surface resistance occurs when the wind or water slides along the craft. Eddy resistance is created

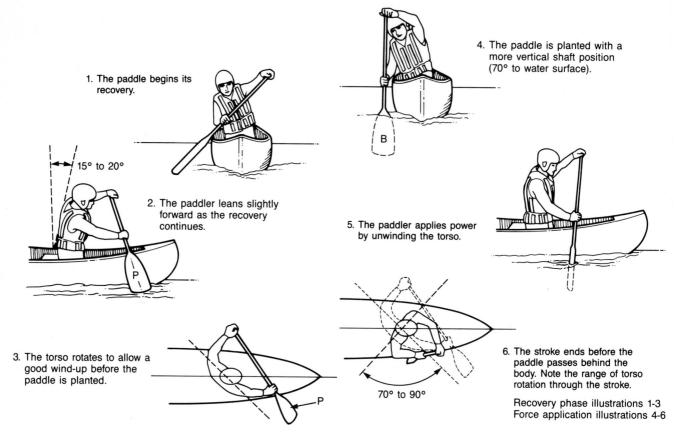

1. The paddle begins its recovery.

2. The paddler leans slightly forward as the recovery continues.

3. The torso rotates to allow a good wind-up before the paddle is planted.

15° to 20°

4. The paddle is planted with a more vertical shaft position (70° to water surface).

5. The paddler applies power by unwinding the torso.

6. The stroke ends before the paddle passes behind the body. Note the range of torso rotation through the stroke.

Recovery phase illustrations 1-3
Force application illustrations 4-6

70° to 90°

Fig. 16-15. Torso rotation in forward stroke.

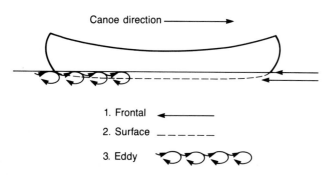

Canoe direction

1. Frontal
2. Surface
3. Eddy

Fig. 16-16. Three types of resistance.

when a craft displaces wind or water at its widest point. The resulting vacuum is filled in by an unstable whirl of displaced water. An understanding of these resistances helps paddlers determine which stroke to use in a given situation. For example, corrective strokes are most effective in the eddy resistance end. When paddling forward, the stern person can best steer the craft. When paddling backward, the bow person can best steer the craft.

Paddling strokes
Power strokes

Forward. The forward stroke is used in solo and tandem canoeing and kayaking. For clarity, the forward canoe stroke is discussed separately from the kayak stroke.

In the catch position the body is wound tightly with the bottom or shaft arm reaching as far forward as possible. Both arms are relatively straight. The top or control arm is across the midline of the body to allow the paddle to be vertical in the water. The torso remains fairly upright with no more than a 20 degree bend (Fig. 16-17). Lunging and straightening the back causes the canoe to bob in the water. The propulsion phase of the stroke involves unwinding the torso. The arms remain relatively straight with the most movement occurring at the shoulder nearest the paddle as it unwinds like a spring. The power of the stroke occurs during the first 5 to 7 inches. Thus, a short stroke with the recovery beginning when the paddle is beside the hip is important. During recovery, the blade should be angled to cut through the air like a knife to reduce air resistance.

The forward kayaking stroke invovles a "push-pull" action against the paddle. Paddlers punch out with their

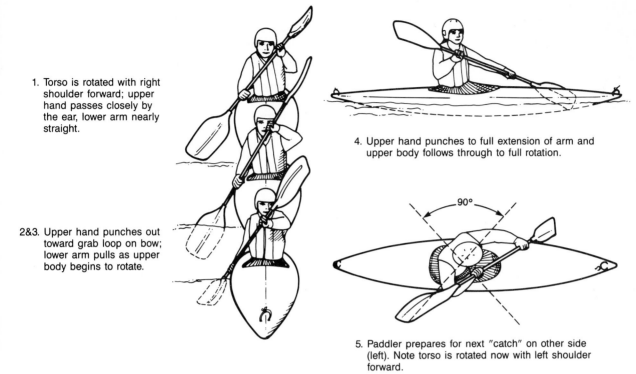

1. Torso is rotated with right shoulder forward; upper hand passes closely by the ear, lower arm nearly straight.

2&3. Upper hand punches out toward grab loop on bow; lower arm pulls as upper body begins to rotate.

4. Upper hand punches to full extension of arm and upper body follows through to full rotation.

5. Paddler prepares for next "catch" on other side (left). Note torso is rotated now with left shoulder forward.

Fig. 16-17. Forward stroke-kayak.

upper arm as the lower arm pulls back. Rotating the body with torso rotation as in the forward canoe stroke is also important. Exit and recovery begins when the lower hand reaches the hip. The paddle blade is removed from the water by lifting the wrist and elbow to shoulder level. This action promotes a clean exit and a quick recovery for the next stroke.

Common inefficiencies include failing to submerge the blade fully, leaning forward or lunging, making the stroke too long, and sweeping the blade in an arc rather than pulling vertically parallel to the keel line. Keeping a boat on a straight course requires timing and power, which may be elusive at first.

Back. The back stroke for canoes and kayaks retraces the forward stroke with the same body techniques. The catch position is just behind the hip nearest the blade and the power phase ends when the upper hand is near the shoulder. The backface of the paddle blade is used. Beginners should look over one shoulder to see where they are going.

Turning, lateral and corrective strokes

J stroke. When using the forward stroke a canoe will begin to veer off course to the soloist's or stern person's off paddling side. For this reason a corrective stroke is needed to keep the vessel on track. The J stroke (Fig. 16-18) is used for this. It is not a kayaking stroke.

Fig. 16-18. "J" stroke.

The initial part of the J stroke, including the catch and beginning of the propulsion phase, resembles the forward stroke. A vertical paddle shaft and torso rotation are keys to success. However, as the paddle comes back to the hip, departure from the forward stroke begins. Rather than an immediate recovery, the paddle or shaft hand grasps the gunwale and simultaneously cups the shaft, as well, creating an anchor point and a first-class lever. The top or control hand with the paddle shaft in a vertical position (blade under the boat), rotates the thumb downward to present the powerface of the paddle to a vertical postion facing away from the canoe. In this position the paddler uses the control hand to curve the

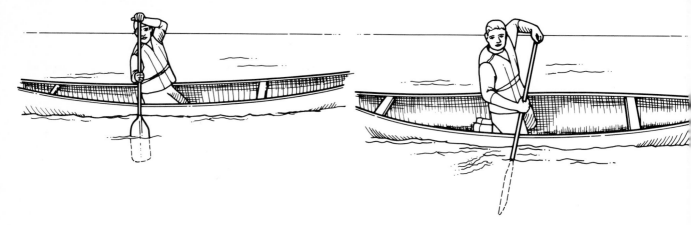

Fig. 16-19. Basic draw stroke.

blade sideways away from the canoe, which corrects the veer and puts the canoe back on track.

This movement is rather quick yet powerful, allowing the paddler to keep an uninterrupted pace or stroke rate. The use of the J stroke will vary according to factors such as solo or tandem paddling and strength/weight ratio of the tandem pair. Sometimes it is used every stroke in combination with the forward stroke, other times every two to four strokes. The trick is to gauge its use to anticipate and counteract the effects of veering.

Draw stroke. The draw stroke is used in canoeing and kayaking to move a boat laterally or to turn a boat, depending on the conditions under which it is applied. The basic draw stroke (Fig. 16-19) is performed at a right angle to the paddler's side. With the arms making a C shape and the paddle in a vertical position extended out away from the boat, the paddle is inserted fully into the water. The boat is then pulled to the blade. Most of the force is provided by the lower or shaft arm as it pulls in to the hip. The hip simultaneously is flipped toward the paddle blade, thereby moving the boat back under the paddler's center of gravity. The stroke ends with the blade parallel to and near the boat. The recovery is initiated with a backward slicing action of the blade above the water or a knifing action of the blade through the water back to the catch position.

Variations on the draw stroke include performing a stationary draw or a dynamic draw (several in a row). The stationary draw is used when the boat has built up some speed and the paddler wants to use one powerful stroke to shift the boat sideways to his or her onside or to initiate a turning action. The dynamic draw is used for lateral or turning maneuvers requiring continuous action or where the boat has no forward momentum. If the draw is used from midships, lateral movement will

Fig. 16-20. Cross draw.

occur. If the paddler is positioned fore or aft or lowers the top hand fore or aft, the draw can be used to turn the boat. Other variations of the draw stroke are bracing strokes and the Duffek stroke, which will be discussed later.

Cross draw. The cross draw (Fig. 16-20) requires the paddler to lift the paddle across the boat to the offside. The body and arms are twisted to face the offside. The top or control hand is kept stationary at or near the armpit. The paddling action is done entirely by the lower or shaft arm. The hand on the shaft is palm down. The grip or control palm faces forward. The power face of the paddle is in a vertical position and is pulled toward the bow. Recovery is above the water. The stroke is used as an alternate to the pry stroke. It is used to turn or move the canoe laterally. It may be used dynamically or from a static position.

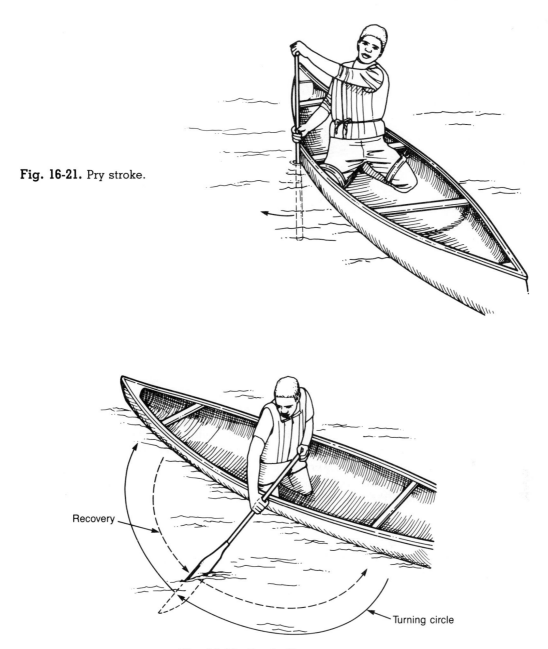

Fig. 16-21. Pry stroke.

Recovery

Turning circle

Fig. 16-22. One-half sweep.

Pry. The pry, sometimes called the pushaway, moves the canoe in the opposite direction of the draw. It moves the boat to the paddler's offside and can be used to turn or move the boat laterally, depending on where the force is applied and whether the canoeist is paddling solo or in tandem. The pry is not a kayak stroke.

To execute the pry (Fig. 16-21) place the paddle in a vertical position with the shaf in contact with the gunwale. The bottom or shaft hand holds the paddle and simultaneously cups the gunwale to stabilize the paddle making it a first-class lever. The top or control hand, knuckles out, pulls sideways toward the midline of the body. A short, quick, powerful action is used with the backface of the paddle used for the stroke. The recovery can be out of or through the water. In each case the paddle is knifed or sliced back to the catch position.

The pry can be used dynamically (several in a row) or stationary. It can be used in combination with other strokes, such as a forward stroke into a pry.

Sweep strokes. Sweep strokes, as the name implies, are wide sweeping arcs of the paddle. Solo sweeps in a canoe or kayak involve a 180 degree arc and are thus called one-half sweeps (Fig. 16-22). Tandem sweeps are intended to account for one's position in a boat and thus

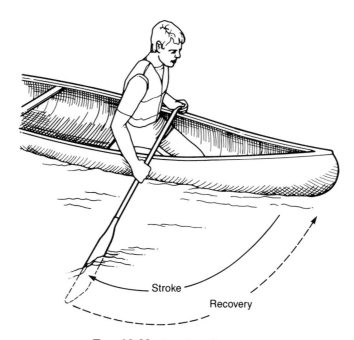

Fig. 16-23. One-fourth sweep.

cover 90 degrees or are referred to as one-fourth sweeps (Fig. 16-23).

Unlike previous strokes in which the paddle was in a vertical position, the paddle position is low and angular. The forward sweeping action is with the powerface of the blade. The reverse sweep is with the backface. Since the stroke's purpose is for turning, the torso of the body twists early for the catch and follows the blade through the exit.

When performed from a solo position at midships, a forward sweep enters at the 12 o'clock position and exits at the 6 o'clock position as the paddler follows with the torso, head, and arms until the shoulders are parallel to the keel line. The forward sweep turns the boat to the paddler's offside. The reverse sweep for a solo boater begins at the 6 o'clock position, ends at the 12 o'clock position, and turns the boat to the paddler's onside.

When paddling tandem the bow paddler's arcs are from the 12 o'clock position to the 3 o'clock position or from the 12 o'clock position to the 9 o'clock position. The stern paddler's strokes are from the 3 o'clock position or the 9 o'clock position to the 6 o'clock position. If the bow does a forward one-fourth sweep and the stern does a reverse one-fourth sweep, the canoe will turn in one direction. If the bow does a reverse one-fourth sweep and the stern does a forward one-fourth sweep, the boat will turn in the opposite direction.

Duffek. The Duffek stroke is a turning stroke. It was first used in kayaking, but can be used in canoeing by a solo paddler or the bow paddler when tandem canoeing. The purpose of the Duffek is to make a 180 degree turn to enter or exit currents and eddys or to turn behind a solid object such as a dock or pier. Since the boat has forward momentum, a sweep stroke (forward or backward) is used to initiate the turn.

A left turn in kayaking, for example, would be initiated by a forward sweep on the right. The Duffek would then be executed on the turning side or left (Fig 16-24). In many ways the Duffek is like the stationary draw. The paddle is vertical in the water. However, in the catch position the blade is opened until it broaches the current. This means that the wrists are cocked to present the power face of the paddle perpendicular to the boat. As the boat turns around the paddle, which is acting as a fulcrum or anchor, the wrists uncock. Other important aspects of the Duffek are a turning of the torso so that one can see the stern at the beginning of the stroke. The top arm is also kept as low as possible (across the forehead). The lower arm is bent, relaxed, and extended slightly forward and over the boat. All of these factors are important to prevent shoulder dislocation. A cross Duffek, like a cross draw, can be executed in canoeing on the canoeist's offside.

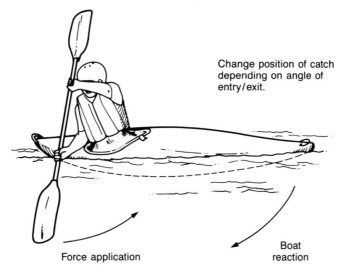

Change position of catch
depending on angle of
entry/exit.

Force application

Boat
reaction

Fig. 16-24. Duffek stroke.

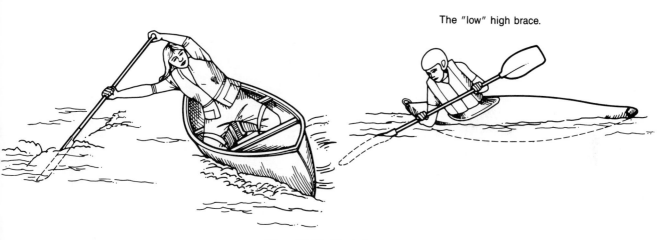

The "low" high brace.

Fig. 16-25. High brace.

Bracing strokes

High brace. Bracing strokes are used to right a vessel and prevent a capsize (Fig. 16-25). The high brace is a variation of the draw stroke. The powerface of the blade is used on the water. Instead of drawing the boat to the paddle from a vertical position, there is more of an angle to the blade. This allows for part of the force to be applied in a downward direction, giving the paddler time to regain balance and reposition the center of gravity inside the boat.

Low brace. The low brace is used in canoeing and kayaking to lean the boat into turns and to correct an impending capsize (Fig. 16-26). In the low brace, lay the backface of the paddle flat in the water behind the hips. The position of the knuckles of both the grip and shaft hand is down. The elbow of the shaft hand is above the paddle. From the entry position the blade is simultaneously pushed down and swept to the side perpendicular to the boat. A quick push down on the paddle will cause the boat to roll to the opposite side, allowing the paddler to regain balance. In an extreme crisis the head and torso can be put into the water and the boat brought around with the knees and hips (hip flip). The body is brought back aboard (over the vessel) only at the end of the recover, just as in an Eskimo roll.

Eskimo roll. The Eskimo roll or modified C to C roll is a two-part process using a sweep stroke combined with a hip snap (Fig. 16-27). The forward sweep brings the paddler's body from under the boat and up to the water's surface in a C position. Then the lower body can snap the boat upright with a hip snap (a high brace maneuver) to the second C position.

Fig. 16-26. Low brace.

The set-up

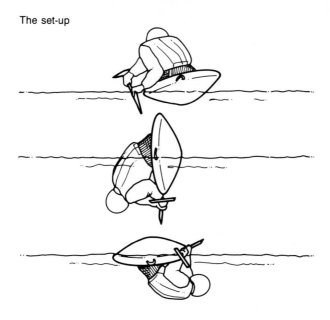

The hip snap

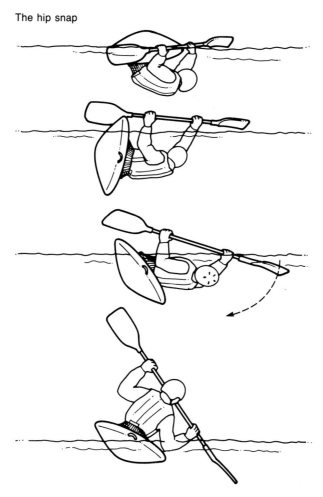

Fig. 16-27. Eskimo roll.

Calm water practice of maneuvers

Boat maneuvers in ponds, lakes, and slow moving rivers involve moving in a straight line, moving sideways, spins, and V turns. Each involves one or more of the strokes previously discussed. The choice of a stroke is often dependent on whether one is in a canoe or kayak and whether one is paddling tandem or solo.

Spins

Spins are discussed first because they can be taught to a group of people and executed under various practice conditions while allowing the group to remain in one place. Spins, full or partial, are used when moving around a bend in a river or positioning around another object such as a boat or dock.

From a kayak or a solo position in a canoe, a forward one-half sweep will turn the bow to the offside of the stroke. A reverse one-half sweep will move the bow to the onside of the stroke. From a tandem paddling position, several combinations of strokes will spin the canoe. If both people draw, the canoe will turn to the onside (Fig. 16-28, A). If both paddlers pry, the canoe will turn to the offside. If the bow paddler executes a forward one-fourth sweep while the stern does a reverse one-fourth sweep, the canoe will spin to the offside (Fig. 16-28, B). If the bow does a reverse one-fourth sweep and the stern does a forward one-fourth sweep, the canoe will spin to the outside.

Moving sideways

Moving laterally in a canoe or kayak is helpful to pull up beside another boat or shore or to move sideways to avoid an object such as a rock or branch in the water.

In a kayak or solo canoe paddling, drawing to the right or left from midships will move the boat sideways in the direction of the onside or paddling side (Fig. 16-29). Use of a pry or cross-draw will move the boat to the offside (Fig. 16-30). In tandem paddling, the use of opposite strokes (draw/pry) will move the boat sideways (Fig. 16-31).

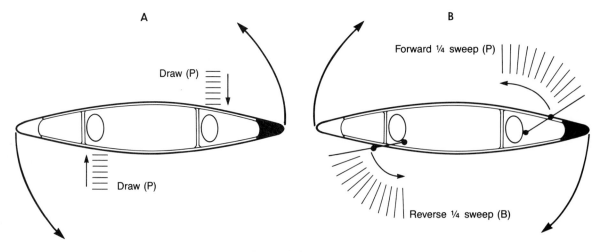

A — Draw (P), Draw (P)

B — Forward ¼ sweep (P), Reverse ¼ sweep (B)

Fig. 16-28. Spins.

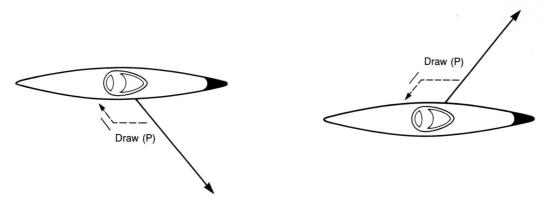

Fig. 16-29. Moving sideways by drawing.

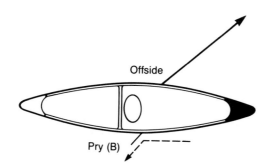

Fig. 16-30. Moving sideways using a pry.

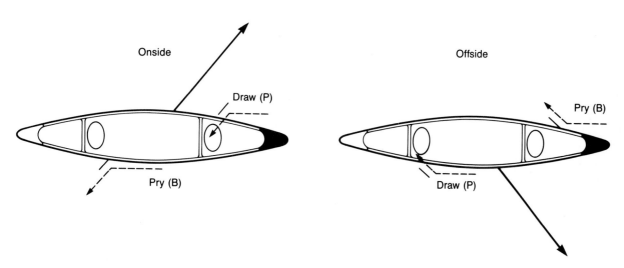

Fig. 16-31. Moving sideways in tandem paddling.

Moving in a straight line

Moving in a straight line (or tracking) is most often the intent of paddling. Going forward is the obvious choice because it is the most powerful and efficient stroke, plus you can see where you are going.

In a kayak, forward movement occurs with the power stroke on alternate sides (Fig. 16-32). Remembering that the boat and paddle are bilaterally symmetrical, equal amounts of force should be applied on each side to enhance going straight ahead. In a solo canoe the J stroke is preferred to go forward. Sometimes a C stroke is used, which is in essence a draw moving directly into a J stroke. Both C and J strokes prevent a canoe from verring to the paddler's offside (Fig. 16-33). When tandem canoeing the bow person uses a forward power stroke. The stern paddler uses a forward stroke with a J or forward one-fourth sweep as needed to keep the boat moving in a straight line (Fig. 16-34).

At times one may also choose to go backwards. This may be done for backing away from shore, another boat or from danger.

In a kayak on would use a backstroke on alternating sides (Fig. 16-35). In a solo canoe one would use a back stroke in combination with a reverse J because the steering is now done at the bow or eddy end of the canoe (Fig. 16-36). In tandem paddling the stern person now does the backstroke, while the bow person steers with a reverse J (Fig. 16-37).

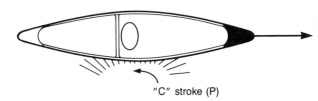

"C" stroke (P)

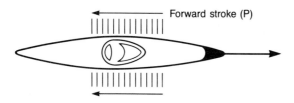

Fig. 16-32. Moving forward in a kayak.

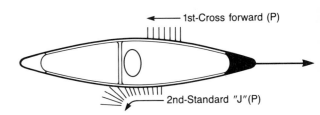

Fig. 16-33. Moving forward when solo in a canoe.

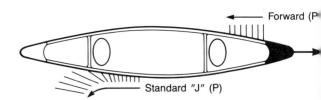

Fig. 16-34. Moving forward when tandem in a canoe

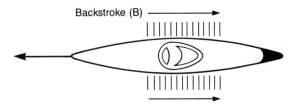

Fig. 16-35. Moving backward in a kayak.

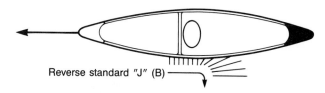

Fig. 16-36. Moving backward when solo in a canoe.

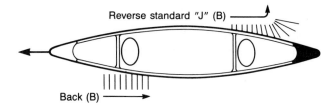

Fig. 16-37. Moving backward when tandem in a canoe.

U-Turns

A U-turn (an abrupt 180 degree turn) in flatwater paddling, though not an essential skill, can be taught to develop proficiency in using combinations of strokes. However, the value of a U-turn becomes apparent when you need to stop behind a rock (eddy turn) or reenter the current (peel out).

In a kayak, a U-turn is done with a sweep on the outside to initiate the turn and carry the momentum forward. Then a Duffek is executed on the inside of the turn. In solo canoe paddling, the choice of strokes depends on the side of the turn. To turn to the onside, combine a reverse sweeping low brace and follow with a Duffek and forward stroke (Fig. 16-38). To turn to the offside, combine a forward stroke followed by a cross Duffek (Fig. 16-39). In tandem paddling, to turn to the onside the stern uses forward one-fourth sweeps while the bow uses a Duffek followed by a forward stroke. To turn to the offside the stern uses a reverse sweeping low brace while the bow uses a cross Duffek followed by a cross forward stroke (Fig. 16-40).

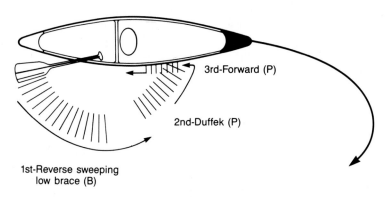

3rd-Forward (P)

2nd-Duffek (P)

1st-Reverse sweeping low brace (B)

Fig. 16-38. Onside U-turn.

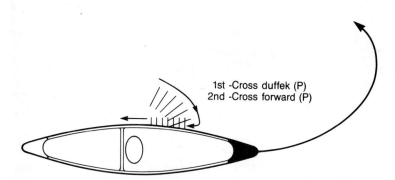

Fig. 16-39. Offside U-turn.

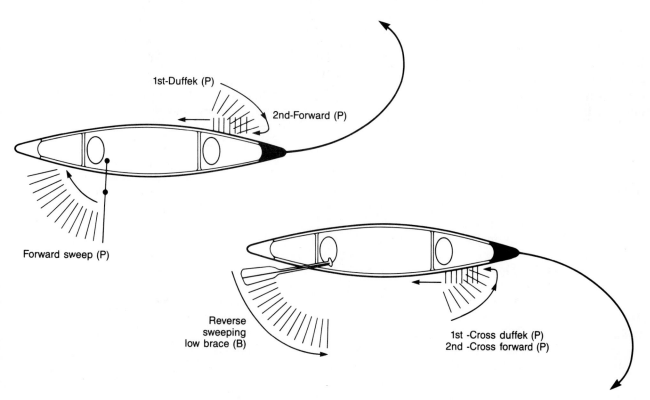

Fig. 16-40. Tandem canoe U-turns.

Rescue

Principles of rescue

Swamping or capsizing a canoe or kayak on flatwater may be caused by wind, waves, wake from powerboats, a paddler's poor balance, or improper trim from improper loading. When a boat does capsize, paddlers must evaluate the situation and determine a course of action. The following guidelines should be observed:

1. Alert other boaters that a capsize has taken place.
2. Victims should initiate self-rescue procedures immediately and be ready to accept assistance from others.
3. Other paddlers can assist in the rescue when it is safe to do so.
4. Paddlers not involved in the rescue should keep their distance and continually evaluate the rescue in the event that more help is needed.

There are rescue priorities to help reduce confusion in a potentially hazardous situation. The first priority is to the paddler in the water. Once in the water, the paddler should initiate self-rescue procedures. Paddlers of decked boats should attempt an Eskimo roll. Once boaters are out of their craft, they should swim to safety if danger exists. If a paddler has a partner, he or she should establish visual and voice contact. Capsized paddlers, after assessing the situation, may elect to stay with their boat and attempt to get back into it using procedures described later. They may choose to swim with their equipment to shore if it is close enough. Boats and other equipment should be rescued only when it is safe to do so.

The second priority in rescue operations is the swamped boat. Paddlers can try a self-rescue of the boat or, when other paddlers are available, use group rescue techniques.

The third priority in rescue operations is other equipment. Objects such as shoes, gear bags, and coolers should be tied in loosely in flatwater situations. They will then bob in the water until paddlers are safe and the boat has been righted. Equipment can then be brought on board again.

Self-rescue

Paddlers can rescue a swamped craft in deep water without assistance from other boats using a Capistrano flip or shake out technique. The Capistrano flip is accomplished by ducking under the capsized canoe and coming up in the air pocket. In unison, the paddlers use a scissors kick and a forceful lifting action to one side to push the craft above the water and roll it upright. A shake out is done while the boat remains upright. One paddler pushes down on an end of the canoe while also pushing forward. The end must then be lifted before the water flows back in. Another way to accomplish the shake out is to rock the canoe from side to side and then quickly pull up on the gunwale before the water flows back in. These techniques rarely get all of the water out of the canoe. The paddler then must decide what to do with the partially submerged boat. The choices are to reenter the boat and paddle to shore or to bail the boat to empty it further. Swamped boats can be paddled, though progress is slow and unbalanced.

Group rescue

Where other boats are available to assist in the rescue, the process changes. Swimming paddlers move to a position where they can help. This may be at the end of the overturned boat where they can push, or at the ends of the rescue boat where they can stabilize. With the boat upside down and perpendicular to the rescue boat, one end is lifted and pulled over the craft. The tipped craft is moved up and over the rescue craft until it is balanced, rolled upright, and slid back into the water (Fig. 16-41). The boat is then moved into position beside the rescue craft and held so that the swimmers can reenter the craft.

SAFETY

Canoeing and kayaking are challenging, adventurous activities with inherent risks. Therefore, it is important to develop an awareness of safety and develop skills which promote safe paddling. Risks in boating cannot be eliminated, but they can be managed to an acceptable level. It is highly recommended that instructors be certified to teach canoeing and/or kayaking by an organization and that participants enroll in certified courses.

The recent increase in popularity of canoeing and kayaking has brought with it an increase in accidents and fatalities. Much can be learned from accident reports compiled by the U.S. Coast Guard. They reveal that most accidents are the result of ignorance. The majority of small craft fatalities involve unknowledgeable, inexperienced boaters. Accident reports indicate five common problems:

1. Paddlers are often not wearing lifejackets. They are either forgotten or used for other purposes such as paddling, sitting on, or kneeling on.
2. Cold water or cold weather is present. Hypothermia inhibits reasoning abilities, the ability to paddle effectively and the ability to self-rescue.
3. Most victims are inexperienced, having had no formal instruction or practice.
4. Alcohol is a contributing factor. Drugs and alcohol affect coordination and judgement. Slow response time and poor decisions in hazardous conditions make accidents predictable.
5. Victims often can't swim. The ability to be at ease in or around water increases the ability to perform well in stressful situations.

Boat-over-boat-rescue

Fig. 16-41. Group rescue.

TEACHING CONSIDERATIONS

1. Always consider the teaching site. Pools, ponds, lakes, and calm places in a river are acceptable. Make sure the site will be free from distractions such as loud noises and groups of other people and free from danger such as trees, branches, debris, broken glass, or other objects.

2. Initial instruction can occur on shore or at the side of the water or pool. It is then possible to work on technique with the paddle and walk about freely to give feedback to people who need correction.

3. Use visuals such as miniature boats and paddles, charts, or mock drawings of boats in the sand to help illustrate points about stroke technique and maneuvers.

4. Move from simple to complex. Boats can actually be paddled by hand to see the action and reaction of strokes on water. With this simple understanding, paddles can be added early and then proceed with more complex drills.

5. Teach spins and turning strokes first so the group can stay close to you. Then, teach power and bracing strokes when the group has beginning control and knowledge of the paddle.

6. Teach and refine for good technique and stroke mechanics. For example, if a stroke is intended to turn the boat it must be applied away from the center at an angle which creates torque. If a stroke is intended to propel a boat in a straight line (forward, backward, or sideways), the paddle must be vertical in the water and pulled in a line opposite the intended motion.

7. Allow students to gain expertise paddling on one side or position before asking them to change. Then, to create versatile paddlers, encourage them to transfer their learning to paddle on the opposite side, to change positions (bow to stern), to paddle with a different person, and to switch from tandem to solo paddling.

8. After students have learned strokes and simple maneuvers, develop drills in which they have to respond automatically. For example, have them respond to commands to turn right, turn left, sideslip right, sideslip left. Mix the commands so their responses become second nature.

9. Move from simple singular maneuvers to combining several maneuvers. Make up a course to be negotiated. For example, enter the vessel, sideslip away from shore, paddle forward, turn left around a bend (obstacle), back up, go between two rocks (obstacles), turn right, paddle forward, etc.

10. Practice safety and rescue procedures along with a paddling sequence. For example, paddle out with another boat and have one capsize (stay near shore). Follow rescue procedures and then paddle back to shore.

11. Instructors should be certified to be aware of standards of practice.

12. If having enough boats is a problem (one boat for every two students) consult local outfitters, YMCAs, canoe clubs, etc. They are often willing to help.

GLOSSARY

amidships The area midway between the bow and stern. Often shortened to midships.

astern Behind the canoe, kayak, or craft.

back paddle Paddling backward to slow or check forward motion.

bail To remove water from a craft.

bar An accumulation of sand, gravel, or rock usually located along the inside bend of a river.

beam The width of a craft measured at its widest point.

blade The broad, flat section of a paddle.

bow The area in the forward end of a watercraft.

bowperson Person who tandem paddles from the bow, front thwart, or front seat.

bracing stroke Paddle stroke providing stability against the capsizing force of a lateral current. May also be used for turning.

broach To turn a craft broadside to oncoming waves or obstructions.

capsize To overturn.

closed boat Boats having the deck as an integral part of the craft.

combination stroke A blended stroke maneuver consisting of two or more simpler strokes.

confluence The point where two or more rivers flow together.

controlhand The upper hand on a canoe paddle which controls turning of the paddle blade.

cross draw A stroke used to move the canoe, or part of the canoe, to the paddler's normal offside.

current General movement of water in a river caused by gradiant differentials.

deck On a traditional open canoe, the triangular piece found at bow and stern to which the gunwales attach at their ends; often called deck plates. On a closed canoe or kayak, a covering for the entire hull.

doubleblade Paddle with a blade at each end; usually used in a kayak and sometimes in an open or decked canoe.

draw stroke A paddle stroke designed to move the craft to the onside of the paddler or toward the powerface of the blade.

Duffek stroke A high bracing stroke first used in the kayak by Milovan Duffek of Czechoslavakia. Used mainly to enter or leave an eddy as an eddy turn (entering) or a peel out (leaving).

eddy Place where the current either stops or moves upstream below obstructions and on the inside of bends.

eddy turn A dynamic technique used by boaters to enter an eddy.

feather Returning the paddle to the "catch" position (ready for a propulsive action) with one edge leading, thus reducing resistance by water or air.

flotation Material placed in a canoe to keep it floating high when upset or swamped.

forward stroke The standard propulsion stroke used in paddling a canoe directly ahead. Also called basic forward or power forward.

freeboard The shortest distance from the waterline to the top of the gunwale of a canoe or to the seamline of any decked boat.

gunwale Strips along the top of a canoe's sides, extending from bow to stern, where the deck and topsides meet.

hull The frame or body of a craft, exclusive of rigging and flotation systems.

hypothermia A serious, life threatening, physical condition caused by a lowering of the body's core temperature.

inside bank In a river bend, the edge of the river with the slower and shallower water.

inverted J A reverse J stroke, used by the tandem bow or solo paddler when canoeing in reverse.

J stroke Stroke used by tandem stern or solo paddler to correct the characteristic swing of the craft to the offside when only a forward stroke is used.

K-1 A kayak with one paddler who sits on the buttocks, keeps the legs extended forward, and uses a double bladed paddle.

keel A thin projecting strip of material running down the exact center of the outer hull of a craft from bow to stern.

lee, leeward, leeway A protected area downwind or downstream of an obstruction which breaks the normal direction and force of the wind or water. Leeward means downwind. Leeway means the drift of a boat downwind.

life vest Personal buoyancy device which is worn like a vest; provides upper body protection and warmth. Also called a PFD (Personal Flotation Device).

low brace Brace stroke in which the entire paddle is nearly flat on the surface of the water.

mouth Area where a river joins another body of water.

nonpowerface The face of a paddle blade opposite the powerface.

offside Side of the canoe on which the paddler is not usually paddling.

paddle The tool used to propel the boat in the desired direction.

painter A length of rope attached to an end of a canoe.

pillow A smooth bulge on the river's surface created by water flowing over an underwater obstruction.

port The left side of a craft when facing toward the bow.

portage The act of carrying a canoe and gear around an obstacle. Also, the place where the canoe has to be taken from the water and carried on land around an obstruction or dangerous spot in the river.

powerface The face of the paddle blade which bears against the water.

pry A type of stroke which uses the craft as a fulcrum to move the boat away from the blade.

recovery The component of a stroke preparing for the next propulsive action.

rocker The upward sweep of the keel line toward both ends of a canoe.

ruddering Holding the paddle blade stationary in the water at a fixed angle to steer.

scull, sculling To propel or align a craft by moving a paddle side-to-side in a continuous figure eight pattern using the same powerface throughout.

sideslipping Situation in which a canoe's center of gravity continues in the initial direction of movement even though the boat is turning.

skirt Garment worn around the waist of closed boat paddlers. It attaches around the coaming to make the cockpit water tight.

starboard The right side of craft when facing the bow.

stem The curved section at the ends of a canoe which slices through the water when paddling forward or backward.

stern The rear section of a watercraft.

swamp When a canoe fills with water but does not capsize.

sweep canoe The last canoe in a group usually containing experienced paddlers, extra equipment, rescue lines, and a first aid kit.

sweepstroke A wide, shallow stroke used for turning or pivoting the canoe.

tandem Two paddlers in a canoe.

throat The flare of the paddle's shaft where it starts to form the blade.

thwart Cross braces, running from gunwale to gunwale, which provide reinforcement for the gunwales. Also known as a spreader or crossbar.

track Paddling in a straight line.

trim The manner in which a canoe rides on the water.

through The low point or hollow found between the crests of two standing waves.

tumblehome The inward-curving upper portion of a canoe which produces a narrowing of the beam at the deck level.

yoke A cushioned shoulder harness that clamps to the gunwales of a canoe permitting the canoe to be carried upside down on the paddler's shoulders.

SUGGESTED READINGS

American Red Cross: Canoeing and kayaking, Washington, DC, 1981. Good coverage of elementary techniques and paddle strokes.

Bechdel R and Ray S: River rescue, Boston, 1985, Appalachian Mountain Club. Focuses on safety and rescue techniques. It is a must for those intending to paddle whitewater.

Evans E and Burton J: Whitewater racing, Bryson City, NC, 1980, John G. Burton. Mostly devoted to downriver and slalom racing technique in decked boats (primarily kayaks).

Evans E and Evans J: The kayaking book, New York, 1988, Viking Press, Inc. Traces the history of the sport and includes information on kayaking in all types of water.

Foster T: Recreational whitewater canoeing, Millers Falls, Mass, 1981, Leisure Enterprises. Includes techniques and instruction for recreational whitewater paddling in open canoes.

Franks CES: The canoe and whitewater, Toronto, 1977, University of Toronto Press. Sets the sport in the contexts of history, technology, geology, and physics.

Gullion L: Canoeing and kayaking: instruction manual, Newington, Va, 1987, American Canoe Association. The instruction manual for certified canoe and kayak instructors and is a must for anyone planning to instruct others.

Mason B: Path of the paddle, Berwyn, Ill, 1983, Blue Heron Enterprises. An illustrated guide to the art of canoeing; a proven handbook for beginners and experts.

Mason B: Song of the paddle, Berwyn, Ill, 1983, Blue Heron Enterprises. An illustrated guide to wilderness travel by canoe.

McNair R, Paul M, and Paul L: Basic river canoeing, (Martinsville, Ind.), 1985, American Camping Association. A good introduction to strokes and tactics.

Rugge J and Davidson J: The complete wilderness paddler, New York, 1980, Random House, Inc. A handbook by two recreational whitewater canoeists; the sections on river tactics and route planning are especially useful.

RESOURCES
Magazines

Canoe, American Canoe Association, The Webb Co., Inc., 1999 Shepard Rd., St. Paul, MN 55116.

River world, World Publications, 1400 Stierlin, Building C, Mountain View, CA 94043.

American whitewater, American Whitewater Affiliation, 1343 N. Portage, Palatine, IL 60067.

American canoeist, Suite 1900, Box 1190, Newington, VA 22122.

Organizations

American Canoe Association, Box 190, Newington, VA 22122. Membership plus a complete book and film library.

American Red Cross, 17th and D Streets NW, Washington, DC 20006. A good source for courses, books, and films.

Canadian Recreational Canoeing Association, Box 500, Hyde Park, Ontario. NOMIZO.

National Paddling Committee, 1750 E. Boulder St., Colorado Springs, CO 80909. Videotapes and training manuals on Olympic flatwater techniques.

Sierra Club, 530 Bush St., San Francisco, CA 94108.

There are many local and state canoe clubs. Consult a phone book under river outfitters to obtain locations and contact persons.

FILMS AND VIDEOTAPES

Fast and clean, videotape, color, sound, 20 min. Nichols Productions, 17000 Carwell Rd., Silver Springs MD 20904. Preparations of the U.S. whitewater slalom team for the 1984 national and world competitions.

Fundamental canoeing, 16 mm, color, sound, 12 min. Sterling Educational Films, 241 E. 34th St., New York, NY 10056. A basic instructional film.

Kayak, 16 mm, color, sound, 20 min. Pyramid Films Productions, Box 1048, Santa Monica, CA 90406. Fundamentals of kayak technique.

Margin for error, 16 mm, color, sound, 25 min., also available on videotape. Nichols Productions, 17000 Carwell Rd., Silver Springs, MD 20904. How to plan for and run a trip down a whitewater river.

One river down, 16 mm, color, sound, 32 min. Paddler Productions, Box 281, Chestertown, NY 12817. Captures the beauty of the land and the experience of wilderness paddling in Labrador.

Path of the paddle: quiet water, videotape, color, sound, 60 min. Blue Heron Enterprises, 6212 W. Cermak Rd., Berwyn, IL 60402. Bill Mason demonstrates basic paddling strokes for solo and tandem paddlers; filmed in rugged Canadian Shield country.

Path of the paddle: whitewater, videotape, color, sound, 60 min. Blue Heron Enterprises, 6212 W. Cermak Rd., Berwyn, IL 60402. How to read the rapids, plan a course, and follow it while in complete control of the boat.

Uncalculated risk, 16 mm, color, sound, 25 min., also available in videotape. American Red Cross, General Supply Office, 17th and D Streets NW, Washington, DC 20006. Concentrates on the risk and dangers of river running.

Whitewater, 16 mm, color, sound, 25 min. NBC Productions, Films Inc., 8124 N. Central Park Ave., Skokie, IL 60076. Contrasts the right and wrong way to run a river.

Whitewater self-defense: the Eskimo roll, videotape, color, sound, 14 min. Nichols Productions, 17000 Carwell Rd., Silver Springs, MD 20904. Slow motion and stop action, using underwater cameras, helps demonstrate the skill and clearly shows components of the Eskimo roll.

17

Mountaineering

Completion of this chapter should enable the reader to:

- Know the importance of physical conditioning and weather considerations in mountaineering
- Select proper mountaineering equipment
- Recognize what backpacking, camping, and other skills are necessary to lead a mountaineering trip
- Demonstrate proper hiking skills for various types of terrain and conditions
- Apply rock-climbing principles
- Practice various rock-climbing holds and descending techniques
- Understand the management and the use of ropes in climbing and descending

Mountaineering as a sport evolved from a desire to fulfill the need for adventure, to satisfy curiosity, for scientific study, and to test abilities and limits. Now that the earth's highest points have been attained, the dream has been extended to space, but even those limits are being reduced. The challenges of earthbound adventurers can be successfully met with the knowledge of the dangers involved and with the training necessary to handle them. A mountaineer shares and appreciates the beauty of nature and at the same time learns to venture into the mountains with respect.

Increasing numbers of people are expressing interest in a variety of outdoor recreation sports that relate to the wilderness, mountains, rivers, and oceans. These would-be adventurers must be made aware of the responsibilities that accompany this interest.

HISTORY

Examples of famous climbs include the Biblical account of Moses receiving the Ten Commandments on Mount Sinai and Hannibal crossing the Alps with his elephants. Military conquests long provided the strongest reasons for passage through and over mountains. One may conjecture that when military needs no longer existed, peoples' adventurous spirit turned in peacetime to the

mountains and to the pursuit of climbing, with scientific or geographical reasons given for the activity.

According to Ronald W. Clark's book, *Men, Myths and Mountains*, in 1492 as Columbus set sail on his history-making voyages, a group of men in France started an assault on a rock bastion that had long been considered inaccessible and inhabited by evil spirits. That this climb was made for the challenge it offered, not for necessity, might mark it as the beginning of climbing as a sport. Actually, climbing was not recognized as a sporting pastime until a century or so later.

In the mid-1500s, Josias Simler, a naturalist professor at Zurich University, published *Concerning the Difficulties of Alpine Travel and Methods by Which They May Be Overcome*. In this same period the clergy and the monks played a significant part in development of mountain travel.

Climbing has never been confined to men only. Clark states that women began to appear as members of climbing groups early in the 1800s. In 1809 Marias Paradis, from Chamonix, became the first woman to climb Mont Blanc. Recent history has also recorded an all-women assault on Mt. Everest.

Military mountaineering played a great and tragic part in the Alps during World War I. After World War I, interest in climbing the world's highest mountains intensified. Membership in the long-established mountain clubs such as the Appalachian Mountain Club and Sierra Club grew quickly, as did the outing clubs of schools and colleges of the United States.

After World War II the U.S. Army Tenth Mountain Division, with many famous skiers and mountaineers in the ranks, brought back their love for and interest in the mountains. They sponsored climbing schools and made many climbs themselves that helped rekindle and generate interest in mountaineering among the youth of the United States.

PHYSICAL CONDITIONING

One should not engage in mountaineering without first attending to one's physical condition. Cardiovascular and respiratory conditioning exercises are appropriate for mountaineers. Stamina and an intense desire to never give up are important in difficult situations. The mountaineer living in the city should consider the many training facilities available. Using stairs instead of elevators and practicing fingerhold chin-ups on the casing over doorways are simple but effective conditioning activities.

WEATHER CONSIDERATIONS

No hiker or climber can afford to disregard the weather. Forecasts are essential, and the normal weather pattern should be known. Local inhabitants may sometimes be helpful, and a rudimentary knowledge of weather signs is necessary. As a general rule the temperature drops 3° to 5° F for every 1000-foot (305 m) gain in elevation. Marginal weather at lower elevations may mean storms at higher elevations. Thunderstorms produce highly dangerous conditions. Lightning follows the ridges along exposed mountain tops. The difference between temperatures in the sun and the shade or in the wind and out of the wind can be as great as 50° F. These facts are essential to hikers and climbers in determining their route or abandoning it.

EQUIPMENT

Boots

A well-fitted pair of leather hiking boots is suitable for both hiking and rock climbing. Sneakers are preferred by some hikers but are suitable only in dry conditions and do not provide the protection or support of leather boots and are not suitable for exposed rock climbs. Lightweight hiking shoes are popular on trails and are kind to both the environment and hikers' feet. Plastic climbing boots are currently state of the art for glacier travel and for snow and ice climbs. They are used almost exclusively on climbs of big mountains. Specialized rock climbing shoes are available for rock climbing. They accommodate jamming and provide excellent traction on rock (Fig. 17-1).

Clothing

Trousers should be somewhat loose fitting to allow the legs freedom to stretch to the fullest without binding, but they must not be so loose as to snag on rock projections. Most are now made of the synthetic materials developed in recent years.

Fig. 17-1. Rock climbing shoes.

Durable hiking shorts of lycra are popular in season. Blue jeans are confining and offer little protection from cold or wet. Wool shirts with long tails provide warmth when wet or dry. Windbreakers and raingear are two items that, as a rule, cannot be used interchangeably but are equally necessary according to the length of the climb or extent of the trip. Warm jackets, parkas, or sweaters might be needed depending on local conditions. Gloves for warmth and protection are needed when handling climbing ropes. Safety helmets are needed for rock climbs. Types of other headgear and socks and underwear are left to individual preference.

FUNDAMENTAL SKILLS AND TECHNIQUES

Backpacking and camping skills should be acquired and should include the following abilities:
1. Make a fire
2. Use gasoline, alcohol, and kerosene compact mountain stoves
3. Read a map and use a compass
4. Use and care for tents
5. Construct an improvised shelter
6. Know first aid
7. Be aware of problems that might be encountered so that the consequences of poor decisions can be avoided

DUTIES OF THE TRIP LEADER

1. Inspect the group's equipment.
2. Make health check: allergies, prior injuries, physical limitations.
3. Group information:
   a. Objective
   b. Direction being taken
   c. Route or trail markers being followed
   d. Return route if different
   e. Time starting and expected return
   f. Weather report and forecast
   g. Orientation via map or guidebook
   h. Action if separated
4. On the trail:
   a. Determine the hiking order and assign numbers so the order can be maintained.
      (1) Put those who tend to hike faster in the rear and the slowest hiker in the front.
      (2) Place weak hiker between two strong hikers.
      (3) Be about second or third for best observation and control.
   b. Assign first aider and assistant leader to the rear and establish that *no one* be behind them. This must be a hard-and-fast rule.
   c. Establish water policy.
      (1) Drink on a regular basis, thirsty or not.
      (2) Do not limit the water intake, as each hiker may have different needs.

(3) Only exception: When refills are not available, practice conservation.
   d. Allow no stragglers. Do not force hikers to hurry to catch up. Slow the pace for them.
   e. Execute a shakedown break after first 15 minutes on the trail.
   f. Inspect at the rest halts (red faces, blueness from cold, possible foot problems, temperament problems between hikers).
   g. Coordinate trail procedures.
      (1) Maintain about 5 feet (1.5 m) between hikers; do not close up tight when column slows down or stops for minor obstacles.
      (2) Avoid accordion action.
      (3) When head of column passes through a difficult area, slow down until the whole column has passed the obstacle.
5. Trail discipline:
   a. Establish trail communications policy.
      (1) Use voice instructions and hand signals.
      (2) Whistle only in emergencies.
      (3) Check off by calling for a numbers count.
   b. Establish behavior policy.
      (1) Get off the trails during rests.
      (2) Put feet up and take packs off.
      (3) Do not litter.
      (4) Purify water that is not obtained from an approved source.
      (5) Conserve energy; restrain excess exuberance.
      (6) Take rest halts often but limit duration (5 minutes every 30 minutes).
6. Other leader responsibilities:
   a. Make all decisions related to safety of party.
   b. Do not let people climb alone even to reconnoiter.
   c. Know the point of no return.
   d. Know when and where help is available.
   e. Know when to stop and make improvised camp in emergencies.
   f. Keep together.
   g. Send no one alone for help.
   h. Be sure all of the group members eat; all need the energy, especially if fatigued.
   i. Keep control in poor visibility; keep in visual or physical contact with the person ahead.
   j. Know when to push on, when to turn back, and when to stop and take shelter.
7. Objective dangers:
   a. Lightning
   b. Rain
   c. Hail
   d. Snow
   e. Ice
   f. Falling rock
   g. Falls
   h. Injuries

i. Poor visibility
j. Difficult terrain
k. Altitude sickness
l. Cold or heat
8. Subjective dangers:
   a. Fatigue
   b. Indecision
   c. Disorientation with surroundings
   d. Hunger
   e. Fear
   f. Lack of necessary knowledge

MOUNTAIN WALKING

The principles of mountain walking evolved from the need to conserve energy on long steep climbs. The normal stride on level ground involves most leg muscles, but especially the muscles of the calf. When one walks naturally the leading foot is planted, then the hiker rises on the ball of that foot, lifting the heel as the rest of the body moves through, bringing the other foot forward. Thus the calf muscles are used continually to help lift the weight at each step. This technique on steep terrain overworks these muscles and is unnecessarily tiring.

The mountain walking technique utilizes the larger thigh muscles predominately and allows a rest at each step. Keep the foot flat and use the full sole; that is, do not step off on the ball of the foot or raise the heel. Straighten the leg completely at each step. Lock the knee momentarily. This places the weight on the skeleton of the body and allows the muscles to relax. This full-sole technique, combined with a slow steady pace, straight back, and body weight over the ball of the foot, is the true mountaineer gait. It requires fewer rests, saves time, covers more ground, and results in arrival at the objective with reserves of energy for other tasks.

A normal pace on flat land for day hikes is about 106 steps a minute or 2½ to 3 miles (4 to 4.8 km) per hour. This rate can be kept up for long periods. In the mountains, distance and time are figured in terms of elevation to be gained or lost. The climb over hard ground, following trails with relatively few obstacles, should take about 1 hour for every 1000 feet (305 m) gained in elevation. This holds whether the climb is straight up or on a series of switchbacks or traverses. Climbing straight up is tiring and thus the pace is slower. The pace may be from 90 steps a minute to 50 or 60 steps a minute. The rate depends on the steepness of the climb, the weight of the pack, and the condition of the climber. At high altitudes (above 12,000 feet [3660 m] lack of oxygen becomes a problem (for some this problem is noticed at elevations as low as 6000 feet [1830 m] above sea level). Descent rates should be about 2000 to 2500 feet (610 to 762 m) of elevation per hour.

TYPES OF TERRAIN
Hard ground

Compact earth or gravel may be mixed with small to medium-sized rocks on well-used trails.

Grassy slopes

Mountain meadows of varying steepness and length are found on the route to many climbs, especially in the Rockies and far west. These slopes are covered with long grass that grows in clumps, with a flat spot on the uphill side of each clump. In the climb, place the full sole of your foot on this flat spot. Climb on a traverse, and switch back and forth for a change. When changing direction, point the lower foot in the old direction and the uphill foot in the new direction to avoid crossing the legs and losing balance. This is the standard herringbone position. A short steep pitch can be climbed with the herringbone step, but this is tiring and should be used only for short stretches. On all types of terrain avoid the tendency to lean into the slope, no matter how steep. Roll the ankles out to help keep the foot flat (Fig. 17-2.)

Descent on grassy slopes

Descend on a traverse often in a jog (depending on the weight of the pack and the condition of the climber). Use a hop-skip technique: weight on the downhill foot and skip with the uphill foot, using it for balance. Drag the uphill foot as if injured. With a little practice a very rapid descent can be made safely. Keep the momentum under control, change direction carefully, keep knees bent and hands low, and keep the weight at right angles to the slope, not forward or back. Do not run straight down grassy slopes, one foot in front of the other. This will result in loss of control. The slope may be taken safely straight down but at a much slower pace. Keep weight back, dig in with the heels, turn toes out, and do a slow skip.

Scree slopes

Scree is a form of loose gravel and small rocks ranging from the size of a pea to stones the size of a fist. Scree is found at the base of high cliffs and forms long scars down mountainsides. Scree may be found in old avalanche paths of either snow or rock and mud slides that took off the top layers down to the gravel, or it may be caused by natural erosion and water runoff. Because of the looseness of the gravel, which rolls under the feet, scree slopes are very tiring and awkward to climb.

Ascent on Scree

Use the full-sole, locked-knee technique. Dig in the toe of the uphill foot and the heel of the lower foot. If everyone in the group steps in the same place a staircase will be formed. Traverse as often as the width of the slope permits. If the terrain is steep, keep a greater distance

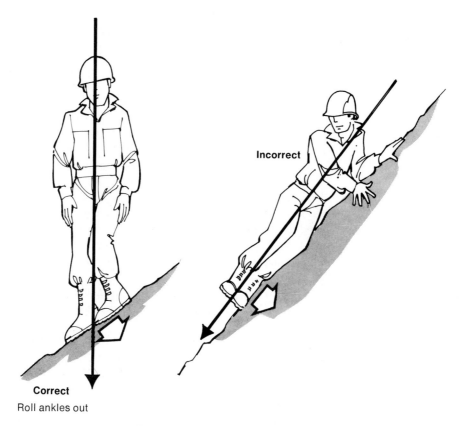

Incorrect

Correct
Roll ankles out

Fig. 17-2. Grassy slope ascent.

between climbers to avoid their being hit by dislodged rocks.

Descent on Scree

Allow extra space between climbers. Use the hop-skip technique on traverses. Straight-down routes are preferred as long as large rocks are not a danger. Hop down, keep the feet shoulder width apart, knees bent, hands low, and shift the weight from one foot to the other, alternating as in a snowplow position. Keep the weight slightly back and dig in the heels, and hop down in low bounds but not with both feet at once like a rabbit. Be careful to keep your speed under control; slow down gradually before you reach the bottom.

Talus rock

Talus is rock lying loose over hard ground. It is composed of boulders of many sizes, from rocks the size of a fist to boulders the size of boxcars. Talus is found at the base of cliffs and above the timberline on mountains. It is deposited through years of erosion and weather effects of freezing and thawing; some talus is the result of the Ice Age's ravages. Talus may be strung over many acres. This loosely anchored rock is often not stable. Great care should be taken when working up, down, or across talus fields. On all types of terrain always step on the uphill

side of the rock. This presses the rock down into the material below and usually stabilizes it. Being careless and stepping on the downhill edge of any loose rock may send it tumbling down the slope, endangering anyone below or resulting in the climber losing balance and twisting an ankle. This use of force applied directly over and down on loose rock must become second nature to climbers. The principle applies to handholds as well.

Low-angle rock

Low-angle rocks are small cliffs with pitches not over 40 to 60 degrees. These usually can be climbed safely with normal precautions, proper technique (Fig. 17-3, A and B), and careful route selection without the aid of climbing ropes. Exposure should be kept to the minimum if possible. Study the rock strata carefully to see which way the slabs run. Layers tilted upward usually offer better handholds and footholds than strata inclined downward.

High-angle rock

High-angle rocks are cliffs with steep pitches and rock faces, some small but others many hundreds of feet high. These rock faces require careful study, expert climbing techniques, and the use of ropes along with trusted partners and the mechanical aids (protection) of pitons, chocks, bongs, wedges, slings, and the assorted hardware

Fig. 17-3. A, Proper form—upright, not leaning in, maximum friction from shoe soles. **B,** Poor form—leaning into rock, little friction from shoes.

of the true rock climber. Because pitons and bongs are rock defacing, there is a tendency now to use other types of metal devices which are placed by hand rather than driven by a hammer. Some of the newer devices are solid while others have moveable parts so they can change in size and therefore be used in different-sized cracks (Fig. 17-4).

Slab rock

Slab rock is smooth and ranges in steepness. It can be climbed without using the hands for balance with proper footgear and technique if the slab does not slope more than 45 degrees and is dry.

ROCK-CLIMBING PRINCIPLES

The techniques of safe rock climbing apply to all degrees of steepness and types of rock. Each climber has four appendages with which to climb: two hands and two feet. The cardinal rules are:

1. Keep three appendages on the rock at all times: one hand and two feet or two hands and one foot.
2. Move one hand or one foot at a time.
3. Test all holds.
4. Let the legs do the lifting. (They are five times as strong as the arms.) Use the hands for balance.

Fig. 17-4. Rack of protection.

5. Try to keep handholds between the shoulders and the waist.

6. Holler "rock" if you dislodge one and it falls. (This warns anyone below to hug the cliff and avoid being hit. If you are below and hear that cry, do not look up; a rock may hit you in the face.)

7. Avoid leaning in and hugging the rock when climbing.

8. Roll the ankles out to get as much of the sole on the rock as the holds permit. Friction is what holds the feet in place.

9. Avoid root and brush holds. They are usually shallow and not safely anchored.

10. Move the head slowly if you have to look down to avoid getting dizzy.

11. Try not to use your knees, elbows, or stomach. Their use makes you hug the rock.

12. Do not pass over small holds (foot or hand) just to find a larger one farther away. If the arms and feet are too far apart, you may find it impossible to recover, and your knees will start to shake.

13. Move loose rock to a safe place. If this is not possible, holler "rock" before tossing it down, thus giving others a chance to protect themselves.

14. Execute a little jump step and change feet if you find that your legs cross when shifting holds, but make sure you have secure handholds before you hop.

15. Keep a buffer zone between what you know you can climb and what you would like to climb. Call this your margin of safety.

16. Stay low and move away from the edge before you straighten up and look down when arriving at the top of a cliff that may be on a ridge line. The wind may be blowing strongly and knock you back over the cliff.

17. Watch out for scree over hard rock. When stepped on, it acts like ball bearings, and the feet slip out from under you in an instant. This is also a danger if there are ledges or hard rock under a thin layer of scree on what looks like a true scree slope. Keep the soles and tread free of rocks and debris for safe climbing.

18. Use the edge of the sole by turning the inside of the foot to the rock to get more of the foot on the rock when traversing across a face.

HOLDS

The following holds and every possible combination of them will eventually be used by experienced rock climbers.

Pull holds

Pull holds are handholds using the fingers. They must be tested carefully. Dig out any loose sand or gravel around the hold. Keep the hands dry (Fig. 17-5).

Friction

Footholds or handholds depend on the climber's weight being forced down on the rock, so the more of the hand or foot on that surface the safer the hold. A combination of pull and friction holds for the feet works best when the body is kept away from the rock. Lean back as far as the hands and feet allow, so that the body weight pushes the feet against the rock, making friction overcome gravity (See Fig. 17-5).

Push holds

Push holds are the most dependable. They work well even on loose rock. As long as the push is directly down and over the rock, the friction generated can support a lot of weight. Push holds in which the hands are palms down and the fingers are pointed down the rock are often used when climbing down. The weight of the body is then held back by friction and muscles. (See Fig. 17-5.)

Pinch holds

Very small projections of rock can be utilized as pinch holds by using the very ends of the fingers. Pinch holds are true balance holds but should only be considered intermediate holds as the body moves to larger holds. The two feet and the other hand must have stronger and larger holds, but pinch holds can be depended on momentarily for balance as the body moves on up or across to a better position. Usually when pinch holds are used the body is in motion, moving to larger holds.

Jam holds

Sometimes a fissure is found in the rock where angles come together or the rock changes direction and small cave-type apertures appear, often only large enough for the hand. Slide the hand into this opening, then try to make a fist, which will act as a chockstone, preventing the hand from being withdrawn as long as the fist is kept clenched. This opening can sometimes be used for the feet. The foot is jammed into the opening as far as it will go. This is a temporary hold, and care must be taken that the angle of climb allows the foot to be withdrawn safely without disturbing balance as the climb continues. (See Fig. 17-5.)

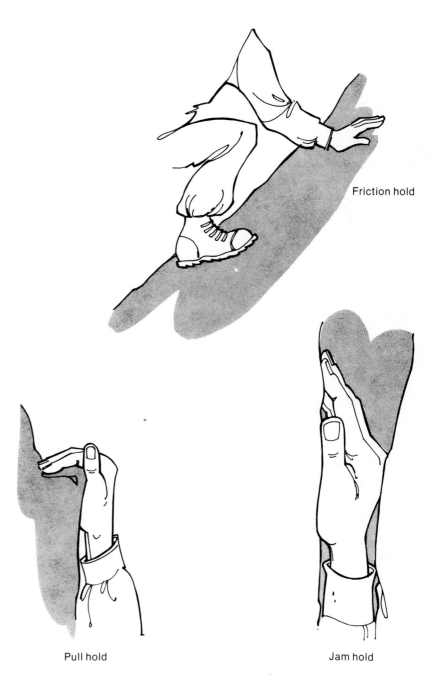

Friction hold

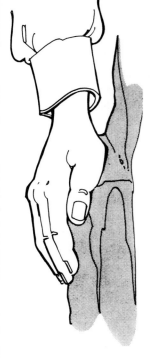

Push hold

Pull hold

Jam hold

Fig. 17-5. Holds.

Fig. 17-6. Chimney technique.

Cross pressure

Cross pressure or chimney technique (Fig. 17-6) is used whenever there are opposing surfaces or rock walls that allow the back and hands to be pressed against one side and the feet against the opposite wall. The body can be inched up as long as the space remains close enough to hold this cross pressure. Friction and the muscle power of the back, legs, hands, and feet will hold the climber in place. One body part is moved at a time, with the hands, back, and feet working together, moving and releasing pressure. Be sure that you do not have gear or equipment around the waist, such as a canteen, to catch on projections and disturb your balance. The key to many spectacular climbs has been use of the chimney technique.

DESCENDING TECHNIQUES

On rock faces, the same route used in climbing up often is followed to climb down, as long as exposure is kept to a minimum. The climb down is more difficult than the ascent because of limited vision. When the climb is relatively easy, face out and climb down. Keep all the principles in mind. Move the hands down before moving the feet. Make full use of push holds to hold the body back as you feel for the footholds. If the climb is moderately difficult move down sideways, and if it is difficult face in and move down backward. Here it is important to always move the hands down first to avoid a stretched-out position. Look between the legs for the footholds. The hands can usually use the holds where the feet were placed. Keep in mind the route you used in climbing up. Again use palm push holds to the fullest with fingers pointed down. Be sure to brush off any debris from the rock and from the soles of your boots before moving up

or down. If you use pinch or pull holds, still try to keep from hugging the rock. Lean back so as much weight as possible is pushing the feet against the rock.

Descent on slab

Well-treated boots or sneakers should be able to hold on slab rock that slopes up to 45 degrees, without your using the hands. To test your footgear, crouch down on the steepest slope on which you feel safe. Then with your feet flat and your weight right over the balls of the feet and the knees forward of the feet, try balancing on one foot. You should find that your position is stable and that you can balance there securely. This will add to your confidence in your footgear. It is important to know at just what angle you can depend on the feet to hold and when they will not. Perform these tests where there is little or no danger if you are wrong.

CLIMBING IN GROUPS ON ROCK

Generally the best climber leads and selects the route. The leader may be stationed at trouble spots to help the weaker climbers, trying to find spots that afford rest and relative safety at intervals during the climbs. Encourage the climbers to help each other, with a boost here and there or a friendly hand grasp from above. Keep the group disciplined enough that they do not crowd each other and that no one steps back on someone else's hands. Always be watchful for falling rock. Discourage jumping down from rock to rock shelves; loose stones may cause a loss of balance. Have an alternate route in case weather or injury requires it. Keep the climb within the limits of the weakest climber.

USES OF CLIMBING ROPES

The safe use of climbing ropes depends on a knowledge of rope stengths, knots, and rope management. A form of nylon rope is best because of its durability, resilence, and strength. Climbing ropes are used to limit the distance a climber would fall, to aid in rapid descents, and to make routes safer.

The decision to climb roped up is made whenever the leader believes there is too much risk of a fall or when any member of the party asks to be roped.

For a two-party climb the leader climbs until a suitable spot for a belay is found. A belay is a hold in which by use of the rope and a braking method of handling the rope, the lead climber can stop the partner from falling more than an acceptable distance (See Figs. 17-7 and 17-8.) The lead climber places protection while ascending and is thus belayed from below. If the lead climber falls, he or she would fall twice the distance to the last piece of protection.

After proper commands, signals, and testing of the position, the leader then safeguards the partner's climb up to the spot. This sequence is repeated, or they can leapfrog, letting the number two climber pass and then lead, as long as both partners have equal ability. Each climber has to be able to climb without pulling or depending on the rope for direct aid. The exceptions would be if the climber above on belay is notified by the partner climbing up that help is needed. Then the belayer would take up any slack between them. The belayer would actually provide tension on the rope so that the climber who is feeling insecure can depend on the belayer to prevent a fall.

There are techniques to be used for most situations in rock climbing, including how to fall safely. These procedures must be practiced and practiced until the reactions of the climbers become reflex actions. Mechanical aids (called protection) such as carabiners, and slings may be placed and used as intermediate anchor points for the climbing rope to pass through on the way up a rock face that does not provide belay spots (See Figs. 17-9 and 17-10.) Protection has a ring or an eye to which the carabiner is attached and through which the climbing rope is snapped. These anchor points limit the distance a climber may fall. If above the protection, the climber would fall only the distance to the protection and the same distance below it plus any distance the belayer allowed. The belayer has a variety of choices. One option is to place protection (Fig. 17-11) with a sling rope anchor to the rock to make it impossible to be pulled off. Another possibility is to snap the climbing rope into protection placed above and then the climbing rope leading to the

Fig. 17-7. Standing belay.

Fig. 17-8. Sitting belay.

Fig. 17-9. Protection placed in a crack.

Fig. 17-10. Protection: spring loaded cramming device.

Fig. 17-11. Placing protection.

climber above would pull the belayer into the rock in the case of a bad fall. The alternative selected depends on the terrain. Climbing teams develop a feel for the rope running between them and can tell what their partner is doing even when the partner is not in sight. When the climb up is finished, the climbing ropes should be inspected as they are recoiled and the route down is determined.

RAPPELLING

Rappelling is a technique of using ropes to slide down steep rock faces or very steep dangerous ground slopes. It is a quick but safe way to descend. The two basic rappel techniques are body rappel (Fig. 17-12) and rappelling with equipment.

Common characteristics of all rappels include the following.

First, an anchor point must be established. Two anchor points are preferred in case one fails. The anchor can be a strong tree or a secure rock around which the rappel rope can run free. It can be established with sling ropes around the anchor point and carabiners to run the rappel rope through. Piton anchors are used on difficult areas by experienced mountaineers. The anchor point must not obstruct the rope, must not contain sharp edges which could cut the rope, or create excess friction that may weaken the rope. The anchor must be solid. The rope must be retrievable from below. Climbing ropes are marked in the center, and the rappel rope is doubled around the anchor point and centered. Both ends are dropped down the face to be climbed. Both ends of the rope must be together and reach the ground or the dismount point, where another rappel can be established if needed.

Second, the rappellers should wear gloves to prevent rope burns. The first person down is responsible for clearing the rope and the route down of any obstructions such as loose rock, brush, or tree limbs if in timbered areas. This person dismounts at the bottom, frees the rope of any tangles, steps away, and yells, "Off rappel" loudly so all at the top can hear and to indicate that it is safe for the next person to come down. The last person down makes sure that the rope at the anchor point can be pulled down when he or she gets to the bottom.

Body rappel

This method should only be used on relatively gradual slopes as it is not as safe as using equipment. After the anchor point is established, face the anchor point with the back to the cliff edge. Straddle the rope, reach behind with the right hand, and grasp both ropes and bring around and across the right hip. Next pass the ropes across the chest and over the left shoulder (for right-handed people). Grasp the rope that is leading to the anchor point loosely in front with the left hand. This is

Fig. 17-12. Body rappel.

the guide hand. Next reach behind the body again with the right hand and grasp the rope that is running down behind the back. Make sure that the rappel rope does not touch the bare skin at any place—neck, shoulder, or legs. The right hand is the brake hand. Grasp the ropes with the back of the hand out and the thumb and forefinger next to the hip. To stop at any point, bring the hand tight to the hip, keeping the back straight, knees bent, and feet apart. Look over the downhill shoulder as the body is turned slightly down the face. To descend, allow slack for the rope to slide around the body as you lean back and walk down the face. Keep the feet flat against the rock if the face is vertical. Lean back at about 75 to 80 degrees but not at right angles on the body rappel. This is a slow controlled rappel. The rope must be flipped free as the brake hand moves away from the hip and the fingers loosen enough to allow the rope to slide through. Body weight and gravity should do the rest. The rappeller can stop anytime but must not let go of the rope in the brake hand. The guide hand may be released if needed to adjust clothing, remove loose rock, or whatever, but *never* the brake hand. When the rappeller is down, the rope should be unwrapped from around the body and untangled, and checked to see that it is free. The rappeller should then step away and holler, "Off rappel."

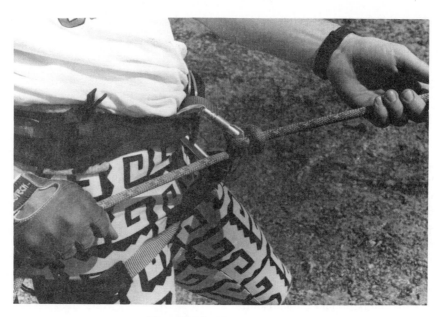

Fig. 17-13. Munter hitch.

Fig. 17-14. Rappelling with a Munter hitch.

Equipment rappel

By the use of a rope or web harness and a Munter (Italian) hitch (Fig. 17-13), the climber can hook into the rappel and with all the friction on the hitch can make a fast, safe, descent (Fig. 17-14). Speed can be controlled, and the descent can be stopped at any time. Nylon web harnesses are manufactured that are adjustable and comfortable, having loops through which the hitch is inserted. For the occasional climber a rope seat is easily fashioned from 1 inch tubular webbing. Tie the two ends together with a water knot (overhand follow-through) or a figure eight follow-through. Next double the webbing forming two loops. With the loops extended by holding them with both hands, make a figure eight with the inside loop by twisting it one turn. This forms a loop for each leg. Next put one leg in each loop. Pull the two loops up around the waist. Grasp the loops around the legs in front and bring all three strands together (the loop around the waist in front and the two leg loops). Next insert a locking carabiner through all three strands.

Seat rappel

Stand facing the rope with the shoulder and brake hand pointed downhill and the guide hand side toward the anchor point. Next pick up the ropes and snap into both strands. With the brake hand take a complete turn around the carabiner and snap in. The two strands leading from the carabiner should be coming off the end of the carabiner toward the anchor point. The other strands run down off the carabiner closest to the body. The ropes are grasped by the brake hand between the thumb and forefinger and allowed to slide along the

Fig. 17-15. Climbing rope.

rope. Place the hand against your nearest hip pocket with the back of the hand out and the thumb side nearest the hip.

To begin the descent, merely move the hand away from the hip, relax the fingers around the rope, and lean back; gravity will do the rest. To stop, place the hand back on the hip and squeeze the rope.

The body position is the same as in the body rappel. Keep the feet apart so as not to pendulum. The knees should be bent to absorb shock. Keep the feet flat against the rock face, keep the back straight, and keep looking down the route being followed. Relax the guide hand so that the descent is not hindered by excess friction.

A minimum friction on the body makes for a smooth, fast, safe descent completely controlled by the climber. An experienced instructor should be at hand to watch every move and correct mistakes immediately as the climbers first learn on a moderately steep ground slope.

Climbers should practice on a short face, about 10 feet (3 m) high, with a safe landing. Beginners will find that the first step down is the hardest. When practicing on vertical rock, there are two safety measures that should be adopted until expertise is acquired. A belay rope is attached around the waist of the rappeller with either a two-loop bowline or a simple bowline. The belay rope is attached to a safety person who is on belay above and who can put tension on the rope if needed, at a signal from the instructor. The instructor should be *beside* the student rappeller. The instructor makes the last check and signals the belayer when ready. The other safety check is to have a person at the bottom who holds the ends of the rappel ropes in both hands. If the rappeller needs to be stopped for any reason this person can pull

on the ropes and the rappeller will brake to a stop. To recover, the rappeller resumes position and signals "okay," and the safety tension is released.

The instructor must insist on a no-nonsense attitude and strict attention during all rock-climbing classes. Carelessness and inattention can quickly lead to serious injury.

Rappelling is not a sport in itself, despite the tendency of some clubs or schools to classify it as a separate activity. It is just one phase of mountaineering.

ROPE MANAGEMENT
General principles

Careful inspection of the rope (Fig. 17-15) for cuts, excess wear, weak spots, and burns must be made constantly. Ropes should not be left with knots in them. Avoid stepping on the rope, because this may grind small pieces of rock into the rope, which will act as an abrasive and eventually weaken and cut the fibers. Rope should be dried carefully if wet but not near an open flame, as nylon ropes melt. Rope should not be hung across sharp objects or nails. If run over rough cliff edges, the edges should be padded with packs or clothing.

Knots

Many manuals cover in detail all manner of knots and how they are tied and used. Familiarity with such skills is obviously a prerequisite for the mountaineer.

TEACHING CONSIDERATIONS

Do not attempt to instruct in mountaineering unless you have completed a qualified program of training and have had a great deal of experience.

GLOSSARY

altitude Same as elevation but usually used in connection with height attained and normally expressed when the elevation is above 12,000 feet (3.66 km).

balance climbing Climbing using only the feet, depending on body position for balance. Done on comparatively easy rock.

belay A method of anchoring a climber with the use of rope for protection against falling.

bivouac A temporary camp-out, usually planned but of short duration (one or two nights).

body harness or seats Web nylon belts that are fastened to the climber that act as seats for support of the body when rappelling or when suspended in space when anchored to the rock while maneuvering for new positions. The climbing rope is attached or hitched to a ring on the seat.

carabiner A metal alloy—aluminum oval ring with a hinged gate that allows a rope to be snapped in at any spot. Gates may have a locking screw for extra safety.

chocks and nuts Small blocks of steel with a cable loop imbedded. The chocks are stuffed into the cracks or fissures to serve in the same manner as the pitons. Carabiners are snapped to the cable sling. These chocks or nuts can be removed, whereas pitons are usually so well driven they cannot be removed without damage.

climbing rope Rope 165 feet (50.3 m) in length, ⁷⁄₁₆ inch (11 mm) in diameter, nylon test about 6200 pounds (2800 kg), tensile strength 150 feet (45.5 m), 9 mm test strength 3500 pounds (1580 kg).

crampons Steel-tooth foot harnesses, attached to the sole of the climbing boots, used on snow and ice climbs.

elevation Usually expressed in feet (meters) above sea level and used in connection with the number of feet (meters) in height to be climbed.

free climbing Climbing with protection but without aid.

frostbite Freezing of exposed flesh or lack of circulation to the extremities; may be superficial or deep, can be severe, and may result in gangrene and amputation if not properly treated.

glissade A technique of sliding down steep, hard-packed snow using ice ax or even ski poles to control the speed. The body faces out from the slope, and the slide is feet first.

grassy slopes Mountains covered with grass that grows in clumps.

high-angle rock Steep rock faces of 70 to 90 degrees.

hypothermia Lowering of the body temperature that, if severe, results in death; usually a result of exposure to cold or wet conditions, not a result of freezing.

ice ax Ax with a head of two parts: a horizontal blade and an end graduating to a point. The shaft is made of metal or a composite, the blade of high-alloy steel. The end of the shaft is a pointed spike for probing and digging into solid snow-packed crevasses or slopes. The ice ax is used to chop steps for footholds. It can be used as an anchor for the belay. It also is used as a brake to stop a falling climber or a roped team of climbers.

low-angle rock Rock where balance climbing is sometimes practiced; not steep.

overhangs Protruding pieces of rock that hang out over the rest of the rock face; require extreme care and skill to negotiate.

piton A steel alloy shaft with a ring or eye at the head. Pitons come in varying lengths and shapes. They are driven into cracks or fissures in the rock and used with snaplinks to act as anchor points for ropes.

piton hammer A short-shafted hammer, blunt on one end and pointed on the other, for driving pitons into the rock cracks. The pointed end is for cleaning out the fissures or testing holds.

rappel A method of sliding down an anchored climbing rope; means of fast descent down cliff.

scree slopes Gravel and loose rock scars running down mountain side.

shakedown break The first rest halt on a hike or mountain walk, which is used to adjust packs, clothing, and so on. It is usually of slightly longer duration than subsequent rest halts.

slab rock Smooth sloping rock faces of varying steepness and length.

sling rope Pieces of rope (Perlon or nylon) in 10- to 15-foot (3 to 4.5 m) lengths, used in various rope installations and for anchoring climber or material; can be used as seats for rappelling.

spread eagle A position resulting when a climber has both feet and arms too far apart for safety. It is difficult to recover from this position.

talus Loose rock lying on mountain slopes; not always stable.

timberline The elevation on a mountain at which trees cannot grow because of high wind, poor soil, and inability to establish anchoring roots. Timberline varies in different parts of the United States and the world.

verglas A thin icy coating over rock caused by cold moist air condensing and freezing on the surface.

SUGGESTED READINGS

Appalachia (semiannual), Boston, Mass., Appalachian Mountain Club.

Clark, R.W.: Men, myths and mountains, New York, Thomas Y. Crowell Co.

Manning, editor: Freedom of the hills, Seattle, 1974, The Mountaineers Books.

Mariner, W.: Mountain rescue techniques, Seattle, The Mountaineers Books.

18

Orienteering

Completion of this chapter should enable the reader to:

- Appreciate the development, values, and objectives of orienteering
- Use maps and a compass for navigation
- Organize a cross-country orienteering event
- Teach others map- and compass-reading skills
- Conduct orienteering lead-up games
- Organize orienteering variations
- Set an appropriate orienteering course

The sport form of land navigation is called orienteering. It is a cross-country race in which participants use a map and compass to navigate between checkpoints along an unfamiliar course. The activity can be a means of enjoying other outdoor pursuits or as a sport it is complete with competition, rules, and organizational structure. Both aspects of orienteering qualify its inclusion in the "environmental sports" family along with running, cross-country skiing, hiking, kayaking, and similar activities.

VALUES

Orienteering has many appealing attributes for modern physical education and recreation. People from 10 to 70 years old can participate in this lifetime sport with no extraordinary physical or mental abilities. Orienteering can be conducted as a coeducational activity; it is appropriate for males and females. Groups, pairs, or individuals may navigate an orienteering course in a competitive or cooperative fashion, involving the participants in a wide range of commitment and challenge. Finally, orienteering can be organized on commonly found, accessible tracts of land. Schoolyards, parks, and town forest preserves are all adequate.

HISTORY

Orienteering began when humans first ventured from their familiar environs into an unmapped world, seeking new horizons. Organized orienteering, however, is a relatively new addition to the sports world, particularly in the United States. The first time an event was labeled an "orienteering race" was in 1900 at a meet organized by Club Tjalve in Oslo, Norway. By 1919, orienteering meets were attracting as many as 200 people, with Capt. Ernst Killander organizing these meets outside of Stockholm and generally being credited as the father of orienteering.

The sport's next boost came in the early 1930s with the invention, by Bjorn and Alvar Kjellstrom, of the one-piece protractor compass, or "orienteering" compass, which provided a simple tool for land navigation. By 1942 orienteering was a compulsory activity in Swedish physical education programs. Orienteering continued to grow, rivaling soccer as the most popular sport in Sweden and spreading to other Scandinavian countries.

In 1946 the same Bjorn Kjellstrom, now living in the United States, sponsored the first orienteering meet in the United States at the Indiana Dunes State Park. However, the sport remained relatively unpracticed in North America until 1965, when Geoffrey Dyson and John Disley introduced orienteering in Canada, where it steadily gained popularity. Since 1967 the sport has grown in the United States, beginning with permanent orienteering groups centered at the Marine Physical Fitness Academy in Quantico, Virginia, in the Delaware Valley, and in New England. The United States Orienteering Federation, which now represents more than 90 clubs and has a membership of 2300, was founded in 1971.

Today some orienteering meets rank as the largest participative athletic events in the world; the Oringen in Sweden attracts over 10,000 competitors for 5 days of competition. In August 1976 more than 1500 orienteers gathered in Quebec for the largest meet in North America to date.

Before organizing an orienteering event, a physical educator or recreation leader should have experience and solid understanding of the following components of the sport: equipment, techniques using map and compass, instructional games, safety precautions, teaching methodology, and sources of information.

OBJECTIVES

Orienteering in whatever setting it might be offered can provide the unique contribution of fostering the attitude that the outdoors is a safe and interesting place. The following objectives are considered outcomes of an orienteering program. The participant will:

1. Gain the basic skills of land navigation using a map and compass
2. Improve his or her physical fitness
3. Learn to be self-reliant in the outdoors
4. Acquire an increased awareness of the environment

EQUIPMENT
Maps

The map serves as the primary tool of navigation to the participant and to the trained eye can yield an enormous amount of information. The most common maps used for orienteering are "topo" (topographic) maps and are produced by the United States Geologic and Geodetic Survey Department. They are available in two scales, 1:24,000 and 1:62,500, the former being preferable for orienteering. Many sporting goods stores, bookstores, and camping stores stock government topographical maps of the local area. An index of maps from which one can order is available from the Map Information Office, United States Geologic Survey, Washington, DC 02042.

As competitive orienteering becomes more popular, specialized orienteering maps (Fig. 18-1) containing greater detail and accuracy are being produced in active areas of orienteering throughout the country. These maps differ from the government topographical maps in that they have a larger scale, usually 1:10,000 or 1:15,000; contain four or five colors; and are drawn from recent, precise aerial photographs. The added detail and accuracy allow course setters to design more demanding orienteering courses and remove the element of luck from the competition.

Both types of orienteering maps contain the same kinds of information

Location. Each map has a title describing a location and contains longitude and latitude coordinates that locate the area on the earth's surface.

Date. The map must be up-to-date; many parts of the United States have dramatically changed during the past 10 years, and government maps may not reflect these changes.

Distance. Every map depicts a portion of the earth's surface in reduced form. The ratio describing the amount of this reduction is called scale. For example, a 1:24,000 topographical map means that one unit of distance on the map equals 24,000 of the same unit of distance on the earth. A graphic of the scale is usually included on the map's border.

Direction. The top border of topographical maps represents the northerly direction, or geographic north. The top of the specialized orienteering maps indicates magnetic north, because such maps are used exclusively by orienteers using magnetic north–seeking compasses. In either case, the righthand border is east, the bottom is south, and the lefthand border is west.

Elevation. The unique feature of topographical maps are their description of elevation in the land mass. This is shown by contour lines in the form of concentric rings. The distance between each contour line, termed the contour interval, represents a vertical change in elevation of the terrain. The center of the rings is the high point of elevation, and the broader circles show progressively lower areas.

Natural terrain features. Important natural features of mapable size are shown. Examples of such features are bodies of water, including lakes, streams, marshes, and swamps; cliffs; woods; and fields. Orienteering maps contain detailed information of this nature.

Other features. Houses, roads, bridges, and power lines are among the other features symbolically displayed on the map. The explanation for each symbol is contained in the map's legend.

Compass

The compass is second only to the map among the orienteer's tools and serves to supplement and confirm information given on the map. The most commonly used compass in orienteering is the protractor compass, the important difference between the protractor or orienteering compass and others is the rectangular base plate that serves as a protractor and assists in determining direction of travel. Protractor compasses are available in the United States from several commercial sources. Models featuring a liquid-filled compass housing that dampers and stabilizes movement of the magnetic needle are well worth the additional expense.

Types of Compasses

A variety of compasses are available, each having features designed for different functions:

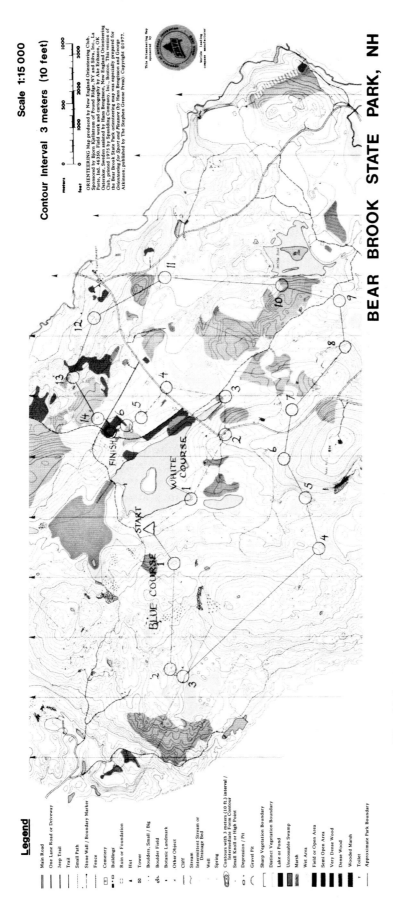

Scale 1:15 000

Contour Interval 3 meters (10 feet)

ORIENTEERING Map produced by New England Orienteering Club. Sponsored by Bjorn Kjellstrom of Pound Ridge, NY and Silva, Inc., La Porte, Ind. 46350. Field work and cartography by Ake Eriksson, OK Osteraker, Sweden assisted by Hans Bengtsson, New England Orienteering Club, printed 1975 by Spaulding Company, Inc., Boston. This version of the Bear Brook State Park orienteering map was especially prepared for *Orienteering for Sport and Pleasure* (by Hans Bengtsson and George Atkinson; published by The Stephen Greene Press) Copyright ©1977.

BEAR BROOK STATE PARK, NH

Fig. 18-1. Orienteering topographical map. (Figs. 18-1, 18-2, and 18-4 to 18-7. From Orienteering for Sport and Pleasure. Copyright © by Hans Bengtsson and George Atkinson. Reprinted by permission of The Stephen Greene Press, a wholly owned subsidiary of Viking Penguin, Inc.)

Legend

Main Road
One Lane Road or Driveway
Jeep Trail
Trail
Small Path
Stone Wall / Boundary Marker
Fence
Cemetery
Buildings
Ruin or Foundation
Hut
Tower
Boulders, Small / Big
Boulder Field
Botanic Landmark
Other Object
Cliff
Stream
Intermittent Stream or Drainage Bed
Well
Spring
Contours with 3 meters (10 ft.) interval / Intermediate Form Contour
Small Knoll or High Point
Depression / Pit
Gravel Pit
Sharp Vegetation Boundary
Distinct Vegetation Boundary
Lake or Pond
Uncrossable Swamp
Marsh
Wet Area
Field or Open Area
Semi Open Area
Very Dense Wood
Dense Wood
Wooded Marsh
Toilet
Approximate Park Boundary

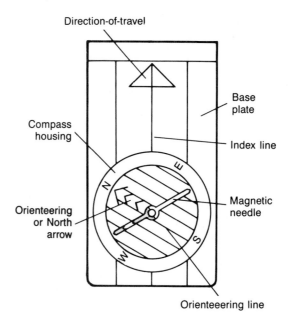

Fig. 18-2. The protractor compass.

Plain watch compass. This compass appears as a pocket watch and is suitable for general travel that requires limited accuracy.

Wrist compass. Similar to a plain watch compass, the wrist compass has a wrist band, allowing the wearer free use of both hands. This is a popular ski orienteering compass but, like the watch compass, does not afford the accuracy required for regular orienteering.

Lensatic compass. Also commonly called the army or the prismatic compass, the lensatic compass features excellent sighting devices but is lacking a protractor base, so it cannot be used to take a compass bearing. Because of its high accuracy, it is popular in map-making.

Mirror compass. The mirror compass is similar to an orienteering compass, but it also has a sighting device that uses a mirror for added precision. The mirror compass is used for course setting, map-making, and backpacking, but is considered too heavy for conventional orienteering.

Protractor or orienteering compass. The following are main components of the orienteering compass (Fig. 18-2).

Base plate. The Plexiglas rectangle under the compass itself is referred to as the base plate or protractor and serves two purposes: measures distance using the scale (in millimeters or inches) on the edges and assists the orienteer in determining a course of travel.

Compass housing. The compass housing is mounted on the base plate and appears as a basic watch compass. It must rotate freely on the protractor and should have a transparent bottom.

Direction-of-travel arrow. The only arrow on the base plate, located in the center of the long end of the protractor, is the direction-of-travel arrow.

Orienteering or north arrow. The north arrow is drawn on the bottom of the compass housing. This arrow is flanked by a series of parallel lines termed orienteering lines.

Magnetic needle. Suspended in the compass housing is a freely rotating, floating needle. The red end of the needle points to magnetic north when not influenced by nearby iron objects.

Strap. Although not shown in the figure, the strap is a necessary part to any compass. A slip knot at the distal end provides the best protection in the event of a fall.

Other equipment

Personal equipment required in orienteering, in addition to the map and compass, simply amounts to functional clothing to be worn in the woods. Hiking boots are used by beginners; "knobby" orienteering shoes are the footwear of experts. Weather dictates the type of clothing necessary, but generally the same worn for a hike is used.

In organizing a meet, several items of equipment (aside from maps and compasses) prove indispensable: score cards, control markers, punches, plastic map cases, red pens for copying courses from master maps onto individual maps, and several clipboards.

CHARACTERISTICS OF A CROSS-COUNTRY ORIENTEERING EVENT

The most commonly practiced form of orienteering is the cross-country event resembling a car rally or treasure hunt. The event occurs in an area of 75 to 2000 acres, ideally consisting of wooded acreage with varied terrain. The meet organizer, using a topographical map (see Fig. 18-1), places from 6 to 15 markers or "controls" in the

CLASS	COURSE					NO.

NAME

CLUB

ATTACH HERE ONLY

CLASS	COURSE	NO.

NAME

CLUB

competition	date		compass

Orienteering ® Control Point Cards courtesy of **SILVA**®	FINISH			
	START			
	TIME			

1	2	3	4	5
6	7	8	9	10
11	12	13	14	15

Fig. 18-3. Orienteering scorecard.

field at distinct terrain features such as trail junctions or hilltops. The positions of the controls are precisely drawn on a master map, numbered sequentially, and connected with a straight line, forming a course or a string of controls for the event. Participants in the cross-country event are then assigned the task of copying the control locations on a personal copy of the map. Individuals are started in a staggered fashion and proceed to locate the markers in the correct sequence, using their skills of navigation in moving from one control to the next in the most efficient or fastest manner. Controls are not hidden but are visibly placed at the listed control description to eliminate the element of luck as much as possible. Route choice, navigational techniques, and rate of travel (running versus jogging) are at the discretion of each participant. Codes or punches at the controls, marked by the competitor on a scorecard (Fig. 18-3) ensure presence at each control. The elapsed time of the orienteers is computed and then placed in rank-order, with the fastest declared the winner. Because of the challenge of locating all the controls on a course, most orienteers consider completion of the race a satisfying goal and position in the meet of secondary importance.

Fig. 18-4. Getting a bearing with map and compass.

BASIC ORIENTEERING TECHNIQUES
Map reading

The map is the primary tool of navigation, with the compass used as a supportive tool to verify and confirm the course when needed (Fig. 18-4). To get the most information from a topographical map, use the following basic techniques of map reading:

1. Before going into the field, be familiar with the map's scale, contour interval, and symbols.
2. Always keep the map "oriented," that is, keep the top facing north regardless of your direction of travel. This will keep the map properly aligned with the terrain. Maps can be read sideways or upside down if necessary, but always keep the map pointing toward north. This can be accomplished in three steps:
   a. Place the compass on the map with its magnetic needle adjacent to a north line on the map.

b. Turn both the compass and the map together until the magnetic needle is parallel to the map's north lines, being certain that the north end of the magnetic needle points toward the north edge of the map.

c. Remove the compass without turning the map and the map is oriented. Now the map corresponds to the surrounding terrain.

3. Fold the map to a readable, holdable size. Concentrate on the part of the map you are using; the remainder will only confuse. Walking or running is best accomplished with a small, neatly folded map that will not get caught on tree branches. Pinch the map between the first two fingers, using the thumb to trace your progress.

4. When reading the map, visualize the terrain through which you will soon be passing. Try to imagine the ground level view that will soon be coming over the horizon, including the slope of the hills, vegetation, and other terrain features. See these things in the mind before seeing them in the field.

Travel by compass

On some occasions the compass must be heavily relied on to determine a direction of travel, usually when adequate terrain features for navigating are lacking, or if the orienteer simply wishes to be absolutely certain of the course of action. This procedure is called taking a "compass bearing" and is accomplished in four steps.

Establishing direction. Place the long side of the compass protractor along the line of intended travel by connecting your present location and your destination with the compass edge. Be sure that the direction-of-travel arrow is pointing from your location to your destination. (See Fig. 18-5).

Setting the north-south lines. While pressing the protractor firmly to the map with your thumb, turn the compass housing around so that the north-south lines of the compass are parallel to the north lines of the map. Be sure that the north arrow of the compass housing is pointing to the north of the map. (See Fig. 18-6).

Reading the bearing. Remove the compass from the map. If the north lines of the map point to geographic north, as in most topographical maps, then an adjustment must be made in the bearing, because there is a difference between geographic north and magnetic north. This difference is called the angle of declination, which meaures the amount that magnetic north deviates east or west from geographic north. If the declination is west, add the angle of declination to your compass bearing. If the declination is east, subtract the angle of declination from your compass bearing. An easy-to-memorize line states: "Declination west, compass best. Declination east, compass least." If the north lines or meridians point toward magnetic north, as in orienteering maps, then no adjustment is necessary. To correct a standard topographical map to magnetic north-south lines, draw new meridians reflecting the angle of declination for that partic-

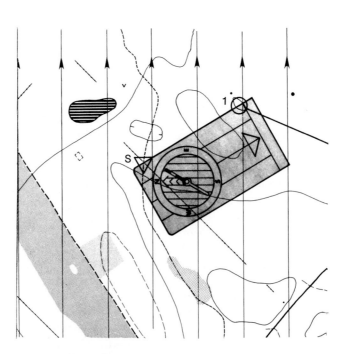

Fig. 18-5. Establishing direction from *S* to *1*.

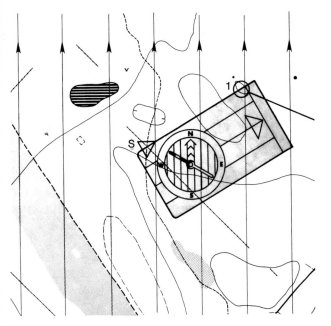

Fig. 18-6. Setting the north-south lines.

ular map. Draw a series of parallel lines tilted at the proper angle of declination from the north-south borders of the map. Now both map and compass speak the same language: magnetic.

Now hold the compass level in your hand with the direction-of-travel arrow pointing away from you. Turn around so that the north end (red) of the magnetic needle coincides with the north arrow of the compass housing. The direction-of-travel arrow is now pointing toward the destination.

Running the bearing. Look down at the compass and focus on the direction-of-travel arrow. Slowly lift your head, sighting directly in line with the direction of travel arrow. Pick out a prominent landmark, which can be a rock or tree about 100 to 200 feet ahead of you in this direction. Take the easiest route to the landmark, avoiding obstacles, and then repeat this step again by sighting new landmarks until you reach your destination.

If there are no prominent landmarks and you are team orienteering, a technique called "leap-frogging" can be used. A teammate is sent out to act as a sighting point.

Remember that the compass is used to supplement the map, so while running on a bearing consult the map to recognize your progress. (See Fig. 18-7.)

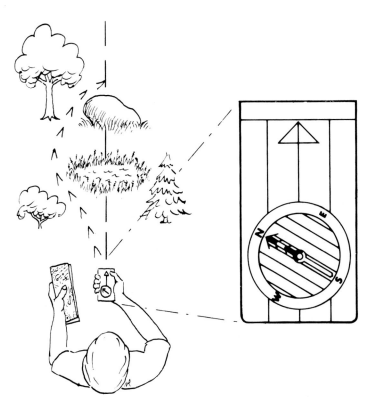

Fig. 18-7. Running the bearing.

Route choice

Route choice is the essence of successful orienteering and must be learned by experience. The fastest route around an orienteering course is different for every individual and is based on fitness, orienteering skill level, and experience. Overriding these factors, however, is the terrain of the course, which ultimately dictates route decisions. Common questions in such decisions are path versus woods travel, elevation gain versus distance, or open fields versus woods.

Aiming off

When taking a compass bearing toward a control located on a linear feature such as a path that is across your direction of travel, you have a 50-50 chance of arriving at the path either to the right or the left of the control. You will not know in which direction your bearing is off, so many orienteers purposely aim slightly to one side of the control and when arriving at the path—knowing the direction of their "error"—they move down the path to the control. The orienteer knows for certain in what direction to turn to seek the marker.

Attack point

Within 165 yards (150 m) of a control, the orienteer should identify an obvious or visible feature to use as the last relocation point on the path to the marker. The larger and more definite the feature and the nearer its location, the more desirable the attack point. Path junctions, corners of fields, and the like provide excellent reference points on the orienteer's last 165 yards (150 m) or less of navigating to a control. Often a course does not provide such luxuries, and the orienteer must adopt another technique.

Precision compass

Precision compass is the precise application of the four-step method of taking a compass bearing cited earlier. Extreme accuracy is required in this technique, which is often employed while traveling from the attack point to the control. This method is time consuming but necessary in parts of the course containing difficult navigation problems and should be used in conjunction with the technique of pace counting.

Precision map reading

Precision map reading is commonly referred to as "aggressive" map reading and is used in areas containing numerous detailed terrain features that can confuse the competitor. The thumb is accurately passed over the map as the orienteer moves through the terrain, checking off each feature along the route. This technique results in slow travel but produces consistency over time.

Control finding

Once in the immediate locale of the control marker, the orienteer must use cautious awareness to quickly find the control. Good skills in this area can save minutes:

1. Always read the control description carefully before searching for its location. Know what you are looking for; for example, the knolltop, the marsh.
2. Choose a good attack point.
3. Slow down as you near the control.
4. Concentrate on your task, ignoring other runners in the area.
5. Use extra caution on the first and last control of the course, as both are critical in finishing the course.

Traffic lighting

Each competitor's pace throughout a course should be controlled by an imaginary "traffic light" in the mind. Through experience, the participant learns the appropriate light for existing terrain conditions, but the following can serve as a general guide:

1. Green light—go. Travel at the fastest speed possible while still maintaining navigational control. This technique is used when traveling along open linear features such as trails, roads, or stone walls.
2. Yellow light—proceed quickly but cautiously under more difficult conditions. More precise navigating is employed. This technique is often used in arriving at an attack point.
3. Red light—stop or go slowly. This technique is used when temporarily lost or disoriented, when a control has been missed, or during particularly critical navigational portions of the course. Good orienteers can sense when to use this light and to slow down, avoiding a major mistake. While traveling from the attack point to the control using precision map reading and compass, use this light.

Collecting features

Any distinct feature across the direction of travel that will aid in navigation is termed a collecting feature. It can be used effectively to funnel the orienteer toward an attack point.

Handrails

These useful terrain features fall parallel to the direction of travel and serve as "handrails" to a control. Objects such as paths or roads serve as excellent tools in this category. Topographic features such as streams or ridges that orienteers can travel beside also serve as excellent handrails.

Rough compass

Frequently an orienteer must travel quickly to get to a large collecting feature or handrail that will be easy to locate. A rough compass bearing coupled with a sense of direction will lead one to the feature. The standard four-step method is used in taking the compass bearing, but it is done quickly. Sightings with the compass along the direction of travel are done less frequently and often on the run.

Distance judging

This essential skill is done with varying degrees of accuracy but is accomplished so that the orienteer knows his or her location at all times. Distance judging requires a two-step approach, first measuring the distance and then pace counting while traveling. To measure the distance to be traveled, place the edge of the protractor along the direction of travel and calculate the number of millimeters on the map beetween current location and destination. Then refer to the map's scale to translate the millimeters on the map to meters on the terrain. This gives the distance to be traveled, but if additional precision is required, this can be translated into the orienteer's paces. By taking repeated trials over a 110-yard (100 m) course in varying terrain, the orienteer should know the number of paces (a double stride) required to cover 110 yards. This personal yardstick of pace counting takes time to develop but is indispensable in precise compass and map-reading situations. Some typical measures for pace count per 110 yards for adults are:

Hiking	60 paces
Running in dense woods	45 paces
Running in flat woods	40 paces
Running on open trails	36 to 38 paces

Orienteers should develop their own pace-count values in using this technique.

INSTRUCTIONAL GAMES

Orienteering teachers rely on their ingenuity in devising orienteering lead-up games, so imagination is the limit. Following are some popular instructional activities that, when done at high speeds, become training exercises for competition.

Follow the leader

There are two main variations of this activity: (1) both leader and followers have a map, and (2) only the leader has a map. In the first case, the leader chooses a point without telling the group where it is. Starting from a known location, the leader orienteers to the point and the rest follow, trying to determine the route on their map. Periodically the leader stops along the route to quiz the group on their location and how they got there. When the destination is reached, the process is repeated with a new leader. The second variation of this game, where only the leader has a map, is similar, but the distances of travel are reduced to 110 to 220 yards (100 to 200 m) and map memory ability is critical. Groups of up to six persons are appropriate. Both activities develop map reading and terrain memorization.

Figures

The purpose of this exercise is to encourage precision compass and accurate pace counting. The game should initially be played in a flat open field and on a small scale, but as students become more proficient the game can be moved into wooded areas and the distance increased.

The task of each student is to walk on an assigned three- or four-sided course and to achieve "closure" at the end, or to finish at the starting point. As an example, the figure of a rectangle will be used (Fig. 18-8.) The

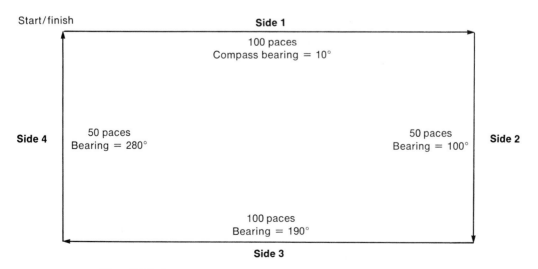

Fig. 18-8. Instructional game diagram for a figures exercise.

student is assigned the following compass bearings and distances:

Side 1—go 100 paces at 10 degrees
Side 2—go 50 paces at 100 degrees
Side 3—go 100 paces at 190 degrees
Side 4—go 50 paces at 280 degrees

A small marker left at the individual's starting point serves as a reference. Instructors can vary the figures to be used as well as distances. Four-sided figures require increments of 90 degrees from the intial compass bearing. Squares require an equal number of paces for all four sides; triangles use only three compass bearings and increments of 120 degrees on each of the two subsequent bearings. Instructors can invent many elaborate courses but should test them for closure before implementation. This exercise can be done individually or in pairs with one person using the compass and the other measuring each side.

Map walks

This informal activity is instructive for beginners in groups of up to a dozen people with one leader and resembles a slow-paced version of "Follow the Leader." At the start, the leader teaches map orienting and basic elements of map reading, such as scale, elevation, and symbols. After this brief lecture and armed with the preceding skills, the group goes for a walk in an area containing many terrain features. During the walk, map orienting and thumbing are stressed and appropriate items discussed as terrain features appear along the route. The length of the walk should be adjusted to the group's attention span and physical abilities. This activity is most successful with novices.

Score orienteering

This activity resembles an Easter egg hunt and is a variation of the cross-country event cited earlier. Ten to 20 controls are placed at terrain features in an area by the instructor prior to the activity. Each control is assigned a point value from 5 to 30, depending on its difficulty and distance from the start. The purpose of the event is for each individual to accumulate points by locating as many high-valued controls as possible within an allotted time. Controls can be located in any order. Whoever accumulates the most points within the time limit wins.

This activity has a number of benefits:

1. Students are encouraged to work efficiently and quickly, making this the sprint race of the orienteering world.
2. The time limit is helpful in working within a class schedule. All participants will be at the finish at a determined time.
3. It is conducive to parks and even school yards, because many controls can be placed in a small area.

Trim orienteering

This is the most educational of all orienteering variations. The activity is simply score orienteering done on a larger scale without a time limit and without competition. Fifty to 100 controls are placed in the woods on a semipermanent basis. Because the markers will remain out in the elements for 1 to 6 months, special small aluminum or wood markers that can be attached to trees are required. Maps are printed showing all the control locations and are made available at local schools, banks, sporting goods stores, or newspaper offices, for example. The course organizer promotes the course and distributes maps.

The advantages of trim orienteering include the following:

1. People can try orienteering at their convenience and at their pace.
2. Families can enjoy orienteering in a noncompetitive fashion.
3. Schools can use parts of the course for instruction.
4. Competitive orienteers can use the course for training.

TRAINING

Orienteering requires mental and physical abilities, so it follows that training should develop one's capabilities in both areas. Unfortunately, in the United States few devote adequate preparation to the mental and technical aspects of orienteering, but many concentrate on the physical training. This deficiency can be corrected by keeping in mind the unique demands of orienteering while planning a conditioning program.

Technique training

The basic techniques previously mentioned can be sharpened through a variety of activities including:

1. Map making
2. Course setting
3. Instructional games (including those previously mentioned)
4. Cross-country orienteering training meets

All of these training activities can produce physical benefits when done at a sufficiently high work load.

Physical training

Orienteering places three distinct physical requirements on the participant: cardiovascular endurance, agility, and running speed.

Physical training should be molded to meet these demands.

Cardiovascular endurance can be improved in a variety of methods, most commonly walking, running, jogging, bicycle riding, and cross-country skiing. This is the most overly trained aspect of all orienteering's components, so keep in mind that the objective of such training tools is the ability to maintain a high work level for 60 to 90 minutes in an orienteering race.

Agility is probably the most ignored physical requirement for successful orienteering. Running at high speeds in the woods places different demands on the body than running at a similar pace on a track. Increased agility can be obtained by training over the same terrain that orienteering meets use—woods, paths, boulder fields, meadows, and hills—adapting the running stride to the undulating, varied footing of the outdoors. Training runs should simulate the specific demands of an orienteering course.

Assignment orienteering

This interdisciplinary approach can incorporate many school subjects into an orienteering format. A standard cross-country orienteering course is used, but once an individual or group arrives at a control, an assignment must be accomplished. The task can be related to other school subjects or to orienteering and may require an instructor at the control.

SAFETY PRECAUTIONS

A few precautions when organizing an orienteering event can eliminate most safety problems:

1. Check the area to be used. Mark on the map all barbed-wire fences, rivers, and cliffs, Avoid running courses over cliffs or across deep rivers.
2. Always employ a check system to register participants. Standard orienteering scorecards contain a stub with the entrant's name, which the organizer retains. On finishing, the orienteer picks up the stub. At the end of the event, the organizer should be left without any stubs. Competitors are reminded to report to the finish regardless of whether they complete the course.
3. Establish a closing time for each course, at which time participants must return to the finish.
4. Place a safety compass bearing on each map or course description that leads from any point on the map to a large collecting feature on the map's border. For example, if a road borders the south edge of the meet area, the safety bearing would be 180 degrees, bringing anyone in need of help to a civilized area.
5. Respect private property and cultivated fields. Always request permission from land owners before designing courses on their property.

COURSE SETTING

For orienteering meets to take place, an organizer or leader must prepare a course and place orienteering markers in the woods. The skill of the course setter along with the quality of the map play a major role in the success of an orienteering meet. The course setter's task is to test the orienteer's running and navigational skills at the appropriate level. Toward this goal, the course setter follows three important rules:

1. Keep the competition fair. The quality of the map should be adequate for orienteering competition and verified by field checking on the part of the course setter. Controls should be correctly placed and not hidden, thus eliminating the element of luck.
2. Design a course to meet the skill level of the orienteers. If a diverse population of orienteers is to attend the meet, several courses must be designed to meet the needs of all levels of orienteers. The difficulty of a course can be controlled by varying the number of controls, course distance, and difficulty of controls (control placement).
3. Design a course that measures both physical and mental skills. Every part of a good orienteering course presents navigational problems that require the orienteer's concentration and awareness. Distances that require merely running skills are a waste.

The course setter should always establish the course well in advance of the competition and preferably have the course checked in the field by another individual. The satisfaction of watching participants enjoy his or her creations is the course setter's reward.

Varied running speeds are developed by changing the pace of training runs or using instructional games that force the participant to travel using the traffic-lights system. Varied pace training runs can include interval training, fartlek, and hill climbing. Instructional games such as "Follow the leader" and "Score orienteering" also encourage the ability and knowledge of varying running speed.

ORIENTEERING VARIATIONS
Night orienteering

Only orienteers with experience should participate in this event. A few modifications of the basic cross-country orienteering format will provide safety.

1. Use a relatively civilized area such as a park or athletic field.
2. Place controls at readily distinguishable features, such as path junctions or fence corners.
3. Shorten the course to a maximum of 1.86 miles (3 km) (less for young participants).
4. Use track relay batons, for example, wrapped with reflective tape as control markers.
5. Insist on everyone checking in at the finish regardless of whether they complete the course.
6. Require flashlights and whistles for all participants.
7. Avoid meet sites containing cliffs, rivers, or busy highways.

Ski orienteering

This is an approved but yet-to-be-implemented Olympic sport that combines orienteering with cross-country skiing. Ski orienteering differs from orienteering primarly in the placement of control markers (nearer paths in the winter version). The meet organizer ensures a number of routes between each control, making route choice the primary navigational problem.

Bicycle orienteering

Requiring road maps instead of topographical maps, this variation of the orienteering theme can be an enjoyable activity. Relatively traffic-free roads are necessary, and participants should be able to find controls without leaving the pavement. Distance of 15 to 30 km are not uncommon. Like ski orienteering, several viable route choices should be allowed per control.

TEACHING CONSIDERATIONS

1. Orienteering is best learned by doing. Encourage beginners to experience navigational problem solving as soon as possible.
2. Limit the amount of lecture time each period to allow additional time for practice of techniques.
3. Use a part-whole approach. Reduce the total activity to three aspects: the map, the compass, and the map and compass together.
4. Begin activities in a familiar setting with a simple orienteering course for a group. Later have individuals attempt more difficult courses in less familiar surroundings.
5. Allow time at the end of each lesson for discussion of route choices, techniques, and strategies.

GLOSSARY

aiming off Plotting a bearing wide of the precise target to avoid false turns near the mark.

angle of declination The angle representing the difference between geographic north and magnetic north.

attack point A feature from which an orienteer begins to navigate carefully to a control.

bearing A direction to travel usually measured in degrees from north and determined by a map and compass.

beeline Straight line.

checkpoint An easily identifiable feature.

collecting feature A distinct feature that is relatively easy to find and recognize.

contour interval The vertical distance between contour lines on a topographical map.

control A prism-shaped, red-and-white (almost always) marker placed in the field prior to an orienteering event and corresponding to a known map point; to be located during the event.

control extension Plotting a course to a larger adjacent feature rather than to the easy-to-miss smaller actual target.

draw A shallow valley with steep sides.

fartlek Swedish word meaning speed play; a form of running training incorporating increased efforts over various distances at different paces.

handrail A feature running parallel to one's direction of travel and thereby serving as a handy navigational aid.

interval training Repeated fast-paced runs of 100 yards to three quarters of a mile interspersed with recovery walks or jogs.

knoll A small hill.

meridian Lines (real and imaginary respectively) running true north to true south on a map or the terrain.

pace count The number of steps traveled

precise compass The following of the compass reading.

reentrant In orienteering, an elongated, sloping valley.

rough compass The following of a general compass route.

saddle A low point on a ridge connecting two summits.

spur A narrow, sloping ridge.

topographical map The graphic delineation of natural and man-made features showing their relative position and elevation.

SUGGESTED READINGS

Bengtsson H and Atkinson G: Orienteering for sport and pleasure, Brattleboro, Vt, 1977, The Stephen Greene Press.

Darst PW and Armstrong GP: Outdoor adventures activities for school and recreational programs, Minneapolis, 1980, Burgess Publishing Co.

Kals W: Land navigation book, San Francisco, 1983, Sierra Club.

Kjellstrom B: Ski-orienteering, LaPorte, Ind., 1974, American Orienteering Service.

Kjellstrom B: Be an expert with map and compass, New York, 1976, Charles Scribner's Sons.

Lowrey R and Sidney K: Orientering skills and strategies, Willowdale, Ontario, 1985, Orienteering Ontario.

FILMS

International Film Bureau, Inc., 332 S. Michigan Ave., Chicago, IL 60604.

Orienteering Service/USA, P.O. Box 547, North La Porte, IN 46350.

Silva, Inc., 2466 State Road 39 N., North La Porte, IN 46350.

ORGANIZATION

United States Orienteering Federation, P.O. Box 500, Athens, OH 45701.

19

Paddle and Platform Tennis

Completion of this chapter should enable the reader to:

- Appreciate the history and development of paddle and platform tennis
- Be familiar with the court dimensions and equipment used in these two games
- Understand modifications of tennis rules that are used in paddle and platform tennis
- Teach the games and their strategies to novice players

HISTORY

The game of paddle tennis was originated in America in 1898 by a 14-year-old boy, Frank Peer Beal, at Albion, Michigan. He observed a game of tennis but could not afford a racquet, nor was his backyard large enough for a full court. He fitted a court to his backyard about a fourth as large as the full-sized tennis court. As a substitute for racquets, he shaped paddles out of a 1-inch maple plank.

The game grew slowly at first, but it eventually spread throughout the country to churches, YMCAs, schools, and similar places where adequate space for tennis was unavailable. Tournaments were held. In 1923 the United States Paddle Tennis Association was organized.

The game became popular indoors as well as outdoors through the efforts of Mr. Beal, Mr. James Mulholland, and others.

The National Recreation and Parks Association is more or less responsible for the promotion and development of paddle tennis, which has become a widely accepted form of recreation and popular on the playground, in the gymnasium, on blocked-off pavement, or in the backyard.

Paddle tennis is like tennis on a small scale or table tennis on a large scale.

In the late 1920s F.S. Blanchard and J.K. Cogswell built an outdoor platform for badminton and deck tennis but later used it for a modified version of playground paddle tennis. That version is now called platform tennis and is played in courts elevated slightly off the ground and surrounded by a wire mesh screen. Nonskid sur-

faces, methods of maintaining tension levels in the surrounding screen, lighting for night play, and portable courts are among the innovations that have popularized the game and allow it to be played in a variety of settings and weather conditions.

PLATFORM TENNIS

The platform is a surface with a playing area 60 feet (18.29 m) long and 30 feet (9.15 m) wide enclosed by a screen 12 feet (3.65 m) high (Fig. 19-1). Centered on the platform are the doubles court which is 20 by 44 feet (6.09 by 13.41 m), and within the doubles court is the singles court measuring 16 × 44 feet (4.87 × 13.41 m) (Fig. 19-1).

Court

Refer to Figs. 19-1, 19-2, and 19-3. The restraining line may or may not be used. This depends on the playing organization and game location.

Equipment
Paddle

There are several types of paddles, and all are made of plywood. The standard paddle (Fig. 19-4, *A*) is recommended because it is the least expensive. It should not be more than 17½ inches (44.5 cm) long by 8½ inches (21.5 cm) wide (Fig. 19-4, *A* and 19-4, *B*).

Ball

A deadened tennis ball is used, which is a regular tennis ball with its internal air pressure reduced so that when

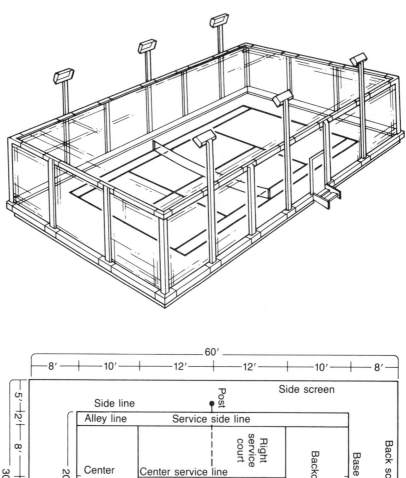

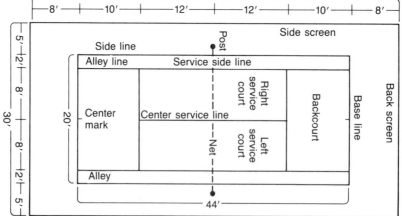

Fig. 19-1. Platform tennis court.

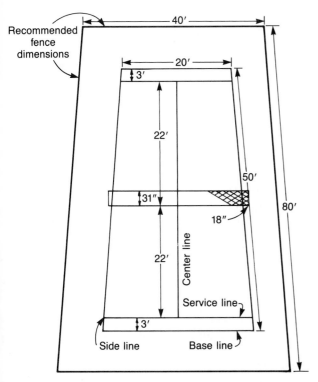

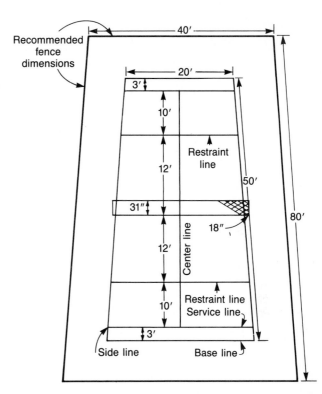

Fig. 19-2. U.S.P.T.A. official court dimensions (without restraint line).

Fig. 19-3. U.S.P.T.A. official court dimensions (with restraint line).

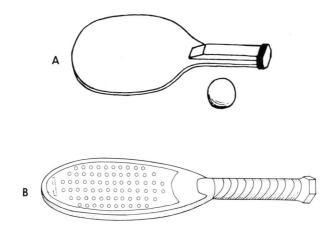

Fig. 19-4. A, Standard paddle and ball. **B,** Platform tennis paddle.

it is dropped from a height of 6 feet (1.83 m) it will rebound 31 to 33 inches (78.7 to 83.8 cm).

Net

The top of the net should be 31 inches (78.7 cm) at the net posts with the cable pulled taut. Not more than 1 inch (2.54 cm) sag is allowed at center. The net extends 18 inches (45.7 cm) outside each sideline.

Fence

Surrounding the court is a fence 10 feet (3.09 m) high, 40 feet (12.19 m) wide, and 80 feet (24.38 m) long.

BASIC RULES OF PADDLE TENNIS
Service

One underhand serve is allowed. If the serve is a fault, the server loses that point. The server stands behind the baseline within the imaginary extensions of the center and side lines and tosses the ball into the air and strikes it with the paddle at a point not higher than 31 inches (78.7 cm) above the court. The server may bounce or drop the ball to the court and strike it with the paddle upon its rebound at a point no higher than 31 inches. The server must use the same type of serve throughout the set. During the serve only one step with either foot is permitted.

Service begins in the right-hand court and alternates courts after each point, regardless of which side gets the point, until the game is completed. The served ball must land in the diagonal court bounded by the service line (not the baseline), the side line, the center line, and the net.

Faults

The service is a fault if:
1. During the service, the ball is contacted above 31 inches high.
2. The server changes from one type of serve to another within the same set.
3. The server does not serve from the proper area.
4. The served ball touches a permanent fixture (other than the net, strap, or band) before hitting the ground.

Service let

The service is a let if the ball touches the net, strap, or band, and is otherwise good, or the ball is served before the receiver is ready. No point is awarded on a let serve.

Server's point

A point is scored if the served ball touches a receiver, or anything worn or carried by the receiver, prior to touching the ground.

Loss of point

A player loses a point if he or she:
1. Returns the ball after a second bounce.
2. Returns the ball so that it hits the ground, a permanent fixture, or other objects outside the opponent's court.
3. Volleys the ball without making a good return.
4. Volleys the ball before it crosses the net.
5. Touches the net.
6. Touches a ball in play.
7. Throws the paddle.
8. Strikes the ball during service above 31 inches from the ground.
9. In doubles, partners both hit the ball in play during one stroke.
10. Violates the restraint (bucket) law where it is authorized.
11. In singles, a player hits the return of a service as a volley.
12. Misses the ball while attempting to serve.
13. Drops the ball, in serving, in front of the baseline.

Good returns

It is a good return if:
1. The ball hits the net and passes over it, and lands in the proper court (a ball landing on a line is still in play).
2. The ball is returned outside the post above or below the top of the net, even if it touches the post, provided it lands in the proper court.
3. A player's paddle follows through over the net after a good return.

Game

The sequential scoring of points is the same as tennis.

1st point = 15
2nd point = 30
3rd point = 40
4th point = game,

If the score reaches 40 to 40, the score is called "deuce". The next score called is "advantage" in favor of the point winner. If the player having advantage ("ad") wins the following point, the game is won. If the player with advantage loses the point, the score returns to deuce. The advantage-deuce sequence continues until the game is won.

Set

A set occurs when a player wins six or more games (up to 12) by a margin of two games. If a set reaches 12 to 12, a tie breaker can be played.

Restraint (in doubles)

During the service both feet of all four players must be behind the "restraint" line [12 feet (3.66 m) from the net] until after the receiver's paddle strikes the ball. If this rule is violated, a point is lost by the offending team.

Singles play

Each player must allow the ball to bounce once on his or her side (exclusive of dropping the ball behind baseline) before the first volley is permitted. For example, the server must allow the receiver's return of serve to hit the floor on the server's side of the court before hitting the ball.

BASIC RULES OF PLATFORM TENNIS

All the rules of paddle tennis are used in platform tennis except the following.

Service

The server tosses the ball into the air in any direction and before it hits the ground hits it with the paddle. The service may be delivered overhand, underhand, or sidearm. The ball cannot be bounced during the serve.

Balls off screen

If a ball in play or on the service hits the deck in the proper court and then touches the back or side screen, both screens, the horizontal top rails, or the snow boards, it may be played as long as it does not bounce on the deck a second time on the same side of the net. The ball must be played off the screen.

Singles

The rules in platform singles play are the same as doubles except the game is played on the 16 × 44 foot (4.87 × 13.41 m) court and two serves are allowed. A hi-bounce ball is recommended for singles.

TECHNIQUES AND STRATEGY

The techniques and strategy of paddle tennis are not different from tennis. For rules, techniques, grips, and learning procedures, refer to the chapter on tennis. The procedures are no different from tennis, even to the use of the popular eastern forehand grip. For backhand shots, there is more of a shift of the hand behind the handle so the face of the paddle is open at an angle and the power of the wrist can produce full strength behind the stroke.

If there is a difference in strategy, it is that in paddle tennis it is best to play the net as often as possible because the court is not as wide as a tennis court.

TEACHING CONSIDERATIONS

1. Because the force requirements for paddle and platform tennis are less than those for tennis, young learners can experience success more quickly. Paddle tennis can be used to teach beginning striking skills to learners, although transfer to the game of tennis will not be complete.
2. The same teaching considerations outlined for tennis are appropriate for paddle and platform tennis (see the chapter on tennis).

GLOSSARY

ball A ball of light sponge rubber, approximately 2½ inches (6.4 cm) in diameter. It is not as lively as a tennis ball.

Frank Peer Beal An American who originated the game in 1898 at the age of 14.

junior court The smaller paddle court used by players under 16 years of age.

nets Junior net: made of white twine, 18 feet (5.49 m) long and 2 feet (61 cm) deep. Senior net: heavier, with its heavy canvas-banded top; 22 feet (6.71 m) long and 2½ feet (76.2 cm) deep.

paddle The hitting instrument (plywood) used in playing the game. The paddle for the senior game is slightly larger.

platform tennis A game of paddle ball played on a platform 30 × 60 feet (9.1 × 18.3 m) that is covered on ends, sides, and top by a wire mesh.

rules Same as for tennis, with a few exceptions.

senior court The larger of the two paddle tennis courts; used by competitors 16 years of age and older.

SUGGESTED READINGS

Lawn tennis annual (published annually), New York, American Lawn Tennis, Inc.

Official paddle tennis equipment and rules (latest edition), New York, The Paddle Tennis Co.

Spalding tennis annual (published annually), New York, Spalding Sporting Goods Co.

20

Physical Fitness

Completion of this chapter should enable the reader to:

- Appreciate the historical development of the concern for physical fitness in the United States
- Understand the meaning of the term "physical fitness" as used in this book
- Recognize the benefits and values of improving one's physical fitness
- Describe factors that affect physical fitness
- Assess one's own physical fitness as well as that of others
- Construct a proper program to improve physical fitness

HISTORY

Since early in the development of *Homo sapiens*, people have realized the benefits of being physically fit. Cultures over time have given greater or lesser emphasis to physical fitness. To the ancient Greeks, being physically fit was of primary importance, equal to intellectual fitness. Until recently, many contemporary societies have placed little emphasis on physical development.

In the United States there is growing awareness of the benefits of being physically fit. These benefits have not always been understood. In 1953 Kraus and Hirschland published an article comparing the performance of American, Austrian, Italian, and Swiss children on a test of minimum muscular fitness.* The results of the comparison were startling to Americans: more than 75% of American children failed the test, as compared to only 10% of European children.

Along with other factors this dismal result led to a revitalization of interest in physical fitness and led President Eisenhower to call a Conference on Fitness of American Youth in mid-1956. Later that year the President's Council on Youth Fitness (now the President's Council on Physical Fitness and Sports) was created. The first nationally normed fitness test was published in 1958. These events set the stage, and for the past 30 years

*Kraus H and Hirschland RP: Minimum muscular fitness test in school children. Research Quarterly 25:177-188, 1954.

American concern and involvement has been slowly but steadily increasing.

DEFINITION

Physical fitness has been defined by the President's Council on Physical Fitness and Sports as "the ability to carry out daily tasks efficiently with enough energy left over to enjoy leisure time pursuits and to meet unforeseen emergencies." The position of the American Alliance for Health, Physical Education, Recreation, and Dance (AAHPERD) is that "physical fitness is a multifaceted continuum extending from birth to death. Affected by physical activity it ranges from optimal abilities in all aspects of life through high and low levels of different physical fitness, to severely limiting disease and dysfunction."

While there is still not agreement on the definition of physical fitness, most authorities agree that an evaluation of physical fitness involves assessment of aerobic endurance, body composition, muscular strength, and muscular endurance. Flexibility, although it is much more difficult to measure due to its specific nature, is also considered by most experts to be a part of physical fitness. As evidence that these components comprise physical fitness, the latest educational fitness program advocated by AAHPERD (called Physical Best) has an assessment portion consisting of the following items: one mile walk/run to test aerobic endurance, a skinfold measurement process to assess body composition, the sit and reach test to evaluate flexibility of the lower back and hamstring muscles, modified sit ups to check abdominal strength and endurance, and pull ups to measure upper body strength and endurance.

Physical fitness, although related, is not the same as health. A world-class athlete can be ill, or a person can be in excellent health (free from disease) but unable to run or swim for more than a few hundred yards. A person's physical fitness level consists of two major aspects: actual and potential. Actual fitness is the state to which one is developed or undeveloped. Potential fitness is determined by genetic factors such as body type, sex, coordination, balance, agility, reaction time, and other inherited factors, and by age and health (no disease).

Physical fitness is a relative concept. There is a minimal fitness level that must be maintained to prevent organic deterioration and ensure proper physiological functions. Beyond this, "proper" level of fitness depends on the daily demands of life. Obviously, a construction worker must be more fit than an office worker to meet the definition of physical fitness as stated by the President's Council.

WHY BE PHYSICALLY FIT?

Although physical fitness and health are different, they are certainly related. Accumulating evidence suggests that physical fitness is inversely correlated to coronary artery disease (CAD). Cardiovascular disease mortality rate increased from the early 1900s to the mid-1960s, but between 1963 and 1989 the trend has reversed. Epidemiologic studies have generally demonstrated a protective effect against CAD from physically active occupations and leisure exercise.

With or without the guidance of the medical community, the public is gradually becoming educated about the value of exercise. Evidence is mounting that the positive relationship between exercise and good health is more than circumstantial.

PHYSICAL VALUES OF EXERCISE
Heart and circulatory system
The effects of proper exercise on the normal heart and circulatory system have been conclusively shown to be beneficial. The normal heart and circulatory system increase in strength and efficiency with exercise. The heart is a muscular organ, and although it differs in type from the muscles of the skeletal system, it responds to exercise in somewhat the same manner as the skeletal muscles insofar as strength, endurance, and growth are concerned. As a result of proper conditioning through exercise, the heart is able to fill with more blood and therefore has a larger volume of blood pumped per stroke. Compared with an untrained heart, a heart conditioned

by exercise relaxes more completely, allowing more blood to enter. The larger and stronger conditioned heart is capable of contracting with greater force, thus pumping more blood per contraction. The trained heart is capable of doing more work with fewer beats, and it can rest longer between beats than the untrained heart. Another advantage is that a heart kept in good physical condition by exercise not only beats slower during strenuous work but also returns to normal more quickly than a poorly conditioned heart.

The belief that strenuous exercise may injure the normal heart has no scientific foundation. The term "athlete's heart," as applied to a weakened or injured heart, has been found to be erroneous. Scientific evidence indicates that an organically sound heart in a child or youth cannot be permanently injured by exercise. The individual will become physiologically and psychologically exhausted before damage is done to the heart muscle. This is not true, however, for a defective heart.

When vigorous exercise is engaged in over time and with regularity, the blood vessels within the muscle tissue itself actually increase in number. Also, the red corpuscles that carry oxygen to the body tissues increase in number, thus increasing the oxygen-carrying power of blood.

Another way in which exercise promotes better circulation is by assisting the heart in moving blood from the body's extremities back to the heart through muscular contractions.

Improved circulation through regular exercise has a beneficial effect on the body's heat-regulating mechanism.

Through increased blood flow and altered blood composition a conditioned person is more able to adjust to environmental heat and cold than an unconditioned one.

Respiratory system
Breathing, or respiration, is the means by which oxygen is taken into the body and carbon dioxide and waste products are eliminated. Respiration increases during exercise. At rest the physically fit person will have slower, deeper respirations and can meet demands placed on the respiratory system with less effort and greater efficiency than the person who is not physically fit. Physical conditioning increases the economy and efficiency of respiratory function. As with heart rate, the respiratory rate of a fit individual returns to normal faster than that of an untrained person.

There is an increase in the flexibility and a strengthening of the respiratory muscles through exercise. It is possible that the the alveoli develop new partitions, increasing the area from which the oxygen can be absorbed.

During exercise the spleen contracts, forcing the blood stored there during rest into circulation, thus increasing the number of circulating red corpuscles and consequently the oxygen-carrying power of the blood.

Flexibility of the joints of the body can be increased through exercise. However, if done improperly exercise can have a negative influence on flexibility as well. For example, if one over-exercised the biceps (the muscle that flexes the upper arm) and failed to also strengthen the tricep (the muscle that extends the upper arm) a reduction in flexibility of the elbow joint could result.

Flexibility is a specific trait. That is, a person who is flexible in one joint may not be flexible in another joint. Therefore it is difficult to assess flexibility with one simple test. However, many physical fitness tests include an assessment of lower back and hip flexibility. This is probably due to the concern in this country with low back pain—a common ailment.

Muscular strength and endurance

The strength of muscle tissue is increased through repeated use when the load it is required to handle is above normal. This is called the overload principle. The overload can be an increase in the number of repetitions performed, the resistance overcome, or both. Muscle tissue increases in size and endurance as it increases in strength. A muscle responds in direct proportion to the extent of demands placed on it. Brief maximal or near maximal exercise develops the kind of strength for efficient, strenuous, short bursts of performance. Repetitive submaximal exercise develops the kind of strength necessary for more prolonged performance. In addition to the increase in size, strength, and endurance of individual muscles, general muscle tone of the entire body is improved through exercise. Good muscle tone is conducive to an erect bearing and good posture. For example, strong abdominal muscles help prevent a sagging, protruding abdomen.

A person with adequate strength to satisfy body needs uses part of the muscle fibers in relays while others rest. This allows some of the fibers to relax and recover while others carry the load. Trained muscles function more smoothly and more effectively than untrained muscles, enabling them to contract more vigorously with less effort.

The gain in muscular endurance from systematic and vigorous physical activity is much greater in proportion than the gain in size. This gain in endurance helps one to continue a relatively hard and difficult task over a long time without fatigue or exhaustion. In a hurried and competitive life with the many varied and continuous demands of daily living, people need to develop reserves of strength and endurance.

Fatigue

The physcially fit person who is skilled and coordinated uses only the muscles that are needed for a task. This is a great saving in unnecessary fatigue. In the trained person smaller amounts of waste products such as lactic acid are formed, and generally these waste products are removed more quickly than in the untrained person.

In combating fatigue, exercise is often stimulating both psychologically and physiologically. The contraction of muscles helps in returning the blood to the heart. Consequently, the heart sends additional blood to fatigued areas of the body, resulting in a psychological feeling of recovery and refreshment. This is one of the main reasons why participation in moderate exercise, particularly in the form of a game, often relieves fatigue after a strenuous workday. As a rule, then, people in good physical condition ordinarily tire less easily, and when they do tire, they recover more rapidly than people in poor physical condition.

FACTORS AFFECTING FITNESS

Many factors can contribute to being unfit. Two important ones are inactivity and overeating.

Inactivity is the major factor in a lack of fitness. Years ago when much of daily human activity (farming, manufacturing, transportation, and so forth) was powered by muscles, inactivity was not a problem and the concern was how to lessen physical labor. Now, when most of the population are engaged in sedentary occupations and do not use their legs for transportation, the problem is one of finding ways to increase physical activity.

When more calories are taken in than expended, the excess calories are stored as fat. Fatness is not only a problem but a preoccupation with many Americans. Countless diet books are on the market, and additional ones are published every month. It is estimated that 40% to 50% of the United States population has excess fat.

Another factor affecting fitness is the inability to relax. This is generally caused by stress and is the body's physiological reaction to external events. Not all stress is harmful. Stressful situations may be pleasant (playing a game), unpleasant (taking an exam), physical (running), psychological (worrying about finding a job), emotional (death of someone close), instantaneous (accident), or prolonged (writing an article).

The general response to stress is "fight or flight," which was once essential when our ancestors were fighting for survival in the wilderness. Now, however, instead of expressing this reaction by fighting or running, we internalize it. This can cause depression, nervousness, and irritability, which can lead to "psychosomatic" illnesses such as hypertension, ulcers, muscle pains, aches, and assorted neuroses. Prolonged stress will wear out the body. The suggestion is that by reversion to the "fight or flight" response (through participation in a socially acceptable physical activity) the internalized stress may be dissipated.

Table 20-1. FITNESS LEVEL DETERMINATION BASED ON DISTANCE (IN MILES) COVERED IN 12 MINUTES

Fitness level	Age (yrs)			
	29 or under	30-39	40-49	50 or over
Males				
Very poor	<1.20	<1.20	<1.15	<1.05
Poor	1.20-1.30	1.20-1.30	1.15-1.25	1.05-1.15
Fair	1.30-1.50	1.30-1.45	1.25-1.40	1.15-1.30
Good	1.50-1.65	1.45-1.60	1.40-1.55	1.30-1.45
Excellent	>1.65	>1.60	>1.55	>1.45
Females				
Very poor	<0.95	<0.95	<0.90	<0.85
Poor	0.95-1.10	0.95-1.05	0.90-1.00	0.85-0.95
Fair	1.10-1.20	1.05-1.20	1.00-1.10	0.95-1.05
Good	1.20-1.35	1.20-1.30	1.10-1.25	1.05-1.20
Excellent	>1.35	>1.30	>1.25	>1.20

ASSESSING FITNESS

Before embarking on a program to improve the level of physical fitness, it is important to have an idea of your actual level of fitness. To determine the current level of cardiorespiratory function the 12-minute walk-run test developed by Kenneth H. Cooper is suggested. A stopwatch or a watch with a second hand and a running track are all that are necessary. If a track is not available, a specific course can be measured out so that the number of laps can be counted and multiplied by the distance for one lap. It is also helpful to divide and mark the course into small distance units so that the exact distance covered in 12 minutes can be determined. A few days before taking the test, jog around the course several times to get an idea of an appropriate pace. If this is not done, it is possible to start too fast and end up walking or start too slow and thus not get an adequate assessment. In either case, an underestimate of your fitness level will be obtained.

Once the stopwatch is started or the watch is set, walk-run as fast as possible for 12 minutes. At the end of 12 minutes stop running, note the distance covered, and walk for a while to cool down. Use the distance run to determine your current level of physical fitness in Table 20-1. Repeat this test every few months to monitor progress.

Body composition or, specifically, percent body fat can be estimated by underwater weighing or by measuring subcutaneous body fat with skinfold calipers. Underwater weighing is more accurate than the skinfold technique but requires the use of expensive and generally unavailable equipment.

Measurement with a skinfold caliper (Fig. 20-1) in-

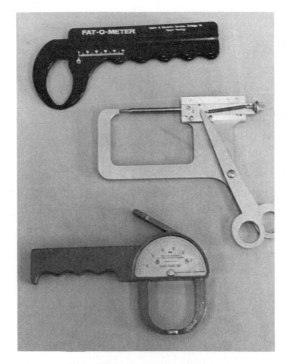

Fig. 20-1. Skinfold calipers.

volves pinching a fold of skin between the thumb and forefinger, pulling the fold from the underlying muscle, and applying the caliper to the fold. This measurement requires a helper and it should be obtained by someone skilled in the technique.

Skinfold measurements are usually taken at several anatomic sites: over the triceps and biceps muscles, below the shoulder blade, above the crest of the hip, at

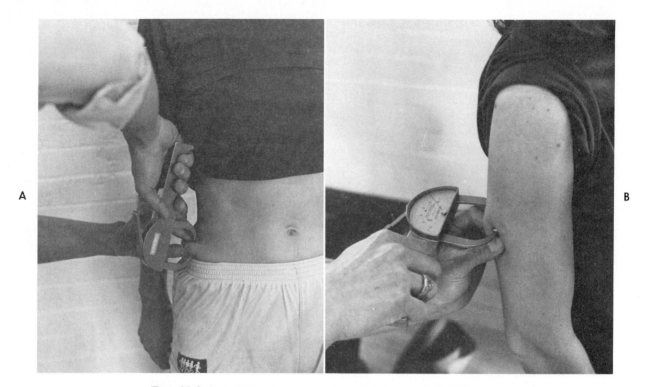

Fig. 20-2. Skinfold sites for females. **A,** Iliac crest. **B,** Triceps.

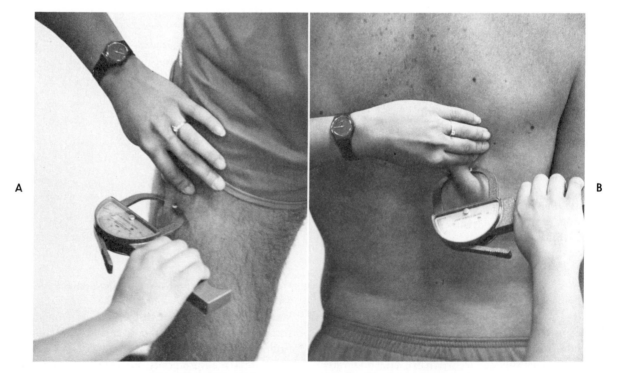

Fig. 20-3. Skinfold sites for males. **A,** Thigh. **B,** Scapula.

various chest and abdominal landmarks, and on the anterior thigh. The sites chosen depend on the equation used for estimating body fat and on the person's sex. The following sites and equations are suggested: for females, the oblique fold just above the iliac crest and the posterior surface of the arm, mid-triceps (Fig. 20-2), for males, the anterior surface of the mid-thigh and the inferior angle of the scapula (Fig. 20-3).

To determine the body density, different equations are used for females and males.

For females:
Body density = [1.0764 − 0.00081 ×
(Skin fold at iliac crest)] −
[0.00088 × (Skin fold at triceps)]

For males:
Body density = [1.1043 − 0.001327 ×
(Skin fold at thigh)] −
[0.001310 × (Skin fold at scapula)]

To determine percent body fat of males or females, substitute body density into the equation:

$$\text{Percent body fat} = \left[\frac{4.570}{\text{body density}} - 4.142 \right] \times 100\%$$

As an example consider that the skinfold thickness for a female at the iliac crest was 25 and at the triceps was 15. Substituting into the body density equation for females gives:

1.0764 − (0.00081 × 25) − (0.00088 × 15)
1.0764 − (0.02025) − (0.0132)
Body density = 1.04295

Substitution of this value into the percent fat equation produces:

$$\left[\frac{4.570}{1.04295} - 4.142 \right] \times 100 = 23.98\%$$

Although there is no agreement on "ideal" percent body fat, 16% for men and 22% for women is generally considered desirable. To estimate the amount of weight (fat) in excess of the desired amount, use the equation:

Excess pounds (fat) = Total body weight ×
(Percent body fat − Desired percent body fat)

For example, if the female in the example above weighs 125 pounds, approximately 2.5 of those pounds are excess fat. That is,

Excess pounds of fat = 125 × (0.2398 − 0.22)
= 125 × (0.0198)
= 2.475 pounds

A minimum level of development of strength and endurance in the abdominal region, lower back, and the

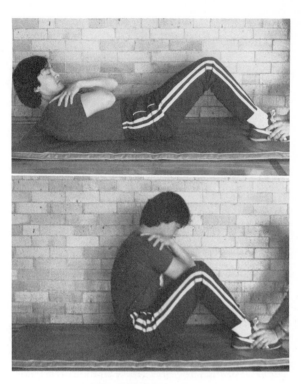

Fig. 20-4. Sit-up test.

upper body, as well as posterior thigh flexibility, are important for the prevention and rehabilitation of lower back problems. To assess the level of fitness in these areas, the following tests are suitable.

The test for abdominal strength and endurance is the modified sit-up. The only necessities for this test are a comfortable surface, a stopwatch or a watch with a second hand, and a partner to hold your feet and keep count and time. To start the test, lie supine on the floor with the knees flexed so that the angle between the thighs and the calves is about 90 degrees. Cross the arms in front of the chest and place the hands on the opposite shoulders. The partner should hold your feet to keep them in contact with the floor, (Fig. 20-4). When timing starts, do as many sit-ups as you can in 1 minute. The sit-up is performed by touching the elbows to the thighs, with the arms maintaining contact with the chest, and returning to the starting position with the middle of the back touching the floor. Use Table 20-2 for comparison purposes, but more important, use the score as a baseline for improvement.

A test for upper body stength and endurance is the pull-up. A variety of areas and equipment may be used such as a pull-up bar in a doorway or a suitable piece of gymnastic equipment. The bar should be about 1½ inches in diameter. Begin by hanging from the bar with the hands in an overhand grip (palms facing outward). From this extended position raise the body with the arms

Table 20-2. ONE-MINUTE SIT-UP NORMS

Fitness level	Age (yrs)			
	29 or under	30-39	40-49	50 or over
Males				
Very poor	<18	<12	<10	<6
Poor	25	18	15	10
Fair	40	23	20	15
Good	48	37	32	26
Excellent	>60	>45	>42	>38
Females				
Very poor	<12	<8	<2	<1
Poor	20	12	6	3
Fair	32	15	10	7
Good	40	34	26	20
Excellent	>50	>40	>35	>25

Table 20-3. SIT-AND-REACH NORMS (IN CENTIMETERS)

Fitness level	Age (yrs)			
	29 or under	30-39	40-49	50 or over
Males				
Very poor	<10	<12	<8	<5
Poor	16	18	13	13
Fair	30	23	25	20
Good	36	43	41	38
Excellent	>42	>48	>48	>43
Females				
Very poor	<18	<20	<15	<15
Poor	22	30	25	23
Fair	32	36	30	30
Good	38	50	48	46
Excellent	>42	>53	>53	>48

until the chin is above the level of the bar and then return to the extended position. Repeat as many times as possible. The test is completed when it is impossible to perform another correct pull-up. There are little normative data available for this test. However, as with any of these evaluative tests, the most important score is your own to use as a baseline for determining improvement.

The test for lower back and posterior thigh flexibility is called the sit-and-reach. A special piece of equipment is needed for this test (Fig. 20-5). To perform the test, remove the shoes and sit down with the feet against the board and the legs fully extended. Extend the arms forward with hands on top of each other and reach forward, palms down, as far as possible. Repeat four times and hold the maximum reach on the fourth trial for 1 second. The score is the farthest reach achieved to the nearest centimeter. When performing this test, do not use a forceful bobbing motion but a smooth forward slide. Compare scores with the norms in Table 20-3 and use your score as a baseline for improvement.

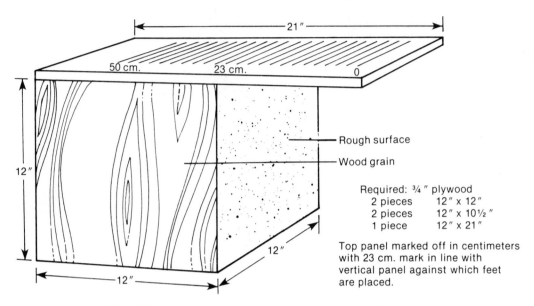

Fig. 20-5. Apparatus necessary for sit and reach test.

IMPROVEMENT OF PHYSICAL FITNESS
Cardiorespiratory fitness

Improvement of cardiorespiratory fitness requires engaging in activities that develop aerobic power. Cycling, running, and swimming employ the type of movement that, when engaged in vigorously, will overload the oxygen transport system and produce an increase in cardiorespiratory endurance. Any activity that involves the body's large-muscle groups in a continuous, rhythmic contraction is generally suitable.

The frequency, duration, and intensity of these exercises are important in developing cardiorespiratory fitness. Authorities agree that for best results it is necessary to exercise at least three times a week for at least one-half hour at an intensity that corresponds to approximately 60% of the heart rate reserve. To determine the rate, use the relationships:

$$\text{Maximum heart rate} = 220 - \text{Age}$$

$$\text{Training heart rate} = (\text{Maximum HR} - \text{resting HR}) \times 0.60 + \text{resting HR}$$

For example, for a 25-year-old with a resting heart rate of 70 beats per minute, the maximum heart rate is 195 (220 − 25); thus the training heart rate is 145, which is obtained from (195 − 70) × 0.60 + 70.

To determine the pulse rate after exercising, turn the left hand palm up and place the first three fingers of the right hand on the left wrist (Fig. 20-6). Count the number of beats for 15 seconds and multiply by 4 to find the heart rate per minute.

Techniques and skills required for the exercises to

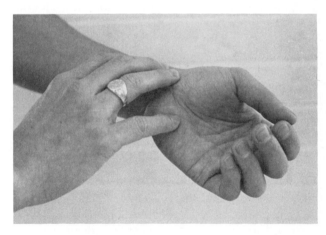

Fig. 20-6. Taking the pulse at the wrist.

accomplish many of the aspects of physical fitness are covered in other chapters of this book. However, some basic considerations should be noted regardless of which exercises or activities are chosen. They are:

1. A thorough physical examination by a physician is recommended, especially if over 35 years of age and previously engaged only in sedentary activities.
2. Begin the program *slowly*. The circulatory and muscular systems will require a period of transition and adaptation. The initial period of 2 or 3 weeks is also important from the viewpoint of motivation. An injury or severe soreness at this point might deter even the most enthusiastic person.
3. From the beginning all sessions should begin with

a short period (10 to 15 minutes) of light stretching and general "loosening up."

4. If a minor illness or injury should occur, refrain from exercising until it passes.

5. Strenuous exercise can be hazardous in extreme heat, humidity, or cold.

6. The cool-down period following the activity should be done in the same environment as the exercise.

7. As progress is made in the level of fitness, it may be desirable to increase the intensity, frequency, or duration of the workouts, or increase all three.

Body composition

To decrease body fat, it is necessary to create a caloric deficit. That is, more calories must be used than are being supplied to the body on a regular basis. One pound of fat is approximately equivalent to 3,500 calories. Exercise combined with a sensible diet is the best way to remove unwanted fat. Also, for some, exercise can suppress the sensation of hunger.

There is no magic diet that will melt away the pounds of fat the body has worked so hard to store. It takes time to accomplish any goal. It is not recommended that anyone try to lose more than 1 to 2 pounds a week. Two pounds of stored fat is equivalent to 7,000 calories, which is a difficult deficit to create. This amounts to running approximately 100 miles (161 km) or consuming 1,000 calories less per day than normal for a week. For most, this amounts to cutting about in half what is eaten per day. Most authorities suggest a combination of diet and exercise as the most sensible way to eliminate body fat.

Abdominal and back exercises

To improve the abdominal strength and endurance and lower back and posterior thigh flexibility, the following exercises (stretches) are recommended. Begin with approximately 5 to 10 repetitions and progress to 25.

Sit-ups. Assume the position for the sit-up test as described earlier. Build up the number that can be done correctly over time.

Sitting stretch. Sit with the knees and hips flexed. The soles of the feet should be touching and pulled as close to the groin as possible. Keep the knees close to the floor. One repetition is accomplished by leaning forward and holding for several seconds. (See Fig. 20-7.)

Straddle stretch. Sit with the legs extended and spread as far as possible. Lean forward and reach for the toes. One repetition is accomplished when this position is held for several seconds. While in the position move both arms to the right leg and hold and then move both arms to the left leg and hold. (See Fig. 20-8.)

Supine hip flexor stretch. Lie flat on the back; draw one knee up to the chest, and with the hands pull the knee tightly against the chest. Keep the other leg in full con-

Fig. 20-7. Sitting stretch.

tact with the floor. Hold this position for several seconds. One repetition is accomplished when this stretch is performed with both legs. (See Fig. 20-9.)

TEACHING CONSIDERATIONS

1. Physical fitness can be taught as a separate unit or integrated into other units of a school or broad-based program. Long-lasting effects, in terms of attitudes and habits, are probably better achieved when a concern for fitness is imparted in programs active enough to both develop and maintain fitness.

2. Teach the "why" as well as the "how to" of fitness components. Make instruction activity based, not "lecture" based.

3. Use preassessment and postassessment to gear the program to individuals and to assess both their and the program's effectiveness. Share information with students about their progress and where they are relative to program goals.

4. Plan lessons to include work in more than one aspect of fitness.

5. Use recovery time from strenuous exercise to teach concepts.

6. Promote responsibility. Encourage work on fitness

Fig. 20-8. Straddle stretch.

Fig. 20-9. Supine hip flexor stretch.

outside of class and give students the ability to design fitness programs using a variety of types of exercise.

7. Testing should be only a small part of a program. Reduce testing time by assigning partners or station work where possible.

8. Choose ways to conduct activity that promote maximum participation. Use space, equipment, and time maximally.

9. Assure that exercises are being done correctly—otherwise they are a waste of time.

10. Be familiar with information on exercises that can be harmful.

GLOSSARY

aerobic exercise Activities that use the oxygen system of the body.

aerobic power The capacity of the heart, lungs, and vascular system to deliver oxygen to working muscles.

anaerobic Energy processes that occur in the absence of oxygen.

arteriosclerosis The formation of plaques on the inner layers of the arterial wall.

basal metabolism rate The energy needed to maintain life under resting, postabsorptive conditions.

body composition The analysis of the body into body fat and lean body mass.

cardiac output The amount of blood pumped by the heart.

cardiovascular endurance The ability of the cardiovascular system to provide enough energy to sustain aerobic activity for an extended period of time.

chronic diseases Diseases that develop over time such as coronary artery disease.

coronary arteries The arteries that supply bood to the heart.

exercise frequency Usually the number of times per week that an individual exercises.

exercise intensity The speed or resistance of an exercise.

fatigue A generalized feeling of tiredness.

flexibility The range of motion of a body joint.

hypertrophy An enlargement of muscle cells.

interval training A training program that utilizes repeated bouts of exercise with periods of rest between repetitions.

jogging Slow running.

lean body mass Muscle, bone, and other nonfat tissues of the body.

Maximal heart rate reserve The difference between maximum heart rate and resting heart rate.

metabolic rate The total energy expended to maintain the sum of chemical and physical activity in the body.

obesity The excessive accumulation of body fat.

overload principle The imposing of a greater than normal stress on one or more body systems.

relaxation The reduction of muscle tension.

skinfold technique A measurement technique used to estimate an individual's percentage of body fat.

strength The ability of a muscle (or muscles) to exert maximal force.

stroke volume The volume of blood pumped by the heart during each beat.

underwater weighing A measurement technique used to estimate an individual's percentage of body fat

warm down A tapering off period following an exercise bout (also called cool-down).

SUGGESTED READINGS

AAHPERD health related physical fitness manual, Washington, D.C., 1980, American Alliance for Health, Physical Education, Recreation, & Dance.

AAPHERD, Physical best: The AAHPERD guide to physical fitness education and assessment, Reston, Va, 1989, American Aliance for Health, Physical Education, Recreation & Dance.

Allsen PE, Harrison JM, and Vance B: Philip Allsen's total fitness for life, ed 4, Dubuque, Iowa, 1989, Wm. C. Brown Group. Contains information on how to appraise, design, and write a fitness program for specific life-styles and initial levels of fitness.

Bompa T: Fitness and body development exercises, Dubuque, Iowa, 1981, Kendall/Hunt Publishing Co.

Brown HL: Lifetime fitness, Scottsdale, Ariz, 1987, Gorsuch Scarisbrick Publishers.

Bucher C and Prentice W: Fitness for college and life, St. Louis, 1985, Times Mirror/Mosby College Publishing. Designed for college students, this book describes the component parts and basic principles of fitness. Each chapter contains objectives, illustrations, self-assessment tools, a summary, a glossary, and references.

Burke E and Humphreys J: Fit to exercise, Ithaca, N.Y., 1982, Movement Publications, Inc. The authors describe the evolutionary, biological, and philosophical reasons for exercise and include chapters on flexibility, motivation, and aging.

Colfer G and Chevrette J: Running for fun and fitness: a self-styled program for aerobic running and physical fitness, Dubuque, Iowa, 1980, Kendail/Hunt Publishing Co.

Corbin CB and Lindsay R: Concepts of physical fitness ith laboratories, Dubuque, Iowa, 1988, Wm.C. Brown Group.

Croce P: Stretching for athletics, Champaign, Ill., 1984, Leisure Press. In addition to basic stretching exercises, presents additional stretches for athletes in various sports.

DiGennaro J: The new physical fitness: exercise for everybody, Englewood, Colo., 1983, Morton Publishing Co. Features include color section on human body systems, more than 100 photos and diagrams, information on how and where to exercise, rewards and problems of exercise, and skill evaluations.

Fox EL: Lifetime fitness, N.Y., 1983, Saunders College Publishing. Covers the essentials of fitness including specific examples of endurance, strength, and nutritional fitness programs.

Franks BD and Howley ET: Fitness leader's handbook, Champaign, Ill, 1989, Human Kinetics Books, Inc. Emphasizes the practical aspects of leading fitness classes.

Garrison L, Leslie P, and Blackmore DL: Fitness and figure control: the creation of you, Palo Alto, Calif., 1981, Mayfield Publishing Co. Uses numerous illustrations to explain the techniques and effects of major types of endurance, flexibility, and strength exercises. Also contains information on nutrition, weight control, and stress management.

Garrison L and Read AK: Fitness for everybody, Palo Alto, Calif. 1980, Mayfield Publishing Co. Written for a coed fitness course; designed to enable the reader to create an individual fitness program.

Getchell B: The fitness book, Indianapolis, Ind, 1987, Benchmark Press, Inc.

Greenberg JS: Physical fitness: a wellness approach, ed 2, Englewood Cliffs, NJ, 1989, Prentice Hall. Focuses on physical fitness from a health and wellness perspective.

Hall JT: Total fitness for men, Glenview, Ill, 1980, Scott, Foresman & Co. Describes specific exercises for improving strength, fitness, endurance, flexibility, power, and coordination. Includes charts for recording individual performance improvement.

Henderson J: Total fitness: training for life, Dubuque, Iowa, 1988, Wm.C. Brown Group. Provides a well-balanced approach to physical activity, health maintenance, nutrition, and mental training.

Hockey RV: Physical fitness: the pathway to healthful living, ed. 6, 1989, St. Louis, The C.V. Mosby Co. Provides scientific yet practical information on the importance of exercise and fitness. Written to enable the readers to evaluate their levels of fitness and then design and implement a personal program to achieve optimal fitness.

Johnson B and Nelson J: Practical measurements for evaluation in physical education, ed. 4, Minneapolis, 1985, Burgess Publishing Co.

Johnson PB: Fitness and you, Dubuque, Iowa, 1988, Wm.C. Brown Group.

Katch F and McArdle W: Nutrition, weight control and exercise, ed. 2, Philadelphia, 1983, Lea & Febiger. Contains information on optimum nutrition for exercise and sport, evaluation of body composition, strength training, and cardiovascular health and aging.

Koch S: Body dynamics: the body shape-up book for women, West Point, N.Y., 1984, Leisure Press.

Lenz H and Murray J: Fit for life: the Annapolis way, West Point, N.Y., 1984, Leisure Press. Step-by-step instructions for developing and maintaining personal fitness are discussed. Contains material on the relationship of fitness to heart disease, flexibility, nutrition, weight reduction, stress, and injuries.

Lindsey R: Fitness for the health of it, ed 6, Dubuque, Iowa, 1989, Wm. C. Brown Group. Covers the health related aspects of physical fitness, nutrition, weight control, body mechanics, and relaxation.

Mazzeo K: A commitment to fitness, Englewood, Colo., 1985, Morton Publishing Co. Includes material on developing a fitness program, posture, body composition, diet, training principles, relaxation, and stress management.

McGlynn G: Dynamics of fitness: a practical approach, Dubuque, Iowa, 1987, Wm. C. Brown Group.

Melby CL and Hyner GC: Exercise and physical fitness: a personalized approach, Dubuque, Iowa, 1988, Eddie Bowers Publishing Co.

Melograno V and Klinzing J: An orientation to total fitness, ed. 2, Dubuque, Iowa, 1984, Kendall/Hunt Publishing Co.

Miller D and Allen T: Fitness: a lifetime commitment, ed. 3, Minneapolis, 1985, Burgess Publishing Co.

Peterson S: The women's stretching book, West Point, N.Y., 1983, Leisure Press. A complete handbook of stretching exercises for women of all ages.

Ramsey F, Paul T, and Murray F: Fundamentals: concepts in exercise and fitness, ed. 3, Dubuque, Iowa, 1982, Kendall/Hunt Publishing Co.

Russell N and Grant R: Concepts in physical fitness: a self-paced program to improved health fitness, Dubuque, Iowa, 1985, Kendall/Hunt Publishing Co.

Sharkey BJ: Physiology of fitness, ed 2, Champaign, Ill, 1984, Human Kinetic Publishers, Inc. Covers aerobic fitness, muscular training, weight control, cardiovascular health, flexibility, and other topics.

Spillman C: The over 40 women's fitness book, West Point, N.Y., 1982, Leisure Press. A guide to all aspects of fitness for women over 40.

Stewart G: Every body's fitness book: a simple, safe, sane approach to personal fitness, Ithaca, N.Y., 1983, Movement Publications, Inc. Includes tips for starting and persisting, information on equipment and supplies, strength and flexibility exercises, weight loss facts and fallacies, and information on low back pain.

Stillwell J and Stockard J: Fitness exercises for children, West Point, N.Y., 1983, Leisure Press. An illustrated guide to more than 100 fitness exercises for elementary school children.

Stokes R and Fars D: Fitness everyone, Winston-Salem, N.C., 1983, Hunter Textbooks, Inc. Contains information on nutrition, sample exercise programs, hints for stress reduction and relaxation, and information on aerobic dance.

Stokes R, Moore C, and Moore A.: Fitness: the new wave, Winston-Salem, N.C., 1986, ed. 2, Hunter Textbooks, Inc. Alternating lectures and laboratories involve students in analyzing their fitness level, setting goals, and working toward achieving optimum fitness. Eleven tests for fitness assessment are included in the appendix along with complete norms for both sexes.

Westcott W: Strength fitness, Rockleigh, N.J., 1983, Allyn & Bacon, Inc. Contains scientifically based principles and step-by-step techniques for setting up an effective fitness program around individual needs.

Williams M: Lifetime physical fitness: a personal choice, Dubuque, Iowa, 1985, Wm. C. Brown Group. Organized around the premise that with the information it contains, the reader can design and implement a healthy life-style. Aerobic exercise, nutrition, relation of flexibility to prevention of lower back pain, and stress reduction are some of the topics covered.

Wilmore JH: Sensible fitness, Champaign, Ill, 1986, Human Kinetic Publishers, Inc. Outlines a comprehensive fitness program for improving strength, muscular endurance, flexibility, and cardiorespiratory endurance.

21

Racquetball, Paddleball, and Handball

Completion of this chapter should enable the reader to:

- Understand the similarities of and differences among racquetball, handball, and paddleball
- Select equipment properly
- Recognize the court markings for these sports
- Understand the rules and scoring procedures for games involving two, three, or four players
- Execute the basic skills including court positioning and various shots and serves
- Display a knowledge of offensive and defensive strategies
- Recognize and use racquetball, handball, and paddleball terms correctly
- Instruct a group of beginning players in the fundamentals of the sports

The popularity of racquetball as a recreational activity increased significantly in the mid-1960s and has been a popular pasttime ever since. The game is a variation of handball and paddleball, activities that have long been popular. The popularity of racquetball can be partially explained by the fact that even beginners can achieve early success in contacting and placing the ball using a stringed racquet, whereas the skills are more difficult to master in handball and paddleball. Although the rules for all three activities are similar, each has its advocates, claiming their favorite to be the best of the three.

HISTORY
Handball

There is evidence that handball originated about the "thermaeor" baths of Rome and that it is one of the oldest of sports. Ireland is credited with first developing the game and holding the first championship tournament. John Kavanagh of York was the leading player and champion in 1840. In this same year handball was introduced in the United States.

The first international match was played in 1887 for a purse of $1,000. The match was between Phil Casey of Brooklyn and John Lawler, the Irish Champion. Casey emerged the winner. The match consisted of 21 games. Of the 10 games played in Ireland, Lawler won 6, and of the 11 played in the United States, Casey won 7 straight games and the championship. The matches were played on a four-wall court. Casey retained the championship for many years and was called the father of the game in America. In 1897 the Amateur Athletic Union (AAU) sponsored the first American tournament, won by Michael Egan.

In the early years of the game, four-wall courts were used. Later, in about 1913, a one-wall court game on the beaches of New York became popular. This was a modification of the four-wall game. The use of one wall brought the game outdoors. A three-wall court is sometimes used for play in which abbreviated side walls abutting the front wall permit corner shots and some sidewall shots.

The first four-wall championship was held in Los Angeles in 1919, and the first one-wall AAU Championship was held in New York in 1924. The first YMCA National Championship was held in Cleveland in 1925.

The AAU, the YMCA, the United States Handball Association (formed in 1951), and the Jewish Community Recreation Association hold joint regional and national championships.

Paddleball and racquetball

The game of paddleball is generally believed to have been formulated at the University of Michigan in the early 1920s. The rules are similar to those for handball except a wooden paddle is used instead of the hand and a different type of ball is used. Racquetball, which developed out of paddleball around the late 1940s, is similar to paddleball except that a stringed racquet is used.

NATURE OF THE GAMES

A rubber ball is batted alternately by the players against the front wall of a one-, three-, or four-wall court. The object is to cause the ball to rebound to such a position and in such a manner that the opponent cannot return it before the second bounce. The ball may be played either on the fly from the front wall or after one bounce from the floor or ground. It is put in play by a serve that must first hit the front wall. A point is scored only by the player or team serving.

VALUES

One of the best of the many features of these great recreational sports is that they combine a vigorous workout in a short time with a great deal of fun. The proper ball, a pair of gloves (or a paddle or racquet), and suitable clothing and shoes are the only equipment needed. Most YMCAs, recreation centers, and athletic clubs have courts. The popularity of these activities grew so fast that commercial racquetball and handball facilities have been built all around the United States. A one-wall court can be marked off in any gym or erected outdoors on a tennis court or similar playing area. The rules are simple and can be learned in a short time. These games require only two, three, or four persons to play, so it is easy to play a game almost any time without getting a lot people together.

These games can be played at any age. However, because they require fast reactions, quick reflexes, and good eye-hand coordination, it is important to play with partners and opponents of comparable ability.

EQUIPMENT
Balls

The balls used for paddleball and racquetball are about the size of a tennis ball. They are manufactured by several companies and come in different colors and degrees of "liveliness." The official racquetball is 2 ¼ inches (5.7 cm) in diameter and weighs about 1.4 ounces (43.5 g). The official handball is black, 1⅞ inches (4.7 cm) in diameter, and weighs 2³⁄₁₀ ounces (65.2 g). It is often suggested that beginners use a softer, larger ball, such as a tennis ball, until some of the basic footwork and shot fundamentals are mastered.

Gloves

In handball, gloves must be worn. The gloves may be made of leather or a soft material and must be light in color. The fingers of the gloves cannot be webbed, and no foreign substance (tape, rubber bands, or the like) can be worn on the gloves. Padded gloves are available and are recommended for beginners. After the hands become toughened and the player's skill increases so that batting the ball does not result in sore hands, tightfitting, unpadded gloves are recommended to allow increased control of the ball.

The racquet

With the increase in popularity of racquetball has come an increase in the number, types, and sizes of racquets available. The phenomenon is similar to the proliferation of types of tennis racquets in recent years. Frames are made of wood, fiberglass, graphite, and various kinds of metals and plastics of differing shapes. The racquet strings may be made of gut, nylon, monofilament, graphite, plastic, metal, or some combination of these.

Of course, prices vary considerably as well. For the beginner, a lightweight metal or plastic frame has advantages. Most importantly, the racquet should feel comfortable when gripped. When selecting a racquet it is important to grip the handle with the safety thong attached in the correct manner.

The paddle

The paddle, while much the same size as the racquet, is made entirely of wood. Some models have a leather-wrapped handle similar to that of the racquet, and all paddles should have a safety thong attached to the handle. Most paddles have regularly spaced holes drilled through the face to reduce air resistance.

Eyeguards

Because of the possibility of eye injury, special eyeguards have been introduced and are highly recommended for both novice and advanced players. In fact, in many tournaments and recreational facilities, lensed eyewear is required.

COURTS
One-wall court

The one-wall court is 20 feet (6.09 m) wide, 34 feet (10.36 m) long, and 16 feet (4.87 m) high, with at least 6 feet

(1.83 m) of clear space beyond the side and long lines. (The 34-foot line is called the long line.) There are no official specifications for playing surfaces. The surface is usually wood, cement, or clay. (See Fig. 21-1.)

The short line is drawn across the court 16 feet (4.87 m) from the front wall and parallel to it. The service line is drawn across the court 9 feet (2.74 m) behind the short line and parallel to it. The space between the service line and short line is the service zone.

Four-wall court

The four-wall court should have a hardwood floor, and sidewalls should be constructed of smooth plaster, tile, concrete, glass, or brick. The court should measure 20 × 20 × 40 feet (6.09 × 6.09 × 12.19 m). (See Fig. 21-2.)

Three-wall court

Three-wall courts are occasionally used and are identical to four-wall courts in dimensions except there is no back wall.

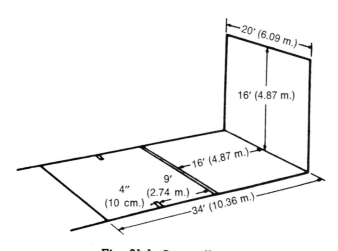

Fig. 21-1. One-wall court.

RULES
One-wall court

The rules for the four-wall court also apply to the one-wall court with the exception of those rules pertaining to sidewalls, back wall, and ceiling plays where there is no ceiling adjoining the front wall, and with the following other considerations.

Serving. The server drops the ball to the floor within the service zone, and on the first bounce strikes it in such a manner that it hits the front wall and returns to the floor beyond the short line and in front of the long line. The opposing side must make a legal return by striking the ball after the first bounce or on the fly.

Following are terms that pertain to serving:

long ball A long ball passes over the long line on the serve.
short ball A short ball does not pass over the short line on the serve.
out An out results from serving two short balls, two long balls, one short ball and one long ball, serving the ball out-of-bounds, or hitting the floor before the wall.

Special rules for paddleball
1. Loss of 3 points for throwing the paddle
2. Loss of 2 points for dropping the paddle
3. Loss of 3 points and serve for throwing the paddle while serving
4. Loss of 5 points and serve for hitting any player with the paddle

Four-wall court
1. The game may be played by two (singles), three (cutthroat), or four players (doubles).
2. In handball, a game consists of 21 points. A match consists of two games of 21 points with a tie-breaker of 11 points if the first two games are split.
3. In racquetball, a game consists of 15 points; a match, two games of 15 points, with a tie-breaker of 11 points if the first two games are split.

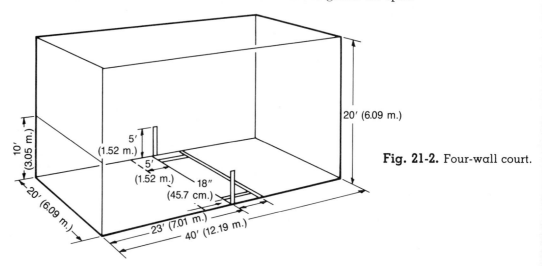

Fig. 21-2. Four-wall court.

4. Only the racquet, paddle, or one hand may be used to strike the ball. The use of the foot or any portion of the body to return the ball is not permitted.

5. In attempting to return the ball, a player cannot strike it more than once.

6. Serving:

   a. To make a legal service, the server drops the ball to the floor within the service zone and strikes it on the bounce, so that it hits the front wall first and on the rebound lands on the floor back of the short line, before or after striking one of the sidewalls.

   b. Drive serve zones in racquetball. The drive serve lines are 3 feet (.91 m) from each side wall in the service box, dividing the service area into two 17-foot (5.18 m) service zones for drive serves only. The player may drive serve to the same side of the court on which he or she is standing, so long as the start and finish of the service motion takes place outside of the three foot line. (See Fig. 21-3.)

   c. The three types of serve are legal serve, out serve, and fault serve. If the serve is legal, play continues; if the serve is an out serve, the server is retired; if the serve is a fault serve, another serve is permitted. What constitutes each of these types of serve is explained under playing regulations.

   d. After the ball has been legally served, the opposing side makes a legal return by striking the ball on the fly or first bounce, causing it to hit the front wall before hitting the floor. The ball may hit the ceiling, back wall, and either one or both sidewalls before it hits the front wall.

   e. The serving and receiving sides alternate in attempting to make legal returns until one side fails. If the serving side fails, it scores an out; if the receiving side fails, a point is scored for the server.

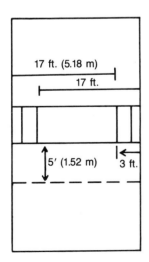

Fig. 21-3. Drive serve zones in racquetball.

Three-wall court

Three-wall handball is played similarly to four-wall with the exception of the back wall. In place of the back wall a line is drawn on the floor parallel to the front wall and is called a long line. A ball, in play, striking behind the long line is a point or a handout depending on the side last to hit the ball. A served ball that lands behind the long line is a long ball. Hitting two long balls or one long and one short ball in succession puts the server out.

PLAYING REGULATIONS
Service

1. The choice for the right to serve is decided by a coin toss, and the player winning the toss has the option of serving or receiving the first game. The player who wins the most points in the first two games has the option of serving first for the third (tie-breaker) game. In informal matches a common procedure to determine who serves is to see which player can rebound the ball off the front wall and come closest to the short line.

2. With the exception of the drive serve, the server may start serving from any place in the serving zone.

3. In serving, the server must start and stay within the service zone; if while serving the server steps outside the service zone, a fault is charged. Stepping outside the service zone twice in succession retires the server and counts as an out. "Stepping over" is the act of putting any part of the foot past the short or service lines. On a lob serve, the server may not back out of the service zone until the ball has passed the back service line.

4. In serving, the ball must be bounced on the floor and struck on the rebound from the floor. The server is out if the attempt to hit the ball on this rebound fails. Not more than three bounces may be used in making a service. Bouncing of the ball by a server in any part of the court before serving is counted as a bounce within the meaning of this rule. Violation of this rule retires the server.

5. In singles, when the server loses the service, the server becomes the receiver; the receiver then becomes the server, and so on alternately in all subsequent services of the game.

6. In doubles, only one player is allowed to serve in the first inning. When this player is put out, each of the opponents is allowed to serve until put out. On resuming service, the player who served first again serves until put out, and then the partner serves.

7. The server may not serve until the opponent has had a chance to get placed or the referee calls play.

8. In doubles, the server's partner must stand within the service zone until the ball passes the service line

on each serve. Two consecutive violations of this rule retire the server.

9. If a player's partner is hit by a served ball while standing in the service box, the serve counts as a "dead ball" without penalty, but any short or fault preceding the service partner being hit with the ball is charged.

10. In doubles, each partner must serve in the regular order of service. Failure to do so counts as a handout, and the points scored on the illegal serve do not count.

11. Every effort should be made to keep the ball dry, particularly on the service. Deliberate violation of the spirit of this rule results in forfeiture of serve. The ball may be inspected at any time during a game, and the referee puts a new ball in play if advisable.

Receiving service

1. In handball and racquetball the receivers must stand at least 5 feet (1.52 m) in back of the short line as indicated by the service or restraining line.

2. In handball the receiver can hit the ball after it passes the short line.

3. In racquetball the receiver may not enter the safety zone [the 5 foot (1.52 m) area between the short line and receiver's line] until the served ball bounces or crosses the receiver's line.

4. A receiver may play the service either on the fly or after the first bounce. In making a fly return, the receiver must play the ball after it passes over the short line in handball and receiver's line in racquetball.

Faults

1. Two consecutive faults retire the server.

2. A serve is considered short when the served ball hits the front wall and fails to strike back of the short line on the fly.

3. A short also occurs when a served ball hits the front wall and two sidewalls before striking the floor back of the short line.

4. A serve is considered long when the served ball rebounds from the front wall and touches the back wall before touching the floor.

5. A serve is also considered a fault if the ball rebounds from the front wall and touches the ceiling.

6. Stepping over the outer edges of the service or short line with any part of the foot in the act of service is considered a fault.

7. Serving the ball in doubles when the server's partner is not in the service box with his or her back against the wall is considered a fault.

Hinders

1. A returned ball that strikes an opponent on its way to the front wall is considered dead even if it continues to the front wall before striking the floor.

2. A player's unintentional interference in such a way as to prevent the opponent from having a fair chance to return the ball is considered a hinder.

3. In doubles, both players on a side are entitled to a fair and unobstructed chance at the ball. The referee should be alert in rendering decision under this rule to discourage any practice of playing the ball where an adversary cannot see it until too late to get into position. It is no excuse that the ball is "killed" or that the adversary "could not get it." A player is entitled to a fair chance to recover any ball.

4. The principle just cited holds true also in singles. It is the duty of the side that has played the ball to get out of the way of the opponent.

5. It is the duty of the referee to decide all hinders and covered balls.

6. When a player is interfered with by his or her partner, a hinder cannot be claimed.

7. When, in the opinion of the referee, a player is hindered intentionally, the referee decides the point against the offending player.

8. A ball off the front wall on a fly or bounce that goes into the gallery or an opening in the sidewall is a hinder, but if it goes into the gallery or opening after a player has touched it (a ball caroming off a racquet, paddle, or hand), it counts as a point or an out against the player attempting the return.

Outs

1. A player intentionally interferes with an opponent.

2. A partner serves out of turn.

3. A served ball touches the server in singles or doubles.

4. A served ball strikes the server's partner when the latter is outside the service box.

5. A legally returned ball strikes the partner of the player returning the ball.

6. A player fails to play a ball properly returned from a service.

7. A served ball hits the ceiling, floor, or sidewalls before striking the front wall.

8. A served ball hits the front wall and sidewall, front wall and floor, or front wall and ceiling at the same time (crotch ball).

9. The server makes two successive faults.

10. The ball bounces more than three times on the serve.

SAFETY

Novice paddleball or racquetball players should be careful to avoid swinging wildly at the ball, because the paddles and racquets can injure a partner or opponent. In fact, paddles and racquets have a thong attached to the handle that must be secured to the player's wrist to prevent a paddle or racquet from slipping from the hand. For this reason, it is illegal to switch the paddle or racquet from hand to hand during play.

FUNDAMENTAL SKILLS AND TECHNIQUES

The beginner watching an experienced player soon learns that there are fundamentals common to most sports. The beginner is often out of position, off-balance, and unable to get a good, accurate shot, while the more experienced opponent seems to always be in the correct position. The beginning student should work on these fundamentals.

Position on floor

Study the possible angles that a ball can travel and rebound within the four rectangular walls of the court as you would in studying angles while playing billiards. Throw or hit the ball at the walls at different angles and heights and observe the rebounds. Try to move to that spot where the ball is expected to be best played. (See Fig. 21-4.)

Footwork

The fundamental skill of correct footwork is essential for proficiency and accuracy in these activities. For a right-handed player the left foot and side should be toward the front wall when a forehand stroke is called for; if a back-hand or a left-hand stroke is called for, the right foot and side should be facing the front wall. While waiting between shots the front of the body should face the front wall, the feet should be about shoulder-width apart, the weight should be evenly distributed on both feet, and the player should be ready to move in any direction. While waiting and when contacting the ball the knees are usually bent and the body is crouched. (See Fig. 21-5.)

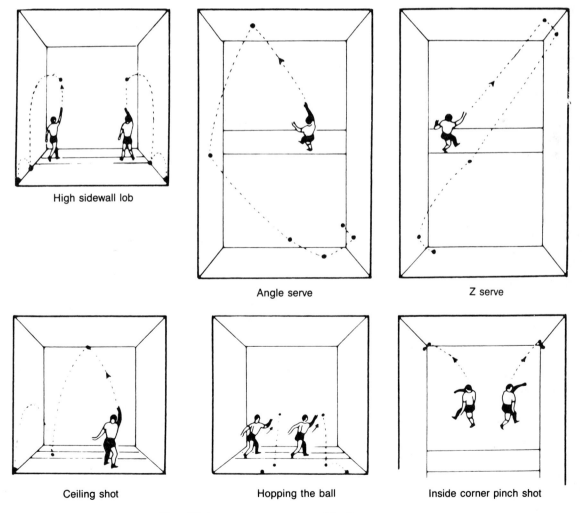

High sidewall lob

Angle serve

Z serve

Ceiling shot

Hopping the ball

Inside corner pinch shot

Fig. 21-4. Floor positions and ball placement.

Fig. 21-5. Stance for an open-hand shot in handball.

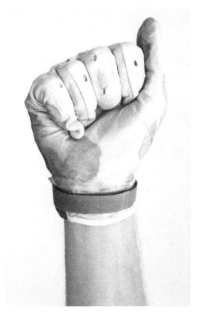

Fig. 21-6. Handball fist shot.

Accuracy of playing shots

Accuracy depends on proper footwork, good balance, and keeping the eyes on the ball with correct arm action and follow-through. The player, by experience, should gain the ability to choose the angle and spot it is desirable to hit without looking at the spot. (The player should be watching the ball.)

Practice low corner shots that have little or no rebound. These shots are called kill shots. The sidearm stroke is most accurate for this shot.

The hand

Snug-fitting gloves should be worn for handball. The tips of the fingers should be slightly squeezed together, and the entire hand slightly cupped like a swimmer's hand. The wrist and elbow should be flexible to accommodate a wrist snap shot or an overarm stroke similar to that of throwing a fast ball. In stroking the ball, the hand should follow through toward the spot where the ball is directed before the arm swings across the body to complete the follow-through. The hand can also be held in a tight fist for certain kinds of shots. (See Fig. 21-6.)

Strokes

The arm strokes used in all three activities are similar except that in racquetball and paddleball a backhand stroke is sometimes employed, whereas in handball the player must develop the ability to use the nondominant hand in striking the ball. In all three activities the overarm, sidearm, and underarm strokes are utilized.

The overarm. The body position for the overarm stroke is similar to that in throwing a ball fast, for example, from a catcher to second base. The arm swings back so that the racquet or the hand begins the stroking action from behind the ear. If a ball is hit from a high reach, the arm is usually held almost straight while stroking. A quick, flexible wrist snap is desirable.

The sidearm. The sidearm stroke on the dominant side of the body is similar to a sidearm throw delivery. If the player is right-handed, the left foot should be in front of the right, and vice versa. Often the stroke is made without changing feet and with a quick, flexible wrist snap. However, the feet should always be ready to react if a more accurate stroke can be delivered by shifting the feet.

The underarm. This stroke is not as common in racquetball or paddleball as it is in handball. In all three activities, the underhand stroke is usually less effective than bending low at the knees and waist and using the sidearm stroke.

In handball, where power is desired, the ball may be contacted with the heel of the hand. This part of the hand is strong and muscular and can withstand constant and repeated contact with the ball.

In all three activities the use of the wrist to impart speed to the ball is paramount. Because of the velocity with which the ball travels, it is not uncommon that a player will not be able to get in the proper position to effectively use the proper body, leg and arm movements, and the wrist snap in these situations is the only re-

Fig. 21-7. Racquetball forehand kill shot position.

maining movement to achieve a decent return. In racquetball and paddleball this motion is aided by the use of light racquets and paddles. In handball it is helpful to contact the ball toward the tips of the fingers, when possible. This permits a longer leverage to the hand, and a wrist whip gives the ball added speed and accuracy. To master this stroke requires a great deal of practice. The ball can be hit with the palm of the hand, but this shot is not so accurate, nor can speed or power be obtained from it.

Kill shots

A kill shot is one that hits the front so close to the floor that there is practically no bounce before an opponent can reach the ball and play it. There are many varieties of kill shots.

Straight kill shot. The straight kill is a shot to the front wall that does not touch either sidewall but hits the wall low (Fig. 21-7).

Outside-corner pinch shot. In the outside-corner pinch shot, the ball first hits the sidewall, bounces to the front wall, and then bounces to the floor. Either the right or left corner may be used.

Inside-corner pinch shot. In the inside-corner pinch shot, the ball first hits the front wall, bounces to the sidewall, and then bounces to the floor. Again, either the right or left corner may be used.

Fly kill shot. In the fly kill shot the ball is hit on the fly from a front wall rebound so fast that the opponent has no opportunity to play the ball.

A player should constantly strive to direct a ball into an area or at such an angle into the sidewalls that the opponent has no opportunity to play the ball. This is a skill that can be mastered only by practice and experience.

Back-wall shot

A hard shot that hits moderately high on the front wall will often rebound all the way to the back wall without hitting the floor. A player sensing such a situation should move into a position to return the ball as it comes off the back wall (or floor) and is moving toward the front wall. By waiting until the ball is near the floor the player can execute a kill shot.

Occasionally a player may not have time to get into the proper position to return a back wall shot as described above. It may be possible to hit the ball hard and moderately high against the back wall to cause it to rebound to the front wall before hitting the floor. This shot should be used only in desperation, because it often results in an easy return for the opponent. The shot should be used only when the player is out of position and needs to buy time to regain proper court position.

Ceiling shot

The ceiling shot is basically a defensive pass shot used when a player it out of position or for a change of pace. It may also be used offensively to move an opponent out of the center court position. It is executed by hitting the ball relatively hard and directing it to contact the ceiling a few feet in back of the front wall. The intent should be to cause the ball to bounce on the floor approximately in the serving area and then come down in a back corner near a side wall. By hitting the ceiling and front wall, the ball develops an overspin and bounces higher than normal, possibly causing the opponent to misplay the ball.

Pass shots

A shot directed in such a way that it travels along the side wall that is farthest away from the opponent is a

Fig. 21-8. Racquetball serve.

pass shot. It should not be hit with so much force that it rebounds off the back wall but instead drops into one of the back corners.

The serve

There are many types and variations of serves (Fig. 21-8). A serve is begun by dropping the ball on the floor behind the service line. On the first bounce, the server hits it with the racquet, paddle, or hand. To be a legal serve, the ball must hit the front wall; it can then either rebound directly back behind the server or from the front wall onto the sidewalls, as long as it rebounds to the floor behind the short line. The server is permitted another serve if a fault is committed. Two faults retire the server.

Drive serve. In the drive serve, the player contacts the ball close to the floor so that it hits the front wall close to the floor and rebounds just behind the short line; it is usually directed at an angle so that when it reaches a receiver it is near a sidewall.

Z serve. In the Z serve, the player serves from the side so that the ball rebounds from the front wall to the sidewall opposite the server at such an angle that the ball lands behind the short line. This serve can also be hit high so that the ball rebounds to the back wall and corner behind the server.

Direct high lob. The server stands close to the right or left sidewall and serves the ball high up on the front wall and close to the sidewall, so that the ball rebounds far back in the court but is very close to the sidewall on its entire flight. This type of serve often drops dead in the back corner and is difficult to return. Some of these serves may just touch the sidewall on their rebound flight, causing the ball to drop dead.

Two-wall serve to back corner. The server takes a position close to the right wall and serves the ball about head high and about 4 or 5 feet from the left sidewall. The ball rebounds to the left sidewall just back of midcourt, rebounds to the floor and on back to the right corner, and hits the back wall and then the right wall before hitting the floor.

The flight of this serve causes the receiver to run around following the ball, looking for an opportunity to play it, which is difficult.

HINTS ON PLAY AND STRATEGY

1. Throughout a game, keep in mind that situations like those described in the various serves may arise, and the ball can be directed and played like a serve. In these situations there is a need to quickly size up an opponent's weaknesses and strong points. Play to an opponent's weakness and disadvantage.
2. Keep your eyes on the ball. Follow it constantly.
3. Protect your eyes by wearing lensed eyeguards.
4. Anticipate—watch your opponent's feet and position. He or she will usually telegraph the return shots.
5. Avoid rushing the ball. It is important to wait before attempting the return shot.

6. Concentrate on your serve. At this time, you have complete control of the ball.

7. Develop several different serves. Analyze your opponent's return of various serves. Concentrate on the serve that is most difficult for your opponent to return.

8. Change from fast play to lob shots and runaround plays to keep an opponent off balance. Strive to place shots accurately.

9. Be constantly on the alert for balls that can be contacted close to the floor or for the opportunity to hit corner kill shots.

10. Constantly work for a desirable position on the court. A good spot is usually the "hole" or "well" near the center of the court and service area. This is also known as the offensive spot, and the backcourt as the defensive spot. Try to keep the opponent out of the "well."

11. Strive to think ahead and set up a series of plays that will keep the opponent off balance and therefore at a disadvantage.

12. Continue to practice your weakest strokes. In handball it is usually necessary to practice hitting with the nondominant hand. In racquetball and handball, regularly practice hitting backhand strokes. On either a serve or rebound, concentrate on hitting a spot on the front wall, but keep the eyes on the ball until it is hit. After a serve, come quickly to midcourt. Continue to maneuver for the offensive position throughout the game.

SKILLS TO PRACTICE ALONE

1. Practice by throwing or hitting the ball to the wall at various angles and receiving the rebounds. Note the angles and directions of the rebounds.

2. Practice hitting lob rebounds and receiving them accurately.

3. Throw the ball so that it hits the floor and then bounces off the back wall and practice returning the rebound from the back wall to the front wall. In practicing this skill, do not rush. Take it easy, keep your eye on the ball, and wait for the ball to reach you.

4. Practice serving and study angles and an imaginary opponent's position.

5. Practice and master these skills and develop the skill of directing the ball to the areas impossible for an opponent to cover.

6. A ball hit low on the wall is difficult to return. Practice this type of return regularly by contacting the ball as close to the floor as possible.

COURT COURTESY

If there is any doubt about any play, it should be played over. It is not good sportsmanship to deliberately hit an opponent with the ball in order to get a hinder on the play. An opponent is entitled to a fair, unobstructed opportunity to play the ball.

TEACHING CONSIDERATIONS

1. Many school situations will be limited to games on one-wall courts. Taped lines on the walls and floor can be used to mark off playing areas.

2. Teach students basic sidearm and underarm patterns beginning with tapping the ball easily against the wall rather than strokes requiring maximum force production. Start with forehand strokes before introducing backhand strokes. Emphasize action of the wrist and open stance as well as returning to a ready position in the play area. Emphasize getting the racquet in proper position.

3. Use partners to practice alternating hits in a cooperative way before introducing competitive strategies. Emphasize interference rules as soon as you introduce partner work. When two players can keep the ball going fairly consistently (at least six hits) without losing control of the ball, begin to increase the demand for greater force levels by increasing the distance of the players from the wall.

4. When players can consistently keep the ball going against the wall, encourage them to begin placing the ball to make their partners move to unused spaces in the playing area. Teach for changing the level of the ball against the wall, changing the angle of the shot, and changing the force level of the ball as offensive strategies. Name the shots and teach for form.

5. Introduce the serve and game rules as players begin to have a need for more formal regulation of play (after some consistency is developed in ability to return the easier shots).

6. Modify and develop rules as necessary to meet the needs of the facilities available.

7. Require all players to wear lensed eyeguards. Include a few moments on eye safety in early instruction.

GLOSSARY

ace A serve that completely eludes the receiver.

crotch ball A ball hitting at the juncture of the front wall and the floor or the ceiling, sidewall, or corner.

dead ball A ball out of play, following a fault not played, a penalty, or a hinder.

fault An infraction of the rules that involves a penalty other than an out.

first service In doubles, only the first player serves to start the game.

handout A handout occurs when a side loses the serve.

hinder An accidental interference or obstruction of the flight of the ball not involving a penalty.

kill A ball returned to the front wall in such a manner that it rebounds from the front wall or sidewall so close to the floor that it is impossible to return.

long ball If on the serve the ball either hits the back wall directly or passes over the long line (three wall) it is called a long ball.

match Winning two out of three games.

out Sometimes called a handout. It is scored against the serving side when the server fails to serve legally. In a doubles game when each of the two partners has been put out, it is a sideout. In a singles game, retiring the server retires the side.

point Scored only by the serving side and made when an opponent fails to play a legal serve or a legally returned ball.

receiver The player or players to whom the ball is served; also called the receiving side.

receiving line The line running parallel with 5 feet (1.52 m) in back of the short line.

receiving zone The back court is the receiving zone for the serve.

server The person serving the ball.

service line The line running parallel with and 5 feet (1.52 m) in front of the short line.

service zone The space between the outer edges of the short and service lines in which the server must remain while serving the ball.

short line The line running parallel with the front wall and dividing the court into two equal parts.

SUGGESTED READINGS

Allsen P and Witbeck A: Racquetball, ed 4, Dubuque, Iowa, 1988, Wm C Brown Publishers. Contains sequential photographs depicting critical movements of various strokes, games strategy, racquetball terminology, questions for self-evaluation, and practice drills.

Dowell L and Grice W: Racquetball, Boston, 1980, American Press.

Edwards LR: Racquetball, Scottsdale, Ariz, 1988, Gorsuch Scarisbrick Publishers. Discusses rules, equipment, terminology, tournament competition, and strategy.

Fabian L, Love P, Hiser J, Larson B, and Lephant S: Racquetball: ten beginning keys to success, Dubuque, Iowa, 1988, Eddie Bowers Publishing Co. Features a section on stretching, over 100 pictures and diagrams, and teaching aids and drills.

Gabert T: Raquetball, Dubuque, Iowa, 1984, Kendall/Hunt Publishing Co.

Gifford P: Racquetball, Edina, Minn, 1985, Burgess International Group, Inc.

Henkin M: The 1985/1986 racquetball primer, Bethesda, Md, 1984, National Press, Inc. Designed for beginners. To be used before and in conjunction with lessons.

Isaacs L, Lumpkin A, and Schroer D: Racquetball everyone, Winston-Salem, NC, 1984, Hunter Textbooks, Inc. Covers the basics from beginning to advanced. Contains chapters on rarer information such as goal setting, mental preparation, injuries, and tournament play. Especially helpful to instructors who teach large groups of students with various levels of skill.

Jones J: Racquetball, Edina, Minn, 1985, Burgess International Group, Inc.

Moore A, Scott T, and Porterfield W: Three-wall racquetball, everyone, ed 2, Winston-Salem, NC, 1986, Hunter Text-books, Inc. Grips, swings, and shots are presented step-by-step with numerous photos. Two chapters are devoted to the modified and the standard three-wall game. Each chapter is followed by an evaluation and assessments of knowledge and skill.

Norton C and Bryant J: Beginning racquetball, Englewood, Colo, 1986, Morton Publishing Co. Contains more than 200 photographs illustrating basic skills. Includes chapters on safety, strokes, serves, strategy, drills, etiquette, and interpreting rules.

Official racquetball rules, Colorado Springs, Colo, 1988-89, American Amateur Racquetball Association.

Pangrazi RP: Racquetball, Glenview, Ill, 1986, Scott, Foresman & Co. Includes activity self-tests and checklists at the end of the text.

Shay A and Leve C: Winning racquetball, Chicago, 1980, Henry Regnery Co.

Smith C: A swinging approach to racquetball, Dubuque, Iowa, 1981, Kendall/Hunt Publishing Co.

Sylvis J: Racquetball for everyone: technique and strategy, Englewood Cliffs, NJ, 1980, Prentice-Hall, Inc.

Turner E and Hogan M: Racquetball, Champaign, Ill, 1987, Human Kinetics Publishers, Inc. Beginning and advanced skills and strategies are presented; includes practice drills and common areas.

The new and official U.S. handball association handball rules, Tucson, Ariz, 1983, U.S. Handball Association.

Tyson P and Turman J: The handball book, Champaign, Ill, 1983, Human Kinetics Publishers, Inc. A comprehensive overview of handball, featuring articles written by the most famous players in the game. More than 200 photos and illustrations.

Verner B: Racquetball: basic skills and drills, Palo Alto, Calif, 1985, Mayfield Publishing Co. Contains a comprehensive introduction to the game, material on strategy, drills following each discussion of a shot or strategy, and boxed information on common faults, hints for improvement, and problem areas.

AUDIOVISUAL AIDS

Introduction to racquetball by John Reznik, 16 mm. Champions on Film, Division of School Tech Corp., Ann Arbor, Mich.

Racquetball and handball stretches chart by Bob and Jean Anderson, drawings with instructions. Stretching, Inc., Box 767, Palmer Lake, CO 80133.

Racquetball basic shots by John Reznik, 16 mm. Champions on Film, Division of School Tech Corp., Ann Arbor, Mich.

Racquetball lessons made easy by Steve Keeley, audio cassette and booklet course. Russell Productions, San Diego, Calif.

Racquetball serving by John Reznik, 16 mm. Champions on Film, Division of School Tech Corp., Ann Arbor, Mich.

Rollout by AMF Voit, full-color. Orange County Film Service, Santa Ana, Calif.

Sports techniques films by Terry Fancher, Janell Marriott, Steve Standemo, and Kathy Williams. Ten-minute sport films on fundamentals of racquetball, racquetball shots, racquetball serves, serve returns, and strategy of singles, doubles, and cutthroat. Available from American Alliance for Health, Physical Education, Recreation, and Dance, 1900 Association Dr., Reston, VA 22091.

22

Rugby

Completion of this chapter should enable the reader to:

- Appreciate the development and values of the game of rugby
- Select rugby equipment and lay out a rugby field
- Describe the rules and scoring procedures of the game
- Practice the fundamental techniques of rugby
- Explain the skills and duties required of the various positions
- Use lead-up activities and other suggestions to teach the fundamentals of rugby

HISTORY

Ball games resembling football have been played for well over 2,000 years. Many descriptions, paintings, and drawings surviving from the Middle Ages show that the game has been played in the British Isles for centuries.

Rugby football was devised accidentally at Rugby School in England in 1823 when one of the players on Rugby's team, William Webb Ellis, tucked the ball under his arm and ran across the goal line, an act recognized as unsportsmanlike conduct. However, this form of the game gained tremendous popularity over the next 40 years, and when the word football was used, some people asked, "Which kind?" Separate rules for rugby and football were formulated in the latter half of the nineteenth century.

Some 20 years after the division from football, a group of clubs in northern England formed what eventually became known as Rugby League. Rugby Union and Rugby League now support two totally distinct games.

Rugby has been played in America since the late nineteenth century but has been overshadowed by gridiron football and soccer, both of which developed from a rugby framework. Walter Camp, a halfback from Yale, changed the course of rugby to gridiron with two basic suggestions. One was to reduce the number of players from 15 to 11. The second was to guarantee possession so that appropriate plans of attack and defense could take place. By 1888, blocking and tackling below the waist were legalized. By 1900, the line-out was abolished and after a threat by President Theodore Roosevelt to ban the game if it was not cleaned up, the forward pass was introduced and rugby was almost gone. Rugby was an official Olympic sport four times from 1896 to 1924. U.S. teams won the gold medal twice (1920 and 1924) defeating the French team both times.

During the 1950s interest was rekindled, and today in the United States there are more than 60,000 players and approximately 1,000 clubs. There are three National Championships and regular International Games. The United States has its own Union (USARFU), as does each region. Rugby has become popular among men and women and is played in many areas of the United States and Canada.

VALUES

Rugby is a team game that requires players to use their skill in conjunction with others to achieve success. It is a running game that requires active involvement of each player for the duration of the game. It develops team spirit and cooperation and affords a high level of satisfaction for the participants.

Because players are moving continually, rugby helps develop cardiovascular endurance. The basic skills of the game require speed, balance, coordination, and strength, important in any physical development program. By virtue of the structure of the game, greatest enjoyment in rugby comes as a result of being fit. It is a contact sport, and players should physically equip themselves to meet this requirement. Fitness and strength training are recommended, and with an organized group most of this can be done using a ball. When training for any sport, it is important to utilize the tools of that sport—in this case the ball—as much as possible.

Preseason conditioning involves building endurance and strength, with emphasis on development of individual skills. During the season much of the time is spent building the team, developing and coordinating plays, and sharpening basic and individual skills. Keeping the body fit and flexible helps prevent injury. Stretching is extremely important before and after training; 10 to 15 minutes should be allowed for gradual loosening up of the major muscle groups in the neck, chest, lower back, arms, abdomen, thighs, hamstrings, and calves.

EQUIPMENT
Clothing

Rugby can be played by persons of all ages and requires little equipment. Proper shoes are most important. They should be high-laced and have leather, rubber, plastic, or aluminum cleats to give the player a secure grip on the ground. Socks, shorts, and a rugby shirt make up the rest of the basic uniform. It is advisable to wear a mouth guard to protect the teeth. Some players (mainly the forwards, who experience a great deal of physical contact) wear shin guards, scrum caps, and headbands.

The ball

The rugby ball is oval in shape and made of four panels of leather or other approved material. It weighs 13½ to 15½ ounces (382 to 439 g).

FIELD

Rugby is played on a rectangular field not exceeding 100.6 m long and 68.4 m wide (110 × 75 yards) (Fig. 22-1). It is often played on a shorter and narrower field depending on the space available and age of the players. A line drawn across the center, the halfway line, divides the field. The goalposts, placed in the center of the goal line, consist of two uprights exceeding 3.4 m (3.7 yards) in height and a crossbar 5.6 m (6.1 yards) wide. The crossbar is attached to the uprights 3 m from the ground. The in goal area between the goal line and the dead ball line must not exceed 22 m.

A 22 m (24-yard) line is marked in each half of the field between the goal line and the halfway line. A player may kick the ball directly into touch from inside his or her own 22 m line and the goal line. The two lines marking the side of the field, the touchlines, mark where the ball goes into touch (out of bounds). The dotted 5 m (5.5-yard) line shows the point where the front player in the line-out stands, and the 15 m (16.4-yard) mark denotes the point beyond which the line out may not extend. A

dotted 10 m (10.9-yard) line drawn across the field enables the referee to decide whether the kickoff has gone the required 10 m.

A 5 m mark in front of each goal line is used for 5 m scrums when the defending team brings the ball over its own goal line and touches it down. Touch flags are placed on each corner where the goal line and touchline meet. Flags are also placed at points along the outside of the touchline to mark the halfway line and both 22 m lines.

RULES
Officials

One referee has control of the game and enforces the rules. Two linesmen (touch judges) watch the sidelines and signal the referee when the ball has gone out of bounds. They also assist the referee where possible regarding infringements of the rules.

The referee keeps the time and the score. Players must obtain permission from the referee to leave and reenter the field during play.

Duration of game

The game is made up of two periods, each 40 minutes in duration. There is a 5-minute interval between periods, during which the teams change ends.

The referee may add on time at the end of each period if necessary. For example, play may be stopped because of injury to a player.

Players and positions

Rugby is played by two teams of 15 players each: eight forwards—two props, one hooker, two locks, two flankers, one No. 8—and seven backs—one scrum half, one fly half, two center three-quarters, two wing three-quarters, one fullback.

Substitutes

Substitutes are allowed only in international games and certain specific games. A maximum of two injured players may be replaced. Players who are substituted for may not rejoin the match.

Basic playing privilege of players

1. A player may catch or pick up the ball and run with it.
2. A player may kick the ball while in possession of it.
3. A player may pass the ball to another player provided the ball is not thrown forward.
4. A player may tackle a member of the opposition who has possession of the ball.
5. A player may not interfere with a member of the opposition who is not in possession of the ball.
6. A player caught in possession of the ball may attempt

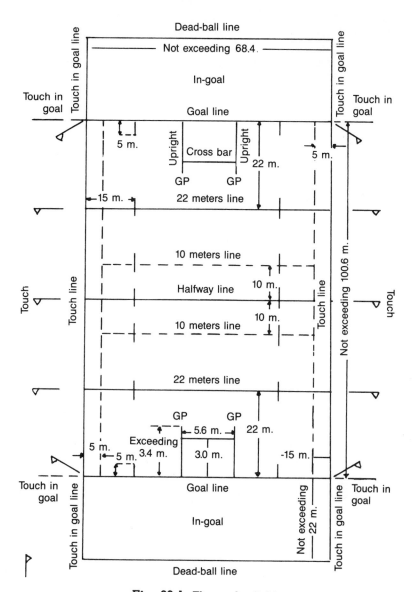

Fig. 22-1. The rugby field.

to transfer it to a teammate provided the player does not come in contact with the ground.

7. A player may not advance forward in front of the ball.
8. A player may kick the ball directly out of bounds when inside his or her 22 m line. If the player is outside the 22 m line the ball must bounce in the field of play before going out of bounds.

Starting the game

The captain of the team successfully calling the referee's coin toss has the option of either kicking off or receiving, or defending one goal or the other. The other captain has the choice in the area not selected by the first captain.

For the kickoff, the ball is placed on the ground in the center of the halfway line. On the sound of the referee's whistle the ball is kicked forward so it travels beyond the opposition's 10 m line. The same procedure is used to start the second period and also to restart play after a team has scored. If the scoring team fails to convert their try, then a drop kick restarts the game.

On the kickoff opponents must stand behind their 10 m line, over which the ball must cross. If the ball crosses the touchline without bouncing, opponents may accept the kick, have it retaken, or scrummage at the center.

Scoring

Try. A try is scored when a player carries the ball over the opposition's goal line and touches the ball on the ground.

Try = 4 points

Conversion. After a try is scored the successful team

has the opportunity to gain 2 additional points (conversion) by kicking the ball between the posts above the crossbar from a point in line with where the try was scored. The ball may be place-kicked or drop-kicked. Team members must be behind the kicker; the opponents must remain behind the goal line until the kicker runs at the ball, when they may charge or jump. If a try is successfully converted, it is called a goal.

Goal = 6 points

Goal = Try (4 points) + Conversion (2 points)

Penalty goal. A penalty is awarded for an infringement of the rules of the game. This allows the team to whom the penalty is awarded an opportunity to score 3 points by kicking the ball through the posts above the crossbar from the point where the infringement occurred. The ball may be drop-kicked or place-kicked.

Penalty goal = 3 points

Drop goal. A drop goal is scored when a player drop-kicks the ball between the posts over the crossbar during the continuous flow of play.

Drop goal = 3 points

Set scrum

When play is halted unintentionally by an infringement of the rules, a set scrum is called. The eight forwards form a scrum, with three forwards (a loose-head prop, a hooker, a tight-head prop) in the front row, two forwards (locks) in the second row, one (the No. 8) in the third row, and the two remaining forwards (flankers) on the sides. The eight forwards bind closely together and push against the opposition. This is called the set scrum (Fig. 22-2). The scrum half puts the ball into the tunnel made where the two front rows of forwards meet, and the hookers from each team try to "hook" the ball back through the scrum onto their side. If the ball goes straight through the tunnel and out the other side, it must be put into the scrum again. No player may handle the ball in the scrum.

Ruck

A ruck occurs in free play when one or more players from each team close around the ball when it is on the ground. Players must remain on their feet and may not handle the ball. The ball is made available from a ruck by players channelling the ball free with their feet.

Maul

A maul occurs in free play when one or more players from each team close around a player who is carrying the ball. A maul ends when the player with the ball breaks loose from the other players or when the ball is released and channelled free. If the ball does not become available, a set scrum is called by the referee.

Line-out

If the ball or the player carrying it touches or crosses the touchline the ball is "in touch" (out of bounds), and play is restarted by a line-out (Fig. 22-3). The ball is thrown in at right angles to where it went into touch between the forwards of both teams, who line up to receive the ball. The two "packs" of forwards line up opposite each other in a line at right angles to the touchline. The team that last touched the ball before it went out of bounds is considered responsible for the stoppage, and the opportunity to restart the game by throwing the ball into the line-out is given to the other team. The

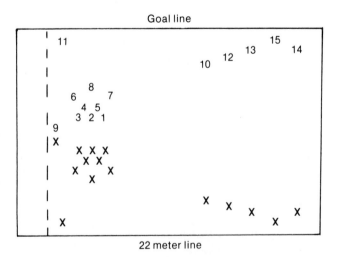

Fig. 22-2. Set scrum position. *X*, Position. Numbers, player's number in each position: *1*, Loose head prop; *2*, Hooker; *3*, Tight head prop; *4, 5*, Locks; *6, 7*, Flankers; *8*, No. 8; *9*, Scrum half; *10*, Fly half; *12, 13*, Center three quarters; *11, 14*, Wing three quarters; *15*, Fullback.

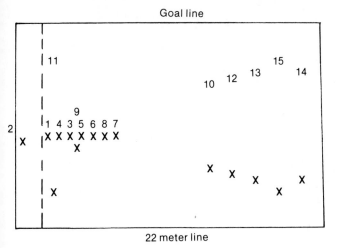

Goal line

11

15
10 12 13 14

9
1 4 3 5 6 8 7
2 X X X X X X X
X X

X
X X X
X
X

X

22 meter line

Fig. 22-3. Line-out position.

scrum half may stand beside the line-out, but all other backs must remain 10 m back from the line-out. If the ball is not thrown straight into the line-out, the referee offers the other team the choice of a set scrum or another line-out. Players must not push, charge, bind, lift, or move within 5 m of the touchline or beyond the farthest player not more than 15 m from the touchline until the ball has passed overhead. Players must also maintain a free channel through the line-out. A line-out is completed when players involved move beyond the line of touch.

Fouls

Players may not:

1. Strike, hack, kick, or trip an opponent
2. Make a dangerous tackle or tackle with a stiff arm
3. Charge, obstruct, or grab an opponent who does not have the ball
4. Obstruct or deliberately waste time
5. Deliberately knock or throw the ball forward

It is not a foul if:

1. The ball bounces forward after hitting the ground or a player
2. A player shoulder-charges a player in possession of the ball
3. The ball is knocked forward in an attempt to catch the ball but is retrieved before it hits the ground

Offside

A player in front of the ball when a teammate is playing it is offside. A penalty may be called if the offside player plays the ball or obstructs or tackles an opponent. Offside is penalized by a penalty kick at the point of infringement, or in free play the option of a scrum is given at the point where the offender last played the ball.

An offside player may be put onside if a teammate

carries or kicks and pursues the ball past him or her. No penalty is given if the offside position is unavoidable and the player retires immediately and without interfering with an opponent. If contact cannot be avoided the player is "accidently offside," and a set scrum is formed.

A mark is awarded when a player who is standing still with both feet on the ground catches the ball and calls, "Mark." The player then has a free chance to kick to touch directly if inside the 22 m line. The player may also kick the ball forward or tap the ball on the boot and run with it. In each case the ball must be played on or behind the mark.

FUNDAMENTAL SKILLS AND TECHNIQUES

All players should practice the fundamental skills of passing, running with the ball, kicking, and tackling. Once proficient at these, it is important to practice the particular skills needed for the position of choice.

Passing

Passing the ball requires a combination of timing, balance, accuracy, and control. The object is to transfer the ball to a teammate as smoothly as possible. It is important to pass in front of the receiver so the teammate can catch the ball easily (Fig. 22-4).

1. Hold the ball in front of the body, in both hands.
2. Look in the direction of the pass and swing the hands across the body. This helps guide the ball accurately in front of the receiver. When passing to the left, transfer the weight from the right foot to the left.
3. As the ball is released, fall away in the opposite direction. If falling to the right, bring the left leg over in front of the right to recover balance.

Receiving a pass

A good pass should be delivered in front of the receiver. The receiver should watch the ball into the hands, which should be in front to receive the ball. This allows an early catch and quick transfer.

Catching

When catching the ball out of the air, it is important to get the body behind the ball. Keeping the eyes on the ball at all times, cradle the arms and pull it into the chest.

Running with the ball

When running with the ball it is as important to be aware of the position of teammates as it is to be aware of the position of the opposition. Be ready to pass the ball to a teammate or to kick where necessary. Try not to run too far off alone, because when tackled by the opposition there will be no support nearby. Run parallel to the

Fig. 22-4. Passing.

touchline when possible. When running and passing, try to create a situation where more teammates than opposition are nearby, and then exploit this position to score.

Side step

The side step is a means of beating an opponent one-on-one by sending the opponent in the opposite direction.

It can be done from either side by a combination of transfer of weight and body movement.

1. For a side step to the right, approach the opponent in a straight line.
2. With the weight on the right leg, drive to the left, taking the opponent with you.
3. Now firmly place the left foot on the ground and drive back to the right, leaving the opponent running in the opposite direction.

Handoff

When there is not time to side step, a handoff might be executed.

1. While approaching the opponent, place the ball under the arm farthest from the tackler.
2. Bend the nearest arm and place it on the opponent's shoulder.
3. Using the opponent's shoulder, move away by straightening the arm and pushing the tackler away.

Kicking

Kicking the ball requires timing, balance, and control. The three basic types of kick are the punt, the drop kick, and the place kick.

The punt

1. Hold the ball with both hands, the left hand under and on the side of the ball and the right hand on top at the back of the ball.
2. Drop the ball while stepping forward with the left foot.
3. Transfer the body weight to the left foot.
4. Keep the head over the ball, and bend the right knee.
5. Swing the right foot forward to contact the ball, keeping the weight on the left foot.
6. Land the ball on the boot at the same angle as it leaves the hand.
7. While following through, the toe should be pointing away. Keep the weight on the left leg and lean backward. (See Fig. 22-5.)

Drop kick

1. Hold the ball upright with one hand on each side of the ball.
2. As the ball is dropped in front of the body, keep the weight on the left foot and the head down looking at the ball.
3. As the ball comes in contact with the ground, strike it with the right instep, keeping the toe pointed.
4. Follow through, keeping the head down and the eyes on the ball. It is important to keep the right foot pointed.
5. While completing the follow-through, keep the weight on the left leg. Some players like to drop

Fig. 22-5. The punt.

A   B   C

Fig. 22-6. Sraight-on place kick. *A,* Front view. *B,* and *C,* Side views.

the ball slightly on the side. When doing so, keep the same basic principles in mind as in the straight-on drop kick, and swing the leg through in a full arc.

Place kick

As with the drop kick, there are different types: straight-on, round-the-corner, and torpedo.

Straight-on

1. Place the ball upright on the ground and steady the right foot directly behind the ball.
2. Retire about 4 to 6 steps and hold steady.

3. Start to run, keeping the head down and the eyes on the ball.
4. Put the left leg down just short of and slightly to the left of the ball.
5. Swing through with the right leg, straightening it on impact and contacting the ball with the toes.
6. Follow through the line of flight of the ball. (See Fig. 22-6.)

Round-the-corner

1. Approach the ball from an angle, with the left foot coming down just short of and slightly to the left of the ball.

2. Swing the right foot through in an arc.
3. With the weight on the left leg and the eyes on the ball, swing the leg through.

Torpedo

1. Place the ball on the ground at an angle pointing toward the goalposts.
2. Use the straight-on method of kicking.

Tackling

Tackling requires a combination of ability, concentration, timing, and confidence. The best way to learn how to tackle is to practice one step at a time and build up confidence. With the correct technique it is possible to knock down the opponent without getting hurt. The three basic types of tackle are head-on, side-on, and from behind. A fourth type, smothering, is sometimes used. In this tackle the arms are wrapped around an opponent to prevent him or her from advancing or passing the ball.

Head-on tackle

1. Judge the approach of the opponent so as to make contact with the shoulder and body weight.
2. As the opponent approaches, drive into the tackle from one leg.
3. Contact the opponent at about waist height, keeping the head to the side. Close the arms tightly around the opponent's legs.
4. Follow through using momentum to bring the opponent to the ground. (See Fig. 22-7.)

Side-on tackle

The basic principles for the head-on tackle apply for the side-on tackle.
1. Line up the opponent.
2. Drive in off one leg and contact the opponent just above the knees.

Fig. 22-7. Head-on tackle.

3. Keep the head behind the opponent's back and wrap the arms around the opponent's legs.
4. The momentum and the arm lock will cause the opponent to fall.

Tackle from behind

1. Drive in off one leg, keeping low.
2. Keeping the head clear, contact the opponent above the knees and close the arms tightly around the legs.
3. The locked legs and momentum will cause the opponent to fall.

PLAYING POSITIONS
Forwards

The eight forwards—known as "the pack"—play as a unit. They are the platform from which the backs play. The forwards are in the front line of attack and are the main source through which their team gains possession of the ball. On gaining possession of the ball the forwards have the option of trying to advance the ball forward among themselves or of transferring the ball to the backs. Physical makeup and natural ability often determine the position one plays.

Although different skills are required for each forward position, forwards as a group need to be strong, powerful, and mobile. The back row of the scrum needs to be fast and aggressive, whereas the front five forwards provide much of the power. The hooker must be quick with the feet in the scrum, and the two locks, usually the largest players on the team, provide useful targets in the line-out.

Backs

Each back position has its particular skills, but in general backs must learn to handle, run, pass, tackle, and kick a ball with ease. Speed, coordination, and ability to read the play are important. The scrum half is the link between the forwards and backs and must be able to transfer the ball to the back line when it is made available by the forwards. The fly half marshals the back line, determines the play, and keeps the backs in position. The back-line players have an important role in halting an opposition attack, because they present the main line of defense.

Offense

The offense should advance forward as a unit, creating gaps in the opposition defense. This may be done by beating the opposition in a one-on-one situation, by creating an extra player situation, or by driving the opposition back by strength. The offense tries to maintain possession of the ball while advancing and to support the player with the ball. They should vary the attack and prevent the defense from organizing.

Defense

Organization is the key to defense. The defense tries to maintain position and to halt the advancing team before they can mount a full attack. Strong decisive tackling, support for the tackler, quick thinking, and ability to adapt to the situation presented will make things difficult for the advancing team.

LEAD-UP ACTIVITIES
Mini-rugby

Mini-rugby is used as an introduction to the 15-a-side game. Its advantages are that it requires a much smaller playing area and fewer players, and it is simple yet exciting and an ideal game for beginners. Participants are afforded an opportunity to play many of the positions of the full game.

The playing area is 69 × 38 m (75.4 × 41.5 yards). Each team has nine players: four forwards—two front row, one lock, one flanker—and five backs—one each scrum half, fly half, center, wing, fullback.

The game may be played on a full-sized rugby pitch, using only one half from touchline to touchline. The game is started from the center and "drop outs" from the existing 15 m (16.4-yard) line.

The adapted rules include the following:

1. There are no line-outs.
2. Kicking is not encouraged.
3. Direct kicking to touch is only allowed inside the 15 m area.
4. There are no kicks at goal for penalties.
5. When a try is scored, a kick at goal is taken from in front of the posts.

When penalties are awarded the opposition retires 7 m (7.6 yards) and the attacking team "tap the ball" and play on. Tackling is unrestricted. The rules for offside, on-side, knock-on, throw forward, and so on apply as usual. Each period lasts 20 minutes.

Touch rugby

Touch rugby may be played during training. The size of the field should correspond to the number playing. The idea of the game is to score a try by touching the ball down behind the opposition's goal line. Players advance the ball by passing and running with the ball.

Tackling and kicking are not allowed. The opposition attempts to touch the player with the ball. Each team has four plays in which to advance the ball. A play is considered finished when a member of the opposition touches the advancing player in possession of the ball. After four plays the other team has four plays in which to score. Each play is started by touching the ball on the foot and passing it to a teammate.

There are no line-outs or scrums, but knock-ons and offsides result in the ball being automatically turned over to the other team.

Grids

Teams of from 2 to 10 players oppose each other in a playing area approximately 5 m (5.5 yards) square. The objective is to develop fundamental skills in a simulated situation. Games in the grids may be organized for drill in a particular skill, such as passing. For example, with five players, three players can attempt to score a try and the other two attempt to stop them. This develops skills for tackling, decision making, passing, use of the extra player, and running with the ball. The number of players and rules of the games can be modified to suit the objective of practice.

TEACHING CONSIDERATIONS

1. Because of safety considerations involved, tackling should probably not be part of the game taught to younger students. Touch rugby with teams of three to ten players and modified rules is probably more appropriate.
2. The weight and shape of the ball make rugby a unique activity, requiring different ball handling and kicking than in soccer and football. Experience in other field sports such as speedball, soccer, and football will help. However, practice time with the rugby ball is a necessity.
3. Practice in ball handling skills should be designed for maximum participation. In most instances this means passing, catching, and kicking skills should be practiced with partners. Distances, directions, and force level requirements should vary as they do in actual games.
4. Offensive and defensive play can be introduced in two-on-one situations. Additional offensive and defensive players may be added as strategies are improved. Actual game play can begin in two-on-two situations.
5. Add scoring options and out-of-bounds rules gradually as the need arises. Maintain off-sides rules to differentiate rugby from football.
6. Stay with the game long enough for skill and appreciation of it to develop.

GLOSSARY

accidental offside A player is offside unintentionally.

attacking team Team that has possession of the ball.

conversion Attempt to gain 2 extra points by kicking the ball over the crossbar after a try has been scored.

dead ball line Line at the end of the field of play.

defending team The team that is attempting to stop the attacking team from scoring while also trying to gain possession of the ball.

drop goal The ball is drop-kicked over the bar during the continuous flow of play.

dropkick Kicking the ball on the half volley.

22 m drop-out Drop kick from the 22 m line to restart the game after the ball has been touched down in the end zone by the defending team or when the ball has crossed the dead ball line.

foul An infringement of the rules.

goal Obtained by scoring a try and a conversion. Worth 6 points.

halfway line Line that marks the center of the field.

in-goal area Area between goal line and dead ball line; end zone.

in touch A ball that goes out of bounds is said to be in touch.

kickoff Used to start the game at the beginning of each period and after a team has scored a try.

knock-on The ball is knocked forward during an attempt to catch it.

line-out Used to restart the game when the ball goes out of bounds.

mark Given to a player who catches the ball cleanly while standing still; player must call, "Mark."

maul One or more players from each side surround and hold the player with the ball and start to struggle for it.

pack The eight forwards.

penalty goal Worth 3 points when a player place-kicks or dropkicks the ball over the crossbar after a penalty given by the referee for an infringement of the rules of the game.

ruck One or more players from each side in the field of play are on their feet and shoving each other, with the ball on the ground between them.

set scrum Used to restart the game after an unintentional infringement of the rules.

throw-in A means of putting the ball into the line-out to restart the game after the ball has gone out of bounds.

try Score when a player carries the ball over the opposition goal line and touches the ball on the ground. Worth 4 points.

SUGGESTED READINGS

The Diagram Group: Rules of the game, New York, 1978, Bantam Books, Inc.

Handbook and laws of the game of rugby, Albany, Calif., 1989-1990, Lampa Printing and Lithograph Co.

Prusmack AJ: Rugby: a guide for players, coaches, and spectators, New York, 1979, E.P. Dutton, Inc.

Robertson I: Success in rugby, London, 1980, John Murray (Publishers) Ltd.

Rugby (newspaper) New York, Rugby Press, Ltd.

Walker P, editor: The love of rugby, London, 1980, Octopus Books, Ltd.

FILMS AND VIDEOTAPES

Mini rugby barbarians style, Rugby Football Union, Twickenham, Middlesex, England.

This is mini rugby, Welsh Rugby Union, 28 St. Marys St., Cardiff, Wales.

Film of the United States—International Games may be obtained through *Rugby* (newspaper), published by Rugby Press, Ltd., 527 Madison Ave., New York, NY 10022.

Video films of international games may be obtained through Trace Video Sports Club, ℅ Brandon Hall, Box 1167, Natchez, MS 39120.

Running Passing Power, *Close Contact Leap*, and *Thinking Boot*. Three rugby videotapes available from "How To" Sports Videos, Box 5852, Denver, CO 80217.

WALL CHARTS

Wall charts may be obtained from the Welsh Rugby Union, 28 St. Marys St., Cardiff, Wales.

23

Self-Defense

Completion of this chapter should enable the reader to:

- Become familiar with the basic principles and strategies of self-defense
- Appreciate the importance of the accuracy, force, speed, and follow-through of self-defense moves
- Demonstrate and execute releases, kicks, and strikes employed in self-defense
- Explain to a group of students when and how to use the techniques described in this chapter

HISTORY

Every society has recorded history of combat. When the working class does not have the advantage of weapons they tend to devise some method of unarmed self-defense and pass it down from generation to generation. One art of self-defense was developed by Chinese monks in the twelfth century. By monastic rules the monks were forbidden to use weapons in combat. Because they were constantly being attacked by nomads and roving bandits, they were forced to devise a defense that did not depend on weapons. During the last half of the twelfth century the Japanese discovered this art, copied it, claimed it as their own, and called it "jiu jitsu." Jiu means *gentle*; jitsu means *art* or *practice*. Many systems of jiu jitsu were developed by the Japanese. In 1882 Professor Jigora Kano, a Japanese instructor who had spent many years practicing many of the systems of jiu jitsu, established the Kodokan, *a school for studying the way*, and labeled his system "judo," which means *the way* or *principle*.

One branch of the Kodokan was established in 1921 in New York City. However, because this system was mainly competitive, young Americans were not interested. In 1925 a group of these young Americans developed their own system of self-defense and called their organization the American Judo Club. They produced a system of self-defense that during World War II proved to be very effective. After the war, interest in judo as a competitive sport started to grow, and today it is recognized throughout the world.

Many school systems throughout the United States are including self-defense against violent crime in the physical education curriculum in junior and senior high schools, colleges, and universities. Classes are also being included in the curricula of various local agencies such as recreation centers, YMCAs, YWCAs, and others.

Modern self-defense is not a martial art. Judo, karate, aikido, and other martial arts require years of training and continual practice, plus speed, balance, coordination, agility, and disciplined mental training. Modern self-defense is simply street fighting combined with common sense. It can be learned in a short time by any person, young or old, weak or strong, coordinated or uncoordinated, and it can be retained for life.

FACILITIES AND EQUIPMENT

No special facilities or equipment are needed for self-defense classes; they can be offered in any room or on any playing field. Football dummy bags, rolled gymnastics mats, and volleyballs can be used for kicking, punching, and jabbing. If such equipment is not available, students can bring pillows and cushions from home.

CLOTHING

Students should wear comfortable, loose-fitting clothing. Gym shoes or sneakers are preferred footwear. However, inasmuch as they may not be wearing gym clothes if attacked, during the last weeks of class students should wear regular street clothing. During practice of self-defense techniques it is recommended that jewelry be removed.

BASIC PRINCIPLES

Self-defense skills should meet the following criteria:

1. They must be so simple that every student can perform them proficiently. Self-defense, unlike tennis or basketball, is a life-and-death skill. If you teach a skill that even one student cannot master, the student may be seriously injured or killed attempting to use it.
2. They must be easily mastered in a short time. Most self-defense classes last between 5 and 15 weeks. In most cases this is the only instruction time the students will ever receive in self-defense.
3. They must be easy to remember without much practice. It is unlikely that students completing a self-defense course will continue to practice the skills. Yet they must be capable of performing them if attacked in 10 days or 10 years.
4. They must be designed to totally incapacitate, not merely hurt, the assailant. There is only one round in self defense—the first one. If the first round is lost, the entire fight is lost.

STRATEGIES

There are three strategies in self-defense. The first two require no skill or ability, just common sense.

1. Eliminate the potential of danger before it begins.
2. Recognize and avoid danger.
3. Fight only when necessary.

Eliminate the potential of danger

Most potential danger can be eliminated by learning to "think safety." Below are listed a few of the hundreds of ways to "think safety."

1. Never hitchhike or pick up a hitchhiker.
2. Have secure locks on all doors and windows and use them.
3. Change all locks when you move into a home or apartment.
4. Keep blinds closed at night.
5. Do not hide keys outside your home or in your car.
6. When walking to your home or car have your key in hand so that you can enter quickly.
7. Be cautious when entering your car, when you are usually looking down and are vulnerable. Look in the back seat before entering a car alone.
8. Walk in well-lighted areas; do not take shortcuts down alleys.
9. If you are a single woman, do not list your first name on your mailbox or in the phone book. Use two initials plus your last name for identification.

Recognize and avoid danger

Even if you eliminate all of the possible dangers you can imagine, you are not totally safe. Therefore, learn to be aware of your surroundings, the dangers that exist, and how to react when necessary. Examples of some ways to recognize and avoid danger are listed here.

1. If confronted by a robber with a weapon, it is almost always best to give up your valuables. Do not fight! Material things can be replaced, but your life and health cannot. However, because many rapes and killings begin as simple robberies, in some cases early and effective resistance may prevent assault.
2. If you are on the street and believe you are in danger, do not stay around to find out. Change your direction and run. If followed, holler "Fire, fire, fire!" Noise of any kind that draws attention to you or your assailant is an effective deterrent. If the assailant continues to chase you, drop your purse or wallet. If that is what the person is after, you are safe.
3. If you receive an obscene phone call, hang up. If the calls continue, tap on the mouthpiece with your fingernail and say, "Officer, this is the call I have been expecting. Now you can trace it." Then hang up.
4. Verify the identity of all callers before you allow them into your home.
5. If you return home and find your door open or windows broken, do not go in. Telephone the police.
6. If you see anything suspect in your neighborhood, do not investigate it yourself. Call the police.
7. If you are followed by another car while driving, do not go home and do not try to outrun the car. Rather, pretend to ignore the driver, keep your hand on the horn, and drive at a safe speed to a gas station, police station, or market.
8. If approached by an exhibitionist, pretend to ignore the person and immediately telephone the police.

Fight only when necessary

The only time you should fight is when your life or health is in danger. There are two major reasons for this:

1. You can lose. There is no assurance that every time you fight, you will win. Therefore, if you fight for a few valuables and lose, you are very foolish, because you may lose your life or health.
2. You must incapacitate, not simply hurt, the aggressor. Therefore, if you are merely verbally insulted and in anger you incapacitate the aggressor, you expose yourself to a lawsuit.
3. Fight to escape. Escape is your primary objective.

BASIC TECHNIQUES

Over the years the approach to self-defense has shifted from the learning of rather formal movements to a less structured and "whatever works" philosophy. The techniques presented here attempt to mirror this progression. The initial movements described have as their basic objective to "turn the tables," allowing the person attacked to gain the upper hand on the assailant. These are followed by techniques primarily for situations in which the assailant is much more powerful than the victim. The goal of these movements is to incapacitate the aggressor. Remember, the primary objective is to escape from danger.

Self-defense has four elements: accuracy, force, speed, and follow-through.

Accuracy

Your self-defense blow must be accurate. Do not aim for the nose and hit the chin. That will only hurt your assailant and you may not have an opportunity to strike again.

Force

Although a physically fit person will deliver the most effective blow, strength is not necessary for self-defense skills. An 80-year-old can successfully deliver a groin pull or eye gouge. Nevertheless, the more force you can generate the safer you will be. Therefore, fight with 100 percent effort.

Speed

Speed is an element of good timing. Because the assailant will most likely be larger and stronger than you, the element of surprise is necessary. This does not mean that you must always react immediately. If you can talk to the assailant, ask "What do you want?" Then pose no threat, and pretend to cooperate. Wait until you can react properly, then employ some of the techniques described later with all the speed you can generate. If you panic and cannot remember what to do, do nothing. Do not struggle. Simply wait until you remember.

Follow-through

If you must fight, plan to follow through with kicks, blows, and jabs until the assailant is totally immobile. If attackers are not incapacitated, they become enraged and more vicious than before. Remember, the primary objective is to escape from danger.

Vulnerable areas and bodily weapons

Six vulnerable areas on a person's body are recommended as targets (Fig. 23-1). A blow to any of these will incapacitate, not just hurt, an attacker. Seven body weapons are recommended for use (Fig. 23-2).

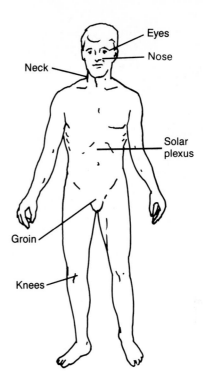

Fig. 23-1. Vulnerable areas.

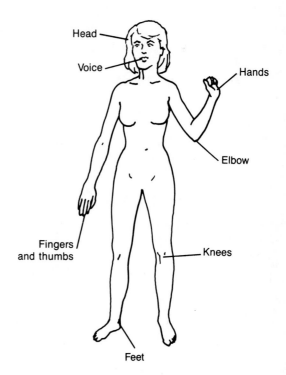

Fig. 23-2. Seven body weapons.

Fig. 23-3. Chest push.

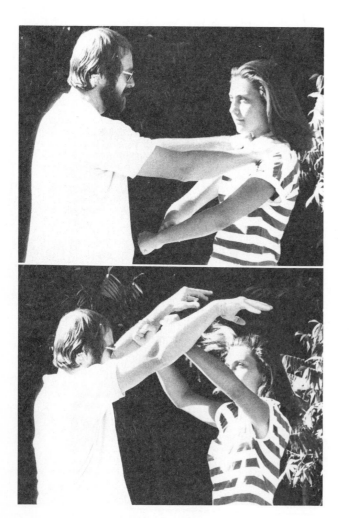

Fig. 23-4. Front two-hand choke.

SKILLS
Release from grips

Chest push (Fig. 23-3). The assailant puts a hand on the victim's chest. The victim immediately places both hands on top of the aggressor's hand at the base of the fingers. Holding the hand tightly against the chest, the victim then flexes sharply at the waist and knees, sending the aggressor to the ground.

Front two-hand choke (Fig. 23-4). The aggressor places the hands around the victim's throat. The victim clasps the hands together, spreads the elbows, and then drives the arms up against the aggressor's arms, forcing them free. If the aggressor has established a firm grip or if the victim is considerably smaller and weaker than the aggressor, this move should be preceded by a knee lift or kick to the groin or leg (described later).

This defense may also be used while lying on the floor.

Another defense against the front choke is the two-hand thumb-grab and twist (Fig. 23-5). The victim reaches up with one hand and grasps the aggressor's wrist, then with the other hand grabs the aggressor's thumb and rotates the hand toward the forearm.

Attack from the rear. If a defender is grabbed from the rear, several defensive moves may be made. The victim may be able to drive an elbow into the aggressor's neck, solar plexus, or groin (Fig. 23-6).

Fig. 23-5. Second defense against the two-hand choke.

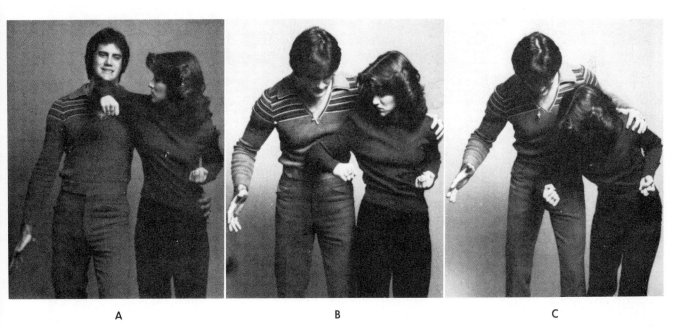

A   B   C

Fig. 23-6. Attack from the rear. **A**, Neck. **B**, Solar plexus. **C**, Groin.

Kicks

The legs are the strongest part of the body. A small person can immobilize a large person with a kick of only 40 pounds of pressure. Kicks should be directed to the front and side of the assailant's knees, groin, and to the head, once the assailant is on the ground.

Front kick (Fig. 23-7). A front kick is used to defend against an assault from the front. Practice this kick in three steps:

1. Lift your knee toward your chest, flex your foot, and bend your supporting leg.
2. Extend your leg straight out, keeping your foot flexed, and contact the target with your heel, not your toes.
3. Bring your leg back to the first position, with your knees still raised. From this position you may kick again if necessary.

After mastering these individual steps, practice delivering them to a single count. They should be directed so quickly that they can hardly be seen. Remember, kick through the target, not just at it.

Side kick (Fig. 23-8). A side kick is used when you are attacked from the side. Practice it in three steps:

1. Lift your leg directly sideward and flex your foot. Keep the supporting leg slightly bent and lean slightly away from the direction in which you intend to kick.
2. Extend your leg out, keeping your foot flexed, and kick through the target with your heel.
3. Bring your leg back to the first position, so that you can kick again if necessary.

Fig. 23-8. Side kick.

Fig. 23-7. Front kick.

Fig. 23-9. Rear kick.

Rear kick (Fig. 23-9). If attacked from the rear, use the rear kick. Learn the rear kick in three steps:

1. Flex your striking leg, turn the foot outward, and flex at the ankle. Bend your supporting knee.
2. Extend your leg backward, with the ankle still flexed, and kick through the target with your heel.
3. Flex your leg back to the starting position so that you can kick again if necessary. Be sure to look at the target (knee) to aim your kick. Do not aim for the shin or instep, as this will hurt rather than incapacitate your assailant.

Supine kick (Fig. 23-10). If you are thrown to the ground roll onto your back and execute supine kicks. Lift your head and shoulders slightly off the ground. Bring your knees to your chest and kick into the assailant's knee or groin. If the attacker moves away, save your energy and stop kicking. Jump to your feet as quickly as you can.

Strikes

Knee lift (Fig. 23-11). A knee lift into the groin will incapacitate a man. This blow has limited value, because the man must be standing directly in front of you. To execute this blow, drive your knee forcefully upward and forward, between the man's legs and into his groin.

Fig. 23-11. Knee lift.

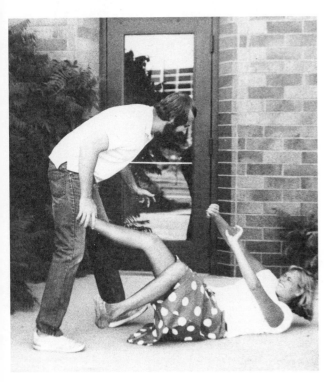

Fig. 23-10. Supine kick.

Groin pull (Fig. 23-12). One of the most simple, effective, and efficient techniques is a groin pull. It is simple because the only action necessary is a squeeze and a pull. It is effective because it will instantly force a male assailant to the ground in pain. It is efficient because with only one hand you can easily grab your target from many positions. To execute a groin pull, simply reach between your assailant's legs, grab the genitals, squeeze, and pull. Unlike the knee in the groin, the groin pull will not be expected by the assailant. This technique works effectively almost any time a person has one hand free. The only time the groin pull is difficult is when a man is wearing tight pants. Then a groin hit must be used.

Groin hit (Fig. 23-13). The groin hit is more difficult than a groin pull, because you can miss the target. Use a groin pull whenever possible. To execute a groin hit, double your hand into a tight fist, bend your arm slightly, and forcefully drive the bony portion of your arm up and through the assailant's groin. Bending your knees will give you additional balance and power. The groin hit can be used when you are attacked from the front or rear.

Fig. 23-13. Groin hit.

Fig. 23-12. Groin pull.

Single-hand blow (Fig. 23-14). The nose, point of the chin, and even the eye sockets are targets for the single-hand blow. Curl your fingers back to the cushioned part of your hand and hold your thumb at the side of your index finger. Flex your wrist backward, and do not clench your entire fist. Bring your hand to your chest, heel up, and thrust your hand up, striking your target at the base of your assailant's nose, contacting the nostrils with the base of your hand. Once again, aim through your target, not at it, to achieve maximum power. Retract your hand to starting position at your chest so that you can hit again if necessary. You should become equally proficient with both your right and left hands.

Double-hand blow (Fig. 23-15). To achieve the correct hitting position for the double-hand blow, clasp your hands together, palms facing inward, as though clapping. Do not intertwine your fingers. This blow is delivered into the assailant's throat or to the back of the neck once the assailant has doubled over from a kick, groin pull, or knee lift.

Thumb gouge (Fig. 23-16). When your life is threatened and both hands are available, execute a thumb gouge. To deliver the thumb gouge, place your hands firmly on either side of your assailant's head to stabilize the head, and gouge your thumbs deeply and directly into the assailant's eyes. If the assailant is wearing glasses, the technique is exactly the same but inside the glasses. This technique is used most effectively against strangulation with the hands or with an object such as a scarf, nylon stocking, or necktie. If you are being strangled from behind with an object, both of the assailant's hands must

be on that object. This allows you to turn (believe it or not) in either direction and perform a thumb gouge. Depending on the amount of pressure that you apply, this technique will temporarily or permanently blind an assailant.

Fig. 23-15. Double-hand blow.

Fig. 23-14. Single-hand blow.

Fig. 23-16. Thumb gouge.

Fig. 23-17. Finger jab.

Finger jab (Fig. 23-17). A finger jab should be used when you have only one hand free. Anytime both hands are free, execute a thumb gouge. To perform a finger jab, round all four fingers slightly and gouge all fingers into the assailant's eyes. Jabbing with four fingers rather than two fingers will increase your chances of contacting the eyes. If the assailant is wearing glasses, direct your fingers to the upper cheeks, just under the lower rim. On striking the cheeks, continue your fingers under the glasses and into the eyes.

Screams

A scream can accomplish three purposes:
1. It can attract attention.
2. It can unnerve even the most determined assailant.
3. It can make you feel much more powerful and aggressive. Any type of noise is a deterrent. The last thing an assailant wants is attention. Do not rely on noise to bring help. The assailant does not want attention and may leave but the public is fickle; help may not come and if someone does investigate he or she may be cautious.

When running from danger, do not scream "Help!" Unfortunately, people may not come to your rescue. Rather, scream "Fire!" When people hear "Fire!" they feel they have a vested interest: their house or car may be on fire. However, when under attack, scream karate-type sounds, like "Seiha, ahhh!" Scream as loudly and forcefully as possible throughout the entire attack. When the assailant is incapacitated, run for the police, screaming "Fire!" Once again, never scream "Help!"

Defense against women

Self-defense against a woman attacker is exactly the same as against a man with the exception of using the groin as a vulnerable area. A hit to the groin or breasts of a woman will hurt but will not incapacitate. Therefore, when fighting with a woman, strike her knees, nose, throat, solar plexus, and eyes.

TEACHING CONSIDERATIONS

1. Only teachers who have received special training themselves should attempt to teach self-defense.
2. If you do not have time to teach the techniques until the students master them, do not teach self-defense. Students may gain a false sense of security about their abilities that may endanger their lives.
3. Initial practice of techniques should include walking through the action with a partner slowly until correct body position is established. Speed and force characteristics can be practiced using objects such as stuffed bags or rolled mats. It is desirable to eventually use mannequins as instructional aids so that accuracy as well as force can be practiced.
4. Space work on strategies throughout the lessons and repeat ideas often. Use situational examples to practice decision making about what to do.
5. Combine moves by having the attacker respond to the victim's moves to simulate an extended fight. Do this in slow motion first and then increase speed.
6. Include short review sessions throughout the curriculum to reinforce skills.
7. Each student will have unique talents and limitations. Develop a strategy to fit each student.

GLOSSARY

accuracy The self-defense maneuver must be "on target."

American Judo Club A club established in 1925 by a number of young Americans.

chest push To shove or push the attacker on the chest with one or two hands.

finger jab Pushing the fingers into the assailant's eyes, nose, or throat.

follow-through To continue a movement to the point of incapacitation.

front choke To attack the windpipe.

front hug To approach the victim and wrap the arms around the body.

groin hit To punch the attacker in the groin or genitals.

groin pull To grab the genitals and pull.

jiu-jitsu "Jiu" means gentle; "jitsu" means art.

kick To use the feet and legs to incapacitate.

knee lift To forcibly lift the knee to the groin or face of the assailant.

modern self-defense This is not a martial art but street fighting combined with common sense. It can be learned in a short time by any person.

potential danger Not to "hit the target."

rear attack The attacker grabs the victim from behind.

scream A basic offensive to alert someone for assistance. Yell "Fire." Yell throughout the attack.

speed To react with expedience to surprise the attacker.

supine kick A kick to the groin when one has been wrestled to the ground.

thumb gouge To use the thumbs to gouge the eyes.

vulnerable areas The areas of the body recommended as targets: eyes, nose, neck, groin, solar plexus, and knees.

SUGGESTED READINGS

Conroy M and Ritvo ER: Common sense self-defense, St. Louis, 1977, The CV Mosby Co.

Grambordella T: Seven days to self-defense, Chicago, 1980, Contemporary Books, Inc.

Hiroshi H and Tow P: Personal self-defense manual for women: mind and body, Dubuque, Iowa, 1982, Kendall/Hunt Publishing Co.

Monkerud E and Heiny M: Self-defense for women, Dubuque, Iowa, 1980, Wm C Brown Group. Covers both the mental and physical aspects of self-defense. Includes sections on striking and kicking, releases from body grabs and holds, weapons, defense, and self-defense for health and exercise.

Pascala LM: Self defense, Glenview, Ill., 1980, Scott, Foresman & Co. Shows how to use rational movements for effective responses to assault. Describes procedures for reporting assault, as well as preventive measures and personal safety.

Peterson SL: Self-defense for women: how to stay safe and fight back, Englewood, Colo, 1989, Morton Publishing Co. A practical, well-illustrated guide on how women of all ages can defend themselves in a variety of situations.

Seabourne T and Herndon E: Self defense, Scottsdale, Ariz, 1987, Gorsuch Scarisbrick Publishers. Presents a highly illustrated overview with the philosophical principles of self-defense for the beginning student. Includes the basic physical techniques and mental strategies necessary to prepare for situations of violence.

Wyness GB: Practial personal defense, Palo Alto, Calif, 1975, Mayfield Publishing Co. Prepares the reader to recognize possible dangers, identify alternatives, and take practical measures in the event of an attack.

FILMS AND VIDEOTAPES

Shattered. MTI Teleprograms, Inc., 3710 Commercial Ave., Northbrook, IL 60062.

This film is about rape. Canadian Filmmakers Dist. Centre, 406 Jarvis St., Toronto, Ontario N44 2G6.

Self-defense and *Self-defense for women,* videotape. "How To" Sports Videos, Box 5852, Denver, CO 80217.

Vulnerable to attack. Professional Arts, Inc., Box 8003, Stanford, CA 94305.

24

Skiing: Alpine

Completion of this chapter should enable the reader to:

- Appreciate the development of skiing and its recent popularity
- Recognize the importance of the selections and care of equipment
- Describe and execute beginning skiing techniques
- Understand intermediate and advanced techniques
- Know the various types of skiing competitions and techniques
- Recognize and use skiing terms correctly
- Instruct a group of students in basic skiing techniques

HISTORY

Skiing started as a form of travel in hunting and war during the Stone and Bronze Ages. Snowshoe-like skis have been found in the bogs and marshes of Finland, Norway, Sweden, and Russia, as well as on rock-wall carvings in Norway and Russia. The primitive toe-strap bindings were too loose for any real control, but a single solid pole acted as a downhill brake and a "pusher" on the flats. The short ski, 6 to 7 feet (182 to 213 cm), for pushing off and the long ski, 9 to 12 feet (274 to 366 cm), for gliding were the first skis commonly used in Scandinavia. As the sport spread to the Alps, skis of equal length evolved.

Skiing as a modern recreational and competitive sport owes much to Sondre Norheim, Mathias Zdarsky, and Sir Arnold Lunn. Norheim, a Norwegian, invented the "stiff" binding in the early 1800s. Zdarsky, in Austria, developed the first dynamic ski technique and started the first ski school. It took a British scholar, Sir Arnold Lunn, to devise slalom and downhill racing. Later he devised the Arlberg-Kandahar races and was knighted for his contribution to skiing and mountaineering and for the improvement of Anglo-Swiss relations.

Although the Americans did not have great ski techniques during the 1850s, they are probably credited with the first professional races. The gold rush in the snow-covered California Sierras attracted many Scandinavians, who could get around on "snowshoes" easily. Skiing be-

came instantly popular and was even used in delivering mail in winter. Records verify that in 1855 a ski competition was held in Onion Valley, California, for a prize of $25,000 in gold nuggets.

The first ski club in the United States was formed in 1872 in New Hampshire and was called the Nansen Ski Club. In 1904 seventeen ski clubs met in Michigan to form the National Ski Association. Again, skiing was supported mainly by Scandinavians. Since then, skiing has become a major American sport and industry (Fig. 24-1). The United States Ski Team is now considered one of the best in the world. Phil Mahre of the U.S. Ski Team attained the highest goal in competitive skiing by winning the World Cup in 1981, 1982, and 1983. His achievement in the 1981 season marked the first time an American had ever won this award.

Once Phil Mahre broke through this barrier, individual members of the United States Ski Team continued to do well in international competition. Some of the most memorable accomplishments include Tamara McKinney's winning of the World Cup in 1983; Steve Mahre's winning of the giant slalom at the World Ski Championships in 1983; Bill Johnson, Phil Mahre, and Debbie Armstrong's winning of gold medals in the downhill, slalom, and giant slalom, respectively, in the 1984 Olympics; Diane Roffe's winning of the giant slalom at the 1985 World Ski Championships, and Tamara McKinney's winning of the gold in the Alpine combined

Fig. 24-1. Downhill skiing is a popular wintertime activity.

and the silver in the slalom at the 1987 World Championships.

Science and technology now make skiing available without an abundance of natural snow. Artificial snow has allowed ski areas to extend their season and provide consistently good surfaces. Snow-making capabilities have provided a boom to the industry, especially for skiers living away from the snow belts.

Preseason conditioning

To enhance the enjoyment of skiing, to speed up the learning process, and to prevent injury, it is important to implement a conditioning program. Perhaps the most enjoyable way to enhance fitness is by participating in activities that incorporate the elements of fitness beneficial to alpine skiing. Alpine skiing is an anaerobic activity. However, the skier must first establish an aerobic base upon which anaerobic fitness can be established. Bicycling, swimming, mountain hikes, and jogging/running/sprinting can be used for aerobic and anaerobic conditioning. Strength and power are best trained in a weight room, preferably using free weights. Tennis, racquetball, squash, volleyball, basketball, and soccer can be enjoyable in addition to contributing to general athletic ability. Waterskiing, windsurfing, trampolining, rollerblading, ice skating, and gymnastics help develop balance, agility, coordination, and ski-specific motor skills.

Total fitness is extremely important in alpine skiing, especially in the prevention of injuries. Conditioning the abdominal area, hips, buttocks, thighs, and lower legs will greatly increase the quality of an alpine skiing experience.

Summer	**Early fall**
Flexibility	Flexibility
Aerobic	Aerobic/anaerobic
Endurance strength	Strength
(higher repetitions/lower	(higher weight/lower
weight)	repetitions)
Sport activities	Sport activities
Motor skills	Motor skills
Late fall	**Winter (ski season)**
Flexibility	Flexibility
Anaerobic	Maintenance
Power	Sport activities
(medium weight/medium	Motor skills
repetitions, explosive	
moves)	
Sports activities	
Motor skills	

Prior to any sports or conditioning activity (including skiing) it is important to warm up the body. Slightly elevate the heart rate on a bicycle or with a light jog, then stretch with a full complement of flexibility exercises.

EQUIPMENT
Boots

Boots are a primary item, demanding a combination of lateral stiffness and proper fit to ensure good control of the skis and happy feet.

Because the price of boots is relatively high, the beginner should first rent a pair of buckle boots carefully fitted at the ski shop. The boots should feel snug with one thin pair of nylon or silk socks plus one pair of thermal socks. If if is possible to lift the heal inside the boot, if the buckles are not tight enough, or if the boots are too soft, turns will lack precision, regardless of how good the skier. Boots that are too small will cut off circulation, causing numbness and possible frostbite. For maximum comfort, it is a good idea to loosely fasten buckles while riding the lifts, then tighten them before the descent. Buy a comfortable pair of plastic, buckle boots because they retain their stiffness, comfort, and appearance longer than do leather boots. A boot press is often used to hold and carry the bulky boots about.

The technologic advances in ski boots have been great during the past few years (somewhat like those in the running shoe). Because of these developments and because so many companies now manufacture ski boots, it is wise to consult a reputable ski equipment retailer to assure proper fit and appropriate boots for your skiing ability.

Table 24-1. CHARACTERISTICS OF SKIS

Type of ski	Characteristics	Recommended length
Sport/Racing	Tracks well but only turns well if precisely controlled	Women: height plus 15-20 cm Men: height plus 20-30 cm
All round compact, mid-length	Turns easily and tracks well	Women and men: height plus 5-15 cm
Short	Turns very easily does not track well	Women and men: height minus 5-10 cm

Skis

Most modern skis consists of a wood laminate. The core is often reinforced with Kevlar, carbon fiber, or ceramic. Fiberglass is used to enclose the construction. Although metal is still sometimes used, it is limited. Solid wood and metal skis are all but gone from the market.

Proper ski length is determined by several factors: height, weight, ability, aggressiveness, and attitude (how badly do you want to improve?). In general, when the skis are held vertically the tips should be about face height for a novice skier. The curve of the ski should wrap around the top of the head for advanced or aggressive skiers.

Most ski shops allow the skier to try various lengths and models prior to purchase. Otherwise, rental skis will give the skier an opportunity to find the correct length and model suited for his or her needs (see Table 24-1).

When planning to purchase new skis, expect to pay approximately $300. Most shops carry used equipment and ski swaps abound during the fall.

Whether buying used or new skis, the bases should be tuned-up, and the edges should be sharpened and beveled. Today's ski bases and edges are so hard, it is next to impossible for a recreational skier to do the job by hand. It is better choose a quality ski shop where the employees are skillful and technicians are available to stone grind the base.

Waxing

Most skis made in recent years incorporate a polyethylene or graphite type running surface. Polyethylene and graphite have somewhat minimized the need for waxing in that these surfaces reduce friction.

Snow temperature, air temperature, humidity, and snow texture affect the amount of friction between the ski base and the snow surface. Racing almost always requires preparation of the ski bases with wax. Very cold, dry conditions or extremely warm, wet situations will call for even recreational skiers to wax the ski bases to enjoy the sport.

Prior to waxing, imperfections in the base should be repaired and the edges sharpened and beveled. It is best to iron the wax onto a warm, dry, clean ski base. The wax should be left on the ski base as long as possible, but scraped off prior to skiing. After the wax has been scraped down to a thin layer (thicker for warm, wet conditions), the base should be brushed or rilled depending on conditions.

Wax companies usually color code waxes for specific snow/air temperatures and snow textures. It is best to buy one brand of wax, read the directions and then experiment. Staying with one brand of wax and learning to use it correctly will allow the skier to make educated choices under varying conditions.

Bindings

Release bindings disengage boots from the skis in a hard fall. They do not guarantee against serious injury, but they do reduce risks. Step-in bindings with the direct release at the toe and heel are the most up-to-date. Be absolutely sure to have the bindings adjusted and tested by a ski shop mechanic. Do not swap skis with friends until the skis have been checked. Bindings that are too loose or too tight are dangerous. They should not release unless the skier lunges forward. Bindings should be mounted in accordance with manufacturers' specifications.

Ski brakes should be used to prevent runaway skis when bindings release. Binding systems using brakes are preferable to those incorporating safety straps.

Poles

Ski poles are built with handles, wrist loops, and metal alloy or bamboo shafts. The rings or baskets attached near the pointed tips of poles prevent the shafts from sinking into the snow too deeply. Prices range according to quality, weight, and flexibility of poles. The expensive thin-walled steel poles with adjustable grips are light and easy to manipulate but can break at the end of their flexibility. The cheaper poles, made of aluminum alloys, are heavier and nonadjustable but usually bend rather than break.

When one is standing on hard ground with boots on and grasping the pole, the elbow should form a right angle with the forearm parallel to the ground. Poles that are too long get in the way and cause bad habits in technique. Ski shops can easily cut down poles to a suitable length.

Ski pole grips

To get the most out of the pole action and to prevent dropping it, the loop of the pole must be in the correct

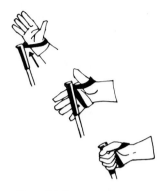

Fig. 24-2. Ski pole grip.

position. With the loop facing you, slip the palm of the hand underneath and entirely through the strap (Fig. 24-2), close the fist around the handle and strap, and slide the hand down so that the loop is snug around the wrist. When skiing, hold the pole firmly in this position.

Ski poles help a skier maintain balance, walk or glide, climb, make turns, get up from falls, and go faster.

BEGINNING TECHNIQUES
Walking and gliding

Walking on skis is the same motion as walking without skis, except for the sliding tendency. Here poles are used for stability and pushing. The change of weight from one ski to another "sets" the ski, making it easy to push off for the next step. Following the natural inclination of the arms, the skier extends the arm and pole opposite the extended leg and pulls against it. As the skier brings the other leg forward he or she braces against the opposite pole. The weight is kept on the balls of the feet so the knees can bend properly. (See Fig. 24-3.)

The exaggerated form of walking is *gliding*. The skier lunges forward and upward from a slight crouch and pulls against the poles to create the momentum for a gliding movement.

The side step

When a hill becomes too steep to walk up, the side step is recommended (Fig. 24-4). With skis pointing across the hill, place the uphill ski a foot above the next, then draw up the lower one. For very steep slopes put pressure on the edges and poles.

Falling and getting up

The best way to fall is to one side. Remember, even the best skiers fall. If you start to lose your balance try to stay up as long as possible. But if gravity gets the best of you, try to relax.

The best way to get up is to place the skis across the hill on the downhill side of the slope. Next tuck the legs

Fig. 24-3. Walking and gliding.

Fig. 24-4. The side step.

up under the hips on the uphill side and push your body up with the hands or poles.

Downhill schussing

The key to the downhill schuss is correct body position and relaxation (Fig. 24-5). Build confidence by starting with a ski teacher on a gentle slope. The run-out should be sufficient to stop safely. Find a fairly flat area and point the skis straight down the fall line. Skis should be parallel and about a foot apart, with weight evenly distributed on them. Lean slightly forward, bending at the

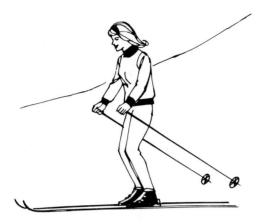

Fig. 24-5. Downhill schussing.

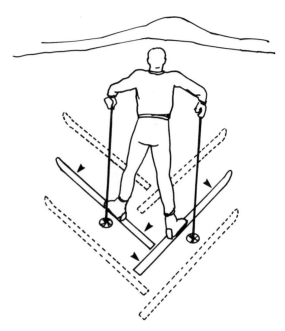

Fig. 24-7. The herringbone.

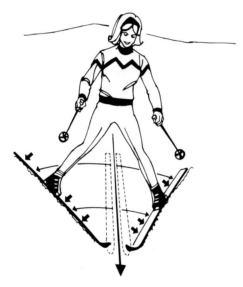

Fig. 24-6. Wedge braking technique.

ankles, knees, and hips. Do not bend forward at the waist. Let the legs absorb bumps by leaning forward and tucking the legs up as you go over the bumps.

Remember, when schussing from deep snow to a hard surface or from packed snow to ice, lean farther forward so that the ski cannot run away with you. In contrast, to schuss from hard snow to powder, lean slightly back.

The wedge

The wedge (Fig. 24-6) is the basic braking technique used by beginners. Facing down the fall line in the downhill schuss position, push off with a brushing motion into a V ski position, with the ski tips together and the tails wide apart. The wider the V, the slower the speed. Low-intermediate skiers brake by sliding both skis to one side.

The herringbone

The herringbone is a faster means of climbing a hill than is the side step, provided the hill is not too steep (Fig. 24-7). Face directly up the hill with skis in a V position, with the tips wide apart and the tails close together. Weight is on the inside edges, and the poles are used to propel upward and prevent backslip as the weight is shifted from one ski to the other.

The kick turn

The kick turn is used not only as a fine balance exercise on flat ground but also for changing direction on dangerous terrain (Fig. 24-8). The turn is actually a stationary 180-degree change of direction. Starting with the skis parallel, poles halfway between boots and ski tips, and weight on the left ski, kick up the right ski high enough that the ski stands on its tail. Next, rotate the raised ski to face in the opposite direction, and bring the pole around as a brace. Transfer weight to the right ski as the left ski and pole shift around next to the right ski. On a steep slope with skis facing across the fall line, the lower leg is always the kick-up leg.

SKIING SAFETY AND ETIQUETTE

1. The best assurance against first-day injury is a lesson from a ski instructor.
2. Have a ski shop mechanic or instructor adjust and check bindings while you have the skis and boots on. Do not swap skis with friends without the same adjustment.

Fig. 24-8. The kick turn.

Fig. 24-9. Traversing.

Fig. 24-10. Stem christie turn.

3. Do not ski on unmarked trails or where avalanche warnings have been placed, even though the snow looks sensational.
4. Do not ski alone.
5. On subzero days, wear thermal underwear or warm-up pants, insulated parka, goggles, and mask or scarf to avoid frostbite. If a white spot appears on the face, place a bare hand on the spot for a minute, but do not rub, then head for shelter.
6. Do some loosening-up exercises before the first run. Warming up prevents strained muscles and may prevent injury.
7. Be a patient learner. *Ski in control* and build up confidence.
8. Be cognizant of the safety of others. Help anyone that needs help.
9. Ski on slopes appropriate to your skill.
10. Obey all the rules of the skiing area.
11. Inform slower skiers you are approaching from behind by calling out "On your left (right)."
12. Do not "cut in" in lift lines.

INTERMEDIATE TECHNIQUES
Traversing

Skiing in a straight line other than the fall line is called traversing (Fig. 24-9). Skis are parallel and slightly apart, weight is over the balls of the feet, with two thirds of the weight on the lower ski and one third on the upper ski. Ankles and knees are rolled into the hill, causing the inside edges of the skis to bite into the snow without slipping. To compensate for this, the upper body leans slightly downhill, but essentially square over the skis. The amount of the bending motion, *angulation*, depends on the steepness of the slope and the radius of the turn. During the trasverse the arms should be slightly forward and about at waist level.

Stem christie turn

The stem turn (stem christie), which combines the wedge turn with the traverse, is useful for a slow turn (Fig. 24-10). The skier enters the turn from a regular traverse

Fig. 24-11. Parallel turn.

position, then stems the uphill ski into a half-V. As the weight transfers, the body angulates over the ski, causing both skis to come around in the turn. As the new direction is established, the skis can run back into the parallel position. Problems in turning usually result from insufficient weight shift to the uphill ski.

ADVANCED TECHNIQUES
The parallel turn (christie)

The parallel turn is a progressive form of stem christie but is more complex because of its dependence on *up-unweighting* and precise edge control (Fig. 24-11). The turn starts from the *traverse* position, standing square over the skis. The skier sinks slightly and plants the pole lightly in the snow on the downhill side between boot and ski tip in anticipation of the turn. As the skier explosively up-unweights, the pressure on the *inside edges* transfers to the *outside edges* and the ankles and knees power the skis around in the turn, ending in a traverse position. The upper torso should be kept as still as possible throughout the turn.

The hop turn

The hop turn is an exercise for coordinating the parallel turn. To execute, thrust the heels of the skis in the direction of the turn, either in quick rhythmic thrustings or subtle hops in between long traverses.

Wedeln

The wedeln is an advanced form of parallel skiing in which the ankles and knees manipulate a series of rhythmic half-turns.

Stepping
Inside-outside (at the end of a turn)

1. Traversing on downhill ski in lowered (knee bent) position on inside edge. Extend downhill knee and transfer weight to uphill ski and back to downhill ski.
2. Same as exercise one, now more weight to uphill ski and transfer to outside edge.
3. Same as exercise two, now extend uphill leg (knee and hip) and glide on outside edge of uphill ski across the slope.
4. Same as exercise three, glide extended for a few yards; roll ski (apply either inclination, angulation or leap) on inside edge; make turn.
5. Same as exercise four in various turns (long, short, wide, tight).
6. All exercises repeated, but stepping (gliding) on a flat ski.
7. Emphasize exercises three and four with a step (glide), not only laterally, but also forward. Foot, however, should not move in *front of knee*.
8. Exercise four after gliding (stepping) on uphill ski,

incline body and roll uphill ski on inside edge; start turn. Careful, you need some speed. (If too slow, application of angulation is necessary.)

9. Same as exercise three, extend uphill knee through a leaping movement and change edges while in the air; touch down combined with the start of the turn. Actually, the body starts to rotate into the turn in the air.

10. Link turns together; completion phase and preparation phase of turn almost become one unit.

Inside-inside (at the beginning of a turn)

1. On flat or easily-descending terrain, with packed snow, standing in wedge position, transfer weight from one ski to the other (inside edge).

2. Wedge position leaping from one ski to the other (weight transfer).

3. Wedge position (stationary), unweighted ski matches pressurized ski and leg.

4. Same as exercise two and three in slow speed (plow-hops).

5. Plow-hops, keeping pressure a little longer on the inside edge to allow the ski to turn.

6. Same as five, make complete turns.

7. In a traverse, skiing on inside edge of downhill ski, lift up uphill ski and bring in wedge position and back to parallel.

8. Same as seven, transfer half of weight to wedged uphill ski; let uphill ski glide on inside edge with most of the weight still on inside edge of the downhill ski.

9. Same as eight, transfer weight completely to wedged uphill ski and start turn.

10. Same as nine, change weight and skis and edges while leaping.

11. Tighten up turning radii and put emphasis on leaping movement to shift weight. Touch down to new ski and edge must be smooth (cat-like), executed with a lot of absorbing motion (lowering knee and bending in all three leg joints).

12. Vary turning radii and ski in different terrain.

13. At especially higher speeds, try to make weight change without a leap.

14. Same as thirteen while extending bring body in position for new turn. Use higher speed inclination and lower speed, hip or knee angulation.

Uphill ski to inside ski (outside-outside: at the beginning of a turn)

1. Standing on a small bump, weight on the uphill ski, scissor downhill.

2. Same as one, move weight from uphill ski to scissored downhill ski and glide down small bumps. Prior uphill ski (outside ski) will be matched to new uphill ski (inside ski).

3. Same as two, move with small leap; weight to new inside ski (scissored) but to outside edge; absorb and pressurize. Ski turns on outside edge. Match outside ski and leg.

4. Same as three, leaping onto outside edge of inside ski. Ski down small bump; let ski turn. Bring outside ski (this was the ski we leaped from) alongside the turning inside ski. Shift weight to the inside edge of this ski and continue turning.

5. Make moves to right and left.

6. Try to link turns together (skating step downhill); moderate speed, not too slow.

7. Apply this move in tactical rhythm changes from long into short turns.

8. Out of the start and around the first gate, if turn to second gate is not too long a turn.

ALPINE COMPETITION
Slalom

The slalom is a course with a vertical drop of 120 to 220 m (394 to 772 ft) for men and 120 to 180 m (394 to 591 ft) for women. The course should be set on a slope with a gradient of 20 to 30 degrees. A slalom course consists of a minimum of 42 gates and a maximum of 63 gates for women and 75 gates for men. The gates are set 4 to 6 meters in width (13.1 to 19.6 ft) and successive gates may not be less than 0.75 m (2.5 ft) and not more than 15 m (49.2 ft) apart. Quickness, power, and agility are prerequisites for a good slalom skier. Slalom skis are usually a little shorter than giant slalom or downhill skis.

Giant slalom

The giant slalom is contested on a longer course than the slalom, and has fewer gates. A giant slalom course should have a vertical drop of 250 to 400 m (820 to 1312 ft) for men and 250 to 350 m (820 to 1148 ft) for women. Giant slalom speeds are higher than those in slalom. The number of gates in giant slalom is figured by computation of 12% to 15% of the course's vertical drop.

Ideal giant slalom terrain is undulating. Strength, agility, and explosiveness are trademarks of the giant slalom skier. Where the slalom is an athletic event, many consider the giant slalom to be more technical.

Downhill

Downhill is the fastest and considered by some to be the most exciting event. Speeds up to 90 mph are reached. Many courses are over 3 miles in length. Gates and terrain are used by the course setter to control the racer's speed. The racer has limited protection other than a helmet and the netting which lines the trail.

Super giant slalom

The super giant slalom combines some of the speed of downhill with the more technical turning aspect of the giant slalom. Speeds are rather high in this exciting event.

NORDIC COMPETITION

Nordic competition includes cross-country skiing and jumping.

SKI ORGANIZATIONS GOVERNING COMPETITIONS
Fédération Internationale de Ski

All races are run according to the rules of the Fédération Internationale de Ski (FIS). This representative body supervises the Olympic Games and World Championships, which are held every 4 years; World Championships follow 2 years after the Olympics.

United States Ski Association

The United States Ski Association (USSA) is the governing body for the sport of skiing in the United States. There are eight geographical divisions, each with its own membership, classification of racers, and schedule of competitions, ranging from juniors through veterans. National, Olympic, and World Championship teams are selected on the basis of qualifying races.

National Collegiate Athletic Association

The National Collegiate Athletic Association (NCAA) is the governing body of intercollegiate ski racing. The top teams and individuals compete at NCAA Championships. The individual winners of the various events, including both alpine and nordic competition, are named to the All-American Ski Team at the end of each season.

National Standard Race

National Standard Race (NASTAR) operates on a handicap system as in golf, using a simple giant slalom course especially designed for recreational skiers of all ages. With the aid of computers and professional pacesetters, skiers can compare their skiing with that of other skiers throughout the country.

TEACHING CONSIDERATIONS

1. Ensure that students are provided with safe equipment, properly fitted. The safety aspects of equipment should be a first priority of instruction.
2. Teach students how to grip poles and maintain the proper stance; emphasize a relaxed, balanced position over the skis.
3. Teach how to fall and how to get up. Have students practice several times.
4. Teach walking and side step patterns. Combine with falling and getting up. Provide enough practice time for students to begin to feel comfortable with problems encountered with the length of the skis.
5. Start downhill schussing on a slight incline, allowing students to come to a natural stop at the end. Add the snowplow braking technique as students increase speed.
6. Gradually increase the slope of the hill when students become confident in schussing, keeping the skis under control, the side step pattern, and the snowplow for both braking on the slope and for stopping.
7. Introduce the stationary kick turn and practice often as a lead-up into more advanced turns. Begin traversing skills as soon as students have control of skis in beginning skills. Start instruction on the side of an incline going across the slope so that you can give continuous cuing on weight distribution.
8. Add the stem turn to the traversing skills, encouraging quick recovery from turn to traversing position.
9. Increase slope and conditions gradually as students master intermediate skills; alter them to techniques used to accommodate changes in conditions.
10. As new techniques are introduced, decrease the difficulty of the practice conditions.
11. Keep instructional sessions active so that students are not standing still in cold weather.

GLOSSARY

angulation When edges bite into the snow from pressure exerted by the ankles and the knees being rolled into the hill, the upper body leans slightly downhill to compensate.

camber Arch of the ski as seen from the side view.

carved turns A form of advanced skiing following the christie turn in which turns are made using the edges without skidding the skis.

chatter Undesirable vibrations of edges while skiing on ice or hard-packed snow.

christie A turn without skidding.

edge control Adjusting the angle between the snow and the running surface of the ski.

fall line The imaginary line of gravity straight down a slope.

groove Indentation running nearly the full length of the bottom of the ski; it helps in control.

inside edges Edges of the skis that grip the snow on the inside of the arc of the turn.

linked turns A series of turns in alternating directions.

moguls Mounds of snow.

outside edges Edges of the skis on the downhill side of the slope, which do not grip the snow.

ruade Movement made by lifting the tails of the skis off the ground and turning, with the ski tips acting as pivots.

schuss boom Ski dangerously out of control.

sitzmark Indentation in the snow made by a skier falling down.

torsion The amount of lengthwise twist in a ski.

traverse Ski on inside edges at an angle to the fall line.

up-unweighting A down-up movement of the ankles and knees to reduce weight on the skis before turning; it facilitates changing of edges.

wedeln Series of rhythmic half-turns in alternating directions.

SUGGESTED READINGS

Coaching Association of Canada: Alpine ski racing skill development model, Ontario, Canada, 1986, National Alpine Ski Team.

Cottrell J: Skiing everyone, Winston-Salem, NC, 1983, Hunter Textbooks, Inc. Includes hundreds of photos to illustrate equipment, exercises, proper techniques, and rules of the slopes. Gives tips on how to correct errors, do's and dont's for the slopes, and drills for practice. A wealth of useful information; especially good for programs where location or time limits actual slope experience and time is spent on conditioning and preparation.

Flemmen A and Grosvold O: Teaching children to ski, West Point, NY, 1983, Leisure Press. For teaching skiing skills to children from tots to preteens. Emphasis on pupils' learning by developing their special talents through a "natural approach."

Hoppichler F: Ski with us, London, England, 1985, Pelham Books, Ltd.

Howe J: Skiing mechanics, LaPorte, Colo, 1983, Poudre Press. Describes the physics of skiing.

Joubert G: Skiing - an art - a technique, LaPorte, Colo, 1978, Poudre Press. This book is considered a classic by many skiing experts.

Kidd B and Grant B: Ski racing, Chicago, Ill, 1984, Contemporary Books, Inc. A fun book to read.

Loudis LA, Lobitz WC, and Singer KM: Skiing out of your mind: the psychology of peak performance, Champaign, Ill, 1986, Human Kinetics Publishers, Inc. Presents material on concentration, awareness, mental rehearsal, and confidence as they relate to skiing.

Major J and Larisson O: World cup ski technique, LaPorte, Colo, 1978, Poudre Press. Good text but the photo essays are exceptionally good.

National Collegiate Athletic Association official skiing rules, Washington, DC, 1989, National Collegiate Athletic Association.

Rothman A: You can ski like a skater, West Point, NY, 1983, Leisure Press. An innovative book for skiers at all levels of ability with simple, easy-to-understand explanations of how to develop alpine skiing skills.

Schaller L: Skiing technique and training, Inspruck, Austria, 1984, M. Theiss Wolfsberg.

Torgerson L: Good glide: the science of ski waxing, Champaign, Ill, 1983, Leisure Press. Written mainly for cross-country skiers; also valuable for alpine skiers and ski jumpers who want to know more about glide waxing and different snow and meterological conditions.

Tucker K and Jensen C: Skiing, Dubuque, Iowa, 1983, Wm C Brown Group. Includes information on fitness, equipment selection, history, racing, cross-country skiing, and opportunities available in skiing. Also includes practice drills and step-by-step photos for the beginner.

FILMS

The great ski chase. Summit Films Productions, Denver.
Incredible skis. Summit Films Productions, Denver.
The moebius flip. Summit Films Productions, Denver.
NASTAR. Joseph Schlitz Brewing Co., Milwaukee.
Ski country USA. Summit Films Productions, Denver.
Ski the outer limits. Summit Films Productions, Denver.

VIDEOTAPES

Downhill skiing basics, alpine skiing with Jeon-Claude Killy. Sports Video, 745 State Circle, Box 1941, Ann Arbor, MI 48106.

Alpine ski school: *Distinctive skiing, Black diamond skiing* and *Fundamentals of skiing.* Karol Video, 22 Riverside Dr., Wayne, NJ 07470.

Fifteen different videos, including *Learn to ski, Advanced ski tuning guide* and *Olympic gold workout.* "How To" Sports Videos, Box 5852, Denver, CO 80217.

25

Skiing: Cross-Country

Completion of this chapter should enable the reader to:

- Appreciate the development of cross-country skiing
- Select and care for cross-country skiing equipment
- Practice proper skiing techniques on various terrains
- Suggest appropriate off-season conditioning activities
- Identify correct cross-country skiing clothing
- Be aware of safety concerns

HISTORY

The history of skiing is deeply meshed with the history of all lands throughout the world that are seasonally covered with snow. The earliest pictorial representation of skiing shows man hunting elk on skis. This picture dates back to approximately 2500 B.C. and was found on the island of Rödöy, off the coast of Norway. The earliest known skis date back to the same era and were found in a bog near Hoting, Sweden. It appears that the early skis were made of bone and were used in Scandinavia for hunting and later for warfare.

Two events in the Middle Ages demonstrate the importance of skiing to the military in the northern countries. In 1206 in Norway, two members of the king's guard carried the king's son, Haken, on skis over the Dovre mountains away from enemy forces. The child later became one of Norway's greatest kings and the event is now celebrated in the famous Norwegian Birkebeiner race. In the 1500s, a similar event occurred in Sweden when Gustav Vasa was leading the battle against Danish rulers. Sensing defeat, Gustav left the town of Dalarna and headed for the Norwegian border. He was later persuaded by skiers to return to fight the Danish army, and the route of his triumphant return on skis is followed in today's most famous cross-country ski race, the Vasaloppet. Gustav Vasa went on to become the founder of modern Sweden.

Interest in skiing spread internationally in the late 1800s as the British discovered skiing in the European Alps and started formal ski competition. The exploits of Norwegian explorer Fridthjof Nansen, written in *The First Crossing of Greenland,* fed British interest in skiing. Gradually, skiing in the alps took on its own technique and style and evolved into the current discipline of alpine skiing. However, cross-country skiing continued to grow in popularity and technical development. The use of metal bindings appeared near the end of the nineteenth century near the Telemark area of Norway, and the use of two ski poles of equal length was substituted for the traditional long single pole at about the same time.

Skiing was brought to the United States by Scandinavian immigrants and became common in the 1800s. Pictures of the California mining camps of the 1840s and 1850s show well-organized ski racing. The most well-remembered American skier of this era was John "Snowshoe" Thompson who, beginning in 1856, began carrying mail from Nevada to California over the mountains on skis. Thompson's trips were legendary, covering 90 miles in about 3 days while he carried 60 to 90 pounds of mail. Interest in skiing in the United States focused in those geographic areas with large concentrations of Scandinavian settlers. By 1872, the first ski club in the United States was formed in Berlin, New Hampshire, and named the Nansen Ski Club. Other clubs shortly followed in the Midwest. The 1932 Winter Olympics in Lake Placid, New York, further heightened interest in skiing because it was the first Olympiad with nordic and alpine skiing competitions (cross-country and jumping). The previous Olympics had carried only nordic events.

Interest in cross-country skiing was sustained in the early twentieth century by a small group of clubs, eastern colleges and universities, and preparatory schools. Competition centered around the winter carnivals of many colleges and universities of the northeast, with ski jumping attracting more spectator attention than cross-country skiing. At the same time, alpine or downhill skiing was growing rapidly in popularity in the United States, led by Hannes Schneider and his distinctive Austrian Alborg technique with its Christina turns.

Skiing in America was greatly advanced by the onset of World War II and the formation of the country's first ski troops—the Tenth Mountain Division. The ski troops proved to be one of the most effective and decorated units of the war, combating German forces in the Battle of Italy. But a lasting side effect of this division was that a cross-section of American men, and not just those graduating from certain eastern colleges, were exposed to the latest in ski and survival techniques. After the war, many of the soldiers of the Tenth Mountain Division continued to follow their interest in skiing by working in the ski industry.

Despite the expanded base for cross-country skiing, participation in the sport remained relatively small through the 1960s, obscured by its downhill relative. This status was dramatically changed by the "discovery" of cross-country skiing in the early 1970s, resulting in the most recent boom in the sport. Cross-country ski sales in the United States amounted to about 14,000 pairs in 1966 and exploded to about 277,000 pairs by the winter of 1971-1972. This twentyfold increase can be partially attributed to the American public's growing interest in fitness and the environment. Cross-country skiing appealed to people who participated in other cardiovascular fitness pursuits such as jogging and cycling and seemed consistent with their sense of concern for the environment. In short, the sport took on the image of being health- and fitness-enhancing as well as environmentally sound.

Recent historical developments

Cross-country skiing has continued to grow in popularity since 1972 but at a reduced rate. Helping this growth has been increased media attention and books such as John Caldwell's *The Cross-Country Ski Book*. First published in 1964, the volume provided much-needed technical information for first-time skiers. Bill Koch's silver medal in the 1976 Olympics in Seefeld, Austria, and his subsequent overall World Cup Title in 1982 brought cross-country skiing further attention.

With the increased popularity of cross-country skiing, the public now has a wider range of skiing opportunities.

Back-country skiing in wilderness parks and on undeveloped lands is still available. In addition, well-developed commercial ski touring centers now exist in most parts of the country with adequate winter snow cover. Cross-country skiing facilities can provide prepared and groomed trail systems, trail maps, and systematic markings, and usually some kind of ski patrol for safety support. This kind of skiing simply was not available in the United States before 1972 and widens the base of appeal to those who would not explore wilderness areas on their own. Now the skier can choose his or her level of involvement in skiing.

In addition, more ski organizations now sponsor and support cross-country ski events. The Ski Touring Council of Troy, Vermont, founded by Rudolph Mattesich, publishes an authoritative list of ski tours and events. The United States Ski Association traditionally sponsors ski races and ski touring opportunities. Ski touring clubs now appear in or near most urban areas of the Snow Belt to provide instruction, tours, and racing experiences for the public.

With the dramatic improvements in snow grooming of cross-country ski trails, the skating technique has become increasingly feasible and practical. Bill Koch popularized the technique in North America with his World Cup victory in the winter of 1981-82. The skating technique on cross country skis closely resembles a speed skater using long ski poles. Skating is considerably faster than the traditional or classical skiing technique which has been used for centuries, but it requires different waxing, equipment, and conditioning.

EQUIPMENT

Recent interest in cross-country skiing has led to more change in ski equipment in the past 14 years than in the previous century. Touring skis have become lighter and more responsive; fiberglass and other synthetic fibers have all but replaced traditional hickory and hardwood skis; ski bottoms either are waxable in the old skiing tradition or have special "no-wax" synthetic bases; ski boot and binding combinations have become more diverse and provide more support. Today's cross-country skiers must become good consumers to purchase the appropriate equipment for their needs, locale, and budget. In sum, the recent advances in cross-country ski technology provide for safer and more enjoyable skiing.

Skis

Cross-country skis are longer, lighter, and thinner than their alpine counterparts. They are designed primarily to allow the skier to slide forward over the snow with a minimum of resistance and effort. Cross-country skis have traditionally been made of thin laminated strips of wood, but in the past decade the trend has been toward fiberglass skis with wood and fiberglass cores and various types of plastic running surfaces. Cross-country skis can be categorized into five distinctive types:

Ski	Width (mm)	Purpose
Mountaineering	60 and up	Skiing with heavy pack; ski mountaineering
Touring	53 to 60	Skiing with light pack; wilderness, ungroomed trail skiing
Light touring	48 to 52	Skiing on prepared track or ungroomed trails
Classical racing	44 to 47	Ski racing
Skating racing	39 to 42	Ski racing

Beginners are advised to use light touring or touring skis depending on their use. The other two types of skis and their usage go beyond the scope of this chapter. Skis for adults (Fig. 25-1) will vary between 185 and 215 cm (74 and 86 in) in length based on the skier's height. The general rule of thumb for a good fit is that skis should be as tall as the skier's outstretched wrist held overhead. Cross-country skis are built with a degree of camber or bow in the bottom running surface. The camber of both skis in a pair should match, and the user should be able to flatten out the entire length of the skis when he or she stands on them on a smooth, hard floor. Bottom camber will help propel the skier forward when flattened on the snow.

Perhaps the most difficult decision when purchasing the first pair of skis is whether to choose waxable or waxless skis. Recently, cross-country skis with machined or mohair bottoms have eliminated the necessity of applying wax to the bottom or running surface of the skis. Such waxless skis have gained popularity with beginning and recreational skiers because of their convenience. The disadvantage of waxless skis lies in their performance. They cannot adjust to the variety of snows and temperatures that the skis will face and as a result will not slide as easily as well-waxed cross-country skis. However, improved technology has narrowed the gap between the performance of waxable and waxless skis.

With the evolution of the skating technique, "skating" skis are now available. They are about 5 to 10 cm shorter than classical skis; have a stiffer bottom camber, particularly in the tail of the ski; and feature reinforced sidewalls to withstand stress.

Poles

Ski poles are important for a cross-country skier because they are used not only for balance but also to push the skier forward. Beginners will quickly learn that downhill ski poles are not adequate for skiing cross-country. Cross-

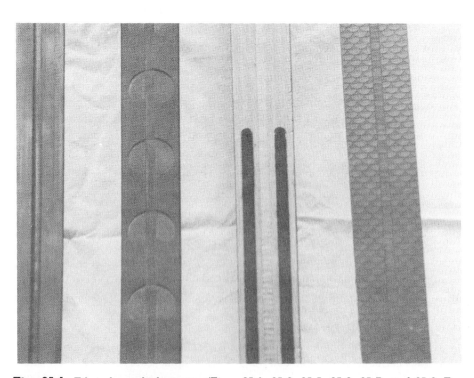

Fig. 25-1. Fiberglass ski bottoms. (Figs. 25-1, 25-2, 25-5, 25-6, 25-7, and 25-8: From *Cross-Country Skiing Today*, by John Caldwell. Copyright 1977 by John Caldwell. Reprinted by permission of The Stephen Greene Press, a wholly owned subsidiary of Viking Penguin, Inc.)

country poles are made of tonkin, metal, or fiberglass and have three distinctive features. They are quite long and should fit comfortably under the skier's armpit while he or she is standing on a floor. Second, the tip of a cross-country ski pole is bent forward to allow for easy removal from the snow when the pole is well behind the sliding skier. Third, cross-country poles have a comfortable grip with an adjustable strap that allows the pole to stay attached to the skier's wrist even when not tightly gripped.

Poles can come with a variety of baskets that are appropriate for different skiing conditions. Wide baskets can support the pole in deep, soft snow while smaller, sometimes triangular baskets work well in packed, prepared-track ski conditions.

Skiers who intend to do much of their skiing using the skate technique should purchase ski poles that come up to their upper lip with the tip of the pole on the floor. The longer poles are mandated by the increased stride length of the skate. The added length of the poles requires them to be much stiffer than traditional poles. Common skating pole materials are aluminum or a graphite and fiberglass blend. Most skis, boots, and bindings can be used for both classical and skating but longer ski poles are essential for proper skating.

Boots

Cross-country ski boots (Fig. 25-2) vary to be compatible with the five types of skis previously cited, with touring and light touring boots the preference for most recreational skiers. Although cross-country boots have long been made of leather uppers with leather or rubber soles, they are now also commonly made with synthetic soles and nylon, plastic, and even Gore-tex uppers. Despite these changes, several rules remain:
1. The ski boot should fit like a comfortable hiking boot or running shoe with the socks of the skier's choice.
2. Higher ski boots should be used because they provide more support and warmth than low-cut models.
3. The ski boot should be compatible with the type of ski and should tightly match the ski binding.
4. Cross-country ski-boot soles should allow for maximum heel-to-toe flexibility while minimizing side-to-side movement.

Light touring boots suffice for most recreational usage because they provide a compromise among support, warmth, and flexibility. Skiers with unique podiatric or circulatory conditions should seek ski boots to accommodate their requirements. Fortunately, a wide variety of quality ski boots is available today.

Boots designed for the skating technique are useful but not necessary. They feature more lateral support in the heel counter, have less flexibility in the heel to toe

plane, and have a higher cut than the classical boots. The boots should be compatible with the binding system of the skis.

Bindings

The modern advances of ski technology are also evident in cross-country ski bindings. Traditional cable and three-pinned "nordic norm" bindings have been challenged. As in many sports, the changes originated in racing skis and later were used in recreational skis. The changes have complicated a once simple decision. Modern bindings appear to work well when matched with the correct boot sole. The skier should carefully examine the compatibility of boots and bindings and check for lateral play between the two. The best boot-binding combinations feature a tight positive attachment.

Many new bindings extend the entire length of the ski-boot sole. They provide a heel plate or locator that keeps the boot stable when flattened to the ski. Although desirable, these full-length bindings are unnecessary when a separate heel plate is used.

CLASSICAL SKI TECHNIQUES
Getting started

Correct cross-country skiing technique allows the skier to cover a wide variety of terrain in an effective and efficient manner. Technique is discussed here to help the skier make the sport more enjoyable and safe. First, the skier should practice putting on the skis and then simply walking about for a short distance with or without poles. Second, while on flat ground the skier should fall, if the snow is soft enough, and practice getting up. This exercise demonstrates the relative safety of cross-country skis. With the skis attached to the ski boots only at the toe, the skier should have little fear of slow-motion falls. Relaxation plays a major part in all ski techniques. The skier should take some time to become comfortable both walking and getting up from a fall.

Flat-terrain techniques
Diagonal stride

The basic stride of cross-country skiing is called the diagonal stride (Fig. 25-3) and is the hallmark of sound cross-country ski technique. Besides being used on flat terrain, it can be adapted, depending on the skier's strength and ability, to uphill sections. The diagonal stride can be broken down into three distinct but overlapping phases: the kick, glide, and pole.

The kick phase begins with one leg kicking or pushing back against the snow and the opposite leg sliding or shuffling forward. The body leans forward from the hips as the skier's weight transfers to the bent front leg. The glide phase extends from this weight transfer until the time the pole in the skier's opposite hand is planted out

Fig. 25-2. A, Light touring/boot binding combination. **B** and **C,** Racing boot/binding combinations. (Figs. 25-2, 25-3, 25-9, and 25-11: From *The Cross Country Ski Book,* by John Caldwell. Copyright 1984, 1971, 1973, 1975, 1977, 1981 by John Caldwell. Reprinted by permission of The Stephen Greene Press, a wholly owned subsidiary of Viking Penguin, Inc.)

Fig. 25-3. Diagonal stride.

Fig. 25-4. Double poling.

in front. Remember that the left arm and right leg will be forward at the same time, just as in walking or running. The poling phase continues until the opposite leg begins to kick, beginning the next cycle. This rhythmic stride allows the skier to shuffle using arms and legs for propulsion forward. The kick should be down into the snow as well as backward. The poling motion should markedly contribute to extending the skier's already initiated glide ahead and will require considerable effort with the arms for the beginner. The diagonal stride, seen as a whole, requires strength, balance, and coordination.

Double pole

Double poling (Fig. 25-4) can be used to maintain forward motion on slight downhills or on flat terrain as an alternative to the diagonal stride. The double pole can be defined as having two phases: the poling phase and the recovery-free glide phase. In the initial poling phase, the poles are planted as far forward as pole length and strength will allow and with the arms in a rigid but flexed position. Then the upper body sinks over the poles, moving the skier forward. The arms push the poles back behind the skier, leaving the skier bent over almost horizontal to the ground with both arms extended behind. In the recovery phase, the poles are retracted from the snow and the body should come back up to the vertical as the arms prepare to reach ahead to begin the next pole. Much of the poling force should be provided by the upper torso, and the abdominal muscles in particular, rather than only by the arms.

Double pole with kick

This maneuver (Fig. 25-5) combines the upper body motion of the double pole with a single kick or "scooter push" of one leg, as in the diagonal stride, and serves as an efficient way to change pace while skiing. Practiced skiers mix these three techniques, depending on their level of fatigue and the demands of the terrain.

The double pole with kick is initiated by simultaneously reaching forward with both arms and pushing backward or kicking with one leg as described in the diagonal stride. The skier's body weight is now all on the forward ski, and the rear or kicking leg is extended. While the skier glides on one ski, both poles are planted as far forward as possible. The glide is now maintained by a double pole. The kicking leg returns to the snow as the body collapses over the poles.

The recovery phase is the same as in double poling. The double pole with kick requires some coordination and practice before mastery, but it is a relaxing technique to use on flat or rolling terrain. The difference between the double pole with kick and the pure double pole is that in the pure double pole the kicking phase is excluded and only the poling motion provides the power to propel the skier down the track.

Uphill techniques

With practice and strength, all of the previously described techniques used on flat terrain can be applied to gradual uphills. Some adaptations must be made, particularly in the diagonal stride, in which the free-glide phase becomes shorter and the pole is planted back further than on the flats. Stride length decreases, and the gliding foot is pushed further ahead of the knee. Again, skiers should measure their capabilities and match them to the terrain. Other techniques exist for steep or otherwise difficult uphill stretches.

Herringbone

Here the skier uses the basic diagonal stride but angles both skis out (Fig. 25-6) to reduce the angle of the hill. The arms are kept low, with the poles forcefully pushed into the snow behind the skier. To help grip the snow, the inside edges of each ski are angled into the snow. A common error of the herringbone is to bend forward at the waist, so the skier should be aware of keeping the head looking up the hill.

Fig. 25-5. Double poling with kick.

Fig. 25-6. Herringbone on uphill.

Fig. 25-7. Sidestep on gradual uphill.

Fig. 25-8. Wedge on gradual downhill.

Side step

On even steeper hills, the side step (Fig. 25-7) is a slower but certain way for beginners to get up. The skier stands with the skis going across (at a right angle to) the fall-line of the hill (the imaginary line down the hill's steepest slope). The skier angles the skis into the hill and lifts the uphill ski, stepping up the hill about 1 foot. The downhill ski follows, and the action is repeated. The skier should be certain that the skis remain perpendicular to the fall line and that the uphill edges of the skis are rolled into the hill.

Downhill techniques
Straight downhill

Cross-country skis are designed to cut through the snow in a straight path with a minimum of resistance and therefore cannot be turned and maneuvered as readily as alpine skis on downhill situations. Velocity and direction can be controlled on cross-country skis using several simple techniques.

The basic downhill position of the skis should be a relaxed position with the weight evenly distributed on both skis. The skier must be conscious that the ski-boot heel is not attached to the ski and must keep some body weight pushing down on the heels. The term "soft knees" has been developed to explain the skier's relaxed, flexible stance that is needed to absorb the bumps in the terrain. The wedge (Fig. 25-8) serves as the basic technique used to control the skier's downhill descent. As the skier descends the hill, the tips of the skis are moved together as the tails are spread apart, forming a V-shaped ski position. To brake from this position the skier wedges out the ski tails and pushes on the inside edges of both skis.

Fig. 25-9. Marathon skate at the end of the kick.

Wedge turn

From the controlled position just described, the skier can initiate a turn by shifting weight onto one ski, which turns the skier in the opposite direction. A good sign of a strong weight shift to one ski will be the shoulder of that same side rotating forward as the skis turn. Wedge turns can be linked together to form a controlled method of traversing and descending a hill.

Step turn

The step turn is the basic maneuver for changing direction on cross-country skis. The technique appears to be a simple movement but requires the skier to commit almost all body weight to one ski and then to regain balance. While in the basic downhill position, the skier picks up the ski in the direction of the turn. The skier then plants that ski in the new direction and shifts the body weight to that ski. The trailing ski is then brought alongside the first ski to regain the basic downhill position. Emphasis should be placed on a smooth and complete weight transfer from one ski to the other. Several quick and small step turns are preferable to one wide-angle step adjustment, particularly at higher speeds.

Advanced downhill turns

Once the skier masters these basic downhill maneuvers, he or she can acquire other, more advanced downhill turns. (Refer to Chapter 24 for an elaboration of other downhill turns that can also be done on cross-country skis.) In addition, the time-honored telemark turn still remains as a classic advanced cross-country ski maneuver.

SKATING TECHNIQUES

Skating requires different rhythms, skills, and strengths from the classical technique previously explained. Many beginners find skating to be more natural and easier to learn than the older kick and glide approach. Keep in mind that the movements explained here require adequate equipment (particularly longer poles) and skis without cross-country kick wax (explained in waxing section).

Marathon skate

Skating (Fig. 25-9) is a recent addition to cross-country ski technique and was popularized in ski racing by Bill Koch in his 1981-82 World Cup victory. The skate has revolutionized cross-country ski racing and since that time has been adopted by successful ski racers. The effects of this revolution are filtering down to citizen ski racers and ski tourers. Skating can be used as a replacement for the double pole with kick and the diagonal stride in situations where the skier wishes to maintain a relatively high velocity. This is most effective on crusty snow conditions or in well-prepared ski tracks.

The skate is initiated with a double pole followed by a single kicking action of one leg. The kicking foot is lifted off the snow, angled out at about 40 degrees and vigorously pushed back as in an ice-skating motion. The tails of the skis will slightly cross before the kick, and at the end of the kick the leg will be extended. In the recovery phase, the kicking leg is brought back completely over the ski track and followed by a glide phase. As a new technique, the skate has many variations, but the skier should practice skating with either leg and mixing it into the other, more traditional techniques. While learning the technique, use existing ski tracks on a level or slightly downhill trail. Practice the marathon skate using both feet as the skating foot.

V-1 Skate

Now the skier does not need set ski tracks but just packed snow. The V-1 skate gains its name from the V pattern that the skis etch on the snow. Here the skier steps out onto one ski and adds a double pole motion. But instead of returning the ski into the track as in the marathon skate, the skier skates off onto the other foot as the arms recover. In total this looks like a speed skater's motion with the lower body combined with a strong double pole. This creates a strong stride on one ski (with the poling) and a recovery step with the opposite leg. Try this on level terrain before moving to slight uphills. Common problems with beginners include not commiting their full weight to the skating ski and allowing the skis to drift farther and farther apart when initiating the skate step. The two boots almost touch one another as they pass in their strides. Strength and coordination are required to use the V-1 on steeper and longer uphills.

Notice in the illustration (Fig. 25-10) how the skier stays fairly erect and straightens the skating leg as he rides over the flat skating ski.

V-2 Skate

As the skating technique evolves, the V-2 appears to be the technique of the future. Now mostly used on flat or slightly downhill terrain by ski racers, future skiers will be strong enough and have enough balance to V-2 on the uphills.

The V-2 is performed in the same fashion as the V-1 except the skier double poles on every skating step. Instead of having a strong and weak side as in the V-1, this is a bilateral motion with a poling action on the left and right strides. The leg tempo must slow down to allow the arms to recover and the poling motion is shorter and quicker.

Skating Summary

Skating is a relatively new innovation in cross-country skiing. In cross-country ski racing events, classical and skating events exist side by side much the same way that different swimming strokes have their own events. They are just different variations of self-propulsion on snow. Skating requires more strength particularly in the upper body yet provides more freedom of motion. Although skating equipment differs from classical skiing equipment, longer ski poles are the only essential difference. Beginners are encouraged to try both versions for the full enjoyment of all skiing techniques.

GUIDELINES FOR THE CROSS-COUNTRY COURSE

A cross-country course must be laid out to be a technical, tactical, and physical test of the skier. The degree of

Fig. 25-10. V-1 skate. **A,** Front view. **B,** Rear view.

difficulty should be in accordance with the ability of the competitors.

The cross-country course should consist of:

1. One third uphill section with a climb between 9 and 15 percent plus some short climbs that would be steeper (10 percent slope = 45 degrees).
2. One third undulating terrain using all terrain features with short climbs and downhill sections, and height differences of 5 to 10 m.
3. One third varied downhill section demanding competence in all downhill skills.

Number of Competitors

Five men and five women from a team may compete in the individual event for the team score, with the highest finishing three in each to count in the team scoring. A relay team consists of three competitors.

WAXING

Cross-country ski wax is a unique chemical compound that allows cross-country skiers to get a grip or "purchase" on uphills. When properly selected and applied, cross-country or "kicker" wax alternately grips the snow crystals when weight is put on the ski and slides when the weight is released from the ski as in the glide phase of the cross-country ski technique. There is both an art and a science to cross-country ski waxing. It requires matching the ski and the skier's weight and technique to the snow conditions and temperature.

Before the revolutionary changes in skis from wood to synthetic-base surfaces, or from straight bottoms to patterned or mohair no-wax surfaces, ski waxing was a reasonably straightforward procedure. Charts matching snow conditions to ski wax color were simple and common. Now, with the wide variety of skis and ski bottoms and wax and no-wax surfaces, waxing has become specific to each type of cross-country ski, and written procedures go beyond the scope of this chapter. Some suggestions will prove helpful for the beginner:

1. Follow the manufacturer's ski base preparation and waxing recommendations. These should come with the skis or be available from the retailer.
2. Adjust these basic waxing rules to your personal technique, needs, and local snow conditions.
3. Consistently use one or two brands of cross-country and alpine wax until you have mastered their entire range of waxes before moving on to other brands.
4. Even "no-wax" skis can perform better with the application of "gliding" or alpine wax on the non-gripping portion of the ski bottoms. This will protect the ski against wear and damage as well as improve its gliding capabilities.

The skating technique simplifies cross-country ski waxing. Since the skier gets purchase on the snow using the edge of the ski, no cross-country or "kick" wax is necessary. A coat of alpine wax is put on the ski bottoms to enhance the ski glide and protect its running surface.

OFF-SEASON CONDITIONING

Since cross-country is a seasonal winter sport, most cross-country skiers turn to other sports and recreational activities for the remainder of the year. Most cross-country participants engage in other outdoor pursuits that are in the same endurance-based, aerobic family of sports. The purpose of off-season conditioning should be to adapt the skier to the physical demands of skiing, allowing the skier to enjoy skiing when the snow arrives. Cross-country skiing can be a demanding experience for those who have been dormant in the off-season! Keep in mind that ski tours, cross-country pursuits, and citizen ski races can extend for a matter of hours or an entire day, depending on the fitness and skills of the skier, so the skier's off-season conditioning should focus on gradually adapting the skier's conditioning for such adventures. Specifically, the skier should prepare for the demands (cardiovascular, muscular, and technical) required for his or her level of involvement. Some conditioning guidelines to remember are as follows:

1. Make cross-country training as enjoyable as possible. Find off-season pursuits that are fun. If possible, find others to train with. This will provide companionship and a support system to maintain a training program.
2. Train in the off-season at the same level of intensity that you will use when skiing. Higher levels of conditioning for skiers require more formal training programs and time. Be realistic in the goals for a cross-country ski season.
3. Conditioning that approximates cross-country skiing is more effective than general conditioning. Gear off-season training specifically to cross-country skiing, if you are serious about ski fitness. An example of this is to train on terrain similar to that which will be skied in the winter.
4. Cross-country skiing is a total body sport in terms of the demands placed on the skier. No individual can excel in all dimensions of skiing. Conditioning programs should place emphasis on the skier's weaknesses to produce more balance.

Cardiovascular endurance training

Cross-country skiing is a member of the cardiovascular endurance family of activites. For that reason, participating in any other endurance-producing activity in the off-season can be beneficial for skiing performance. Bicycling, jogging, orienteering, hiking, skulling, and rowing are common off-season alternatives. Canoeing, kayaking, and swimming, although not as commonly used,

Fig. 25-11. Off-season conditioning on roller skis.

will still be beneficial to off-season recreational skiers. The use of roller skis (Fig. 25-11) or roller blades is the most sport-specific form of off-season cardiovascular training.

Muscular strength and endurance training

Cross-country skiing places demands on the strength and endurance of all the major muscle groups of the body. Besides the weight-lifting, weight-training, and circuit-training methods cited in Chapter 39, the use of Universal and Nautilus exercise devices is helpful. The skier should not overlook basic hard physical labor as in wood splitting, gardening, and chain sawing as a means for developing muscular endurance. Cross-country trail clearing in the late fall can be a foundation to snow skiing fitness.

The skating technique places a premium on muscle endurance and strength. Therefore, skaters should place emphasis on strength and muscle endurance training relative to their cardiovascular fitness.

Skill training

As previously mentioned, off-season conditioning should closely approximate snow skiing. Skill training is a com-

ponent that helps the skier master the technical aspects of skiing while in the off-season. Skill training minimizes the difficulty of the transition from off-season or dry-land training to snow skiing. Many ingenious forms of skill training have been developed by ski racers. Some are appropriate for the recreational athlete (such as roller skiing). The simple addition of ski poles in hiking or jogging can improve both endurance and technique. Ski bounding and ski striding on gradual uphill slopes are other examples of excellent skill training activities.

The recent development of roller blades or hockey skates on in-line wheels has been a great asset to cross country skiers. Roller blades, when used with skating length ski poles provides excellent skill, cardiovascular, and muscle endurance training.

CLOTHING

The correct clothing for cross-country skiing can vary as widely as skiing and weather conditions. Few formal rules can be stated, but several guidelines are offered:

1. Dress in about the same clothes you would wear if hiking in similar weather.
2. Wear loose-fitting, nonbinding clothing, which will allow a wide range of motion.

3. Wear several light and warm layers, which provide more ventilation than a few heavy bulky layers (e.g., a ski parka).
4. Always remember hats, ear band, and gloves or mittens as essential.
5. Bring a change of dry shirts, socks, and footwear for after a ski tour.

Many ski tourers have found some of the new synthetic fibers that can provide warmth and windproofing to be ideally suited for the sport. A small backpack or fanny-pack can hold additional clothing and a trail snack.

SAFETY CONCERNS

While cross-country skiing remains a relatively safe sport, the participant should exercise caution, ski within his or her limits, and use common sense. When on a day-long tour, the following equipment should be included:

Small backpack	Screwdriver
Extra ski wax	Matches
Spare ski tip	Map and compass
Adhesive tape	Ample fluids
Knife	Extra food

Injuries are rare in cross-country skiing, but two emergency situations should be recognizable to all skiers: frostbite and hypothermia. Frostbite is the freezing of the surface layers of skin cells on exposed extremities of the body: usually ears, nose, chin, fingers, or toes. Frostbite can be prevented by keeping hands and feet—and face, in extreme cold—properly covered. Partners can check each other's faces to reveal any area lacking in circulation and appearing white or gray. Frostbite victims should be removed from the wind and cold as quickly as possible. Treatment for serious frostbite requires medical personnel.

Hypothermia is the gradual lowering of the core temperature of the body and can occur when a person is exposed to much wind, cold, and wetness. Hypothermia is most likely to occur when a skier is hungry, tired, and inexperienced about how to behave in the outdoors in the winter. Symptoms of hypothermia include lethargy, slurred speech, poor coordination, and shivering. Efforts must be made immediately to warm the person both by removing him or her from the cold and feeding hot fluids, if the person is conscious. Medical care is advised in serious cases. Hypothermia can be avoided by proper clothing, adequate feeding, and traveling within one's limits.

TEACHING CONSIDERATIONS

1. Initial practice should include just walking with skis on flat terrain. Practice lowering the body to the ground in a slow fall and getting up again until the skier is comfortable maneuvering the length of the skis.

2. Instruction should be consistent with the perceived purposes of the learner. Beginning recreational skiers will need only basic skills to make their initial experiences safe and satisfying. Do not attempt to teach all techniques in one period. Come back to more advanced techniques after participants have had an opportunity to use what they have learned. If possible, teach techniques on a "need-to-know" basis as students encounter conditions needing more advanced techniques. Consider the endurance level of participants when planning lessons. Beginners use more energy than skilled participants. Make beginning trails short.

3. Begin with flat-terrain techniques. The diagonal-stride and double-pole techniques should be sufficient for the beginner to enjoy a flat-terrain experience. Later lessons can incorporate the double pole with a kick or marathon-skate technique for students who are interested in speed.

4. Most cross-country experiences require only minor adjustments to the basic cross-country skiing techniques, which can be taught and practiced quickly on the appropriate terrain. Skiers who will experience steeper slopes will need basic instruction in how to get up and down a hill safely on their skis. The side step and herringbone should be taught as methods of getting up a steep hill. The straight downhill ski technique will be sufficient for moderate inclines, but the wedge technique will need to be mastered to control speed on steeper inclines. These skills are not easily performed without practice or instruction on sloped terrain, and beginners should be encouraged not to attempt downhill skills on large slopes. The side step can be taught as a safety skill to get down a slope that is beyond the skier's skill level.

5. Keep instruction sessions short. Minimize listening time; maximize practice and opportunity to participate in a cross-country experience right away.

GLOSSARY

cardiovascular fitness The ability of the body to process oxygen to do work using the heart, lungs, blood vessels, and muscles.

citizen ski races Ski races designed for mass participation by recreational skiers. Citizen ski racers are considered skiers between elite ski racers and recreational ski tourers.

glide wax Sometimes referred to as alpine or speed wax; it can be applied to the tips and tails of skis to enhance ski speed. Used exclusively in skating.

kicker wax Sometimes referred to as cross-country wax; it is applied to a waxing zone of varying length in the middle of the ski. Kicker wax produces the grip allowing the skier to move uphill.

ski bounding An uphill running exercise designed to simulate the movement of skiing uphill. This is done in the off-season for skill and cardiovascular training.

SUGGESTED READINGS

Barnett S: Cross country skiing downhill, ed 3, Seattle, Wash, 1983, Pacific Search Press.

Bergh U: Physiology of cross-country ski racing, Champaign, Ill, 1982, Human Kinetics Publishers, Inc. Presents an overview of exercise physiology, reports the physiological data drawn from elite skiers, and explains various training techniques used by elite Swedish skiers.

Brady M and Skjemstad L: Waxing for cross country skis, ed 6, Berkeley, Calif, 1981, Wilderness Press.

Borowski L: Ski faster, easier, Champaign, Ill, 1986, Human Kinetics Publishers, Inc. Includes step-by-step instructions on how to perform the diagonal stride technique.

Borowski L: The simple secrets of skating, Broomfield, Wis, 1988, (published by author).

Caldwell J: The new cross-country ski book, ed 8, New York, 1987, Viking Penguin, Inc. Updated to include both skating and classical techniques. The book provides advice from buying and maintaining equipment to basic through advanced techniques.

Endestad A and Teaford JK: Skating for cross-country skiers, Champaign, Ill, 1987, Human Kinetics Publishers, Inc. Combines the technique and training principles of skiing and speed skating.

Flemmen A and Grosvold O: Teaching children to ski, Champaign, Ill, 1983, Human Kinetics Publishers, Inc. Provides instructions for teaching children of all ages basic skiing skills and fundamentals of cross-country and alpine skiing and ski jumping.

Gaskill S, editor: A coaches field guide to cross country skiing technique, Park City, Utah, 1982, United States Ski Coaches Association.

Gaskill S, editor: Summer and winter training for cross country ski racing, Park City, Utah, 1982, United States Ski Coaches Association.

Gillette N and Dostal J: Cross country skiing, ed 3, Seattle, Wash, 1988, The Mountaineers.

Hall M: One step ahead: an expert's guide to cross-country skiing, Tulsa, Okla, 1981, Winchester Press, Inc.

Lederer W and Wilson JP: The new, complete cross country ski book, ed 2, New York, 1983, WW Norton & Co, Inc.

NCAA men's and women's skiing rules book, Mission, Kan, 1989, National Collegiate Athletic Association Publishing Department.

Satterfield A and Bauer E: The Eddie Bauer guide to cross-country skiing, Reading, Mass, 1983, Addison-Wesley Publishing Co, Inc. Offers advice on how to choose skis, how to get in shape, and how to perform basic maneuvers and emergency first aid.

Sharkey BJ: Training for cross country ski racing: a physiological guide for coaches and athletes, Champaign, Ill, 1984, Human Kinetics Publishers, Inc. A new technical discussion of the physiological systems involved in cross-country ski racing and a systematic plan for their development. Also contains information on nutrition, monitoring overtraining, tips on plyometrics and other dry-land training techniques, and fitness tests.

Tjeda-Flores L: Back country skiing, San Francisco, 1981, Sierra Club.

Torgerson L: Good glide: the science of ski waxing, Champaign, Ill, 1985, Human Kinetics Publishers, Inc. Written mainly for cross-country skiers, this book is also valuable for alpine skiers and ski jumpers who want to know more about glide waxing and different snow and meteorological conditions.

Woodward R: The cross country ski technique book, West Point, NY, 1983, Leisure Press.

FILMS AND VIDEOTAPES

Cross country skiing, Nordicross, Performance skiing - cross country skiing advanced, Telemarking and World of cross country skiing - for beginners. "How To" Sports Videos, Box 5852, Denver, CO 80217.

Cross country ski skating. The Athletic Institute, 200 N. Castlewood Dr., North Palm Beach, FL 33408.

Skating and striding: cross country skiing and skiing cross country with Jeff Nowak. Karol Video, 22 Riverside Dr., Wayne, NJ 07470.

RESOURCE

United States Ski Association, 1726 Champa St., Denver, CO 80202.

26

Skin and Scuba Diving

Completion of this chapter should enable the reader to:

- Appreciate the development of skin and scuba diving
- Understand the need for preliminary safety precautions
- Describe features of the equipment used in skin and scuba diving
- Understand the principles of diving physics and diving medicine

The underwater world is relatively unexplored and filled with beauty beyond description. It is a world of greater depths than the highest mountain peaks and covers nearly seven tenths of the surface of the earth. It is inhabited by uncountable varieties of animal and plant life. It is a restless, dynamic, changing world possessing rhythm, design, movement, and power. Humans are inexplicably drawn to this underwater world. They must, however, proceed with care and skill. This new world can be hostile and sometimes cruel. For these reasons the following information, though brief, is explicit, definite, and important for those who venture below the water's surface. Learn these lessons well, then enjoy the underwater world with confidence and skill.

HISTORY

Exploration of the land surface and surfaces of the world's water masses dates from the beginning of human history, but exploration of the underwater world is a relatively recent adventure. Although Aristotle wrote about diving devices as early as 360 B.C., and the great historian Pliny in 77 A.D. described the use of breathing tubes for underwater activity, real opportunity for extended underwater movement and investigation did not occur until introduction of the scuba regulator in 1943 by Jacques-Yves Cousteau and Emile Gagnan of France.

The forerunners to modern methods of underwater exploration and sport are many. Early Greek and Roman strategists, in an effort to perfect the art of warfare, trained and equipped soldiers of strong swimming ability to approach enemy craft from below the water surface. They were supplied with air through a short length of

hollow reed. Soldiers of the fifteenth and sixteenth centuries were fitted with surface-breathing bags connected to the diver by means of a hose and leather hood arrangement and wore weighted shoes. These divers were restricted to the shallow depths because of their crude equipment. In his autobiography, Benjamin Franklin described his making of hand and foot fins to facilitate faster swimming. In the early 1800s, William Forder developed a metal helmet that covered half of the diver's body and was supplied with air from the surface by a hand-operated bellows. In 1837 Augustus Siebe developed a full dry diving suit with a rigid helmet. In the latter part of the 1800s the French developed a rubber diving suit and mask, supplied with air from a metal canister carried by the diver. A mechanical regulator was employed to control the flow of air. An American, C.J. Lambersten, patented a successful closed-circuit rebreathing unit in 1942. This unit was adopted by the Navy for underwater demolition teams, because with this equipment the diver's expired air did not bubble to the surface to reveal his position as he worked underwater.

Recently the design of the scuba has been refined and sophisticated, but the basic principle remains the same as the Cousteau-Gagnan design.

PRELIMINARY CONSIDERATIONS

The term "skin diving" is used to describe diving activity when the diver uses mask, snorkel, and fins and holds the breath while swimming underwater. The term "scuba" comes from self-contained underwater breathing apparatus and refers to underwater swimming when the diver adds to the basic skin diving items equipment designed to take an air supply beneath the surface. "Sport

347

diving" is commonly used to include both skin and scuba diving activities.

Prerequisites

The student who wishes to learn scuba diving should locate a scuba instructor who holds *current certification from a recognized national agency* (NASDS, NAUI, PADI, or YMCA). Qualified instruction and subsequent certification in scuba diving are mandatory for the diver who wishes to purchase compressed air from a dive shop or diving resort. In addition, the student benefits from the experience of a qualified instructor and is covered during instruction of the liability insurance carried by the instructors of national certification agencies.

Swimming test

The following test must not show only the minimum level of swimming competency but should be executed with a high level of skill and with relative ease.

1. Swim 200 yards using overarm stroke, sidestroke, and breaststroke
2. Swim 50 feet underwater without swim aids
3. Tread water for 10 minutes
4. Rest on the back for 10 minutes with little or no movement
5. Execute surface dives to 10 feet

Medical examination

In addition to being a strong swimmer, the student must be in sound medical health. The physician should carefully examine for functional or structural deficiencies in the following:

1. Cardiovascular system
2. Pulmonary system
3. Neurological system
4. Otolaryngological system
5. Gastrointestinal system
6. Metabolic and endocrinological function
7. Hematological properties
8. Orthopedic considerations
9. Behavioral health

In addition, because venous gas emboli formed during decompression may result in fetal malformations, diving should not be done during any stage of pregnancy.

SKIN DIVING
Equipment

Items essential for skin diving are the mask, snorkel, and fins. (See Fig. 26-1.) When diving in cold water, the diver should wear a neoprene-rubber wet suit or a dry suit. When a wet suit is worn, a weight belt must also be used to overcome the suit's buoyancy. Diving authorities insist that a personal float, such as an inflatable vest or belt, is absolutely essential for safe diving.

Supplementary items of equipment are the surface

Fig. 26-1. Curved snorkel, *left;* straight snorkel, *right;* silicone, hypoallergenic medium-volume, panoramic mask, *upper left;* medium-volume, multipurpose mask, *upper right;* two low-volume masks, *bottom;* open heeled, adjustable, vented fin, *left;* full-footed snorkeling fin, *center;* open heeled, adjustable, nonvented fin, *right.*

float, such as a tire tube or paddle board, knife, game and collecting bags, diver's flag, compass, depth gauge, pressure gauge, watch, and photographic equipment. Some of these items are required by law in some states.

Mask

The mask, sometimes called a faceplate, keeps water from coming in contact with the eyes and eliminates distortion, thereby enabling the diver's vision to be limited only by the light and clarity of the water. It also prevents water from being inhaled through the nose. The mask should fit the face with comfort and provide a watertight seal when the diver is submerged. The lens should be made of safety glass, not plastic, and secured in the mask by a metal or molded-plastic retaining ring with a tension screw. The adjustable strap should attach on or near the front of the mask to assure a snug watertight fit. Some models have a one-way purge valve that enables the diver to clear water from the mask without changing the swimming position. Masks with molded depressions that permit the diver to close off the nostrils by pressing with the fingers, facilitating easy clearing of the ears, are required.

Snorkel

The snorkel is a tube that is held in the diver's mouth and extends above the surface of the water. It enables a diver to swim and breathe without lifting the head from the water. Although several types are available, a J-

Fig. 26-2. Skin divers in proper underwater swimming position.

shaped semirigid rubber or plastic tube is the most advisable and popular among experienced divers. Those with ping-pong valves and rubber flutter valves are inefficient and not recommended for sport diving. A rubber or silicone mouthpiece allows the diver to maintain control of the tube and breathe with the head submerged for easy underwater viewing. The snorkel should have a soft rubber or silicone mouthpiece that is comfortable to the diver's mouth, permitting extended use without undue mouth fatigue.

Fins

Fins are mainly of two types: open heeled and full footed. Either is satisfactory, depending on the diver's preference, but an adjustable strap model is usually preferred. The purpose of the fins is to give extra power in swimming, not to increase speed. The fin should fit comfortably to allow circulation and prevent the feet from cramping, but be snug enough to be secure when going through the surf. Fins of extra large design can cause undue fatigue, particularly when used by an untrained diver. Beginning divers should use a medium-sized fin of medium flexibility.

Exposure dress

Wet suits made of cellular foam neoprene rubber and designed to fit snugly over the whole body are superior and preferred to the old dry suit model. A small amount of water enters the wet suit, is quickly warmed by the diver's body, and then serves as insulation between the body and the surrounding water. The suit increases the diver's buoyancy significantly, so weights must be worn to enable the diver to submerge and swim with ease.

Weight belt

The weight belt deserves special attention. Lead weights attached to a web belt are used to overcome buoyancy. Most important is the quick-release buckle, which must be designed to operate with one hand. When any situation that could possibly lead to an emergency occurs, the diver must be able to release the weight belt and allow it to fall away free and clear.

Accessory equipment

Information about other equipment for skin diving may be found by consulting the references at the end of the chapter. However, no one should dive without a personal flotation device (PFD), such as an inflatable vest, in addition to a surface float. A good automobile inner tube with attached line makes a practical surface float for resting. A canvas or burlap bag tied to it serves to carry the diver's equipment.

Skin diving skills

All basic swimming strokes except the breast stroke are used for diving; however, the open, enlarged flutter kick with very loose knee action is the most common source of propulsion. Many divers alternate the dolphin kick with the flutter kick to help prevent fatigue. A strong kick allows the diver freedom for the hands and arms to carry equipment, take pictures, and pick up interesting objects. When the diver is swimming, the arms are usually trailed in a comfortable position at the sides and are not specifically in use. (See Fig. 26-2.) This position allows for maximum balance and relaxation. However, when swimming in turbid, murky water with poor visibility, the diver should extend both arms forward at full length to ward off undetected obstructions. When underwater, the diver should always swim as effortlessly as possible, conserving oxygen and thereby extending the length of "down time."

Diving down

When in open water, the diver should use either the tuck or pike surface dive to submerge. If the dive must be made through kelp or other plant life or into unfamiliar water, a feet-first dive should be executed.

Hyperventilation

Some divers extend their down time by means of rapid and deep breathing with exceptionally full exhalations just before submerging. No other practice in diving is more hazardous. Hyperventilation, combined with the exertion of swimming under water and a change in the normal regulatory responses of carbon dioxide and oxygen caused by the pressure changes, can cause anoxia (lack of oxygen) and result in drowning. Instead, the diver should take two or three deep breaths and hold the final one at about two-thirds capacity to start the dive.

Clearing

When the diver submerges, the snorkel will be filled with water, but the air pressure in the diver's mouth prevents the water from entering it. Upon surfacing, the diver can blow out the water in the tube by a short forceful exhalation while keeping the face submerged.

Sometimes a small amount of water seeps into the face mask during the dive. This water should be evacuated to prevent it from being inhaled through the nose. To clear the mask, the diver should roll to one side, press the upper edge of the faceplate inward, and exhale through the nose into the mask. The water pooled in the bottom side of the mask is forced out by the air pressure. Care should be taken to release hand pressure on the mask while still blowing; otherwise water will flood into the mask through the released seal. Another method is for the diver to tilt the head back, press on the top of the mask, and exhale through the nose.

If the mask has a purge, make it the lowest point, seal the mask against the face, and exhale through the nose. (See Fig. 26-3.)

Equalizing pressure

To provide for comfort and prevent injury, it is essential that pressure inside and outside the eardrum always be equal. When the diver descends, pressure on the eustachian tube side of the drum and that developed by increasing pressure of water on the outside must be equalized. Swallowing and sliding the jaw from side to side will sometimes accomplish this. Pinching the nose while blowing gently against the closed nostrils can also equalize the pressure. However, other methods should be tried first because mucus can be forced into the middle ear with this technique. The diver must never use earplugs or place anything in the ears while diving.

Entries

Always enter the water from as close to the surface as possible. When the entry is from a point well above the surface, such as the side of a boat that is not equipped with a diving platform, the entry should be made with a giant-stride feet-first jump. When executing this entry, cover the face mask with one hand to prevent it from

Fig. 26-3. Clearing mask—head tilted to side; head tilted back.

being dislodged by the impact of the water. Keep other gear, such as cameras, well away from the body. Take a giant stride well away from the takeoff point, keeping the body erect and eyes looking forward. After settling in the water, level off and make an approach swim to the diving area. Another important rule is to breathe continuously (never hold the breath).

Ascending

When ascending, extend one hand and arm overhead, look up, and keep turning 360 degrees. This method should always be used to ensure the diver from coming up headfirst under another diver's tank, a boat, a floating object, or any obstruction that could cause injury.

Performance techniques

When beginning a dive, snorkel on the surface, pushing a tube in front with the face submerged until reaching the diving location. Swim easily and relaxed, conserving energy and strength for the dive. The dive should be planned so that both buddies know the intentions of the other. A well-planned dive is the first step toward a safe dive. Surface dives should be made steep to the bottom; then, when underwater, divers should swim slowly.

Buddy diving

Never dive alone. This and remembering to breathe continuously are the most important rules of safe diving. Diving together and staying together take practice between partners but must be done to ensure enjoyable and safe diving. You enter the water together, dive together, and leave the water together.

DIVING PHYSICS

As the diver goes beneath the water surface, he or she is aware of an increase in the surrounding pressure. This has an important effect on parts of the diver's body and the air the diver breathes.

The air mixture compressed in a scuba tank is atmospheric air, never pure oxygen, and contains the same gas percentages (78.62% nitrogen, 20.84% oxygen, 0.04% carbon dioxide, and 0.5% water) as atmospheric air. When these gases are breathed under pressure, as in scuba diving, several basic laws of physics must be carefully considered.

Boyle's law states that if temperature is constant the volume of a gas will vary inversely with the absolute pressure, while the density varies directly with the pressure. If the pressure of a gas is doubled, the volume is decreased by one half, but the density is doubled. This simply means that when a skin diver is descending, the air in the lungs is compressed and as the diver surfaces it expands. This phenomenon is important only to the skin diver diving to exceptional depths. If the scuba di-

ver, breathing air at the ambient pressure (pressure equal to the surrounding water), does not exhale and breathe normally when ascending, the volume of air taken into the lungs at depth is going to expand as the pressure of the surrounding water is lessened during the ascent. This gas expansion can cause serious medical problems and might result in a fatal injury.

Henry's law states that the quantity of gas that goes into solution in any liquid is directly proportional to the partial pressure of the gas. This means that if a quantity of liquid is capable of absorbing 1 quart of gas at 1 atmosphere of partial pressure, the same quantity of liquid would absorb 2 quarts of gas at 2 atmospheres. An understanding of gas absorption by the blood while diving is important to the diver in appreciating the need for computing a decompression dive.

Generally, we live under a constant pressure of 14.7 pounds per square inch (1.013×10^5 N/m^2), or 1 atmosphere (pressure decreases slightly as altitude increases); but when we dive beneath the surface of the ocean, we add about 0.445 pound per square inch for every foot depth. When we reach the 33-foot (12.1 m) depth, we have added another 14.7 pounds per square inch (1.013×10^5 N/m^2) and are at 2 atmospheres of absolute pressure. For each additional 33 feet (12.1 m) we add another atmosphere of pressure. The diver must understand and appreciate the effects of this pressure of water and atmospheric pressure above the water. It is this pressure that causes pain in the diver's ear during descent, drives gas into solution, and presses the face mask against the face.

Sight and hearing are dramatically affected by the water. Because of the water's refraction and absorption of light, underwater objects appear to be about one third closer than their actual distance and about one fourth larger than their actual size. Sound travels much more rapidly in water than in air. When a tank is struck with a hard object such as a knife, the noise can be easily heard for quite a distance; however, it is more difficult to determine the direction from which the sound came in water than it is in the atmosphere. Communicating by voice underwater is very unsatisfactory, so divers must develop a system of hand signals that all divers in the party understand and are able to use.

SCUBA DIVING

Several types and arrangements of self-contained underwater breathing apparatus enable the diver to take a supply of air below the surface. Scuba has been the greatest advance in the effort to explore the underwater world. Assuming a consumption rate of 0.5 cubic feet per 1 minute, such equipment extends diving time to 140 minutes on the surface, 70 minutes at 33 feet, or 35 minutes at 99 feet. Scuba also frees the diver to swim with relatively complete freedom and to roam the depths at will. Although time and depths can be extended dramatically over skin diving limits, the novice scuba diver is cautioned to limit the dive time to 90% of tank capacity and to restrict depth for his or her first 25 or 30 dives to 60 feet. For normal sport diving a limit of 100 feet should be used and the absolute limit of 130 feet is recommended. However, this should not be done without consulting U.S. Navy standard decompression tables. (One standard tank provides approximately 1 hour of diving time depending on dive depth, water temperature, and breathing pattern.) Not until well after a year of regular sport diving at the depths and times just listed should the diver move into depths approaching 100 feet. These may seem to be unduly restrictive diving limits, but it is interesting to note that many amateur and recreational divers find their most interesting and enjoyable diving in about 35 feet of water. Remaining within this depth limit enables the diver to avoid a decompression dive even though several dives may be made during a 12-hour period.

Equipment

Two general classifications are recognized: the closed-circuit, or rebreather, scuba and the open-circuit scuba. Although other equipment is sometimes used, only the open-circuit scuba is recommended for sport divers. Open-circuit scuba means that all exhaled air is exhausted into the water and none is reused. In closed-circuit scuba the breathing gas is recirculated; the carbon dioxide is absorbed by granulated chemicals and the oxygen is added to a breathing bag as needed from a high-pressure supply tank. Open-circuit scuba uses compressed atmospheric air and never pure oxygen as in closed circuit, because 100% oxygen becomes toxic when breathed under pressure greater than 29 pounds per square inch (even less for some people). This pressure is reached when diving deeper than 33 feet. The three main components of open-circuit scuba are the regulator, the tank, and the valve. (See Fig. 26-4.)

Regulator

The regulator is the heart of the scuba, as it is responsible for delivery of the diver's air at exactly the correct pressure and whenever the diver inhales. For this reason the regulator is often referred to as a *demand* regulator, because it permits air to flow into the diver's mouth each time the diver demands by the slightest inhalation. This inhalation causes a drop in the pressure on one side (dry side) of a rubber diaphragm. The water pressure on the other side (wet side) of the diaphragm is then able to push the diaphragm inward, which in turn activates a level that opens a valve and allows air to flow through the diver's air hose. When the pressure on both sides of the diaphragm again becomes equal, the valve closes and

Fig. 26-4. *Left,* Steel tank (70.2 cubic feet) equipped with a K valve, a single-hose regulator with an octopus, a 3-gauge console (pressure, depth, and compass), and a buoyancy vest with a push-button inflator. *Right,* Steel tank (80 cubic feet) with a J valve.

the air flow is shut off. This pressure balance is regained when the diver discontinues inhaling.

Modern regulators are designed with a single hose. A detailed reference for specifications should be consulted to become familiar with their operation. At present the two-stage, single-hose regulator is the most widely used because of its reliability, ease of repair, and ease of breathing with it.

Valve

The valve is located between the tank and the regulator. Basically, there are two types of tank valves: the constant reserve (J type) and the nonreserve (K type). The J valve mechanism is preset to provide air as long as tank pressure remains above 300 pounds per square inch (20.67 × 10⁵ N/m²), but below this pressure a spring-activated piston restricts the diver's air and breathing becomes difficult. This is a signal to the diver that the air supply is low and the reserve lever should be pulled to open the reserve valve and allow the last 300 pounds of air to flow freely. The diver should end the dive at this time by returning to the surface station for another tank and rest period. Never continue diving when on reserve air, and always check to make sure the reserve lever is in the up or loaded position before entering the water.

The nonreserve or K-type valve has no reserve feature and is simply an on-off valve control. Divers using this valve usually attach an air pressure gauge to their regulators to keep themselves constantly informed as to the air remaining in the tank. The K valve with a pressure gauge is the most widely used type.

Tank

Air cylinders for diving are available in many sizes and in single, double, and triple units. The size and air pressure of the tank generally determine the time a diver can remain submerged. However, breathing rate, water temperature, depth, and working rate are also important determinants of underwater time. The tank size usually recommended is the "standard 80." This means the tank contains 80 cubic feet of air when filled to 3000 pounds per square inch.

Backpack

The backpack must be fitted with quick-release buckles or safety hitches and must never be put on over the weight belt. The backpack must secure the scuba to the diver with comfort and allow freedom of movement in all positions, but it must also be designed to be "ditched" without hesitation or fumbling.

Scuba diving skills

Swimming skills used in scuba diving are fundamentally the same as those used in skin diving; however, one point of caution should be noted. No one should attempt scuba diving until well skilled and experienced in skin diving.

Entries

When entering and exiting through the surf while wearing a scuba, the diver must remember that although carrying a supply of unrestricted air, he or she is also more vulnerable to wave action in the surf and can be easily tumbled and thrown about when attempting to stand. When exiting through the surf, the diver should remain in an extended swimming position until well up on the beach before attempting to stand, then quickly turn about and shuffle backward until clear of all surge and water action.

When entering from an elevated point, boat dock, or land, the diver should use a feet-first entry but never into unknown water. The diver should grasp and protect the mask with one hand as in the skin diving entry, and with the other hand hold the weight belt buckle to prevent it from releasing accidentally.

When entering unknown water, the diver should make a feet-first drop or slide-in entry. This method also reduces the chances of frightening game from the diving area. Other methods, such as forward and backward rolls, may be used when appropriate for conditions.

Scuba drills

These drills should be practiced only with a partner and with a trained instructor observing.

Submerging and swimming without a mask. Replace and clear the mask without surfacing. (See skin diving skills for clearing.)

Mouthpiece clearing. Remove the mouthpiece underwater. Return it to the mouth, give a short sharp exhale to clear it of water, and resume breathing. Use the purge valve if available. Always take the first breath slowly after clearing the snorkel or mouthpiece of the regulator.

Buddy breathing. Two divers share one air supply. The diver with air passes the regulator mouthpiece to the buddy, who receives and clears the mouthpiece and takes two breaths before returning it. The diver with the air supply always retains control of the mouthpiece. The second diver uses the hands to help swim and keep the two divers close together. Although all divers should learn the buddy breathing system, an octopus setup on the regulator (Fig. 26-4), if used, allows the out-of-air diver to breathe through an auxiliary second stage.

Free ascent. Practice of this skill will help the diver remain calm if his or her air supply is lost. In this situation the diver looks up, starts a controlled ascent with one arm extended over the head, and exhales continuously for entire ascent. The diver's instructor, with air functioning and mask in place, must always accompany the free-ascending diver to the surface.

Buoyancy testing. Buoyancy testing is essential because the addition of scuba equipment adds several pounds of weight that tends to overcome the buoyancy of the diver. Weights should be added or subtracted to allow the diver to gradually sink after a full exhalation on the surface.

DIVING MEDICINE

Most diving disorders or medical problems in diving are classified as barotrauma, or a change in normal conditions because of changing pressure. Usually it is an injury resulting from unequal pressure between a space inside the body and the outside water pressure. The cavities of the middle ear and the sinuses are most susceptible to changing pressure, but serious problems can also develop from pressure on the breathing gas. Nitrogen narcosis, oxygen toxicity, and carbon monoxide poisoning are examples of these disorders. Some of these problems and their causes, symptoms, and treatment appear in Table 26-1.

TWELVE BASIC RULES

1. Be in top physical condition and have an annual medical examination.
2. Be comfortable in the water.
3. Secure certified training in the use of scuba from a recognized agency.
4. Use safe. time-proven equipment of reputable manufacturers.
5. Be familiar with the diving area *before* diving.
6. Know the basic laws of diving physics and physiology.

Table 26-10. DIVING DISORDERS

Disorder	Cause	Symptoms	Treatment
Drowning	Physical exhaustion; running out of air; loss of mask or mouthpiece; flooding of apparatus; entanglement	No respiration; blueness of skin	Immediate artificial respiration, preferably by mouth-to-mouth method; start at once
Air embolism	Failure to breathe normally or holding breath while ascending results in blockage of circulatory system by excessive pressure rupturing lung tissues and allowing air to enter bloodstream	Weakness; dizziness; loss of speech; paralysis of extremities; visual disturbance; staggering; bloody frothy sputum; unconsciousness; death could occur within seconds after reaching surface, if not before.	Recompress immediately to 74 pounds per square inch (165 feet); medical care; lower head to allow bubbles to go to feet rather than head
Decompression illness (bends or caisson disease)	Bubbles of nitrogen expand in bloodstream and tissues of body from inadequate decompression following exposure to pressure; nitrogen absorption depends on depth, time, and working rate; nitrogen more soluble in fatty tissues	Skin rash; itching; pain deep in joints, muscles, and bones; choking; visual disturbances; dizziness; convulsions; weakness in arms and legs; loss of hearing or speech; paralysis; unconsciousness; death	Recompress by Navy treatment tables; if caught in time, there are usually no serious aftereffects
Nitrogen narcosis	Intoxicating effect of nitrogen when breathed under pressure; no prevention except to avoid deep diving; occurs usually at about 130 feet, though reported at 30 feet	Loss of judgment and skill; feeling of intoxication; slowed mental activity; fixation of ideas; similar to alcohol intoxication	Stop work; reduce pressure; effects disappear when ascending; no aftereffects
Oxygen poisoning	Using pure oxygen below 33 feet for longer than 30 minutes; depends on carbon dioxide tension and work rate; not probable on compressed air until about 132 feet	Nausea; dizziness; headache; twitching of muscles around mouth and eyes; disturbance of vision (tunnel vision); numbness; unconsciousness	Surface; rest; medical care; never dive below 30 feet on pure oxygen; use only compressed air in tanks
Carbon monoxide (CO) poisoning	Contaminated air supply from internal combustion engines; improperly lubricated compressors; carbon monoxide combines with blood, causing internal asphyxiation; improper exhalation	Lips and mouth are bright cherry red; 10% in blood causes headache and nausea; 30% causes shortness of breath; 50% causes helplessness	Surface; artificial respiration if not breathing; oxygen; medical care; may seem to be all right on bottom but lose consciousness on ascent
Apnea	Hyperventilation and extended dives in skin diving	No warning symptoms to speak of (perhaps moment of blackness before total unconsciousness)	Fresh air; artificial respiration; do not hyperventilate excessively
Squeeze	Pressure differential over concerned area; middle ear and sinuses usually first place where pain felt; also face mask, suit, lung (thoracic) squeezes	Usually sharp pain due to stretched or damaged tissues; damage can occur without pain, however	Equalize pressure on affected areas

7. Always use a float with surface identification, usually a diver's flag.
8. Join a reputable diving club.
9. Never dive alone.
10. Practice skin diving frequently *before* scuba diving.
11. Heed all pains and strains as warning symptoms.
12. Know basic first aid.

TEACHING CONSIDERATIONS

1. Scuba diving should not be taught by anyone who does not hold current certification as an instructor by a recognized national agency. Information needed goes beyond that described in this text.
2. Scuba diving should not be taught to anyone who cannot pass the swimming test or medical examination.
3. Beginning skin diving skills can be taught in a pool. Students should be cautioned, however, that practice in the pool is not adequate for skin diving in large bodies of water.
   a. Maintain the buddy system.
   b. Familiarize students with use of equipment before diving. Practice using the equipment on the surface.
   c. Practice dives using proper ventilation techniques.
   d. Practice diving, clearing and equalizing pressure, and ascending techniques.
   e. Practice surface snorkeling, diving, clearing and equalizing pressure, swimming to a point, and ascending.

GLOSSARY

absolute pressure True pressure; gauge pressure plus 14.7 pounds.

air embolism Air bubble in the bloodstream that occurs when the diver attempts to surface while holding the breath.

anoxia Oxygen deficiency.

aqualung Tank containing compressed air.

atmospheric pressure Air pressure at sea level is 14.7 pounds per square inch (1 atmosphere). It increases at the rate of 0.444 pounds per square inch for each foot of depth in seawater.

bends Too much nitrogen in the bloodstream. It expands as the diver ascends.

Boyle's law At a fixed temperature, the volume of a given quantity of gas varies inversely with its absolute pressure.

buoyancy Upward force exerted on the immersed or floating body by a fluid.

compressor Used to fill scuba tanks with air.

decompression Release from pressure.

dry suit Waterproof rubber exposure suit used by divers.

face mask A mask so equipped with faceplates as to increase a diver's vision.

fins Devices worn on the feet to increase kicking power.

hyperoxia Too much oxygen in body tissue.

hyperventilation Respiratory activity in excess of that required to meet the body's normal requirements.

nitrogen narcosis Diving ailment resulting when the diver goes too deep and the nitrogen in the air supply begins to have a narcotic effect.

recompression Treatment of decompression sickness or air embolism by use of a recompression chamber.

regulator Device used for the adjustment and automatic control of air flow.

scuba Self-contained underwater breathing apparatus.

skin diving Diving without the use of underwater breathing apparatus.

snorkel J-shaped tube that projects above water at one end and terminates with a mouthpiece underwater.

tank Air cylinder used by divers.

tidal volume Volume of air inhaled and exhaled normally.

toxic Poisonous.

weight belt Belt of lead weights used to overcome buoyancy.

SUGGESTED READINGS

Ascher S and Shadburne W: Scuba handbook for humans, ed 2, Dubuque, Iowa, 1977, Kendall/Hunt Publishing Co.

Navy Department: United States Navy diving manual (current edition), Washington, DC, U.S. Government Printing Office.

PADI open water diver manual, 1988, Santa Anna, Calif, Professional Association of Dive Instructors.

Strauss R: Diving medicine, New York, 1976, Grune & Straton, Inc.

PERIODICAL

Skin diver magazine, 8490 Sunset Blvd., Los Angeles, CA 90069.

VIDEOTAPES

Ghost fleet, How to use dive tables, Learn snorkeling, and *Scuba refresher course.* These four programs available from "How-To" Sports Videos, Box 5852, Denver, CO 80217.

27

Soccer

Completion of this chapter should enable the reader to:

- Appreciate the history and values of soccer, the most widely played and watched game in the world
- Describe the correct field dimensions and understand the rules of the game
- Demonstrate the fundamental skills of soccer, including kicking, passing, dribbling, trapping, heading, and tackling
- Understand the system of play
- Construct drills enabling beginning players to learn and practice appropriate skills
- Demonstrate a command of soccer terminology

HISTORY

The true origin of soccer is difficult to determine. One theory traces the game back to 600 B.C. in Japan, where a game called *kemari* was believed to have been played. Another historian reports that soccer originated in Greece where it was called *harpaston*. The Romans obtained the game from the Greeks and, in turn, passed it on to England.

The early games were rugged and irregular. Two towns 3 to 5 miles apart sometimes engaged in a game, with no rules enforced. Occasionally a river had to be crossed. The marketplace of the town was the goal.

In 1848 the advocates of football met in Cambridge to draw up a list of rules that became known as the Cambridge Rules. This meeting was unsatisfactory, because some schools favored carrying the ball as permitted in rugby. The result was a meeting in 1863 of the group that favored the kicking game. This group voted to confine play entirely to kicking and later became known as the London Football Association. To distinguish between the two types of football, they called one "rugby" and the other "association." Later this was shortened to "assoc," and finally to its present designation, soccer.

Soccer has been played in American colleges since 1830. In 1868 Princeton challenged Rutgers, and the first intercollegiate soccer game was played in New Brunswick, New Jersey. Rutgers won, but Princeton asked for a return game and won.

Soccer became a national sport in 1913 with the organization of the United States Football (Soccer) Association. In 1919 soccer was introduced at Bryn Mawr, a women's college. It was not until 1927, however that the National Association for Girls' and Womens' Sports published the first soccer rules for women.

In terms of participation and spectator interest, soccer is the world's most popular sport. It has been estimated that more than 100 million people play the game. The World Cup in soccer, which is played every 4 years, attracts a world-wide audience and is rivaled in attendance only by the Olympic games.

Soccer first appeared in the Olympics in 1900 in Paris as a competition among club teams rather than national teams. The British teams dominated early Olympic competitions. The United States first entered the Olympics in soccer in 1924 (won by Uruguay). South American teams dominated the sport until 1952 when Eastern European teams began to emerge, with Hungary winning the Olympic gold. Teams from Hungary, Poland, Czechoslovakia, and East Germany still remain competitive in international soccer. Brazil and some of the Arabian Gulf countries are becoming competitive at this level.

In fact, the 1984 Olympic silver medal went to Brazil as they lost 2-0 to the French team. It was the first medal for France in Olympic soccer competition.

The 1986 World Cup was captured by Argentina. Although in the past decade there has been a tremendous increase in the number of youths in the United States playing soccer, United States teams are not yet competitive at the international level. From the 1924 through 1988 Olympics, the United States has won only two of 16 matches (with three ties) and has been outscored 59-11.

VALUES

Soccer should be taught in every basic physical education program from the elementary grades up through high school and college if for no other reason than to teach boys and girls the skillful use of their legs. Soccer is a running game and thus it helps develop cardiovascular endurance. Little equipment is required, making soccer one of the least expensive athletic activities.

No particular body size or physical build is necessary. Training for and playing soccer develop leg strength, body coordination, speed, and muscular endurance. The game can be played equally well by both sexes.

GENERAL DESCRIPTION

The game is played by two teams of 11 players, each of whom attempts to advance a ball toward the opponents' goal with the object of scoring (getting the ball between the goalposts and under the crossbar) by propelling the ball with the head, feet, or body. Handling the ball with the hands is prohibited for all players with the exception of the goalkeeper.

THE FIELD

Soccer is played on a rectangular field not more than 120 yards (109.73 m) nor less than 110 yards (100.58 m) in length. The width should not be more than 80 yards (73.15 m) nor less than 65 yards (59.44 m). (See Fig. 27-1.)

The side field boundary lines are called touchlines.

Corner flags not less than 5 feet (1.52 m) high are placed at each corner. At each corner of the field a quadrant with a 1-yard (30.4 cm) radius is drawn. Corner kicks are taken from this area.

In front of each goal a goal area is drawn, 6 yards (5.49 m) along the goal line from each goalpost and 6 yards into the field of play. A larger area is also marked out in front of each goal 18 yards (16.46 m) along the goal line from each goalpost and 18 yards into the field. This is called the penalty area. A penalty kick mark 2 feet (61 cm) long is made 12 yards (10.97 m) out from the goal line directly in front of the goal. An arc is drawn (radius 10 yards [9.14 m]) using the middle of the penalty kick mark as the center. In addition the field has a centerline (or halfway line) drawn across it and a center circle with a 10-yard (9.14 m) radius.

The goals

The goals are placed centrally on each goal line and consist of two upright posts 8 yards (7.3 m) apart joined by a horizontal crossbar, the bottom edge of which is 8 feet (2.43 m) from the ground. Goalposts are usually made of 4 × 4 inch pieces of wood or from tubular metal. Nets should be attached to the back of each goal and should extend behind the goals so as not to interfere with the goalkeeper.

Coaching box

The coaching box is marked parallel to the touchline. It is at least 5 feet (1.53 m) from the touchline and extends 20 yards (18.29 m) in both directions from the halfway line (see Fig. 27-1). Coaches and players must remain inside the coaching box, except for players warming up in preparation to enter the field.

RULES
Clothing

Shoes are the most important part of a player's equipment. Regulation shoes are high-laced and have cleats to protect the player against slipping.

Cleats and studs cannot be less than one-half inch (1.26 cm) in diameter or width and cannot project from the sole or heel more than three-fourths inch (1.91 cm). Aluminum, leather, rubber, nylon, or plastic cleats are legal if they conform to width and length specifications.

Shin guards are worn inside knee-length socks. A gym suit completes the necessary equipment.

Officials

One referee and two linesmen control the game, enforce penalties, and decide disputed goals.

All linesmen are under the direct supervision of the game referee. The linesmen also indicate when the ball is out of bounds and which side is entitled to the corner kick, goal kick, or throw-in, and assist the referees in controlling the game.

One scorekeeper and one timekeeper are also required.

Duration of game

Two equal periods of 45 minutes are played, with 10 minutes between halves. Teams change ends at the half. The score stands as official with the following exception: time is extended to permit a penalty kick to be taken. The clock is stopped when a goal is scored. It is started on the kickoff. In case of a tie two extra 15-minute periods are played.

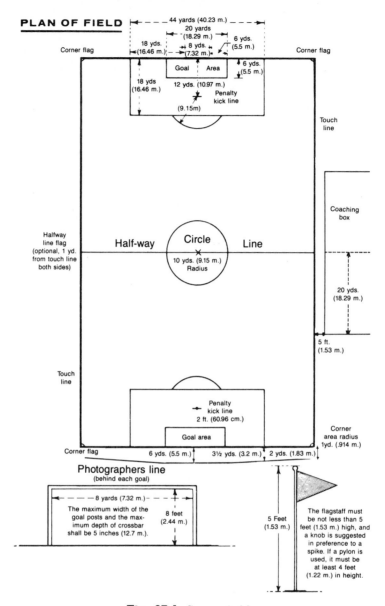

Fig. 27-1. Soccer field.

Players

The game is played by two teams of 11 players each. Generally the lineup includes one goalkeeper, two to four defensive players (backs), one to three midfield players (halves), and two to five strikes (forwards).

Lineups sometimes used consist of one goalkeeper, three backs, three halves, and four forwards, or one goalkeeper, four backs, two halves, and four forwards.

Playing privileges of goalkeeper

A goalkeeper within the penalty area has the following playing privileges:

1. The goalkeeper may throw, drop-kick, punt, pick up, or bounce the ball once.

2. The goalkeeper when in possession of the ball may not carry it more than four steps before releasing it into play.

3. The referee will remove without caution any player who intentionally charges the goalkeeper.

4. The goalkeeper must not be interfered with.

5. The goalkeeper outside the penalty area has no more privileges than any other player.

Playing privileges of other players

1. A player may dribble, shoulder, or head the ball.

2. A player in possession of the ball may place himself between his opponent and the ball.

3. A player may stop the ball by trapping it under his

feet, between his feet, or between the front of his legs and the ground.

4. A player may kick the ball while it is trapped by an opponent, provided he does not commit a foul.
5. A player may stop the ball by blocking it with any part of his body except the hands or arms.

Play

At the beginning of the game a coin is tossed to decide the kickoff and which goal each team is to defend. The ball is put in play by a place kick (a kick at the ball while it is stationary on the ground) taken from the center of the field by the center forward at the start of the game, at the start of the half, and after each goal. After a goal is scored, the team scored against kicks the ball. Opposing players must stand at least 10 yards (9.14 m) away at the time of the kick. The ball is in play after it has rolled forward at least 27 inches (67.5 cm). A goal cannot be scored directly from a kickoff. The kicker cannot play the ball again until it has been played or touched by another player.

Ends must be changed after each half, and the team that received the kickoff in the first half kicks off.

When resuming the game after a temporary suspension of play, except on a free kick, the referee drops the ball at the place where it was when play was suspended, except in the penalty area. If suspended in the penalty area, the ball is dropped in the nearest point outside of the penalty area. A goal may be scored directly from the dropped ball.

Ball out of bounds (restarts)

The boundary lines are considered part of the field of play. Thus a ball is not out of bounds until the whole ball completely crosses the goal line or touchlines.

A ball that goes out of bounds over a touchline is thrown in by a player of the team opposite to that of the player last touching the ball. The *throw-in* is made with both hands and must be from behind and over the head. The ball may be thrown in any direction. Both feet must be in contact with the ground at the moment the ball is released and each foot must be either on or outside the touchline.

When a ball goes out of bounds over the goal line without resulting in a goal:

1. If last touched by an offensive player the game is restarted by a *goal kick* taken by a defender. The ball may be placed in that half of the goal area nearest where the ball went out. The ball must be kicked to clear the penalty area. A goal cannot be scored directly from a goal kick. Opponents must be outside the penalty area.
2. If last touched by a defensive player, the ball is put back into play by a *corner kick* taken at the corner

nearest where the ball went out. The kick is taken from within the quarter circle by a member of the attacking team. A goal may be scored directly from a corner kick. Members of the opposing team must be at least 10 yards (9.14 m) away until the ball travels the distance of its circumference (27 inches; 67.5 cm). The kicker cannot play the ball a second time until it has been touched by another player.

Throw-in

When a ball passes completely over the touchline it must be brought back into play by an opposing player by a two-hand overhead throw-in. (See ball out of bounds, above.) If the throw-in is improper, it must be taken over by a player on the opposing team.

Goal kick

When the ball is sent over the goal line, except that part between the posts, by the attacking team, it is kicked back into play by the defenders.

Corner kick

When the defending team plays the ball behind its own goal line outside of the goalpost area, the opposing team takes a corner kick. Opposing players must not be within 10 yards (9.14 m) of the kicker. A goal may be scored directly from the corner kick.

Offside

A player is offside if he is nearer his opponent's goal line than the ball at the moment the ball is played unless:

1. He is in his own half of the field.
2. There are two of his opponents nearer to their own goal line than he is.
3. The ball last touched an opponent or was last played by him.
4. He receives the ball direct from a goal kick, corner kick, or a throw-in, or when it is dropped by the referee.
5. An indirect free kick is given to the opponents if the offside player has interfered with the play or with the opponent. Otherwise, an offside player is not punished.

Note: A player not ahead of the ball when it is last played cannot be offside.

Direct free kick

A goal may be scored directly from a direct free kick. Opposing players may not be within 10 yards (9.14 m) of the ball. Offenses for which a direct free kick is given include:

1. Handling the ball
2. Kicking, tripping, striking, charging from behind, jumping at, holding, or pushing an opponent

3. Goalkeeper handling the ball outside the penalty area
4. Spitting at an opponent

Note: If either of the first two infringements occurs in the penalty area and is committed by a defending player, a penalty kick is awarded.

Indirect free kick

A goal may not be scored directly from an indirect free kick. Opposing players may not be within 10 yards (9.14 m) of the ball. The following are the offenses for which an indirect free kick is awarded:

1. Charging illegally (not violent or dangerous)
2. Attempting to play the ball when it is in possession of the goalkeeper
3. Touching the ball a second time before another player touches it after a free kick, throw-in, corner kick, or penalty kick
4. Goalkeeper carrying the ball more than four steps within penalty area without releasing it

5. Goalkeeper delay in getting rid of the ball
6. Illegal coaching after warning by referee
7. Unsporting behavior
8. Dangerous play
9. Offside
10. Obstruction

Penalty kick

A penalty kick is taken from the penalty kick mark. All players with the exception of the kicker and the goalkeeper must be outside the penalty area until the ball is kicked. The goalkeeper must stand on his goal line without moving his feet until the ball is kicked. The ball remains in play if it rebounds from the goalposts or goalkeeper. The kicker may not play the rebound until the ball has touched another player.

Scoring

A goal counts as 1 point. The ball must have been legally propelled between the goalposts and under the crossbar (Fig. 27-2).

Fig. 27-2. Official soccer signals.

FUNDAMENTAL SKILLS AND TECHNIQUES

Soccer is a physical game requiring endurance, speed, and skill. On the field of play, complex situations may arise that require quick thinking, speed, and maneuvering, which are not always covered by rules or techniques. This makes the game interesting and challenging.

The modern game of soccer is primarily a kicking game. The players should therefore become proficient in the techniques required to control the ball with the feet, including kicking, passing, dribbling, and trapping. Other skills to be mastered include heading and tackling. When these fundamentals are learned, attention can be focused on field position, team play, and strategy.

Kicking

The ball can be kicked with any part of either foot, and game conditions call for various kicks to be made. The instep and inside of the foot are most often used, but the sole, toe, outside of the foot, and even the heel occasionally are required. Beginning soccer players should concentrate on becoming proficient with both feet and avoid the natural desire to favor the dominant leg.

1. Volleying is contacting the ball before it hits the ground, generally with the instep, although the knee or thigh may be used. If a long pass or a shot at the goal is called for, a powerful leg swing, contacting the ball near the ground with the instep, is most effective. With the long pass the force should be directed more vertically than for the shot at the goal. Contacting the ball as it hits the ground is sometimes called a half volley. The direction and force of a half volley are determined by the body position at the instant of contact.
2. Driving the ball with the instep is a common kicking technique in soccer (Fig. 27-3). At contact the knee should be directly above the ball. If the knee is behind the ball, the ball will be lifted into the air; if the knee is too far forward, the ball will be driven into the ground. Planting the body weight firmly on the nonkicking foot, watching the foot contact the ball, and extending the kicking leg through the point of contact will help increase accuracy of the drive.

Passing

Most short passes in soccer are made with the inside or outside of the foot. Much practice is required to be able to flick the ball over to a teammate while dribbling it down the field. On occasion it is desirable to pass the ball over an opponent. To accomplish a relatively long lifted pass, it is necessary to plant the nonkicking leg firmly, swing the kicking leg forcefully, contact the ball below its center, and follow through. To loft the ball quickly (chip shot) but for a relatively short distance, the player should plant the nonkicking leg close to the ball

Fig. 27-3. Kicking.

with the body weight ahead of the ball. Then stab the toe of the kicking leg under the ball, making contact very close to the ground, and the ball will be vertically scooped into the air. Little or no follow-through is possible because of the body position.

Trapping

Trapping is a means of bringing the ball under control with any part of the body except the arms. Trapping a ball in flight is accomplished by keeping the heel of the shoe on the ground and bringing the sole of the shoe down on the ball the instant it strikes the ground. A ball may be stopped by stepping on it lightly if it is rolling slowly, getting it between the foot and leg and the ground if it is moving fast, or clamping it between the legs and the ground if it is a high bounder or fly ball. It may be trapped between the knees or in the midsection of the body by jackknifing over it (Fig. 27-4).

Dribbling

Dribbling the ball down field is generally accomplished through a series of short controlled pushes made with the inside and outside of the foot (Fig. 27-5). While learning to dribble it is important to watch the ball, but as the player becomes increasingly skilled the eyes must

Fig. 27-4. Trapping.

Fig. 27-5. Dribbling.

be used more to assess the positions of teammates and opponents, and dribbling must become increasingly a kinesthetic skill. Once this level is reached the soccer player must add various moves to become a proficient dribbler. For example, opponents can be kept off balance by varying the speed of the dribble. Slowing down and then accelerating in a random pattern disrupts an opponent's timing. Changing direction, sometimes quickly and sometimes subtly, can accomplish the same disruption. Other techniques include faking a pass to a teammate or pretending to move the ball in one direction and then going another.

Fig. 27-6. Heading.

Heading

Heading is a skill unique to soccer and must be learned with care to prevent injury. A playground ball or Nerf soccer ball should be used until proper techniques and confidence are obtained. The important skills to practice include:

1. Getting the body into position as early as possible before heading the ball
2. Keeping the eyes on the ball as long as possible
3. Striking the ball with the front of the forehead
4. Using the whole body by arching the back just before contact and then flexing at the hip and neck so that the forehead is moving forward as fast as possible at the instant of contact (Fig. 27-6).

The ball is sometimes headed sideways with the same type of action except the ball is played off the side of the head.

Tackling

Tackling may be accomplished by several methods. The object in tackling is to get possession of the ball from an opponent. This method is accomplished by the use of the legs alone. A side tackle is made with the inside of the foot and inside of the leg. This method involves playing the ball instead of the player. The split tackle is made by dropping to one knee and kicking the ball forward with the toe of the other foot.

Playing the player instead of the ball involves contact with the opponent passing the ball, which is accomplished by charging the offensive player in possession of the ball and hitting the opponent with the shoulder below the shoulder. The idea is to force the opponent from the ball.

Goalkeeping

The goalkeeper (usually called keeper) has privileges not afforded the other players. The keeper may use his or her arms and hands to control the ball; take up to four steps while in possession of the ball; dropkick, throw, or punt the ball; and is free from interference by opponents when in possession of the ball. The keeper does not have these privileges when outside the penalty area.

Playing positions

The forwards are the offensive line. The center forward is usually the shooter of goals and the pivot of the forward line. The inner forwards play slightly behind the center, roving back and forth to cooperate with the outside forwards, who usually attempt to kick the ball across the field for the center or inner forwards to shoot. The forwards must be good feeders to the forward scoring zone and must therefore be good passers. The halves back up the forward line, feed passes to the forwards, and cover the opposing outside forwards and center forward.

The halves are the backbone of the soccer team. They must learn to dribble, tackle, and pass accurately and cleverly.

The backs assist the goalkeeper in defending the goal and seldom advance very far in front of the penalty zone. They usually take the goal kicks. The backs must learn to kick well and accurately. The goalkeeper rarely leaves the zone immediately in front of the goalposts. The goalkeeper is permitted to use the hands or arms and to catch, throw, hit, or kick the ball, or to use the body to prevent goals from being scored. When the goalkeeper catches the ball, it is usually kicked or thrown out to the wings.

PRACTICE TECHNIQUES

Practice dribbling around the field, in and out of obstacles. Practice with two or more players dribbling down the field. Form a small circle or have partners face each other to practice heading the ball. Learn to tackle with the feet only. Study and learn to play your position properly. In passing, time the pass, make it accurate, and look for openings and uncovered teammates to whom to pass. Develop teamwork. Be alert.

In dribbling, keep as close to the ball as possible. Strike the ball below its center with the foot. Do not dribble too much or come too close to an opponent. Keep your eyes on the ball. Be deceptive. Learn the technique of trapping the ball.

Offense

A successful soccer team is one in which the 11 individual players coordinate their talents. Many hours of practice are necessary to learn the offensive plays that can be employed and to learn to anticipate teammate reactions to various situations. Space does not permit description of offensive formations; general principles are mentioned here for the beginning soccer player.

1. Play your position and move with the flow even when you do not have the ball.
2. Move in an unpredictable pattern. Do not always play next to the touchline or run down the middle.
3. Keep the forwards at various depths on the field. If the forwards operate as a straight line across the field, the number of passing opportunities is limited.
4. Position the defensive players over the entire width and depth of the field. It is tempting to always focus on going toward the goal area, but dribbling down the side may free up the middle by causing the defense to come out, thereby opening a possible shot by a teammate.
5. Always work to penetrate the opponent's defense. Look for weaknesses.

Defense

A combination of one-on-one and zone defense is used by most soccer teams. Often an excellent defensive player is "assigned" to mark the other team's best offensive player while the rest of the defenders maintain a specific field area and are responsible for opponents who enter it. The key to good defense is teamwork and playing in depth rather than straight line formation.

Key elements on defense are (1) slowing down the attacking player so teammates can make the transition from attack to defense, (2) supporting and providing cover for defenders, (3) restricting the amount of space that can be attacked, (4) concentrating on defense and funneling back to the penalty area to prevent goals, and (5) keeping as much pressure on the offense as possible.

SYSTEMS OF PLAY

Systems of play are not solutions to poor teamwork or problems with individual team members. The system should be adapted to the level of the players' skills. All players should understand their role in a system of play and each player should link with other players on the team to make a good system work. Some of the most popular systems are illustrated in Fig. 27-7.

TEACHING CONSIDERATIONS

1. Use smaller balls for younger students.
2. Introduce passing, dribbling, and receiving skills as the basic skills of soccer. Develop these alone and in combination. Players should be able to move at a fairly high speed with the ball alone and in combination with another or others before they learn the more difficult skills of heading, trapping, or tackling. Have them practice individually or with a partner to provide more practice opportunities. Add changes in speed and direction as well as passing to the right and left. Be firm about not using hands from the beginning of practice.
3. Offensive and defensive play should begin with small groups three-on-one or three-on-two, giving the advantage to the offense until the skills are developed sufficiently to maintain possession. Teach tackling in two-on-one situations at this level. Offensive concepts of opening up space for passes, passing ahead, and combining the dribble and pass effectively should be taught until they are used with consistency.
4. Shooting can be introduced as part of three-on-two or three-on-one combinations. Basic defensive positions should be taught using these combinations. Emphasize cutting off the offense's passing and shooting opportunities.
5. Gradually add offensive and defensive players. For unskilled players numbers on teams should be kept small (six or eight on a team) and space adjusted accordingly until players can handle the complicated relationships between players and can deal with the force requirements necessary to play a large field effectively.
6. Add special skills of heading, throw-in, and penalty and corner kicks only after playing with more basic skills and rules is somewhat continuous.

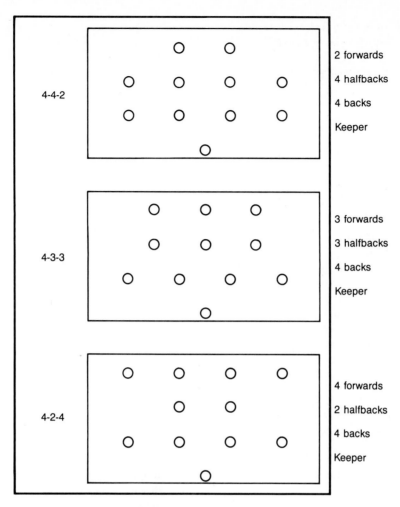

Fig. 27-7. Popular systems of play.

GLOSSARY

attacking team Team that has possession of the ball.

blocking Stopping the motion of the ball with some part of the body.

carrying An infringement of the rules when the goalkeeper takes more than four steps while holding the ball.

center-back The defender who plays in the middle of the defense.

chip To lift the ball into the air with a quick instep kick causing the ball to back spin.

clear To send the ball by foot or head a good distance.

cover To make, guard, or provide support for teammates.

cross To kick the ball from the wings (outside) toward the goal or a player in the penalty area.

defending team The team that is trying to get possession of the ball.

direct free kick A free kick from which a goal may be scored directly.

dribbling A succession of forward kicks in which the player keeps the ball under control.

drop ball Ball held waist high and dropped by an official. Used to put the ball in play at certain times.

drop kick A ball that is dropped on the ground and kicked just as it bounces.

feint A deceptive move (fake) with or without the ball.

holding Impeding the progress of a player by placing the hand or extended arm in contact with the player.

indirect free kick A free kick from which a goal cannot be scored.

mark To stay close to an opponent for defensive purposes (mark-a-person).

own goal The goal a team is defending.

passing Moving the ball from one player to another.

place kick A kick made while the ball is stationary on the ground.

punt A ball kicked by the goalkeeper within the team's penalty area.

restart The starting of play whenever the ball is out of play or the game is stopped.

striker An attacking player in the center of the forward line.

square pass A pass played to either side of a player.

through pass A pass that goes between and past defenders.

throw-in To put the ball in play from the side line by a two-hand overhead method.

trapping To stop the progress of the ball. Done with the foot, between both feet, or between the legs or legs and the ground.

volley Meeting the ball in the air with some part of the body and directing it to a teammate.

SUGGESTED READINGS

Athletic Institute: Youth league soccer: coaching and playing, North Palm Beach, Fla, 1988, The Athletic Institute. Explores techniques and discipline of coaching and playing.

Brown EW: Youth soccer: a complete handbook, Carmel, Ind, 1990, Benchmark Press, Inc. Written for volunteer coaches, the book provides detailed descriptions of how soccer should be taught to children of all ages.

Clues A and David J: Soccer for players and coaches, Englewood Cliffs, NJ, 1980, Prentice-Hall, Inc.

Ford G and Kane J: Go for goal, Rockleigh, NJ, 1984, Allyn & Bacon, Inc. Contains more than 200 drills for every age level, which are designed to teach the rules of the game, maintain fitness, and encourage enthusiasm. Each drill begins by specifying the required number of players, appropriate ages, playing area, and duration. Also includes instructions for constructing and running preseason training programs.

Hopper CA and Davis MS: Coaching soccer effectively, Champaign, Ill, 1987, Human Kinetics Publishers, Inc. Designed for coaching beginning players, the book provides direction on how to teach soccer skills and playing strategy and features 50 practice activities.

Hughes C: The football association coaching book of soccer-tactics and skills, London, 1980, British Broadcasting Corporation and Queen Anne Press.

Kovalakides N: Soccer officials manual, West Point, NY, 1983, Leisure Press. Presents the step-by-step instructions and guidelines for effective soccer officiating.

Luxbacker J: Fun games for soccer training, Champaign, Ill, 1987, Human Kinetics Publishers, Inc. Details enjoyable games to develop fitness, skills, and tactical awareness in players at all levels.

Luxbacker J: Soccer: winning techniques, Dubuque, Iowa, 1986, Eddie Bowers Publishing Co. Inc. Contains over 80 photos and diagrams illustrating basic concepts.

Mullins C: Parent's guide to youth soccer, West Point, NY, 1983, Leisure Press. Contains a wealth of information about every aspect of youth soccer. Written to help parents enjoy soccer as much as their children.

Nelson R: Soccer, Dubuque, Iowa, 1986, WMC Brown Group. Presents information on skill development, conditioning exercises, practice formations, team strategies, hints for learning, equipment, rules for the game, and a section on goalkeeping skills.

Official NCAA soccer guide, New York, 1985, National Collegiate Athletic Association.

Official soccer guide, Washington, DC, 1984, American Alliance for Health, Physical Education, and Recreation, National Association for Girls' and Women's Sports.

Reeves JA and Simon JM: Coaches' collection of soccer drills, West Point, NY, 1981, Leisure Press. Contains a collection of more than 100 drills designed to improve all basic skills.

Simon JM and Reeves JA: The soccer games book, Champaign, Ill, 1982, Human Kinetics Publishers, Inc. Presents instructions and diagrams of games that can aid in teaching and coaching soccer.

Thompson W: Teaching soccer, Edina, Minn, 1980, Burgess Publishing Co.

VIDEOTAPES

Forty soccer videotapes covering all aspects of the game. "How To" Sports Videos, Box 5852, Denver, CO 80217.

Soccer series: *Basic Individual Skills; Offensive and Defensive Maneuvering* and *Goal Keeping.* The Athletic Institute, 300 Castlewood Dr., North Palm Beach, FL 33408.

Soccer series: *Juggling, Dribbling and Passing, Shooting, Goal Keeping.* NCAA instructional video tapes. Karol Video, 22 Riverside Dr., Wayne, NJ 07470.

Soccer by Messing S, Klivecka R, and Mulroy T: *The Winning Kick, Championship Ball Skills, The Art of Goalkeeping,* and *Coach to Win.* The Athletic Institute, 300 Castlewood Dr., North Palm Beach, FL 33408.

28

Softball

Completion of this chapter should enable the reader to:

- Appreciate the development of softball and the popularity of its many variations
- Know the basic rules of the game and some of their modifications
- Demonstrate the basic softball skills of throwing, catching, batting, pitching, and baserunning
- Execute effective offensive and defensive softball strategy
- Modify the game of softball to meet local conditions and needs
- Teach softball skills and strategies to a group of students

HISTORY AND GENERAL DESCRIPTION

The YMCA perhaps did more than any other organization to inaugurate softball by transferring the game of baseball from the outdoors to the indoors. This took place about 1900. Softball is an adaptation of baseball. Because of limited indoor space and the hardness of the ball, the YMCA directors originally made the ball softer, the bat smaller, and the baselines and pitching distances shorter. The pitcher throws the ball with an underhand motion.

Several years later the Playground Association of America, now known as the National Recreation and Parks Association, needed such a game that could be adapted to small outdoor spaces and could be played by all ages, especially by young boys and girls. It took on different names at different times, such as playground ball, kitten ball, recreation ball, and ladies' ball, but in 1933 softball was adopted as the official name by the Amateur Softball Association. That year a national tournament was held at the World's Fair in Chicago. At the same time this organization set up and standardized rules that are the basis for rules today. In the years after 1929, when thousands were unemployed, the game was a great source of recreation at community centers.

Before World War II, public interest in softball grew so much that teams were organized into leagues all over the country, and it was estimated that well over 5 million people engaged in this popular American game. Because

of its great appeal to all ages, and because little equipment is needed and any ordinary playground is adequate, this game has become among the most popular of all activities at playgrounds and is now played by over 35 million Americans. The game has even been modified for the blind by use of a ball that emits a beeping sound.

Modifications of the basic rules have produced many types of games and leagues, such as fast pitch and slow pitch; leagues for men's teams, women's teams, and coed teams; games using the regulation-sized softball (12 inch [30.48 cm]) and games using a much larger ball; rules forbidding the use of gloves; and many other interesting variations. Presented here are the abridged rules and techniques of fast-pitch softball followed by a common set of rules for slow pitch. As mentioned, many variations are enjoyed in different parts of the country.

EQUIPMENT AND FIELD

The bat should be round and made of hardwood or aluminum, no more than 34 inches (86.36 cm) long, 2¼ inches (5.72 cm) in diameter at its largest part, and weigh no more than 38 ounces (1.07 kg).

The ball should be a smooth-seamed, leather-covered sphere containing yarn and kapok, measuring no less than 11⅞ inches (30.16 cm) and no more than 12⅛ inches (30.8 cm) in circumference (although some women's

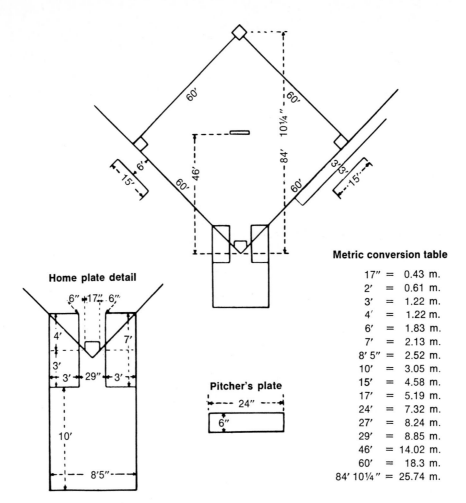

Metric conversion table

17"	=	0.43 m.
2'	=	0.61 m.
3'	=	1.22 m.
4'	=	1.22 m.
6'	=	1.83 m.
7'	=	2.13 m.
8' 5"	=	2.52 m.
10'	=	3.05 m.
15'	=	4.58 m.
17'	=	5.19 m.
24'	=	7.32 m.
27'	=	8.24 m.
29'	=	8.85 m.
46'	=	14.02 m.
60'	=	18.3 m.
84' 10¼"	=	25.74 m.

Home plate detail

Pitcher's plate

Fig. 28-1. Softball playing field for men. Pitching distance for women's fast pitch is 40 feet (12.2 m) and bases are 65 feet (19.83 m) apart for men's and co-ed slow pitch. Official distances from home plate to the fence are 225 feet (68.63 m) and 200 feet (61.0 m) for men's and women's fast pitch, respectively. In slow pitch it is 275 feet (83.88 m) for men and 250 feet (76.25 m) for women.

leagues now use an 11-inch [27.94 cm] ball) and weighing from 6¼ to 7 ounces (177.19 to 198.45 gm).

The home plate should be made of solid rubber or other suitable material. (See Fig. 28-1, *inset.*) The distance to the pitcher's box is 40 feet (12.2 m) for women and 46 feet (14.02 m) for men for fast pitch. For both men's and women's slow pitch the distance from home plate to the pitcher's place is 46 feet (14.02 m).

Gloves may be worn by any player, but mitts are limited to first basemen and catchers. The pitcher's glove may not be white or grey and must be a solid color. Other players may use multicolored gloves.

A mask, throat guard, and chest guard must be worn by catchers in fast pitch and are recommended in slow pitch. Spikes or any other type of sharp projections on the shoes are usually prohibited except in higher levels of competition.

All players on a team must wear identical (e.g., color,

trim, style) uniforms, including caps. Helmets may, and under some local rules must, be worn by catchers, batters, and baserunners.

Playing field dimensions are given in Fig. 28-1.

ABRIDGED RULES (FAST PITCH)
Teams, players, and substitutes

A team shall consist of nine players, whose positions shall be designated as pitcher, catcher, first baseman, second baseman, third baseman, shortstop, left fielder, center fielder, and right fielder. Ten players are allowed if a designated batter is used. Except for the pitcher (who must be positioned as defined in the pitching rules), the catcher (who must be within the lines of the catcher's position), and the designated hitter, players in the field may be stationed at any points on fair ground.

A substitute may take the place of a player whose name is in the team's batting order. Any starting player (except the designated hitter) may be withdrawn and reentered one time as long as the player remains in the same position in the batting order. A player other than a starting player may not reenter the game after being removed. The designated hitter may bat for any player provided it is made known before the start of the game. The designated hitter must always occupy the same position in the batting order, cannot enter the game on defense, may be substituted for by a player who has not yet been in the game, but may not reenter the game once replaced.

The game

1. A regulation game consists of seven innings, unless the team second at bat scores more runs in the six innings than the team first at bat has scored in seven innings.
2. It is a regulation game if the team last at bat in the seventh inning scores the winning run before the third player is out.
3. It is a regulation game if it is called by the umpire because of darkness, rain, or other cause, provided five or more innings have been played by each side or the team second at bat has scored more runs at the end of its fourth inning or in any part of its fifth than the team first at bat has scored in five complete innings.
4. When a game is called in any inning after the fifth, the score is what it was at the time the game was called if the team second at bat has more runs than the first team at bat. Or, if the team second at bat has fewer runs than the team first at bat when the game is called, the score is that of the last inning completed by both sides.

Pitching

1. Preliminary to pitching, the pitcher must come to a full stop for at least 1 but not more than 10 seconds, facing the batter with the ball held in both hands in front of the body and with both feet on the ground and in contact with the pitcher's plate.
2. The pitcher is not considered in pitching position unless the catcher is in position to receive the pitch.
3. In the act of delivering the ball to the batter, the pitcher may not take more than one step, which must be forward and toward the batter. The step must be taken simultaneously with the delivery of the ball to the batter.
4. A legal delivery is defined as a ball delivered to the batter underhand and with follow-through of the hand and wrist past the straight line of the body before the ball is released. The pitcher may use any windup desired, provided no motion to pitch is made without immediately delivering the ball, no rocker action is made, there is no stop in or reversal of the forward

motion, no more than one revolution of the arm is made in the windmill motion, and the windup is not continued after the forward step is taken as the ball is released.
5. At no time during the progress of the game may the pitcher use tape or other substance on the pitching hand or fingers or on the ball. Powdered resin may be used to dry the hands.

"No pitch" is declared whenever the pitcher pitches during a suspension of play or when a quick return of the ball is attempted before the batter has taken position or when the batter is off-balance as the result of a previous pitch.

Illegal pitches

An illegal pitch, entitling the base runners to advance one base, is called by the umpire as follows, and in each of the cases cited a ball is also called in favor of the batter:

1. Any delivery of the ball to the batter without the pitcher's previously taking position as defined in the pitching rules
2. Taking more than one step before releasing the ball
3. Final delivery of the ball to the batter with the hand above the hip and the wrist of the pitching arm farther from the body than the elbow as described in point 4 of the pitching rules
4. Failure to follow through with the hand and wrist past the straight line of the body as described in point 4 of the pitching rules
5. Rolling the ball along the ground or dropping the ball while the pitcher is in pitching position
6. Making any motion to pitch without immediately delivering the ball to the batter
7. Delivery of the ball to the batter when the catcher is outside the lines of the catcher's position
8. Continuing the windup after taking the step described in point 3 of the pitching rules
9. Taking a pitching position on or near the pitcher's plate without possessing the ball

In each of these cases the ball is considered dead and not in play until again put in play at the pitcher's box. If, however, the batter strikes at and hits into fair territory any of the illegal pitches just mentioned, there is no penalty for such illegal pitch; the ball remains in play, and the base runners may run bases or be put out as though the ball had been legally pitched.

Foul tip

A foul tip is a ball that is batted by the batter while standing in the lines of the batter's position and that goes sharply and directly to the hands of the catcher and is legally caught. A foul tip caught is a strike and the ball remains in play. A foul hit ball that rises higher than the batter's head is not a foul tip under this rule.

1   2   3

4   5   6

Fig. 28-2. Overhand full-arm throw.

Out

An out is declared as follows:

1. The batter makes a foul hit other than a foul tip as just defined and the ball is caught by a fielder before touching the ground, provided it is not caught in the fielder's hat, cap, protector, pocket, or other part of the uniform or does not strike some other object before being caught.
2. The ball is batted illegally.
3. A bunt is fouled after the second strike.
4. The batter attempts to hinder the catcher from fielding or throwing the ball by stepping outside the lines of the batter's position, or in any way obstructs or interferes with that player; the exception to this rule is that if a base runner attempting to steal is put out, the batter is not out.
5. Immediately after three strikes, whether there are no outs, one out, a runner on first base, runners on first and second bases, runners on first, second, and third bases, or runners on first and third bases.
6. The third strike is swung at and the ball does not touch any part of the batter's person.
7. Before two players are out, while first and second, or first, second, and third bases are occupied, the batter hits a fair fly ball that is handled or, in the opinion of the umpire, could have been caught by an infielder with reasonable effort.
8. The batter steps from one batter's box to the other while the pitcher is in position ready to pitch.

FUNDAMENTAL SKILLS AND TECHNIQUES

The basic skills of softball, like those of any other sports activity, must be learned and practiced often. The techniques necessary for good performance are given here.

Throwing

Although throwing is a natural activity, some skills in throwing the ball in softball differ from the natural way of throwing.

Overhand full-arm throw

In the overhand full-arm throw (see Fig. 28-2), the ball is grasped with two fingers on the top (a small hand may require three fingers on top) and the thumb underneath. The hand is swung down, ending well behind the shoulder below shoulder height. The left side of the body is turned in the direction of the throw. The left foot is in front, the toe touching the ground. The weight of the body starts on the right foot and is brought forward with the forward motion of the arm (see Fig. 28-3). While the elbow is leading the arm movement, the wrist is cocked to increase the range of motion of external rotation. The ball is released with a downward snap of the wrist, which increases the speed the ball receives from the arm motion.

Short-arm throw

In the short-arm throw (see Fig. 28-4) the hand is brought into position above the right shoulder, elbow pointed

Fig. 28-3. Stance for overhand full-arm throw.

Fig. 28-4. Short-arm throw.

Fig. 28-5. Underhand windmill pitch.

backward and down. The ball is propelled forward by elbow extension and a sharp wrist snap. The right shoulder, arm, and wrist do most of the work, inasmuch as it is impossible to get very much body weight behind the throw. The catcher uses this throw.

Underhand windmill pitch

The windmill pitch starts below the shoulder with the arm fully extended. The hand is turned with the palm down at the start and then is brought forward with a pendulum swing of the arm to the front. The elbow is slightly flexed throughout. The follow-through brings the hand, with the palm up, about chest high. (See Fig. 28-5.)

From this underhand throw several kinds of pitches can be made: drop, curve, change-up, rise, and knuckle. Speed, balance, and relaxation are necessary in pitching.

Catching

Fielding flies

There are two methods for fielding flies: (1) with the thumbs together and the fingertips up (see Fig. 28-6) and (2) with the little fingers together and letting the ball drop into the nested hands (basket catch).

The advantage of the first method is that the throw can be made faster; the advantage of the second is that the catch is more sure. The ball is visible, and if it spins it is more likely to remain in the hands. The fielder

should be at the spot at which the ball is descending to get set for it.

If the ball is hit deep over the head, turn and run (never run backward) to the spot where the ball is expected to drop, glancing over the shoulder while running.

When the ball drops into the hands, let them give slightly with the impact. Shield the eyes from the sun with the gloved hand. Do not hold the ball after catching it. Be careful that revolving balls do not spin out of the glove.

Back up other fielders when possible.

Fielding ground balls

A bouncing ground ball should be fielded at the height of its bounce. For quick play, advance to meet the ball. Time the speed of advance with the speed and bounce of the ball. The success of this play lies with the fielder's judgment and timing with the moving ball.

If the bouncing ball is above the waist, catch it with the fingertips turned up. The waist-high ball can be caught either way, depending on whether the ball is dropping or coming up.

To maintain balance when running in for a ball, run with the legs and feet apart. Meet the ball out in front of the body with the left foot slightly advanced. Keep the eyes on the ball until it is in the hands.

A ground ball may take unexpected hops to the right or left, and these should be fielded with the feet apart, the knees slightly bent, and the body crouched. In fielding fast and hard-hit balls, it is proper to close the feet or block balls by dropping on one knee (see Fig. 28-7).

Fig. 28-6. Fielding flies.

Fig. 28-7. Fielding hard-hit ground balls.

Fig. 28-8. Batting grip and stance.

Batting

Good batting ability and clever baserunning are the keys to successful offensive softball. It is therefore essential that beginners practice and observe the following skill fundamentals. (Because this is written for beginners, it is assumed that the player throws and bats with the same side of the body; therefore, switch hitting is not described.)

1. Select a bat that feels comfortable in weight, grip, and balance.
2. Use a grip that best controls the bat.
3. Assume a natural and comfortable position at the plate, with the feet well apart and with the nondominant side of the body toward the pitcher. The elbows should be well away from the body to allow for freedom in swinging the bat. The nondominant elbow is on a level with the hand and slightly below the shoulder. (See Fig. 28-8.)
4. Start the swing with the hips by rotating them forward. Take a step forward and swing the bat parallel to the ground, and follow through.
5. If the ball is coming into the strike area, keep the bat poised at shoulder height, ready to swing. Never rest the bat on the shoulder while waiting for the pitch.
6. Keep the eyes on the ball from the moment the pitcher starts the windup until the ball reaches the plate.
7. Observe pitches carefully, and swing only at the good pitches in the strike zone.
8. Swing forward on a horizontal plane. Do not swing too hard.
9. Run quickly to first base as soon as the ball is hit.
10. A quick eye, muscle control, strong forearms, and quick wrist action are the keys to good hitting.

Power and choke hitters

A power hitter stands farther back of the plate, with the feet well apart and parallel to the side of the box. The power hitter grips the bat near the small end, the dominant hand above the other hand.

A choke hitter stands closer to the plate when first learning. Later a position can be taken with the feet together and a stride taken forward when the hitter swings. The trunk should be slightly inclined toward home plate. The choke hitter grips the bat several inches from the small end of the bat.

Bunting

Bunting is just as effective an offensive weapon in softball as in baseball.

The arms and elbows are held well out from the body; the nondominant hand holds the bat and the other hand acts as a steering hand. The bat recoils slightly when it meets the ball.

There are two kinds of bunts: (1) the sacrifice, and, (2) the drag (or push) bunt, pushing the ball between the pitcher and first base. As the pitcher lets go of the ball, run the dominant hand about halfway down the bat. Hold the bat loosely to deaden the bunted ball and at an angle to lay the ball down either the first or third base line.

Catching

The catcher should be in a half-squat position to move quickly and reach out to the right or left or to jump up and move forward for a throw. Practice a quick snap throw. (See Fig. 28-4.) Work as close under the bat as possible. Keep the eyes on the ball.

Pitching

Assume the pitching position with both feet on the rubber plate. Throw an underhand pitch to the batter (see Fig. 28-5.) Preliminary movements may be taken by the pitcher as long as the final delivery to the batter is underhand and parallel to the body.

The pitcher should develop a wrist snap and a finger flip with a complete follow-through. A pitcher should be able to throw a slow ball for a change of pace.

Practice putting spin on the ball to create a curve that will cause the batter to hit a pop-up. (See Figs. 28-9 through 28-12 for various pitches.)

To prevent a successful bunt, pitch high in the strike zone.

Fig. 28-9. In-curve and out-curve releases.

Fig. 28-10. Drop grip and drop release.

Fig. 28-11. Grip and release for fast ball in-curve and out-curve.

Fig. 28-12. Grip release for rise.

Fig. 28-13. Hook slide.

Baserunning

In softball the runner must hold the base until the ball leaves the pitcher's hand. Readiness to start for the next base requires assuming a stance facing the next base with one foot on the side of the base ready to sprint for the next base the instant the pitcher releases the ball. If the ball is hit to the right side of the field, a runner leaving first base should watch the third-base coach to determine whether to stop at second base or try for third base. The base coach has a better view of the entire field of play and can make a better judgment than the runner. Run straight at the base until you are 10 to 15 feet (3 to 4.5 m) from it. If it appears you might be able to go on to the next base, move out to the right and circle in order to push off and run straight toward the next base. If it appears the base you are heading for will be as far as you can advance, continue on the straight line and slide if necessary.

A runner on occasion must be able to slide correctly. An excellent slide is the hook slide. (See Fig. 28-13.) This is performed by sliding on the thigh and hip and hooking the bag with the toe of the foot or sliding past the base and tagging it with the hand, depending on the position of the defensive player. The runner slides to the right of the bag, making it difficult to be tagged. The slide should be started soon enough in front of the bag so that the runner can slide to the bag and not plunge onto it.

Playing bases
First base

The first baseman should cover the base in a way that does not cause interference with the runner but allows balls from all directions to be played. The first baseman should be able to handle high and low throws. It is correct to push the hands toward the ball in receiving balls bouncing close to the feet and come up in the same movement. The first baseman should play the base on the inside when receiving throws from the infield. If no runner is on the base, the first baseman normally stands about 6 feet (1.83 m) off the base and a few feet toward home plate. In softball this distance from home to first base is relatively short. This makes the bunt an effective offensive weapon. The first baseman must always be ready to charge forward in case of a bunt.

Second base

The second baseman must have the ability and agility to run to the left or right for ground balls. The best position is a little nearer second base than first and back of the baseline. It is important to tag runners quickly, when possible, while maintaining a good grip on the ball in the glove. The second baseman should back up other infielders when possible.

Third base

The third baseman should play about 6 feet (1.8 m) inside the diamond from the base and in front of the baseline toward home plate.

In tagging a runner, the infielder must be alert at all times, should the runner attempt to get around the baseman with a hook slide. Worry the runner, but do not leave an opening in your position. The third baseman should not compete with outfielders for flies and should not run in until the batter is seen to go into a bunting motion by sliding the hand down the bat.

The outfielders

The outfielders must have running speed, must be able to accurately judge the flight of a fly ball, and must be able to throw accurately and hard. A throw must be long, with smooth execution of a full arm swing rather than a wrist snap. Outfielders should study hitters to know where they hit. In playing a ground ball, the outfielder should place the body in front of the ball to block it. An outfielder should watch every pitch and be ready to move in any direction at each pitch.

Team offensive strategy

Players should sacrifice individual record performances for team success. A batter should sacrifice getting on first to move a runner to second so that a possible hit can score the runner on second.

The hit-and-run play is good offensive team strategy. The squeeze play is an offensive weapon that may be used with a runner on third. When the game is in the late stages and there are fewer than two outs, it is good strategy to bunt in an attempt to score the runner. The runner starts for home on the pitch and the batter bunts.

The double steal is another excellent offensive play used to catch the defensive team off balance. This play can be attempted with runners on first and second but most often is attempted with runners on first and third, the idea being to score the runner on third if the catcher throws the ball to second base in an effort to retire the runner coming from first base.

Almost any offensive or defensive strategy that is effective in baseball is also good for softball.

Defensive strategy

Good defense involves meeting any crucial situation that may arise. For example, to break up a double steal, the shortstop or second baseman runs over behind the pitcher and in front of second base, receives the throw from the catcher, and throws it back to the catcher.

The infield can draw in for a play at the plate. A double play is always an excellent defense if it can be executed.

Always get the runner nearest the plate if possible. Good team defense requires that infielders help and cooperate with the other infielders.

An intentional pass or a pitch out to make a play at second or first can be good defensive strategy in the proper situation.

SLOW-PITCH SOFTBALL

Slow-pitch softball is becoming popular in high school, college, and city recreation programs. In fact, there are probably more participants now in slow-pitch than in fast-pitch softball.

Playing field

The playing field is basically the same as that for fast-pitch softball. Differences between slow-pitch and fast-pitch field dimensions are noted in Fig. 28-1.

Equipment

Equipment specifications for the bat and ball are identical to fast pitch although many local leagues have begun using 14-inch (35.58 cm) and 16-inch (40.66 cm) softballs. Although not required and seldom used, catcher's masks are recommended. Spikes are prohibited.

Players

A team consists of 10 players: pitcher, catcher, first baseman, second baseman, third baseman, shortstop, left fielder, center fielder, right fielder, and short fielder.

A starting player may reenter the game in the same position after being substituted for. A substitute may not reenter the game. A starting player may reenter once.

The game

A regulation game consists of seven innings. In case of a tie game more innings are played. A forfeited game is awarded to the team that is ready to play.

Pitching regulations

The pitching arm must come to rest holding the ball in front of the body, with one or both feet in contact with the pitcher's plate. This position cannot be held longer than 10 seconds. The pivot foot must remain in contact with the pitcher's plate until the ball leaves the hand. It is not necessary to take a step but if taken, it must be toward the batter and must be within the area bounded by the edges of the pitcher's plate. The pitch must be released at moderate speed (umpire's judgment). The hand must be below the hip. The ball must be delivered with a perceptible arc of at least 6 feet (1.83 m) from the time it leaves the pitcher's hand until it reaches home plate. The pitched ball may not be higher than 12 feet (3.66 m) from the ground during its flight to home plate.

In slow pitch, a batter may be walked by notifying the home plate umpire.

Batting

The batter shall take position within the lines of the batter's box. The batter has 1 minute to take the place after the umpire calls "Play," or the batter is *out*. All batters must bat in their batting order, or an out is called on the person at bat. However, if this error is discovered in time, an adjustment can be made.

A *strike* is called (1) for each legally pitched ball, (2) for each pitched ball missed by the batter, (3) for each foul tip—the batter is out if the tip is on the third strike, (4) for each pitched ball struck at and missed that touches any part of the batter, and (5) for hitting a batter positioned in the strike zone.

A *ball* is called for a pitched ball that does not enter the strike zone. The strike zone is over any part of home plate between the highest shoulder and the knees of the batter when in a natural batting stance.

A *fair ball* is one that (1) lands in fair territory—between first and third bases, (2) lands on any one of the bases with the exception of home base, or (3) falls on fair ground beyond first or third base.

The batter is out immediately when an *infield fly* is hit with base runners on first and second, or first, second, and third with less than two outs. This is called the infield-fly rule.

A *foul ball* is a legally batted ball that (1) settles on foul ground outside the first or third baseline or behind home plate or (2) bounds past first or third base on foul ground or outside of bases. *If a foul fly is caught, the batter is out.* The batter is out if there are two strikes and the next batted ball is a foul tip. A foul tip is a batted ball that goes from the bat, not higher than the batter's head, to the catcher's hands and is legally caught. A legally caught foul tip on the third strike is a dead ball. Baserunners may not advance.

The batter is out under the following circumstances:

1. On three strikes
2. When the ball is bunted or chopped downward
3. When a fly ball is legally caught
4. On an infield fly rule
5. When the batter interferes with the catcher

Intentional interference puts a runner out plus the batter who hit the ball.

Baserunning

1. All bases must be touched in order.
2. If two base runners are on the same base, the last runner on can be tagged out.
3. The batter becomes a base runner when four balls are called.
4. When a fair ball bounds or rolls into a stand or over, under, or through a fence or other obstruction marking the boundaries of the playing field, the ball is dead and all base runners are awarded two bases from the time of the pitch.
5. There is no base stealing. Only after the pitched ball has passed home plate and has been batted can the base runner leave a base.
6. The base runner is out if running outside the 3-foot (0.91 m) line. But the base runner is not out if it is necessary to run around a fielder taking the ball.
7. The base runner is out if he or she passes another base runner.
8. The base runner is out if off base and struck by a fair ball before it passes a fielder.

TEACHING CONSIDERATIONS

1. Establish a reasonable level of consistency in fielding and throwing skills before using these skills in game or gamelike conditions.
   a. Consider beginning with a softer ball.
   b. Start with fielding slow balls thrown directly to the fielder. Increase the speed gradually and cause the fielder to move to either side, forward, and back to receive the ball.
   c. Include throws of different distances and directions from the fielder. Acknowledge appropriate throwing patterns for different situations.
   d. Include fielding of batted balls as soon as learners are ready for balls coming with more force.
2. The basics of the game can be taught without batting a pitched ball (by replacing batting with a throw or batting off a tee) and with fewer numbers of players. There are many lead-up and modified games that permit more practice and have much higher levels of participation than the official game. Teachers should consider using these. Baserunning and defensive strategies are best taught without batting to permit more offensive play opportunities.
3. Practice pitching as a separate skill. Give all students

opportunities to play all positions. Do not permit weak players to be "left out in the field."

4. Teach batting in small groups including a pitcher, a catcher, and several fielders. Practicing against a high fence or wall helps where other facilities are not available.

5. For less skilled players, slow down the pitching or give the batter the option of throwing the ball or batting off the tee.

6. Start with only basic rules. Add more technical rules as learners are ready for them.

7. Give students the responsibility for leadership (being captain or in charge of equipment) but teach them what is expected of these people, and maintain those expectations.

GLOSSARY

appeal play A play on which an umpire cannot make a decision until requested by a player. The request must be made before the next play.

assist Throwing or deflecting, by a player, of a thrown or batted ball by which a possible out could be made.

base on balls Reaching first base after four balls are called.

base path An imaginary line 3 feet (0.91 m) to either side of a direct line between bases.

battery The pitcher and catcher.

batting average Number of hits made by a batter divided by the times at bat.

batting order The official listing of the sequence of the players to bat.

beanball A ball thrown at the batter's head.

bunt A ball softly touched by the bat and landing within the infield.

designated hitter A player who does not take the field defensively but bats in the batting order in the place of another player.

double play A play in which two players are legally put out on the same hit ball.

error A play that fails to cause the out of a runner or that allows advancement of a runner.

fair territory The part of the playing field within or including the first- and third-base foul lines from home base to the bottom of the extreme playing field fence and perpendicularly upward.

foul tip A ball that goes directly from the bat to the catcher's glove.

infield That portion of the field within the baselines.

infield-fly rule The batter shall be declared out when hitting an infield fly with runners on first and second or first, second, and third with fewer than two outs.

inning That portion of a game in which a team plays both offense and defense, starting with the first team at bat.

passed ball Failure of the catcher to hold a pitched ball and the runner advances. An error is charged against the catcher if the third strike is dropped and the runner reaches first base.

pivot foot The foot that the pitcher must keep in constant contact with the pitcher's plate until the delivery of the ball.

play "Play ball" means to resume play or to begin the game.

sacrifice bunt A bunt for the purpose of advancing a runner.

sacrifice fly A fly ball hit to the outfield, allowing a runner to score after tagging up when the ball is caught.

stolen base A player on base advances to the next base without the ball being hit.

strike zone The area between the batter's knees and armpits.

switch hitter A batter capable of batting either right-handed or left-handed.

Texas leaguer A looping ball hit between the infield and outfield.

wild pitch A ball thrown in such a way that the catcher cannot catch it.

SUGGESTED READINGS

Craig S and Johnson K: The softball handbook, Champaign, Ill, 1985. Human Kinetics Publishers, Inc. Contains tips and techniques for developing softball techniques.

Drysdale SJ and Harris KS: Complete handbook of winning softball, Rockleigh, NJ, 1984, Allyn & Bacon, Inc. Covers teaching fundamental skills such as throwing, catching, and backing-up. Describes how to develop winning team strategies and how to consider the catcher and pitcher as a unit, and offers tips on bunting, run-down, pick-offs, and coaching.

Elliot J: Youth softball: a complete handbook, Carmel, Ind, 1990, Benchmark Press, Inc. Contains information on fundamental skills, safety, equipment, facilities, legal liability, conditioning, coaching, nutrition, injuries, and motivation.

Houseworth SD and Rivkin FV: Coaching softball effectively, Champaign, Ill, 1985, Human Kinetics Publishers, Inc. Contains guidelines for teaching softball skills, daily practice plans for three age groups, and information on common errors to watch for. Other features include history, glossary, rules, and methods of preparing players for competition.

Johnson CP and Wright M: The woman's softball book, Champaign, Ill, 1984, Human Kinetics Publishers, Inc. Details women's fast-pitch softball and offers over 40 drills for developing basic skills.

Kneer ME and McCord CL: Softball: slow and fast pitch, Dubuque, Iowa, 1987, Wm C Brown Group. Covers equipment, rules, and techniques for both fast- and slow-pitch softball.

Meyer RG: The complete softball book: the loonies' guide to playing and enjoying the game, Champaign, Ill, 1984, Human Kinetics Publishers, Inc. Includes material on developing fundamental skills and the physical and psychological steps to an improved performance.

Official softball guide, Reston, Va, 1989, American Alliance for Health, Physical Education, Recreation, and Dance.

Potter DL and Brockmeyer G: Softball: steps to success, Champaign, Ill, 1989, Human Kinetics Publishers, Inc. In 25 chapters the authors identify the keys to correct technique, describe common errors, provide practice drills, and suggest performance goals for softball skills.

Reach J, Schwartz B, and Van Wyk K: Softball everyone, Winston-Salem, NC, 1989, Hunter Textbooks, Inc. Coverage of both slow- and fast-pitch softball. Includes history, equipment, terminology, scoring, rules, and building skills. Individual and team offensive and defensive skills are presented.

Stockton B: Coaching baseball: skills and drills, Champaign, Ill, 1984, Human Kinetics Publishers, Inc. Contains more than 100 drills and includes diagrams, stick figures, and charts covering fundamentals of hitting, defensive play, baserunning, coaching, drill systems, and strategies.

Whiddon NS and Hall LT: Teaching softball, Minneapolis, 1980, Burgess Publishing Co.

VIDEOTAPES

Five individual videotapes and one series of seven videotapes available from Cambridge Physical Education and Health, P.O. Box 2153, Charleston, WV 25328-2153.

Fast-pitch series (five videotapes: *Hitting and bunting, Offensive strategies, Pitching mechanics, Pitcher development,* and *Team defense*) available along with four others from "How To" Sports Videos, Box 5852, Denver, CO 80217.

Pitching and *Hitting.* Karol Video, 22 Riverside Dr., Wayne, NJ 07470.

Softball hitting and a series of three videotapes (*Basic skills in softball, Better hitting and baserunning,* and *Better pitching and defense*). The Athletic Institute, 200 N. Castlewood Dr., North Palm Beach, FL 33408.

29

Speedball

Completion of this chapter should enable the reader to:

- Appreciate the wide variety of skills that can be developed in this game, which is a combination of basketball, touch football, and soccer
- Understand scoring procedures and rules for men's and women's versions of the game
- Demonstrate the many physical skills involved in speedball
- Modify the game to fit specific circumstances
- Instruct a group of students in the fundamentals of speedball
- Be familiar with the terminology

HISTORY

Before 1920 the main team sports used for fall outdoor participation in physical education classes and intramural programs were touch football and soccer. Many recreation directors, physical education teachers, and coaches felt the need for a vigorous outdoor game through which participants could develop many basic skills. After much experimentation, Elmer D. Mitchell of the University of Michigan developed the rules for speedball, combining many of the fundamental elements and skills found in basketball, touch football, and soccer. Because speedball is designed to permit all players on a team to participate in all phases of the game, including catching, throwing, and kicking, it developed rapidly and is now widely used in recreation and physical education classes and in intramural programs throughout the United States.

Speedball gradually became popular with men and women. However, because basketball and soccer rules for women differed from those for men, in 1933 the National Section of Women's Athletics of the American Association for Health, Physical Education, and Recreation revised and adapted speedball rules for girls and women. Rules for girls' and women's speedball are published periodically.

As rules for men's and women's basketball and soccer become increasingly similar, and with the passage of legislation mandating coeducational physical education classes, two sets of speedball rules will be unnecessary. In the meantime, we suggest that recreation leaders, physical educators, or coaches select the rules, field dimensions, and player position names that best fit their needs.

GENERAL DESCRIPTION

Speedball is played by two teams. Although 11 players constitute a regulation team, the game can be played with fewer members. A variety of techniques are used in speedball, including kicking and dribbling the ball with the feet as in soccer, catching and throwing the ball as in basketball, and punting and passing the ball as in football. Because speedball combines the elements of basketball, soccer, and touch football, generally the soccer rules apply when the ball is on the ground, basketball rules apply to aerial or fly balls, and football rules usually apply in the forward passing of the ball and in scoring. The playing positions for men and women are listed in Table 29-1 as well as in Figs. 29-1 and 29-2.

The object of the game is for the team in possession of the ball to advance the ball down the field toward the opponent's goal line and attempt to score. The opponents of the team in possession of the ball try to intercept and obtain possession of the ball to move it toward the opposite goal line in an attempt to score.

Table 29-1. PLAYING POSITIONS OF MEN AND WOMEN

Women	Men
Left wing	Left end
Left inner	Left forward
Center	Center
Right inner	Right forward
Right wing	Right end
Left halfback	Left halfback
Center halfback	Fullback
Right halfback	Right halfback
Left fullback	Left guard
Right fullback	Right guard
Goalkeeper	Goalkeeper

FIELD AND EQUIPMENT

Although fields of varying sizes can be used for speedball, the one most commonly used by men is the size of a football field. Figs 29-1 and 29-2 show the dimensions of speedball fields for men and women. A middle line divides the playing area in half. Two restraining lines run parallel to the middle or halfway line. There is a penalty area at each end of the field that extends the width of the field. The end-zone penalty area is 10 yards (9.14 m) for men and 5 yards (4.57 m) for women. The ball used for speedball is slightly larger than a soccer ball. Although the regulation ball is recommended for use, many schools prefer to use a soccer ball. No special equipment other than the ball and the playing field is required.

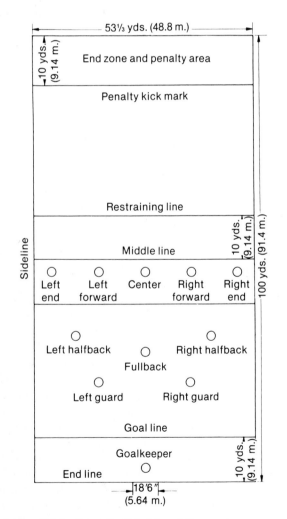

Fig. 29-1. Speedball field and lineup for men.

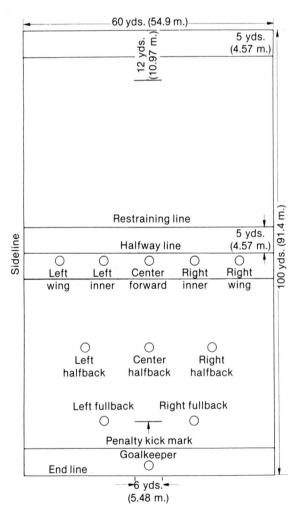

Fig. 29-2. Speedball field and lineup for women.

SCORING

Points may be scored as follows.

Field goal. A field goal is scored when a ball that has been kicked or legally played with any part of the body passes between the goalposts and under the crossbar. A field goal counts 3 points in men's rules and 2 points in women's rules.

Drop kick. A drop kick is made when the ball passes over the crossbar after having been drop-kicked from the field of play outside the penalty area. A drop kick counts 2 points for men and 3 points for women.

Touchdown. A touchdown is scored when an offensive player passes the ball to a teammate who catches it behind the opponent's goal line. A touchdown counts 1 point for men and 2 points for women.

Penalty kick. A penalty kick is scored when the player awarded the try kicks the ball between the goalposts and under the crossbar. A penalty kick counts 1 point for men and 1 point for women.

End goal. The end goal applies to men's rules only. An end goal is scored when an offensive player who is in the end zone legally causes the ball to pass over the endline but not between the goalposts. An end goal counts 1 point.

The values of different types of scoring are given in Table 29-2.

FUNDAMENTAL REGULATIONS
Officials

The officials for a game of speedball consist of two umpires, two timekeepers, and two scorers. The umpires have final authority in all decisions pertaining to the conduct of the game. Two linesmen may assist.

Duration of game

A men's regulation speedball game consists of four 12-minute quarters with a 10-minute rest period between halves and a 2-minute interval betwen quarters. Each team is allowed three time-outs during a game. Each additional time-out taken by a team constitutes a technical foul.

The women's game is made up of four quarters of 8 minutes each with a 10-minute interval between halves and 2-minute intervals after the first and third quarters. Each team is allowed three time-outs during a game. Each additional time-out taken by a team constitutes a team foul.

Beginning the game

The game and each quarter are started by having one team kick off (place kick) into its opponent's territory from the center of the field. The members of the kicking team line up on the middle or halfway line. They remain

Table 29-2. VALUES OF DIFFERENT TYPES OF SCORING

	Points	
	Men's rules	Women's rules
Field goal	3	2
Drop kick	2	3
Touchdown	1	2
Penalty kick	1	1
End goal	1	

behind the ball until it is kicked. The opponents of the kicking team must remain behind their restraining line until the ball is kicked. In men's rules the kickoff must travel 10 yards (9.14 m) or be touched by a member of the receiving team before the kicking team can touch it. In women's rules the kickoff must travel the length of the circumference of the ball and may be lifted by the foot to a teammate. It may not be touched by the kicker until another player has touched it. Goals are changed at halftime. After a score the team that did not score kicks off.

Playing the game

When the ball is in play, it is referred to as an aerial or fly ball or a ground ball.

Aerial or fly ball

A ball has been kicked into the air is referred to as a fly ball in the men's rules and an aerial ball in the women's rules. A fly ball that has been caught may be passed from one player to another as in basketball or moved by a forward pass as in football. It can continue to be played in this manner until it again touches the ground, becoming a ground ball. A player catching an aerial or fly ball is allowed to take one step in making a pass if the ball is caught while the player is standing still, or two steps if the player caught the ball while running.

Ground ball

A ball that is in contact with the ground is called a ground ball, whether it is stationary, rolling, or bouncing. The ball remains a ground ball, even though it may bounce into the air, until it is lifted into the air by a direct kick. A ground ball can be kicked, headed, or played with any part of the body except the hands and arms.

Dribbling the ball

A player may dribble a ground ball with the feet using a succession of short kicks. A player may use one overhead dribble; that is, after catching the ball, the player may toss it into the air and catch it again. The player may toss it in any direction and run to catch it before it strikes the ground. Any number of steps may be taken before catching the ball after tossing it. Only one overhead dribble is permitted before passing to another player. A touchdown cannot be scored by an overhead dribble.

Goalkeeper

The main work of the goalkeeper is to keep the ball from going through the goal. The goalkeeper has no privileges or restrictions but is governed by the same rules as other players.

Illegal play

Although defensive play is allowed in speedball, blocking and tackling as in football are illegal. A player must attempt to secure the ball legally and without undue body contact or roughness.

In women's rules, striking the ball from the hands of a player is considered a foul, but in men's rules a player may legally take the ball from an opponent.

Tie ball

A tie ball is called when two opposing players catch the ball simultaneously, hold the ball without gaining possession, or commit a double foul or when the officials are in doubt as to which side last touched the ball before it went out of bounds. In case of a tie ball, the official puts the ball into play by a jump ball as in basketball. All players must remain at least 5 yards (4.57 m) from the spot where the ball is being put into play as a jump ball until it is touched by one of the jumpers. Following a jump ball, the ball may be played as a fly or aerial ball. A score may not result from a jump ball that is caught in the end zone, even though the ball is still in play. A jump ball at the center of the field is used to begin play after a double foul or at the beginning of an overtime period in men's rules. In women's rules the jump ball is used at the spot of the foul in the case of a double foul. If the ball drops to the ground after the jump, either jumper can kick it.

Out of bounds

When a player causes the ball to go out of bounds over the sidelines, it is put into play with a pass by a player of the opposing team. In returning the ball to the field of play, the player can use either an underhand or overhand pass and can use one or both hands. In the case of a double foul over the sideline, a jump ball is used 5 yards (4.57 m) in from where the foul was committed. When a player causes the ball to go over the end line without scoring, the opponents put the ball into play by a pass or a kick.

Penalty kick

A place kick is used in making a penalty kick in the men's game, while a drop kick is used in the women's game. A penalty kick is awarded as the result of a foul. In men's play the kick is made from the 10-yard (9.14 m) line; in women's play the kick is made from the 12-yard (10.97 m) line. In the men's game the defensive players must line up on the end line until the kick is made. In women's play the defensive players may be behind the goal or on the field so long as no one is within 5 yards (4.57 m) of the kicker.

Free kick

The free kick is part of the women's game and is awarded in the following cases:

1. For an individual or personal foul committed on the field outside the penalty area
2. For a personal foul behind the goal line committed by the attacking team

When a free kick is awarded, the ball is placed at the spot where the foul was committed. The ball may be kicked in any direction and must travel at least the full circumference of the ball. No opposing player may approach within 5 yards (4.57 m) of the kicker. The ball must be kicked, but it may be turned into an aerial ball.

MEN'S RULES
Violations

The following infractions of rules are considered violations:
1. Traveling with the ball
2. Touching a ground ball with the hands or arms
3. Dribbling overhead more than once
4. Kicking or kneeing a fly ball before catching it
5. Causing the ball to go out of bounds
6. Interfering with a kickoff or jump ball
7. Illegally interfering with a penalty kick
8. Illegally interfering with a player returning the ball from out of bounds

Violation penalties

The penalty for a violation committed on the field of play outside of the end zone is that the opponents are awarded the ball out of bounds for a throw-in. If a violation is committed within the penalty area, one penalty kick is given the opponents. If the penalty kick is missed, the ball continues in play.

Technical fouls

The following infractions are considered technical fouls:
1. Illegal substitutions
2. Unsportsmanlike conduct
3. Unnecessary delay of the game
4. Taking more than three time-outs

5. Having more than 11 players on the playing field at one time

Technical foul penalty

A penalty kick is awarded for a technical foul committed outside the penalty area. Any member of the team may make the penalty kick. If the penalty kick is not successful, the ball is dead and a touchback is awarded the opponents.

Personal fouls

Personal fouls include the following infractions:
1. Pushing, holding, kicking, tripping, charging, or blocking an opponent
2. Unnecessary roughness

Personal foul penalties

If a personal foul is committed by a player within his penalty area, the offended team is given two penalty kicks. If the second kick is missed, the ball remains in play. If a player commits a personal foul outside his penalty area, the opponents are given one penalty kick. If the penalty kick is not successful, a touchback is declared.

WOMEN'S RULES
Individual fouls

The following infractions are individual fouls:
1. Kicking, tripping, holding, hacking, or blocking an opponent
2. Charging, pushing, or obstructing an opponent
3. Tagging and repeated touching of an opponent with head, elbow, or body
4. Entering the game illegally
5. Delaying the game
6. Traveling with the ball
7. Touching a ground ball with the hands or arms
8. Juggling the ball more than once
9. Holding the ball more than 3 seconds
10. Attempting a drop kick within the penalty area
11. Drop kicking for a goal or attempting a forward pass for a touchdown within the penalty area
12. Unnecessary roughness, including knocking the ball out of an opponent's hands after it had been legally caught, kicking the ball in the hands of a player who is in the act of converting a ground ball into an aerial ball, or using any other form of rough or dangerous play
13. Air dribbling the ball more than once

Penalties for individual fouls

1. For an individual foul occurring outside the penalty area:
    a. A free kick where the foul was made during play of a ground ball

    b. A free unguarded throw if the foul was made during the play of an aerial ball
2. For a defensive player making a contact foul within her penalty area or behind her team's goal line, a penalty kick is awarded. For a noncontact foul one indirect free kick is awarded.
3. For an offensive player within her own penalty area making a foul, an indirect free kick is awarded.
4. For an offensive player committing a foul while behind the opponent's goal line, a free kick or throw is taken on the goal line opposite the place where the goal occurred.
5. In the case of a double foul made anywhere on the field including the penalty areas, a toss-up is used between the two offenders and occurs at the spot of the fouls. For a double foul occurring behind a goal line, the toss-up between the two offenders occurs on the 5-yard (4.57 m) line opposite the place where the fouls occurred.

Team fouls

Team fouls include the following infractions:
1. Taking more than three time-outs
2. Having more than 11 players on the field of play at one time
3. Failing to report to the officials before going into the game

Penalties for team fouls

One penalty kick is awarded for each team foul. In the case of a double foul two opposing players jump for toss-up.

FUNDAMENTAL SKILLS AND TECHNIQUES
Dribbling with the feet

Dribbling with the feet is used in moving the ball toward an opponent's goal line, most often in situations where it is not advisable to kick up or kick to a teammate. In dribbling the ball it is extremely important to control the ball at all times, which means that it must not be kicked with force. In most cases, the inside surface of the foot should be used for best control, although experienced players may use the outside of the foot along the area of the little toe. Ordinarily, for best control the ball should be kicked from an even run about every third step.

Passing

Many types of basketball passes may be used. Any kind of one- or two-hand throw is acceptable depending on the particular situation. The baseball-type pass is used extensively in speedball because of the wide playing field available. A player with the ball may pivot as in basketball if one foot is stabilized. This sometimes helps in finding a teammate open to receive a pass.

Overhead dribble

Only one overhead dribble is allowed. The overhead dribble is made by tossing the ball into the air and running to catch it before it strikes the ground. There is no restriction on the number of steps that may be taken after tossing the ball and before catching it again. The overhead dribble is particularly useful when a closely guarded player tosses the ball over the head of the opponent to get free.

Place kicking

The place kick is used in an attempt to score after a foul. The ball is placed on the penalty kick line or 10-yard (9.14 m) line for men and on the 12-yard (10.97 m) line for women. The object is to kick the ball past the goalkeeper, between the goalposts, and under the crossbar. The goalkeeper is the only player on the opposing team who is permitted to defend against the place kick.

Drop kicking

For the best control of the ball in drop kicking, hold the ball just above the knees, flex at the waist, drop the ball to the ground, and kick it just as it bounces; take one step with the left foot and kick the ball with the right foot, or vice versa.

Punting

Punting in speedball is used to advance the ball toward the opponent's goal line as quickly as possible. Techniques of punting in speedball are similar to those in football. The ball should be kicked with the upper surface of the instep. Take one step forward with the left foot, drop the ball from extended arms, and kick the ball with the right foot. The ball should be dropped as the foot starts its upward swing. If the player kicks with the left foot, the reverse technique should be used.

Catching

The ball should be caught with the entire hand, because many passes are vigorously thrown. After the catch, the ball should be held with the fingers. Inasmuch as catching a speedball is similar to catching a basketball, the same technique should be practiced in perfecting this skill.

Blocking

Any part of the body, except the hands and arms, may be used to stop or slow the ball. Women should cross their arms in front of the chest in trying to stop the ball at shoulder level. To prevent the ball from rebounding too vigorously off the body, the player should move back slightly at the instant of impact.

Trapping

Trapping with the feet

In trapping the ball with the foot, the player extends the leg forward toward the ball with the heel 4 to 5 inches above the ground and the toe pointing upward. The sole of the foot is presented to the ball as it approaches. When the ball comes within reach of the foot, the player presses down and traps the ball between the sole of the foot and the ground.

Trapping with the legs

In trapping the ball with the right leg, the player slightly advances the left leg diagonally forward and outward and flexes the right leg as though intending to kneel. The flexion should be inward over the right toe. The ball should be trapped between the lower leg and the ground. In double-leg trapping, the feet are close together as the rolling ball approaches from the front. The player traps the ball by kneeling on it. However, the weight of the body should remain over the feet. More advanced players may stop a rolling ball by rotating either leg outward, contacting the ball with the inside of the foot and "giving" as contact is made.

Kick-up

In many situations in the game of speedball a ground ball may be played more advantageously by converting it into an aerial or fly ball. A player may convert a ground ball into a fly ball by kicking it into the air.

Kick-up with two feet

With the ball held firmly between the insides of the feet and ankles, the player jumps into the air, lifting the ball upward (Fig. 29-3). After releasing the ball from the ankles and feet, the player catches it before it touches the ground. Because the kick-up is one of the easiest ways to pick up a ground ball, players should practice and develop considerable skill in its use.

Kick-up with one foot

The play can be made on a rolling ball by flipping the ball into the air with the foot and catching it after it leaves the foot but before it touches the ground. As the rolling ball approaches, the player should extend the leg forward with the pointed toe touching the ground. As the ball rolls onto the instep of the foot, the player flips the ball into the air and catches it.

The one-foot kick-up can be made on a stationary ball by placing the foot on top of the ball and drawing it backward to start the ball rolling toward the player. Then the toe is quickly placed under the ball so that it will roll onto the instep. When it rolls onto the instep, the player quickly flips the ball into the air and catches it

Fig. 29-3. Kick-up with two feet.

Fig. 29-4. Kick-up with one foot.

before it touches the ground (Fig. 29-4). The kick-up technique on both a rolling ball and a stationary ball can also be used to lift the ball to a teammate.

OFFENSIVE PLAY

In moving the ball down the field, the forward line should be spread and the players should attempt to stay in front of the ball. As the ball approaches the goal line, the wings should go across the endline to receive a forward pass. The halfbacks should remain in a position to back up the forwards or try to score if an opportunity presents itself. Also, the halfbacks should be ready to guard against the opposing team if the ball is intercepted and lost. In the men's game a long kickoff deep into the opponent's territory usually is best. The kicking team should move rapidly down the field after the kickoff to prevent the opponents from returning the ball toward their goal line. In the women's game a long kickoff downfield is not always the best strategy, depending somewhat on the ability of the players. Inasmuch as the kickoff in the women's game need not travel more than the circumference of the ball, the best strategy often is to keep control of the ball by dribbling it along the ground or converting it into an aerial ball, or to gain possession of the ball by a kick-up or by using a short control pass.

DEFENSIVE PLAY

One-on-one player defense is most often used. Fullbacks, guards, and halfbacks guard the opposing forwards. The goalkeeper may leave position to assist in stopping a touchdown play when necessary.

TEACHING CONSIDERATIONS

1. Decide on the rules applicable for coed situations. Most students will have had some experience with basketball, soccer, and football: teach speedball as a combination of these sports. Be clear about how to score and how to legally play aerial and ground balls. Use a modified soccer ball for young learners.
2. If soccer is part of the school curriculum, less time need be spent on dribbling and passing skills with the feet. If soccer is not a part of the curriculum, this part of the game will need more work than passing and throwing skills using the hands.
3. Teach students how to move the ball down the field (both aerial and ground balls) and how to convert ground balls to aerial balls. Practice until these skills are developed with some consistency. Work with the punt and catching punts as a way to move the ball down the field. Help students to understand that dribbling with the feet is the slowest way for groups to move the ball. Use small groups of partners or groups of three to practice moving the ball.
4. Add defensive players only after students have some control of both aerial and ground balls. Start with two-on-one, three-on-one, and three-on-two situations to introduce defensive and offensive play of both aerial and ground balls. Gradually add additional offensive and defensive players. Practice the types of scoring possibilities first without defense and then with defense, again initially giving the offense the advantage.
5. Use smaller fields and fewer players (four, six, or eight) on a team when play begins. This will allow offensive and defensive strategies to be better understood and practiced and will give students more practice opportunities with basic skills.
6. Introduce penalty kicks only after continuous play has been achieved.

GLOSSARY

aerial ball A ball that has been raised into the air by either a one- or two-foot kick; a punt, drop kick, kick-up, or thrown ball that has not touched the ground.

air dribble A ball that is tossed or tapped into the air and caught by the same player.

attackers The team in possession of the ball.

blocking the ball Intercepting the ball with any part of the body. A player cannot block a ground ball with the arms or hands unless they are in contact with the body.

closely guarded Being guarded within 3 feet.

dead ball A ball no longer in play; out of bounds, after a score, after a foul, during time out, or a tie ball.

defenders The team not in possession of the ball.

double foul Fouls committed at the same time by both teams; a toss-up is awarded.

dribble Advancing the ball by a series of kicks.

drop kick Dropping the ball to the ground and kicking it just as it bounces from the ground.

end goal Passing the ball over the endline but not between the goalposts; counts 1 point for men but does not apply to women's rules.

field goal Passing the ball between the goalposts and under the crossbar; 3 points for men, 2 for women.

foul An infringement of the rules for which a free kick, free throw, or penalty kick is awarded the opponents.

free kick A place kick from which a goal can be scored directly.

free throw A throw taken by any player on the team that has been fouled during the play of an aerial ball.

goalkeeper A player whose duty it is to defend the goal.

ground ball A stationary, rolling, or bouncing ball that is in contact with the ground.

handling the ball Putting the hands or arms on a ground ball.

indirect free kick A free kick from which a goal cannot be scored directly.

kick-up The play converting a ground ball into an aerial ball.

own goal The goal one's team is defending.

own half The half of the field in which one's own goal is located.

passing Means of moving the ball by passes or batting with the hands to another player.

penalty kick A free kick awarded as the result of a foul; men use a place kick from the 10-yard (9.14 m) line and the ball must go under the crossbar; women use a drop kick to pass the ball over the crossbar.

place kick A stationary ball kicked by a player.

punt A play in which a player drops a caught ball and kicks it before it touches the ground.

trapping Stopping the motion of the ball by placing the sole of the foot on it, by kneeling on it, or by catching it between the front of the legs and the ground.

volley A play in which a player fields a fly or aerial ball with some part of the body, such as the head, hip, or shoulder.

SUGGESTED READINGS

American Alliance for Health, Physical Education, Recreation, and Dance: Speedball for men, Reston, Va, 1980, American Alliance for Health, Physical Education, Recreation, and Dance.

Meyer M and Schwarz M: Team sports for girls and women, ed 4, Philadeophia, 1980, WB Saunders Co.

Official soccer and speedball rules and guide, Washington, DC, 1980-1982, American Alliance for Health, Physical Education, and Recreation, National Association for Girls' and Women's Sports.

FILMS

Speedball for girls, 11 minutes, color. Coronet Films, 65 E.S. Water St., Chicago, IL 60601. Appropriate for junior and senior high schools and college. Explains positions, rules, techniques of developing team cooperation, and some individual skills.

30

Springboard Diving

Completion of this chapter should enable the reader to:

- Know the origins of diving and the few standardized diving rules
- Be familiar with a progression of activities to be used as a lead-up to spring-board diving
- Recognize the groups of dives and the fundamental skills of the approach hurdles and entry
- Teach, in a logical progression, jumping from the diving board, the basic required dives, and a few more difficult optional dives

HISTORY

Diving is a form of aerial acrobatics. It is an outgrowth of gymnastics. Instead of landing on a mat, the diver dives into water, either headfirst or feetfirst.

At its beginning diving into water was more or less a feat, such as a high dive from a bridge, from flying rings suspended over a pool, or from a rope suspended from a branch to swing the performer far out over the water.

The competitive sport of diving is believed to have originated in the early 1900s in England, Germany, and Sweden. At that time only a few simple dives were perfected. The dives were named after their originators, such as the Mollberg, which was later changed to the full gainer and is now known as the reverse somersault. The half reverse was first called the flying Dutchman, was later the half gainer, and now is known as the reverse dive. However, competition was the needed impetus to challenge youth. During the past 40 years of competition, diving has developed into one of the most beautiful, thrilling, and spectacular of aerial acrobatics. It is fun and great sport.

Men's springboard and platform diving has been dominated by divers from the United States. The gold medal in the springboard event has been won by a United States diver in 14 of the 18 Olympics since it was introduced in 1908 and in the platform event 12 of the 20 times since 1904. Although not quite as dominant, the United States women divers have also enjoyed great success.

They have captured the gold in the springboard event in 11 of 16 Olympics and in the platform event 8 of 17 times.

In fact, between 1920 and 1976 (the United States boycotted the 1980 Olympics) we won 106 of a possible 156 Olympic medals in men's and women's springboard and platform events.

Greg Louganis continued domination in the sport by U.S. men by being the first male diver in 56 years to win the gold in both the springboard and platform events in 1984 and then topped this achievement by being the first male ever to repeat this performance at the 1988 Olympics. Chinese divers have improved, however, as they captured the silver and bronze in both springboard and platform diving in the men's event and dominated the women's events with the exception of United States diver Kelly McCormick's bronze in the springboard event.

RULES

A few simple rules are now standardized internationally. They are as follows:

1. A dive is executed from either a standing or a running position.
2. It is executed from either a backward or forward starting position.
3. It can be performed from either a rigid platform or a springboard.

Fig. 30-1. Dive in pike position.

4. It must be executed in one of four body positions:
   a. Tuck, in which the body is flexed at both hips and knees.
   b. Pike, in which the body is flexed at the hips (Fig. 30-1).
   c. Straight, in which the body is held straight throughout the dive (Fig. 30-2).
   d. Free, which is some combination of the other positions (usually pike and straight) and is used only in certain twisting dives.
5. The legs must be held together at all times, with toes pointed.
6. Entry can be either headfirst or feetfirst.
7. Competitive springboard diving must be performed from either a 1- or 3-m (3.3- or 9.9-foot) height from the water.
8. Platform diving must be performed from a height of 10 m (32.8 feet).
9. A springboard must be either 14 or 16 feet (4.26 or 4.88 m) long by 20 inches (50.8 cm) wide.

ELEMENTARY DIVING TECHNIQUES (PROGRESSIVE LEARNING FOR BEGINNERS)

Before attempting springboard diving, the beginner should start in the water at the shallow end of the pool, pushing off from the side wall and gliding as far as pos-

Fig. 30-2. Dive in straight position.

sible on the surface, with the entire body stretched out straight, arms and legs held together, head down between the arms, and toes pointed. By experimenting, the beginner will discover how some positions are more streamlined than others. This principle applies to entering the water following a dive.

Undersurface dive

Push off as described, but direct the arms and head at a shallow angle toward the bottom. When nearing the bottom, turn the hands and head upward and the body will again glide to the surface.

Shallow-water surface dive to handstand

Stand away from the wall in waist-deep water. Execute a light spring upward, then quickly bend at the hips (pike) and thrust and direct the arms to the bottom about 8 to 10 inches in front of the feet.

Be careful in executing this maneuver, making sure to keep the arms extended over the head. Then lift the legs up over the head out of the water and balance in a handstand. To resurface give a slight push backward with the hands and raise the head up sharply, with the arms trailing at sides.

Deep-water surface dive—pike

This dive requires considerable skill in the use of the hands and arms, inasmuch as one cannot push with the feet from the bottom or sides of the pool as in the shallow water dive. But it is not too difficult for the beginner. It teaches the diver to pike with the legs straight at the knees and with the ankles stretched and held together. This is a swimming and lifesaving skill. It is performed from the surface of the water in a breaststroke swimming position.

Take a deep breath, duck the head sharply, pull the arms laterally to the hips as in the breaststroke, face the palms down and press the water downward, and sweep the arms forward. When the trunk is vertical, or upside down, the body is in a jackknife position with the legs lying on the surface. Now lift the legs vertically above the hips, using the hands and arms for support. The weight of the legs above the water will push the body down toward the bottom. Tuck, rotate, place the feet on the bottom, and push up to the surface, with the arms trailing at the sides. Repeat several dives continuously, getting a breath above the surface between each dive.

Deep-water surface dive—tuck

The deep-water surface dive—tuck is performed exactly as the pike, except that the knees as well as the hips are bent. This teaches a closely bunched tuck for somersault dives. Note that the body turns down more easily than in the pike position.

ELEMENTARY DIVING FROM POOL DECK

The student should now be prepared with pool deck diving before attempting diving from the springboard. For each of the three elementary dives from pool deck described, start at the deep end of the pool. Be sure that in each dive the legs are higher than the head at the instant of entry to avoid a "belly flop."

Sitting dive

Sit on the edge of the pool with the feet on the top of the gutter. Join thumbs, arms straight, and sight the hands at a point on the bottom of the pool, 4 feet out from the takeoff wall. Lean forward, take a deep breath through the mouth, guide the arms and hands to the sighted spot, lower the head between the arms, and push gently with the legs until the knees are straight. Continue to hold the knees and ankles straight and the legs together. As soon as the body has entered the water, direct the hands upward toward the surface, thumbs still locked, and permit the body to glide until the momentum is spent.

At the entry, the water should hit the top of the head, not the forehead. When the head hits the water, do not let reflex bend the knees.

Standing squat dive

Stand on the edge of the deck, toes of both feet gripped over the edge of the pool deck. Assume a full squat position with the buttocks close to the heels. Extend the arms and direct them at a spot on the bottom of the pool, 4 feet out from the takeoff wall. The eyes are only a few inches higher from the water than in the sitting dive. Take a deep breath, lean forward, and push with the feet until the knees are straight, and continue as in a sitting dive.

Standing semicrouch dive

Stand on the edge of the deck, toes hooked over, knees slightly bent, trunk bent at the hips to a horizontal position. The arms are held back at hip level. Spot the water as explained in the descriptions of the previous two elementary dives to determine where to hit the water. Raise the trunk and arms slightly by straightening the knees, take a deep breath, drop the knees, and swing the arms forward in a "pump-handle" swing. As the arms pass the knees, push with the legs. As the feet leave the takeoff, lower the head between the arms. Close the eyes for entry. Glide as far as possible.

TECHNIQUES OF SPRINGBOARD JUMP DIVES

The beginner should progressively advance to the next category of elementary dives, the jump dives.* In all of these, the diver enters the water feet first. The dives are first executed from a standing position at the takeoff end of the board to give the student the sensation of a springing takeoff from slightly higher than the side of the pool.

Front jump—straight

As the body leaves the board, reach the arms upward, shoulder width apart, fingers and thumbs squeezed together. Press the head and shoulders slightly backward to keep the body from falling forward and to keep it aligned erect for entry. Just before the entry, swing the arms down along the sides of the body. Spot the water straight ahead. At takeoff lean slightly, not more than 2 or 3 degrees from the vertical. Stretch the toes toward the bottom, legs straight and tightly squeezed together. When the body has entered the water, flex the feet at the ankles toward the knees to prevent injury on the bottom of the pool. Repeat dive often to work on balance and "get the feel" of how much to lean to end up with

---

*See Springboard diving fundamentals in Armbruster DA, Allen RH, and Billingsley HS: Swimming and diving, ed. 6, St. Louis, 1973, The C.V. Mosby Co.

Fig. 30-3. Standing or running front dive—straight position.

Fig. 30-4. Standing or running front dive—pike position.

a vertical entry not too far away from the end of the board (See Fig. 30-3.)

Front jump—pike

Reach the arms toward the ceiling as in the straight front jump. Just before the body reaches maximum height, with the legs held together straight at the knees and toes pointed, flex the body at the hips. Hold the head erect and spot with the eyes straight ahead. Lower the arms to the legs, hands touching the toes. Unpike immediately and slide the hands along the legs to the side of the body for the entry. Entry is the same as in the straight front jump. Considerably more skill, balance, and control are required to achieve a vertical entry when performing a front jump—pike than when performing a front jump—straight. (See Fig. 30-4.)

Front jump—tuck

This dive is easier to perform than the pike, but it teaches the fundamentals of tucking and untucking. The diver reaches high at the takeoff and, instead of piking, tucks the body. To execute this dive, the knees are brought up to the chest, and the knees and ankles are held together and the ankles extended. The arms are lowered, the hands grasping the lower legs and pulling them in so that the heels are brought toward the buttocks in a tight tuck. The hip and knee joints must be relaxed. The head is held erect throughout the dive, with eyes directed forward. The tuck is held until after the diver has

Fig. 30-5. Standing or running front jump dive—tuck position.

passed the peak of height. As legs are untucked, they shoot downward and are pressed backward in line with the trunk. The hands slide down to the sides of the body. On all foot-entry dives, the arms are to be held at the sides of the body, not overhead. (See Fig. 30-5.)

Fig. 30-6. Standing backward jump dive—straight position.

Fig. 30-7. Standing backward jump dive—pike position.

Fig. 30-8. Standing backward jump dive—tuck position.

Back jump

As the diver jumps from the board, the arms swing up in front of the body, while kept straight, to an overhead position. The arms are stretched upward. As the diver jumps upward and backward from the board, the head and body must be held erect to avoid a falling takeoff. As the diver descends from the peak, the hands are lowered to the thighs, and a vertical entry is made. The eyes should remain focused on a spot on the wall at eye level at the rear wall. The eyes then aid the body to control itself during the dive. The back jump may also be executed in pike and tuck. (See Figs. 30-6 to 30-8.)

FUNDAMENTAL TECHNIQUES OF RUNNING SPRINGBOARD DIVING
Approach

There are many different skills to be learned in the art of diving. Two of the most essential are good body control and coordination. This means proper movement of arms in the hurdle and proper handling and straightening of knees and ankles in dropping on and springing from the board. Obtaining adequate height above the water is one of the essential prerequisites for becoming a good diver. The trampoline is an excellent training apparatus for developing height in dives, for losing the fear of height, and for learning to maintain balance.

The approach is a skill consisting of the stance, walk, hurdle, and takeoff.

Fig. 30-9. Series of ideal forms for executing standing takeoff.

Fig. 30-10. Series of ideal forms for executing three-step run, hurdle, and takeoff.

Stance

Assume an erect position, with the chest and chin up, stomach drawn in, and arms along the sides of the body, feet together. (See Figs. 30-9 and 30-10 for the progressive stages of the approach.)

Walk

The approach for running dives must consist of at least three steps. The hurdle is not a step. Most divers prefer four steps and a hurdle. The steps should be of moderate speed and natural. During the walk, focus the eyes on the tip of the board until just before the feet land on the board; then raise the eyes to a focal point on the water several feet in front of the board.

The steps in the walk should be natural rather than long.

Hurdle and takeoff

The hurdle should be approximately 2 feet long. If using the four-step approach, and assuming that the left foot is the best takeoff foot, start the approach with the right foot. As you step onto the takeoff foot, the shoulder girdle and head should pull up erect from the forward lean of the walk, eyes focused on the end of the board. The hands are slightly behind the hips, fingers and thumbs straight and squeezed together. From this position the arms are lifted above the head. The knee opposite the takeoff leg is sharply raised to aid the takeoff leg and arm to reach maximum height in the hurdle for a longer drop onto the end of the board. Both ankles are depressed during the hurdle. During the drop, the body is stretched straight with both legs together. Just as the feet are about to contact the board, raise the toes slightly to drop onto the balls of the feet and bend the knees. The arms are now moving downward toward the hips in preparation for the landing. As the diver lands and the board bends for the body weight, the arms swing past the hips, as straight as possible, and up in front of the body to an overhead position at the point of takeoff. As the arms swing up, the legs extend against the board, and both of these actions aid in gaining left into the arc. Finally the board recoils, sending the diver into the air. The diver must stay with the board until it is through bending down and until it rebounds. The takeoff should not be hurried. A great deal of practice is required to acquire an accurate hurdle and line of flight from the takeoff.

Height and line of flight

Height in diving is the vertical distance of the highest peak reached by the body's center of motion in the line of flight. The line of flight is the path described by the center of body weight from the takeoff to the entry. Height and correct line of flight are a natural result when the walk, hurdle, and takeoff are well controlled and timed. Too much effort or muscular power in the walk and take-off will result in jerky and unbalanced motions.

Some persons have a natural springing ability and can obtain greater height than others.

Entry

The point of entry of a dive should be at a spot on the surface directly under the center of body weight, on a line with the descending flight of the body, and projected downward to the bottom of the pool. The diver should follow the line of flight well below the surface of the water. Arching the body upward too soon under the surface can result in a bad back sprain.

For headfirst entries, the arms should be sharply closed several feet above the surface and held in line with the spine. The head is held between the arms so that the water hits the head on the top of the forehead. The legs must be stretched and closed tightly, the ankles and toes stretched and pointed in line with the legs. The feet should pass into the same hole in the surface that the head entered. The body should not be arched at entry.

On foot-entry dives, the body is held erect, the arms are closed snugly along the sides of the body, and the head is held erect.

Back approach

Dives in the back and inward groups and some dives in the twisting groups require the diver to start from a position on the end of the diving board with the back facing the water.

Approach

The diver takes the initial position on the board as if doing a forward approach, however, after a momentary pause, he or she walks confidently to the end of the board keeping the head up, exaggerating the arm swing slightly and taking medium sized steps. The approach should end approximately 18 to 24 inches from the end of the board with the left foot leading (the following directions can be reversed if the diver prefers to pivot in the opposite direction). The right foot is then crossed in front of the left leg and placed at the end of the board. As the weight is shifted to the ball of the right foot the diver simultaneously raises both arms so that they extend directly forward from the shoulder (parallel with the diving board) and executes a one-half turn to the left. This movement results in a position with the front part of the right foot on the board and the back part of the right foot off the board over the water. Then the left foot is brought into place next to the right foot and with the arms still extended the feet are adjusted to secure proper balance with the heels parallel to the water. Finally, the arms are lowered to the sides. The diver must keep the center of gravity over the relatively small base of support (front half of the feet) and there is a slight feeling of leaning forward. For inward dives the center of gravity should be slightly more forward than for backward or backward twisting dives.

Take-off mechanics

The first motion is to lift the arms (extended) laterally and slightly forward from the sides of the body (Fig. 30-11). The arms may be raised to shoulder height or above, depending on the divers' preference. As the arms move upward the body is also raised up on the toes. This action causes a reaction by the board and it is important to time the rest of the take-off with the rhythm of the board. Most divers take a deep breath during this initial movement as well.

The initial arm movement is crucial to the success of the take-off. If done too forcefully, the movement can cause the entire body to lose contact with the board (called a crow-hop) and destroy the rhythm of the take-off.

Next, the arms are brought down as the knees bend to push the diving board down. The driving action of the arms continues to about the hips, where it quickly changes direction and the arms begin to move upward again. Just before the arms change direction from downward to upward the knees and ankles extend against the board and the arms reach up into the intended line of flight of the dive.

Except for the time the arms are changing from downward to upward, they should remain fairly straight during

Fig. 30-11. Series of ideal forms for executing the back take-off.

the take-off movement. During the downward phase of the take-off, the hips actually move slightly down and back to compensate for the knees bending slightly forward. It is important, however, not to bend the trunk forward at the waist but rather to keep the back vertical above the hips.

GROUPS OF DIVES

Competitive dives are categorized into five groups:

Group I—Forward dives
Group II—Backward dives
Group III—Reverse dives
Group IV—Inward dives
Group V—Twisting dives

All are combinations of the forward or backward dive with either a somersault or a twist in one of the straight, pike, tuck, or free positions. The dives described here are listed in group order, but the following sequence is recommended for teaching them to beginning divers.

1. Forward dive—straight
2. Forward dive—pike
3. Backward dive—straight
4. Inward dive
5. Forward dive—half twist
6. Backward somersault—tuck
7. Forward somersault—tuck
8. Forward dive, full twist—straight
9. Reverse somersault—tuck
10. Reverse dive
11. Forward one and one-half somersault

Group I: forward dive—straight

This dive is commonly known as the swan or plain front dive. It is, in reality, a half somersault. The difficulty of this dive lies in the amount of body control required to maintain the body in good alignment while in the air. As the feet come in contact with the board at the end of the hurdle, the eyes are lifted from the board and are focused straight ahead. The face is held directly forward

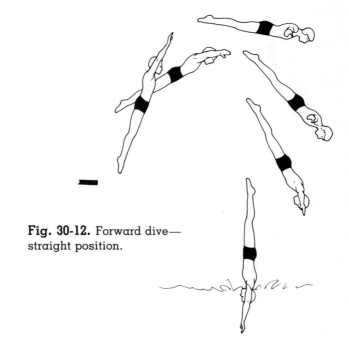

Fig. 30-12. Forward dive—straight position.

until after the peak of the dive has been reached. When the diver leaves the board, the body should be stretched. The hands are lifted from the hips and are spread out straight from the shoulders with a slight angle forward. A line across the upper back should follow along the top of the arms when the body is in the straight position. From the head down, the body should be straight and the legs held close together with the toes pointed.

As the peak of the dive is reached, the body rotates forward around its center of weight, which is just above the hip joint. This rotation lifts the legs upward and levels the trunk, so that the heels are just above the head level when the body is at its peak.

The rotation continues as the body falls from the peak, and the head is slowly dropped between the arms as the eyes are shifted to the point of entry. The hands are brought close together as the vertical entry is made.

The diver should reach for the bottom as the entry into the water is made. (See Fig. 30-12.)

Group I: forward dive—pike

Takeoff is made with the hands held close together in an overhead reach. The pike is started at the end of the reach. The feet are pressed forward, the arms are moved downward, and the hips are lifted above the head as the body rises into the peak of the dive. The eyes are spotted well down the course of the pool. As the peak of the dive is reached, the hands are brought into contact with the feet. The legs at this point are in a vertical position, with the toes pointing downward.

As the body drops below the peak of the dive, it has rotated slightly forward, so that its position resembles an inverted **V**. The legs are then lifted slowly as the body starts to open up, and the continued rotation of the body places it in a vertical position for the entry. As the legs lift upward, the arms reach forward to a position along the sides of the head, and the hands are held close together at the entry.

Group II: backward dive—straight

Although the backward takeoff dives are blind dives, they are easy to perform in that the body is simply levered backward and additional movements are then made.

As the body lifts from the board in the backward dive—straight, the eyes are first focused overhead. The arms reach upward and slightly backward and are spread in line with the back of the spine. At the height of the lift, when the head is about at the peak of the dive, the head is stretched backward and the eyes begin to look for the entry spot in the water behind the diver.

During this head and arm action, the hips and legs should be lifted and the knees and ankles must be stretched. The arms are brought together when the body has dropped to a point opposite the board, and the entry is made with the hands close together and the head between the arms. (See Fig. 30-13.)

Group III: reverse dive—straight

As the body drops onto the board preliminary to the takeoff for this dive, the weight should remain over the toes, and the diver should not shift the weight backward as the heels contact the board. As the board lifts the diver, the center of body weight (in the hips) should be shifted just in front of the base of support (balls of feet), so that the body is easily projected forward and upward.

The reverse dive is one of the most graceful of all dives. It is essentially a backward dive from a forward takeoff. The diver actually gains distance in a forward direction; thus the name "gainer" or "reverse" dive.

At takeoff, the arms lift to an overhead position, then spread laterally to shoulder level as the eyes look upward and the head is tilted back. When the body reaches the position at the end of the lift from takeoff, the head,

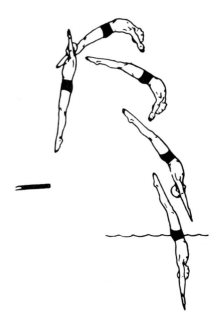

Fig. 30-13. Back dive—straight position.

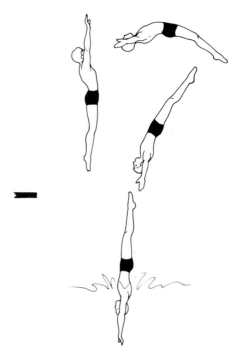

Fig. 30-14. Reverse dive—straight position.

arms, and shoulders are levered backward and the chest, hips, and legs are lifted as well as stretched. When the body reaches the horizontal position at the peak, the legs remain lifted as if anchored, because backward rotation causes the head and shoulders to drop. The arms are closed, the head is brought between the arms, and the body is straightened as it drops in a vertical entry. (See Fig. 30-14.)

Group IV: inward dive—pike

While the body is poised over the end of the board, the center of weight is over the balls of the feet. During the preliminary arm movements of the takeoff, the center of weight moves vertically but should not move forward or backward.

At the time of takeoff from the board, the arms are straight and reaching overhead and slightly forward of a vertical line with the palms facing forward.

At the end of the reach, the hips are flexed and raised, the arms are brought forward and downward, and the hands touch the front of the feet at the peak. The hips have lifted above the head to the peak of the dive. The legs are vertical when the pike is completed. The eyes sight over the toes to the entry point as the touch occurs. After the diver touches the feet, the body begins to straighten as the arms are moved laterally to an overhead position in preparation for the entry. (See Fig. 30-15.)

Group V: forward dive, half twist—straight

The takeoff is similar to the forward dive—straight with the twist initiated just before leaving the board by turning the shoulders in the desired direction of the twist. The arms are spread to a T position as the body lifts to the top of the dive. To twist to the right, as the diver is ascending, the left arm and shoulder are rotated forward while the head remains stationary with the eyes focused forward. As the diver rotates in a somersaulting direction, the water should come into view directly below the left hand. (See second position in Fig. 30-16.) The arms move as in turning a large steering wheel counterclockwise. The legs constantly bear upward during the twist and the drop of the trunk.

The head should not resist the downward movement of the dive by pulling backward but should be allowed to follow the downward rotation movement. Once the eyes focus on the entry point at the peak of the dive, they should not lose sight of it during the rest of the dive. Following this rule aids in obtaining the necessary arch to rotate the body.

The hands are closed slowly above the head, and the arms are pressed to the ears as the body is straightened for the headfirst vertical entry. (See Fig. 30-16.)

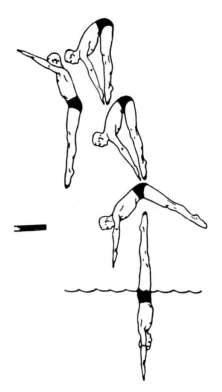

Fig. 30-15. Inward dive—pike position.

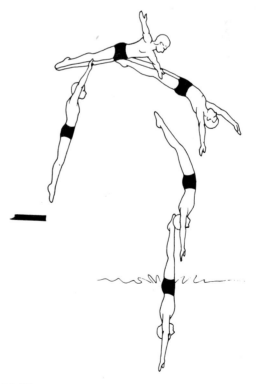

Fig. 30-16. Forward dive, half twist—straight position.

Fig. 30-17. Forward somersault—tuck position.

Fig. 30-18. Forward somersault—pike position.

Group I: forward somersault—tuck or pike

The body leaves the board in the same manner for both the forward somersault tuck and pike except more rotational force is needed to successfully complete the pike somersault. Somersaulting rotation is achieved by throwing the head, trunk, and arms outward and downward just before leaving the board.

In the tuck, the heels are brought toward the buttocks while the diver bends at the knees and waist and grabs the legs with the hands. When the diver's back is approximately parallel with the water, the legs are extended. This produces a "sitting in air" appearance. (See fourth position in Fig. 30-17.) Complete extension follows, with the same entry as for all feetfirst dives.

In the pike, the actions are the same except that the body is bent at the waist only. The pike should be held slightly longer than the tuck, because the velocity of the rotation is slightly less.

The angle of entry can be adjusted in both dives by remaining either tucked or piked or by opening. This adjustment is learned quickly with practice. (See Figs. 30-17 and 30-18.)

Group II: backward somersault—tuck

The tuck is started just after the upward and backward swing of the arms on takeoff and is done by lifting the thighs to the chest and drawing the heels toward the buttocks while grabbing the shins with the hands.

During the somersault the diver should maintain the tuck position while looking upward to sight the water at approximately one half revolution. The focus should remain on the entry point until the opening from the tuck begins, when the diver can look at the water under the tip of the board or at the tip of the board itself.

Because the motions of the backward somersault push the diver in the direction of the board, it is important that when springing the board he move his balance backward to ensure the dive is accomplished at a safe distance from the board.

When the chest is horizontal to the surface and well above the board, the legs are thrust to full extension and the toes are kept pointed. The head and shoulders are held erect so that the body is perfectly aligned at the entry.

As the body is opened the hands simply slide from the shins to the front of the thighs. (See Fig. 30-19.)

Group III: reverse somersault—tuck

At the takeoff, the eyes are focused upward and the reach is made slightly in back of vertical. The arms will move forward slightly in reaction to the legs' coming toward the chest when going into tuck position. (See first position of Fig. 30-20.) The tuck is held until the chest is parallel to the water, at which time the legs are thrust

Fig. 30-19. Back somersault—tuck position.

Fig. 30-20. Reverse somersault—tuck position.

out, the hands ride up the legs to the thighs, and the body is readied for a feetfirst entry. (See Fig. 30-20.)

Group V: forward dive, full twist—straight

The diver leaves the board as in the forward dive, half twist—straight. If the twist is to the right, the shoulders turn to the right just before the diver leaves the board. Just after the takeoff, the left arm is moved across the chest with the elbow bent 90 degrees. The right arm is bent 90 degrees and the forearm is positioned just above the head. The legs bear upward during the whole movement. A quarter twist is started, and the eyes hold a spot on the point of entry until the twist is far enough to pull the head away. The half twist has been made during the ascent to the peak, and the diver is now in a horizontal position. The twist is fairly rapid and is continuous.

The head is now turned sharply to the right as the right elbow drives toward the water and the hand reaches for the entry, while the eyes focus on the entry point. The left arm is then extended and joins the right arm in stretching for the entry. This stretching action should be emphasized in this dive because it squares the body so that the hips and shoulders are straightened at the entry.

All movements in this dive should center around the longitudinal axis of the diver. Movements of the shoulders must be loose in order to avoid any lateral action caused by strained movements of the arms.

Common errors in performing this dive are failure to bear the legs upward during the twisting movements and too much somersaulting action at the takeoff by starting the twisting mechanics of the arms too early. (See Fig. 30-21.)

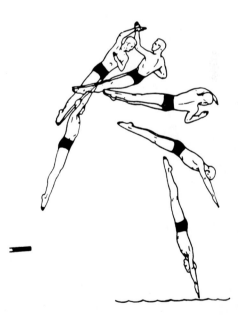

Fig. 30-21. Forward dive, full twist—straight position.

Group I: forward one and one-half somersault—tuck or pike

This dive is very similar to the forward somersault—tuck, except an additional half forward somersault rotation is made while the body is in the tuck or pike position.

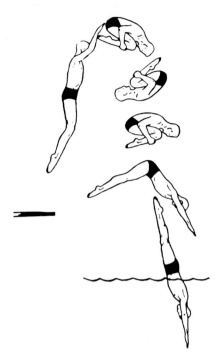

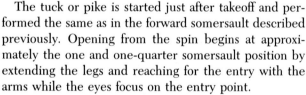

Fig. 30-22. Forward one and one-half somersault—tuck position.

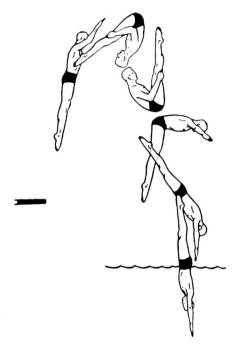

Fig. 30-23. Forward one and one-half somersault—pike position.

The tuck or pike is started just after takeoff and performed the same as in the forward somersault described previously. Opening from the spin begins at approximately the one and one-quarter somersault position by extending the legs and reaching for the entry with the arms while the eyes focus on the entry point.

The arms reach for the point of entry, and the body slides down the parabolic line of trajectory and into the water. (See Figs. 30-22 and 30-23.)

TEACHING CONSIDERATIONS

1. Students should feel secure in deep water before attempting diving skills.
2. Before teaching springboard diving, work on surface dives and dives from pool deck as indicated in the chapter. Stress form (clear body positions) in all beginning diving experiences. Make clear the desired form by demonstrating and practicing position on the deck.
3. Begin springboard diving with jump dives (feet entering first). Give students an opportunity to get the feel of the board by bouncing and stopping momentum through flexion as the toes retouch the board on landing. Students can have more opportunities to practice control and good form if they practice jumping onto mats into the desired body position (with or without the use of a minitramp or trampoline) rather than only diving into the water.

4. The hurdle is an essential skill for running springboard diving. Practice it on the deck and then on the board without an actual dive. After students start on the board, focus on essential beginning points and visual spotting techniques. Work for an integrated, natural production of force in the takeoff.
5. Start with basic dives in each of the five groups of dives. Work for good form and consistency before moving to more advanced dives. Divers should have a clear idea of takeoff, flight, and entry positions. Use audiovisual aids to freeze the critical parts of the dive and to stress learning cues. Provide learners with videotaped and verbal feedback if possible after some consistency is established.
6. Organize large group instruction for maximum practice. Avoid long lines at the board. Include review and repetition of work. Do not permit students to move to more advanced dives unless a high level of consistency is established with the less difficult ones.

GLOSSARY

approach The stance, three or more steps, and hurdle taken before the takeoff.

award A score ranging from 0 to 10 given by each judge signifying how well the dive was performed.

balk Beginning the approach but stopping before leaving the board.

degree of difficulty A number assigned to each dive that ranks the dive according to difficulty.

final score The sum of the scores awarded for each dive.

free position Any combination of the layout, pike, and tuck positions used in executing twisting dives.

fulcrum The bar located near the middle of the board, which is usually adjustable to permit varying the amount of spring obtained from the board.

hurdle The jump during the approach just preceding the takeoff.

low board The 1 m board.

long Rotating past a vertical line of entry.

optional dive Any official dive performed in a competition which is not required by the rules governing the contest.

peak The place in a dive where the diver's center of gravity reaches its highest point.

pike position A diving position in which the body is bent at the hips but not at the knees.

required dive The first dive listed in each of the five groups: the forward dive, the back dive, the reverse dive, the inward dive, and the half-twist dive.

save A movement made during the entry of a dive to cause the legs to enter the water vertically even though the dive was long or short.

score The number obtained when the sum of the judges' awards is multiplied by the degree of difficulty for a dive.

short An expression denoting that a diver entered the water before the desired amount of rotation was achieved.

straight position A diving position in which the body is straight, not bent at the hips or knees.

takeoff The period of a dive between the end of the hurdle and the time the diver loses contact with the board.

tuck position A diving position in which the body is bent at the hips and the knees and is as compact as possible.

SUGGESTED READINGS

National Association for Girls and Women in Sport: Competitive swimming and diving, Reston, Va, American Alliance for Health, Physical Education, Recreation, and Dance.

NCAA men's and women's swimming and diving rules, Mission, Kan, 1989, National Collegiate Athletic Association Publishing Department.

Official NCAA swimming guide, New York, 1989, National Collegiate Athletic Association.

Swimming and diving rule book, Kansas City, Mo, (current edition), National Federation of State High School Association.

VIDEOTAPES

Competitive diving series, including *Fundamentals of diving, The required dives, Optimal dives, Parts I and II*. The Athletic Institute, 200 N. Castelwood Dr., North Palm Beach, FL 33408.

Diving techniques. Karol Video, 22 Riverside Dr., Wayne, NJ 97470.

31

Swimming

Completion of this chapter should enable the reader to:

- Be familiar with the evolution of swimming and the various strokes
- Orient a group of students to being in water
- Instruct novice swimmers in basic swimming skills such as floating, gliding, and beginning propulsion
- Teach beginning and advanced swimming strokes
- Recognize the proper progressions for teaching beginning, intermediate, and advanced swimmers

HISTORY AND EVOLUTION

Early man probably learned swimming by observing animals that used a running motion to move about on or in the water. Water is an unnatural medium for humans because it interferes with the breathing mechanism; animals are usually better equipped anatomically for swimming. Humans cannot easily keep the nose above water while horizontal.

Carvings showing people swimming have been found dating as early as 9000 B.C. In the Middle Ages, accounts in the Greek, Roman, Anglo-Saxon, and Scandinavian classics dealt often with great feats of swimming of the heroes of the day.

In 1538 Nicolaus Wynman, a German professor of languages, wrote the first book on swimming. In 1696 M. Thevenot, a Frenchman, wrote a more scientific treatise.

The strokes listed here are still fundamental and seaworthy for utility purposes but have been considerably refined for competitive swimming.

These strokes evolved in the following order:

1. The "doggy" or human paddling strokes.
2. The breaststroke (sailor stroke), the first scientific stroke taught.
3. The underarm sidestroke. This stroke was still too slow for speed because both arms recovered under the water as they did in the breaststroke. The kick was scissorslike.
4. The side overarm or English overarm stroke. This stroke was faster than either the breaststroke or the side underarm stroke because the uppermost arm recovered above the surface and thereby reduced undesirable resistance.
5. The trudgen stroke, discovered in South America in 1860 by an Englishman, John Trudgen. This stroke employed the method of recovering both arms above the water hand-over-hand and further reduced resistance to water and created greater speed. It was similar to the side overarm stroke except that the body turned over to the uppermost side to also permit the under arm to lift out of the water for recovery. In this stroke the scissors kick was used.
6. The Australian crawl, introduced to England by Richard Cavell of Australia in the 1902 championships. This was the first true hand-over-hand stroke with vertical thrash of the legs. Cavell explained the stroke as "crawling through the water." The scissors kick was eliminated for speed swimming because recovering the legs caused great resistance.
7. The American six-beat leg kick crawl. The Australian stroke was scientifically refined by American coaches. This style broke all existing freestyle records in speed swimming and became known as the fastest human stroke in water.
8. The inverted breaststroke. This is the breaststroke executed upside down while swimming on the back.

9. The back crawl. About 1910 the crawl was turned upside down and was much faster in competition than the inverted breaststroke. Here again there was no recovery of arms or legs underwater as in the inverted breaststroke. It, too, minimized resistance and created faster speed on the back.

10. The butterfly breaststroke.* This stroke was beginning to make its appearance in competition about 1934. The kick remained the same as in the breaststroke, but the arms recovered above the water simultaneously. They lifted out of the water at the hips and were swung laterally forward to the entry, resembling a butterfly in flight; thus the name.

11. The dolphin fishtail breaststroke. The newest of all the swimming strokes was created by Armbruster through the ability and skill of Jack Sieg. The purpose of this stroke is to obtain greater speed with the breaststroke by eliminating the recovery underwater of the legs in the kick. This is accomplished by beating the legs up and down in unison. This kick actually creates greater speed when used without arms than does the alternating crawl flutter kick. It synchronized beautifully with the butterfly arm stroke and created greater speed.

Not only have all of these strokes been developed and refined, but they have been put to practical use by the average swimmer and are expressed in many different categories of water activities, usually called aquatics. Some of the categories of aquatics are:

1. Recreational
2. Lifesaving
3. Competition
4. Synchronized or ballet
5. Springboard diving
6. Water games—polo, basketball, baseball, and the like
7. Water safety
8. Survival
9. Skin and scuba diving

Most of these skill activities in water have as a basic background the fundamental skill strokes.

It is strongly recommended that the beginner be taught all of the basic strokes to gain an assurance of self-preservation, an at-home feeling, and the joy and relaxation in recreational swimming. To accomplish this, the beginner must know the fundamental skill strokes. This method of learning is the "Armbruster all-stroke method for beginners." (See Fig. 31-1.)

*See Armbruster DA, Allen RH, and Billingsley HS: Swimming and diving, ed 6, St Louis, 1973, The CV Mosby Co.

UNITED STATES OLYMPIC SWIMMING HISTORY
Men

In 1896 at Athens, there were only four swimming events, and competitors could use any stroke. The event took place outside in a lake. Over the years the competitions became increasingly organized in terms of distances, strokes, and facilities. By 1912 there were seven men's events and three women's events.

The first outstanding United States swimmer was Duke Kahanamoku of Hawaii who won the 100 meter freestyle in 1912 and again in 1920. His new style of kicking (the flutter kick) was later adopted by most freestyle swimmers. In 1924 Johnny Weissmuller, the next dominant U.S. swimmer, emerged. He was the first person to swim the 100 meter freestyle under a minute and won a total of five gold medals at two Olympiads.

In 1932 the Japanese men swimmers won five of six events and they won three of six events in 1936. Following these games the Australian men became the swimming power until 1964.

Don Schollander of the United States matched Johnny Weissmuller's feat of five gold medals by winning four in 1964 and one in 1968. Schollander's gold in 1968 was in the 4 × 200 meter relay, and Mark Spitz, a team member on that relay team, was destined in 1972 to win seven gold medals. At that time it was the most gold medals ever won at a single Olympic Games in any sport and each medal involved a world record (four were individual events and three were relays).

One of the most dominating team performances occurred at the 1976 Olympics when the U.S. men's team won 12 of 13 possible golds and 10 silvers in the 11 individual events. In 1980, when the United States boycotted the Olympics, the Soviet men's team dominated by winning seven of the 13 gold medals. In 1984, when the Soviets boycotted, the U.S. men returned to dominance by taking 9 of the 15 gold medals.

In 1988 a record 21 different nations earned medals in swimming (both men's and women's) but the men's events were once again dominated by a U.S. swimmer. Matt Biondi gathered five golds, one silver and a bronze for a performance eclipsed only by Mark Spitz.

Women

The first Olympic women's swimming events were held in 1912, and the next several Olympics were dominated by swimmers from Australia, Great Britain, and the United States.

In 1920 Ethelda Bleibtrey of the United States won the 100 meter freestyle, the 300 meter freestyle, and anchored the 4×100 meter freestyle relay to sweep all three events at the Antwerp Olympics. In 1932 the U.S. women's swim team, led by Helene Madison, won six of the seven swimming and diving events but won only three bronze medals in 1936.

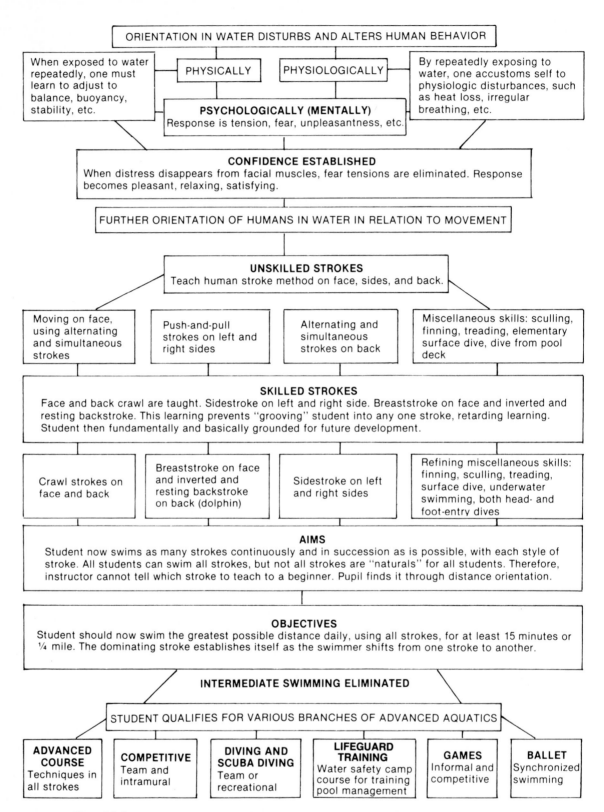

Fig. 31-1. The Armbruster all-stroke method—a progressive learning procedure chart for swimming.

As with the men's swimming events, the Australian women's teams, led by Dawn Fraser, dominated the Olympics after World War II. The U.S. women began to reemerge as a swimming power in 1968 when Debra Meyer won three gold medals. In 1972, when Mark Spitz was winning seven golds, the dominant women swimmer was Shane Gould of Australia with four golds, one silver, and one bronze. However, Melissa Belste of the United States also won three golds in two individual events and a relay.

In 1972, when the U.S. men had the great team performance, the U.S. and Australian dominance in the womens events continued, but it came to an end in 1976 as the East German women won 11 of the 13 golds. Shirley Babashoff of the United States did manage a gold and three silvers, giving her eight Olympic medals in her career and establishing her as one of the United States' great female swimmers.

When the United States boycotted in 1980, the East German women repeated their feat of garnering 11 of the 13 gold medals. In 1984, when the East Germans boycotted, the U.S. women swimmers returned to power with 11 of the 14 golds.

In the 1988 Olympics, the stars of the women's swimming competition were Kristin Otto of East Germany and Janet Evans of the United States. Otto's six gold medals broke the record for most golds won by a woman in any sport at one Olympics. Seventeen-year-old Janet Evans won the 400 meter individual medley, the 800 meter freestyle and the 400 meter freestyle in a world record time of 4:03:85.

ARMBRUSTER ALL-STROKE METHOD FOR TEACHING BEGINNERS

The Armbruster all-stroke method begins by adjusting students to water; then several skilled and some low-skilled techniques are learned. When the student is comfortably adjusted to water and basically "stanced," the basic skill strokes can be learned quite rapidly.

Beginners can learn the strokes and make reasonable progress; however, not everyone can swim all strokes equally well. Therefore by teaching all of the students all of the strokes, everyone will naturally find the stroke most comfortable and suitable through a distance orientation program after the stroke skills are learned. People differ anatomically. If students are taught all strokes, in the distance orientation program, the stroke that takes the least effort will naturally be selected most often. Each student will find the stroke that gives the most self-satisfaction and pleasure, even though basically "grounded" in every stroke. The students are not first "grooved" in one or two strokes but are basically grounded for advanced swimming, lifesaving, or any other form of aquatic interest. The idea, too, is to do away with the intermediate level of swimming.

The secret of this method is really to work the legs by drilling them in the different kick skills. Ordinarily legs are clumsy and awkward, being composed of big muscles that in everyday living are trained only to walk, run, jump, and perhaps dance. To get legs to relax in water and become skilled, and to get the feel of the unnatural medium water, the swimmer must train and overlearn.

Correct breathing habits are the next essential skill to teach. One must breathe to swim. Water interferes with the breathing mechanism of the human being. Even the quadruped holds its nose at the highest point of its body in relation to the surface level in order to swim. It, too, must breathe to swim. The human being has learned to exhale under the surface and inhale above the surface.

Instructors should emphasize skill learning by constant drill and action. Action creates interest and results in interested students who will work hard if they know they are learning. Swimming taught progressively and intensively accomplishes that. If students become fatigued (not exhausted) from constant exercise, they will naturally take it easy, and when they take it easy, the response is relaxation. Relaxation is learned through constant repetitions.

OBJECTIVES

1. To orient students to water, a medium that disturbs a person physically, physiologically, and mentally and brings about the following:
   a. Unstableness
   b. Apparent loss of body weight
   c. Loss of sense of balance
   d. Change in body position for locomotion
   e. Change in heat-regulatory mechanism
   f. Change in respiration
   g. Change in normal muscle tonus
2. To give confidence, using drills that have the following objectives:
   a. To eliminate mental hazards
   b. To teach the proper techniques of inhalation and exhalation
   c. To bring about relaxation in the water
   d. To encourage enjoyment of swimming
3. To teach self-reliance for self-preservation
4. To teach an appreciation of distance over water no matter how short or long
5. To teach respect for water generally while swimming
6. To impart confidence in skill and ability of accomplishment
7. To teach strokes in such a way as to motivate the student to persistent practice

8. To encourage swimming as a source of lifelong pleasure
9. To teach distribution of effort and conservation of strength
10. To teach how to delay fatigue
11. To teach how to dive into water

BASIC SKILLS AND TECHNIQUES
Adjustment to water

1. Examine the pool markings to know its depth at all locations before entering the water.
2. Wade waist deep into the pool and submerge repeatedly to chin level, rinsing up and down and washing the face.
3. Hold onto the splash gutter and allow water to lift the legs and body to the surface. Stay relaxed.

Breath control

Depending on the level and maturity of swimmers, the following activities can be performed while holding on to the pool gutter, holding on to a partner, or without support.

1. Standing in waist-deep water with the body inclined forward, practice breath holding; inhale through the mouth, close the mouth, shut the eyes, and submerge the face flat beneath the water. Hold for 3 seconds and recover. Repeat several times, lengthening the time of holding the breath underwater.
2. Inhale through the mouth, submerge the face with the eyes closed, exhale through the nose, and recover. Repeat several times.
3. Inhale through the mouth, submerge the face with the eyes closed, and exhale through the nose, mouth, or both, steadily but as slowly as possible. Recover and repeat several times.

Use of eyes underwater

Inhale, close the eyes, submerge, open the eyes, count the number of fingers visible on a partner's hand, and recover. Repeat.

Shipping water with mouth

Submerge, open the mouth, recover, and ship out water into splash gutter. Repeat several times.

Balance and control of the body

The following activities are designed to aid the student in developing confidence in the water. To ensure that confidence is generated and fear is not reinforced, it is important to discuss and practice (with partners) the procedures of returning to a stable position before assuming the various floating and gliding positions.

Jellyfish float. This float may be performed in either the pike or tuck position. Take a deep breath, submerge the face, raise the knees to the chest or extend the legs, and hold with the arms for 3 seconds. Release the hold, allow the legs to extend to the bottom of the pool, let the arms float up a little, and then push them down and toward the hips while at the same time raising the head. The instructor should pay close attention to the swimmer in these initial floats as individual differences, especially in amount of leanness and fatness, will result in large differences in ability to float. (See Fig. 31-2.) Repeat.

Prone floating position. The prone floating position is taken by lifting and extending the arms forward beyond the head beneath the surface, with the head held low in the water, and extending the legs (this is the only difference between the prone float and the jellyfish float). (See Fig. 31-3.) To recover to the standing position, pull the knees to the chest, round the back, then simultaneously press firmly downward with the extended arms, extend the legs to the bottom of the pool, and lift the face from the water. With the legs extended downward, the feet will settle on the pool floor. (Water must be at least waist deep.) Keep the eyes open. After recovery, exhale through the nose, open the mouth, inhale, and flutter the eyes open.

Prone glide and stand. For the prone glide, bend forward at the waist, with the arms extended forward. Lay the upper body and arms in the water, just under the surface. Take a deep breath at the side, bend the knees, and roll the face under the surface. Straighten the knees, push the feet off the bottom, and slide into a prone position and the glide. At the end of the glide, draw the knees into the chest and recover as in the prone float.

Back floating position. With a partner standing directly behind, assume a back floating position by submerging to the chin and, with the partner supporting the back of the neck with one hand and the small of the back with the other, lift the hips and extend the arms sideward. The ears will be under water. The partner gradually removes support, first from the small of the back and then from the neck. The body will not necessarily stay horizontal to the water. Some swimmer's legs have a tendency to sink. The important elements are to relax, keep the arms extended, and hold the neck back to keep the face above water. The partner should help you recover the first few times. To gain recovery from the back float, move the arms downward and forward in the water, round the back, bring the knees to the chin, and lift the head slowly forward. When the body moves to a vertical position, extend the legs to the bottom and stand. (See Fig. 31-4.)

Back glide and stand. For the back glide, sit back so the shoulders are submerged, push off with the feet, glide until forward motion stops, and then recover as in the back float. In the glide, keep the arms at the side and the legs straight and together.

Fig. 31-2. A, Jellyfish float, pike, and tuck positions. **B,** Recovery from jellyfish float.

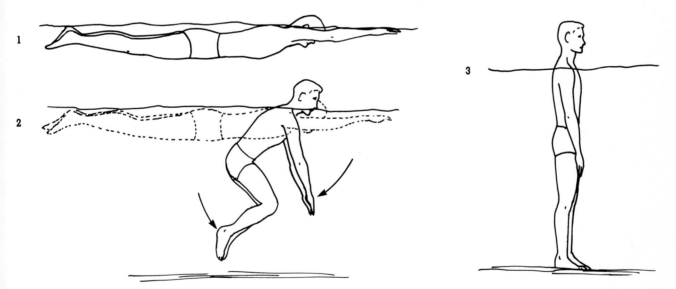

Fig. 31-3. Prone float and recovery.

Fig. 31-4. Back float and recovery.

Simple leg movements to keep body horizontal and to aid propulsion

Kick glide, prone position. For the kick glide, prone position, start in the same manner as in the prone glide, but as the body straightens out on the surface, move the legs in an alternate up-and-down maneuver, delivered with the knee fairly loose; continue to the limit of breath-holding ability. (For additional practice, hold onto the splash gutter or a kickboard and kick the legs as above.)

Kick glide, back position. In the kick glide, back position, assume a back floating position but with the back flat and chin tucked well into the throat. Move the legs in a slightly bent-kneed flutter kick. Snap each knee into extension when finishing the kick. (For additional practice, hold onto the splash gutter and execute the flutter kick.)

Simple arm movements for support, propulsion, and balancing of body

Arm stroke on the front. For the arm stroke on the front (dog paddle or human stroke), assume the prone position in the water and extend the arms alternately forward and downward, following with a press backward under the body. Cup the hands slightly on the pull backward. In the recovery forward of each arm, straighten the hand, draw it up under the chin, and extend it to a forward position; cup the hand and repeat the stroke.

Arm stroke on the back. The arm stroke on the back (finning) is a paired movement of the hands and arms in a back position. The arms are first extended by the sides and then drawn up about 1 foot, at which point they are thrust outward and then toward the feet in a sort of pushing movement, supplemented by a sort of fishtail flip of the hands and wrists.

Coordination of breathing with leg and arm movements

Combined stroke on the front. The combined stroke on the front is composed of up-and-down alternating beats of the legs and the dog paddle with the arms, with breathing done entirely above the surface or alternately inhaling above and exhaling below the water. Two or more beats of the legs should accompany each cycle of arm strokes.

Inhalation should be done with the head turned to the side. If the head is turned to the left to get air, inhale when the right arm is extended forward. Rotate the head into the water on this cycle, and when the left arm is extended, exhale under water through the mouth. To inhale to the right side, the left arm should be extended, and on this cycle, as the right arm is extended rotate the face into the water and exhale.

Combined stroke on the back. The combined stroke on the back consists of finning with the hands and flutter kicking with the legs. Assume the back floating position with the back flat and the chin tucked well into the throat. First, the leg beat is started using greater speed and more flexibility than is used in the front kick. The thrust of the hands (finning) is put into the stroke at regular intervals. Breathe naturally.

Turning, right and left. Begin the front stroke (human stroke), maintaining the body nearly horizontal, and execute a right turn and then a left turn. Try executing a complete turn. Extend the hands and pull in the opposite direction of the turn.

Change positions. In changing position or turning over from the front to the back, start swimming, keep the body nearly horizontal, and at the point of changing positions, roll the body either right or left to a back floating position. Keep the shoulders and head low in the water. The head, arms, hips, and legs will aid in rolling the body. In changing from a back float to the front, roll in a similar manner to a front position and resume the stroke.

SKILLED STROKE TECHNIQUES
Resting backstroke

The resting backstroke (Fig. 31-5) should be the first stroke taught to beginners. It requires little coordination and gives the student a sense of motivation. This is principally a resting stroke for an emergency or for easy swimming while resting, and it lays a sound foundation for the breaststroke and elementary backstroke as well as for treading water. The face is never underwater, and thus breathing is not a disturbing factor.

Whip kick (inverted breaststroke kick)

The recovery is executed by spreading the knees but holding the heels together. Press the heels down as they

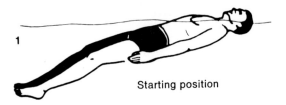

Starting position

Recover arms and legs together

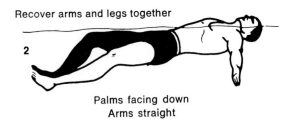

Palms facing down
Arms straight

Kick and pull together

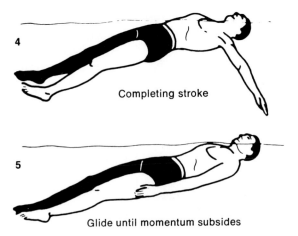

Completing stroke

Glide until momentum subsides

Fig. 31-5. Progressive steps in swimming the resting backstroke—the first skill stroke to learn.

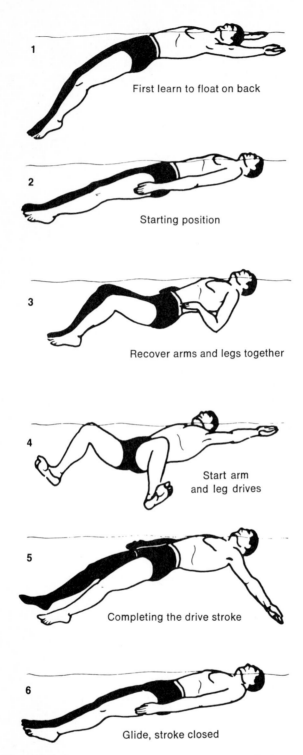

1. First learn to float on back

2. Starting position

3. Recover arms and legs together

4. Start arm and leg drives

5. Completing the drive stroke

6. Glide, stroke closed

Fig. 31-6. Progressive steps in swimming and elementary backstroke.

recover toward the buttocks so that the knees do not lift out of the water, and at the same time lift the hips to prevent the drop. Separate the heels and cock the feet outward toward the knees. Start the drive by sweeping the legs out and together, and engage the water with the soles of the feet, extending the feet as they kick. During this kick, when the knees are not quite straightened, squeeze the thighs together forcefully with the knees relaxed to give a whiplike motion to the foreleg and feet, resulting in increased propulsion. This stroke can also be introduced using a flutter kick first, as the whip kick can be difficult for some students to master.

Arm stroke

The arm recovery starts from the sides of the thighs by turning the palms downward and slightly at an angle in the direction of recovery, the little finger side of the hand leading and knifing through the water. The arms are held straight. The arms move outward away from the thighs to a point just above the shoulders.

The pull is executed by turning the palms to the rear and slightly downward and moving the straight arms forcefully to the sides of the thighs.

At no time during either the recovery or the pull of the hands or arms should they be above the surface.

Whole stroke

This stroke is easy to execute because the arms and legs work in unison. The arms and legs recover at the exact moment and kick and pull at the same moment. When the stroke is closed, stretch out straight and pause until momentum from the previous stroke is spent. Repeat.

Elementary backstroke

This stroke (Fig. 31-6) should be taught after the resting backstroke has been mastered.

This style affords a little more speed than does the resting backstroke and is still restful and easy to learn. However, more coordination is required to execute it because the arms are partly recovered before the legs recover.

Whip kick

The kick is executed exactly the same as in the resting backstroke kick.

Arm stroke

The arm recovery in the elementary backstroke differs from that in the resting backstroke. The arm recovery is executed by bending the elbows downward and sliding the hands from the sides of the thighs up along the sides of the body toward the shoulders. Then the hands, palms facing up, reach out diagonally from the armpit under the water until the arms are straight. Turn the palm facing backward and pull, straight-armed, to the sides of the thighs. Pause until the momentum from the pull subsides.

Whole stroke

In the recovery phase, hold the legs straight while the arms recover to about armpit level; then start the leg recovery at the same slow speed as the arms recover. When the arms have reached the pulling position, the legs have recovered to the kick position; that is, the knees and heels are apart, feet pointed outward. The kick and pull must start at the same instant. Stretch the body and legs straight, though relaxed, and pause for the momentum to spend itself. Breathe regularly.

Underarm sidestroke

The underarm sidestroke (Fig. 31-7) is easy to learn. It is the foundation stroke for lifesaving. Breathing is not difficult, because the nose and mouth are turned to the rear and the water passes by the side of the face. This is not one of the modern competitive strokes.

Scissors kick

The scissors kick is perhaps the most powerful of all kicks in the water, which is why it is used so much in lifesaving.

First the kick is learned on both sides by holding onto the sides of the pool. The body is held straight on its side, legs straight, feet extended, and one leg on top of the other. To start the recovery movement, flex at the knees and slowly draw the heels backward. Both legs are held together and move simultaneously. This drawing of the heels backward gives just the proper amount of flexion at the hip joint. In this position, if an imaginary line were passed through the midpoint of the shoulder and hip joints, it would project out over the legs at a midpoint between the knees and ankles when the legs are in a full recovery position. The scissors is now opened by moving the underleg back and the top leg forward, still maintaining the fully flexed knees. The foot of the top leg cocks itself, or flexes toward the knee. The under foot remains extended. From this position the legs start the drive, sweeping outward and together by extension of the knees and the foot of the top leg. The under leg hooks the water and acts in the same manner as kicking a ball, whereas the top leg has a whip motion similar to a horse's pawing. The legs come together stretched straight and relaxed and pause long enough for momentum to be spent in the glide.

Arm stroke

While the body is on its left side, with the shoulder girdle in a true vertical plane, the under left arm is extended forward directly under the head, with the palm facing down and the hand just under the surface. The upper

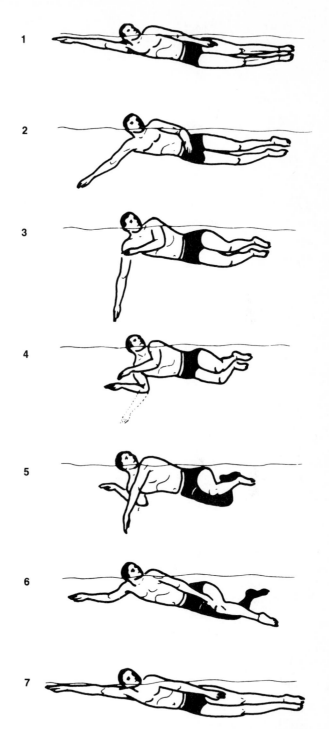

Fig. 31-7. Progressive steps in swimming the underarm sidestroke.

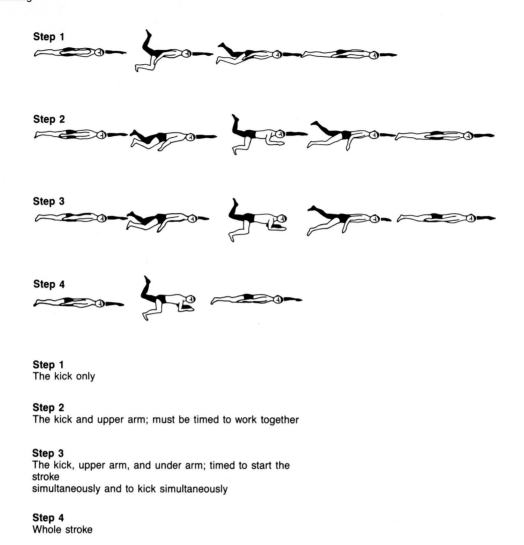

Step 1
Step 1
The kick only

Step 2
Step 2
The kick and upper arm; must be timed to work together

Step 3
Step 3
The kick, upper arm, and under arm; timed to start the stroke
simultaneously and to kick simultaneously

Step 4
Step 4
Whole stroke

Fig. 31-8. The four steps of learning the sidestroke.

right arm is pulling back, hugging closely along the upper front part of the body with the palm of the hand resting on the front side of the upper leg—never on the top of the leg.

The learner should first get a clear mental picture of the arm stroke from the starting position, that is, both arms moving simultaneously along the longitudinal plane of the body. They meet just under the head, change direction, and simultaneously extend again to their starting position. The under arm moves forward; the upper arm moves backward. The student can "singsong," "Everything drawn in, everything thrust out." Actually, as the upper arm slides forward to recover to meet the under arm, the under arm should pull diagonally downward and backward to a line under the head. Here it changes direction and starts the recovery movement, with the hand and fingers pointing forward to its starting position. Even though the hands move in and out to-

gether, the under arm is always pulling on the "in" movement, while on the "out" movement the upper arm is pulling, or vice versa.

Whole stroke coordinated in four steps

It is recommended that each of the four steps be learned thoroughly before advancing to the next step. (See Fig. 31-8.)

Step 1—scissors kick only. Take a deep breath and lie on the left side floating position with the body straight and the left under arm extended in a line with the body. Turn the face into the water on top of the under arm and hold the breath. The upper right arm is in front of the upper thigh. Take at least four kicks in succession and pause between each stroke for the glide. The upper hand is in front of the upper thigh and remains on it during these kick exercises. This trains the upper arm to work in unison with the kick, as it must do in the whole stroke.

Step 2—the kick and upper arm. The body is still on its extended left side, with the face under water as in step 1. To execute step 2, the upper hand and arm recover at the same time as the legs. The hand planes forward beyond the face, with the elbow and hand submerged to a point beyond the face. The arm pull starts at the same time as the kick. Here again, as in the resting backstroke, the upper arm and legs recover at the same time, and the kick and pull occur at the same time.

Step 3—the kick, upper arm, and underarm. The body and face are still in the same position as in step 1. To execute step 3, press—do not pull—the underarm diagonally down and backward to a point under the face. At the same instant that the underarm starts its press, the legs and upper arm are recovered. The hands meet, cross over, and repass as the underarm hand recovers and thrusts forward to guide the glide. At the same time the underarm recovers, the upper arm and legs start the kick and pull. Pause and glide. Repeat the singsong, "Everything in, everything out," as in the underarm sidestroke. Glide. This makes the arms and legs simple to coordinate into the whole stroke. Repeat at least four strokes before stopping for air.

Step 4—breathing. Take one or two strokes in the step 3 position and then turn the face out of the water and face to the rear with the chin in line with the upper shoulder. Breathe in at the same time that the arms and legs come in; breathe out at the same time that the arms and legs go out. Remember, "Everything in, everything out." Once four or five strokes are correctly timed and coordinated, you have learned the skill of coordinating the whole stroke. Now repeat the same four-step procedure on the right side. The water level should remain constant at the face, leveling at the corner of the lower eye and lower corner of the mouth.

Note: These four-step procedures can also be performed with flotation devices such as kickboards.

Breaststroke*

The breaststroke was the first competitive stroke and is still used in competitive events. However, it is also an excellent utility stroke and is used in many lifesaving skills.

Kick

There have been many modifications of the breaststroke kick in recent times. These modifications have resulted primarily from an interest in increasing the speed of the entire stroke. In general, the main characteristic of these modifications has been to reduce unwanted resistance

---

*For the breaststroke and the dolphin butterfly stroke, see Armbruster DA, Allen RH, and Billingsley HS: Swimming and diving, ed 6, St Louis, 1973, The CV Mosby Co.

by narrowing the knee spread and increasing the desired resistance by adding a slightly downward thrust in the propulsive phase of the kick. However, for the beginner the traditional kick is probably easiest to learn initially.

The breaststroke kick (whip) is almost the same as used in the inverted or the resting backstroke. The body is prone, arms extended, face under. The recovery begins with the heels close together and then drawn toward the buttocks just under the surface. This results in the knees being brought forward; however, the angle of the thighs to the upper body should be slightly greater than 90 degrees. In other words, the knees should not be drawn up quite so far as to be directly below the pelvis. (See Fig. 31-9, 4.) When the heels are fully drawn up to the buttocks, the feet separate outward and the ankles are cocked, or the feet are flexed outward at the ankles and toward the knees. The legs are now in position to drive. The drive is made with an outward and together sweep, extending the ankles until the legs are again closed to the starting position, with the legs straight and the toes pointed. Pause with the legs fully extended until momentum from the kick is spent. During the propulsive phase of the kick, you should feel as though water is being pushed backward by the soles of the feet. Also attempt to get a whiplash to the legs during the kick phase. This is accomplished by driving the thighs in toward each other before the knees have fully extended. This movement gives the powerful whiplash kick.

Arm stroke

In the starting position, the arms are extended forward, hands close together, palms facing away from each other. The arms spread out and pull simultaneously in a lateral downward and backward movement, and the elbows bend as the hands reach shoulder width apart. The hands continue to a point under the chin. Pulling them farther removes the support from under the shoulders and head, causing them to drop and sink, which disturbs the body balance. At the completion of the arm pull, the face is lifted to breathe and the knees begin their flexion for the kick recovery. The recovery of the arms begins under the chin as the hands join each other and are thrust forward to the starting position. At this point, pause to allow for a glide. The entire arm stroke is a continuous, uninterrupted movement. Practice walking across the pool and coordinating the breathing with arm action technique.

Whole stroke

Push off from the side of the pool with the body prone on the surface, fully extended, the face underwater. The arms pull as just described to a point under the chin, at which time the breath is taken and the legs are recovered with the feet spread and cocked for the drive. By this

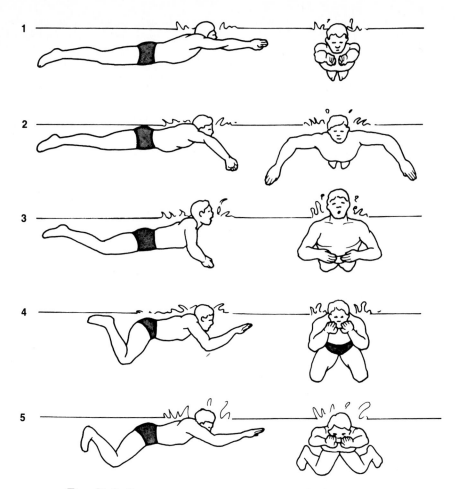

Fig. 31-9. Progressive steps in swimming the breaststroke.

time the arms are already thrusting forward. When the arms are almost fully extended, the legs start the drive. The arms pause for the glide when they have reached full extension. The legs also pause for the glide when they have closed at the end of the drive. The body is now fully extended. Exhale slowly during the glide. Repeat several strokes to time the movements smoothly and continuously from the start of the stroke to the end of the leg drive. (See Fig. 31-9.) The breaststroke can easily be executed with the face out of the water, as may be required in some lifesaving situations. To accomplish this the glide is shortened and the stroke requires more effort than normal.

Crawl stroke

The crawl stroke (Fig. 31-10) is the speed king of all strokes. Neither arms nor legs recover underwater, which accounts for its greater speed. The modern speed crawl is truly one of the most refined and specialized of all sports skills.

Flutter kick

The body is prone, with arms and legs fully extended, face under, and ankles stretched and close together. From this position the flutter kick is executed by alternately oscillating the legs vertically from the hips, forcefully and regularly. On each downward beat the foot turns inward (pigeon-toed). This occurs naturally if the ankles and feet are held loosely. This increases the surface area of the foot. In the upward beat the foot is extended, not pigeon-toed. Beginners should first attempt this kick while learning to hold the legs straight yet not rigid. This originates the movements from the hips. When this is learned and the thighs move up and down, the knee action can be learned. For example, look at the action of one leg only. In some ways it is similar to pedaling a bicycle. As the leg drives up, the sole of the foot pushes upward and remains there until the knee is almost straight on the downward beat. (See action of right leg in Fig. 31-10, *1* through *3.*) This movement results in a quick down-up whiplash of the foreleg and foot at the

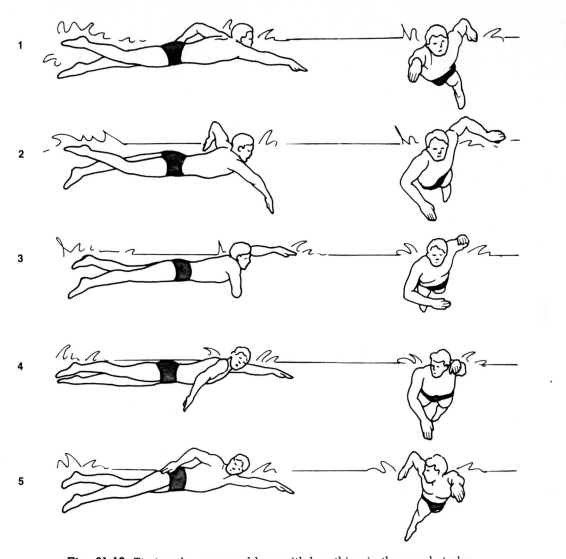

Fig. 31-10. Timing the arms and legs with breathing in the crawl stroke.

end of the downbeat, the same principle used in the breaststroke kick. This skill can be learned by daily drills with the aid of a kickboard.

Arm stroke (alternating)

This stroke is executed by alternately reaching hand-over-hand forward into the water and pulling the body forward over the surface. The arm stroke has seven components: (1) entry, (2) support, (3) catch, (4) pull, (5) push, (6) release, and (7) recovery.

For the entry, place the hand in the water at a natural arm's length, directly in front of the shoulder. The hand should enter the water before the elbow or shoulder. A comfortable reach should be made; never overreach. (See Fig. 31-10, *1* through *3.*)

In modern speed swimming, as well as in teaching the crawl stroke to beginners, an opposition rhythm type of stroke is prevalent. "Opposition-type stroke" means that the arms are nearly opposite each other at all times. However, if speed is desired, the fundamental mechanics of the stroke become quite complex and highly technical in obtaining the ease and balance necessary for good performance as well as speed. These technical essentials can be obtained once the fundamentals of the stroke have been mastered.

The beginner should not be concerned with speed in learning but should merely be able to execute the arm stroke with reasonably good opposition timing.

The catch and pull should start, first in the hand and then bending the elbow slightly for good leverage. (See Fig. 31-10, *2.*) The pull shifts into a push as the arm passes under the chest toward the opposite hip. Then the push continues the drive to the release with the forearm and hand. At this point the shoulder begins to lift in preparation to recover the arm until the hand clears the surface at the hip.

The arm is then recovered to the entry by lifting the shoulder, bending at the elbow, and turning the hand so that the palm faces to the rear and gradually faces the water at entry. The arm recovery movement is up and outward, away from the hip, and forward to the water. The shoulder is held high while the hand and forearm enter the water. The desired high elbow position on the recovery, entry, and catch is made easier if the shoulders and hips are allowed to roll to both sides during a complete stroke. The rolling action should be symmetric, with the head held in a relatively stable position. (See Fig. 31-10.)

Whole stroke*

While the arms execute a complete revolution, the legs complete some number of evenly measured beats. In walking, the arms and legs move in a 1 : 1 ratio, an opposite arm and leg counterbalancing movement. In swimming the crawl, a preferred (though not mandatory) leg to arm ratio is 3 : 1; that is, the legs perform three beats to each arm stroke, or six beats to each complete cycle of both arms. This ratio gives the stroke a counterbalancing movement like that in walking or running.

Breathing

Breathing in the crawl stroke is executed as follows: just as the arm opposite the breathing side is put into the water for support, the head is turned to inhale and then immediately returned in line with the body. When turning the head for air, keep the chin in close to the throat and look to see if the mouth is inside the trough of the bow wave formed by the head. Take a quick breath as the mouth is opening; do not pause after opening the mouth. Curl the lips out away from the teeth when opening the mouth. (See Fig. 31-10, *4* and *5*.)

Back crawl stroke

The back crawl stroke (Fig. 31-11) is the crawl stroke inverted. However, it differs somewhat from the crawl in that the face is not under the water during the stroke, so that breathing is simplified.

Inverted flutter kick

Essentially the kick is the same as the flutter kick in the crawl stroke. The body is extended on its back, legs held

---

*For a critical analysis of the crawl stroke, see Armbruster DA, Allen RH, and Billingsley HS: Swimming and diving, ed 6, St Louis, 1973, The CV Mosby Co.

closely together, ankles and toes pointed, chin low on the throat, water level at the lower earlobes and around, not over, the chest. The legs move alternately up and down with action originating from the hips. On the upward beat the toes turn in, and on the downward beat they are extended. At the end of the upward beat the kneecap should not break through the surface and the foot should throw some water above the surface without projecting out of the water. To accomplish this skill, the thigh, as in other styles of kicks, forcefully drives down just before the knee has straightened. This action gives the foreleg and foot an effective propulsive up-down whip. The ratio of leg kicks to one complete stroke revolution is 6 : 1, the same as in the crawl stroke.

Arm stroke

The arms move in opposition to one another as if the swimmer has a broomstick across the back of the neck and shoulders with the arms extending out along the broomstick.

The moment the arm has finished its pull along the side of the thigh, the hand gives a final downward press as the shoulder is lifted out of the water and the hand is turned to face outward. The arm is bent slightly at the elbow at the beginning of the recovery phase, but it is straightened for the entry. The arm recovers to the entry with an upward swing and continues to the entry at a point not more than 6 inches outside the shoulder line. The hand and forearm should not be slowed as they near the point of entry but should accelerate so that they are in the water before the shoulder can sink under.

The power or pull phase of the stroke can be done with either a bent arm or a straight arm. The bent-arm stroke is used by high-level competitive swimmers but is more difficult to learn than the straight-arm pull, which is generally recommended when learning the backstroke. In the initial part of the straight-arm pull, the arm is shallow, about 2 to 6 inches underwater. As the arm reaches a point directly out from the shoulder the depth should be about 6 to 10 inches. From here, the arm continues until it reaches the leg and begins the recovery phase. (See Fig. 31-11.) The bent-arm pull is initiated slightly deeper than the straight-arm pull. As the pull progresses, the arm is drawn in toward the body by bending at the elbow. Just before the hand reaches a point directly out from the shoulder, the pull changes to a push. The arm and hand continue and finish near the leg, as in the straight-arm pull, to begin the recovery phase. In both types of pulls the arm stroke should be smooth and relaxed throughout. A slight hip and a more pronounced shoulder roll permit an easier recovery and catch, as well as more efficient action of the opposite arm.

Fig. 31-11. Progressive steps in swimming the back crawl showing the six leg beats and one revolution of the arm cycle.

Breathing

Breathing should be continuous and rhythmic. Hold the head with the chin always lined up on dead center, never moving from side to side. Try to keep the body stretched to prevent sagging at the hips. (See Fig. 31-11.)

Dolphin butterfly stroke

The dolphin butterfly stroke was created by Armbruster at the University of Iowa in 1935 with the aid of one of his swimmers, Jack Sieg. The legs in this stroke move in unison in an up-and-down wavelike action that resembles the tail of a dolphin in swimming. The arms also move in unison in both the propulsive and the recovery phases. The arms recover low above the surface, are held nearly straight, and resemble the wings of a butterfly in flight.

The stroke is definitely dominated by the kick. This dolphin wavelike kick by the legs only has become the fastest means of kicking through water. It is even faster than the alternating flutter kick used in the crawl and back crawl strokes, yet the basic characteristics of the dolphin kick are the same as those of the alternating flutter crawl kicks.

The dolphin butterfly stroke is very exhausting to the untrained individual. Except for use as a competitive swimming stroke, it has little, if any, value to humans. However, the stroke is included here because many students desire to learn it, if for no other reasons than for its rugged, challenging action and for the satisfaction of being able to perform it.

Kick

It is essential that before learning the dolphin kick the beginner thoroughly master the crawl flutter kick, because the basic characteristics of the two are the same. When the flutter kick is learned and performed with ease, the student is well conditioned to attempt the dolphin kick. In daily training drills the practice of this kick works in well with the other stroke kicks in the all-stroke practice method.

As practice progresses, the student should lie face down on the surface of the water, kicking only, with the hands finning at the sides of the hips. As a final step of conditioning and training, and before the whole stroke is attempted, the student should submerge and practice the kick underwater during breath-holding intervals. The hands should be finning at the sides of the hips rather than extended in front of the head. By practicing the kick underwater, the student is able to determine that the progress is true forward and not down or up. If either occurs, adjustment should be made to equalize the up-and-down beat in relation to the forward plane of progress. It is also essential while performing underwater to stress relaxing the entire spine from the shoulders through all the joints to the end of the toes. To help beginners become familiar with this movement, it is often practiced with the aid of swim fins. When the true shortened up-and-down beat of the kick and the up-and-down action of the hips have been mastered, the student has been properly trained and conditioned for learning the arm action.

Arm stroke

The student should first practice the arm stroke by walking across the swimming pool, bent at the hips, chin at water level, stroking with the arms. The stroke can also be practiced while stationary, in the same position.

The arms start the stroke from the point of entry, just outside the shoulders, pressing downward into a short lateral spread. The hands and forearms continue the pull backward with a quick inward action, elbows bending, until they reach a point just under and ahead of the shoulders. From this point the power drive is completed backward to the sides of the hips until the arms and hands have cleared the surface of the water. This final emphasis is delivered by straightening the elbows until shoulders, arms, and hands have cleared the surface of the water. From this action the arms also derive the impetus to swing laterally forward through the recovery phase to again reach the correct point of entry. During the recovery the arms are held nearly straight, palms facing the surface. The recovery should be executed without hesitation at the end of the power drive. The arms should enter the water with a soft plunge, the wrists slightly flexed toward the surface as they enter. Actually, the hands and forearms should enter the water slightly ahead of the upper arms and shoulders. At this point, without hesitation, the catch of the next stroke is started.

When walking or swimming across the pool practicing the arm stroke, the student should imagine the body moving toward the face of a large clock; the left arm should enter the water pointing to 11 o'clock and the right arm should point to 1 o'clock.

There is no pause in the entire stroke turnover. This is what is known in swimming terms as a fast turnover stroke; that is, the moment the arms complete the power drive, they go into the recovery to start the next stroke. Not only must the arms recovery quickly, but the power drive of the arms must also be rapidly executed. It is this fast turnover cadence that makes the stroke so strenuous for the beginner, especially if the beginner is poorly conditioned. However, most students skilled in other strokes have an urge to learn the challenging, complex skills involved in performing this stroke.

Whole stroke

The stroke is started by moving the arms forward laterally to the point of entry. The hands enter the water just

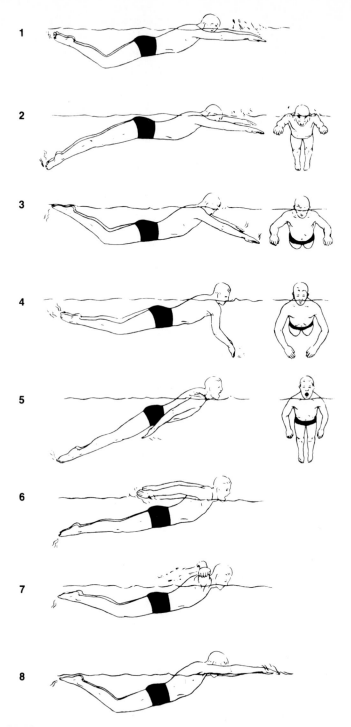

Fig. 31-12. Progressive steps in swimming the dolphin butterfly stroke.

outside the shoulders simultaneously, pointing to the 11 and 1 o'clock positions, respectively. As the hands execute the catch, with a slight spread and downward press, the first downward beat of the kick takes place. (See Fig. 31-12, *1* and *2*.) This downbeat of the kick is a natural counteraction caused by the powerful downward catch and pull of the forearms, similar to the counterswing of the arms and legs in walking or running. While the hands and arms execute the inward drive or pull to a point just ahead of and under the shoulders, the first upbeat of the kick has taken place. (See Fig. 31-12, *3* and *4*.) From this point the arms continue to complete the final power drive as the second downbeat of the kick takes place. (See Fig. 31-12, *4* and *5*.) This action is again a natural counterbalancing movement of legs and arms. As the arms drive out of the water at the hips and move into the recovery phase, the legs execute the second upbeat. (See Fig. 31-12, *6* through *8*.) Note that during the entire arm recovery phase there is but one beat of the legs, which is up, and none supporting the body. For this reason it is essential that the swimmer move the arms quickly from the end of the drive to the entry. This quickened movement will prevent the body from sinking below swimming level. The most troublesome part in learning the stroke is this latter phase. If the arms move too slowly or hesitate at any point between the final drive and the entry, rhythm and timing are lost.

In executing the entry, the arms plunge lightly into the water and immediately go into the catch to start the next stroke. The stroke should first be practiced without breathing until reasonably satisfactory timing is attained. Then too, in learning, beginners often make the mistake of starting the recovery of the arms prematurely before the arms and hands have cleared the surface of the water well back of the hips and straightened elbows. (See Fig. 31-12, *5* and *6*.)

Breathing

Correct breathing in the dolphin butterfly stroke is not too difficult, providing the beginner does not develop a tendency to climb too high to get a breath. In learning this skill, the student should again walk the arm stroke across the swimming pool with the face submerged while executing the breathing and correct timing action of the head in the arm stroke cadence. Taking a breath every stroke should be practiced. Correct breathing habits in this stroke are essential to obtain ease of performance of the entire stroke.

To inhale, the swimmer should lift the head just far enough for the mouth to clear the surface of the water. This action takes place just as the arms have passed backward from under the shoulders and are completing their drive. Air is actually taken just as the arms clear the water and move into the recovery phase. (See Fig. 31-12, *4* through *6*.) Note how the finishing "kick" of the arm stroke gives the head the necessary lift to inhale. Emphasis is placed on dropping the head quickly into the water (but not too deeply) after air has been taken and before the arm recovery has reached the point of entry. (See Fig. 31-12, *7* and *8*.) It should now be easy for the beginner to visualize why it is essential to quickly recover both the head and the arms to give support to the body during this phase of the stroke. Both the head and the arms are above the surface of the water during

the second upward beat of the kick. If this phase of the stroke is not well timed and executed, the beginner will tend to sink too deep in the water and then have to climb too high to get air. With practice, proficiency is acquired and the tiring unnecessary movements are minimized.

LEARNING PROGRESSION FOR BEGINNERS

1. Review swimming pool landmarks regarding pool depths, any unique features of the natatorium, and personal safety rules.
2. Orientation and adjustment to water in order to overcome loss of body weight, loss of balance, and loss of body heat, all of which disturb the beginner psychologically, physiologically, and physically
   a. Submerging the face, opening the eyes, and holding the breath
   b. Shipping water with the mouth
   c. Breathing with bobbing exercises
   d. Floating, tucked and body straight, on both the face and back
3. Adjustment of the hands and feet to paddling in shallow water
   a. Sculling with and without the feet
   b. Finning with and without the feet
   c. Treading water with and without the feet
4. Unskilled strokes on the face, sides, and back
5. Skilled strokes (basic strokes)
   a. Kicks
      (1) Flutter
      (2) Scissors (both sides)
      (3) Whip
   b. Arm strokes (basic strokes)
      (1) Alternating stroke with breathing
      (2) Sidestroke with breathing
      (3) Breaststroke
      (4) Resting inverted breaststroke
6. Synchronizing or timing of arms and legs in all strokes—part-whole method, that is, breaking down each stroke from the whole into its component parts and by progressive stages building it again into the whole stroke
7. Orientation in distance swimming

LEARNING PROGRESSION FOR INTERMEDIATE SWIMMERS

Instruction in intermediate swimming is given to those who have taken and passed the beginner's course; those who have never had instruction but can pass the beginner's test, although they have no knowledge of stroke technique; or those who can swim in deep water.

1. Study pool sanitation and personal health and hygiene.
2. Review strokes, and review techniques of proper breathing.

3. Practice and drill on the techniques and timing of the leg action in all the stroke kicks.
4. Coordinate and time the technique of the arm action with the leg action and breathing action; review the diving techniques.
5. Start orientation to distance swimming, emphasizing relaxation and natural breathing.
6. Practice fundamental dives from the springboard.
7. Learn and practice safety factors for self and others, such as tired swimmer's stroke, a simple rescue, simple carries in towing, and resuscitation.
8. Swim distances, stressing ease in breathing, relaxation, and the distribution of effort over distance comfortably.

LEARNING PROGRESSION FOR ADVANCED SWIMMERS

Instruction in advanced swimming is given to those who have passed the intermediate course or have achieved the ability to swim ¼ mile (0.4 km) and have demonstrated all of the standard strokes.

1. Practice timing the strokes to develop ease of performance with added power and speed, thereby gaining confidence.
2. Swim each stroke 100 yards (90 m) with correct timing.
3. Swim 25 yards (22.5 m) on each side, holding the upper arm out of the water fully extended.
4. Swim 25 yards (22.5 m) on the back, holding both hands out of the water.
5. Swim ¼ (0.4 km) mile in 8 minutes or less.
6. Learn a good racing start and good technique in turning at the end of the pool.
7. Be able to do at least three dives from the springboard in good form.
8. Learn safety factors in small craft.
9. Swim safely for 20 minutes.
10. Learn how to wade properly in water of unknown depth.
11. Learn how to swim out of a swift current.
12. Learn how to assist another person temporarily in distress in deep water.
13. Learn how to swim for two people.
14. Swim under water for a distance of 25 yards (22.5 m).
15. Learn how to conserve strength.
16. Learn how to rest while tired in deep water.
17. Learn boatmanship:
    a. Paddling and rowing.
    b. What to do when capsized.
    c. How to land safely when capsized.
18. Be able to teach others how to swim.
19. Learn how and when to make a safe rescue.
20. Be able to demonstrate proper resuscitation.

TEACHING CONSIDERATIONS

1. Skilled lifeguards should be on duty in the pool for all instructional sessions.
2. Beginning classes should contain fewer students than intermediate or advanced classes. All classes should be ability grouped as specified in the chapter.
3. Include review and practice in all sessions.
4. Basic stroke technique is easier to understand if demonstrations and initial practice take place out of the water.
5. Consider using a "buddy" system for safety and skill feedback.
6. Work first for technique and then using strokes for distance.
7. With intermediate and advanced swimmers, consider why students are taking the course. Competition, endurance, and recreational goals require different teaching orientations.

SUGGESTED READINGS

Armbruster DA, Allen RH, and Billingsley HS: Swimming and diving, ed 6, St Louis, 1973, The CV Mosby Co. A classic book.

Forbes MS: Coaching synchronized swimming effectively, Champaign, Ill, 1984, Human Kinetics Publishers, Inc. The six skill units progress from strokes, transitions, and skills through complex figures and include teaching methods, execution techniques, illustrations, common mistakes and their corrections, and practice swimming sequences.

Hudson D: Advanced swimming, Dubuque, Iowa, 1982, Kendall/Hunt Publishing Co.

Hudson D: Introduction to swimming, Dubuque, Iowa, 1981, Kendall/Hunt Publishing Co.

Intercollegiate and interscholastic swimming guide, official rules of swimming and diving (published annually), New York, National Intercollegiate Athletic Bureau.

Lewis DP, Piper CL, and Sutton K: Aquatics, Englewood, Colo, 1983, Morton Publishing Co. Provides descriptions, illustrations, methods, and suggestions for selected aquatics activities. Among others, the chapters include scientific principles, beginning and intermediate swimming, advanced lifesaving, adapted aquatics, and water polo.

Maglischo E: Swimming faster: a comprehensive guide to the science of swimming, Palo Alto, Calif, 1982, Mayfield Publishing Co. Brings together recent research on the biomechanics of stroke technique and the physiology of swimming. Extensively illustrated.

Maglischo E, and Brennan C: Swim for the health of it, Palo Alto, Calif, 1984, Mayfield Publishing Co. Written to be used in a self-directed or coached swim conditioning program. Includes an overview of the principles of conditioning for flexibility and endurance, a clear step-by-step progression through stroke principles, and complete information on how to set up a self-paced program, including interval training.

Messner YJ and Assman N: Swimming everyone, Winston-Salem, NC, 1989, Hunter Textbooks, Inc. Coverage for beginning through advanced swimming classes, including step-by-step presentation of skills, background of the activity, equipment used, safety, injury prevention, self-evaluation techniques, and values of the sport.

Midtlyng J: Swimming, ed 2, Dubuque, Iowa, 1982, Wm C Brown Group.

Official NAGWS aquatic guide, Washington, DC, 1989, American Alliance for Health, Physical Education, Recreation, and Dance.

Official NCAA swimming guide (1989), Collegiate-Scholastic, Shawnee Mission, Kan.

Shank C: A child's way to water play, West Point, NY, 1983, Leisure Press. Explains how parents can expose their children to a variety of water play experiences to help them feel comfortable around water and be more prepared to learn how to swim.

Taylor B, and Pettine A: Underwater techniques in teaching the beginning swimmer, West Point, NY, 1983, Leisure Press. Describes in detail the underwater technique used successfully by the authors in teaching beginning swimmers.

Thomas DG: Swimming: steps to success, Champaign, Ill, 1989, Human Kinetics Publishers, Inc.

Thomas DG: Teaching swimming: steps to success, Champaign, Ill, 1989, Human Kinetics Publishers, Inc.

Torney J, and Claton R: Teaching aquatics, Edina, Minn, 1981, Burgess International Group, Inc.

Vickers BJ and Vincent WJ: Swimming, ed 5, Dubuque, Iowa, 1989, Wm C Brown Group. Contains illustrated material on elementary diving, special water activities, competitive swimming and diving, cardiopulmonary resuscitation, and artificial respiration.

PERIODICAL

Swimming technique (quarterly), Swimming World Publications, PO Box 45497, Los Angeles, CA 90045.

VIDEOTAPES

Freestyle techniques and *Starts, turns and individual medley*. Karol Video, 22 Riverside Dr., Wayne, NJ 07470.

Thirteen videotapes, including several on the various strokes, drills, and baby water safety. "How To: Sports Videos, Box 5852, Denver, CO 80217.

Swimming, Different strokes and *Getting better* are among several available from Sports Videos—Champions on Film, 745 State Circle, Box 1941, Ann Arbor, MI 48106.

Excellence in swimming stroke technique—three programs (*Freestyle and backstroke, Breaststroke and butterfly* and *Starts and turns*). The Athletic Institute, 200 N. Castlewood Dr., North Palm Beach, FL 33408.

32

Table Tennis

Completion of this chapter should enable the reader to:

- Appreciate the historical development and social values of table tennis
- Describe the proper equipment for the game
- Apply the rules for singles and doubles play
- Execute and demonstrate proper grips, footwork, and table tennis shots
- Explain singles and doubles strategy for table tennis

HISTORY

It is generally agreed that table tennis originated about 1890 as a game called Ping-Pong. It had a brief popular following throughout the United States and then fell into obscurity. Around 1920 it was revived as a popular parlor game. The International Table Tennis Federation was established in Berlin in 1926, and in 1933 the United States Table Tennis Association (USTTA) was established.

Table tennis is now considered to be the world's second largest participation sport and is a major sport in the Peoples Republic of China and in Japan. It is the number one racket sport in America. It has been estimated that about one in every six Americans plays the game.

Although world championships have been held in table tennis since 1927, it did not become an Olympic event until 1988. Early years of international competitions were dominated by Central European countries, especially Hungary and Czechoslovakia. In the mid 1950s the dominance in table tennis shifted to Asia and it has remained there with a few notable exceptions. China captured six of the possible seven titles at the world championships in New Delhi in 1987. South Korea spoiled the sweep by winning the women's doubles. In the 1988 Olympics, the Chinese and the South Koreans split the four gold medals with China winning the women's singles and the men's doubles and South Korea winning the men's singles and the women's doubles.

VALUES

Table tennis is an excellent home game for the entire family. One of the reasons for its popularity is that per-

sons of any age and either sex can play the game the year round. It is popular at recreation and community centers. Table tennis causes little or no damage or injury indoors because a small racket and "light as a feather" ball are used.

Finding opponents to play singles or doubles is usually easy. If unequal in ability, the better play can "spot" an opponent a few points to increase the competitive enjoyment of the game.

EQUIPMENT

Any type of clothing and shoes allowing freedom of movement and comfort is acceptable. However, in tournament play USTTA rules specify that the attire should be a uniform color other than white.

The racket (blade)

Although a variety of satisfactory rackets are available from commercial sources, a wooden rubber-faced racket is mandated by the rules. The striking surface of the racket blade must be covered with a pimpled rubber with the pimples facing inward or outward. A single layer of cellular (sponge) rubber may be located underneath the rubber surface. The two surfaces of the blade shall be black on one side and bright red on the other.

The ball

The ball is small, celluloid, spherical, white or yellow in color, 38 mm in diameter and 2.5 g in weight. It is fragile but quite hard to break unless stepped on. The USTTA-approved standard ball has a uniform bounce. If it is

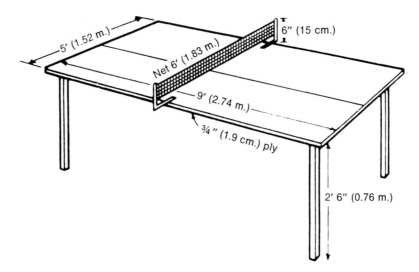

Fig. 32-1. Table and net for table tennis.

dropped from a height of 12 inches (30.5 cm) on a ply-wood table, it should bounce up 8¾ to 9¾ inches (22 to 25 cm).

The table

The table should be constructed of ¾ inch (1.9 cm) ma-terial, usually plywood or particle board, and be 9 feet (2.74 m) in length and 5 feet (1.52 m) in width. The playing surface should be dark (usually green) and non-reflecting and should lie in a horizontal plane 2 feet 6 inches (76 cm) above the floor. The sidelines and endlines are white and should be ½ to ¾ inch (2 cm) wide. The centerline is also white, but only ⅛ (3 mm) wide. (See Fig. 32-1.)

The net

The net is lightweight. It is stretched taut across the center of the table and attached to the outside by vertical standards. The top of the net should be 6 inches (15.3 cm) above the table and extend to attached posts 6 inches (15.3 cm) outside of the sidelines.

RULES* (ABRIDGED)
Singles

A game is won by the player who first scores 21 points, unless both players have scored 20 points, in which case the one who first scores 2 points more than the opponent is the winner.

The choice of playing position at the table and order of service are determined by the toss of a coin. If the winner of the toss prefers to have first choice of playing

*The official rules of table tennis (latest edition), United States Table Tennis Association, U.S. Olympic Complex, 1750 E. Boulder St., Col-orado Springs, CO 80909-5769.

positions, the opponent then has the choice of whether to serve first or receive first, and vice versa.

The change of service takes place after 5 points have been scored. The receiver then becomes the server and the server becomes receiver, and so on, after each 5 points until the end of the game or the score 20-all. At the score 20-all, the receiver becomes the server and the server the receiver, and so on, after each point until the end of the game.

In the start of a new game, the player who served first in the previous game becomes receiver and the receiver becomes server, and so on, alternating after each game.

The players also exchange ends after each game, and if play consists of more than one game, in the deciding game of the match the players change ends when one player reaches a score of 10. A match is the majority of three (or five) games.

Service

A good service is delivered by projecting the ball from the free (nonserving) hand and the projection starts from above the playing surface. The ball must be resting in the palm of the free hand which is flat and the thumb free of the fingers. Without imparting spin to the ball it is projected upward within 45 degrees of the vertical. As it starts to descend, the ball is struck so that it touches the server's court first and then, passing directly over or around the net, touches the receiver's court. At the in-stant of contact of the racket on the ball in service, both handle and ball must be behind the endline of the serv-er's court.

A good return of a served ball must be struck by the receiver on the first bounce so that it passes directly over or around the net and touches directly on top of the opponent's court.

Points

A point is awarded to the opponent in the following circumstances:

1. Failure to make a good service, unless a let is declared
2. Failure to make a good return of a good service or a good return made by the opponent, unless a let is declared
3. If the player, the racket, or anything that the player wears or carries touches the net or its supports while the ball is in play
4. If the player, the racket, or any wearing apparel moves the playing surface while the ball is in play or touches the net (or its supports)
5. If the player's free hand touches the playing surface while the ball is in play
6. If, before the ball in play has passed over the endlines or sidelines, not yet having touched the playing surface on the player's side of the table after being struck by the opponent, it comes in contact with the player or anything the player wears or carries
7. If at any time the player volleys the ball, except as provided in number 1 under Let
8. If a player strikes the ball twice in succession
9. If the server (or partner) stomps a foot during the service

Let

A let ball, which is then replayed, is called in the following cases:

1. If the served ball, in passing over the net, touches it or its supports, provided that the service would otherwise have been good or volleyed by the receiver
2. If a service is delivered when the receiver is not ready, provided always that the receiver may not be deemed unready if an attempt to strike at the ball is made
3. If either player is prevented by an accident not under his or her control from serving a good service or making a good return
4. If either player gives up a point, as provided in number 3 to 7 under Points, owing to an accident not within his or her control

Scoring

A point is scored by the side that makes the last successful return prior to the end of a rally. In an unsuccessful return the ball is missed, struck with the side of a racket blade having an illegal surface, hit off the table, sent into the net, or hit onto the player's own half of the court on the return. Failure to make a good serve also scores a point for the opponent unless it is a let.

In play

The ball is in play from the moment it is projected from the hand in service until one of the following has occurred:

1. It has touched one court twice consecutively
2. It has, except in service, touched each court alternately without having been struck by the racket intermediately
3. It has been struck by either player more than once consecutively
4. It has touched either player or anything that the player wears or carries, except the racket or the racket hand below the wrist
5. On the volley it comes in contact with the racket or the racket hand below the wrist
6. It has touched any object other than the net and supports

Doubles

Good service

The service is delivered as previously described, except that it must touch first the right half of the server's court or the centerline on the server's side of the net and then, passing directly over or around the net, touch the right half of the receiver's court or the centerline on the receiver's side of the net.

Choice of order of play

The official rules specify that the team winning a coin toss has (1) the choice of ends, (2) the right to receive or serve first, or (3) the right to require the losing team to make the first choice. After choice 1 or 2 has been made, the other team makes the remaining choice.

The pair who have the right to serve the first five services in any game decide which partner shall serve, and the opposing pair decide similarly who will first be the receiver.

Order of service

The first five services must be delivered by the selected partner (1) of the pair who have the right to do so and must be received by the selected partner (3) of the opposing pair (Fig. 32-2, A). The second five services must be delivered by the receiver of the first five services (3) and received by the partner of the server (2) of the first five services (Fig. 32-2, B). The third five services must be delivered by the partner of the first five services (2) and received by the partner of the receiver (4) of the first five services (Fig. 32-2, C). The fourth five services must be delivered by the partner of the receiver (4) of the first five services and received by the server (1) of the first five services (Fig. 32-2, D). The fifth five services must be delivered as the first five services, and so on, in sequence until the end of the game or a score of 20-all, at which point each player serves only one service in turn until the end of the game.

The team (or player in singles) who served first shall receive first in the next game. In each game the initial order of serving is the opposite of the preceding game.

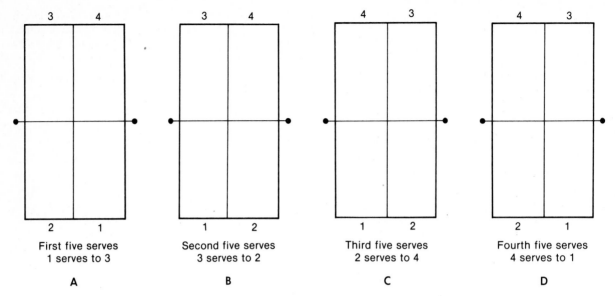

Fig. 32-2. Order of service for table tennis doubles.

In a one-game match or in the deciding game of a match of more than one game, the pair that served the first five services have the right to alter their order of receiving or that of their opponents at the score of 10.

FUNDAMENTAL SKILLS AND TECHNIQUES
The grips
The forehand and backhand grips are similar to the shakehand grip used in tennis.

Both must be learned unless the penhold grip is used, in which case the ball is always struck with only one face of the racket. Either gripping technique can be used successfully. However, the wrists should not be bent but rather the forearm may be rotated to adjust the angle of the racket face.

Forehand grip
In the forehand grip the short handle of the racket is gripped very closely to the blade, with the blade itself partially held in the hand and the forefinger and thumb bracing opposite sides of the blade. The index finger is positioned behind the blade for support. (See Fig. 32-3, *A.*)

Backhand grip
The backhand grip is the same as for the forehand, except that the thumb is usually placed on the back of the blade. (See Fig. 32-3, *B.*)

Penhold grip (Fig. 32-3 C and D)
Because the same blade surface is used for all shots, the grip position remains unchanged.

Points to remember
1. Do not grip the racket too tightly; relax.
2. Hold the wrist firm and rotate the forearm as needed to obtain the correct blade angle.
3. Whenever possible, face somewhat to the side in forehand and backhand shots as in tennis.
4. Constantly check the racket head, making sure that it is not dropped because the wrist is bent.
5. Regularly check the thumb and index finger to keep them in the proper place.

Serving
For a topspin serve with either a forehand or backhand stroke, the ball is put into play by projecting it upward from the flat free hand. As the ball is descending it is met by the racket which is swung forward and upward and the racket face is closed (facing toward the table top and net).

For a backspin (chop) serve, the ball is struck with a downward, forward motion of the racket. The racket face is open (facing upward from the table top and net). The player will need to practice adjusting the angle of the racket to find the most effective one.

For a forehand side-spin serve, the racket is brought across the ball from right to left (if right handed) just as the racket strikes the ball, with the racket head moving to a nearly vertical position and the ball being struck directly in front of the server.

For a backhand side-spin serve, the racket is swung across the ball from left to right and (if right handed) the ball is released from the left hand just as the racket passes in front of the server. Effective spin serves require giving the ball considerable spin.

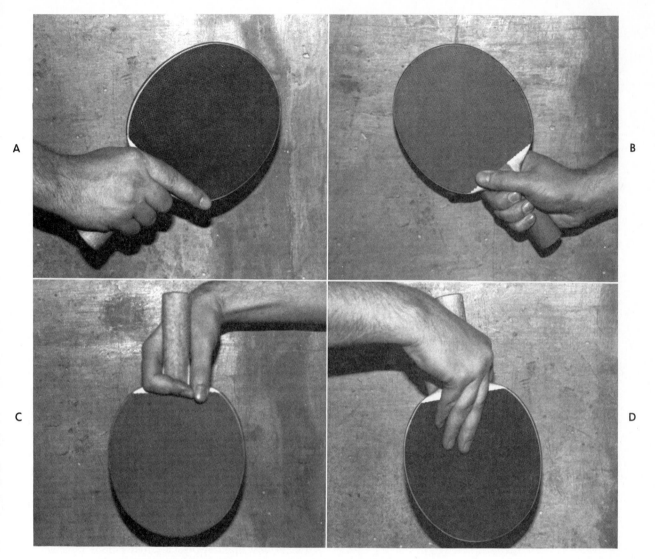

Fig. 32-3. Grips for table tennis (as seen from behind the player). **A,** Forehand. **B,** Backhand. **C,** Penhold grip. Striking surface side. **D,** Backside.

In putting the ball into play, the server must keep the fingers straight and together and the thumb free. No cupping or pinching of the ball is permitted. If this rule is violated, a let is called and the server warned. If the violation is repeated, a point is awarded to the opponent.

Footwork and stance

Proper stance and footwork in serving or receiving are just as important in learning table tennis as they are in tennis, badminton, or any sport skill that requires a constantly alert player. (See Fig. 32-4.)

A good beginner's stance in serving the ball is a position from about 1½ to 2 feet (45 to 160 cm) directly behind the centerline of the table. Face slightly to the right side with the feet well apart and the left foot forward (for a right-handed player). Remember the service rule

stating that at the moment of impact, both the racket and ball must be behind the endline on the table. In addition, the service toss must start at table height or above.

A good stance position in receiving is from about 2 to 2½ feet (60 to 75 cm) directly in back of the centerline of the table. The feet are spaced well apart, the knees slightly bent, and the body is inclined forward in an alert position. From this position one can quickly step forward, backward, or to the side to make either a backhand or forehand shot. After the shot is made, recover to this position in preparation for the next return.

For a forehand or backhand return, the feet should be placed, at the moment of contact of the racket with the ball, so that they are perpendicular to the line of flight of the ball. The feet should be well spread in order to

Fig. 32-4. Stance.

shift weight forward and backward in delivering a shot.

Whenever possible, attempt to be moving forward when striking the ball. In going after a ball for an effective shot, remember to face the ball as you play it. Also remember to get back to midcourt quickly after the shot is made. Watch the ball at all times.

Stroke techniques
Half volley or push shot
The half volley or push shot is the basic defensive shot. It is accomplished by meeting the ball as it touches the table and gently hitting it back over the net with the racket, which lifts and carries it forward at the same time. To add deception, the racket can be turned to either a forehand or backhand stroke.

Forehand top-spin hot
The forehand top-spin shot is the basic offensive drive and is similar to the tennis drive. This drive is accomplished by striking the ball vigorously with an upward forward motion on either the maximum height of the bounce or as the ball begins to descend. The racket is tilted or angled forward at the point of contact with the ball. The upward motion imparts the overspin. This shot is best played on deep or high-bouncing returns. As skill and accuracy are required, learn to shift body weight forward to add power to the shot.

Backhand drive
The backhand drive is similar to the forehand drive except that it is often shorter because the arm may cross in front of the body if not turned sideways. The ball is hit preferably on the rising part of the bounce. The racket is held with the thumb supporting the blade, and the wrist may be snapped at contact.

Forehand chop
The forehand chop is primarily a defensive stroke. It is executed with a hatchet-chopping motion. The stroke starts from nearly shoulder height, whenever possible, hitting forward and downward with the top of the racket blade open (tilted back away from the ball). The stroke is finished with the arm almost fully extended in front of the body. Cutting with the blade down behind and under the ball gives the ball a backspin as it leaves the face of the racket. This stroke should be executed with considerable speed. Chop shots are primarily defensive returns.

Backhand chop
The backhand chop also requires that the racket be tilted backward (open). It is like the forehand chop, except that it is a shorter stroke and employs stronger use of the forearm and wrist. The stroke is started at about chest height and ends at about waist height. This shot, like most shots, requires a great deal of practice to acquire a worthwhile degree of control and accuracy.

Drop shot
The drop shot is executed by moving the racket as if beginning a drive but stopping the forward motion of the racket and opening its face just before hitting the ball and letting the ball hit the racket, returning the ball just over the net. This shot should be used only occasionally as a change of pace, to catch an opponent off guard or when an opponent has moved back from the table on a preceding shot.

Smash shot
The smash shot is actually what its name implies. It is used on a higher-than-net-bounce—the higher, the better. It is high straight forward and downward without spin on the opponent's court. Attempt it only when an advantageous situation presents itself. Play it accurately and put weight behind the smash. It is a kill, or point, shot. Make it good when used, and remember to avoid contact with the table.

Points to remember
1. Vary your shots and strategy—make your opponent guess what stroke you will make.

2. Exploit your opponent's weaknesses and work toward strengthening yours.
3. Practice spins for control and accuracy.
4. Do not smash when a drive is more desirable and safer.
5. Concentrate on the ball.
6. Do not smash too soon or be overanxious.
7. Do not telegraph your intentions or your shot.
8. Do not try to return a chop with a chop.
9. If shots are hitting the net too often, try an upward lifting motion instead of a straightforward swing.
10. In a drive be sure to follow through.
11. Vary your serves and returns.
12. Do not hit harder than your form justifies.
13. Always strive to perfect form.
14. Always assume that the opponent will return the ball.
15. Adhere to form and do not sacrifice it for speed or power; speed and power will naturally follow well-executed form and good technique.

Strategy

For singles play

Probably the best strategy for the defensive as well as offensive game is similar to that of tennis—relying on the opponent to commit an error. Concentrate on returning the ball safely to the opponent's court. Vary the speed of returns. Try different shots and study the opponent's weaknesses or strong points. Size them up quickly and play to an opponent's weaknesses. Keep the opponent guessing and avoid setting up easy shots. Keep the ball in play.

For doubles play

Essentially, strategy in doubles play is the same as in singles play. Alternating successive shots between team partners makes the doubles type of play actually a singles game. Offensive strategy therefore consists of keeping the opponents running and off balance as in tennis. Do not drift into a slow, deliberate game, but mix the type of shots and tempo of the game.

If one wins the toss at the start of the game, it is good strategy to take the choice of serving first. This causes the opponents to determine who is to serve first, and the receivers can then choose wisely as to who is to receive, inasmuch as the same player must receive from the same opponent throughout the game. Receiving first puts one in a strategic position in the possible crucial closing moments of a close game. Keep the eyes on the ball. Learn to react quickly in choosing which type of shot to make in each game situation. Use cross-court angling shots and keep opponents off balance. Constantly strive for a versatile, deceptive attack and defense to keep opponents from anticipating your shots in advance.

It is especially important to assume the correct playing position between shots. Ordinarily the player, after hitting a shot, moves backwards away from the table to avoid blocking the partner's pathway to the ball while also remaining as close to the playing area as possible. Moving to one side or the other often results in being out of position when it is your turn to hit the ball.

TEACHING CONSIDERATIONS

1. Begin practice with two students to a table when possible.
2. Teach the grip and a simple courtesy serve (hitting the dropped ball as it bounces up from the table) to beginners. The objective is that they be able to put the ball into play. Later come back to the legal serve and spin.
3. Teach the ready position and forehand and backhand racquet positions. Let beginning students practice hitting the ball back and forth in a cooperative way before introducing specific offensive strokes. When the ball crosses the net at least eight times consecutively, students should be ready to begin keeping the ball low to the net and placing the ball to various spots on the table in game situations.
4. After basic ball control has been mastered, teach specific offensive and defensive shots and introduce spin shots.
5. Teach singles rules before doubles rules.
6. Include an opportunity for game play or gamelike play in each lesson. Give game play a focus in the beginning of the unit by changing the scoring or rules to encourage skill development (e.g., "Keep ball less than 6 inches above net" or "The ball must bounce in the alternate side of the opponent's court").
7. Match students of equal ability for game play. In large groups play for time rather than points so that games finish at the same time for rotation.

GLOSSARY

ace A point scored on a shot that is impossible for the receiver to return.

ad Advantage.

all Equal score (as in 12-all).

angle shot Moving a shot diagonally across the table.

backhand Hitting the ball with the back of the hand facing the direction of movement.

backspin Revolving the ball the opposite way of its flight (counterclockwise spin).

blade The face of the racket.

chop Hitting the ball downward on the back of the ball, giving the ball a backspin.

deuce A tie game at 20-all; 2 points scored consecutively are needed to win.

drive Giving a stroke topspin by turning the racket slightly forward as the ball is hit. Hitting the ball with a closed racket face.

drop shot A shot that barely crosses the net.

endlines White stripes on the ends of the table.

fingerspin Spinning the ball with the fingers on the serve; illegal.

flick A short return.

follow-through Continuing the swing after hitting the ball.

forehand Hitting the ball with the back of the hand turned toward the body.

half-court Either half of the table.

let Playing the ball over; occurs when the ball hits the top of the net and passes over it on the serve, when the receiver is not ready, or when an accident prevents a good service or return.

mixed doubles A game in which two teams of one male and one female play.

score The server's score is always called first.

slice Striking the ball in such a manner as to impart a spin to it.

smash Executing a "kill shot," usually after receiving a high bounce.

topspin A forward-rotating ball (clockwise spin).

volley Illegal stroking of the ball while it is in the air before it hits the table.

SUGGESTED READINGS

Official Sports Library for Women: Official recreational games and sports (published biennially), National Association for Girls' and Women's Sports, Washington, DC, American Alliance for Health, Physical Education, and Recreation.

United States Table Tennis Association: ITT handbook (current edition), U.S. Olympic Complex, 1750 E. Boulder St., Colorado Springs, CO 80909-5799.

PERIODICALS

Table Tennis Topics and *U.S. Table Tennis News*. Published for the United States Table Tennis Association by Corporate and Marketing Communications, Inc, 1055 Washington Blvd., Stamford, CT 06901.

VIDEOTAPES

Play table tennis with the Swedish national team. "How To" Sports Videos, Box 5852, Denver, CO 80217.

33

Team Handball

Completion of this chapter should enable the reader to:

- Appreciate the evolution, development, and values of an activity that is gaining popularity in the United States
- Construct a team handball court
- Demonstrate knowledge and understanding of handball rules
- Execute the fundamental skills of passing, running, dribbling, and shooting
- Demonstrate offensive and defensive principles of the game
- Teach a group of students how to play team handball

HISTORY

Team handball, as it is called in the United States to distinguish the fast-paced and popular Olympic sport from the four-wall court sport that is played in in United States, developed in Europe (Bohemia, Germany, Denmark, and Sweden) during the early 1900s. Handball, as it is known in the rest of the world, evolved from combining several middle-Euopean games, including German raffball and torball and Danish handbold, which resulted in a new sport (field handball) that could be contested across international boundaries.

In 1928 the Amateur Handball Federation was formed by the representatives of 11 countries with the inaugural rules calling for 11 players on a side and for the sport to be played outdoors on soccer fields. In 1933 this version of handball, "field handball," was included in the events in the 1936 Berlin Olympics. This was the only time that this version of handball was included as part of the Olympic program. When the Olympics were resumed in London in 1948, field handball was not included, and the sport, for the most part, laid dormant until the Games returned to Munich in 1972.

Handball, as it is played today, developed in the Scandinavian countries, where the sport moved indoors to escape the severe winters of northern and eastern Europe. Due to a lack of indoor facilities that would accommodate the 11-person teams, the number of players on each team was reduced to seven—a goalkeeper and six court players. This is the version of handball that the International Handball Federation (IHF) embraced at its seminal meeting in 1946. At that time the IHF was comprised of 54 nations representing almost 3 million players. Handball was recognized as an international sport by the International Olympic Committee in 1965 and was included as a "new" Olympic event for men in 1972 at Munich and for women in 1976 at the Montreal Games.

In general, the most powerful handball teams have been from the Eastern European countries and the Soviet Union. Since 1972, the gold medal in men's handball has been won by Yugoslavia (1972), the Soviet Union (1976), East Germany (1980), Yugoslavia (1984) and the Soviet Union (1988). The women's handball gold medal has gone to the Soviet Union (1976 and 1980), Yugoslavia (1984) and South Korea (1988). Asian countries, notably China and South Korea, are beginning to serve notice in the sport, as indicated by South Korea's gold in the women's and silver in the men's competition at the 1988 Seoul Olympics.

The United States Team Handball Federation (USTHF) was formed in 1959 and is a member of the IHF and the Pan-American Handball Federation. The USTHF falls under the jurisdiction of the USOC and has its administrative offices at the United States Olympic

Training Complex in Colorado Springs, Colo. It publishes *Team Handball-USA,* the official publication of the federation.

While rapidly expanding into more than 80 countries worldwide, team handball has grown at a modest but steady rate in the United States. During the past decade, it has gained a large number of participants and enjoys its most avid following on the East Coast. Team handball's growing popularity is due to its fast, exciting action and low cost of participation in comparison with other team sports.

VALUES

Team handball is an excellent sport for physical education and recreation programs. The equipment required is minimal and relatively inexpensive. Existing facilities, such as basketball courts, can be modified to accomodate the sport.

Team handball is a fast-moving sport that can provide an intense cardiovascular workout. It requires motor skills common to other popular sports, including running, jumping, throwing, and catching. The rules are simple and when played competitively, it ranks as one of the fastest and most demanding of team sports.

The sport may be played with as few as five and as many as seven players on each team, as well as both indoors and outdoors. It is similar in concept to basketball, lacrosse, soccer, and water polo. The objective is to score a goal by moving the ball past the defensive team and throwing the ball past the goalkeeper into the goal. Dribbling, passing, and defensive techniques are similar to those used in basketball. A goal counts as 1 point.

Team handball can be modified to be played by 5 to 15 players on a team, depending on available space. It can be played by elementary school students (where it lends itself well to coed activity) as well as those at the junior high, secondary, and collegiate levels. Additionally, it is a tremendous intramural, collegiate, and recreational sport.

In summary, team handball is a sport for all seasons, ages, and those who are enthusiastic to participate in a vigorous and exciting game. It is easily learned, may be played indoors or outdoors, is adaptable to almost any location or environmnent, and can be modified to meet the needs of special populations.

EQUIPMENT

The equipment required is minimal. A basketball-type shoe may be used for indoor and outdoor play, and a cleated shoe may be used on grass. Team uniforms with special identification for the goalkeepers are necessary. Players may wish to wear knee and elbow pads, and goalkeepers may want to wear additional protective equipment.

The only other piece of equipment needed is a ball. The USTHF ball requirements for men are a weight of 15 to 17 ounces (.43 to .48 kg) and a circumference of 23 to 24 inches (58 to 60 cm), while, for women and juniors, the ball must weigh 11½ to 14 ounces (.33 to .40 kg) and have a circumference 21 to 22 inches (54 to 56 cm). Balls may be constructed with 12, 18, or 32 panels. At least two balls should be available at the beginning of a game. (When handballs are not available for physical education and recreational use, appropriately sized playground balls can be substituted.)

THE FIELD

The following discussion of the playing area reflects dimensions established by the USTHF, which allows for variation from the standard IHF rules. Precise international mesurements can be found in the IFH rules, which may be obtained from the IHF or USTHF.

The official indoor or outdoor field may be not more than 147 × 75 feet (44 × 22 m) and no less than 126 × 60 feet (38 × 18 m). (See Fig. 33-1.) The field for international competition is 131 feet 4 inches × 65 feet 8 inches (40 × 20 m). An indoor basketball court can be modified without difficulty (Fig. 33-2).

Located centrally on each goal line is a goal 6 feet 8 inches (2 m) high and 10 feet (3 m) wide. The goal is usually made of 3- × 3-inch wood and pipe, fitted with a net tensioned so that the ball cannot immediately rebound (Fig. 33-3). In front of each goal are two semicircles. The inside arc (the goal area line or the 6 meter line) is the goal area and is a solid line drawn at a radius of 20 feet (6 m) from the goal. The next arc is the freethrow or 9-meter line. It is drawn as an interrupted line parallel to and outside the goal area line, 3 meters farther from the goal. Directly in front of, and at a distance of 23 feet (7 m) from each goal, the penalty marks are drawn. Marks are also drawn at 13 feet (4 m) in front of each goal to identify the closest that a goalkeeper may approach a player attempting a penalty throw (10 feet or 3 meters). Midway between the goal lines a centerline is drawn, and on the sideline closest to the players' benches each team's substitution area is delineated by a 6-inch (15 cm) hash mark that is 14 feet 7 inch (4.45 m) from the centerline. A complete diagram of court dimensions with all markings is illustrated in Fig. 33-1.

RULES
Officials

There are two referees who are in charge of the game. Both have the right to warn and disqualify players, and their decisions are final. The most frequently used referee signals are illustrated in Fig. 33-4.

The field referee is stationed behind the play, whose duties are to announce penalties, give warnings, and order suspensions. The field referee concentrates on the

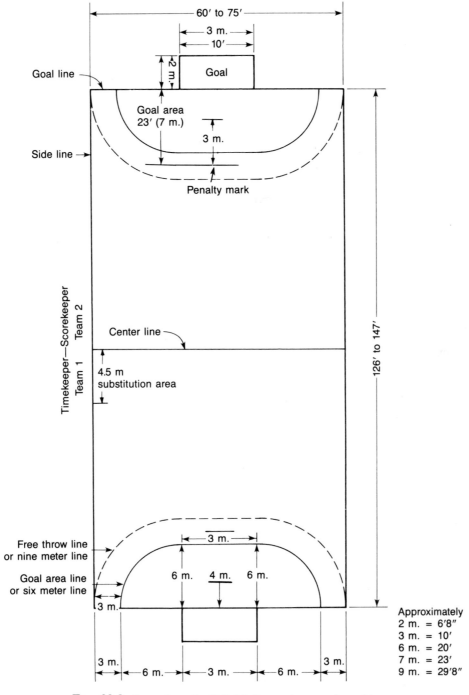

Fig. 33-1. Team handball field dimensions and markings.

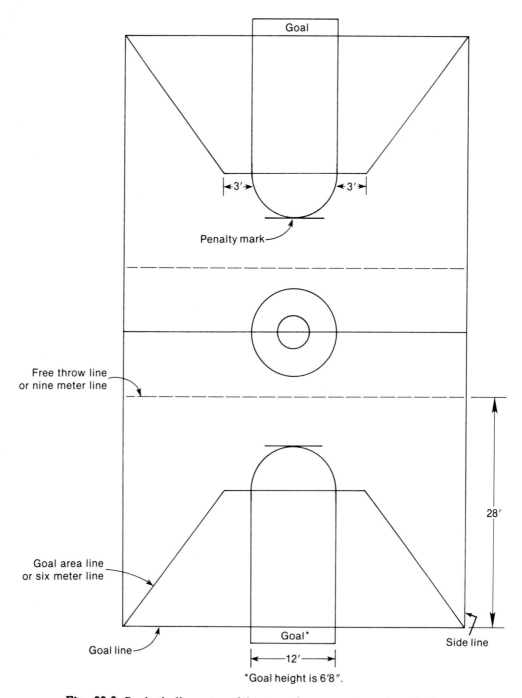

Fig. 33-2. Basketball court modifications for use as team handball court.

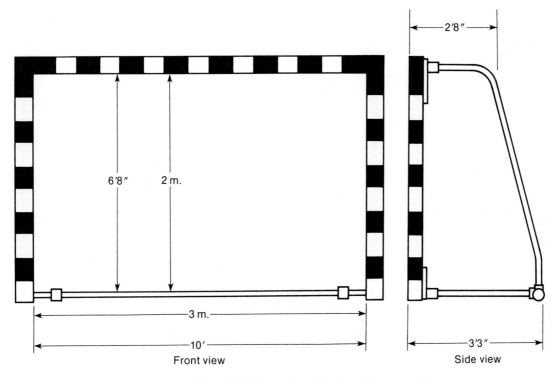

6'8"   2 m.

3 m.

10'

Front view

2'8"

3'3"

Side view

Fig. 33-3. Team handball goal.

Fig. 33-4. Team handball referee signals.

player with the ball and that player's opponent. Responsibilities also include checking the proper distance of the defense on free throws. The decision of the field referee prevails over the goal referee on contradictory decisions.

The goal referee's positioning should be ahead of the play and on the goal line. His or her duties include enforcing goal area rules; whistling penalty throws, goals scored, and corner throws; and supervising throw-offs and throw-outs.

In addition to the two referees, a scorekeeper and a timekeeper are required. These officials are responsible for controlling time, monitoring substitutes entering and leaving the field of play, keeping the time for suspensions, and generally helping the referees by keeping them abreast of these concerns.

Duration of game

Game duration can be set to accommodate conditions. However, USTHF official game periods are as follows. For men, two 30-minute periods are separated by an intermission of 10 minutes. In tournament play, there are two 15-minute periods with no intermission. Male juniors play two 25-minute periods with a 10-minute intermission, with the exception of junior tournaments which consists of two 10-minute periods with no intermission. All other teams play two 20-minute periods with a 10-minute intermission, with tournament rules specifying two 10-minute periods with no intermission.

In case of a tie at the end of regulation play, there is a provision for two 5-minute halves or 2- to 3½-minute halves for overtime. A coin toss determines the team that takes the throw-off. If before the start of the game it was determined that there should not be a tie, then overtimes shall continue until a winner is determined. No players may be added to the roster.

Number of players, substitutions, and suspension

The game may be played with 5 to 15 players of either or both sexes. An official USTHF team has 12 players— 10 court players with only 6 playing at a time, and 2 goalkeepers with only 1 playing at a time. The positions of the players are goalkeeper, center halfback, right and left backs, center forward, and right and left wings.

Substitution is from the bench area near midcourt. Once a court player is off the playing field, a substitute may enter. Substitutes need not notify the timekeeper. The procedure is the same for the goalkeeper, but the goalkeeper substitute must have a distinctive uniform. Illegal substitution may result in a free throw or penalty throw for the opponent.

Players may be suspended from play for 2 minutes, 5 minutes, or permanently, depending on the severity of the foul. With suspension, the opposing team receives a penalty throw.

Playing privileges of court players

1. A player may hold the ball for up to 3 seconds, pass, shoot, dribble, or run three steps with the ball.
2. Players may not double dribble, hold the ball for more than 3 seconds, kick the ball, or take more than three steps with the ball (penalty: free throw).
3. Stalling is not permitted (referee's judgment).
4. A defensive player may obstruct an opposing player by using the body or arms. A player is not permitted to strike, grab, or tackle an opponent, and the ball must be the object of attack by defensive players.
5. No player except the goalkeeper may dive for a ball lying or rolling on the ground.

Playing privileges of goalkeeper

1. The goalkeeper may defend the goal in any way using the hands, feet, and body.
2. Usual time and step restrictions are placed on the goalkeeper with possession of the ball.
3. The goalkeeper is free to move outside the goal area anytime without the ball but must then abide by the rules for other players.
4. The goalkeeper is prohibited from leaving the goal area when in control of the ball (penalty: free throw).
5. When the goalkeeper recovers a blocked or missed show for a throw-out, opponents can block it from outside the 6-meter line, a goal can be scored directly from it, and the goalkeeper cannot touch the ball again until it has been touched by another player.
6. The goalkeeper is prohibited from picking up a ball outside and carrying it into the goal area (penalty: penalty throw).
7. A court player substituting for a goalkeeper must notify the official before entering the goal area (penalty: penalty throw). This court player cannot enter the goal area until the goalkeeper is off the court (penalty: penalty throw).
8. The ball may not be thrown to a player's own goalkeeper while the goalkeeper is in his or her goal area (penalty: penalty shot).

Start of play

The game officially must be started with seven players per team: six court players and one goalkeeper. A coin toss determines the option of side or throw-off which places the ball into play. The game starts within 3 seconds after the official blows the whistle. All players must begin on their own half of the court. A goal cannot be scored from a throw-off.

A throw-off is taken from the center of the field in any direction. All players must be in their respective halves of the field when the throw-off is taken, the opposing players being at a distance of at least 10 feet (3 m) from the ball. When taking a throw-off, throw-in, free throw, or penalty throw, the thrower must keep part of one foot in constant contact with the ground. The player may, however, repeatedly lift and put down the other foot.

Ball out of bounds

A ball is not out of bounds until the entire ball crosses the goal line or sideline. A ball crossing the sideline is put back into play with a throw-in by the team that did not last touch the ball before it went out of bounds. A throw-in must be executed from outside the sidelines, with one foot remaining stationary during the throw. The ball may be thrown with one or two hands. A goal cannot be scored from a throw-in.

A ball crossing the goal line outside the goal and last touched by the offensive team, or touched by the goalkeeper on a shot on goal when the goalkeeper was the only defender touching the ball, results in throw-off. The goalkeeper executes the throw-off from within the goal area in whatever manner is desired. A goal cannot be scored directly from a throw-off. Opposing players must stay behind the 9-meter (9.9-yard) line on a throw-off.

When a ball crosses the goal line outside the goal and was last touched by a member of the defensive team other than the goalkeeper, a corner throw is awarded to the offensive team (Fig. 33-5). The ball is placed in play similar to a throw-in from the intersection of the goal line and sideline.

Fouls—common (penalty: free throw)

Common fouls are called for such violations as faulty substitution, faulty throw-in, intentionally playing across goal line or sideline, and body contact or striking an opponent that results in loss of possession or failure to complete the play. Furthermore, the defender must be between the player and the goal. If contact is not too blatant or the defender had good defensive position, a foul is not always called. Free throws are also awarded for double dribbling; taking more than three steps; holding the ball more than three seconds; offensive player charges; illegal picking, holding, or pushing; or unnecessarily rough play.

Fouls—flagrant (penalty: penalty shot)

Flagrant fouls are called for violations, such as taking the ball away from a player; obstruction with arms, hands, or legs; grabbing an opponent; pushing or forcing an opponent into the goal area; and shooting or throwing the ball at an opponent intentionally. If the foul is severe, by the referee's judgment, the player may be suspended from the game.

Free throw

In a free throw the ball is put into play at the point of the infraction. If the foul occurs between the 6- and 9-meter (6.6- and 9.9-yard) lines, however, the ball is put into play from the 9-meter line closest to the point of infraction. All offensive players must be outside the 9-meter line, and all defensive players must be at least 3 meters (10 ft) from the ball. A direct shot at the goal or a pass are the options for a free throw.

Penalty shot

This is a free shot at the opponent's goal from the penalty mark, with only the goalkeeper defending and being at least 3 meters from the thrower until the shot is taken. Any player may take the shot, and one foot must be stationary at all times. The shot must be taken within 3 seconds after the referee blows the whistle. All other plays must be outside the 9-meter line (Fig. 33-6).

Referee's throw

Although rarely used, the referee's throw is warranted in certain game situations. If there are simultaneous infractions or interruptions to the game, such as from an injury, a referee's throw is the only fair way to put the ball back into play. The referee stands in the area where the double foul was committed and bounces the ball back into play. All players must remain at least 3 meters (10 ft) away until the ball has been bounced.

Goal area
Legal entry
1. Goalkeeper is legal in the goal area.
2. A court player after playing the ball when no advantage is gained may enter the goal area.

Penalties for illegal entry
1. A court player in possession of the ball in the goal area (penalty: free throw).
2. A court player not in posession but gaining an advantage (penalty: free throw).
3. A court player gaining defensive advantage (penalty: penalty throw).

FUNDAMENTAL SKILLS AND TECHNIQUES

Inasmuch as team handball is similar to basketball in terms of running, dribbling, passing, and taking shots on goal, many of the basic skills that should be practiced parallel those of basketball.

Passing

Passing is basic to the game and is a good skill with which to begin a program. Beginners should master the chest or push pass, bounce pass, overhead pass, shovel or underhand pass, baseball pass, and hook pass. A handball is about the size of a softball, and beginning players tend to want to grip the ball, which is an incorrect technique for control. The ball should rest in the hand on the fingertips, and considerable wrist snap should be used in passing. Players should be reminded to make short, crisp passes, and to pass frequently. Just as in basketball, a

Fig. 33-5. Player taking a corner throw.

Fig. 33-6. Player taking a penalty shot.

Fig. 33-7. Player taking a shot at the goal.

good passing team will have a distinct advantage over a group of individuals.

Shooting

Although team handball shots are for the most part different than those in basketball, there are many similarities and several of the shot names are the same. Shots that are similar to those in basketball and may be practiced with some technical changes are set shots, jump shots, dive shots, lob shots, underhand shots, and any of the twisting moves that might be used with dunk shots. Changes in technique include not gripping the ball, and using a great deal of wrist snap and strong lower arm moves similar to those used in throwing a softball. Ad-

Fig. 33-8. Player driving toward the goal.

ditionally, players should be taught to shoot at the high and low corners of the goal (Fig. 33-7).

Dribbling

Dribbling is basically the same as in basketball. It is important to keep the body low for protection and ease of movement while keeping the ball low and the head up to watch for an opening in which to pass or shoot. Remember that a pass can move the ball down the court much faster than a dribble, so one should look for the pass before taking the dribble (Fig. 33-8).

Running

Running and being in sound condition are key components of team handball. The player able to help the team with or without the ball is the best kind of team player. Agility drills for quickness in changing directions and lateral movement are important, but time should also be devoted to promote aerobic and anaerobic endurance as well as overall strength and flexibility.

Offensive play

The three basic offensive player positions in team handball are the wing player, circle runner, and back-court player. Each position has responsibilities.

The wing player (usually two) should be quick and agile and able to lead the fast-break attack. This player attacks the goal when shooting and should be able to protect the ball. The circle runner is usually the biggest and strongest player on the court and is generally a blocker, setting picks for the wing players and back-court players. The circle runner (usually only one) needs strength to handle the ball in heavy traffic and coordinates moves with the other players. The back-court players (usually three) should be strong, hard throwers who can pass, run, dribble, and shoot well. These players should be the best all-around athletes on the court and usually provide most of the team scoring.

Just as in basketball, there are set plays in team handball, and it relies heavily on players setting screens and picks for one another to take shots at the goal. Offensively, players should focus on total team movement, remain spread out, think pass before dribble, move the ball quickly, and always pose a scoring threat.

Because defensive teams employ either a one-on-one or zone defense and follow many of the principles of basketball defense, the offensive team should practice against both of these defensive systems.

Defensive play

The basic defense patterns are the one-on-one defense and the zone defense. In one-on-one defense, each player is responsible for one opponent. In zone defense, each player is responsible for a zone or area on the court. A zone defense is designed to give the opponent longer shots and prevent close shots at the goal. Team members must continually communicate to make each system successful.

In summary, each defender should strive to stay between the goal and his or her designated opponent; the defense should shift as a unit; no defense will fit all offensive systems; the defender should not jump too soon when attempting to block a shot or pass (See Fig. 33-9); and constant communication between defenders is necessary.

Goalkeeper

Goalkeeping is probably the most important and difficult position in team handball. A goalkeeper should be quick, unafraid of the ball, possess good hand-eye and foot-eye coordination, and be able to throw the ball to start the fast break. The goalkeeper should not catch the ball unless thrown directly at him or her, but should block shots by knocking them down, to the side, or over the goal line. The team that has a talented and well-trained goalkeeper has a great advantage during match play (Fig. 33-10).

Fig. 33-9. A defensive block.

Fig. 33-10. Goalie blocking a practice shot on goal.

TEACHING CONSIDERATIONS

1. The basic skills of team handball are essentially those of basketball with the exception of shooting. Shooting strategies are more similar to those of soccer, as are some field placement strategies. See the chapters on basketball and soccer for additional suggestions.

2. Keep team size small for maximum opportunity for practice and play. Use several small courts (or outside areas) with fewer players rather than a large area with many players.

3. Since the ball is lighter and smaller than a basketball, more students will be able to throw longer and harder passes than in basketball. Practice passing ahead of moving players and moving into open spaces to receive a pass in consort with two or three players. Stress the pass (rather than the dribble) as the quickest way to move the ball down the court.

4. Gradually add defensive players to practice moving the ball down the court (three-on-one and three-on-two situations). Initially, scoring can include passing the ball across the endline or into an undefended goal. Later a goalkeeper should be included and three-on-three and four-on-four games can be played.

5. Supplement goaltending practice with play around the goal area line. Students must become familiar with the unique skills and strategies that are required by the sport.

6. When teams get above four-on-four players, introduce specific player roles (other than goalkeeper) if they have not begun to emerge from four-on-four play (wing, circle runner, and back-court player).

7. Introduce zone defense (particularly on larger courts) after students have mastered the basics of person-to-person play. Place as much emphasis on defense as on offense.

8. Provide opportunity for gamelike play each lesson (modified in the beginning). Encourage skill and strategy development by modifying the rules to reinforce the lesson content (e.g., no dribbling, or scoring from the sides only).

9. Match-condition scrimmages should be frequent with positive feedback on each player's technique and tactical understanding of the game.

GLOSSARY

common foul Violations such as illegal substitutions, illegal throw-in, illegal body contact, double dribble, and more than three steps with the ball (penalty: free throw).

corner throw A throw taken by an offensive team player after a ball crossed over the goal line last touched by a defensive player other than the goalkeeper, except when a shot was taken, to put the ball back into play.

court player A team player other than the goalkeeper.

defensive player A player whose team does not possess the ball.

flagrant foul Violation such as rough body contact and unsportsmanlike play (penalty: penalty throw and possible suspension).

free throw Results from a common foul and is used to put the ball back into play from the point of the infraction, unless infraction occurs between the 6- and 9-meter (6.6- and 9.9-yard) lines, in which case the ball is put in play on the 9-meter line nearest the point of infraction.

goalkeeper The only person who can legally play the ball in the goal area and use the feet.

held ball A ball held more than 3 seconds.

offensive player A player whose team possesses the ball.

penalty throw Results from a flagrant foul and is a free shot at the goal from the penalty mark with one foot remaining stationary during the throw and only the goalkeeper in the goal are defending.

referee's throw Does not occur often, but is the result of simultaneous infractions of disruptions to the game and is executed by the referee's bouncing the ball back into play from the point of infraction while all players are at least 3 meters away.

throw-in Used by the team that did not cause the ball to go across the sideline to put the ball back into play.

throw-off Taken from the center of the field to start the game.

throw-out When the goalkeeper blocks or catches a shot that does not cross the goal line, he or she uses the throw-out to put the ball back into play.

traveling Illegal progression in any direction with the ball.

SUGGESTED READINGS

Bennett JP: Elementary school team handball, J Phys Ed 76(5): 113, 1979.

Bennett JP: Modified team handball, J Phys Ed 49(57):57, 1978.

Hattig F and Hattig P: Handball, Niedernhausen/TS, Federal Republic of Germany, 1979, Falken-Verlag.

Klussow NP: Handball, Berlin, 1986, Taktik.

Team handball: rules of the game, 1985 edition (1989 update), United States Team Handball Federation.

Toomey B and King B: The Olypmic challenge 1988, Costa Mesa, Calif, 1988, HDL Publishing.

Trosse HD: Handball training, ed 2, Reinbek, Germany, 1988, Taktik.

Trosse HD: Trainingslehre handball, Berlin, 1985, Bartels and Wernitz

34

Tennis

Completion of this chapter should enable the reader to:

- Have a basic knowledge of the historical development of tennis
- Be informed about the proper selection of equipment
- Know the rules and scoring of tennis, and understand the etiquette of play
- Perform and demonstrate the fundamental skills for effective playing technique
- Know the principles of strategy for competitive play
- Teach others by using sound instructional and practice techniques

HISTORY

There is evidence that a form of tennis was played in the ancient Greek and Roman Empires, and that a game in which a ball was batted back and forth with a type of racquet may have been played in the Orient more than 2000 years ago. Still other indications are that tennis may have begun in Egypt and Persia 500 years before the Christian era.

Despite these obscure ancient origins, there is no doubt that a tennislike game was played in thirteenth-century France. Called *jeu de paume* (literally, game of the hand), it was first a bare-handed game of hitting a stuffed cloth bag over a rope. When paddles, and later racquets, were added, the game grew steadily in popularity. By the close of the fourteenth century it was also well established in England.

It is believed the game received its present name when English visitors heard French officials called *tenez*, which meant to resume play, an expression similar to "play ball" used by baseball umpires. The English thought tenez was the correct name for le paume. In time the English word tennis was substituted.

At the beginning of the fifteenth century there were 1400 professional players in France, and yet the first standardized written rules of tennis did not appear until 1599. The game reached a peak of popularity in England and France during the sixteenth and seventeenth centuries; Paris alone having built 1800 courts. But the French Revolution virtually obliterated the sport (Paris

was left with only court), and a civil war did much the same in England.

What remnant of the game was left in England seems next to appear at a particular garden party given in 1873 by British Army Major Walter C. Wingfield. His guests were introduced to a game called "sphairistike," later to become more descriptively referred to as "lawn tennis." In attendance at the party was an army officer who took the game with him to Bermuda as a diversion for the British garrison stationed there. Miss Mary Outerbridge, who was vacationing on the island during the winter of 1873-74, became intrigued with the game and brought equipment with her upon returning to her New York home.

As a member of the Staten Island Cricket and Baseball Club, Miss Outerbridge received permission to lay out a court in an unused corner of the grounds. Within a few years tennis was included as an activity at nearly every major cricket club in the east, and soon it became a sport of the masses. But the rules were diverse, so in 1880 a brother of Miss Outerbridge called a meeting in New York to establish a standard code. An outcome of that meeting was the establishment of the United States Tennis Association (USTA), still the ruling body of American tennis today.

Later that same year the first tournament for the National Championship of the United States was held at Newport, Rhode Island. The site was moved in 1915 to Long Island, and in 1978 it was relocated to its present site at the National Tennis Center in Queens, New York City.

This tournament, now called the U.S. Open, is considered one of the four most prestigious in the world. It joins with the Australian Open, the French Open, and (the most venerable of all) the Wimbledon, named for the London suburb where it is played. A winner of all four tournaments in the same year will have accomplished the "grand slam" of tennis, the rarest feat in the game.

In 1988 tennis returned to the Olympics as an official sport for the first time since 1924, and it was open to professional players. The women's singles was won by Steffi Graf of Germany (who also had won the grand slam that year and had won in the Olympic competition in 1984 when tennis was a demonstration sport). The men's singles was won by Miloslav Mecir and the United States went home with both gold medals in doubles with Ken Flach and Robert Seguso winning the men's competition and Pam Shriver and Zina Garrison triumphing in the women's contest.

VALUES

Tennis is, without a doubt, one of the most popular of universally accepted games. There are many reasons:
1. It can be played by everyone.
2. It is a coeducational recreational game and is well suited for mixed competition.
3. It requires only two or four people to play.
4. It can be played indoors or outdoors.
5. Only a short time is needed to play either an easy game or a strenuous game that taxes the players' ability, endurance, speed, and agility.
6. It is an excellent game of eye-hand coordination.
7. It is a noncontact sport.
8. It can be adapted as a team sport in addition to being suitable for individual competition.

REASON FOR POPULARITY

The main factors to which tennis owes its popularity are:
1. Availability of court.
2. Availability of teachers.
3. Relatively low cost of equipment.
4. Stimulus of tennis associations and tournaments.
5. Trend toward individual sports.
6. Suitability of the game to both sexes and to a wide range of ages.
7. Onset of indoor tennis so that the sport is no longer seasonal.
8. Commercialization and publicity.
9. Growing demand in high schools and colleges for athletic programs for women.
10. Suitability as a sport for intramural as well as interschool competition.

For these and many other reasons, it is one of the best basic skill sports for carryover. All children should learn to play sometime within their school experiences, for its social values have a far-reaching influence on achievement of a full, rich life.

EQUIPMENT
Clothing

Tennis attire has evolved into multicolored clothing that is flexible in all the right places and has enough aesthetic appeal to be worn at a lawn party after a match. Orthopedic shoes have eliminated the plight of skidding around the court in discount sneakers, inviting self-inflicted hotfoot. Be sure, however, to buy only tennis (or "all-court") shoes, which are designed to support the constant changes of direction that tennis demands.

The ball

Tennis balls are made of two rubber cups molded together, covered with synthetic and wool felt, and inflated with compressed air. To maintain internal pressure, they are packed in pressurized containers and should be opened just before play. Once the can is opened, the ball will slowly lose its pressure. All tennis balls that have "Approved by the USTA" indicated on their packaging have met standards of constructions and playability.

The racquet

Racquet heads vary in size and shape for the purpose of affecting the sweetspot (the area on the strings that will produce the most reliable shot). Midsize racquets have around 85 square inches of strung surface, and oversize racquets have 100 or more. There is no "bigger is better" relationship. Overall, the midsize racquets offer the best combination of power and control.

Better racquets are composites—a crossbreed of several materials. The most satisfactory material is fiberglass, generally regarded as the best companion material for other fibers, such as graphite, boron, Kevlar, and even wood.

In general, a stiff racquet will produce more power and control than a flexible one. However, some are so stiff they will vibrate considerably on impact with the ball and could be tough on sensitive elbows. Still, a general rule is that the stronger your game becomes, the more likely it is that you will appreciate a stiff racquet.

The "weight" of a racquet is misleading, for what one manufacturer calls light another may call medium. Moreover, racquets can be head-heavy or head-light, or have the weight evenly distributed. The real test is how it feels in your hand.

Also, there is no absolute way to measure your hand for the right grip size. Grips range from 4 to 5 inches

(10.1 to 12.7 cm) (the extremes being rare) in steps of 1/8 inches (0.31 cm). The main factor is what feels comfortable.

Most strings are 15- or 16-gauge diameters, with 16 gauge being thinner and livelier. Conveniently, manufacturers have established recommended tension ranges for each of their products, varying from 55 to 80 or more pounds of tension. If you are a power hitter, opt for the upper end of the range. Otherwise, stay more toward the middle. Racquets that are prestrung will be in the middle of the recommended range.

The net

The net should be 3 feet (0.915 m) high at the center and 3 ½ feet (1.07 m) high at the posts, with the bottom touching the ground or held down at the center by a net band. The posts should be located 3 feet (0.915 m) outside the sidelines and be equipped with a winch to raise or lower the net to desired height.

Cotton nets are best for indoor courts. The tarred hemp-type nets are best for outdoor courts because they are waterproof.

Courts

The surface of the court should be smooth, firm, and level. It may vary from grass to cement. Hard-surfaced courts afford play soon after rain. Most clay courts in the United States are composition or Rubico and not the red clay of European courts. Clay is particularly suited for match play (from the spectator's point of view) because the ball tends to hit and bounce rather than skid as on a hard-surfaced court, thus producing longer and more involved points. Although hard-surfaced courts cost more to build, they cost less in upkeep. For information regarding types of construction, see the suggested readings found at the end of this chapter.

Dimensions

1. Singles court: 78 × 27 feet (23.8 × 8.24 m)
2. Doubles court: 78 × 36 feet (23.8 × 10.98 m) (4½-foot [1.37 m] alley added to each side)

3. Height of net at center: 3 feet (0.915 m), commonly measured by taking the length of the racquet plus the width of the racquet head (using a normal-size racquet).
4. Height of the net at the posts: 3 ½ feet (1.07 m)
5. Height of the posts: 3 ½ feet (1.07 m)
6. Distance of the posts away from the sidelines: 3 feet (0.915 m)
7. Distance between the baseline and the service line: 18 feet (5.49 m)
8. Distance between the service line and the net: 21 feet (6.41 m).

The endlines are called baselines, and the sidelines are called sidelines. The forecourt is near the net, and the backcourt is near the baselines. (See Fig. 34-1.)

RULES AND SCORING
The singles game

1. One player remains the server for all points of the first game of a match, after which the receiver becomes the server for all points of the second game, and so on alternately for subsequent games of the match.
2. To start a match, the player who wins a "toss" may choose (a) to serve or to receive for the first game, whereupon the other player shall choose the end of the court on which to start, or (b) the end, whereupon the other player shall choose to serve or to receive. The "toss" is typically a spin of a racquet where one player guesses if an identifying mark will land up or down.
3. The server must take up a position behind the base line without touching that line, and between an imaginary extension of the center mark and the singles side line. From that position the server must project the ball into the air by hand and strike it in any fashion (underhand serve is legal) before the ball hits the ground.
4. For each point the server is given two opportunities to make one good service into the proper court. To start a game, the server stands to the right of the

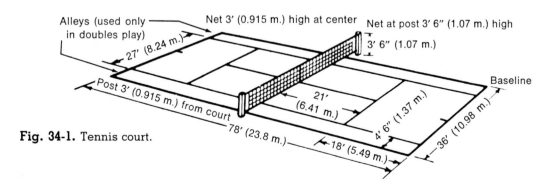

Fig. 34-1. Tennis court.

center mark and attempts to deliver the ball diagonally across the net into the receiver's right service court. When the first point has been completed, the server then stands to the left of the center mark and serves diagonally. Thus, when the total number of completed points is an even number, service attempts are made from the right of the center mark, and from the left when the completed points are an odd number. If a player inadvertently serves from the wrong side of the center mark, play resulting from that service is to be counted, but the improper position of the server must be corrected as soon as it is discovered.

5. A fault is an invalid serve, and is counted as a service attempt. The *foot fault* occurs when the server steps on the base line or into the court before the racquet contacts the ball, or when the server is in contact with the imaginary extension of the center mark or singles side line. However, the serve may legally be made while the server is completely in the air. Another service fault occurs when the server swings with the intent of hitting the ball but misses (although the ball may be tossed and then caught without penalty, so long as no serve is attempted). Finally, the service is a fault if the delivered ball does not land in the proper service court or on a line bounding that court. If the ball touches the net and then lands within the proper service court (including its lines) it is not a fault but a *let*.

6. Any service that is a let does not count as an attempt, and is retaken. In addition, a let may be called by a receiver who was not ready to receive the serve, unless the receiver makes an attempt to return the ball. Any other interruption in normal play from an outside source is also a let, and the point is replayed. For example, if a ball from a neighboring court interrupts a rally or either of the services, the entire point is replayed, including the two service opportunities for the server.

7. There are no rules that govern the position of the receiver; a station may be taken anywhere, including within the service court. However, the receiver may not strike the served ball until after it has bounced.

8. With the occurrence of a legally served ball, play is continuous as long as the players succeed in making legal returns, even though a returned ball may strike another ball lying within the boundaries of the court. As is true with the service, a ball which lands on a line is considered to have landed in the court bounded by that line. After the service, it is not necessary for either player to allow the ball to bounce before making an attempted return.

9. After the service, a player has made a good return and play continues:

a. When the ball lands from flight within the proper court.
b. If the ball strikes and passes over the net and then lands within the proper court.
c. When a player strikes a ball on his or her side of the net, even though the follow-through carries the racquet over the net without touching it. Note, however, that if a ball has bounced on a player's side of the net, and the spin of the ball causes it to rebound or it is blown back over the net again, that player may then reach over the net to strike the ball, provided the player does not touch the net or the opposing court.

10. The server wins a point when a legal service is not returned, or when a service hits the receiver or the receiver's racquet before it touches the ground. The receiver wins a point when the server commits two consecutive faults (double fault) or otherwise delivers the ball in an illegal manner. After the service, a player loses a point:

a. When the ball bounces twice before the player strikes it.
b. When a returned ball lands outside the opposing court.
c. When a ball lands within a player's court then strikes a permanent fixture before its second bounce.
d. Any time a player strikes a ball before it has bounced and fails to make a good return, no matter where the player was standing when the ball was struck.
e. If the player or the player's clothing or racquet touches the net or net post while the ball is in play.
f. If the player hits a ball from flight before it has passed to that player's side of the net.
g. If the ball in play touches a player or anything the player wears or carries except the racquet. A return may legally be made off any part of the racquet.
h. If the player throws the racquet at and hits the ball.
i. If the player intentionally interferes with an opponent.

11. Players change sides of the court at the end of the first, third, and every subsequent odd game of each set, and at the end of each set unless the total number of games in a completed set is an even number, in which case the change is not made until the end of the first game of the next set.

Scoring

A player must win at least four *points* to win a game, then at least six games to win a set, and usually at least two sets to win a match. When a player has no points in a game the score is called *love;* the first point is called 15; the second point 30, the third point 40; and on winning the fourth point, that player has won the game, provided that the player is ahead by at least 2 points at that time.

When both players have won 1 point, the score is called 15-all and when both players have won two points, the score is 30-all, but when both players have won three points, the score is called *deuce*. A score of deuce means that one player must win two consecutive points to win the game. The first point won by a player after a deuce score is called *advantage* for that player (often shortened to *ad*). If that point was won by the server it is called *ad in*, and if that point was won by the receiver it is called *ad out*. If the same player who won the advantage point also wins the next point, the game is won by that player. However, if the other player wins the next point, the score returns to deuce, and so on until one player wins two consecutive points after a deuce score.

When a player wins six games and has at that time a lead of at least two games, that player wins the set. If a player wins six games and the opponent has won at least five games, traditional scoring requires that the set be extended until one player has a two-game lead. However, this custom has been replaced by playing a tie-breaker game if the set becomes tied at six games each. In this game the first player to win 7 points with a 2-point advantage wins the set. To start the tie-breaker game, if it is player A's turn to serve the thirteenth game (with the set tied at six games each), that player serves for the first point. Then, player B serves for points 2 and 3. Note that player B serves from the left of the center mark for point 2, then from the right of the center mark for point 3. Next, player A serves points 4 and 5, left then right of the center mark. Player B then serves point 6, then the players change sides, followed by player B serving for point 7. The game continues with players alternately serving for 2 points each until one player has won at least 7 points with the necessary 2-point advantage. Players continue to change sides whenever the total number of points played is any multiple of 6.

Points won in a tie-breaker game are called by their numerical value rather than the traditional scoring. After the tie-breaker game, player B becomes the server for the first game of the next set, and the players stay on their sides of the court for that game.

The doubles game

1. The server may stand anywhere between an extension of the center mark and the doubles side line, behind the base line. One player serves for the first game of the set, then a player on the opposing team serves for the second game. The partner of the player who served for the first game then serves for the thrid game, and the partner of the player who served the second game then serves for the fourth game, and so on for all subsequent games of the set, each player serving every fourth game. A team may elect to change its order of service for the next set.

2. Should a partner serve out of turn, a correction must be made as soon as the mistake is discovered, but play that has been completed before the discovery must be reckoned. If a game has been completed before the erroneous serving order is discovered, the order as altered must then remain for the continuation of the set.

3. One player of each team must receive all serves in the right service court, and that player's partner must receive all serves in the left service court for the entire set. At the end of any set a team may change its order of receiving for the next set. The order of receiving is not determined by the order of serving.

4. Should a team receive out of turn, the altered receiving order must remain as is until the end of the game in which the discovery is made, whereafter the partners must resume their original order for the next game they receive.

5. If a served ball strikes the server's partner (including that partner's racquet) it is a service fault, but if a served ball strikes the receiver's partner or racquet before it touches the ground, it is a point for the serving team.

6. If both partners strike the ball for any return, it is a point for their opponents.

7. To play a tie-break game, the player whose turn it was to serve for the thirteenth game of the set (with the score tied six games each) serves for the first point of the game. Thereafter each player serves for 2 points, holding to the same rotation as was used in the set, and following the same change of ends after every 6 points as it true for singles.

ETIQUETTE

There is an ethical code in tennis that obliges every player to maintain a certain spirit within the rules, including giving an opponent the benefit of doubt on line calls, avoiding foot faults during serving, never intentionally distracting an opponent, never stalling in an effort to upset an opponent, and always conducting oneself in a fashion that makes the game enjoyable for everyone. Specific situations are:

1. Any call of "out" on an opponent's ball must be made as soon as possible, before you have sent the ball back across the net.

2. You cannot ask for a replay of a point where you are unable to make a sure call. The rules do not

allow it, so the doubt must be resolved in favor of your opponent.

3. You may, however, ask your opponent to make the call on a ball that lands on your side but which you did not clearly see.

4. If you hit a point-ending shot that you see as clearly out, but your opponent thinks is good, you should make the correct call. This applies also to your own serve.

5. However, if you hit a first serve that you saw as out and the receiver, nevertheless, returns the ball for a point-winning placement without making an out call, you must assume the receiver made the return in good faith; therefore, the point counts and you cannot make an out call (which would then allow for your second serve).

6. Whenever a player realizes he or she has committed a violation, that player should make the call immediately. This includes such things as hitting the ball after two bounces, touching the net, or hitting the ball before it has crossed over the net.

7. The server should announce the score of the game prior to serving each point, always calling the server's score first and the receiver's second.

8. If there is a disagreement as to the score and it cannot be resolved, the score should revert back to the last score on which there was agreement.

9. The server should never hit a serve until the receiver has had time to assume a ready position.

10. A serve that is clearly out should not be returned by the receiver.

11. After a point has been placed, return balls directly to the server; do not hit them back carelessly.

12. If your ball goes into the adjoining court, wait until the players on that court finish their point before calling for the ball.

13. If a ball from an adjoining court comes into your court, return it to the owners as soon as possible. If it interferes with your point, play a let.

14. In doubles, call service faults for your partner when he or she is the receiver.

15. Try for every point. Tossing points and playing to the audience are insulting to your opponent.

16. In nontournament play, insist on furnishing the balls half of the time, and perhaps more often if you are much the inferior player.

17. Do not damage the court unnecessarily.

FUNDAMENTAL SKILLS AND TECHNIQUES

All strokes in tennis depend on a solid foundation of hitting techniques which give substance to every shot. These are the basic skill performances that should become automatic for any court situation, as follows:

Stay Relaxed. Tense muscles produce rigid shots that are scattered and faulty. The first requisite for smooth, coordinated hitting is to remain relaxed—not lethargic, but calm. Stay loose, yet alive and energetic.

Think rhythm and timing. Give each swing a fluid motion with an unhurried start, a solid middle, and an unrestrained finish.

Be ready to respond. Between shots, maintain a ready-to-react position with a low center of gravity, feet shoulder-width apart, knees bent, weight mostly on the toes, and buttocks down. Relax your shoulders, and ease your grip in the racquet.

Pivot the whole body. From the ready-to-respond position, as soon as you sight the oncoming ball, begin to rotate your entire body by turning shoulders, arms, and hips, all together in a neat, packaged backswing that coils the body ready for uncoiling into the foreswing. This is especially critical for hitting a backhand, in which the shoulders play an important power role.

Go forward at impact. At contact with the ball, your weight should be going forward—toward the direction of the intended shot. Bring everything (racquet, arm, shoulders, hips, and knees) forward with the stroke. Feel the energy of your body driving the ball where you want it to go.

Hit the ball early. Contact the ball in your groundstrokes diagonally in front rather than alongside or behind your body. Intercept the ball early in its flight during a volley. Reach up and forward for serves.

Hit through the ball. Make sure the racquet is not quitting its forward speed as it meets the ball. Keep your racquet alive, actively moving through the hitting zone for all shots, including a volley or a lob.

Bend your knees. Never lock your knees when hitting, waiting to hit, serving, or receiving the serve, or playing the net. Flexed knees will allow a smooth shift of weight and provide a uniform, rhythmical swing.

Keep you eyes on the ball. Focus on the ball as it leaves your opponent's racquet, then refocus again after the bounce. Notice how much the ball slows down from its bounce, giving you time to clearly set your sights and organize the coordination of your swing. And on the serve, keep your chin up to see the actual contact.

Coil and uncoil. Every swing is a continuous motion of wind and unwind—coiling into the backswing then uncoiling for the foreswing. No matter how strong the swing, every shot should be a flowing coil-uncoil of effortless energy in motion.

GRIPS

It is important to develop a "feel" for the racquet in your hand—a sensory awareness of the relationship of the racquet to the position of your hand. (see Fig. 34-2). There is no exact way for every person to hold the racquet,

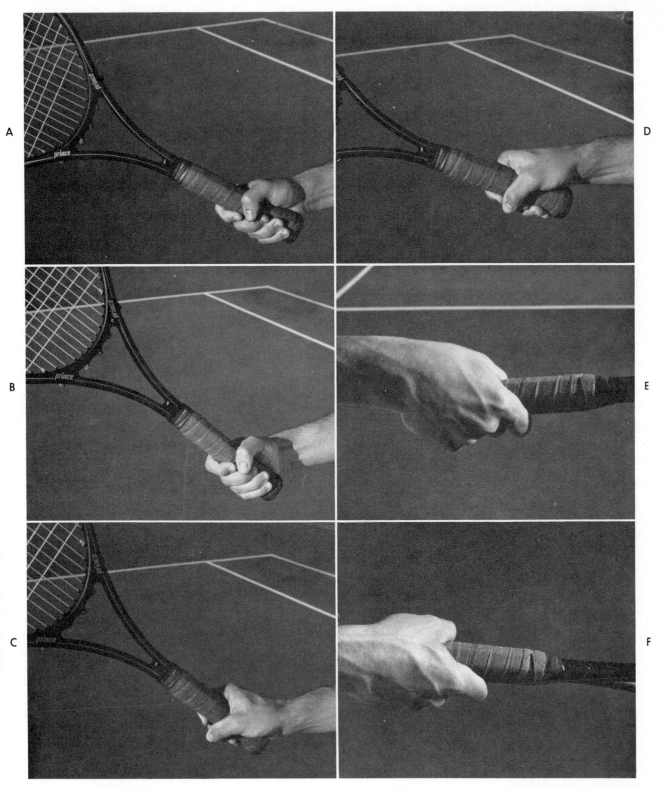

Fig. 34-2. Various grips for tennis. **A,** Eastern forehand. **B,** Western forehand. **C,** Eastern backhand. **D,** Continental, top view. **E,** Eastern, top view.

although a grip called the "eastern" offers utility for most players. The "western" grip is seldom used.

Eastern

To achieve the eastern forehand grip (Fig. 34-2, *A*), extend a racquet to you with the face perpendicular. Clutch the handle of the racquet as you would when shaking hands. Your palm should be in the same plane as the racquet face. Spread your fingers comfortably wide, and extend your index finger into a "trigger finger" position under the handle. Your thumb will wrap around the handle to contact or lie adjacent to the inside of your middle finger.

The eastern backhand grip (Fig. 34-2, *C*) has the palm on top of the handle, a quarter-turn from the forehand grip. There's less spread of the fingers, and the thumb runs at a 45-degree diagonal across the back of the handle.

Continental

The continental grip (Fig. 34-2, *D* and *E*) is halfway between the eastern forehand and backhand. There is some logic to employing this grip for the backhand, since it more properly aligns the wrist to provide for a stronger grasp than the eastern backhand.

Two-handed backhand

Players who hit a two-handed backhand can grasp the racquet with both hands effectively in an eastern forehand, or with the lead hand in a continental grip.

GROUNDSTROKES

Backhands (see Fig. 34-3) and forehands (see Fig. 34-4) are collectively called groundstrokes. They are the framework upon which all other aspects of the game are built. Effective groundstrokes have the following characteristics:

1. Keep the grip loose to start, firm to hit. Between shots, ease your grip. You'll automatically squeeze the racquet harder as you come into the ball.
2. Get a good shoulder turn for the coil into the backswing, especially for backhand shots, and emphatically if hitting a two-handed backhand.
3. When coiling for a backhand, look over the forward shoulder to sight the approaching ball. Pretend that an arrow extended through both shoulders would point at the ball. Bring the front shoulder down low for a low ball, high for a high ball.
4. Watch the ball all the way into the hitting zone. You do not need to see the ball actually hitting the strings, but keep a keen focus on the ball as it approaches the area of contact.
5. Take your weight off your front foot as you coil into the backswing so that you can step forward into the shot.

6. Point the handle of the racquet at the target (the area you want to hit the ball into) in your backswing.
7. Get all your weight into the shot. Accelerate the racquet into the contact point and have your weight going toward the target.
8. On two-handed backhands, keep the trailing arm directly behind the handle at contact, not lifted up with a hunched shoulder. (See Fig. 34-5.)
9. Extend your swing fully through the ball without hesitation, easing up only after contact.
10. Try to carry the ball on the strings as long as you can. Imagine that each ball has three other balls behind it. Try to thread the racquet through all four as you swing.

THE SERVE

Serving is a truly enthralling part of tennis. It's enlivening, arousing, and catalytic of the rest of one's game. However, the act is hardly more difficult than throwing a ball. (See Fig. 34-6.)

1. Serving is a dynamic, whole-body act. Start with an attitude of mental and physical freedom. If you hold back, you tighten your muscles and the swing has a cement-arm feeling. Instead, relax your whole self. Let your arm go limber.
2. To prepare for the serving motion, take up a throwing stance behind the base line. Stand as if you are going to toss a ball over the net.
3. Image the spot, in the air, where the racquet will meet the ball. Hold the ball in your tossing hand directly beneath that spot. Cradle the ball in the fingers, not in your palm, and point your thumb toward the imagined spot of contact.
4. Hold the ball and racquet in front of you, together, more-or-less pointed toward the target service court.
5. Start the serving motion with both arms, then continue into the windup without pause or hesitation. There is no hurry at the start, but no static halt at any point in the windup.
6. Lift the ball up unhurriedly, using your thumb as a guide to point toward the final destination of the toss.
7. Coil your body, similar to preparing for a forehand, and bring the racquet around behind you with the handle pointing toward the tossed ball.
8. Most or all of your weight should come to the back foot as you toss and wind up. Add some bend to your knees.
9. Start your foreswing into the ball from the ground up. That is, the knees rebound from their bend, the backbone uncoils, the hitting shoulder catapults toward the ball, and the arm thrashes up and over with the elbow unbending and the wrist adding a final vigorous snap that makes the racquet feel like a whip.

Text continued on p. 458.

Fig. 34-3. Backhand drive.

Fig. 34-4. Forehand drive. **A,** Straight—without a cut.

Fig. 34-4, cont'd. B, Circular—with top spin.

Fig. 34-5. Two-handed backhand drive.

Fig. 34-6. Service.

10. Build speed as you go. Feel like at the moment you hit the ball your swing is still gaining momentum. The whole swing is upward and forward in a clean arc that starts slow and finishes fast.

RETURN OF SERVE

There is no more neglected phase of tennis than the return of serve. Yet the techniques for success are surprisingly simple.

1. Stand in the middle of the widest possible area into which the server can hit, and as far in as you can and still feel confident in being able to hit under control.
2. Hold the racquet loosely, directly in front of you, with your body flexed and your weight on the front of your feet.
3. Go to meet a wide serve by moving diagonally forward, on a path 90 degrees to the flight of the ball. Move toward the ball, not away from it.
4. The harder the serve, the more the swing for the return must be compact, with less backswing, but no restriction on the follow-through.
5. Keep a solid, firm wrist as you come into the ball, especially on hard serves.
6. Have a "scrambling" attitude. Do anything to get the ball back.

PLAYING THE FORECOURT

The liveliest tennis occurs at the net. Go up to the net often, not only for the tactical advantage it presents, but also because it adds dimension to the game. However, approach the net only after your opponent hits a ball that lands shallow in your court or when you hit a ball that you believe will force your opponent to reply with a weak return. Once at the net, your two offensive weapons are the volley and the overhead.

The volley

1. A volley is a short stroke. It's a compact and firm block of the ball—a punch rather than a swing.
2. However, the weaker the opponent's return is, the more your volley stroke can resemble a regular groundstroke.
3. The ball should be contacted early, before it gets to the side of your body.
4. Generally, keep a vise-tight grip for the stroke and *drive* the racquet into the ball rather than just using the strings as a trampoline.
5. Reach for a wide ball by quickly turning your shoulders and pushing into a short step with you lead foot and, if necessary, following with a cross-over step with your trail foot.
6. Stay ready with your racquet head chin-high, in front of you.

7. Defend the net like an ice hockey goalie. Attack the ball! Hit every ball you can reach, aggressively when you can.

Overheads

1. You must get under and *in back* of the lofted ball. Skip-step into position. Keep your legs alive, with knees unlocked, for last-minute adjustments.
2. The overhead is like a serve, but the windup is more compact. Forget any fancy windup. Just get the racquet up and over your shoulder, like you were an archer reaching back to pull an arrow out of the quiver.
3. Turn sideways as you arrive at your hitting place and rivet your eyes on the ball.
4. Make contact with the ball more in front of you than for a serve.
5. Hit the ball with as much power as you can control. The overhead is not a push or a punch, so crack off a point winner.

THE LOB

Use a lob to loft the ball over an opposing net player, or when you need time to recover court position.

1. Let the racquet do the work. There is no need to lift your whole body into the shot.
2. Shorten the backswing. Get the racquet *under* the point of contact, then hit upward and forward in the same plane as the height you want to give to the ball.
3. Try to hold the ball on the strings as long as possible, and follow through into the path of the ball.
4. Keep a firm wrist for the stroke.
5. Whenever you can, hit the ball just over the reach of your opponent's racquet. Always provide enough clearance—hit too high rather than too low.
6. When under pressure, do anything to get the ball up and give it extra height.

HALF VOLLEY

This is a difficult shot and should be avoided by playing either at the net or in the backcourt. When this shot is necessary, use the following techniques.

1. Bend the knees to get down to the ball.
2. Watch the ball all the way to the racquet.
3. Use no preliminary swing but execute a full follow-through, hitting with a great deal of lift to make the ball drop into the court.
4. Stop and balance the weight forward at contact.
5. Use a firm rigid twist and get the proper angle to the racquet. This angle is somewhat over the ball.
6. After hitting the shot, move to the net rather than remaining in the middle of the court.

SPIN

A topspin (forward spin) causes the ball to drop rapidly and hence may be hit hard and fairly high above the net and still fall in court.

A cut or slice (backward spin) causes the ball to float or sail; it has a short, low, slow bounce. It may cause the net player to hit the ball into the net or out of bounds.

On service, a right-hand slice bounces to the left and curves to the left. An "American" service curves to the left and down but bounces to the right and high.

GENERAL REMINDERS

At any level of play, there are on-court behaviors which are important parts of quality play.

1. Think positively about your game. Be in command of your physical responses.
2. Think of the racquet as part of you—an extension of your hitting arm.
3. Make every stroke a continuous, rhythmical, fluid action.
4. Hit the ball with your entire body, not just your arm.
5. Keep your style somewhat freelanced and not bound by a compulsion to have perfect, picture-book form.
6. Focus your attention on the ball in play, not your opponent, the net, the base line, or a previous errant shot.
7. Play dynamic, aggressive, spontaneous tennis.
8. Relish every chance to hit the ball. Enjoy the sheer physical pleasure of playing the game.

EFFECTIVE PRACTICE

Practice is the basis of improvement. It is the time to discipline your muscles so that in the next match your mind can focus on the enjoyment of the game instead of the mechanics of your swing.

Create muscle memory. If there is no structure to practice it becomes too easy to slip into lethargic habits such as not bending the knees or failing to transfer the weight properly. Keep your thoughts on the fundamentals of the game, looking first at your grip, then checking your pivot and backswing. Give special attention to accelerating the racquet into the ball. Try to train your muscles with free-flowing strokes.

Rehearse offense and defense. Offensive tennis is built around hitting the ball consistently deep into your opponent's court and hitting powerful serves. Practice these with flair, trying to land every ground stroke behind the opponent's service line, and hitting serves with extra flamboyance. But also rehearse the defensive shots you'll need in competition, such as a well-lofted lob and returns of strong serves.

Make practice like a game. Part of every practice should simulate the game or segments of the game so that it's not merely hitting the ball back and forth without purpose. Creating gamelike circumstances makes practice more interesting and gives incentive to do well.

Practice specific shots. Have a partner feed you the type of shot you want to practice. For instance, if you want to rehearse overheads ask to have lobs hit to you. Often it's better if your partner hits a bucket of balls to you, without attempting to return your shots. After the bucket is exhausted, switch roles so that you can aid your partner's practice.

Play specific points. Try to stage playing situations. Be inventive with these drills, but make them as close to reality as possible. For example, you can play a three-ball rally whereby your partner feeds a ball to you that you hit for a deep shot and then follow with a charge to the net. Your partner, not bothering to flag down your shot, hits another ball to you that you can volley, and then lifts another ball for you to hit as an overhead. Or, while your partner is practicing serves, you could practice returns by attempting to return every serve, in or out, while your partner does not chase your returns but attends only to serving.

Include aerobic conditioning. Practice can be arranged to incorporate rehearsal of skills and aerobic conditioning for tennis play. A good drill is an all-court scramble where your partner has a bucket of balls and hits a variety of placements to any part of your court. You chase down and return every ball you can, and your partner continues to act as a feeder without retrieving shots.

Practice in logical sequence. Warm up properly, then hit easily for the first few minutes. Next, give your shots plenty of depth, then try for placements into a particular area of the court. Play some "rapid fire," when you and your practice partner stand across the net from each other, just inside the service line, and hit volley after volley to each other. Then hit serves and returns of serve. Play match situations. Then do drills that include aerobic conditioning and finish off the session with free hitting in which you focus solely on rhythm and form.

Make practice fun. Add variety to the sessions. Experiment with different techniques or add spin to the ball. Or, play some points when the only rule is that the ball must cross over the net. Let practice be therapeutic and spark renewed interest in the game. Remember that tennis is a game. Its purpose should be to add enjoyment to your life.

STRATEGY

The strategy for effective play in tennis is remarkably uncomplicated. Most situations in a game have automatic answers or, at least, sensible responses.

Singles

Keep the ball in play. The first rule of tennis strategy is to hit the ball over the net, land it in bounds, and do this one more time than an opponent on each point. The worst mistake is to hit the ball into the net. It's a dead loss, never giving an opponent a chance to commit an error. Rather than trying constantly for point winners, loft the ball with enough room to clear the net by several feet. Give your opponent opportunities to misplay the ball.

Keep the ball deep. An associated tactic is to consistently place the ball deep. This will compel an opponent to stay back, hitting incessantly from behind the base line, with little chance to come up to the net to hit point winners. You'll also give yourself more time between points as the longer returns from your opponent allow you to move into a better hitting position on each ball and to collect yourself for a rhythmical, free-flowing swing.

Know when to use angles. When your opponent offers a shallow ball, take advantage of the expanded angles for placing your return. The further inside the court you can move to hit, the greater the potential is for hitting an angled shot toward either side line. If you are also pulled off to one side of your court for this shallow ball, the situation then becomes more favorable for hitting a cross-court return.

Use the forecourt often. Go up to the net as often as you can, even if you're still uncertain about your ability. Your presence alone may be enough to force a jittery opponent into committing errors. And once at the net, finish the point off as quickly as possible. Try to hit every ball out of your opponent's reach.

Get the first serve in. Too often players assume they should bash away at the first serve and, upon failure, push the second. Instead, slow down the pace of the first serve and increase the pace of the second. This makes first serves successful more often, and keeps your opponent from stepping up to hit winners off your second serve.

Play percentage tennis. An overall guide is to ask (1) What do you do best? and (2) Where is your opponent weakest? Use your strengths. Note what an opponent cannot do well and play to that flaw often. That way you'll win instead of trying to avoid losing.

Doubles

Take the net. Doubles is a net game. The basic and overriding objective is to gain control of the net, from where most points are won. Both players should get into the forecourt at every opportunity to take command of the point.

Hit high percentage serves. Control the pace of your serve. If you can, hit it mostly to the receiver's backhand side where it will generate a softer return, giving your net-playing partner more time to reach the ball and volley a winner.

Hit away from a net player. When one opponent is at the net and the other back, hit the ball past the net player. It is especially important to return a serve back toward the server, deep if you can. Alternatively, lift a lob over the net player.

Exploit open space. Doubles teams are often overprotective of the alleys and thus play too far apart. Send the ball up the middle often, where the two of them may hesitate an instant due to uncertainty over who will take the ball. However, when given a chance to hit cross-court, take advantage of the wide doubles court. Use the angle opportunity, but provide a margin for error by aiming to land the ball on the singles side line.

Cover the empty space. Tie an imaginary rope between you and your partner. If your partner is forced off the side of the court, let the rope pull you over to cover the now-wider area of return space that is presented to your opponents. Always stay in the middle of the court space that's left over when your teammate is pushed out of position.

TEACHING CONSIDERATIONS

1. The techniques of skilled hitting have a common denominator of physics. Regardless of how contradictory different players' styles appear to be, at the critical microsecond when racquet and ball are in contact, everyone must impart the same force to achieve the same end. Learn the physics that apply to hitting a tennis ball, then help students to understand those laws and evaluate how well they are doing in relation to them.

2. Keep instructions simple. It's easy to become overloaded with instructional facts about each stroke. At some point a learner will no longer handle all the information while simultaneously trying to organize commands about what the muscles should do. The best method is often the simplest. Focus on only the most important aspects of hitting.

3. Attend mostly to the rhythmical patterns of the swing. Encourage learners to first develop smooth, flowing motions for each swing, without necessarily judging their swings on the basis of where the ball goes. Emphasize the coiling and uncoiling and the position of the body relative to the ball. Have them think of the *art* of tennis. Make them "look good" as they hit. Focus their attention on the sensation of rhythm and timing for every swing.

4. Play lots of "mini-tennis" games to emphasize rhythm and proper position. Have one partner stand at the net and toss the ball on one bounce to the hitter; then switch roles. Or have partners stand on

opposite sides of the net at the service lines and rally the ball trying to keep it within the boundaries of the service court. Provide students with games in which they can have instant success by making it possible to develop a "feel" for the game.

5. Become target oriented. Introduce rallying for specific targets. For example, to improve the depth of everyone's shots, stretch a piece of cord across the court several feet inside the base line to act as an aim point for deep groundstrokes. For the serve, stand a ball can inside each corner of the service court as targets. Or exchange groundstrokes using the alley as in the in-bounds area.

6. A common mistake is to turn the head prematurely, looking up to see where the ball is going before it's hit. Have players attend to all the dimensions of the ball as they follow it into the hitting zone. Focus on the spin, trying to actually see the seams of the ball. Or, note the color the ball and try to heighten its hue as it approaches. Create the habit of refocusing on the ball after its bounce. Then play "bounce-and-hit" whereby both partners say "bounce" every time the ball bounces (including on the opposite side of the net), and "hit" every time a player strikes the ball. This will help players to refocus after the bounce and to concentrate on the ball rather than on mechanical parts of the swing.

7. The service toss is a major headache for many players. Too often they throw it, or force it into the air with an exaggerated lift of the knees. Isolate the toss by practicing it alone, perhaps starting with the tossing hand resting against the inside of the forward thigh, then lifting and releasing the ball as if settling it on a shelf at hitting height. Place a racquet on the ground, the head in front and inside the forward foot. Toss the ball to proper height and allow it to drop to see if it will land on the racquet face.

8. Teach beginners to serve with a four-part but continuous sequence, as follows: (1) start with both hands held together, elbows bent, racquet pointed in the direction of the target court; (2) drop both hands down at the same time, toward the forward thigh; (3) bring both arms up together to release the ball and arc the racquet behind the hitting shoulder; then (4) deliver the racquet into the back of the ball with an accelerating forward swing. Have students say "down-together, up-together, swing" as they practice the motion of the serve.

9. Arrange from variants of the game to encourage certain skills. For example, play a ground stroke game without the serve in which each point begins with one player hitting a ground stroke and the ball must cross the net three times before a point can be scored (this will encourage controlled rallies). Or, practice

second serves by playing games in which only one serve is allowed. Or, play games in which the server hits half-speed and only backhands are allowed thereafter.

10. Make practice fun. Add variety to the sessions, sometimes doing such things as hitting the ball with the racquet held in the nondominant hand. Play some points where the only rule is that the ball must cross over the net and land before the fence. Or, have a rule that after every shot players must run up and touch the net with their racquets. Try a game in which, on each side, a player hits a shot and then must hand the racquet off to another play for the next shot.

GLOSSARY

ace A point-winning serve that is hit beyond the reach of a receiver.

ad court The left service court; also that court into which the serve is hit when the total number of points played in a game is an odd number.

ad in When the server has a score of advantage.

ad out When the receiver has a score of advantage.

advantage The next point after a deuce score. The player who wins the point is said to have the "advantage" and if that player also wins the following point the player will have won the game; if not, the score returns to deuce.

alley The area on either side of the singles court that is included as in bounds for doubles play.

approach shot A groundstroke hit by a player to prepare the way for an approach to the net.

backcourt An undefined area in the vicinity of the base line.

backhand A stroke used to play a ball on the opposite side of a player's dominant hand.

base line The line marking the end of the court.

break (service break) To win a game that the opponent serves.

center mark A short line extended inward from the base line as a continuation of the center service line that marks the two halves of the court and indicates the sides of the court in which the server must stand.

chop stroke A forward, downward motion giving the ball backspin.

cross-court shot Hitting the ball from one side of the court across the net to the side diagonally opposite.

decue An even score in a game after six or more points have been played. Or, an even score in games after 10 or more games have been played.

deuce court The right service court; also that court into which the serve is hit when the total points played in a game is an even number.

double fault Failure of a player to get either of the two service attempts into the proper service court.

down-the-line shot A ball hit across the net parallel to a side line.

Fault A served ball that does not land within the proper service court. Or, any other violation of the rules of service.

forecourt That area of the court between the net and the service line.

foot fault A service delivery that is illegal because the server stepped on the base line or into the court before the racquet contracted the ball.

forehand A stroke used to play a ball on a player's dominant side.

game A unit of a set completed when one side wins four points before the other side wins three or, if both sides have won three points, when one side thereafter gains a two-point margin.

groundstroke A forehand or backhand stroke used to hit the ball after it has bounced.

let Any point that must be replayed. Most often it refers to a serve that hits the top of the net, then lands in the proper service court.

lob A high, arching shot that lands near the opponent's base line.

love A score of zero. In a love game, one side wins no points; in a love set, one side wins no games.

match A contest between two or four players in which one side must win a predetermined number of games or sets to be declared the winner.

match point Term used when a side needs but one more point to win the match.

overhead (smash) A free-swinging stroke used for a ball that is over the player's head.

rally The exchange of shots between opponents after the serve, usually referring to prolonged play.

serve The stroke used to put the ball into play at the start of each point. The more inclusive term "service" applies to the right to be the server and the served ball itself.

service break A game won by the receiver.

set A unit of a match completed when one side wins six games or when one side wins the tie-breaker game.

set point When a side needs only one more point to win the set.

side line The line that marks the outside edge of either the singles or the doubles court.

tie-breaker A scoring system designed to eliminate prolonged sets in which one player must win seven points with a two-point advantage to win a set. Played when a set becomes tied at six games each.

volley A short punch stroke used to hit the ball before it bounces.

SUGGESTED READINGS

American Alliance for Health, Physical Education, Recreation, and Dance: Tennis, Waldorf, Md, 1988, National Association for Girls' and Women's Sports.

Assaiante P: Championship tennis by the experts, Champaign, Ill, 1981, Human Kinetics Publishers, Inc. Presents ideas from some of the most successful tennis players and coaches.

Becker B and Kaiser U: Boris Becker's tennis: the making of a champion, Champaign, Ill, 1987, Human Kinetics Publishers, Inc.

Bollettiori N: Tennis your way, North Palm Beach, Fla, 1982, The Athletic Institute. Easy reading, no dogmatic method, puts the reader in the position of the pupil. Author is one of foremost teachers of tennis.

Brody H: Tennis science for tennis players, Philadelphia, 1987, University of Pennsylvania Press. Explains how the laws of physics work in the game of tennis; based on thorough laboratory testing.

Brown J: Teaching tennis: steps to success, Champaign, Ill, 1989, Human Kinetics Publishers, Inc.

Brown J: Tennis: steps to success, Champaign, Ill, 1989, Human Kinetics Publishers, Inc.

Bryant JE: Game-set-match, ed 2, Englewood Colo, 1990, Morton Publishing Co. Written especially for first-time tennis players. Contains sections on learning experience suggestions, elimination of errors, mental aspects of competition, and physical aspects of the game.

Burwash P: Tennis for life, New York, 1981, Times Books. Offers checkpoints for all basic strokes and reviews strategies for different playing conditions.

Burnwash P and Tullus J: Total tennis: a complete guide for today's player, New York, 1989, Macmillan Publishing Co. A fresh look at the game. Uses nonclassical style of instruction that attends to individual differences. Comprehensive treatment of strategy.

Claxton D and Faribault J: Tennis, Scottsdale, Ariz, 1988, Gorsuch Scarisbrick Publishers. Includes a task-mastery workbook and learning sequences for tennis skills.

Collins B: My life with the pros, New York, 1989, EP Dutton. An anecdote-filled history of the pro game and its players.

Collins DR, Hodges PB, and Haven H: Tennis: a practical learning guide, Bloomington, Ind, 1985, Caroline House Publishers, Inc. Sound, basic, beginner-oriented instruction.

DeGroot WL: Tennis and you, Englewood, Colo, 1984, Morton Publishing Co. Geared toward the beginning player, but does contain information on intermediate and advanced techniques.

Douglas P: The handbook of tennis, New York, 1982, Alfred A Knopf, Inc. Illustrated; with foreword by John McEnroe.

Eddy R and LeBar J: Learning tennis together, Champaign, Il, 1982, Human Kinetics Publishers, Inc.

Elliott B and Kilderry R: Tennis: a scientific approach, New York, 1983, Saunders College Publishing. Thoroughly illustrated; covers all aspects of the game. Designed to help instructors teach more effectively and players to improve their performance.

Gallwey W: The inner game of tennis, New York, 1974, Random House, Inc. Still the best available book on the mental side of tennis. Especially valuable for novice players who are experiencing little progression.

Gensemer R: Intermediate tennis, Englewood, Colo, 1985, Morton Publishing Co. Using more than 150 photos, this book concentrates on intermediate skills such as spin and power for the serve, returning the serve, playing the lob, strategy, and realistic practices.

Gould D: Tennis anyone?, ed 4, Palt Alto, Calif, 1985, Mayfield Publishing Co. Includes material on the background of tennis, the basic strokes, the serve, net play, receiving the serve, rules, scoring, etiquette, singles and doubles strategy, drills, and conditioning activities.

Groppel JL, Loehr JE, Melville DS, and Quinn AM: Science of coaching tennis, Champaign, Ill, 1989, Human Kinetics Publishers, Inc. A collaborative work to combine the sciences of biomechanics, motor learning, exercise physiology, and sport psychology as they apply to tennis.

Groppel JL: Tennis for advanced players and those who would like to be, Champaign, Ill, 1984, Human Kinetics Publishers, Inc. Explains how to use basic mechanics to improve strokes and select equipment to fit individual needs.

Johnson J and Wxanthos P: Tennis, Dubuque, Iowa, 1981, Wm C Brown Group. Gives attention to official as well as unwritten rules of the game.

Luszki WA: Winning tennis through mental toughness, New York, 1982, Everest House, Publishers. Describes a psychological approach to winning tennis.

Moore C and Chafin MB: Tennis everyone, ed 3, Winston-Salem, NC, 1986, Hunter Textbooks, Inc. Contains hundreds of photos and covers practice drills, officiating, development of the sport, the National Tennis Rating program, the two-handed backhand, and up-to-date listing of films and where to obtain them.

Payne G: A tennis manual for beginning and intermediate players, Dubuque, Iowa, 1983, Kendall/Hunt Publishing Co.

Pelton BL: Tennis, Glenview, Ill, 1986, Scott, Foresman & Co. Information on fundamental strokes, patterns of play, strategy, rules, and recent champions. Also includes a performance checklist to evaluate course objectives.

Richmond MB: Total tennis, New York, 1980, Macmillan Publishing Co, Inc.

Smith C: An individualized instructional approach to tennis, Dubuque, Iowa, 1981, Kendall/Hunt Publishing Co.

United States Tennis Association: Official tennis guide and yearbook with official rules (published annually), New York, AS Barnes & Co, Inc.

Wright B: Aerobic tennis: how to get fit and play better, Bolinas, Calif, 1983, Shelter Publications, Inc. Cleverly written, with solid instructional base. Second half of text focuses on conditioning and practice.

Zebas CJ and Johnson HM: Tennis, back to the basics, Dubuque, Iowa, 1987, Eddie Bowers Publishing Co. Inc. Includes over 100 photograhs and diagrams and a chapter on how to analyze the basic tennis strokes.

VIDEOTAPES

Series including *Forehand and backhand stroke fundamentals, Applying forehand and backhand strokes, The serve,* and *Net play*. The Athletic Institute, 200 N. Castlewood Dr., North Palm Beach, FL 33408.

Thirteen videotapes, many about famous tennis professionals. Corbin House, 227 Corbin Place, Brooklyn, NY 11235.

Series including *Serve and return of serve, The volley, The forehand,* and *The backhand*. Karol Video, 22 Riverside Dr., Wayne NJ 07470.

Six series of tennis videotapes. *Complete tennis from the pros* (4 programs), *Dennis Van Der Meer* (12 programs), *How to win at doubles and stay the best of friends* (2 programs), *New Dennis Van Der Meer* (3 programs), *Play your best tennis* (2 programs) and *Tennis to Win* (2 programs) plus 7 miscellaneous programs. "How to" Sports Videos, Box 5852, Denver, CO 80217.

Fourteen tennis programs available from Sports Video, 745 State Circle, Box 1941, Ann Arbor, MI 48106.

35

Touch Football and Flag Football

Completion of this chapter should enable the reader to:

- Appreciate the historical development of touch and flag football
- Know the rules for each of these activities
- Practice and demonstrate the basic skills of blocking and touching opponents and kicking, passing, and receiving a football
- Be familiar with fundamentals of offense and defense for touch and flag football
- Correctly execute several offensive and defensive formations used in the two activities
- Teach the fundamentals of touch and flag football to a group of novice players

Touch football

Touch football is similar to regulation rugby football and to a modified form of American football except that the ball carrier is stopped by being touched rather than by being tackled, and blocking as in regulation football is eliminated. These changes lessen the danger of injury and encourage an open style of game. Forward passing is the principal offensive weapon, with all players eligible to receive the pass.

HISTORY
Football as it is played today is derived from soccer and rugby. Harvard, Yale, Princeton, and Rutgers were the schools that made early attempts at playing this game. The early attempts at football were not much more than gang fights over a round ball.

However, since 1869 rules have been formulated, equipment has been adopted and qualified, and coaches and members of the medical profession have worked toward making football a relatively safe game.

Touch football has been modified so that it can be safely played without pads. Playing the game without costly equipment has enabled children and young adults to participate. Touch football is an interesting and beneficial game for all who desire fun and competition.

In 1932, the Intramural Sports Section of the College Physical Education Association drafted and adopted rules for school and college play.

The National Touch and Flag Football Rules were first developed after considerable study of the variations of the game as played in the colleges and universities throughout the United States and Canada by a National College Touch Football Rules Committee of the College Physical Education Association. In 1950 this committee, in addition to an advisory committee and subcommittees, submitted questionnaires to more than 100 schools concerning the rules and recommended their standardization. The recommendations were presented to the Intramural Section of the College Physical Education Association and were approved by that professional group. Through cooperation with the Athletic Institute, the first rules book was published in 1952. The rules of this chapter reflect the eighth edition of the Official National Touch and Flag Football Rules published in 1984.

EQUIPMENT
Playing Field. The field is 40 yards (36.6 m) wide by 100 yards (91.5 m) long. (See Fig. 35-1.)

Ball. A regulation American football is used.

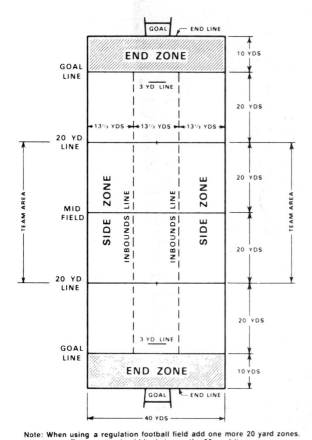

Note: When using a regulation football field add one more 20 yard zones. Team areas should be between the 30 yard lines.

Fig. 35-1. Football field.

Uniforms. No special uniform is necessary; however, a gym uniform can be used. Basketball, tennis, or suitable gym shoes should be worn. Teams should be equipped with distinctively colored jerseys.

THE GAME

1. The game consists of four 12-minute periods, with 1 minute between quarters and 10 minutes between halves.
2. An overtime period is played in case of a tie. Each team is given four downs from the same 20-yard line; the team advancing the ball farthest in the four downs is the winner.
3. A team failing to appear within 2 minutes after the appointed time forfeits the game.
4. Time-outs of 1½ minutes may be called three times in each half of the game by each captain. Additional time-outs result in a yard penalty. The time clock is stopped in the following instances:
   a. When the ball goes out of bounds
   b. When the referee calls time out at a captain's request

c. After a score is made
d. At the discretion of the referee

Scoring

1. Touchdown—6 points
2. Field goal—3 points
3. Safety—2 points
4. Point after touchdown—1 point for kick; 2 points for running or passing
5. Forfeited game—1 point
6. Tie-breaker—1 point

Players and substitutions

1. A team consists of 7 to 11 players. The offensive team must have at least three players on the line of scrimmage.
2. Any number of substitutions may be made during the game. Substitutes must report to the referee before entering the game.

Playing regulations

1. Start of game: The game is started by the following procedure:
   a. Choice of goals and kickoff: A coin is tossed, and the winner gets the choice of goals, of kickoff, or of receiving. The loser of the toss has choice of a remaining option. These privileges of choice are reversed at the beginning of the second half.
   b. Putting the ball in play: The ball is put in play at the beginning of the game, at the beginning of the second half, and after a score by a place kick or a drop kick from the kicker's 20-yard line.
   c. Recovery of a kickoff: If a member of the kicking team recovers or catches a kickoff beyond the receiver's restraining line (which is 20 yards away), the ball becomes dead and belongs to the team making the recovery. No member of the kicking team is eligible to touch, recover, or catch the ball until it crosses the receiver's restraining line. No member of the kicking team may interfere with the receiving team's opportunity to catch the ball. A kickoff ball that is first touched by the kicking team before it reaches the receiver's restraining line goes to the receiving team. If the ball is caught by the receiving team in the field of play, the ball continues in play.
2. Ball kicked over opponent's goal line on kickoff: If the ball is kicked over the opponent's goal line on the kickoff, it goes to the opponents for scrimmage on their 20-yard line.
3. Ball going out of bounds on kickoff: If the ball is kicked out of bounds on the kickoff, the receiving team gets the ball where it went out of bounds.
4. Fumbled ball: At any time the ball is fumbled—dur-

ing scrimmage, after lateral passing, or after a kick or a run—the ball is a live ball and belongs to the team that recovers it. If the offensive team regains possession, the down advances unless recovery gives them a first down. If the defense recovers the fumble, it is a first down.

5. Necessary gain in downs: If in four consecutive downs a team fails to advance the ball to the next zone, it goes to the opponents at that point.

6. Downed ball: The player is downed and the ball is dead when an opposing player touches the first player with one or both hands in an area from the knees to the shoulders. The use of a one- or two-handed tag must be determined before the game begins.

7. The following regulations apply to passing:
   a. All players of the offensive team are eligible to receive passes. Any member of the defensive team may intercept passes.
   b. Forward passes may be thrown from anywhere in back of the line of scrimmage, and lateral passes may be thrown anywhere on the playing field.

Note: To increase passing and receiving proficiency, the instructor may stipulate that passes can be thrown anywhere on the field in any direction.

Fouls and penalties

1. It is a foul to tackle, trip, push, or rough another player, and these result in a 15-yard (13.7 m) penalty.
2. It is a foul to use the hands or to leave the feet in an attempt to block an opponent. The penalty for making an illegal block is loss of 15 yards (13.7 m) from the spot of the foul.
3. It is a foul for a player to be offside before the ball is put in play. The penalty is loss of 5 yards (4.57 m) from where the ball was put in play.

Officials

1. The referee has absolute charge of the game, and decisions made by the referee are final.
2. The umpire pays particular attention to holding and interference on forward pass plays.
3. The linesman measures distance and reports offside and personal fouls such as holding and roughness. The linesman may also be the timekeeper if no special individual is assigned this duty. (See Fig. 35-2 for official football signals.)

FUNDAMENTAL SKILLS AND TECHNIQUES
The stance

The player must be positioned within 1 foot (30 cm) of the scrimmage line.

Offensive line stance. The stance used by players on the offensive line must enable them to move forward, backward, and laterally; therefore, it must be a position with the feet comfortably apart and staggered, knees bent, with the body in balance to facilitate a quick movement in the desired direction.

Defensive line stance. This stance is similar to the offensive stance, but the body is closer to the ground. Weight must be forward so a lineman can charge forward.

Offensive backfield stance (two-point stance)
1. The feet are about shoulder width apart, with the toes pointed straight ahead.
2. Weight is equally distributed on the balls of both feet and the knees are slightly flexed.
3. The hands or elbows are on the knees, arms are slightly flexed, thumbs are on the inside of the knees, the head is up, and the eyes are straight ahead.

Defensive backfield stance. Players should stand in a natural but alert posture, feet apart and staggered. A semierect body position facilitates quick movements yet affords an effective position to observe movements of the offense.

Blocking

The object of blocking in touch football is to keep a defensive player from moving into a particular spot on the field or to move a defensive player out of a certain area. Blocking may be accomplished by contacting the opponent with any part of the blocker's body (see Fig. 35-3). Blockers must be on their feet before, during, and after contact. The blocker may not use the hands in any way.

Blocking techniques
1. Assume the two-point stance.
2. Make contact with the defensive player as quickly as possible to gain an advantage from momentum.
3. Stay relatively low.
4. Keep the back straight and parallel to the ground.
5. Keep the head up.
6. Keep the feet wide to provide a base of support.
7. Use short steps to help maintain balance.
8. Know your assignment—whom to block and which way the play is going.
9. The block should be executed so that the blocker's head will be between the opponent and the ball carrier.

Touching

Touching is used as a substitute for tackling. The location of the ball carrier when touched by a defensive player will determine the location for start of the next play.

1. Pursue the ball carrier quickly but with controlled speed and be ready for a change of direction by the ball carrier.
2. Touch the opponent between the knees and shoulders.

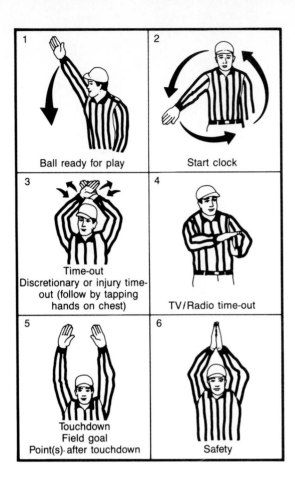

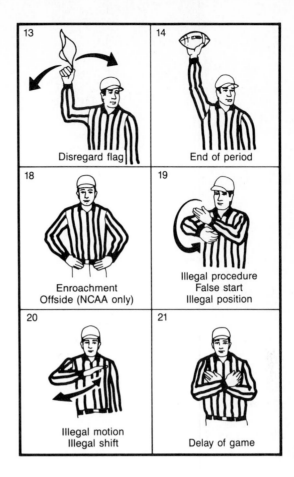

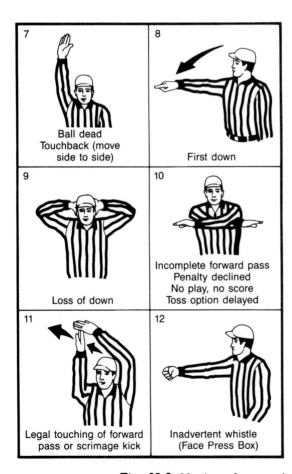

Fig. 35-2. Men's and women's touch and flag football signals.

Continued.

31 Ball illegally kicked, batted or touched

32 Invalid fair catch signal (High School only) Illegal fair catch signal

33 Forward pass interference Kick catching interference

34 Roughing passer

35 Illegal pass Illegal forward handing

36 Intentional grounding

37 Ineligible downfield on pass

44 Helping runner Interlocked interference

45 Grasping face mask or helmet opening

46 Tripping

47 Player disqualification

38 Personal foul

39 Clipping

40 Blocking below waist Illegal block

41 Chop block

42 Holding or obstructing

43 Illegal use of hands or arms

Fig. 35-2, cont'd. Men's and women's touch and flag football signals.

Fig. 35-3. Shoulder block.

Kicking

Punting. The punt is one of the most important plays in football. It can determine the outcome of the game. The punt is used to gain yardage or to better a team's position on the field. Punting is highly specialized, and constant practice is necessary to develop into a good kicker.

1. Stand with the feet slightly apart and staggered, legs flexed at the knees, and weight equally distributed on the balls of both feet.
2. Incline the body forward from the waist, arms and hands extended in front of the body, fingers spread, and palms up.
3. Have the kicking foot ahead at the start of the kick.
4. Follow the ball with the eyes from the center and after the ball is caught; keep the eyes on it until it has been kicked.
5. Hold the ball with both hands, laces up and with the long axis of the ball cocked slightly to one side.
6. Hold the ball on the kicking foot side just below the chest.
7. Take a maximum of three steps before contacting the ball.
8. Keep the toe of the kicking foot pointed inward.
9. Release the ball so that is remains in its long axis until after being kicked.
10. Contact the ball between the toe and upper part of the kicking foot.
11. Swing the leg from the hip through the perpendicular arc, the center of the long axis of the ball meeting the instep approximately 2 feet (60 cm) above the ground.
12. As the foot meets the ball, extend the lower leg and lock the knee joint.
13. Follow through.
14. Kick the ball high as well as far.
15. When advantageous, kick out of bounds.

Catching punts
1. Keep the eyes on the ball.
2. Form a basket with the arms, forearms nearly parallel, and give slightly with the impact of the ball.
3. Catch the ball with the fingers and hands, not by trapping it against the body.
4. Run up to the ball so that after you catch it you can continue on to complete the play.

Place kick

The traditional and soccer styles of place kicks may be used. The soccer-style kick is a popular form that has evolved in recent years.

Traditional style
1. The kicker should stand so that the path of the kicking leg will be in line through the point of the kick and over the center of the crossbar (Fig. 35-4).

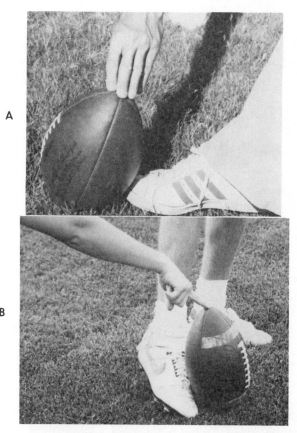

A

B

Fig. 35-4. Place kick. **A,** Traditional style. **B,** Soccer style.

2. A spot slightly below the center of the ball should be picked in advance and the eyes kept focused on this spot throughout the kicking action.

3. The feet should be comfortably spread, knees slightly bent, and body slightly inclined forward from the hips.

4. For the kickoff, any number of steps may be taken in the approach to the kick, but for a field goal or point after the touchdown, only two- or three-step approaches are valid.

Passing or throwing

Forward pass or overhand pass. The forward pass is an offensive technique used to advance the ball and to hold the secondary defensive players deep enough to make the running game function.

1. Grip the ball slightly behind the middle with the fingers on and across the lace.

2. The fingers and thumb should be relaxed and well spread.

3. In the event that the front part of the ball fails to drop in flight, the index finger should be extended toward the rear point of the ball.

4. The right foot should be firmly planted on the ground and the left foot pointed in the general direction of the pass.

5. The ball should be raised toward the right shoulder with both hands, and as the delivery starts, the right hand should come back with the ball to a

position behind the ear. The upper arm should then be approximately parallel to the ground. (See Fig. 35-5.)

6. The ball should be delivered directly over the right shoulder with the index finger pointing the direction of flight.

7. The passer should lead the receiver just a little and should throw with sufficient speed to get the ball to the target quickly, but not too hard to be caught.

8. Body weight transfer should be used in the throw.

Lateral pass. The lateral pass is one of the most successful methods of producing touchdowns, provided a few general rules are followed.

1. Use for passes under 5 yards (4.57 m).

2. Use when you are prevented from breaking away.

3. Do not wait for a lateral pass when you are in a position to block for the ball carrier.

4. Use a lateral pass as late as possible.

5. Do not throw lateral passes indiscriminately.

6. Practice either the basketball-type lateral or the one-handed underhand lateral pass.

   a. Basketball pass:
      (1) The ball is delivered by both hands with arm and wrist action, so that it turns relatively slowly end over end.
      (2) There is very little arch on the ball.

   b. One-hand underhand pass:
      (1) The ball rests in the right hand and is held there by the left hand until the toss is made, the ball rolling off the fingertips with a slight spiral action.

Centering. Centering is much like a forward pass, but upside down.

1. Hold the ball on the ground with the right hand.

2. Have the fingers on the laces.

Fig. 35-5. Forward pass.

Fig. 35-6. Centering.

3. Use the left hand to guide the ball.
4. Spread the feet as far apart as is comfortable. (See Fig. 35-6.)
5. With the quarterback right behind center, pass the ball with only the right hand.

Pass receiving or catching the ball

1. The receiver should keep the eyes on the ball and catch it with the hands rather than trap it against the body.
2. The arms and hands should be loose and relaxed before actual reception of a pass.
3. As the ball touches the hands, a slight giving movement should occur.
4. The ball should then be brought against the body and moved to a carrying position.
5. The receiver should try to catch the ball over the left or right shoulder.
6. The receiver should be under the ball as much as possible.
7. The receiver should try not to change stride unless necessary.

LEARNING SEQUENCE

1. Learn the positions, including duties and conventional formation. (See Figs. 35-7 and 35-8.)
2. Work on the kick formation and assignments involved.
   a. Protection.
   b. Getting downfield quickly.
   c. Kicker acting as safety.
3. Practice forward passes and related plays.

a. Numbers system. Teacher numbers each player and calls number in designating approximate assignment; for example, "No. 3, flat to strong side."
   b. Other members decoy or act as secondary receivers.
   c. Always be alert for lateral.
4. Practice running plays.
   a. Buck—for short but essential yardage.
   b. End run.
   c. Simple reverse.
   d. Laterals.
5. Run with ball.
   a. Carry the ball securely.
   b. Wrap the hand around the visible end of the ball.
   c. Be alert at all times and ready to out guess defensive players.
   d. Be able to sidestep to either the right or left.
   e. Be able to pivot in either direction.
   f. Break when you catch a defensive player off-balance.
   g. Follow your interference.
6. Try various defenses.
   a. Regular line defensive positions. (See Figs. 35-9 and 35-10.)
   b. Backing up fast on running plays.
   c. Pass defense.
      (1) Rushing the passer.
      (2) Covering receivers by zone, one-on-one, or combination.
   d. Punt defense.
      (1) Rushing the kicker.
      (2) Assuming offensive tactics as soon as the ball is in the air.

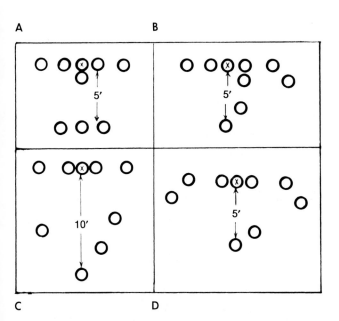

Fig. 35-7. Offense for nine players. **A,** T formation. **B,** Single wing. **C,** Punt. **D,** Double wing.

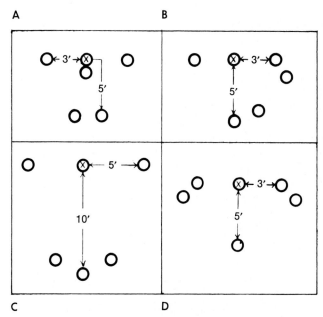

Fig. 35-8. Offense for six players. **A,** T formation. **B,** Single wing. **C,** Punt. **D,** Double wing.

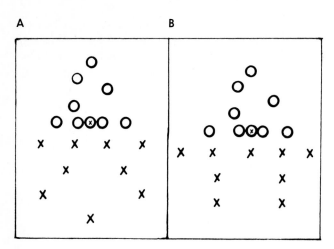

Fig. 35-9. Defense, *X*, formation for nine players. *A*, 4-2-2-1. *B*, 5-2-2.

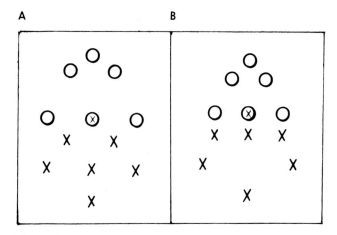

Fig. 35-10. Defense, *X*, for six players. *A*, 2-3-1. *B*, 3-2-1.

7. Playing suggestions:
   a. Assignments should not be tipped off by players' leaning or pointing the eyes, head, or body or by changing facial expression.
   b. Remember that the passer is a ball carrier as long as the ball is in his or her hands.
   c. Vary your style of defense play when flanked by an offensive player. Move out and set, move out and come back in motion, and move and dart through the split if it is wide enough.
   d. Early in the game discover which defense players are weak in covering passes.
   e. Set up plays by sacrificing one or two downs to make future plays function properly.
   f. Plays should be set up in a sequence, including both pass and running plays.

Flag football
FLAG FOOTBALL FOR MEN
In the game of flag football each player has two flags: one is worn on each side of the body. To "tackle" a player carrying the ball means to remove a flag. The rules of touch football are used.

FLAG FOOTBALL FOR WOMEN (MODIFIED)
Equipment
An intermediate-sized football is used. Two flags are worn by each player, one on each side of the body. They should be easily detachable.

Players and positions
There are nine players on each team, plus substitutes. The offensive team should have five line players and four backfield players. The defensive team can line up in any formation, but none of the players should be closer than 3 yards from the line of scrimmage. Anytime the ball is dead a substitute may enter the game without reporting to an official, provided her name is entered on the scoresheet. (See Figs. 35-7 to 35-10.)

Scoring
Touchdown. A touchdown is made when a runner carries the ball across the goal line or a pass is completed in the end zone.

Conversion. One point is given for a run, 2 points for a pass. A team is given one scrimmage play from the conversion line to complete a pass in the end zone or to carry the ball over the goal line. The ball must be caught in the end zone to be good.

Safety. A safety counts 2 points. A safety is scored when the ball legally in the possession of a player becomes dead behind her own goal line. The team scored on restarts the game with a kickoff from its quarter line.

Length of game
The game consists of four 10-minute quarters with 2 minutes between quarters and 10 minutes between halves. No quarter is ended until the ball is dead. In the case of a tie, the team with the greatest number of earned downs is declared the winner.

Start of game
A toss-up decides choice of goals and of kickoff or receiving. At the beginning of the second half the kickoff is alternated. The sides of the field are exchanged at the end of the first and third quarters.

A punt or place kick puts the ball in play at the beginning of each half, after the try for extra points, or after a safety. Team kickers must remain behind their quarter line until the ball is kicked. The receiving team must remain behind the centerline until the ball is kicked.

When a kickoff is caught in the field or end zone the player may run, hand off, or throw a lateral pass. The ball remains in play until the carrier's flag is pulled. The line of scrimmage is the point at which the flag was detached. When a kickoff is fumbled in or lands in the end zone, it is declared a touchback and the receiving team starts its series of four downs on its quarter line. On a kickoff, if the ball lands on the playing field beyond the centerline, the receiving team starts its first down where the ball landed. If the ball is fumbled by the receiving team, it is declared dead and is played from where it touched the ground. If the ball does not cross the centerline on the kickoff, the receiving team has the option of having the kick repeated or putting the ball in play on the centerline. If the ball goes out of bounds, the receiving team may ask that it be kicked over or may play it from where it went out.

Scrimmage play

Line-up. The offensive team must be behind the line of scrimmage, and the defensive team must be 3 yards away from the line of scrimmage. When the ball is centered only one player of the offensive team can be in motion behind the line of scrimmage. The offense may not have more than four players in the backfield.

Centering the ball. When the referee declares the ball ready, the ball must be centered within 25 seconds. The ball must be centered under the legs in one motion by the center to any backfielder. It is a dead ball and a down if the ball is fumbled or touches the ground.

Downs

Each team has four downs to advance into the next zone or to score. If the team advances into the next zone, a first down is earned. Failure to advance the ball to the next zone results in loss of possession.

Scrimmage kick

Any backfielder may punt or place kick on any down. The receiver of the kick may run with or hand off the ball or throw a lateral pass. If a member of the kicking team touches the ball first, it becomes dead where it was touched. If the ball is kicked into the receiving team's end zone, it is brought out to the receiver's quarter line. On a kick, the ball is dead where it first touched the ground.

Offensive play

The team receiving the kick may use any number of lateral passes or handoffs anywhere on the field. Forward handoffs may be used only behind the line of scrimmage. Handoffs in front of the scrimmage line must be parallel to the scrimmage line or to the rear and can be made by anyone. A forward pass must be thrown from behind the line of scrimmage. Any player may catch it. A player who intercepts a pass in her own end zone may ground the ball, resulting in a touchback, or she may run with it.

Defensive play

A defensive player must have one or both feet on the ground when taking a flag. The ball becomes dead where the flag is detached. The ball carrier must not attempt to stop a player from taking the flag.

Dead ball

The ball becomes dead:
1. When the carrier falls down.
2. When the carrier's flag is detached.
3. Following a touchdown, try for a point, safety, or touchback.
4. When runner or ball goes out of bounds.
5. When a scrimmage kick hits the ground.
6. On a kickoff, when the ball hits the ground.
7. On an incomplete forward pass.
8. When a fumbled ball touches the ground.
9. When a player of the kicking team touches a scrimmage kick before a member of the receiving team does.

Fouls

Fouls on kickoff
1. Member of kickoff team crossing quarter line before kickoff. Ball may be kicked again from 5 yards in back of quarter line.
2. Member of receiving team crossing the centerline. Ball may be kicked again from 5 yards in front of the quarter line.

Fouls on scrimmage line
1. Failure of team to announce punt to referee. Penalty: 5 yards and punt repeated.
2. Offside on scrimmage line. Penalty: 5 yards.

Fouls occurring as or before the ball is centered
1. Failure to center the ball within 25 seconds. Penalty: 5 yards.
2. A false start by the center. Penalty: 5 yards.

Fouls during the forward pass
1. A pass thrown after crossing the line of scrimmage. Penalty: loss of 5 yards from the point of forward pass.
2. A passer intentionally grounding the ball. Penalty: 5 yards.
3. A player interfering with another player who is attempting to catch or intercept a pass. Penalty: 15 yards from the line of scrimmage and down advances.

Illegal wearing or pulling of flag
1. It is illegal for the ball carrier to use her hands or

clothing to hide or prevent an opponent from pulling off the flag.

2. Pushing, holding, or hitting the ball carrier while pulling her flag is illegal. Penalty: 15 yards from the spot where the foul occurred.

Illegal handoff

1. It is illegal for the ball to be handed forward in front of the line of scrimmage. Penalty: 5 yards from the point of foul and down advances.
2. A backfield player may not hand the ball forward to a line player. Penalty: loss of 5 yards from point of foul and down advances.

Personal contact

There should be no body contact between players. Penalty: loss of 15 yards from point of foul and down advances if foul committed by offense team. Down remains the same if committed by the defense.

Unnecessary roughness

The penalty for unnecessary roughness is 15 yards. The down advances if the foul is committed by the offense. The down remains the same if the foul is committed by the defense.

Double and multiple fouls

Two fouls cancel each other. When a multiple foul is committed, the captain of the offended team decides which penalty to accept.

SAFETY PRECAUTIONS

1. Inspect all equipment to ensure safety and minimize injuries.
2. Provide competent officials.
3. Inspect the field and clear it of all obstacles that might cause injuries.
4. Give immediate medical attention to injured players.

TEACHING CONSIDERATIONS

1. Use a modified ball (smaller, lighter) for young learners and women. Consider using a foam or plastic ball to establish skills.
2. In most school programs, contact blocking or tackling of any sort should not be permitted because of safety. Flag football is an acceptable substitute.
3. Passing and receiving skills should be taught first. Partner work can be used, first with stationary receivers from short distances and then with moving receivers from longer distances.
4. Two-on-one play can begin a player's introduction to defense. Encourage players to break up passing plays by staying with the receiver between the goal and receiver.
5. All players should practice kicking skills. This can be done in partners, with one partner kicking and the other receiving the ball.
6. When passing, kicking, and receiving skills have be-

come somewhat consistent, modified games can be played, beginning with two-on-two and moving toward more players on each side. Having six players is adequate for the game and encourages more participation. Teach a few basic offensive and defensive plays and then encourage students to design their own plays.

7. Increase the size of the playing field as the number of players increases. Add centering and specific positioning as students begin to understand, through their play, the need for differentiated positioning. Keep rules at a minimum. Enforce no-contact rules consistently.

GLOSSARY

backfield The players behind the line who usually handle the ball.

backward pass A pass that travels toward the goal line a team is defending; may be made by any player.

balanced line Same number of players on each side of the center.

block Using the shoulder, but not the arms, to intercept a defensive player or to stop a defensive player from touching the ball carrier.

bootleg play Faking a handoff or a pass to another player, then running with the ball shielded with the body from the defensive team's view.

button hook A pass route in which the receiver turns and runs back to catch the ball.

centering The act by the center of putting the ball in play from the ground by handling or passing the ball between the legs to a backfield player.

clipping Landing on the back of the leg(s) of a player not carrying the ball.

cross-back An offensive play in which two backs cross, one of them taking a handoff from the quarterback.

cut back To change direction; usually done by the receiver or ball carrier.

disqualifying foul Unnecessary roughness, for which a player is removed from the game.

double wingback An offensive formation: two backs are placed about 1 yard outside of their ends, one back is placed either to the right or left behind a guard, and the tailback is about 5 yards behind the center.

down A unit of game that starts with the entering of the ball and ends when the ball is declared dead.

end zone The 10-yard area between the goal line and end line.

fair catch A catch designated by the player receiving a kicked ball by raising the hand.

flag guarding Using the hands, arms, or clothing or spinning more than once to prevent another player from pulling the flag. Penalty: 15 yards and loss of down.

flanker An offensive player lining up closer to the sideline than the team.

handoff A play in which one back hands the ball to another back.

lateral pass Passing the ball backward or sideways.

line of scrimmage An imaginary line marking the position of the ball at the start of each play.

offsides Advancement of a player beyond the line of scrimmage before the ball is snapped.

safety A score made when a free ball, or one possessed by a player defending his or her own goal, becomes dead behind the goal, provided the impetus that caused the ball to cross the goal was supplied by the defending team.

shotgun offense A formation, used primarily for passing, in which the quarterback lines up 5 to 6 yards behind the center.

SUGGESTED READINGS

AAHPERD rules for coeducational activities and sports, Reston, Va, 1980, American Alliance for Health, Physical Education, Recreation, and Dance.

American Alliance for Health, Physical Education, and Recreation: NAGWS guide, Washington, DC, 1980-1982, American Alliance for Health, Physical Education, and Recreation.

Menke FG: Encyclopedia of sports, ed 4, New York, 1972, AS Barnes & Co., Inc.

The official national touch and flag football rules, North Palm Beach, Fla, 1986, Athletic Institute.

Stanbury D and DeSantis F: Touch football, New York, 1979, Sterling Publishing Co.

36

Track and Field

Completion of this chapter should enable the reader to:

- Become familiar with the events included in a track and field competition and the equipment and facilities required
- Analyze the various skills involved in the running, jumping, vaulting, and throwing events
- Be aware of the rules governing competition in these events
- Teach basis skills in these events to a group of students

HISTORY

The equivalent of track and field events originated almost with the beginning of humanity. To survive, humans had to be both gymnasts and sprinters. Survival depended on the ability to outperform the challenger, human or animal. When not in search of sustenance or being pursued, early humans kept physically fit by engaging in running, jumping, or throwing activities with families or groups.

Games involving the fundamentals of track and field were formulated by the Greeks during their Golden or Homeric Age. The most famous of these games were the Olympics, which began in 776 B.C. and were held every 5 and then 4 years until 392 A.D., when they were abolished by the Romans. In 1896 they were reorganized again by Baron Pierre de Coubertin of France, and since then have been conducted as an international festival. The United States Olympic teams have done well in most track and field events.

Research is constantly being conducted to improve techniques so that the competitor will realize better time for a sprint, a little better distance in the long jump, or a greater height in the high jump. With the application of scientific principles, records are constantly being broken.

EVENTS

Track and field consists of four types of events: running, jumping, vaulting, and weight throwing. The track events are running, sprinting, and hurdling; the field events are long jump, triple jump, high jump, pole vault, shot put, discus, javelin, and hammer throw.

Running Events

Sprints. Outdoor sprints include 100 to 400 meter dashes. Indoor sprints vary with the facility and range from 50 to 70 yards.

Middle distances. Outdoors or indoors, any race that falls within 600 yards to 1 mile is considered middle distance. The most common races are the 800 meter (half mile) and the 1500 meter (1 mile).

Distances. Common distance running events include the 2 mile and 5000 meter indoors, and 3000 meter (women), 3000 meter steeplechase (men), and 5000 and 10,000 meter (men and women).

Hurdles. A confusing array of races is run using hurdles over the total race distance. The height of hurdles and distance between them vary for indoor and outdoor races and for men and women. Outdoors, men run 110 meters for the high hurdles (42 inches high for men and 39 inches high for boys) and 400 meters for the intermediate hurdles (36 inches high). Outdoor races for women are 100 meters for the high hurdles (33 inches high) and 400 meters for the intermediate hurdles (30 inches high). Indoor races vary between 50 and 60 yards for both men and women.

Relays. Relay teams consist of four members, each of whom (except in the shuttle hurdle relays) carries a baton, passing it to the next runner (within a marked zone) until the last runner carries it across the finish line. The relays include 4 x 100 meters, 4 x 200 meters, 4 x 400 meters, 4 x 800 meters, and 4 x 1500 or 1600 meters. The medley relays are the sprint (200, 400, and 800 meters) and the distance medley (400, 800, 1200, and 1600 meters).

Steeplechase. The steeplechase is a 3000 meter event for men that includes 28 hurdle jumps and 7 water jumps. The hurdles are 3 feet (0.914 m) high, and the water jump is 12 feet (3.66 m) long with a regular downward slope resulting in a depth of 2.3 feet (0.7 m) for the final 1 foot (0.3 m). The water-jump pit is filled with water to track level and has a 3-foot (0.914 m) hurdle at the front of it. The competitors must go over or through the water. They may jump or vault over each hurdle or place a foot on each hurdle and on the hurdle at each water jump.

Race walking

Race walking is advancing through a progression of steps so taken that unbroken contact with the ground is maintained. The walker must progress in such a manner that the lead foot (preferably the heel) makes contact with the ground before the rear foot leaves the ground. The leg must be extended momentarily, and the support leg must be extended vertically.

Violations include:
1. Lifting—failure to maintain broken contact. Penalty: disqualification.
2. Creeping—failure to extend the leg. Penalty: disqualification.

The race walk is generally conducted over a distance of 5 and 10 kilometers on the track and 20 to 50 kilometers on the roads.

Jumping events

Long jump and triple jump. The runway generally varies from 120 to 160 feet (39.6 to 48.8 m) for men and 90 to 120 feet (29.7 to 39.6 m) for women. The styles of long jumps used are the sail, hitch kick, and hang. The triple jump has three phases: the hop, the step, and the jump.

High jump. The two primary styles of jumping are the straddle and the "Fosbury flop."

Pole vault. The modern pole vaulter must be a sprinter, weight lifter, and gymnast. The combination of speed, strength, and coordination makes this a spectacular event. Since the introduction of the fiberglass pole, tremendously increased performances have been recorded. The runway varies from 125 to 140 feet in length.

Weight-throwing events

Shot put. For college, Athletic Congress, and Olympic competition, 16 pounds (7.25 kg) is used; for high school, 12 pounds (5.44 kg) and for women, 4 kg. The shots are made of a cast-iron, bronze, or brass shell with a lead center. The indoor shot has a plastic shell. The shot is thrown from a circle 7 feet (2.13 m) in diameter.

Discus. The collegiate discus is wooden with a metal rim, measures 8.622 inches (21.6 cm) in diameter, and weighs 4 pounds 6.548 ounces (2 kg). It is thrown from a starting circle 8 feet 2½ inches (2.5 m) in diameter. For women the minimum weight of the discus is 2 pounds 3.25 ounces (1 kg), and the diameter is 7⅛ inches (17.6 cm). For high school the discus must weigh not less than 3 pounds 9 ounces (1.6 kg).

Hammer. The hammer consists of a round weight attached to a triangular handle by a wire. It weighs 16 pounds (7.25 kg), and its total length may not exceed 48 inches (1.2 m). It is thrown from a circle 7 feet (2.13 m) in diameter. The indoor equivalent of the hammer-throw event is the 35-pound-weight throw.

Javelin. The javelin is a metal alloy spear, tapered at the tail end, with a reinforced steel tip. The length is approximately 8½ feet (2.6 m), and the weight is 1.765 pounds (0.8 kg). It has a cord grip 6.3 inches (16 cm) wide around the center of gravity. For women the minimum weight of the javelin is 1 pound 5½ ounces (0.61 kg). It is 7 feet 2½ inches (2.2 m) in length and has a cord grip 5⅞ inches (14.9 cm) wide.

Other track and field events

In the Olympic games some events are not always standard in United States competition. The 20 kilometer and 50 kilometer walks are examples. The tests of all-around skill and ability are the decathlon for men and the heptathlon for women.

The decathlon consists of 10 events that are run over 2 days in the following order: first day, 100 meter dash, long jump, shot put, high jump, and 400 meter dash; second day, 110 meter hurdles, discus, pole vault, javelin, and 1500 meter run. The heptathlon consists of seven events that are scheduled over 2 days in the following order: first day, 100 meter hurdles, high jump, shot put, and 200 meter dash; second day, long jump, javelin, and 800 meter run.

FACILITY

A satisfactory facility for track and field is the combination football area surrounded by an oval 400 m track. (See Fig. 36-1.) Usually eight running lanes are marked off. Around the periphery of the field are pits and circles for the field events. A good layout is one in which two or more events can be conducted simultaneously.

SHOES

With the advent of new training and racing surfaces in the past few years, many types of shoes have been introduced. There now seems to be a specific shoe for every event in the sport of track and field. Most shoes have interchangeable spike plates and are built for protection

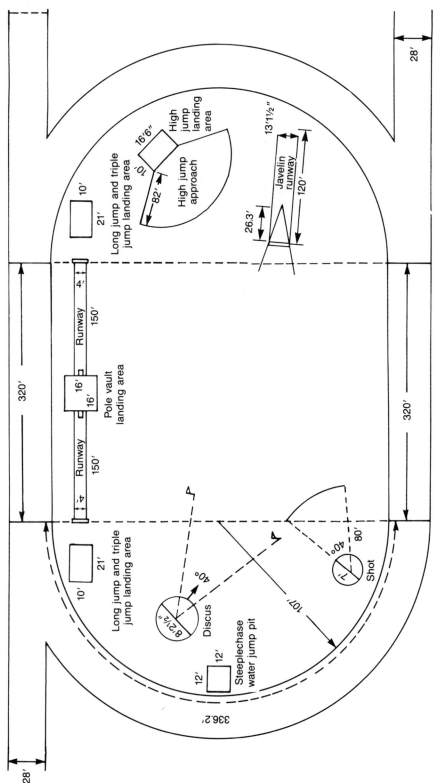

Fig. 36-1. Track and field facility.

Fig. 36-2. "On your mark"—medium starting position.

and comfort as well as style and fit. The type of shoe worn can make a great difference in terms of traction on a racing surface and therefore can represent the winning edge.

MECHANICAL ANALYSIS OF TRACK AND FIELD EVENTS
Running events
Starting blocks

Starting blocks are essential to the sprinter, providing a solid base from which to push off and preventing unnecessary slipping or injury to the runner. Adjustable blocks that can be used either indoors or outdoors are the most satisfactory.

Starting positions

Because of a wide difference in anatomic proportions among participants, there is a variance in starting positions. However, three main positions are recognized: the bunched, the medium, and the elongated. The bunched position is seldom used. The medium starting position is the most widely used; and the elongated start is sometimes used by tall competitors.

"**On your mark.**" For the bunch start, the front foot is placed approximately 19 inches in back of the hands and the rear foot about 29 inches from the hands. In the medium starting position the front foot and rear foot are approximately 15 inches and 34 inches, respectively, from the hands. (See Fig. 36-2.) In this position the rear knee bisects the front foot. For the elongated starting position, the front foot should be approximately 13 inches

and the rear foot approximately 41 inches from the hands. In all three starting positions the fingers and thumbs are placed like a tripod on the starting line and about shoulder width apart.

"**Set.**" To get set means to distribute the weight of the body in the best possible position from which to take off. In the bunch start, this means raising the hips to a position approximately 25 degrees higher than the shoulders. This is decreased to about 20 degrees for the medium start and even less for the elongated start. Concentration should be on the rear leg and the opposite arm. (See Fig. 36-3.)

"**Go**"—**discharge of pistol.** Push off forcefully on the front block. Step forward with the rear foot and throw the arm opposite the rear foot forward down the track while blasting out of the blocks. This reaction takes practice. The action is to fall as far forward as possible without leaving the feet. The moment of force should be as far in back of the center of gravity as possible. Concentration should be on the first 20 yards. The runner should not shorten the steps or use strides that are too extended or too short. (See Fig. 36-4.)

Sprinting

The sprinter should be relaxed while running to maintain the greatest speed. Many stand too straight or hold the head too high, which causes fatigue and tension in the back and neck and causes an unnecessary expenditure of energy.

Rhythm must be mastered by coordinating all body parts. The arms should be flexed and should swing freely

Fig. 36-3. "Set"—medium starting position.

Fig. 36-4. "Go"—discharge of pistol.

at the sides, making an arc from the waist to the shoulders. The hands should be open and relaxed. While the sprinter is running, the weight of the body should fall on the balls of the feet. The heels sink, but not entirely to the ground. As the center of weight moves over the feet, the legs straighten. As the leg is flexed and brought forward, all the extensor muscles should be at rest. The length of the stride is determined by the speed attained. Maintenance of a parallel line of gravitation is most important for achieving smoothness and rhythm.

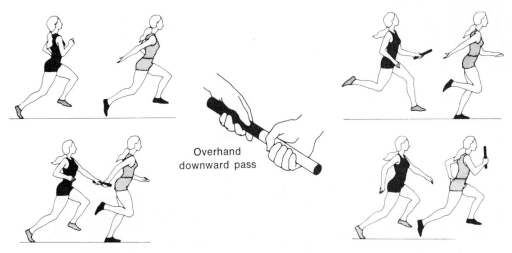

Fig. 36-5. Nonvisual baton pass—overhand downward pass.

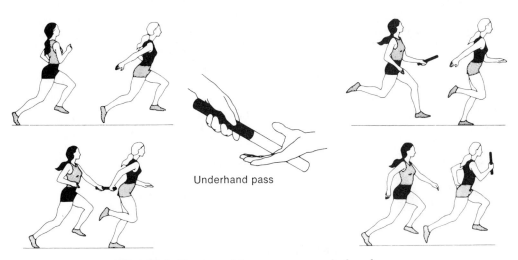

Fig. 36-6. Nonvisual baton pass—underhand pass.

Running the 400 meters

As the distance increases, the runner assumes a more erect posture, the strides become shorter, and the heels assist in supporting the weight.

A good rule to follow in preparation for competition is to run repetitions of more than 400 m to develop endurance and to run repetitions of less than 400 m to develop speed. Alternate these workouts. Rest a day before a meet.

Relays—passing the baton

The *visual pass* is a pass that is seen by the receiver, and it is the receiver's responsibility to make sure of the pass. It is used primarily in the long relays when the fatigue of the runner may lessen coordination, decreasing the runner's ability to pass accurately. The baton may be passed from the left hand to the right hand or from the right hand to the left hand.

In sprint relays, this will normally alternate with the first and third runners carrying the baton in the right hand and the second and fourth runners carrying it in the left hand.

The *nonvisual pass* or blind pass is a pass that is not seen by the receiver. In this pass the responsibility for a successful pass lies with the runner. This pass is used in sprint relays and must be practiced by the runners. It is a quick, highly coordinated movement, the baton going from the runner to the receiver at top speed. The baton is carried in the extended left hand of the runner and received on the run in the right hand of the receiver. (See Figs. 36-5 and 36-6.)

Hurdling

Good hurdling depends on the ability to start fast and to generate top sprinting speed.

The action between the hurdles should be that of a

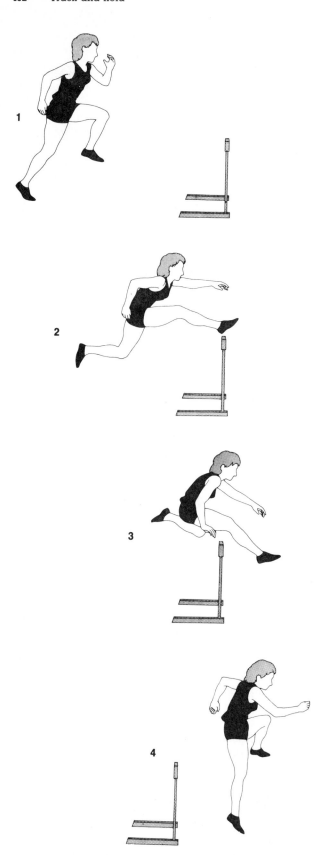

Fig. 36-7. Running the hurdles.

sprinter. The steps should not be elongated to reach the next hurdle; this slows the hurdler down. The lead knee should start the hurdling action. The arms should follow, with the upper part of the body lowering to meet the upcoming knee. Next the trailing leg is flattened out and then picked up as close to the under arm as possible. This facilitates a sound landing position and good first stride once over the hurdle. The landing should be made on the ball of the foot for a continuous print action. When there is proper weight distribution, the center of gravity will be ahead of the touchdown point, and this will ensure forward momentum and a return to sprint form.

The technique for clearing the intermediate hurdles is slightly different because the hurdle is lower. The pivot over the hurdle rail is slower. In the 400 meter intermediate hurdle race, economy of effort becomes an important factor. Because the horizontal speed is slower than in the high hurdles, the stepping-down action once over the intermediate hurdle is less violent. In all hurdling, flexibility is very important. (See Fig. 36-7.)

Running the steeplechase

The key to the steeplechase lies in mastering the barriers. Running workouts combining long distance, intense distance intervals, and speed work are necessary, but the method for jumping the barriers deserves special attention. The key to jumping the barriers is momentum. It is important not to slow down in front of the hurdles or the water jump. Lack of momentum causes landing with the center of gravity far behind the lead leg and coming to a near halt on the far side of the barrier. The usual method for attacking the water jump is to place the lead leg on the barrier, allow momentum to move the body across the barrier, push off the barrier, and land in the water on the other foot far enough out so that the leg that pushed off the barrier can land next on the track beyond the water. It is important to get back to proper running form as quickly as possible.

Jumping events
Long jump

Success or failure in the long jump depends on the ability to get into the optimum takeoff position with as much speed as can be controlled during this phase of the jump. The distance for the approach to the takeoff board varies with the speed and size of the athlete but generally is between 110 and 130 feet. The jumper should establish the takeoff foot and starting mark by "running through" the jump a few times and checking for accuracy. In most cases the method of setting up two or three checkpoints is recommended to enable the jumper to adjust the stride before reaching the takeoff board.

Takeoff. The first step is to plant the takeoff foot (usually heel contacts first) on the takeoff board. The center of gravity at this point is behind the takeoff foot. Midway through the takeoff the body weight is shifted directly over the takeoff foot, and just before loss of contact with the takeoff board the center of gravity is moved ahead to the takeoff foot. The takeoff leg remains fairly straight throughout the takeoff. The other leg is flexed at the knee, and the arms swing in opposition to the legs. The head is up and the eyes focused forward. (See Fig. 36-8, *1* through *4*.)

Hang. The jumper reaches forward with the leading leg and then sweeps it downward until both legs are together somewhat behind the line of the body. This sweeping movement produces an opposite reaction in the upper body, thereby extending the body. The cir-

Fig. 36-8. Hitch kick form.

cular swing of the arms continues until both arms are high above the head. The knees are then bent and the legs brought forward in preparation for landing.

Hitch kick. Once airborne, the jumper extends the leading leg forward and then sweeps it downward and backward. Coordinated with this movement is a pulling through of the takeoff leg (knee bent) and a downward and backward swinging of the arm on the side opposite the lead leg. At the end of this in-the-air stride the legs are in a position opposite that at takeoff. Next the rear leg is brought forward in a bent-knee position (to minimize forward rotation). The hitch-kick style aids in balancing the jumper in the air and provides an advantageous landing position. It does not propel the jumper through the air.

Triple jump

As in the long jump, linear velocity is important. However, unlike in the long jump, this velocity must be controlled, conserved, and evenly distributed over all three phases: the hop, the step, and the jump.

The strongest leg should be used for the takeoff. The knee of the other leg should come up and forward at takeoff. Balance is important, so the long jumper should keep the line of vision straight ahead. The takeoff angle should be about 20 degrees. Inasmuch as the first jump (the hop) is just one of the three jumps, it should not be made too long. The landing should be on the entire foot, with the knee and the ankle immediately flexing and the center of weight slightly behind the landing foot.

Of the three jumps, the step is the most difficult in terms of gaining distance. The arms are important for balance and momentum. They must be held waist high and pump vigorously. The knee should lead first in the step phase.

On the jump phase, height is most important. Both arms should be brought forward and upward to creat momentum. For beginners, the hang style is the best technique for the jump.

High jump

The two basic styles of high jumping currently in use are the straddle and the flop.

Straddle. The approach is from a 20-or 30-degree angle to the plane of the uprights. Done properly, the approach should allow maximum vertical velocity and provide sufficient horizontal motion for crossing the bar and the required body rotation for bar clearance. The approach is made from 12 to 14 strides out. The jumper jogs the first few steps, then strides hard the final eight, with the last three the longest. Swinging upward toward the bar together, the free leg and arms accelerate to create takeoff momentum. Early arm action helps to initiate the twisting of the trunk necessary for bar clearance. After takeoff the arm opposite the lead leg reaches toward the bar, the jumping leg flexes, and the rotation of the body increases, using the bar as the axis. The rotation continues so that the jumper lands on the back. (See Fig. 36-9.)

Flop. Because the movements are simple and natural, the flop seems to be easier to learn than the straddle. The approach is J shaped. Because it begins with a straight line, it allows for development of speed, which is transferred to the slight curve at the end (the last three or four steps). Centrifugal force is a major component at the end of the approach, so this phase must be smooth to enable the jumper to plant at the proper angle and initiate the desired rotations.

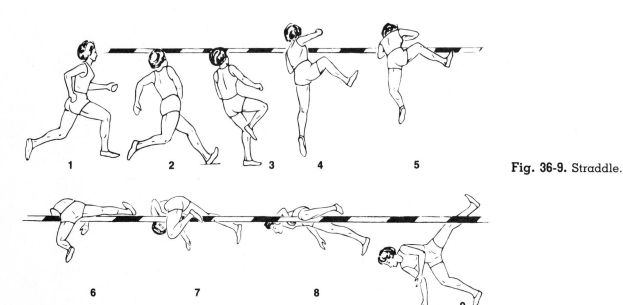

Fig. 36-9. Straddle.

During the approach the jumper gradually lengthens the stride. On the third-to-last step the arms become synchronized with the lead leg. As the bent-knee lead leg begins its upward and forward movement, the arms are brought forward and upward. The jumping (outside) foot should be planted almost parallel to the bar, 3 to 4 feet directly in front of the near standard.

As jumpers experiment with this relatively new high jump technique, two styles are emerging—the power and the speed flop. A speed flopper uses a sharper knee angle than the power flopper with the leg closest to the high bar. This action causes the drive knee to be faster for the speed flopper than for the power flopper. The last step is a heel-toe action. The jumper crosses the bar in the middle, and momentum will cause the jumper to land in the far corner. (See Fig. 36-10, *A* and *B*).

Pole vaulting

The advent of the fiberglass pole changed the event of pole vaulting tremendously. Not only did the performances improve markedly, but coaching techniques required change. The fiberglass pole does for the vaulter

Fig. 36-10. The flop. **A,** Progression of movement. **B,** The body passing over the bar.

what the parallel bars and the horizontal bar do for the gymnast. In both cases the resiliency of the apparatus actually aids the performer. There are five phases in vaulting.

Approach. The vaulter should use an approach allowing the greatest buildup of controlled speed. The handhold should be slightly wider than the shoulder width.

Pole plant. The pole should be planted early and out in front of the body. The upper arm is extended as straight as possible overhead or slightly in front of the head. The vaulter should continue to drive into the pole. The plant foot should be directly under or slightly behind the upper hand at takeoff.

Swing. After the takeoff the lower arm should be locked. This aids in the transfer of linear velocity to angular velocity. The knee opposite the plant foot should be driven up, whereas the plant foot is left hanging until the next phase, the rollback.

Rollback. During the rollback phase the hips should be brought higher than the head and the knees flexed into the chest. The vaulter should remain in the rollback position until the pole is well into its recoil.

Pullup-pushup-pushoff. The final phase starts with a pullup and should be done when the pole is almost straight for maximum efficiency and greatest height potential. The pushup is done much like the handstand pushup. After maximum height is realized the vaulter pushes off, dropping the legs and rotating around the bar. (See Fig. 36-11.)

Weight-throwing events
Shot put

A common technique used for throwing the shot is a modified version of the Perry O'Brien shift, named after the man who first used it. The thrower starts at the back of the circle facing the opposite direction of the throw with the right foot on a line bisecting the circle. (See Fig. 36-12.) The shot is held at the base of the first three fingers and is placed in the neck or under the chin. The knees should be flexed and the trunk bent forward. The nonthrowing arm is raised at an angle and used for balance. The hips and shoulders at this point are square to the back of the circle, and the weight is over the right foot. The left leg starts in the direction of the throw. This action causes a falling backward in the direction of the throw. At the same time the right leg should begin a driving action. The line of movement of the shot is nearly horizontal during this phase.

The right foot lands near the exact center of the circle and the left leg near the front of the circle. (See Fig. 36-12.) The hips and body begin to rotate in the direction of the throw. The forearm and elbow should remain directly behind the shot. The arm is extended and chases after the shot, and the wrist is snapped. The eyes should follow the shot during the follow-through.

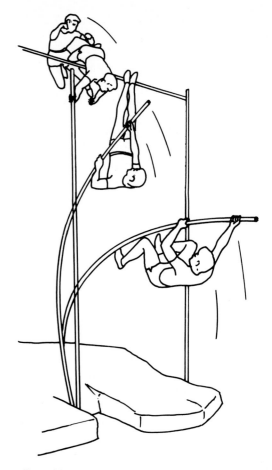

Fig. 36-11. Flexibility of fiberglass pole.

Discus

Most beginners are under the mistaken impression that the discus is thrown with the arm. It should be made clear that the force is generated primarily by the hips, legs, and trunk.

The hand is placed on the discus with the fingers slightly separated and the first joint of each finger curled slightly over the rim. The thumb rests on top of the discus, and the wrist is slightly cocked toward the little finger. At the release the discus should spin clockwise (right-handed thrower), and the index finger is the last finger to lose contact with the discus.

To achieve the greatest force the thrower starts in the extreme back position of the circle and will eventually complete 1 ¾ turns before the release. Usually the beginning of the spin is preceded by a few preliminary swings of the discus back and forth to establish a rhythm. The beginning position of the spin should be with the feet slightly wider than the shoulder width and the top part of the body rotated more than 180 degrees to the right. (See Fig. 36-13, *A* for position of feet.)

The spin is then initiated by the legs and the hips as

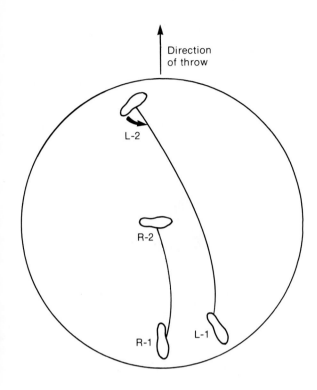

Fig. 36-12. Foot movement for shot put.

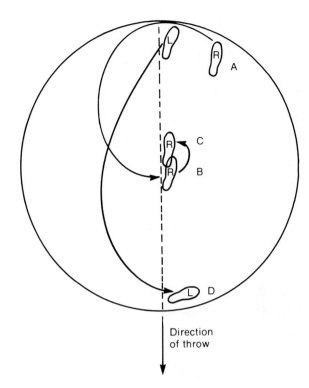

Fig. 36-13. Foot movement for discus.

the weight is shifted to the left. The upper body remains relaxed, and the throwing arm trails behind with the discus at shoulder height. A key here is to keep the feet in contact with the ground as long as possible.

As the weight continues to shift to the left, the right foot will be lifted off the ground and should be driven forward toward the center of the ring to establish a new support. Before the right foot contacts the ground the thrower will face the front of the ring, pass through this position, and again face the back of the ring. (See Fig. 36-13, *B*.) Once the right foot contacts the ground the performer pivots on this foot. (See Fig. 36-13, *C*.) The left foot comes off the ground to eventually be placed at the front of the circle a little past the centerline. (See Fig. 36-13, *D*.) Once the left foot makes contact the thrower enters the explosive part of the throw.

With the right foot planted now in the center of the circle and the left foot planted in the front of the circle, the thrower explodes and acelerates the turning of the upper body against the firmly anchored lower body. The discus at the beginning of this explosion should be about at shoulder height, dropped to hip height, and then released at shoulder height.

Javelin

In competition the method of throwing the javelin is the over-the-shoulder style, using a crossover step in the last stage of the approach. The average runup is about 110 to 130 feet. The crossover style allows the thrower a long last stride and a quick pushoff with the free leg. (See Fig. 36-14.)

Because of the design of the javelin, air resistance causes it to follow flight curves that are not parabolic. By making adjustments in the center of gravity and the surface configurations, aerodynamic javelins were produced that sailed better and farther than the older type.

Recently, however, another design change occurred to reduce the possible danger from the javelin traveling too far. The center of gravity has been moved forward and javelin distances are now somewhat less than in the past.

The optimum angle of release is a function of the type of javelin used: for the nonaerodynamic javelin the angle is probably between 42 and 50 degrees; for the aerodynamic javelin it is probably between 30 and 40 degrees.

Hammer throw

From a position facing the opposite direction of the throw and toward the edge of the circle, the hammer thrower begins with the feet approximately shoulder width apart, arms extended, and body weight over the leg on the side of the hammer. Before the release of the hammer the thrower will swing it around the head twice while facing the starting position and then turn 3½ complete circles with the hammer in order to build its velocity to a maximum. While rotating through the 5½ circles the path of the hammer is gradually changed from one approxi-

Fig. 36-14. Sequence of javelin throw.

mately parallel with the ground to one describing a diagonal direction at an angle of approximately 45 degrees to the ground.

The most successful hammer thrower is the one who can move the feet, hips, and shoulders progressively farther ahead of the hammer to maximize the muscular forces acting to increase the hammer's velocity.

BASIC RULES

Sprinting

1. A false start may be called if the runner does not comply with the command "On your mark" or "Set."
2. A false start is declared if the runner jumps the gun. In NCAA competition, one false start disqualifies the runner. In IAFF/international competition, a runner is disqualified after the second false start.

Hurdling

1. The entire body must pass over each hurdle.
2. The hurdler cannot run around a hurdle.
3. The hurdler must stay in the lane.

Relay races

1. Disqualification of one runner disqualifies the entire team.
2. The baton must be passed inside the 20 m passing zone.
3. The baton must be carried in the hand.
4. If the baton is dropped, it must be recovered legally.
5. The last runner of the race must have the baton.
6. After passing the baton, the runner must not interfere with the opponent.

High jump

The crossbar must be cleared without displacement.

Pole vault

The crossbar must be cleared without displacement caused by either the body or the pole.

Long jump and triple jump

1. The jumper's shoe must be extended over the scratch line.
2. The foot must not drag during the stop phase of the triple jump.

Shot put

1. A legal shot must be used.
2. The shot must land within the sector.
3. The put must be from within the circle.
4. The competitor must exit from the rear of the circle under control.

Discus

1. The throw must land within the sector.
2. The competitor must stay within the circle until the distance is marked.
3. The complete throw must be from within the circle.
4. The proper discus must be used.

Javelin

1. The throw must land within the sector.
2. The javelin must be held by the cord grip.
3. A regulation javelin must be used.

Hammer throw

1. The throw must land within the sector.
2. During the throw the competitor must not leave the circle.
3. The implement must be legal.
4. Gloves may be used.

SAFETY PRECAUTIONS

1. Run through a few flexibility and conditioning exercises.
2. Wear properly fitting shoes.
3. Be serious about practice jumps and runs.
4. Do not jump from wet surfaces or with wet soles.
5. Take proper care of equipment.

TEACHING CONSIDERATIONS

1. Basic running, jumping, and throwing events can be taught without a great deal of equipment. Jumping events require some kind of jumping pit. Other facilities can be adapted from those usually present in school situations.
2. It is a challenge for the teacher to organize maximum activity and practice for track and field. Beginning with running and jumping events that can accommodate more participants and then organizing the class by stations usually avoids much standing around. However, students must have clear guidelines as to what to do at stations and must be able to practice good form independently of the teacher. In classes for which good working skills have been established, peer teaching also works well for student feedback.
3. Try not to do only one type of event in one period (e.g., all running, all throwing, or all jumping).
4. Divide the class by ability and run a meet to culminate the unit. Keep school or class records and post them to motivate good performance.

Sprinting events

1. Homemade starting blocks can be made if others are not available.
2. Provide for practice of the start and teach the strategies of sprinting as well as ideal sprinting form.

Relays

1. Practice batons can be easily made from broomsticks or scrap tubing.
2. Start with one type of pass and teach it until runners show no loss of speed in the pass.
3. Group relay teams for class competition into equal teams, but provide opportunity for the fastest runners to work together as well.

Long-distance runs

If conditioning programs have preceded or been part of a unit, long-distance running can be included. If not, distances beyond a quarter mile or mile (depending on age) should not be included in the unit.

Hurdling

1. Adapt equipment for initial learning of hurdling form so that the learner is not hurt when contacting the "upper rail." Use commercial adjustable hurdles (some have Velcro).
2. Work to the side of the hurdle on either the trail or forward leg before putting both together. Make sure learners understand the correct position going over the hurdle (assume it on the floor).
3. As soon as form is established, begin using more than one hurdle and push students for time.

Long jump

1. The long jump can be taught effectively using backward chaining (start with the middle part of the action—the takeoff). Spend time on the takeoff before working on the approach.
2. Visual aids of the flight pattern in the air are helpful.

Triple jump

1. Walk through the sequence of hop-step-jump with the students slowly until the pattern is established. Then increase speed and distance.
2. Help students to get as much distance on each phase as possible by practicing not only what the legs do, but the total body action including the arms. Have students place markers where each phase lands and try to increase the distance between the markers.

High jump

1. Modify equipment for beginners by using a rope stretched between the poles that will not hurt if contacted. Mats or landing pads piled up high on the landing side of the poles will also take the fear out of jumping.
2. Teach both the straddle and flop, and have students choose early which style they would like to develop.

Shot put, discus, javelin, and hammer throw

1. Equipment is usually available for the shot put and discus. Beginners can master rudimentary technique using softballs (shot put) or weighted Frisbees (discus) to provide more equipment for initial instruction. Students will develop bad habits if equipment with the proper weight is not provided after they master initial form.
2. Both skills are more easily learned if the approach is left until after the release is learned.

GLOSSARY

acceleration zone An area the width of one lane, 10 m (11 yards) long, which may be used by a relay runner to begin running before receiving the baton in the exchange zone.

alley May consist of two or three lanes used as a single lane for running the 800 meter run or 3200 meter relay from a one-turn stagger when more runners are competing than the number of lanes available.

anchor The last runner on a relay team.

approach Run used by the competitor before the actual takeoff in the jumps and the javelin throw.

apron Area in front of the high-jump pit.

baton The stick carried and passed on by the runners of a relay team.

breaking for the pole Cutting over to the inside lane of the track.

course Path of the runner.

crossbar Bar over which the high jumpers and pole vaulters jump.

curb Inside border of the track.

curved starting line An involuted (waterfall) staring line used in 1500, 3000, 5000, and 10,000 meter races.

dead heat A race in which two or more runners cross the finish line at exactly the same moment.

exchange zone An area the width of one lane 20 m (22 yards) long used in relay races. The baton must be passed from one runner to a teammate while they are in this zone. (See passing zone.)

false start Leaving the starting blocks or starting line before the gun sounds or making a movement from the set position.

finish line A line drawn on the track, the edge nearest the runner marking the legal completion of the distance raced.

finish posts Posts on each side of the finish line to which the finish yarn or tape is attached.

finish yarn or tape The cord stretched across the track directly above the finish line to aid the finish judges in determining the winner of a race.

flight The breaking down of a large field of competitors into smaller competitive groups. Used in the horizontal jumps and the throwing events so that competitors may warm up and compete within a reasonable time. Also can refer to a lane or row of hurdles.

foul jump or throw A jump or throw counted as a trial but not measured because of some violation of the field event rules.

grip The handhold on a baton, discus, shot, or javelin, or specifically the cord wrapping on the middle of the javelin.

heat A preliminary round of a race from which the designated places advance to the next round.

high-jump standards Uprights used to hold the crossbar for the high jump.

IAAF International Amateur Athletic Federation.

jostle To run against or to elbow; a form of crowding or bumping together that may hamper or impede a runner.

Kelly pool balls Small numbered balls used in drawing for lanes; also called shake balls.

lane The path marked on the track for a race or that part of a race during which a runner must stay in a prescribed path.

lap One complete circuit of the track.

leg of a relay Distance over which one member of a relay team must run.

medley relay A relay race in which the members of the relay team run different distances.

pass Voluntary giving up of one of a competitor's preliminary or final jumps or throws. Also refers to the actual exchange of a baton or the overtaking of one runner by another in a race.

passing zone A zone the width of one lane 20 m (22 yards) long used in relay races. The baton must be passed from a runner to a teammate while they are in this zone. (See exchange zone.)

pole Inside or curb lane of the track.

qualifying round Competition in which performances qualify the athlete for positions in the trials but time or distances are not considered for final placing. Marks can be considered for record purposes.

recall Calling back of runners after a false start.

scratch Decision not to compete in an event after confirmation or declaration.

scratch line Curved or straight line behind which throws must be made.

sector lines Boundary lines within which a throw must land to be a fair throw.

staggered start Start of a race in which runners do not start on a straight line. Used in races run around a curve up to and including 800 meters (800 yards).

starting block An implement against which runners may place their feet in order to get a faster start at the beginning of a race.

straightaway Straight area of the track between one curve and the next.

stride Distance covered by one step.

TAC The Athletic Congress; governing body for most United States amateur track and field competition.

takeoff board A board from which a long jumper begins the jump.

takeoff mark A spot at which a competitor leaves the ground, as in the high jump and long jump.

TFAUSA Track and Field Association of the United States of America.

toeboard A curved piece of wood or metal used as a foul line for the shot put and the javelin.

trail leg Takeoff leg or rear leg in hurdling.

trial An attempt in a field event.

turn Curved portion of the track. A standard 400-meter (440-yard) track has two turns or curves in one lap.

visual exchange A baton exchange in which the receiver watches the incoming runner until the pass is completed.

warm-up Preparation of the body through light exercise for more vigorous exercise.

SUGGESTED READINGS

Brooks C: Women's hurdling: novice to champion, Champaign, Ill, 1981, Leisure Press. Discusses hurdling techniques along with efficiency of body movement, techniques of training, and psychological concerns.

Crawford T and Bertucci B: Winning track and field drills for women, Champaign, Ill, 1985, Human Kinetics Publishers, Inc. Offers comprehensive description of the track and field drills used by America's most successful women's track coaches.

Cretzmeyer FS, Alley LE, and Tipton CM: Track and field athletics, ed 8, St Louis, 1974, The CV Mosby Co.

Dintiman GG: How to run faster, Champaign, Ill, 1984, Leisure Press. Includes details on scientifically based training program including strength, power, plyometric, anaerobic, and form training.

Foreman K: Coaching track and field techniques, ed 4, Dubuque, Iowa, 1982, WC Brown Group.

Foreman K: Track and field, ed 2, Dubuque, Iowa, 1983, WC Brown Group.

Gambetta V: The Athletics Congress' track and field coaching manual, Champaign, Ill, 1981, Human Kinetics Publishers, Inc. Presents training methods and techniques for all track and field events.

Jacoby E: Applied techniques in track and field, Champaign, Ill, 1983, Human Kinetics Publishers, Inc. Gives a comprehensive overview of how to achieve maximum performance in track and field events.

Official collegiate track and field guide, New York, 1989, National Collegiate Athletic Association.

Randolf J: Championship track and field: by the experts, vols. 1 and 2, Champaign, Ill, 1982, Human Kinetics Publishers, Inc.

Track and field guide, Reston, Va, 1983-1985, National Association for Girls' and Womens' Sports.

VIDEOTAPES

Five series of videotapes on track and field by the following experts: Bill Dellinger (6 programs), Ken Foreman (6 programs) and Meg Ritchie (2 programs). "How To" Sports Videos, Box 5852, Denver, CO 80217.

Running events, Jumping events, and *Throwing events.*The Athletic Institute, 200 N. Castlewood Dr., North Palm Beach, FL 33408.

Thirty track and field videotapes available from Sports Video, 745 State Circle, Box 1941, Ann Arbor, MI 48106.

Sprinting techniques, Hurdling techniques, The long jump, The triple jump, and *The discus.* Karol Video, 22 Riverside Dr., Wayne, NJ 07470.

37

Volleyball

Completion of this chapter should enable the reader to:

- Appreciate the development of volleyball and describe the general rules and equipment used
- Practice the fundamental skills of passing, setting, spiking, serving, and blocking
- Explain aspects of team play and offensive and defensive strategies
- Teach the fundamentals of volleyball

HISTORY

Volleyball was invented in 1895 by William J. Morgan, who was physical education director of the YMCA in Holyoke, Massachusetts. He developed the game to provide an indoor game for the winter months in which relatively large groups of men could participate in a small gymnasium. The principal features of tennis were employed, but the net was raised and the players struck the bladder of a basketball with their hands instead of racquets.

The YMCA is chiefly credited with promoting this very fine game throughout the United States and in many foreign countries. In America volleyball is played regularly on playgrounds and in recreation centers, camps, and school and college classes and intramural programs. It recently has become one of the most popular sports in high school and college women's athletic programs. Also, it has become an excellent recreational game in the armed services and was used in both World War I and World War II.

The YMCA held its first National Volleyball Championships in 1922. The annual YMCA tournaments and the addition of the United States Volleyball Association (USVBA) Open Championships in 1928 further popularized the game, not only as a pleasurable sport but also as a competitive game.

Volleyball was adopted as an Olympic sport in 1964 at Tokyo. While at the time it was a sport played around the world, it was the Soviets and Japanese who took it most seriously. The Japanese women's teams introduced tenacious defense and increased the level of play by scraping and diving for every ball hit by an opponent. The Soviet's contribution to the game was the power offense. With the exception of 1976, when the Polish men's team defeated the Soviets for the gold medal, the Soviets or the Japanese won every men's and women's volleyball gold medal through 1980 (Soviet men three gold, women three gold; Japanese men one gold, women two gold). In fact, in the women's competition from 1964 through 1980 the only time the gold or silver medal failed to go to the Soviets or Japanese was in 1980 when the Japanese boycotted the Olympics (silver to East Germany).

Until 1984 the highest finish by a U.S. men's team was seventh in 1968 and the highest placement by a U.S. women's team was eighth, also in 1968. But in 1984 (when the Soviets boycotted) the U.S. men won the gold and the U.S. women won the silver (China won the gold). In 1988 the Soviet women's team regained the gold by beating Peru (with China capturing the bronze) but the U.S. men's team repeated its gold medal performance, this time by beating the Soviets 13-15, 15-10, 15-4 and 15-8.

Today the game of volleyball requires team strategies involving offensive and defensive plays and highly refined individual skills. Another modification that has become popular, especially on sand courts and beaches, is played with just two players on each side.

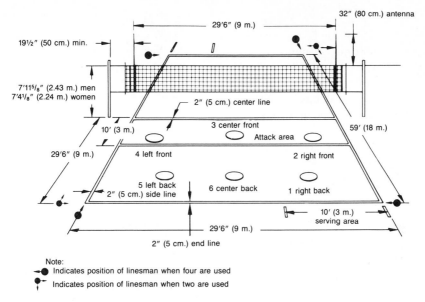

Fig. 37-1. Volleyball court.

DESCRIPTION AND EQUIPMENT

Volleyball for men and women is played on a rectangular court divided by a tightly stretched net. The top of the net is 7 feet 11⅝ inches (2.43 m) from the floor for men and 7 feet 4⅛ inches (2.24 m) from the floor for women. (See Fig. 37-1). A backcourt spiking line is drawn across the court 9 feet 10 inches (3 m) from and parallel to the centerline. Two lines, each 6 inches (15 cm) long, are drawn behind the endline to designate the serving area. One line is an extension of the right sideline. The other is 9 feet 10 inches (3 m) to the left of the first line. Six players constitute a team: three frontline players and three backline players.

An inflated leather ball 25⅝ inches (65 to 67 cm) in circumference and weighing between 9 and 10 ounces (260 to 280 g) is used. It is somewhat smaller than a basketball and resembles a soccer ball or water polo ball in size.

The play begins with a serve by the right back player. The server stands with both feet in the service area, which must be at least 6 feet 6 inches (2 m) deep and is 9 feet 10 inches (3 m) wide to the right and in back of the endline. The right boundary line of this area is an extension of the right sideline of the court. The serve consists of hitting the ball with the hand (open or closed) or any part of the arm so that it goes clearly over the net and within the boundries designated by vertical extensions of the sidelines called the net antennae. The receiving team must return the ball over the net before it touches the floor. Each team may hit the ball a maximum of three times in returning it across the net (a block is not considered one of the three hits). The ball is returned

back and forth until one team makes an error. Only the serving team may score points. If the receiving team commits a fault a point is scored. If the serving team makes the error or commits a fault, side-out is called and the other team serves following the rotation of players.

The ball must be cleanly hit in volleyball; it may not come to rest momentarily in the hands or on the arms. A player may not hit the ball twice in succession (*exception:* blocking rule). The server continues to serve until loss of serve or completion of the game. Following a side-out, the opposite team must rotate clockwise one position before serving. This rotational system is used so that every player rotates not only in serving but in position on the floor. Both teams must be in correct rotation order at the time the ball is served. However, after the serve players may exchange court positions.

ABRIDGED RULES AND REGULATIONS

USVBA rules and regulations are described here.

Playing area and court specifications

The height of the net is the only difference between court specifications for men and women. For the official measurements of the court and playing area for men see Fig. 37-1.

Officials and their duties

1. The first referee is the superior official and decides whether the ball is in play or dead and when point or side-out is made and imposes penalties for rule infractions.

2. The second referee, stationed beneath and at the op-

posite end of the net from the first referee, assists the first referee wherever possible but is primarily responsible for net and centerline violations and for supervision of substitutions.

3. The scorer, seated on the side of the court opposite the referee, keeps the record on points scored, substitutions made, and time-outs called and supervises rotations of servers.

4. When two linesmen are used they are stationed diagonally opposite each other. (See Fig. 37-1.) They are responsible for decisions concerning boundary plays and serving errors.

Players and substitutes

1. In official matches each team must consist of only six players. Player positions along the net are designated right front, center front, and left front; those in the backcourt are called right back, center back, and left back.

2. When the ball is served, players must be in their positions. In the front line the center front must be between the right and left front. In the back line the center back must be between the right and left backs. Also, the back row players may not overlap with the front line players. As soon as the serve is contacted, players may move anywhere on their side of the court.

3. A substitute may replace any player when the ball is dead, provided the player has reported to the scorer and received permission of the referee. A player taken out of a game may reenter once but must return to the original position in the serving order.

4. A substitute who enters the game and is then removed cannot reenter until the next game.

Service and rotation of positions

1. Choice of playing area or service at the start of a match is determined by the toss of a coin. After each game the teams alternate who serves first. When teams are tied in the number of games won, the first serve in the deciding game is determined by a coin toss.

2. The player in the right back position makes the serve and continues as the server until side-out is called. After side-out is called, an opponent becomes the server.

3. Each member of a team, on receiving the ball for service, rotates clockwise one position and remains in this new position until side-out has been called on an opponent's serve.

4. When a game is completed, teams change courts, and alterations in rotation of players must be made at that time. During the deciding game of a match when the score is tied, the teams change courts when one team reaches 8 points.

5. The server must stand entirely outside the court in the service area until the ball is struck. The server must bat the ball with one hand clearly over the net so that, if untouched, it will land within the opponent's court. A serve is good if it clears the net and is touched by an opponent, regardless of where it might have fallen.

Returning the ball

1. A return may be hit in any direction. A player may use any part of the body above and including the waist to hit the ball.

2. A return that passes over that part of the net between the net posts or their imaginary extensions is in play even if it touches the top of the net while in flight.

3. A return may be recovered from the net, provided the player avoids contact with the net.

4. After once contacting the ball, a player may not touch it again until it has been touched by some other player. (*Note:* After the ball has been blocked at the net, any of the blockers may make the next contact.)

Restrictions in the play of backline players

1. Backline players may not participate in the action of blocking.

2. Backline players may not spike from the attack area but may from behind the attack line.

3. Inasmuch as the attack line extends indefinitely, a backline player may not hit a ball into the opponents' court from above the height of the net while outside the court and within such limits of the attack area.

Infractions

If any member of the receiving team commits any of the infractions listed, 1 point is credited to the serving side; if the infraction is made by the serving team, side-out is called.

1. Serving illegally or serving out of turn.

2. Catching or holding the ball or failing to make a legal return.

3. Touching the ball twice in succession.

4. Contacting the net. A player is not considered to have contacted the net if a hard-driven ball causes it to touch him or her. (*Note:* Should two opponents contact the net simultaneously, neither player is penalized, and the serve is repeated.)

5. Touching the ball when it has already been played three times without passing over the net.

6. A player's foot completely touching the floor on the opposite side of the centerline. (*Note:* A player's foot or feet may contact the opponents' side, provided that some part of the foot or feet remains on or above the centerline.)

7. Reaching under the net and touching the ball or an opponent while the ball is in play.

8. Changing player positions before the serve has been made. Until the serve is made, players on each team must be in their relative playing positions.
9. Violating substitutions or time-out regulations.
10. Unnecessarily delaying the game.

Time-out

1. Time-out can be called only by the referee on request of a team captain or coach when the ball is dead.
2. Time-out for substitutions is not charged against a team, provided play is resumed immediately.
3. Time-out for rest is limited to twice in each game, and play must be resumed in 45 seconds, except that if a player has been injured but is to remain in the game, the rest period may last 3 minutes.
4. Time-out between games is 2 minutes.

Scoring

1. Failure of the receiving team to return the ball legally over the net into the opponent's court scores 1 point for the team serving.
2. A game is won when either team scores a 2-point lead with 15 or more points.
3. The score of a forfeited game is 15-0.
4. A match is won by the team that first scores two of three or three of five games. The three-of-five format is most common among college and international matches. Courts are changed in the middle of the third or fifth game.

FUNDAMENTAL SKILLS AND TECHNIQUES

Volleyball is a game that challenges the participant's skill in the use of the hands and agility in jumping, twisting, reaching, and hitting. Hitting motions that require the use of proper body control and muscular coordination are constantly demanded.

Passing

The most fundamental skill to be learned is the ability to pass the ball to a teammate, which is required on almost all plays.

Forearm pass

A forearm pass should be used to receive serves, low balls, and spikes. (See Fig. 37-2.) The forearm pass used to recover the opponents' attack is called a "dig." The official rules do not permit carrying the ball, which occurs during any open-handed hit below the chest. If the ball is hit underhanded, the player should clasp the hands together in any one of three methods: (1) clenched fist, (2) curled fingers, or (3) thumb over palm. (See Fig. 37-3.)

When possible the passer should move quickly to a

Fig. 37-2. The forearm pass.

position behind the ball, with knees bent, feet shoulder width apart, and trunk slightly forward. The hands and arms should be extended and together and parallel, with the elbows locked during contact. The hands should point toward the floor and the ball should be contacted on the forearm above the wrist. The arm movement should be an arc from the shoulders, with the legs actively involved.

One-arm pass

One-arm passes should not be used except at times when it is impossible to use both arms. In an emergency the player should hit the ball with a one-arm underhand fist, but when possible should be hit with the forearm.

Setting

The setter moves to a position so that the forehead is in line with the descending ball and faces the direction of the intended set. The setter's hands "form a window" 6 inches in front of the face with the upper arms nearly horizontal, wrists cocked, and fingers spread. The ball should be contacted with the inner surface of the thumb and fingers. A synchronized springing action of the fingers, wrists, and arms, as well as extension of the legs, pushes the ball forward. (See Fig. 37-4.)

Spiking

Spiking is the act of striking the ball with great force in a downward direction into the opponents' court. To ac-

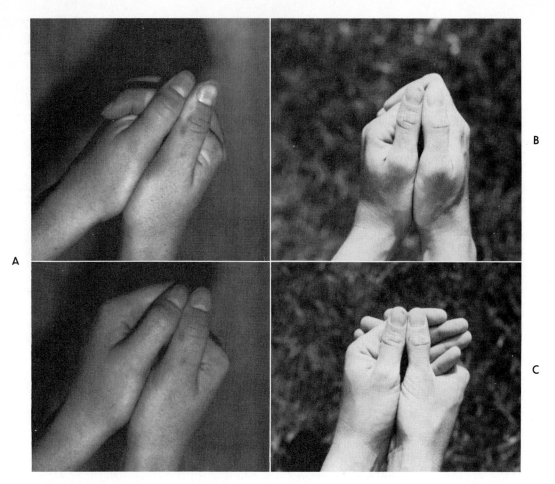

Fig. 37-3. Hand positions for the forearm pass. **A,** Clenched fist. **B,** Curled fingers. **C,** Thumb over palm.

Fig. 37-4. The set.

Fig. 37-5. Spiking.

complish this powerful offensive skill, the player must learn to coordinate the approach, takeoff, and arm movements. The spiker's preliminary position is near the sideline and attack line. Three or four steps are taken during the approach, with the last step taken with the stronger leg.

The step-close takeoff is one method of transferring the momentum of the body into a vertical direction. During the last steps the heels of both feet contact the floor, and then the weight is shifted forward to the toes.

Both arms swing backward to shoulder height when the heels contact the floor. The arms are swung forward and upward during the takeoff. The left arm extends directly upward above the shoulder, and the right arm bends into a throwing position. The left elbow leads the swing, followed by an extension of the spiking arm, contacting the ball with the heel of the open hand. The wrist should snap quickly over the ball to impart a topspin. (See Fig. 37-5.)

Tip

A tip is a soft shot contacted with the fingertips. The arm action is similar to the spike, but the attacker reduces the speed of the swing. The ball is contacted high above the net so that the tip is just over the opponent's attempted block.

Serving

Serves should never be missed at the beginning of a game, after a time-out or substitution, or near the end of a close game. Players should study the opposing team and serve to deep corners, weak players, areas between players (seams), and substitutes. Players should always concentrate on keeping the serve in bounds.

A player should learn to serve accurately and carefully, avoiding trick serves, because a team cannot score unless the serve is made good. The success of a serve therefore depends primarily on accuracy, control, and consistency. Regardless of the type of serve used, the server should attempt to place the ball in the opponents' backcourt, preferably in the corners or to the opponents' weakest receivers.

Types of service

The underhand serve is the easiest to learn and control. The use of the overhand serve will give greater speed to the served ball as well as a twisting line of flight deceptive to the opposing receivers. Sidearm serves can also be made.

Underhand serve. The underhand serve is the easiest and simplest for beginners to use to start the play.

In executing this serve, the player faces the net with the left foot in front (if right-handed) of the right, rests the ball in the left hand at about knee height, and hits it off the holding hand, which swings forward and upward during the hit. The hitting arm swings as in bowling a ball. The hand follows the ball straight through in the direction of the flight of the ball. (See Fig. 37-6.)

Overhand serve. There are two types of overhand serves—the floater and the top spin. The chief asset of the floater is its speed and its weaving line of flight, making it difficult for opponents to return. The top spin serve, while resulting in a more predictable path than the floater, tends to dive toward the floor after it crosses the net.

The overhand serve is executed by tossing the ball 2 or 3 feet in the air above and in front of the right shoulder. The left side of the body faces the net; with the feet in a stride position. As the ball falls to the desired hitting spot, the arm extends from a cocked position to contact the ball. The heel of the hand should be used. Contacting the ball momentarily at its midpoint and with little follow-through results in a floater, while contacting the ball on its lower midsection, snapping the wrist, and rolling the hand over the top of the ball imparts the top spin. The overhand serve is the one most used by players participating in power volleyball. (See Fig. 37-7.)

Sidearm serve. The sidearm serve is infrequently used. Its chief assets are its deceptive curves and the twist that the line of flight often has. Consistent use requires practice, but the serve can be used as a change of pace.

The ball is held at about hip level and is tossed about a foot into the air while the arm swings parallel to the floor. The left side of the body faces the net, left foot forward as in a forehand stance in tennis, and the swing of the arm is similar to the forearm swing.

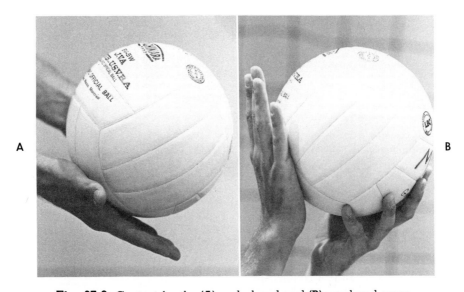

Fig. 37-6. Contact for the **(A)** underhand and **(B)** overhand serve.

Fig. 37-7. Overhand serve.

Jump serve. A recent development is the jump serve. Hitting the serve while jumping allows the server to contact the ball at a higher point, thus permitting a steeper angle. The similarity of the body actions of this serve to the spike (except the angle of contact with the ball) makes this serve a natural and its use is increasing in high level competition.

Receiving the serve

The ball should be advanced from the backcourt to the front line in preparation for either spiking or placement in the opponents' court. The success of the receiving team depends on anticipating the flight of the serve and then on accurate passing.

Because the overhand serve is such a potent offensive weapon, formations for receiving the serve are necessary. An effective approach called the W formation is for the two front-line outside players to move back and toward their respective sidelines and the front-line center player stay near the net with the right shoulder turned slightly toward the net. The back-line center player becomes the primary serve returner by being positioned in the center of the court approximately 12 feet ahead of the back line.

The back-line outside players move back to about 6 or 7 feet from the back line. In this formation the receiving team is best prepared to react to the rebound from the center back player, whose job is to nullify the effects of the opponents' serve.

Blocking

Blocking is a defensive play by an opponent or opponents against the spike or any other placement play near the net. Essentially, the block consists of a defensive player or players' jumping into the air directly in front of the spiker, with arms extended in an effort to block the ball and at the same time to rebound it off the arms back into the spiker's court. (See Fig. 37-8.) This results in the receiver's forming into a W arrangement as shown in Fig. 37-9. To block effectively, one should time the jump with that of the spiker. Multiple contacts by a player(s) participating in a block are legal provided they are during one attempt to intercept the ball.

Retrieving the ball from the net

To play the ball from the net, crouch low, legs spread and bent, with the body facing the sideline. As the ball

Fig. 37-8. Blocking.

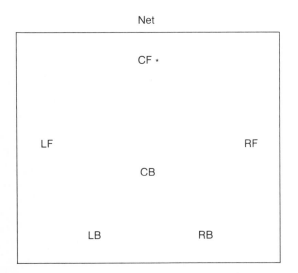

Net

CF *

LF   RF

CB

LB   RB

Fig. 37-9. Formation for receiving a volleyball serve (back toward net).

rebounds from the net, use a forearm pass and an upward-backward striking motion so that a teammate may be able to play the ball. If the ball hits the net near the top, it will drop almost straight down. If it hits low in the net, it may rebound several feet, and the retriever must be stationed accordingly.

Team play

The idea of the game of volleyball is not merely to hit the ball back and forth over the net. Essentially, the game offers many opportunities for team play, both offensive and defensive. When these skills are smoothly developed and executed, a real sense of enjoyment is derived by all players.

Offense or attack

The basic offense consists of passing the ball from the back line to a setter at the net. The setter delivers the ball above and within 2 or 3 feet of the net to the spiker for the attack plays selected to take advantage of the opponents' weaknesses.

The attack is used to develop and establish a playing situation that will deliver to the opponents an unplayable ball. This requires team play. The spiker should aim the ball into an unguarded area of the opponents' court. Sometimes as a surprise play the spiker tips the ball just over the blockers' heads or directs it to either side of the blockers' hands.

The four-two is a simple, basic offense. Four players are designated as attackers and the two best ball handlers as setters. In this system a setter always switches to the center of the front line. Success depends on the ability of the five remaining players to pass the ball to the designated setter. The service order should be arranged so that the two setters and two best spikers are diagonally opposite each other.

Defense

Primarily, good defensive methods are formation plays to most effectively block or recover a hard-hit or well-placed ball. A block is usually set up by grouping two (or occasionally three) front-line players. The back-line players are the secondary line of defense. The diggers must crouch low with hands held waist high, ready for a low, fast, spiked ball.

Return quickly to original position when drawn out on a play. The server should assume position immediately after a serve.

TEACHING CONSIDERATIONS

1. The overhead set is the basic skill upon which continuous play can be built. Therefore it should be the first skill taught. Teach the set using the following guidelines:
   a. Establish consistent good form in simple conditions from either a self-toss or a partner toss.
   b. Build the progression from:
      (1) Stationary setting to moving to receive the ball (stress getting into position before contacting the ball)
      (2) Returning the ball to the same direction, to returning the ball to a different direction
      (3) Simple tosses, to balls tossed across the net
2. Once the set is established one-on-one, two-on-two, and four-on-four, cooperative and competitive play can be introduced to teach positioning and basic offense and defense strategy. Offensive strategy includes:
   a. Playing the ball to an empty space on the opponents' court (back and to the sides).
   b. Changing the direction of the ball.
   c. Changing the dynamics of the hit (tip or spike).
      Defensive strategy for beginning players includes primarily returning to home base to cover space.
3. The serve can be introduced as court size increases. Introduction of the serve requires introduction of the forearm pass. Progression for the forearm pass is similar to that of the set.
4. Combine practice of the forearm pass with the set and serve until students can receive a serve with the forearm pass from different directions and can set it to different directions.
5. Introduce the spike and dig only after consistency with the set and forearm pass is established.
6. Build new skills into the basic game gradually. Provide opportunities to play the game in modified form through the unit, increasing the number of players, size of the court, and skills used gradually as students develop consistency. Do not permit students to swing at the ball with one hand (make it illegal in game play if necessary). Modify rules to encourage good play (e.g., must be three hits on a side, or as many hits as needed).

GLOSSARY

ace A serve that lands in the opponent's court without being touched.

actual playing time Time from the service to dead ball; 8 minutes constitutes a timed game.

blocking A defensive play; attempting to block or stop the returning ball over or near the net.

carrying the ball It is illegal to hold the ball. It must be batted.

catch Allowing the ball to come to rest on any part of the body.

cover Being positioned behind a spike or a block to field a ball glancing off a team member.

dead ball Ball that is out of play.

defaulted game Game in which one team does not have six players to start.

delaying the game Deliberately slowing down the game.

dive A defensive maneuver to recover a ball by extending to a prone position to contact it.

double foul Simultaneous fouls.

foot fault To step on or over the endline before or during the serve, or to step completely over the centerline.

game point The last point in the game.

held ball The ball coming to rest momentarily in the hands or arms.

kill A spike that is impossible to return.

liner A ball that lands on the court boundry line. It is considered in bounds.

match To win two of three or three of five games.

point Awarded the serving team for any infringement of the rules by the receiving team or for an unreturned shot.

rotation Shifting positions clockwise just before the next person serves.

service Putting the ball into play by the right back.

service area Area 6 feet 6 inches (2 m) deep and 9 feet 10 inches (3 m) wide at the right rear of the court, from which the ball is served.

set A high pass that is generally the second play by a team to relay the ball for a spiker.

side-out Ending of a team's right to serve because of an infringement of a rule.

spike A ball hit forcibly from a height above the net.

switch A change of playing positions on the court for strategic reasons.

term of service Serving the ball until side-out is called.

time-out Stopping the game for rest, substitutions, or injuries.

tip A fake spike.

violation A foul, such as a lift, double hit, or four hits on one side.

SUGGESTED READINGS

Bertucci B: Championship volleyball: by the experts, ed 2, Champaign, Ill, 1982, Human Kinetics Publishers, Inc. Gives an extensive overview of all aspects of volleyball, including skills, drills and strategies.

Bertucci B and Bertucci T: Championship volleyball drills, vol 2, Champaign, Ill, 1985, Human Kinetics Publishers, Inc. Contains more than 100 drills designed to develop advanced skills.

Bertucci B and Hippolyte R: Championship volleyball drills (vol 1: individual training), Champaign, Ill, 1984, Human Kinetics Publishers, Inc. Offers a comprehensive description of volleyball drills designed to develop individual skills.

Cox R: Teaching volleyball, Edina, Minn, 1980, Burgess International Group, Inc.

Egstrom, GH and Schaafsma F: Volleyball, ed 3, Dubuque, Iowa, 1980, WC Brown Group. Describes rules and philosophy of play, basic and advanced skills, strategy, offensive and defensive concepts, and coeducational play.

Fraser SD: Strategies for competitive volleyball, Champaign, Ill, 1988, Human Kinetics Publishers, Inc. Presents various strategies for service, receiving the serve, and offensive and defensive plays.

Kluka DA and Dunn PJ: Volleyball, Dubuque, Iowa, 1988, WC Brown Group. Presents the unique characteristics and qualities of volleyball with clear photographs of sequential movements, visual skill enhancements, a chapter on officiating, and a discussion of volleyball's history.

Odeneal W: Winning volleyball drills, Champaign, Ill, 1982, Human Kinetics Publishers, Inc. Shows volleyball drills designed to develop all basic skills.

Official volleyball reference guide, Colorado Springs, Colo, 1989, United States Volleyball Association.

Official volleyball rules and guide, Reston, Va, 1989, American Alliance for Health, Physical Education, Recreation, and Dance; National Association for Girls' and Women's Sports.

Schaafsma F, Heck AJ, and Sarver CT: Volleyball for coaches and teachers, ed 2, Dubuque, Iowa, 1985, Wm C Brown Group.

Scates A: Winning volleyball, ed 3, Boston, 1984, Allyn & Bacon, Inc. Contains individual and team fundamentals, detailed teaching procedures, drills, offensive and defensive plays, philosophy and tactics of coaching, and conditioning and training procedures.

Scates A: Winning volleyball drills, Boston, 1984, Allyn & Bacon, Inc. Includes more than 130 drills for players at all levels. Each drill includes purpose, description, coaching tips, and equipment.

Slaymaker T and Brown VH: Power volleyball, ed 3, Dubuque, Iowa, 1983, WC Brown Group. Intended as a manual for beginning or intermediate levels; analyzes skills in terms of performance improvement and recommends specific remedial actions.

Stokes R and Haley M: Volleyball everyone, Winston-Salem, NC, 1984, Hunter Textbooks, Inc. Includes hundreds of illustrations; reference materials including films, checklists, drills, and quizzes; and information on mental as well as physical readiness.

Viera BL and Ferguson BJ: Teaching volleyball, Champaign, Ill, 1989, Human Kinetics Publishers, Inc.

Viera BL and Ferguson BJ: Volleyball: steps to success, Champaign, Ill, 1989, Human Kinetics Publishers, Inc.

VIDEOTAPES

Two series: *Coaching women's volleyball* (7 programs) and *Gold medal volleyball* (10 programs). "How To" Sports Videos, Box 5852, Denver, CO 80217.

Volleyball and *Volleyball drills*. Sports Video, 745 State Circle, Box 1941, Ann Arbor, MI 48016.

Serving, blocking and individual defenses and *Passing, setting, and spiking*. Karol Video, 22 Riverside Dr., Wayne, NJ 17470.

38

Water Polo

Completion of this chapter should enable the reader to:

- Describe the history of and equipment and facilities for water polo
- Know the rules and officiating practices
- Execute the swimming skills required of a water polo player
- Demonstrate defensive and offensive skills and tactics
- Teach a group of students how to play water polo using proper drills and teaching techniques

HISTORY

Bored with conventional swimming races and stunts, a group of British aquatic athletes during the 1860s created a new type of game. Played originally in lakes, with 11 players per side and rafts as goals, water polo has undergone numerous refinements until today it ranks as perhaps the most demanding of all aquatic sports.

Introduced to the Olympic Games in 1900, water polo has always appealed to swimmers throughout the world, especially in Europe. Until recent years, however, it remained a rather obscure sport. Britain and Belgium dominated early Olympic competition (Britain won four gold medals in the five Olympics between 1900 and 1920, whereas Belgium won four silver and a bronze in the six Olympics between 1900 and 1924). Incredibly, beginning in 1928 Hungary won a medal in every Olympics through 1980, amassing six golds (1932, 1936, 1952, 1956, 1964 and 1976), three silvers (1928, 1948, and 1972) and three bronzes (1960, 1968, and 1980).

With the increase in swimming pools and the availability of well-trained professional swimming coaches, resulting in the tremendous increase in the number of competent swimmers around the world, water polo is one of the fastest growing sports. In fact, of the 30 sports on the Olympic agenda, the United States Olympic Development Committee rated water polo as the third fastest growing sport in the United States.

In the past and for various reasons, the United States did not conform to the rules used by most other nations, that is, the FINA (International) rules. Now, however, the United States type of water polo follows almost exactly the FINA rules so that our teams can gain experience to enable them to do well in international competition.

Earlier in this century the United States promoted what was called "softball" water polo, in which a soft, semi-inflated ball was used; the ball could be taken underwater, and much of the action occurred beneath the surface. This game attracted few spectators because no one could see what was happening underwater. Furthermore, the referee, who was situated at poolside, could not see what was taking place, and, therefore, an increasing number of underwater injuries occurred. Most swimmers and swimming coaches were disinterested because there was little relationship between swimming on the surface, as the swimmers did, and wrestling underwater, as the poloists did.

In the late 1940s and throughout the 1950s a small group of California swimming coaches brought United States water polo back to the surface of the water and created a style of play that appealed to California high school and college swimmers and that, during the 1960s, spread rapidly across the country.

Until 1984 the United States had managed only three bronze Olympic medals (1924, 1932, and 1972) in water polo. The United States did win the gold, silver, and bronze medals in 1904 but the only foreign team (Germany) withdrew because of the "strange" rules adopted in St. Louis. In both 1984 and 1988, however, the United States teams finished with the silver medal, losing in both cases to Yugoslavia in close games. The 1984 final score was 5-5 but the gold medal went to Yugoslavia because they had scored more total goals in the tournament. In 1988 the Yugoslavia team defeated the U.S. team 9-7 in the first overtime game in Olympic history.

EQUIPMENT

Each team must have two sets of caps:

The goalkeeper on the visiting team must wear a cap with alternating colored and white quarters with the number 1 or 1A clearly marked on it; the teammates must wear white caps numbered 2 through 21.

The goalkeeper on the home team must wear a quartered colored cap with the number 22 or 22A clearly marked on it; the teammates must wear colored caps numbered 23 through 42.

The ball is made of rubber with a rough-textured waterproofing substance that makes it easier to handle, even with one hand. It is yellow and approximately the size of a volleyball.

NCAA RULES

Play is based on two popular sports: swimming and lacrosse.

Playing is done on the surface of the water by teams of seven players each. NCAA water polo is now considered legal in both 100-foot (30 m) and 75-foot (25 m) pools, with the 100-foot (30 m) field preferred and championships played in a 100-foot (30 m) by 75-foot (25 m) pool. The deeper the water the better. If the entire playing area is deep—6½ feet (2 m) or more—it is ideal, but most indoor pools have a shallow end. (See Fig. 38-1.) The goalposts must be 10 feet (3 m) apart, and the crossbar must be 3 feet (0.914 m) above the water surface when the water depth is 5 feet (1.52 m) or more; when the water depth is less than 5 feet (1.52 m) the crossbar must be 8 feet (2.44 m) from the floor of the playing area. Canvas backing and sides must enclose the goal area. The depth of the goal space must be a minimum of 18 inches (46 cm). The boundaries of the penalty throw zone extend along the 4-yard (4 m) line a distance of 22 feet (6.6 m). (See Fig. 38-1.)

At the start of the game each team consists of six field

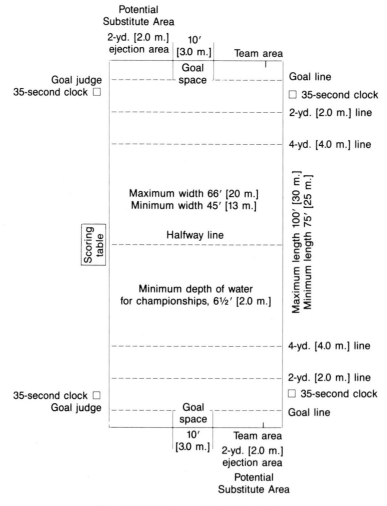

Fig. 38-1. Water polo field of play.

players and a goalkeeper, each wearing a swimsuit and a cap with ear protectors. The captain of each team must be a player in the water. Substitutions may be made only during time outs or dead time.

The goalkeeper is the only player on the team who can stand or jump from the bottom (if the water is shallow enough to permit this), or catch and pass the ball with both hands at the same time, or hit the ball with a clenched fist provided he or she is inside the 4-yard line.

The guards and forwards on each team may swim freely up and down the pool as they see fit, interchanging positions as often as they wish. They may not stand on or jump from the bottom, nor may they touch the ball with more than one hand at a time when catching, passing, or shooting it, nor may they enter inside the opposing team's 2-yard (2.0 m) line unless preceded by the ball.

Over the years water polo rules have changed frequently because of influences of the NCAA, AAU, and FINA. The rules are beginning to stabilize, as demonstrated by the fact that the AAU and NCAA rules are now identical except for a few minor differences for the goalkeeper. A current rule book from both organizations should be consulted to ensure that players are familiar with the difference.

PLAYING TIME

In intercollegiate competition the game consists of four 7-minute quarters, the teams changing ends after every period of play. In high school competition the game consists of four 5- or 6-minute quarters, depending on the ages of the participants, and the teams change ends after every period. There is a 2-minute interval between each quarter and a 5-minute interval between halves.

STARTING THE GAME

At the start or restart of a game, one player (usually the goalkeeper) must be in position between the goalposts and the field players must take up their positions at least 1 yard apart on their respective goal lines. They may grasp the wall of the pool, ready to push off. (See Fig. 38-2.)

The game is started with a blast of the whistle by the referee, who then drops or throws the ball at the halfway line into the lane closest to the referee. If the ball is not dropped or thrown properly, it may be done again. If the player on one team jumps the whistle, the ball is given to the opposing team on the 2-yard line where the infraction occurred.

OFFICIALS

The head referee walks along one side of the pool, watching for infractions, and is aided by the assistant referee, who patrols the opposite side of the pool. The referees are both equipped with shrill whistles and official flags. These flags must be 12 inches (0.3 m) square and correspond in color to the color of the caps worn by the

Fig. 38-2. Line up and start of a game just after referee's whistle.

Fig. 38-3. Water polo signals.

opposing teams. The white flag will be fastened to one end of a 36-inch (0.9 m) stick, and the colored flag to the other end.

Whenever one of the referees sees an infraction committed by a player, the referee blows the whistle and signals the flag. For example, if a player wearing a white cap commits a foul, the referee will blow the whistle, point with one hand to the spot of the foul, and extend the colored flag overhead. This means the nearest player on the team wearing the colored caps, against which the foul was committed, may take possession of the ball. (See Fig. 38-3.)

Anticipation is the name of the game, and unless there is obvious doubt as to whose ball it is, which requires the players to look up to see which color flag is being extended, the players must react to change of possession almost instinctively.

In addition to the two referees, other necessary officials include a timer and a scorer, both of whom should be seated at the scorer's table at poolside. For important competition, there should be goal judges situated at each end of the pool, whose primary duty is to help the referees determine whether the shots taken by the players enter the goal for a score or do not enter the goal.

As in all sports, it is important that the officials be skilled and competent. This is especially true in water polo, in which the players are somewhat submerged and out of sight, thus inviting underwater holding and kicking unless the referees are adept at interpreting what is happening beneath the surface.

TECHNICAL FOULS

The following are common technical fouls:

1. Starting before the referee blows the whistle to begin the quarter
2. Holding onto or pushing off from the sides of the pool during play
3. Taking or holding the ball underwater when "tackled" by an opposing player (tackled meaning to have made body contact)
4. Swimming inside the opposing team's 2-yard (2 m) line unless preceded by the ball
5. Touching the ball with both hands at the same time (goalkeeper excepted)
6. Standing on, walking on, or jumping from the bottom when taking an active part in the game (goalkeeper excepted)

When a technical foul occurs, the referee blows the whistle and by proper extension of the flags awards possession of the ball to the team against which the infraction was committed. The player on the team awarded possession who was nearest the point of infraction then has 3 seconds to put the ball back into play; this may be done by passing to a teammate or by dropping the ball into the water and swimming with it. The ball must visibly leave the hand.

PERSONAL FAULTS

The following are personal faults:

1. Pulling back a player who does not have the ball
2. Any penalty shot foul
3. Interfering with a free throw
4. Entering the water incorrectly
5. A dead-time technical foul

Each personal fault is accompanied by a 35-second ejection for the offending player (except for making a foul resulting in a penalty shot). The ejected player must swim to the ejection area and exit the water. The player should be ready to reenter the water correctly when the 35-second ejection flag of the player's color is raised and waved from the scorer's table. Play can continue immediately after the fault is called, but if the offending player interferes or is too slow in leaving the pool, another personal fault may be charged at the referee's discretion. The player who is ejected may be substituted for at the coach's discretion or must be substituted for if it is the third fault. Accumulating three personal faults results in "fouling out" of the game.

PENALTY SHOT

A penalty shot can be awarded by either of the referees when (1) an offensive player inside the opponents' 4-yard (4 m) line but not touching the ball is held, ducked, pulled back, kicked, or struck, and (2) a player other than the goalie uses two hands to block a shot. When one of these infractions occurs, the head or assistant referee should immediately blow the whistle and, by holding the two-flagged stick with both hands in a vertical position above the head, signal that a penalty shot has been awarded.

A penalty shot is taken from the 4-yard (4 m) line in front of the goal. (See Fig. 38-1.) All players except the defending goalkeeper must leave the 4-yard (4 m) line until the shot is taken, and no player can be within 2 yards of the shooter.

After ascertaining that the shooting player is on the 4-yard (4 m) line and ready to shoot and that the goalkeeper is on the goal line, the referee gives a sharp, quick blast of the whistle. At the whistle, the shooter must shoot without delay and without faking at the goal. The goalkeeper may try to block the shot; if the shot is blocked or is otherwise missed, the ball is immediately in play and action continues.

WHEN A GOAL IS SCORED

When a goal is scored, either from a shot taken by a player out in the field or by virtue of a penalty shot, all players line up at the center of the pool on their respective sides. The player whose team has just been scored on and who is closest to the center throws the ball back to either the goalkeeper or another player at the referee's signal. Both teams should be "ready to go" almost immediately after a goal has been scored; there should be no let up in the action.

SWIMMING SKILLS

The better one can swim, the better chance one has at becoming a competent water poloist. It is practically impossible for a swimmer of limited ability to play a respectable game of water polo because the rules place a premium on speed, clean play, and continual action.

The ordinary *freestyle* or *crawl stroke* is used most commonly in water polo. However, because each player must remain alert to the positioning of other players and the location of the ball, it is necessary to swim with the head raised. This results in a type of crawl stroke in which the arms are a bit higher and the legs a little lower than normal, but by and large, there is not too much dissimilarity to the regular racing crawl stroke used by competitive swimmers; basically the same muscles propel the body through the water.

The second most important stroke for the water poloist is the *breaststroke*, in which a whip or frog kick is used. This type of kick, especially when refined into the "eggbeater" kick, does the best job of enabling the player to raise the body high out of the water. The higher a player rides in the water, the more advantageous it is.

To perform the *eggbeater kick* the poloist simply uses the familiar breaststroke whip or frog kick but moves the legs alternately rather than simultaneously; in short, when one leg is bent in the frog position, the other is extended, and vice versa. This kick, when mastered, enables the player to raise the body several inches and sometimes as much as a foot up out of the water.

The *sidestroke kick* is also important because a single sidestroke or scissors kick, done from a prone, stationary position, will quickly provide momentum with which the player may get started, after which the crawl stroke is usually used.

The *backstroke* is useful because there will be times in every game when the player is sprinting downpool ahead of the ball. By turning over on the back, the player can look and see where the ball is while continuing to swim down the pool on the back.

The *butterfly stroke* is not used much in actual water polo competition, but many coaches use it during practices to help the players build up their shoulder and arm muscles.

Normally the first 30 or 40 minutes of every water polo practice is devoted to the swimming skills just discussed because a poloist must be able to perform several different strokes with finesse and speed. Inasmuch as a game lasts 20 or 24 minutes in high school competition and 28 minutes in college competition, not including the time used for changing ends after each quarter or for timeouts, during all of which the player remains in the water either swimming or treading, a high degree of stamina is necessary. A poloist participating in a water polo game from start to finish will usually be in the water twice as long as a swimmer competing in a mile-long race! Furthermore, the necessity for making continued stops, pivots, and directional changes in midpool adds to the requirement for stamina.

Many champion swimmers have used water polo for conditioning purposes, and an increasing number of swimmers are finding that they enjoy the tactics provided by water polo more than mere swimming up and down the pool.

DEFENSIVE SKILLS AND TACTICS

Recent rule changes have resulted in changes in defensive tactics. For example, the full-pool press is seldom employed now because of the new method of starting the game after each goal is scored (all players moving to the center of the pool). Because the goalkeeper can now throw the ball anywhere in the pool, the offensive team has increased forward mobility. The standard defense is the half-pool one-on-one, but with the new ejection rule (personal faults) the zone defense must be employed at times as well.

Half-pool one-on-one. The defensive team members fall back into their half of the pool area whenever the opponents capture possession of the ball. As soon as the opponents swim past midpool, the defenders pick them up and guard them one-on-one. The half-pool one-on-one is effective at shutting off the opposing team's fast break, but it allows the opponents to take their time setting up their attack, and it also removes all defensive players from the opposing team's goal area and, therefore, eliminates a quick counterattack in case the ball is intercepted or stolen.

Zone defense. The defensive team members fall back into a cluster around their goal and defend a particular segment of the goal area rather than a player on the opposing team. Thus the defensive team shuts off almost all close-in shots that the attacking team might want to take, but challenges the attackers to shoot freely from far out. This necessitates good goaltending by the defensive goalkeeper.

When an ejection occurs, the zone defense becomes a necessity because of the six-on-five situation. The typical defense for an ejected player situation is a 3-2. Three players shift back and forth on the 2- or 3-yard (2 or 3 m) line while the ball is passed back and forth. The two outside players guard the two outside offensive players and sluff (leave their assignments and move toward the ball) when the ball goes inside.

Slow-swimming teams have used the zone defense successfully to stop faster-swimming opponents, but it places an emphasis on defense rather than offense and does not lend itself well to much scoring by the team relying on it.

No matter the tactics used by a team defensively, each player must possess individual skills. Guarding an opponent is not easy. Each player when guarding must determine whether the opponent likes to swim around a lot or remain in one position, handles the ball with the right or left hand, is intimidated by close breathing-down-the-neck guarding, or uses illegal underwater tricks to gain an advantage.

A good player stays close to the opponent, prepared to execute a "tackle" whenever possible. It is permissible to tackle an opponent by impeding the arm or leg movement, by swimming over, or by ducking the opponent, *provided the opponent is touching the ball*. This makes water polo a rough, tough sport at times.

Many beginning water poloists are competent swimmers and have enough ball-handling ability to do a good job offensively at the start, but good guarding is a separate skill that must be practiced endlessly. The poloist who can keep a particular opponent from scoring while causing some bad passes to be thrown and some good passes to be fumbled is an asset to any team.

GOALTENDING

As in soccer, field hockey, and other sports, the goalkeeper in water polo has special privileges and restrictions. The goalkeeper's position in the field of play and duties are unique.

In water polo the goalkeeper should play about 2 or 3 feet (0.6 or 0.9 m) in front of the goal being defended. A good goalkeeper can block at least half the good shots taken at the goal. In short, a skilled goalkeeper's value cannot be underestimated; the goalkeeper is the backbone of the team, always being in the position to compensate for errors being made by teammates and often positioning teammates when on offense.

It is true that a goalkeeper needs swimming speed less than the other players, but there will come times when a loose ball falls in front of the goal, and the goalkeeper's speed in swimming to it might save a score by the opposition. Furthermore, the goalkeeper must tread water throughout the entire game. Inasmuch as a game can last as long as 45 minutes, including between-quarter breaks and time-outs, stamina is necessary.

From the position in front of the goal, the goalkeeper can see all that is taking place in the pool and should not hesitate to shout directions to teammates.

The goalkeeper should be able to move quickly from side to side across the goal when opposing players swim in from various angles to shoot, and should also be able to stand up to strong shots without flinching. More than any other player, the goalkeeper's ability to execute the eggbeater kick and raise the body high out of the water is important; a goalkeeper who is high in the water, with outstretched arms and a confident expression, can be an imposing sight to a player swimming in and preparing to shoot.

The goalkeeper should be an adept ball handler. The goalkeeper is the only member of the team allowed to catch and pass the ball with both hands at the same time, and poor ball handling is inexcusable.

To summarize, the goalkeeper should have some swimming speed and stamina, a good eggbeater kick, the ability to "talk it up" to teammates, fast reactions, better than average ball-handling skill, courage, and enough strength to withstand a degree of physical contact, because the goalkeeper, like any other player, can be tackled when touching the ball.

Goalkeeper is a demanding position to play, and only the best athletes can succeed at it.

OFFENSIVE SKILLS AND TACTICS

The team in possession of the ball has one objective: to advance the ball down the pool by dribbling and passing and then to score by shooting the ball into the opposing team's goal.

Dribbling is done by controlling the ball between the arms while swimming the crawl stroke with the head raised. The arms are carried a bit higher than normal in the recovery to protect the ball from opponents. Profi-cient poloists can dribble with amazing speed, but a better way to advance the ball is by passing. This seemingly simple skill is actually difficult to perform. The passer can pick up the ball with only one hand, and when doing so can immediately be tackled by an opponent. Therefore the passer must first assume a position to make the pass without being grabbed, ducked, or otherwise impeded; this requires adroit body maneuvering.

Because the players are usually low in the water, the passer frequently has a tough time seeing a teammate to whom to pass with all the splashing that is taking place, so sharp eyesight can be helpful. (See Fig 38-4.)

Finally, the passer must lift the body up out of the water with a powerful kick so that the passing arm clears the surface of the water and the ball, when thrown, clears the outstretched arms of the opposing team members.

It is essential that the pass arrive on target; if it is even a foot or two off target, the receiver may have trouble catching it, because just one hand can be used, and the catch must be made in such a manner as to avoid being tackled.

If the pass receiver is stationary in the water and has secured an advantageous position over an opponent, the pass thrown to the receiver should be a dry pass, one that travels from the passer to the receiver entirely in the air without touching the water (See Fig. 38-5).

If the pass receiver is swimming down the pool or is closely guarded by an opponent, the pass thrown to the receiver should be a wet pass, one that lands in the water in front of the receiver if the receiver is swimming or at the side away from the opponent if the receiver is closely guarded.

Whether wet or dry, the pass must be thrown with accuracy and must then be caught and handled adeptly. The mark of a good water polo team is its ability to advance the ball down the pool with accurate passes and without losing control or possession.

As with defensive tactics, offensive play in water polo has recently changed dramatically because of the new rules. Two commonly used attacks involve the fast break and a motion type of offense.

Fast break. If all players on a team are in top physical condition, the team is likely to use a "fast break" offense. When the team gains possession of the ball, all the players break as swiftly as possible toward the opposing team's goal. This takes some practice and coordinated effort so the players do not swim into each other. But when these techniques are executed properly, one or two players are almost assured of breaking into the open and will have a good shot at the goal if given an accurate pass.

A fast-breaking team can often run up many goals against an inferior opponent, but this type of attack requires a whole team of swift, well-conditioned athletes,

Fig. 38-4. Water polo game in progress.

Fig. 38-5. Passing into the hole.

Fig. 38-6. Fast break (white caps) after an intercepted pass.

much practice, and accurate passing. Furthermore, if the attack does not result in a score, the team members will have to use their speed to get back on defense hurriedly (See Fig. 38-6).

Motion offense. In the motion type of offense, one or two players drive to the 2- or 3-yard line. They set the "hole." When the ball comes to them, a foul usually occurs. Then the other players make a break to get free for a shot. If a good shot does not result, the ball is returned to the hole and worked again for a foul, pass, and shot. The hole guard's fouls often result in an ejection and a six-on-five situation. The offense now works greatly off the fouls.

Whether a team uses a fast-breaking offense, or depends on a single shooter stationed near the opposing team's goal to do most of the scoring, or uses two or three players breaking in and around the player on the 2- or 3-yard line, no scores can be recorded without some strong, accurate shooting.

SHOOTING SKILLS

The goal at which the players are shooting is large: 10 feet (3.05 m) across, with the crossbar 3 feet (0.915 m) above the water surface when the water is 5 feet (1.52 m) or more in depth and 8 feet from the floor of the playing area when the water is less than 5 feet (1.52 m)

in depth. Yet when a goalkeeper is positioned in front of the goal, with the body held high and the arms outstretched, the goal looks surprisingly small to the attacking player. Furthermore, whenever the attacker touches the ball or lifts it up in preparation for taking the shot (see Fig. 38-7), opponents can tackle the attacker.

Thus it takes much practice to become a good shooter, one who can handle the ball easily with one hand, outmanuever opponents to avoid being tackled, and shoot past a waiting goalkeeper. A player who under these conditions can score on 50% or more of shots over a season of competition is doing well.

Water polo players should take at least 50 practice shots daily and should learn to master as many different shots as possible. Every player should be able to score through hard, accurate shooting when the opportunity presents itself.

Frequently used shots

Power shot. When unguarded and unhurried, the shooter can simply assume a vertical position in the water, rear back, and shoot as hard as possible toward the goal.

Bounce shot. From the same unguarded and unhurried vertical position, the shooter can throw the ball so that

Fig. 38-7. Attacker preparing to shoot at goal.

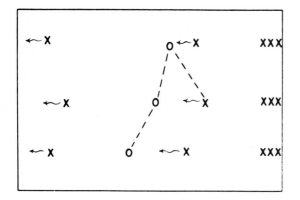

Fig. 38-8. Three-player passing drill.

it hits the water in front of the goal and bounces up into the goal.

Lob shot. Taken from almost any position facing the goal, the lob shot is designed to be thrown high into the air so that it sails gently over the goalkeeper's outstretched arms into the corner of the goal in the rear.

Pop shot. When swimming in toward the goal and closely pursued, a player often cannot stop and shoot without being caught from behind and tackled; therefore from the swimming position the player can bat the ball a few inches into the air with the underwater arm and then slap the ball goalward with the other arm as it swings forward on the recovery.

PASSING DRILLS
Circle drill
The circle drill is excellent for practicing the dry pass. Catching the ball softly with the fingers spread wide

should be emphasized. All of the players should practice with both the left and right hands. If the group is large enough for two or more circles, competition can be easily established by having each circle count the number of good passes and receptions without the ball touching the water.

A keep-away drill could also be used by having three or four defenders in the center of the circle try to intercept the ball. Such a drill emphasizes sharp, quick passes to the open player on the part of the offense and quick reaction and hustle on the part of the defense.

Three-player passing drill
The three-player passing drill is good for practicing the wet pass. (See Fig. 38-8). Leading the receiver should be emphasized, but not so much that the defense has a chance at the ball. Have all players vary positions and use both hands.

TEACHING CONSIDERATIONS
1. Water polo requires highly conditioned players with skilled swimming techniques. If students do not have the stamina to participate with official rules, consider modifications that permit resting on the side of the pool, two-hand ball handling, no-tackling rules, or free substitution for a tired swimmer. Excessive fatigue in an unconditioned or unskilled swimmer can be dangerous.
2. Include conditioning and practice of the basic swimming strokes used in water polo as a large part of all classes (crawl, breaststroke, sidestroke kick, and backstroke).
3. Teach passing as a basic individual skill in shallow and then deep water, first to stationary receivers and

then to moving receivers. Add a passive defender (no tackling) and a moving receiver as soon as basics are established. As the technique becomes consistent, give tackling privileges to the defender.

4. Teach tackling as a separate skill, first with a passive offensive player and then with an active offensive player.

5. Combine practice of dribble and pass, dribble and shoot, and receiving a pass and shooting, first without defense, next with passive defense and then with active defense. Move from practice situations utilizing one individual moving the ball to a partner and then three players moving the ball. When adding defensive players, give the offense the advantage initially.

6. Teach shooting skills first without a goalkeeper, then with a goalkeeper, and then with a defender.

7. Teach man-to-man defense intially as the basic defense. Later teach zone defense around the goal, and zone defense as a basic defense.

8. Begin game play in two-on-one, three-on-two, and three-on-three situations using a smaller play area.

9. All practice situations should be organized to permit maximum ball-handling opportunities. Waiting for a turn should be avoided.

10. Skills involving positioning in game play should be gradually integrated into practices as defense is added and the number of players increases. Because swimmers can tire easily and cannot quickly recover from poor positioning, strategies on player movement in the play area are critical and should be taught specifically.

GLOSSARY

backing Canvas backing to enclose goal space.

caps Each team must have two sets of caps, one white and the other a contrasting color. The visiting team wears white. All caps must have plastic ear guards.

corner throw A throw taken by the offensive team when the defense causes the ball to go over its goal line.

ejection Penalty accompanying personal fault. Offending player must swim to ejection area, exit the water, and remain out for 35 seconds (or less if a goal is scored).

faceoff In cases of a double foul or if the ball is thrown in at the start to the advantage of one team, a faceoff is used to put the ball into play.

flag Home team must supply two referees with flags. These flags must have a white flag at one end of a 36-inch (91.4 cm) staff and a dark blue flag at the other end. These flags are used for signals.

free throw A throw used to put the ball in play after a foul, goal, ball out of bounds, or any other situation in which one team is directly given the ball. The free throw is later taken at the point of infraction. The player has 3 seconds to get rid of the ball. It may not be thrown directly at the goal.

game 28 minutes of actual play, in four periods of 7 minutes each. There should be 2-minute intervals between quarters and a 5-minute period at the half.

goal throw A free throw taken by the goalkeeper after the offensive team causes the ball to go over the goal line outside the goal.

illegal player A player who has committed a third personal foul or has been ejected for the entire game.

penalty throw A throw taken by any member of the offended team from the penalty line. A one-hand, over-the-shoulder shot is taken.

signals The flag positions used by the referee to denote the game situations.

technical fouls Infractions committed that are not of a personal nature, such as stalling, striking the ball with the fist, or being within 2 yards (2 m) of the opponents' goal line.

35-second possession It is a technical foul for a team to retain a ball for more than 35 seconds without shooting the ball at the opponents' goal.

time-outs There may be three time-outs of not more than 2 minutes each per team in the first four quarters. In overtime each team may have one time-out.

SUGGESTED READINGS

Cutino P and Bledsoe D: Polo, the manual for coach and player, Los Angeles, Calif, 1979, Swimming World Publications.

NCAA official water polo rules, 1989 (revised annually).

PERIODICAL

Water polo scoreboard (monthly), La Puente Calif

VIDEOTAPE

Water polo. Karol Video, 22 Riverside Dr., Wayne, NJ 07470.

39

Weight Training, Circuit Weight Training, and Weight Lifting

Completion of this chapter should enable the reader to:

- Describe the history of weight lifting and distinguish the differences among the activities in this chapter
- Set up a personal weight training and circuit weight training program
- Recognize the importance of safety in these activities
- Identify appropriate exercises for various parts of the body
- Explain the competitive and power lifting events
- Teach basic weight lifting techniques to a group of beginning students

HISTORY

In its earliest form, weight lifting was a part of everyday life; however, the exact period in history when weight training became a practice or part of a training regimen is not known. There is, however, evidence that the first physical training programs were geared toward the development of only the strength component of fitness.

Ancient myth and folklore include accounts of strong men, such as Samson, Hercules, and the Greek warrior Milo. A lengendary figure, Milo was said to have carried a calf up to a hayloft each night and then retrieved it each morning. As the calf gained weight Milo gained strength, until he was carrying a full-grown cow up and down a ladder daily.

In the days of the Greeks, Egyptians, and Romans, weight training played an important role in preparing soldiers for battle. During the Middle Ages, Romans trained their soldiers by marching them over long distances with heavier than normal loads. Throughout the seventeenth to nineteenth centuries, most of the empires and armies of Europe followed the Greek and Roman examples and trained with overloaded packs.

Weight lifting was introduced to the United States between 1859 and 1872, when Dr. G.B. Winship toured the United States and Canada giving lectures and exhibitions.

Weight lifting soon found its way into the carnivals, circuses, and vaudeville stages, where men and women performed unbelievable feats of strength that in fact were gimmicks and tricks, and which probably are responsible for most of the myth and mystery that has surrounded weight training until recent times. Weight lifting survived this era and went on to find its way into YMCAs and athletic and health clubs. With these organizations promoting the activity, evidence of the value and worth of weight training began to grow.

Weight lifting has been included in the Olympic games since 1896. At first there were two events—a one-handed lift and a two-handed lift—and the lifter's body weight was not considered. In 1920 the press, snatch, and clean and jerk were introduced, and this system remained until 1972, when the press was eliminated. In the early Olympics weight lifting was dominated by the European nations. In the United States an organized program for competition was not begun until the AAU held its first American National Championships in 1929. In 1932 the United States entered its first team in Olympic competition, and won the team championship for the first time in 1948 by winning four of the six weight categories. In the 1952 and 1956 Olympics, all the gold medals were won by United States or Soviet weightlifters. However, since the 1960 Olympics the Soviet and

Eastern European countries (primarily Bulgaria, Hungary and Poland) have dominated the competitions.

In recent years the sport of powerlifting has been the most popular form of competitive lifting in the United States. Since the AAU held its first American National Championships, the United States National team has won the Pan-Am and World Team titles with surprising regularity. In less than 10 years the sport has grown to the extent that more than 40 nations now compete in the International Powerlifting Federation World Championships. Although a comparatively new form of competition, the sport of powerlifting is now being considered as an additional event in Olympic competition.

Weight training is constantly increasing in popularity in colleges, health clubs, and YMCAs across the country. It is not uncommon to find a set of barbells in the recreation room of many American homes. In an age that has provided us with countless labor-saving devices, weight training has provided the much needed vigorous exercise that our push-button life-style has taken away.

Weight training
GENERAL CONSIDERATIONS

Frequency. Lifting should be done three times per week, with at least 1 day of rest between sessions. More advanced programs often follow different weekly schedules concentrating on specific areas on set days during the week. However, most basic programs start with working every body part equally, 3 days per week.

Logical order. Exercises should progress from multi-jointed muscle group exercises (bench press, squat) to single-jointed intrinsic muscle group exercises (arm curls, calf raises).

Beginning poundage. By trial and error one selects starting amounts of weight that can be lifted with proper form for 10 to 12 repetitions of an exercise.

Rest and recovery. During exercises one should allow 1½ to 2 minutes between each set to recover fully before proceeding to the next set. One exercise (all sets) should be completed before moving to the next exercise.

Sets and repetitions. A basic program usually consists of three sets of 10 to 12 repetitions, with proper recovery between sets.

Last set. The last set of each exercise should be difficult to complete using proper form. The weight should be such that a "momentary failure" is reached during the last set of each exercise.

Partners. It is important to lift with a partner and always consider safety first.

GENERAL TECHNIQUES FOR ALL LIFTS

Stretching. Basic overall stretching should precede any lifting, with particular attention to the muscle groups to be exercised. For example, before the bench press one should concentrate on stretching the chest, shoulders, and triceps. Many experts suggest that stretching activities should be used at the end of a workout as well.

Warm-up. Warm-up activities should be specific to the exercise; for example, a light bench press should be done in preparation for the bench press exercise. Usually a warm-up consists of 10 repetitions with a light, comfortable weight.

Breathing. One should inhale during the negative or lowering phase of all lifts, and exhale during the working or positive phase. One should never hold the breath during any part of a lift.

Full range. One should always complete the full range of motion during any lift, and never do any partial or half movements while learning the basic exercises.

Spotting. For any exercise culminating with the lifter in a fatigued state and still supporting the weights, a spotter should be used. See Fig. 39-1 for an example of correcting spotting technique.

FUNDAMENTAL SKILLS AND TECHNIQUES
Exercises for the upper body
Free-weight bench press (for chest, shoulders, and upper arms)

Starting position. Lie on the bench with feet flat on the floor and arch the back slightly. The spotter lifts the weight from the rack and gives it to the weight lifter. The weight lifter should take the weight with the arms extended and the hands slightly wider apart than the shoulders. (See Fig. 39-1.)

Movement. Lower the bar to the middle of the chest. (See Fig. 39-2.) Then recover to the straight-arm starting position.

Technique and safety tip. Once the bar is pressed up approximately 12 to 14 inches from the chest, strive to angle the bar slightly back toward the head and shoulders. This places the bar at an advantageous angle for the shoulders and triceps to finish the lift.

Universal gym bench press

The technique for this exercise is the same as for the free-weight bench press but no spotter is required. The body should be positioned so that handles cross the middle of the chest.

Universal gym lat pull (for upper back, biceps, and posture muscles)

Starting position. Grasp the bar with a wide overhand grip. Kneel on one knee, with the head up and the back straight. (See Fig. 39-3.)

Movement. Pull the bar down behind the head until the bar reaches the base of the neck. (See Fig. 39-4) Return the bar to the starting position.

Fig. 39-1. Free weight bench press—starting position.

Fig. 39-2. Free weight bench press.

Fig. 39-3. Universal gym lat pull—starting position.

Fig. 39-4. Universal gym lat pull.

Technique and safety tip. Return the bar slowly to avoid any loss of control or stabilization. No spotter is necessary.

Free-weight bent rowing (for posture muscles, biceps, and upper back)

Starting position. Stand with the feet shoulder width apart and the toes pointed out slightly. Bend over until the torso is parallel to the floor, and bend the knees slightly. Grasp the barbell with an overhand grip, with the hands at about shoulder width.

Movement. Pull the barbell up until it reaches the lower rib cage. (See Fig. 39-5.) Then return it to the starting position.

Technique and safety tip. Concentrate on raising the elbows as high as possible. No spotter is necessary. Always keep the knees bent to avoid lower back injury.

Fig. 39-5. Free weight bent rowing.

Free-weight overhead press (for shoulders and upper arms)

Starting position. Stand with the feet shoulder width apart and the toes pointed out slightly. Keeping the head erect, bend down and grasp the barbell with an overhand grip, with the hands also shoulder width apart. Return to the standing position and lift the barbell shoulder high. (See Fig. 39-6.)

Movement. Push the barbell straight up until the arms are fully extended. (See Fig. 39-7.) Return to the shoulder-high position. The knees should remain straight.

Technique and safety tips. Never bend or arch the back. Always look straight ahead or down during the lift to prevent lower back arching.

Fig. 39-6. Free weight overhead press—starting position.

Fig. 39-7. Free weight overhead press.

Free-weight arm curls (for biceps)

Starting position. Stand with the feet shoulder width apart and the toes pointed out slightly. Bend at the knees, grasp the bar with an underhand grip, then return to the standing position. (See Fig. 39-8.)

Movement. With the elbows tucked tightly against the rib cage, pull the bar up to the chest, and return to the starting position. (See Fig. 39-9.)

Technique and safety tip. To avoid arching the back, keep the head down and the eyes on the bar, or stand with the back against the wall.

Fig. 39-8. Free weight arm curls—starting position.

Fig. 39-9. Free weight arm curls.

Parallel bar dips *(for lower chest, shoulders, and upper arms)*

Starting position. Use an overhand grip on the parallel bar, and jump up to an arms-extended position. (See Fig. 39-10.) Cross the legs and arch the back slightly.

Movement. Bend or "dip" until the chest touches the crossbar or the elbow is bent 90 degrees. (See Fig. 39-11.) Push back up to the starting position.

Technique and safety tips. Keeping the back arched and the eyes forward helps prevent swinging and rocking during the movement.

•   •   •

Three additional exercises for the upper body—side lateral raises, bent lateral raises, and sit-ups—are described under Circuit Weight Training.

Fig. 39-10. Parallel bar dips—starting position.

Fig. 39-11. Parallel bar dips.

Exercises for the lower body

Free-weight parallel squats (for thighs, hips, lower back, and buttocks)

Starting position. Stand with feet shoulder width apart and the toes pointed out slightly. Grasp the bar with a comfortable, wide overhand grip. (The distance between the hands will vary with the individual.) Position the bar across the shoulders just below the base of the neck. (See Fig. 39-12.)

Movement. With the head up and the back slightly arched, squat until the tops of the thighs are parallel to the floor. (See Fig. 39-13.) Then extend the legs and return to the starting position.

Technique and safety tips. To avoid bending forward at the waist, keep the head up and the eyes focused ahead. The knees should be aligned directly over the toes while in the squat position. The rate of descent should be slow and controlled. Never try to bounce out of the squat position. Always use at least one spotter when doing this exercise. If it is difficult to keep the feet flat on the floor, use a heeled running shoe or stand with a 2- by 4-inch board under the heels. Straddling a bench during the exercise is one way to avoid squatting too far down.

Fig. 39-12. Parallel squat—starting position.

Fig. 39-13. Parallel squat.

Universal gym leg press *(for thighs and buttocks)*

Starting position. Sit up straight at the station and place the feet on the lower pedals of the carriage. Grasp the handles on the sides of the chair. (See Fig. 39-14.)

Movement. Push until the legs are fully extended, and then return to the starting position. (See Fig. 39-15.)

Technique and safety tips. Position the seat so that the knees are flexed at least 90 degrees at the start of the exercise. Control the weight in the extended position. However, try to "pop" the weight up at the top of the stroke. Return slowly to the starting position.

Fig. 39-14. Leg press—starting position.

Fig. 39-15. Leg press—movement.

Universal gym knee flexion *(for hamstrings)*

Starting position. Lie face down on the knee flexion table with the back of the ankles touching the carriage pads. The knees should be extended over the edge of the table.

Movement. Pull the carriage as far up toward the buttocks as possible. (See Fig. 39-16.) Then return to the starting position.

Technique and safety tips. The hips and buttocks have a normal tendency to rise during the movement, but this can be corrected by using a flexed table.

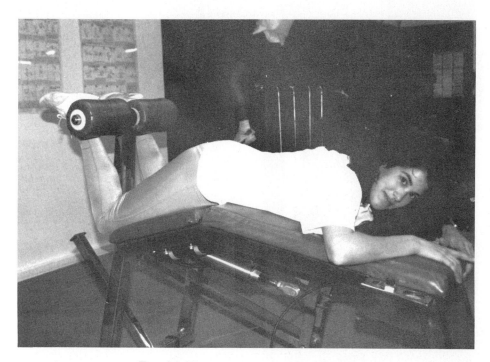

Fig. 39-16. Universal gym knee flexion.

Free-weight heel raises (for calves)

Starting position. Grasp a dumbbell in each hand and position the balls of the feet over a board or stair step.

Movement. Stretch the calves by lowering the body until the heels are lower than the toes, then extend to a "tip-toe" position. (See Fig. 39-17.)

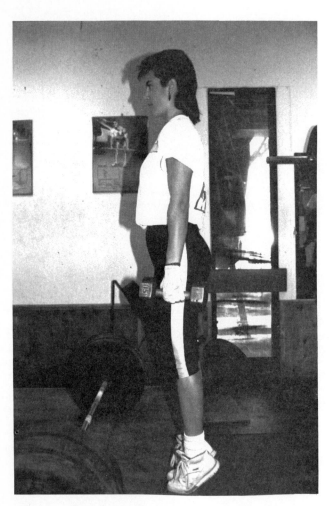

Fig. 39-17. Free weight heel raises.

KEEPING A RECORD

When beginning a weight training or circuit training program, set down goals and chart the progress toward them. Fancy charts and printed graphs are not necessary. However, to keep track of current status and future plans, a diary or log is often helpful.

Most diaries start with the date and personal observations, such as body weight and current condition (for example, tired, energetic, strong, weak). This is followed by a renewal of goals (e.g., "Add two more repetitions to every exercise this week"). Next entered are the exercises to be done, and finally, the number of sets, number of repetitions, and amount of weight used for each exercise. Use one page for each workout session. When doing circuit weight training (described in the next section), list the exercise to be done and the heart rate at the completion of each circuit.

Circuit weight training

Circuit weight training has become an increasingly popular form of weight training because it is believed to be one of the best forms of total body conditioning. Circuit weight training involves aerobic (using oxygen) as well as anaerobic (not using oxygen) work capacities. Normally, circuit weight training consists of 8 to 12 stations, with different weight training exercises at each. The participant moves from one station to another continuously. This provides the aerobic phase, with only enough time to get ready for the next exercise. Usually 10 to 15 repetitions are completed at each station. This provides the strength and local muscle endurance components. Rest time between stations is normally 10 to 15 seconds. The exercises should progress from the large, major muscle groups to the smaller groups and alternate between the upper and the lower body.

TYPICAL PROGRAM

1. Frequency: Program should be done 3 days per week on alternate days.
2. Intensity: 30 seconds at each station.
3. Repetitions: 10 at each station.
4. Rest time: 15 seconds between stations.
5. Order of exercises:
   a. Parallel squat
   b. Bench press
   c. Universal gym leg press
   d. Universal gym lat pull
   e. Back hyperextensions (see Figs. 39-18 and 39-19)
   f. Overhead press
   g. Leg curls
   h. Arm curls
   i. Leg extensions
   j. Side lateral raises (see Fig. 39-20) or alternate exercise (see Fig. 39-21 and 39-22).
   k. Sit-ups (see Fig. 39-23)

After the circuit is completed, the participant should fully recover before starting another cycle.

Fig. 39-18. Back hyperextensions—starting position.

Fig. 39-19. Back hyperextensions.

Fig. 39-20. Side lateral raises.

Fig. 39-21. Starting position.

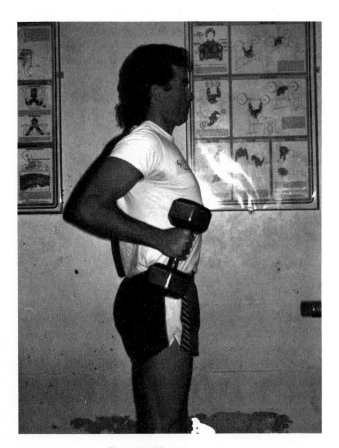

Fig. 39-22. Movement.

Fig. 39-23. Sit-ups.

SETTING UP A PERSONAL CIRCUIT

Below are a few stations, listed by body part. When setting up a circuit, choose one or two exercises from each section. (Be sure to choose exercises that can be done with available equipment.) Next, decide time intervals to be used; and finally, determine how many repetitions will be used at each station.

Another technique is to complete as many repetitions as possible in a chosen time limit (e.g., 30 to 45 seconds). If this procedure is adopted, items 2, 3, and 4 above change to (2) Intensity: desired time limit; (3) Repetitions: maximum; and (4) Rest time: longer than 15 seconds to accommodate recovery. Also, only one cycle may be necessary when using this technique.

As an alternate exercise to side lateral raises, start with the arms at the sides with the elbows flexed at 90 degrees. Move the elbow backward until the weights are next to the hips and then return to the starting position. The arms remain flexed 90 degrees at the elbow throughout the exercise. This exercise is less stressful on the shoulders and elbows than side lateral raises. (See Fig. 39-21 and 39-22.)

Section 1—lower body (large-muscle group)

1. Free-weight parallel squat
2. Universal squat
3. Squat jump (see Fig. 39-24); remember, do not bounce or sag in squat position; jump as high as possible; alternate which foot is forward in the squat portion of the exercise

Fig. 39-24. Squat jumps.

Section 2—upper body (large-muscle group)

1. Bench press
2. Incline bench press
3. Resistance push-ups (see Figs. 39-25 and 39-26)

Section 3—lower body (small-muscle groups)

1. Back hyperextensions
2. Universal leg press

Fig. 39-25. Resistance push-ups—starting position.

Fig. 39-26. Resistance push-ups.

Section 4—upper body (small-muscle groups)

1. Overhead press
2. Parallel bar dips
3. Bent rowing
4. Lat pull-down
5. Pull-ups (wide overhand grip) (see Fig. 39-27)

Fig. 39-27. Pull-ups (wide overhand grip). **A,** Starting position. **B,** Movement.

Section 5—lower body (single muscle group)

1. Knee extensions (see Fig. 39-28)
2. Calf raises
3. Leg curls

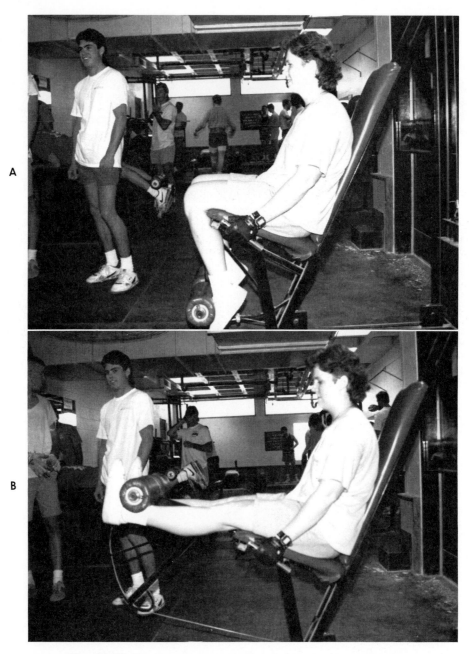

Fig. 39-28. Knee extensions. **A,** Starting position. **B,** Movement.

Section 6—upper body (single muscle group)

1. Arm curls
2. Sit-ups
   a. Unanchored
   b. Standard bend knee sit-ups
3. Side lateral raises
4. Shoulder shrugs (see Fig. 39-29)
5. Bent lateral raises (see Fig. 39-30)

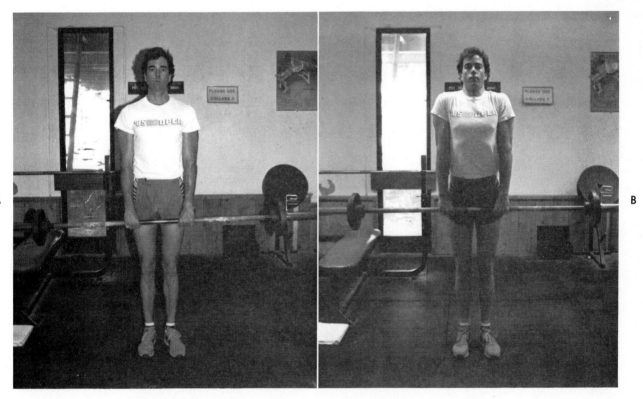

Fig. 39-29. Shoulder shrugs. **A,** Starting position. **B,** Movement.

Fig. 39-30. Bent lateral raises.

Weight lifting
COMPETITIVE LIFTING (OLYMPIC AND POWER)
Weight classification

Flyweight	114½ pounds (52 kg) and under
Bantamweight	123½ pounds (56 kg) and under
Featherweight	132¼ pounds (60 kg) and under
Lightweight	148¾ pounds (67.5 kg) and under
Middleweight	165¼ pounds (75 kg) and under
Light heavyweight	181¾ pounds (82.5 kg) and under
Middle heavyweight	198¼ pounds (90 kg) and under
	220½ pounds (100 kg) and under
Heavyweight	242½ pounds (110 kg) and under
Super heavyweight	275 pounds (125 kg) and under
Power lifting only	Unlimited

GENERAL RULES

Each competitor has the privilege of three trials for each scheduled event. In no case can a weight once tried be replaced by a lesser weight. The athletes themselves decide on the weight with which they will begin each event. The greatest amount in each event is then totaled, and the contestant with the highest total is the winner.

OLYMPIC LIFTS
Clean and jerk

Place the bar horizontally in front of the legs. Grip the bar with both hands and pull it up in a single, distinct motion from the ground to the shoulders while splitting or bending the legs. While resting the bar on the chest or arms, bring the feet back to the original position, that is, on the same line. Bend the legs, then extend the legs and the arms suddenly, thus jerking the bar to the arm's length above the head. The weight must be held in the final motionless position until the referee's signal to replace the bar on the platform. (See Fig. 39-31.)

Fig. 39-31. The clean and jerk.

Fig. 39-31, cont. The clean and jerk.

Fig. 39-32. The snatch.

Snatch

Place the bar horizontally in front of the legs. Grip the bar with both hands and pull it in one motion from the floor to the end of the arms vertically above the head, either splitting or bending the legs. The bar should pass with a continuous nonstop movement along the body, of which no part other than the feet may touch or graze the floor during execution of the movement. The lifted weight must be held in the final motionless position, arms and legs stretched and feet on the same line, until the referee gives the signal to lower the weight. (See Fig. 39-32.)

POWER LIFTS
Squat

Place the bar horizontally across the back of the shoulders. Assume an upright position with the hands gripping the bar and the feet flat on the platform. After the referee's signal, bend the knees and lower the body until the surface of the legs at the hip joint is lower than the tops of the knees. Then recover to the standing position. (See Figs. 39-12 and 39-13.)

Bench press

Assume a supine position on the bench, with the feet flat on the floor. The proper lift does not officially start until the bar is brought down and is absolutely motionless on the chest. The referee's signal is given, and the bar must be pressed vertically to arms' length. (See Figs. 39-1 and 39-2.)

Dead lift

Place the bar horizontally in front of the feet. Bend at the knees, grip the bar with both hands, and lift it upward with one continuous motion, with the arms remaining extended until standing erect with the knees locked and shoulders thrust back.

TEACHING CONSIDERATIONS

1. The decision to include weight training or circuit weight training in a program should be based in part on the availability of equipment in relation to the number of students involved. Unless a vigorous workout at least three times a week for a minimum of 6 weeks can be provided for each student, training effects are likely to be minimal.
2. For a school program, consider circuit weight training because of the total body effect. For units with specialized training goals, teach students the principles and possible effects of both weight training and circuit weight training.
3. Individual pretesting to assist with individual programs should be conducted before a full program is

begun. Students can design their own programs if they are taught the principles of program design and if the teacher checks the programs before the students begin. Goal setting should be part of each program with periodic checks of progress in relation to goals.
4. Use exercises for which sufficient equipment is available to maintain the aerobic nature of the program.
5. Partner work is almost a necessity for many exercises.
6. Do not allow students to perform exercises incorrectly at any time. Insist on proper form and safety.
7. If students are kept off the equipment when they aren't using it for exercising, accidents are less likely to occur.

GLOSSARY

barbell A specialized steel bar 4 to 7 feet long with one or more disks of various weights.

cheat Do an exercise improperly.

circuit weight training A type of weight training done in a continuous manner until an entire cycle of exercises is completed.

clean Raise the barbell in one explosive motion to the standing bent-arm press position.

dumbbell A short-handled barbell used in one hand.

isokinetic exercises A type of resistance exercise in which the amount of resistance offered is regulated by a mechanical device to be proportional to the effort applied.

isometric exercises A type of exercise involving the static contraction of a muscle or muscle group. Resistance is greater than force applied.

isotonic exercises Exercises involving muscle contraction that produces movement through a partial or complete range of motion. Resistance remains constant.

power lifts Squat, bench press, and dead lift.

press Push a barbell or dumbbell to arms' length.

Olympic lifts Snatch and clean and jerk.

repetitions (reps) Number of times an exercise is repeated without stopping.

resistance Amount of weight or pressure the muscles work against.

set A specific number of repetitions.

weight lifting A competitive sport. Olympic weight lifting or power lifting.

weight training A form of exercise in which muscle groups are worked against resistance. Apparatus is usually a barbell, dumbbell, or weight machine.

SUGGESTED READINGS

Allsen PE: Strength training: beginners, body builders and athletes, Glenview, Ill, 1986, Scott, Foresman & Co. For beginners who want to improve their general fitness and athletic ability for specific sports or start a lifetime body-building program.

Fleck SJ and Kramer WJ: Designing resistance training programs, Champaign, Ill, 1987, Human Kinetics Publishers, Inc. Overview of scientific research as well as practical guidance for developing individualized programs.

Hesson JL: Weight training for life, Englewood, Colo, 1985, Morton Publishing Co. Contains a lifetime approach to weight training, including goal setting, stretching, guidelines for all ages, exercises for women, setting up a personal program, and advanced techniques.

International Powerlifting Federation: Official rules, 1988.

Johnson M: Weight lifting and conditioning exercises, Dubuque, Iowa, 1989, Eddie Bowers Publishing Co. Inc. Contains a wide variety of exercises for all the major body parts.

McHugh TP: Weight training for fitness and sports, Dubuque, Iowa, 1984, Kendall/Hunt Publishing Co.

O'Connor R, Simmons J, and O'Shea P: Weight training today, St. Paul, 1989, West Publishing Co.

Payne H: Weight training for all sports, New York, 1987, Viking Penguin, Inc. Contains a special section geared toward the disabled sportsman explaining the therapeutic value of weights to aid recovery.

Rasch PJ: Weight training, ed 5, Dubuque, Iowa, 1990, WC Brown Group. Includes material on weight training for men and women, safety precautions, and the physiology of weight training.

Riley DP: Strength training by the experts, Champaign, Ill, 1982, Human Kinetics Publishers, Inc. Includes information on organizing a program, equipment, muscle structure and physiology, and strength training fundamentals and techniques.

Riley DP: Maximum muscular fitness: strength training without equipment, Champaign, Ill, 1982, Human Kinetics Publishers, Inc. Guidelines and illustrations of manual resistance exercises for the lower body, upper body, arms, abdominals, and neck.

Schwarzenegger A and Hall DK: The education of body builders, New York, 1981, Simon & Schuster, Inc.

Smith C: Conditioning and weight training, Dubuque, Iowa, 1981, Kendall/Hunt Publishing Co.

Stewart GW: Everybody's fitness book, New York, 1980, Doubleday & Co, Inc.

Stone WJ and Kroll WA: Sports conditioning and weight training, ed 2, Dubuque, Iowa, 1986, WC Brown Group. Contains nearly 200 photographs; shows how to apply strength and conditioning exercises to most major sports for men and women. Scientific principles, in-depth training programs, flexibility, warm-up, stretching, and sports nutrition are covered.

Thomas TR: Muscular fitness through resistance training, Dubuque, Iowa, 1986, Eddie Bowers Publishing Co. Inc. Contains over 135 illustrations, nutrition information, resistance training for women, and normative information.

Tuten R, Moore C, and Knight V: Weight training everyone, ed.2 Winston-Salem, NC, 1986, Hunter Textbooks. Written specifically for the college activity program; contains a chapter of questions and answers, hundreds of illustrations, suggestions for developing personal programs for strength development, and sample programs for specific sports.

United States Weightlifting Federation: Official rules, 1988, Colorado Springs, Colo.

Wescott WL: Strength fitness: physiological principles and training techniques, ed 2, Dubuque, Iowa, 1987, WC Brown Group.

VIDEOTAPES

Series of six videotapes for strength and conditioning: *Strength training techniques, Circuit strength training, Training for speed, Plyometrics training, Strength program design for football* and *Strength program design for basketball*. Sports Video, 745 State Circle, Box 1941, Ann Arbor, MI 48106.

40

Wrestling

Completion of this chapter should enable the reader to:

- Display a knowledge of the various forms of wrestling and the equipment and facilities used
- Know the rules of the sport and differences that exist between high school and college wrestling
- Demonstrate fundamental skills, including starting positions, takedowns, escapes, reversals, and pinning holds
- Teach a beginning group of students the fundamental skills of wrestling
- Be familiar with wrestling terminology

HISTORY

Wrestling is one of the oldest sports known. In the ancient Olympic Games, wrestling was an integral part of the pentathlon, a form of all-round althetic championship featuring running, jumping, wrestling, and throwing the discus and javelin. The ancient Greeks were not the first to engage in the sport: the Babylonians, Egyptians, and Hindus taught their youth a form of wrestling as a matter of military need.

Although in various countries there have been minor differences in rules and objectives of wrestling, making about as many systems as nations engaging in this sport, there is no basic difference in the various systems.

Today the value of wrestling is universally recognized. There are several distinct styles of wrestling, including the catch-as-catch-can, the Greco-Roman, judo, and sumo. Catch-as-catch-can, the style used in the United States, permits any holds except those believed dangerous, the main objective being to bring the opponent's shoulders to the mat. The Greco-Roman, used in Europe, is restricted to holds only above the waist and employs the flying fall, the object of which is to touch both of the opponent's shoulders to the mat for a fraction of a second. The freestyle, a compromise between catch-as-catch-can and Greco-Roman, permits any holds not dangerous. In judo, a style used in Japan, the objective is to throw the opponent cleanly or pin the back to the mat for a period of 30 seconds. Sumo, another Japanese

style, has become a national sport in Japan. The primary requisite is great strength.

From the first modern Olympic games until 1924 wrestling rules varied greatly, usually favoring the country hosting the event. In Paris in 1924, some order was achieved and both freestyle and Greco-Roman events were contested. Over the years many countries have produced great Olympic individual wrestlers and wrestling teams. Turkey, Sweden, the United States, West Germany, and the Soviet Union all were successful until around 1960. Since 1960 the sport has been taken more seriously by the Eastern block countries than other parts of the world. With a total of 20 gold medals (10 categories in each of the two styles) it is a sport worth concentrating on to gain international attention.

In 1972 in Munich, 15 of the golds were won by Eastern block wrestlers (nine by the USSR). The United States won three golds, including one by Dan Gable, who did not give up a point in six matches. Between 1972 and 1980 the Soviet wrestlers continued to dominate the sport. In 1984 in Los Angeles the U.S. wrestlers put together a competitive team and did well (7 golds and 2 silvers in freestyle and the first ever golds [2] in Greco-Roman events), but the performance was somewhat tainted by the Soviet boycott. In 1988 the United States captured only two gold medals and five medals overall. The USSR captured nine medals, four of them gold.

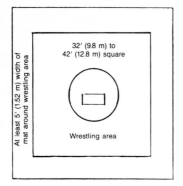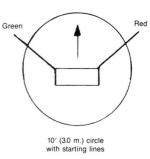

Fig. 40-1. Recommended mat sizes.

Fig. 40-2. Front and rear view of official uniform. Front view shows 4-inch inseam. Rear view shows pinning area.

THE MAT

The wrestling area of the mat is no less than 32 feet (9.8 m) square or, if circular, 32 feet in diameter and not more than 42 feet (12.8 m) square or a circular area 42 feet (12.8 m) in diameter. There should be at least a 5-foot (1.52 m) width of mat around this area. The mat should have the shock quality of a 2-inch (5 cm) thick hair felt mat. In the center of the mat there should be painted a circle 10 feet (3.05 m) in diameter.

Two 1-inch (2.54 cm) starting lines are placed in the center of the mat. One of the lines lies on the diameter of the 10-foot circle and the other starting line is parallel to the first line and 10 inches (25.4 cm) from it. One inch (2.54 cm) lines close the ends of the starting lines, forming a box in the center of the mat. One starting line should be green (toward the home team) and one red (toward the visiting team). (See Fig. 40-1.)

EQUIPMENT

The uniform (see Fig. 40-2) consists of full-length tights, close-fitting outside trunks, and a sleeveless shirt without fasteners at the shoulder and fastened down at the crotch. A properly cut one- or two-piece uniform is optional. A minimum 4-inch inseam is required. Lightweight over-the-ankle wrestling shoes, without heels and laced through eyelets, must be worn, and a protective earguard is required. In addition, contestants must be clearly identified by some means (such as red or green anklets).

ABRIDGED RULES
Weight classification
Intercollegiate
The classes for intercollegiate wrestling are as follows:

118 pounds (53.5 kg) and under
126 pounds (57.2 kg) and under
134 pounds (60.8 kg) and under
142 pounds (64.4 kg) and under
150 pounds (68.0 kg) and under
158 pounds (71.7 kg) and under
167 pounds (75.8 kg) and under
177 pounds (80.3 kg) and under
190 pounds (86.2 kg) and under
175-275 pounds (80.2-124.7 kg)

In all dual college meets there is no weight allowance at weigh-in.

High school modification

103 pounds (46.7 kg) and under
112 pounds (50.8 kg) and under
119 pounds (54.0 kg) and under
125 pounds (56.7 kg) and under
130 pounds (58.9 kg) and under
135 pounds (61.2 kg) and under
140 pounds (63.5 kg) and under
145 pounds (65.7 kg) and under
152 pounds (68.9 kg) and under
160 pounds (72.5 kg) and under
175 pounds (77.5 kg) and under
189 pounds (85.7 kg) and under
275 pounds (124.7 kg)

High school competition is governed by the NCAA Wrestling Guide high school modification.

Major differences between scholastic and collegiate rules
Injury time
HIGH SCHOOL: Three minutes to recover.
COLLEGE: Two minutes to recover.

Riding time
HIGH SCHOOL: No riding time.
COLLEGE: One point for 1 minute or more accumulated time advantage more than opponent.

Fall
HIGH SCHOOL: Two seconds.
COLLEGE: One second.

Number of matches
HIGH SCHOOL: No wrestler shall compete in more than five full-length matches in any day.
COLLEGE: No similar rule.

Weight allowance
HIGH SCHOOL: No allowance.
COLLEGE: Three-pound (1.4 kg) allowance in November and December, 2 pounds (0.9 kg) in January, 1 pound (0.5 kg) in February, except in qualifying tournaments, which are scratch weight.

Weigh-in
HIGH SCHOOL: Maximum of 1 hour and minimum of 30 minutes before dual meet is scheduled to begin.
COLLEGE: Maximum of 5 hours and minimum of 30 minutes, unless otherwise mutually agreed on.

Duration of bout
HIGH SCHOOL: Three 2-minute periods (tournaments—overtime, two 1-minute periods; consolation—three periods: first period, 1 minute; second and third periods, 2 minutes each).
COLLEGE: Three periods: first period, 3 minutes; second and third periods, 2 minutes (tournaments—overtime, three 1-minute periods; consolation—three 2-minute periods).

Sweatbox
HIGH SCHOOL: Prohibited.
COLLEGE: Permissible.

Weight class restriction
HIGH SCHOOL: May wrestle one weight class above actual weight at time of weigh-in; unlimited contestant must weigh a minimum of 184 pounds (83.4 kg).
COLLEGE: May wrestle any weight class above actual weight; unlimited contestant must weigh a minimum of 177 pounds (80.3 kg).

Conduct of match
The first period starts with the wrestlers opposite each other on their feet, one standing on the green area and the other on the red. The wrestlers will first come forward and shake hands and then go back to their 3-foot starting lines. When the referee blows the whistle they begin wrestling. A fall during this or one of the other periods terminates the match. If no fall occurs in the first period, a coin is tossed and the winner of the toss chooses either the bottom or top position. The third period starts with the wrestlers in the alternate positions. The referee starts all wrestling with the whistle. If during

the match no falls occur, the winner is decided by the point system. Wrestlers must return to and remain in their respective areas until the winner is declared or a penalty (Table 37-1) will be imposed. In case of a tie in tournaments, there will be three overtime periods of 1 minute each. Wrestlers' positions will be the same as when beginning a match and decided in the same way, by the toss of a coin. If there is still a tie at the end of overtime, criteria are applied to the overtime periods to determine the winner. These include (in the following order) abusive and unsportsmanlike conduct penalties, near falls, takedowns, reversals, escapes, riding time, stalling, illegal holds, technical violations and unnecessary roughness, time advantage, and then these criteria applied to the normal match. If none of these criteria produce a winner, the referee shall determine the winner by deciding the superior wrestler.

In college and high school wrestling, if the wrestlers go off the mat they are brought back to the center of the mat with the wrestler that had advantage on top. If neither had control, they start again on their feet.

Scoring for high school and college
Point-scoring system for matches in which no fall occurs

1. For "takedown," or bringing the opponent to the mat from standing—2 points
2. For escaping from a defensive position on the mat—1 point
3. For reversal of position from a defensive position on the mat—2 points
4. For a near fall or a situation in which the offensive wrestler has control of the opponent and a fall is imminent—2 points when near fall criteria held for 2 seconds, 3 points when held for 5 seconds
5. For 1 minute or more of superior, accumulated time advantage behind an opponent—1 point, 1 point being the maximum awarded for the match

Tournament scoring (team points)

1. First place in each weight—10 points
2. Second place in each weight—7 points
3. Third place in each weight—4 points
4. Fourth place in each weight—2 points
5. For each fall secured throughout the meet—1 additional point
6. Default scores—1 point
7. Forfeit scores—1 point
8. Advancement scores—1 point; consolation—½ point
9. Disqualification—1 point
10. Decision—½ point

Dual meet scoring (team points)

1. Fall (any part of both shoulders held in contact with the mat for 2 seconds in high school and 1 second in college competition)—6 points
2. Decision
   a. Five points if winning wrestler has 15 match points more than losing wrestler (technical fall)
   b. Four points if winning wrestler has between 8 and 14 match points more than the losing wrestler
   c. Three points if winning wrestler has 7 or less match points than losing wrestler
3. Draw—2 points for each team
4. Forfeit—6 points
5. Default—6 points
6. Disqualification—6 points

Illegal holds

The following holds are illegal: hammerlock above the right angle, the twisting hammerlock, front headlock, headlock without the arm, the straight head scissors, over scissors, full nelson, strangle holds, all body slams, toe holds, twisting knee lock, key lock, overhead double-arm bar; bending, twisting, or forcing of the head or any limb beyond its normal limit of movement; locking the hands behind the back in a double-arm bar from a neutral position; full back suplay from a rear standing position; and any hold used for punishment alone.

FUNDAMENTAL SKILLS AND TECHNIQUES

Descriptions are given from one side only. However, the techniques may be applied from the other side by changing the approach from right to left and left to right.

Wrestling positions
Square stance

Feet should be comfortably spread and turned out with the weight centered on the balls of the feet and distributed evenly on both feet so that movement is free and easy. The knees should be bent, back rounded, head up, and arms extended forward but elbows close to the body. (See Fig. 40-4.)

Starting position on the mat (referee's position)

Defensive wrestler. The defensive wrestler must be kneeling with hands in the center of the mat. The wrestler must keep both knees on the mat and must not spread them more than the width of the shoulders. The legs must be parallel, with the toes turned neither out nor under in an exaggerated position. The heels of the hands must be on the mat and not less than 12 inches (30 cm) in front of the kees. (See Fig. 40-5.)

Offensive wrestler. The offensive wrestler may be kneeling or on one knee with a foot at the side of the opponent

Table 40-1. INFRACTION PENALTY TABLE*

Infraction	Rule, section	Warnings, cautions	First penalty	Second penalty	Third penalty	Fourth penalty
Unnecessary roughness[1]	6-5	No	1 match pt.	1 match pt.	2 match pts.	Disqualify
Illegal holds[1]	6-8	No	1 match pt.	1 match pt.	2 match pts.	Disqualify
Technical violations,[1,2]	6-10, 6-18	See Note 2 and Summary	1 match pt.	1 match pt.	2 match pts.	Disqualify
False starts and incorrect[3] starting positions	6-17, 6-18	Yes (two)	1 match pt.	1 match pt.	1 match pt.	1 match pt.
Unsportsmanlike conduct[4] Nonparticipating team personnel; Contestants before and after match	6-4	No	Deduct 1 team pt.	Deduct 1 team pt.; disqual- ify, remove from prem- ises		
Unsportsmanlike conduct[4] contestants	6-4	No	1 match pt.	1 match pt.	2 match pts.	Disqualify
Flagrant misconduct	6-6	No	Disqualify; de- duct 1 team pt.; remove from premises[5]			
Foreign substances on skin or illegal uniform or equipment	6-7	No	Disqualify if not removed or corrected within contes- tant's remain- ing injury time[7]			
Control of mat area and Questioning the official[6]	4-11 4-13 8-5	Yes (verbal)	Warning	Deduct 1 team pt.	Deduct 2 team pts.	Deduct 2 team pts.; remove from premises

*Note A—Any combination of four penalties, excluding false starts and assuming incorrect starting position, accumulated during a regular match or during an overtime match will result in disqualification.

Note B—Disqualification due to technical violation, illegal holds, unnecessary roughness or unsportsmanlike conduct does not eliminate a contestant from further tournament competition. Disqualification for flagrant misconduct eliminates that contestant from further competition in that tournament, and he forfeits all points and placement earned in the tournament.

[1]Points for unnecessary roughness, technical violations, and illegal holds will be awarded in addition to points earned by the offended wrestler.

[2]Stalling (including delay of match) is a technical violation with penalties awarded for such action being preceded by a visual warning.

[3]The first two violations will result in visual cautions.

[4]The penalties are accumulative throughout a dual meet or a tournament session for coaches, trainers, managers, and physicians. They are accumulative for a contestant for a match or dual meet. These penalties are accumulative per institution.

[5]Removal is for the duration of the dual meet or tournament in which it occurred.

[6]A verbal warning and a warning precede the first penalty. These offenses are cumulative per institution throughout each dual meet and for the duration of triangular meets, quadrangular meets and tournaments.

[7]Referee may declare an official's timeout to correct equipment or uniform that becomes illegal or inoperative during use.

SUMMARY OF TECHNICAL VIOLATIONS

Stalling (6-10-a)—First, warn

Holding legs (6-10-b)

Delaying match (6-10-f)—(treat under stalling)

Interlocking hands (6-11)

Figure four scissors (6-12)

Leaving mat without permission (6-13)

Going off wrestling area (6-14)

Toweling off (6-15)

Grasping clothing, etc. (6-16)

False starts (6-17)

Incorrect starting position (6-18)

Fig. 40-3. Official wrestling signals.

Fig. 40-4. Square stance.

Fig. 40-5. Basic starting position on the knees.

Fig. 40-6. Optional offensive starting position.

and the head along the midline of the opponent's back (Fig. 40-5). The palm of the right (or left) hand must be placed loosely against the defensive wrestler's navel at the waistline and the left (or right) hand must be placed loosely on the back of the opponent's left (or right) elbow. The knee or leg must not touch the near leg of the opponent and must be even with or ahead of the defensive wrestler's foot.

Optional offensive starting position. The offensive wrestler may be positioned on either side or to the rear of the opponent with all weight supported on both feet, one knee, or both knees. The offensive wrestler must place the hands on the opponent's back with thumbs touching. Only the hands can touch the defensive wrestler's back. The defensive wrestler must be positioned as described above. (See Fig. 40-6.)

Fig. 40-7. Drop step.

Wrestling objectives

Offensive

1. Takedown—to take the opponent to the mat
2. Controlling—to keep the opponent under control on the mat
3. Breaking—to force an opponent off-balance when down on the mat
4. Pinning—to bring the opponent's shoulder blades in contact with the mat for 2 seconds.

Defensive

1. Reverse positions—to change from a defensive position on the mat to an offensive position
2. Escaping—to free oneself from the grasp of an opponent while in a defensive position on the mat

Takedown skills

In preparation for a takedown, the wrestlers move around, tie up, and use various set ups attempting to gain an advantage. The eyes should be focused ahead but past the opponent so that one can be aware of anything that moves in the range of vision. An example of a tie-up is to hook the back of the opponent's head with your right hand and at the same time put your left hand on the opponent's bicep. Pull with the right hand and push with the left hand. A set-up is any movement or act that distracts the opponent to make him vulnerable to a takedown move.

The drop step is a penetration move for a takedown attack. Bend the knees to lower the hips, drive off the inner edge of the back foot, and step as far forward as possible but keeping good balance. Keep the head up and the arms in, close to the body. Concentrate on getting your hips close to the opponent. (See Fig. 40-7.)

Duck-under. From the standing position, grasp the opponent's right elbow with the left hand, drop to the right knee, and force the arm up. Grasp one or both of the opponent's legs and force the opponent off-balance. (See Fig. 40-8).

Counter. Defensive wrestler resists by moving the feet back, dropping to the knees, and forcing the opponent's head to the mat.

Arm drag and go behind. Start from the standing position. The objective is to get behind the opponent while standing. Grasp the opponent's left wrist with the right hand, and then with the left hand grasp opponent's left arm above the elbow and pull with both hands to the left until the opponent is partly turned. Then slip the right arm around the opponent's waist and with the right foot step behind the opponent. Lock the hands around the opponent's waist. (See Fig. 40-9.)

Counter. Resist and keep facing the offensive wrestler when the opponent attempts to pull your arm.

Drop with leg trip. The objective is to take the opponent down from a position behind. Lock your hands with the arms around the opponent's waist and the head resting on the opponent's left hip. Drop to the left knee and

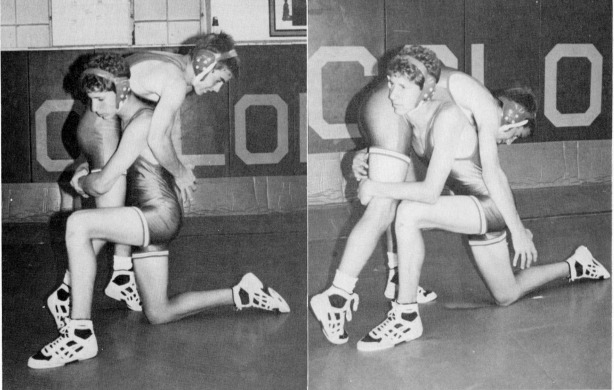

Fig. 40-8. Duck under and takedown.

Fig. 40-9. Armdrag and go behind.

grasp the opponent's left ankle with the left hand. Place your right leg in front of the opponent's right leg. Then force your right shoulder to the opponent's buttock and force the opponent forward while pulling the opponent's ankle.

Counter. Open the body lock by tearing the opponent's hands apart.

Fig. 40-10. High crotch position.

High crotch to single-leg takedown. From a tie-up position, lift the opponent's elbows and simultaneously step in quickly. Once in close, duck the head and shoulder under the opponent's left arm, reach behind the opponent's back with your right arm, and bring it between his legs. Grasp the right hand with your left hand and pull up. This is the high-crotch position. (See Fig. 40-10.) This can be followed by a single-leg takedown by moving down on the opponent's left leg while dropping to the mat on your right knee. By pulling the opponent's left leg and foot toward you and pushing forward with your shoulders, the opponent can be dumped backward for the takedown. (See Fig. 40-11.)

Counter. Keep the leg the attacker is trying to control between his legs to prevent him from lifting it.

Fireman's takedown. From the collar-biceps tie up, move the left hand from the biceps to the opponent's triceps. Step the right foot between the opponent's legs and drop to the left knee. Move your head under the opponent's right arm and pull down (See Fig. 40-12). Move your right hand from the opponent's neck and go between his legs and reach up the back. Drop your left hip to the mat, pull down with your left hand or arm and lift the opponent's body with the right arm. Pull your head out and reach across the opponent's body with your right arm to hold under his left shoulder with your right hand. (See Fig. 40-13.)

Counter. Free up the right arm (being held at the tricep by the attacker) and cross face and get the left arm under the attacker's midsection or between his legs to avoid being lifted off the mat.

Fig. 40-11. Single leg takedown.

Fig. 40-12. Fireman's takedown—initial move.

Fig. 40-13. Fireman's takedown—completion.

Fig. 40-14. Bar-arm and waist lock.

Fig. 40-15. Far arm and far ankle.

Breakdowns and rides

To break a wrestler down means to put the wrestler on hands and knees on the mat from the starting position. Because of the low center of gravity and the four points of support, this is difficult. The technique is to disengage one of the points of support.

Bar arm and waist lock. From the starting position, pull the near arm out from under and force the opponent to the mat by pulling the opponent down with the arm that is around the waist. (See Fig. 40-14.)

Counter. After the tie-up, the bottom wrestler rolls toward the top wrestler. Then the bottom wrestler takes the left arm, which is free, wraps it over and around the top wrestler's arm, and grasps the top wrestler's wrist and pries it loose.

Far ankle and far arm. The object is to quickly reach under the wrestler and grasp the far arm above the el-bow. Now pull this arm to you, and at the same time grasp the far ankle with the other hand. Turn the opponent over by applying body leverage. (See Fig. 40-15.)

Counter. The best way to counter this move is for the bottom wrestler to pull the right arm away (or the left arm if the approach is from the other side).

Grapevine and arm bar. This can be accomplished only if the top wrestler is extremely fast. The top wrestler must quickly move on the bottom wrestler's back and wrap the right leg between the bottom wrestler's arm and leg. The top wrestler then places the body across the bottom wrestler. While in this position the top wrestler grasps, from above, the bottom wrestler's arm.

Counter. The bottom wrestler should expect this and not allow the top wrestler to place a foot between arm and leg. However, if the top wrestler's leg does go

Fig. 40-16. Grapevine and arm bar.

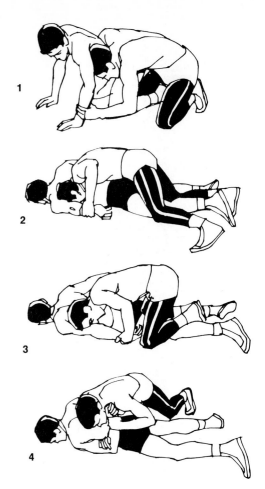

Fig. 40-17. Head pry and near arm.

through, the bottom wrestler should push it through farther than opponent wanted it to go. (See Fig. 40-16.)

Head pry and near arm. To execute this breakdown the top wrestler moves the right knee to a position between the bottom wrestler's legs. The top wrestler then slides the left hand down to the wrist of the bottom wrestler. While lifting the bottom wrestler's arm up and slightly to the side, the top wrestler places the head in back of the bottom wrestler's arm and applies pressure. This pressure and the pressure forward of the right thigh force the bottom wrestler to the mat. (See Fig. 40-17.)

Counter. The bottom wrestler should try to pull arm forward as the top wrestler moves the hand from the elbow to wrist.

Grapevine and bar nelson. Execute a grapevine as previously described, placing the right forearm behind the opponent's neck, pushing the left arm under the opponent's left arm, and locking hands (bar nelson).

Grapevine and half nelson. Execute a grapevine as described previously, placing the left arm under the opponent's left arm and the forearm behind the opponent's neck (half nelson).

Body scissors and half nelson. Place the right foot between the opponent's right arm and right thigh with the left foot in a similar position, locking the feet (body scissors). Execute a half nelson as before.

Spiral breakdown. The top wrestler moves the right hand to inside the bottom wrestler's right thigh and pries

outward. The top wrestler also moves the left forearm behind the bottom wrestler's left forearm and pushes forward. At the same time the top wrestler is circling in a clockwise direction.

Escapes and reversals

Stand-up. The wrestler in the defensive position pushes off the mat with both hands, brings the elbows back and toward the ribs, raises the head and trunk, and steps out with either foot. By sitting on the rear foot and leg, which are still on the mat, the wrestler prevents the opponent from grasping this ankle or stepping over the near leg. Next the defensive wrestler grabs the opponent's hands, pulls them apart, and pushes back with the back. The opponent is forced to resist this action (which helps the bottom wrestler to stand) or else be pushed over backward. Finally, when both wrestlers are standing, the defensive wrestler continues to pull the opponent's hands apart and then turns to face the opponent. (See Fig. 40-18.)

Counter—far-ankle pick-up. The offensive wrestler

1

2

3

Fig. 40-18. Stand-up.

Fig. 40-19. Far-ankle pick-up.

Fig. 40-20. Forward jam.

Fig. 40-21. Near-ankle pick-up.

Fig. 40-22. Body lock and forward trip.

releases the arm that is around the defensive wrestler's wrist and moves this arm to grasp and lift the far ankle of the bottom wrestler. (See Fig. 40-19.)

Counter—forward jam. Remaining in the referee's position, the top wrestler jams the defensive wrestler forward and down to prevent a stand-up. (See Fig. 40-20.)

Counter—near-ankle pick-up. The offensive wrestler releases the near arm in the referee's position, moves behind, and grasps and lifts the near ankle of the bottom wrestler. (See Fig. 40-21.)

Counter—body lock and forward trip. If the defensive wrestler gets to a standing position, the offensive wrestler should keep the hands tightly clasped around the defensive wrestler's body, step outside and in front of the bottom wrestler's leg, and push forward, thus tripping the defensive wrestler back to the mat. (See Fig. 40-22.)

Side roll. The wrestler in the defensive position locks the opponent's right wrist by pressing the arm close to his body, then rolling to the right, bringing the opponent over and under (side roll) or showing the right arm between the opponent's legs (crotch hold).

Fig. 40-23. The sit out and turn in.

Sit out. Step the right foot forward first. Then shoot the left foot out and forward. At this point (Fig. 40-23, *2*) the defensive wrestler can turn out (to the right) by pushing down with the right elbow to break the offensive wrestler's grasp around the waist and swinging the left arm forcefully forward, or turn in (as illustrated).

Counter. Top wrestler should break the left arm down as the bottom wrestler attempts to execute the kick out with the left leg.

The switch. Begin the switch by crossing the right hand over the left (if the referee's position is on the right side). Now place the weight on the left foot. Kick the right foot forward and to the left. Keep the hips off the mat. With the left arm reach over the top wrestler's left arm and grasp the left thigh from the inside. Lean back and apply

Fig. 40-24. The switch.

force to the opponent's shoulder. Now pivot on the right foot and grasp the top wrestler around the waist. (See Fig. 40-24.)

Counter. Break down the bottom wrestler's right arm as the opponent attempts to pivot just after kicking out.

Fig. 40-25. Side roll.

Pinning holds

Side roll. This move is executed from the referee's position. (See Fig. 40-25.) The bottom wrestler straightens the left leg and at the same time grasps the top wrestler by the wrist (right). The bottom wrestler then brings the right leg to the left, drops on the right shoulder, and rolls the top wrestler over. As the top wrestler hits the right side, the bottom wrestler turns to face the opponent. The bottom wrestler now places the left arm over the top wrestler's right shoulder and around the head to a half nelson. Finally, the bottom wrestler inserts the right arm between the opponent's legs, raises the left leg, and then locks the hands. Locking the hands or arms around the opponent's leg and head is called the cradle.

Arm bar and half nelson. The top wrestler uses the near arm breakdown described earlier. Then bring the left hand up and put it on the bottom wrestler's back. Apply a half nelson with the right hand, move to the right side and "sink" the half nelson in as far as possible. Circle counter clockwise on knees to turn the bottom wrestler on his back. This combination of moves is called the "chicken wing." (See Fig. 40-26.)

Three-quarter nelson. This also is executed from the referee's position. The top wrestler places the right knee behind the bottom wrestler. The top wrestler then moves the right arm from the bottom wrestler's waist, reaches under the bottom wrestler with the right hand, and locks hands over the back of the bottom wrestler's head. Next the top wrestler pulls the bottom wrestler's head under and moves to the left. To keep the bottom wrestler from rolling out, the top wrestler retains control of the bottom wrestler's leg with the right leg. (See Fig. 40-27.)

Half nelson and crotch hold. Starting in the referee's position and using a breakdown, the offensive wrestler puts the defensive wrestler flat on the mat. The offensive wrestler then secures a half nelson on the bottom wrestler by moving the arm closest to the bottom wrestler's head under the near arm and behind the neck. With the other arm, the offensive wrestler grasps the defensive wrestler's top leg, lifts it up, and pushes the bottom wrestler over to the back. The top wrestler continues to maintain a helf nelson with one arm and an inside crotch hold with the other. (See Fig. 40-28.)

Near cradle. Assume the wrestlers are in the referee's position, with the top wrestler on the left side of the bottom wrestler. If the bottom wrestler tries to stand up by raising the left knee off the mat, the top wrestler should release the right arm from around the bottom wrestler's waist and move that arm behind the opponent's left knee. At the same time the top wrestler should shift to a position in front of the bottom wrestler and move the left arm from the bottom wrestler's left elbow to a position around the head and try to lock hands under the bottom wrestler's chest. By pulling the hands together and pushing the bottom wrestler to the right and forward, the top wrestler should be able to move the opponent into a pinning position. (See Fig. 40-29.)

Guillotine. This is done from either the kneeling or the referee's position. Starting from the cross-body ride, the top wrestler reaches over the body of the bottom wrestler and places the right hand on the mat for support. Then the top wrestler grasps the bottom wrestler's left wrist with the left hand. The top wrestler then lifts the bottom wrestler's left arm up over the head and then falls back, pinning the bottom wrestler's shoulders. (See Fig. 40-30.)

Counter. The bottom wrestler should not allow the top wrestler to lift the left arm.

Fig. 40-26. Chicken wing.

Fig. 40-27. Three-quarter nelson.

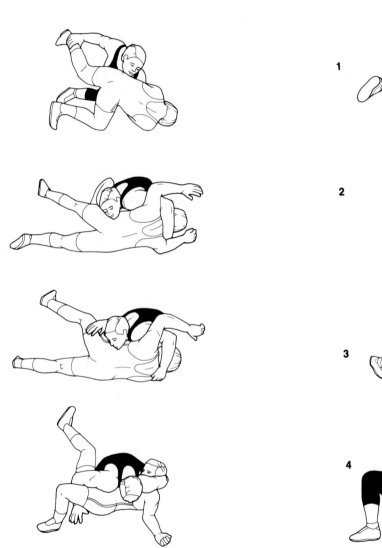

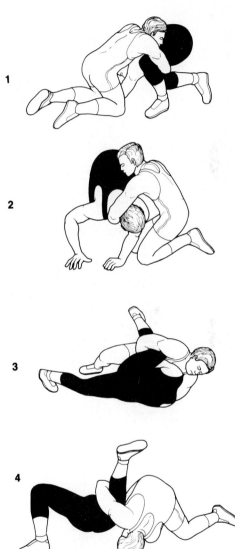

Fig. 40-28. Half nelson and crotch hold.

Fig. 40-29. Near cradle.

Fig. 40-30. Guillotine

PERSONAL STRATEGY

1. *Live right*. Watch how you eat, drink, and party. Consistently maintain your class weight. Retain your maximum strength by not undertraining or overtraining. Get sufficient rest. Keep clean even when just working out.
2. *Train right*. Challenge your coach. Set up a training schedule and follow it. Always attempt to practice with a superior wrestler. *Hurt* sometime during your training program.
3. *Watch and ask*. Do not fool around when not wrestling. Try to pick up new skills. Get into the middle of the action. Ask questions about new moves that you might see, and then learn them.
4. *Be prepared*. Know the scientific principles involved in wrestling. Know all the skills of wrestling so you can successfully counter them. Know the method of scoring points. Be aware of the penalty system.
5. *Wrestle*. Plan ahead what move you are going to make and what you will do if your opponent successfully counters it. Try to outguess your opponent. Watch your opponent's center of weight and move quickly.
6. *Shake hands*. Be courteous when the match is over whether you win or lose.

TEACHING CONSIDERATIONS

1. Match students for weight.
2. Begin with holds from the referee's position before the standing position.
3. Walk through beginning holds with a passive defense until proper technique is established. Increase resistance gradually.
4. Combine offensive and defensive moves in practice. Give both offense and defense a choice of several moves in drill-like practices, focusing the wrestlers on the decision-making process involved in selecting a move.
5. Introduce illegal holds as they may occur in drills, and be firm about calling them.
6. As soon as several offensive and defensive skills have been developed, provide opportunities for mini-matches in each lesson. Use these times as opportunities to teach rules and scoring. Structure the matches to require or encourage the use of particular moves as part of the lesson (e.g., giving more points for a particular move).
7. Go back to basics when students revert to poor technique. Provide for repetition. Continually return to earlier moves as you introduce advanced moves.
8. Modify the rules as needed to make illegal any move beginners cannot perform safely, either because of skill level or conditioning.
9. Change matched partners as often as possible within a weight class.

GLOSSARY

arm drag A preliminary move to execute a takedown from behind.

breakdown From the referee's position, the wrestler on top forces the bottom wrestler off the hands and knees to a position flat on the mat.

bridge A position on the mat in which the wrestler is supported on the head and feet with the back arched.

counter Stop a move made by the opponent.

cradle A move made to force the opponent's head and knees together.

decision If no fall occurs in a match, the wrestler with the greatest number of points is declared the winner.

default Winning a match through the inability of an opponent to continue the match.

disqualification A situation in which a contestant is banned from participation in accordance with the Infraction Penalty Table. (See Table 37-1.)

escape Gaining a neutral position by the defensive wrestler while the supporting points of either wrestler are within the wrestling area.

fall Holding both of an opponent's shoulders to the mat simultaneously for 1 or 2 seconds; also termed a pin.

forfeit Winning a match through failure of an opponent to appear.

half nelson A hold executed from the rear by reaching either the left or right arm under the opponent's corresponding arm and using the hand behind the head to apply pressure.

hammerlock Holding the opponent's arm behind the back. This is illegal if the hand is pulled away from the body or if the angle at the elbow is less than 90 degrees.

near fall Position in which the offensive wrestler holds the opponent's shoulders or the scapula area in contact with the mat for a designated time, less than that required for a fall.

neutral position Position in which neither wrestler has control.

out of bounds The supporting parts of either wrestler outside the boundary lines.

pin Synonymous with fall.

position of advantage Having control of an opponent.

reversal Act of moving from a defensive position to an offensive position.

sit out A maneuver executed from the referee's position, in which the bottom wrestler throws the legs forward to a sitting position.

stalemate Neither wrestler is able to improve the situation; the referee stops and restarts the match.

stand-up A breakaway (escape) move resulting in getting up to the feet quickly.

starting position on the mat Position in which the defensive wrestler is kneeling with hands in the center of the mat. The offensive contestant is kneeling at the side of the opponent, with the nearest arm around the opponent's body perpendicular to the long axis with the palm of the hand placed on the navel and the other hand placed on the back of the opponent's nearest elbow.

takedown Bring an opponent from a standing position to the mat and under control.

technical fall Occurs when a wrestler has earned a 15-point advantage over the opponent.

time advantage Accumulated time during which a wrestler is in a position of advantage over the opponent; no more than 1 point may be awarded in any one match. (Not used in high school.)

SUGGESTED READINGS

Banach L and Chapman M: The new breed: living Iowa wrestling, Champaign, Ill, 1985, Human Kinetics Publishers, Inc. Describes what it was like to wrestle for renowned coach Dan Gable; by an Olympic gold medalist.

Chapman M: Encyclopedia of American wrestling, Champaign, Ill, 1990, Human Kinetics Publishers, Inc. A detailed chronicle of the people and places that have made wrestling history.

Chapman M: Nick and the Cyclones, Champaign, Ill, 1988, Human Kinetics Publishers, Inc. The story of how hard work, perseverance, and a strong belief in his wrestlers brought six national championships to coach Harold Nichols and Iowa State University.

Combs S: Coaching youth wrestling, North Palm Beach, Fla, 1987, The Athletic Institute.

Keith A: Successful wrestling, Champaign, Ill, 1990, Human Kinetics Publishers, Inc. Step-by-step instruction for 30 wrestling techniques, from simple to complex.

Martell B: An illustrated guide to teaching kids to wrestle, Champaign, Ill, 1985, Human Kinetics Publishers, Inc. Step-by-step instructions for developing wrestling techniques and skills in young wrestlers.

Martens R: Parent guide to kids wrestling, Champaign, Ill, 1980, Human Kinetics Publishers, Inc.

Mysnyk M: Wrestling fundamentals and techniques. The Iowa way, Champaign, Ill, 1982, Human Kinetics Publishers, Inc. Describes a wrestling program based on the procedures and techniques used at the University of Iowa—the perennial NCAA champions.

Official wrestling guide, New York, 1989, Amateur Athletic Union of the United States.

Official wrestling guide, New York, 1989, National Collegiate Athletic Association.

Schalles W: They call it wrestling, Champaign, Ill, 1983, Human Kinetics Publishers, Inc. Over 300 pictures describing the efforts, experiences, and accomplishments of American wrestlers.

VIDEOTAPES

Takedowns, Escapes and reverses, and *Riding and pinning*. Karol Video, 22 Riverside Dr., Wayne, NJ 07470.

Three videotape series on kid's wrestling, including *Organizing a kid's wrestling club, Basic skills and better techniques*, and *The keys to fitness, nutrition and safety*. The Athletic Institute, 200 N. Castlewood Dr., North Palm Beach, FL 33408.

Two part videotape series showing over 25 basic moves. Sports Video, 745 State Circle, Box 1941, Ann Arbor, MI 48106.

Series of three videotapes: *Fundamentals, Advanced*, and *Free style*. "How To" Sports Videos, Box 5852, Denver, CO 80217.

Wrestling classic and *Wrestling's greatest heroes*. Corbin House, 227 Corbin Place, Brooklyn, NY 11235.

Miscellaneous Field and Court Dimensions

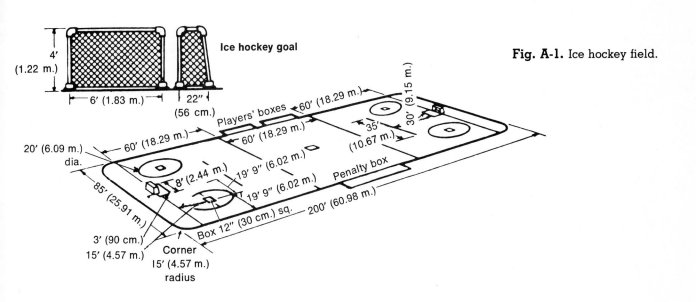

Fig. A-1. Ice hockey field.

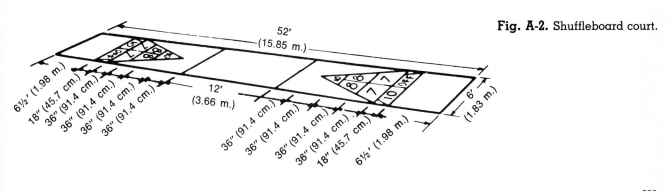

Fig. A-2. Shuffleboard court.

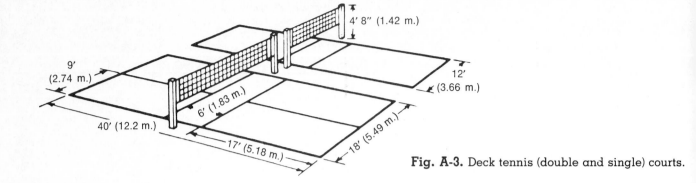

Fig. A-3. Deck tennis (double and single) courts.

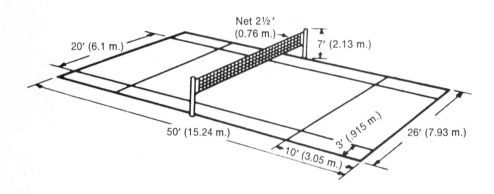

Fig. A-4. Aerial tennis court.

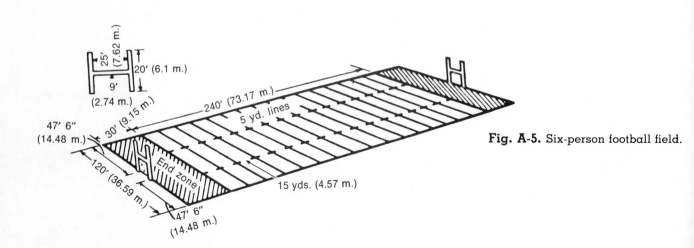

Fig. A-5. Six-person football field.

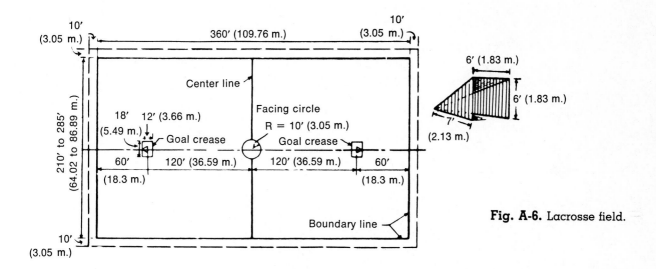

Fig. A-6. Lacrosse field.

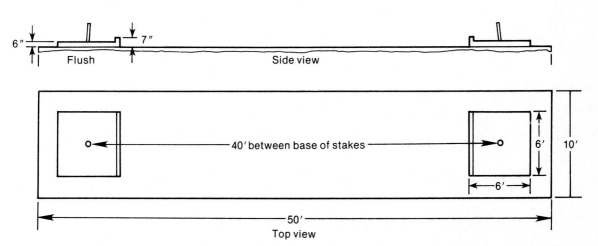

Fig. A-7. Horseshoe pit. The 1-inch x 3-foot stakes extend 14 inches above ground and incline 3 inches toward each other. Stakes are 30 feet apart for women and boys under 16 years.

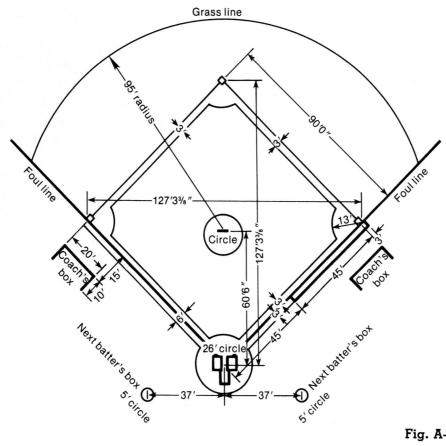

Fig. A-8. Baseball diamond.

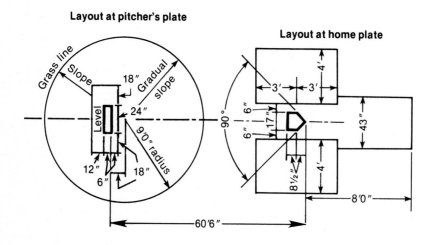

Equipment Manufacturers and Distributors

Accusplit
2290A Ringwood Ave.
San Jose, CA 95131

Manufacturer and distributor of sportswatches, stopwatches, fitness products, pedometers, and jogmeters.

ADA Tennis
3904 Clark
Kansas City, MO 64111

Badminton, squash racquets, and tennis and racquetball products.

AFW of North America
Exchange National Bank, Suite 311
Olean, NY 14760

Producer of moveable swimming pool floors, stainless steel removable access ramps, parallel bars and other pool components.

Alpha Factor—Division of Tighe Industries, Inc.
Valley View Rd., Box 6246
York, PA 17406

Women's and men's gymnastic apparel, accessories, and rhythmic gymnastic equipment.

American Athletics, Inc.
200 American Ave.
Jefferson, IA 50129

Manufacturers of gymnastic, physical education, strength, conditioning, and home exercise equipment.

American Timing Systems
12755 E. Western Ave.
Garden Grove, CA 92641

Manufacturers of high-visibility sports timing and scoring equipment, including scoreboards, game clocks, printing timers, and pace clocks.

Ampro Corp.
1340 N. Jefferson St.
Box 6300
Anaheim, CA 92806

Aerobest exercise flooring and exercise mats.

ATEC
P.O. Box 1317
Santa Cruz, CA 95060

Baseball and softball pitching machines, batting cages, field maintenance equipment, equipment bags and other related training aids.

Athletic Safety Products, Inc.
167 Willis Ave.
Mineola, NY 11501

Developer of "Flexguard," a football facemask designed for strength, lightness, and safety.

Baden Sports, Inc.
1120 S.W. 16th
Renton, WA 98055

Athletic inflatable products, baseballs, and softballs.

Bear Archery

Archery manufacturer: bows, arrows, quivers, targets, broadheads, arm guards, and scents.

BigToys
2601 S. Hood
Tacoma, WA 98409

Playground and movement education equipment.

Bollinger Industries
19401 Londelius St.
Northridge, CA 91324

Institutional sporting goods: inflatable balls, weight lifting equipment, and baseball, basketball, tennis, and track equipment.

BSN Sports
Box 7726
Dallas, TX 75209
Manufacturer and distributor of athletic, physical education, and recreation equipment and supplies.

Cannon Sports
P.O. Box 11179
Burbank, CA 91510-1179
Sporting goods for activities for aerobics to wrestling.

Capezio Dancewear—Ballet Makers, Inc.
33 W. 60th St.
New York, NY 10023
Manufacturers of dance shoes, leotards, tights, and accessories for dance, theatre, and recreation.

Champion Products, Inc.
3141 Monroe Avenue
Rochester, NY 14618
Athletic workout gear.

Cosom/Mantua
Grandview Ave. / P.O. Box 10
Woodbury Heights, NJ 08097
Floor hockey, baseball, softball, bowling, frisbees and foam products.

Cramer Sports Equipment
618 S. Main St.
Wellsville, KS 66092
Physical education products and track and field equipment.

Dayton Racquet Co., Inc.
302 S. Albright St.
Arcanum, OH 45304
Manufacturer of steel frame, steel strung racquets for tennis and badminton and racquetball racquets.

Dekan Athletic Equipment Corp.
2 N. 610 Fair Oaks Rd.
West Chicago, IL 60185
Gymnastics, physical education, and track and field equipment.

Dudley Sports Co.
120 Mill St., P.O. Box 388
Dublin, PA 18917
Manufacturer of softballs, baseballs, and gloves.

Fisher Athletic Equipment, Inc.
Route #8, Box 602
Salisbury, NC 28144
Gymnastics mats, team and travel bags, pole vault and high jump pits, volleyball posts, and guide wire pads.

Flaghouse, Inc.
150 North MacQuesten Parkway
Mt. Vernon, NY 10550
Items for movement education, aquatics, and outdoor education; items for coach's aides, and school furniture and game tables.

GameTime, Inc.
101 Kingsberry Rd.
Fort Payne, AL 35967
Manufacturers of playground, sports, and park products.

General SportCraft Co.
140 Woodbine St.
Bergenfield, NJ 07621
General sporting goods and team athletic equipment.

Gibson, Inc.
P.O. Box 1444
Englewood, CO 80150
Manufacturer and supplier of gymnastics equipment and soccer supplies.

Gold Medal Recreational Products
20 Blue Mountain Rd.
Blue Mountain, AL 36201
Nets, accessories, and recreational products.

Graves-Humphreys Co.
1948 Franklin Rd., S.W.
Roanoke, VA 24014
Physical education, recreation, and sporting goods equipment and supplies.

GSC Sports
15672 Producer Lane
Huntington Beach, CA 92649
Full line of gymnastics equipment, sporting goods, early child development products, and mats.

Gym-Thing, Inc.
6310 Blair Hill Ln.
Baltimore, MD 21209
Manufacturer and importer of movement education and gymnastics equipment.

Hillerich and Bradsby Co.—Louisville Slugger
200 W. Broadway
Louisville, KY 40232
Baseball and softball bats, fielding and batting gloves and accessory items.

H.L. Corporation
P.O. Box 3327
Manhattan Beach, CA
Rackets, shuttles, accessories and teaching aids for badminton, tennis and racketball.

Jayfro Corp.
976 Hartford Turnpike
Waterford, CT 06385

Manufacturer of athletic, recreational, physical education, playground, special education, exercise, and gymnastics equipment and games.

JUGS Pitching Machines
19460 S.W. 84th Street
Tualaton, OR 97062

Pitching machines for softball, baseball, soccer and football.

Kast-A-Way Swimwear, Inc.
9356 Cincinnati-Columbus Rd.
Cincinnati, OH 45241

Speedo swimwear, training equipment, digital watches, trophies, medals, books, and heart rate indicators.

Kenko Sports International, Inc.
242E Route 109
Farmingdale, NY 11735

Air-filled rubber baseball for ages 4 years to adult, rubber-covered softballs in four sizes, and new "Softee" ball in three sizes.

Kwik Goal
140 Pacific Drive
Quakertown, PA 18951

Manufacturer of goal posts and soccer accessories.

Leo's Dancewear, Inc.
1900 N. Narragansett Ave.
Chicago, IL 60639

Manufacturer of dance and gymnastics shoes and garments.

Louisville Badminton Supply
1313 Lyndon Ln., Ste. 103
Louisville, KY 40222

Indoor badminton equipment and supplies.

Mikasa Sports
17500 Red Hill Avenue, Suite 180
Irvine, CA 92714

Mikasa athletic balls and ragball textile athletic balls.

Molten American Co.
3325 Kashiwa St.
Torrance, CA 90505

Inflated athletic balls, basketballs, soccer balls, volleyballs, footballs, and playground balls.

Muehleisen Mfg. Co.
1100 N. Johnson Ave.
El Cajon, CA 92020

Gymnastics, aerobics, and exercise mats, and protective athletic equipment.

National Golf Foundation
200 Castlewood Dr.
North Palm Beach, FL 33410

Support and identification items for golf teachers and coaches. Educational publications, films, videotapes, annual seminars, and local inservice programs.

Nautilus Sports/Medical Industries, Inc.
151 E. Ohio Ave.
Lake Helen, FL 32744

Full range of conditioning and exercise equipment.

New England Camp & School Supply Company
P.O. Box 20
Newton Centre, MA 02159

Equipment for most sports and recreational activities.

Nissen/Universal
930 27th Ave., S.W.
Cedar Rapids, IA 52404

Manufacturers of physical fitness equipment, gymnastics equipment, and electronic signs.

Orienteering Services, USA
Box 1604
Binghamton, NY 13902

Information on orienteering, the map and compass sport for fitness and recreation. Program development, lesson plans, teaching aids, games, audiovisual materials, and compasses.

Paramount Fitness Equipment Corp.
6450 East Bandini Blvd.
Los Angeles, CA 90040

Fitness products, including selectorized weight resistance machines, Olympic benches and racks, sit-up boards, and dumbbells.

Passon's Sports
P.O. Box 49
Jenkintown, PA 19046

Physical education and athletic supplies and equipment.

Polvonite Corp.
Van Wyck Lane
Wappingers Falls, NY 12590

Foam safety equipment, wrestling mats, gym mats, wall padding, and landing mats.

Porter Equipment Co.
9555 Irving Park Rd.
Schiller Park, IL 60176-1983

Gymnasium and playground equipment of all types.

Price Mfg., Inc.
P.O. Box 2031
Princeton, NJ 08540

Manufacturer of tennis racquets, ball machines, stringing machines, and clothing.

Rackets International
24572 La Cienega
Laguna Hills, CA 92653

Racketball, tennis and badminton rackets.

Rip Flag—Mason City Tent & Awning Co.
408 S. Federal
Mason City, IA 50401

"Rip Flag" football belts.

George Santeli, Inc.
465 S. Dean St.
Englewood, NJ 07631

Manufacturer of fencing equipment for classes, teams, and individuals. A full line of uniforms, masks, gloves, bags, and teaching plastrons made in the United States.

Select Service & Supply Co., Inc.
2905 E. Amwiler Rd.
Atlanta, GA 30338

Equipment and supplies for physical education, athletics, recreation, camping, health education, and dance.

Snitz Manufacturing
P.O. Box 76
East Troy, WI 53120

Specialize in products for physical education, recreation and team activities.

Sportime
One Sportime Way
Atlanta, GA 30340

Equipment for physical education, recreation, athletics, dance and aquatics.

SSK America, Inc.
17101 S. Central Ave., Unit 1C
Carson, CA 90746

Baseball and softball gloves and accessories.

STX, Inc.
1500 Bush Street
Baltimore, MD 21230

Lacrosse equipment and teaching aids.

The Swim Shop
742 Fesslers Ln.
Nashville, TN 37210

Everything for an aquatics program.

Tachikara-Arch Billmire Co., Inc.
9742 Pflumm Rd.
Lenexa, KS 66215

Tachikara volleyballs, basketballs, footballs, soccer balls, and playground balls for competition and physical education.

Things from Bell, Inc.
230 Mechanic Street
Princeton, WI 54968

Physical education and recreation equipment.

Tr
101-B Cuvier St.
San Francisco, CA 94112

"Real Bounce" foam balls, short regulation tennis racquets, short court tennis, "Nerf" footballs, and soccer balls.

Triple Threat Flag Belts
614 Ruth St.
Prescott, AZ 86301

Flag belts.

Universal Racquets
4420 Jarobe, Suite 4D
Kansas City, MO 64111

Tennis, badminton, racquetball and squash racquets.

Urethane Products, Inc.
200 S. Jackson Rd.
Venice, FL 33595

Products for physical education programs, featuring foam balls, soccer balls, volleyballs, and foam saucers.

U.S. Games, Inc.
P.O. Box 117028
Carrollton, TX 75011-7028

Physical education, athletics, and recreation products.

Voit Sports, Inc.
P.O. Box 7726
Dallas, TX 75209

Athletic balls, swim products, and exercise equipment.

West Coast Netting, Inc.
8978 Haven Ave.
Rancho Cucamonga, CA 91730

Sport nets and related game standards, table tennis tables, and portable time clocks.

Wham-O, Inc.
835 E. El Monte St.
San Gabriel, CA 91776

"Frisbee" discs, "Hacky Sack" footbags, and educational materials on flying disc and footbag sports, games, and activities.

Wittek Golf Supply Co., Inc.
3650 N. Avondale Ave.
Chicago, IL 60618

Golf clubs; golf balls; tee mats; golf teaching aids,
accessories, bags, and carts; grips, cages, and nets; jackets,
gloves, personalized bag tags, and towels.

Wolverine Sports & Champions on Film
P.O. Box 1941, 745 State Circle
Ann Arbor, MI 48106

Manufacturer and distributor of sports instructional films
and a quality line of athletic, playground, body building,
and exercise equipment for all ages.

Yonex Corp.
350 Maple Ave.
Torrance, CA 90503

Distributor of "Yonex" tennis and badminton equipment and
accessories.

York Archery
P.O. Box 110
Independence, MO 64051

Bows, arrows and accessories.

Credits

Figs. 2-1 thru 2-6. Photos by Lorna Francis

Figs. 3-1 and 3-2. Courtesy Bear Archery

Fig. 3-7. From Archery & Fencing Rules by NAGWS of the American Alliance of Health, Physical Education, Recreation and Dance. Copyright 1980.

Fig. 3-8. From The Archer's Bible by Fred Bear. Copyright 1968, 1980 by The Fred Bear Sports Club. Reprinted by permission of Doubleday & Company, Inc.

Figs. 3-11, 3-12 and 3-14. From Bear, F.: Fred Bear's world of archery, NY, 1979, Doubleday & Co., Inc. Photos by George Bing.

Fig. 5-4. Redrawn from Badminton, Sports Techniques Series, Chicago, 1969, The Athletic Institute.

Fig. 5-6. From Badminton, Educational Sports Techniques Series, Chicago, 1969, The Athletic Institute.

Figs. 6-1, 6-2 and 6-3. Reprinted with permission of The National Collegiate Athletic Association.

Fig. 7-1. From Greg Lemond's complete book of bicycling by Lemond, G. and Gordis, K., 1987, Putnam Publishing Group.

Figs. 7-2, 7-5, and 7-6. Photos by David Bassett, Jr.

Figs. 8-5 thru 8-10. Photos by Raili Mood.

Fig. 10-1. Reprinted by permission of The American Alliance for Health, Physical Education and Dance, 1900 Association Dr., Reston, VA 22091.

Fig. 11-1. Photo by Raili Mood.

Fig. 12-1. From Rules of golf by United States Golf Association, P.O. Box 708, Far Hills, NJ, 07931.

Fig. 12-13. Photo by Raili Mood.

Figs. 13-62 thru 13-64. From Brown, J.R., and Wardell, D.B.: Teaching and coaching gymnastics for men and women. NY, 1980, John Wiley & Sons, Inc., pp. 406-408.

Fig. 14-1. From Klafs, C.E., and Lyon, M.J.: The female athlete, ed. 2, St. Louis, 1978, The C.V. Mosby Co.

Figs. 15-3 thru 15-8. Photos by Rick Schmidt.

Figs. 17-1, 17-3, 17-4 and 17-7 thru 17-9. Photos by Norman Gilchrest.

Figs. 17-10, 17-11 and 17-13 thru 17-15. Photos by Tresa Gilchrest.

Figs. 18-1, 18-2 and 18-4 thru 18-7. From Orienteering for sport and pleasure. Copyright 1977 by Hans Bengtsson and George Aktinson. Reprinted by permission of The Stephen Green Press, a wholly owned subsidiary of Viking Penguin, Inc.

Fig. 18-3. Courtesy of Silva Company, Orienteering Services, U.S.A., Box 547, La Porte, IN 46350.

Fig. 21-7. Photo by Raili Mood.

Fig. 23-6. From Seven days to self-defense. Copyright 1980 by Ted Gambordella, used with permission of Contemporary Books, Inc., Chicago.

Fig. 24-1. Photo by Raili Mood.

Figs. 25-1, 25-4, 22-5, and 22-6 thru 22-8. From Cross-country skiing today by John Caldwell. Copyright 1977 by John Caldwell. Reprinted by permission of The Stephen Greene Press, a wholly owned subsidiary of Viking Penguin, Inc.

Figs. 25-2, 25-3 and 25-11. From the cross country ski book by John Caldwell. Copyright 1984, 1981, 1977, 1975, 1973, 1971 by John Caldwell. Reprinted by permission of The Stephen Greene Press, a wholly owned subsidiary of Viking Penguin, Inc.

Figs. 25-9 and 25-10. Photos by George Atkinson.

Fig. 27-1. From National Collegiate Athletic Association: NCAA Men's Soccer Rules, Mission, Kansas, 1984. Specifications subject to revision annually. Reprinted with permission from the National Collegiate Athletic Association.

Fig. 32-3. Photo by Raili Mood.

Fig. 33-4. From United States Team Handball Federation: Rules of the game, 1981-1985 edition. Colorado Springs, CO.

Fig. 35-2. From Grambeau, R.J. The official national and touch football rules, North Palm Beach, FL, 1986. The Athletic Institute. Used with permission of the Athletic Institute.

Fig. 35-4B. Photo by Raili Mood.

Figs. 36-2 thru 36-4. Photos by Raili Mood.

Figs. 36-7 thru 36-11, 36-12A, and 36-14. From Wakefield, F., Harkens, D., and Cooper, J.M.: Track and field fundamentals for girls and women. ed. 4, St. Louis, 1977, The C.V. Mosby Co.

Fig. 36-10. From Cretzmeyer, F.X., Alley, L.E., and Tipton, C.M.: Track and field athletics, ed. 8, St. Louis, 1974. The C.V. Mosby Co.

Figs. 37-3, 37-4, and 37-8. Photos by Raili Mood.

Figs. 38-1 and 38-3. Permission to reprint granted by The National Collegiate Athletic Association. Specifications subject to revision annually.

Figs. 38-2 and 38-4 thru 38-6. Photos by George Weiny.